04/10/15

P

REDCAR & CLEVELAND COLLEGE LIBRARY

Redcar & Cleveland College

D0533892

WITHDRAWN
11/4/23
SM

HE

The Age of the Dictators

A Study of the European ... mps, 1918–33

David G. Williamson

PEARSON
Longman

Harlow, England • London • New York • Boston • San Francisco • Toronto • Sydney • Singapore • Hong Kong
Tokyo • Seoul • Taipei • New Delhi • Cape Town • Madrid • Mexico City • Amsterdam • Munich • Paris • Milan

To Luca and Marco

PEARSON EDUCATION LIMITED

Edinburgh Gate
Harlow CM20 2JE
United Kingdom
Tel: +44(0)1279 623623
Fax: +44 (0)1279 431059
Website: www.pearsoned.co.uk

First edition published in Great Britain in 2007

© Pearson Education Limited 2007

The right of David G. Williamson to be identified as author of this work has
been asserted by him in accordance with the Copyright, Designs and Patents Act
1988.

ISBN: 978–0–582–50580–3

British Library Cataloguing in Publication Data
A CIP catalogue record for this book can be obtained from the British Library

Library of Congress Cataloging in Publication Data
A CIP catalog record of this book can be ontained from the Library of Congress

All rights reserved; no part of this publication may be reproduced, stored in a
retrieval system, or transmitted in any form or by any means, electronic,
mechanical, photocopying, recording, or otherwise without either the prior
written permission of the Publishers or a licence permitting restricted copying in
the United Kingdom issued by the Copyright Licensing Agency Ltd, Saffron
House, 6–10 Kirby Street, London EC1N 8TS. This book may not be lent,
resold, hired out or otherwise disposed of by way of trade in any form of
binding or cover other than that in which it is published, without the prior
consent of the Publishers.

10 9 8 7 6 5 4 3 2 1
10 09 08 07

Set by 3 in 10pt Sabon
Printed and bound in China   EPC/01

The Publisher's policy is to use paper manufactured from sustainable forests.

Contents

Preface

The object of this book is to provide for students, and indeed all who are interested in this period, a concise and up-to-date study of the 'era of the dictators'. Its emphasis inevitably falls on the history of the three main dictatorships of Soviet Russia, Fascist Italy and Nazi Germany, but the Spanish Civil War and the establishment of Franco's dictatorship in Spain is also analysed and there are shorter chapters on the establishment of authoritarian regimes in many new states that came into being after the defeat of the Central Powers in 1918.

The book is divided into four main sections dealing with the origins of the dictatorships and then their development up to 1945 – and beyond, in the case of Stalinist Russia and Francoist Spain. Each chapter starts with an introduction, which outlines its major themes and indicates the main topics that it addresses. Focus boxes and brief notes in the margin help explain points made in the text by providing background information or summaries of historiographical debates, while a timeline at the beginning of each chapter provides a guide to the key dates of the relevant material covered in the chapter. At the end of the book there is also a comprehensive glossary of technical terms. The text is cross-referenced so that readers can explore the origins and consequences of events they are studying, as well as the similarities and differences between the dictatorships. In places, bullet points are used to help readers grasp simply and speedily key developments of complex events. At the end of each chapter there is a collection of documents, which both serve as a basis for further discussion and illustrate more fully some of the issues

referred to in the main text. At the end of the book there are suggestions for further reading of books in English on the dictators,
which are divided into sections and enable readers to explore
issues raised in this study in greater depth.

Finally I would like to thank Heather McCallum, Christina
Wipf Perry and Natasha Dupont for all their help and encouragement while writing this book.

Maps

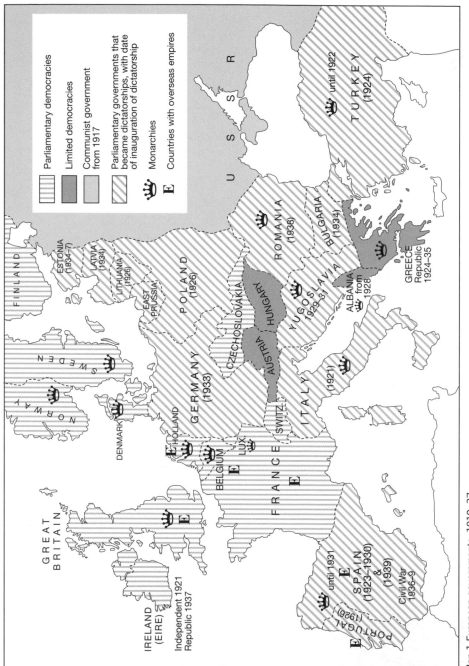

Legend

	Parliamentary democracies
	Limited democracies
	Communist government from 1917
	Parliamentary governments that became dictatorships, with date of inauguration of dictatorship
♛	Monarchies
E	Countries with overseas empires

FINLAND

SWEDEN

NORWAY

ESTONIA (1934–7)

LATVIA (1934)

LITHUANIA (1926)

EAST PRUSSIA

U · S · S · R

GREAT BRITAIN ♛ E

IRELAND (EIRE)

Independent 1921
Republic 1937

DENMARK ♛

♛ HOLLAND E

BELGIUM E

LUX

GERMANY (1933)

POLAND (1926)

CZECHOSLOVAKIA

AUSTRIA

HUNGARY

ROMANIA (1938)

BULGARIA (1934) ♛

FRANCE E

SWITZ.

ITALY ♛ (1921)

YUGOSLAVIA ♛ 1929–31

ALBANIA ♛ from 1928

GREECE Republic 1924–35 ♛

TURKEY (1924)

♛ until 1922

SPAIN (1923–1930) & (1939)

Civil War 1936–9

♛ until 1931 E

PORTUGAL (1926) ♛ E

Map 1 European governments, 1919–37

Source: © M. Gilbert, 1966, *Recent History Atlas*, London, Weidenfeld, London, 1967, p. 48. Reproduced by permission of Taylor & Francis Books UK.

Map 2 The Russian Civil War, 1918–20

Source: © Gilbert, 1966, *Recent History Atlas*, p. 39. Reproduced by permission of Taylor & Francis Books UK.

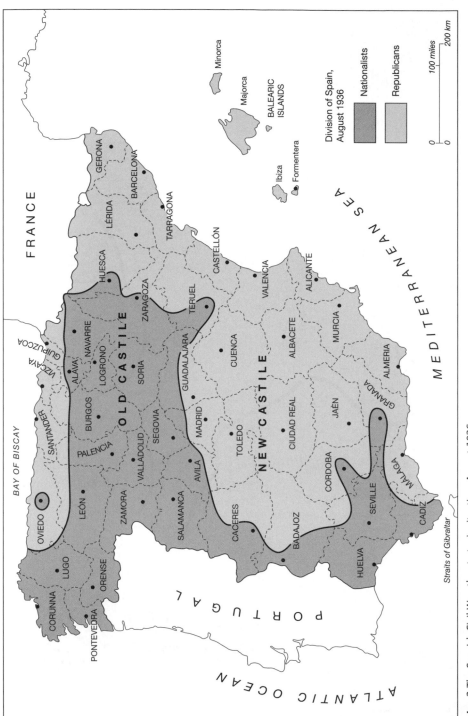

Map 3 The Spanish Civil War: the strategic situation, August 1936

Source: H. Browne, *Spain's Civil War,* London, Longman, 1983, p. ix.

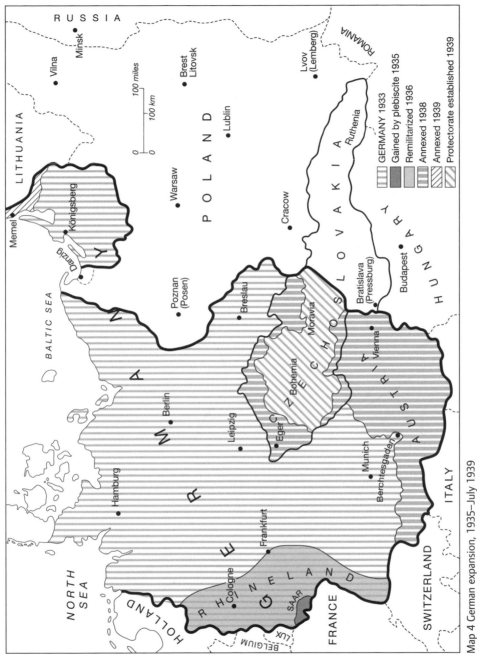

Map 4 German expansion, 1935–July 1939

Source: © Gilbert, 1966, *Recent History Atlas*, p. 50. Reproduced by permission of Taylor & Francis Books UK.

Map 5 The German invasion of the USSR, 1941
Source: D. Evans, *Stalin's Russia*, London, Hodder, 2005, p. 129.

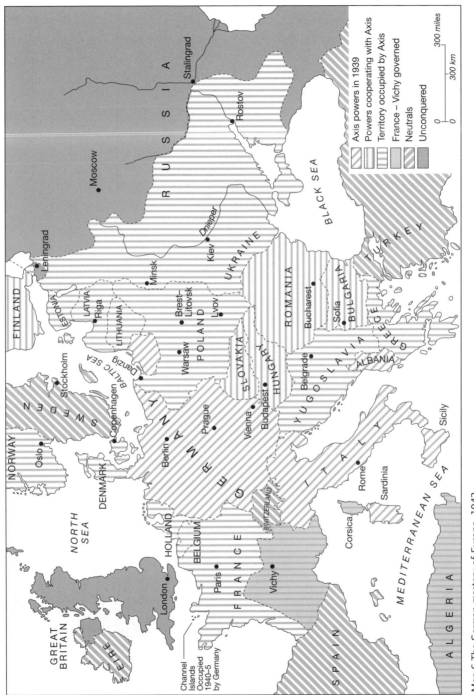

Map 6 The German mastery of Europe, 1942

Source: © Gilbert, 1966, *Recent History Atlas*, p. 72. Reproduced by permission of Taylor & Francis Books UK.

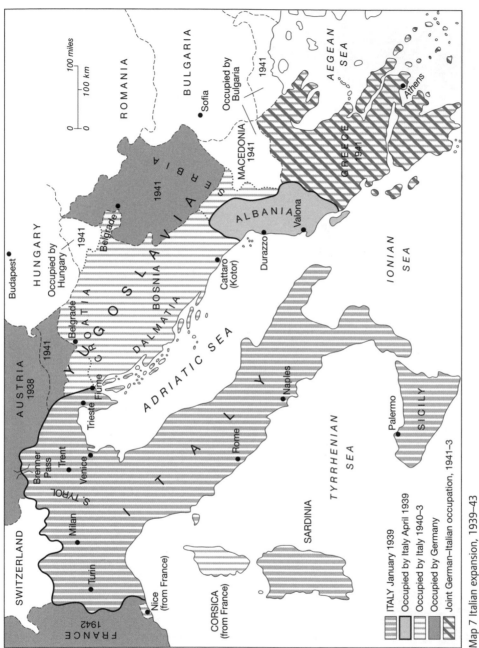

Map 7 Italian expansion, 1939–43

Source: © Gilbert, 1966, *Recent History Atlas*, p. 56. Reproduced by permission of Taylor & Francis Books UK.

Map 8 Central Europe, 1955

Source: D. Williamson, *Europe and the Cold War, 1945–91*, London, Hodder, 2006.

Acknowledgements

We are grateful to the following for permission to reproduce copyright material:

Maps 1, 2, 4, 6 and 7 redrawn from *Recent History Atlas* by Martin Gilbert, ISBN 00297764357, published by Weidenfeld 1966, reproduced by permission of Taylor & Francis Books UK (Gilbert, M. 1966); Chapter 2, Box 'Goods supplied by private traders in the NEP' from Private Trade and Traders during NEP in *Russia in the Era of NEP* edited by S. Fitzpatrick *et al.*, reprinted by permission of Indiana University Press, Bloomington and Indianapolis (Ball, A. 1990); Chapter 3, Box 'Social or professional background of National Fascist Party Members' and Chapter 12, Box 'The Nazi New European Order' from *A History of Fascism, 1914–45*, pub Routledge, reprinted by permission of Thomson Publishing Services (Payne, S. G. 2001); Map 3 redrawn from *Spain's Civil War* (Seminar Studies in History series), reprinted by permission of Pearson Education Ltd. (Browne, H. 1983); Chapter 5, Box 'Inflation: dollar quotations for the mark, 1914–23' from *Germany 1866–1945*, reprinted by permission of Oxford University Press (Craig, G. 1978); Chapter 5, Box 'German industrial production, 1913–28' adapted from *Perspectives on Modern German Economic History and Policy*, reprinted by permission of Cambridge University Press (Borchardt, K. and Lambert, P. 1991); Chapter 5, Box 'National election results in the Weimar Republic, 1919–30' from Inflation, stabilization and political realignment in Germany, 1924 to 1928 in *The German Inflation Reconsidered: A Preliminary Balance* edited by G. D. Feldman *et al.*, reprinted by permission of Verlag

Walter de Gruyter & Co. GmbH (Childers, T. 1982); Map 5 redrawn from *Stalin's Russia* (Teach Yourself History series), pub Hodder, reprinted by permission of David Hancock, Perception Design (Evans, D. 2005); Chapter 8, Box 'The standard of living, 1929–39' from *Fascism in Italy: Society and Culture 1922–1945*, pub Allen Lane 1973, reproduced by permission of Penguin Books Ltd. and *The Fascist Experience* by Tannenbaum, Copyright © Basic Books, Inc., 1972, reprinted by permission of Basic Books, a member of Perseus Books Group (Tannenbaum, E. R. 1973); Map 8 redrawn from *Access to History: Europe and the Cold War 1945–1991, 2nd Edition*, pub Hodder, reprinted by permission of Gray Publishing (Williamson, D. 2006); Chapter 10, Boxes 'Peasant holdings' and 'Productivity targets' from *Stalin and Khruschev*, © 1990 Lynch, published and reproduced by permission of Hodder & Stoughton Ltd. (Lynch, M. 1990); Chapter 12, Box 'Occupied territories" from *Geschichte der Deutschen Kriegswirtschaft, 1939–1945, Volume 2*, reprinted by permission of Akademie Verlag GmbH (Eichholtz, D. 1985); Chapter 13, Box 'Comparison between the British and German war economies' from *War and Economy in the Third Reich*, © R. J. Overy 1994, reprinted by permission of Oxford University Press (Overy, R. J. 1995); Chapter 13, Box 'Food consumption in Germany 1939–45' redrawn from Albert Speer and Armaments Policy in Total War in *Germany and the Second World War, Volume V, Part II* edited by Research Institute for Military History, reprinted by permission of Oxford University Press (Muller, R.-D. 2003); Chapter 15, Box 'The Soviet war economy' from *The Soviet Home Front, 1941–45: A Social and Economic History of the USSR in World War II*, reprinted by permission of Pearson Education Ltd. (Barber, J. and Harrison, M. 1991).

Photographs: Figure 2.1 Getty Images/AFP; Figure 2.2 Getty Images/Hulton Archive; Figure 2.3 Russia On-Line; Figure 2.4 RIA Novosti; Figure 2.5 Russia On-Line; Figure 2.6 Empics; Figure 3.1 Empics; Figure 3.2 Estate of Kimon Marengo/ Centre for the Study of Cartoons & Caricature, University of Kent; Figure 4.1 Getty Images/Hulton Archive; Figure 5.1 Snark International; Figure 5.2 Mary Evans Picture Library; Figure 6.1 Getty Images/Hulton Archive; Figure 6.2 Corbis/Bettmann; Figure 7.1 Corbis/Bettmann; Figure 8.1 Getty Images/Time & Life

Pictures; Figure 8.2 Getty Images/Hulton Archive; Figure 8.4 Corbis; Figure 8.5 Getty Images/Time & Life Pictures; Figure 9.1 Corbis/Bettmann; Figure 9.2 Corbis/Hulton-Deutsch Archive; Figure 9.3 Getty Images/Roger Viollet; Figure 10.1 RIA Novosti; Figure 10.2 RIA Novosti; Figure 10.3 RIA Novosti; Figure 10.4 Mary Evans Picture Library; Figure 12.1 'You Too! Your Comrades are Waiting in the French Division of the Waffen', Second World War poster, c.1942 (colour litho), French School, (20th century) / Giraudon, Private Collection / The Bridgeman Art Library; Figure 12.2 Getty Images/Hulton Archive; Figure 13.1 Getty Images/Hulton Archive; Figure 13.2 Corbis/Bettmann; Figure 15.1 RIA Novosti; Figure 16.1 Society for Co-operation in Russian and Soviet Studies.

We are grateful to the following for permission to reproduce texts:

Chapter 5, Documents 5 and 7, Chapter 6, Documents 1, 4, 9 and 10 extracts from *Nazism 1919–1945. Volume 1: The Rise to Power 1919–1934* edited by J. Noakes and G. Pridham, ISBN 0 85989 598 X, University of Exeter Press, 1998, reprinted by permission of University of Exeter Press (Noakes, J. and Pridham, G. eds 1998); Chapter 7, Documents 2, 3 and 4 extracts from *Nazism 1919–1945. Volume 2: State, Economy and Society 1933–1939* edited by J. Noakes and G. Pridham, ISBN 0 85989 599 8, University of Exeter Press, 2000, reprinted by permission of University of Exeter Press (Noakes, J. and Pridham, G. eds 2000); Chapter 12, Documents 1 and 4 extracts from *Nazism 1919–1945. Volume 3: Foreign Policy, War and Racial Extermination*, edited by J. Noakes and G. Pridham, ISBN 0 85989 602 1, University of Exeter Press, 2001, reprinted by permission of University of Exeter Press (Noakes, J. and Pridham, G. eds 2001); Chapter 13, Documents 3, 4 and 5 extracts from *Nazism 1919–1945. Volume 4: The German Home Front in World War II* edited by J. Noakes, ISBN 0 85989 311 1, University of Exeter Press, 1998, reprinted by permission of University of Exeter Press (Noakes, J. ed 1998).

In some instances we have been unable to trace the owners of copyright material, and we would appreciate any information that would enable us to do so.

Introduction

The 'era of the dictators' is a convenient label to describe the period of dictatorships, which dominated Europe between 1918 and 1945, but on closer analysis, like all historical labels, it can prove simplistic. Dictatorships in Europe were not unique to the inter-war period. The period 1918–45 certainly encompassed the rise and fall of the dynamic dictatorships in Germany and Italy, but the Spanish and Portuguese dictatorships continued on into the 1970s, and the Soviet dictatorship remained virtually intact until 1990.

Is the logic of this chronology then that there is no clear-cut era of the dictators? In retrospect it can be argued that up to 1939, or perhaps still more 1942, Europe was being recast by the new 'totalitarian' dictatorships. By 1939 18 regimes can be described as dictatorial. During the period of German occupation, with the exception of Switzerland and Sweden, the remaining Continental democracies were replaced with authoritarian regimes. Although the defeat of Italian Fascism and German Nazism in 1943–5 destroyed the most dynamic of these movements, paradoxically this opened up the way not only for the democratic reconstruction of Western Europe, but simultaneously also to the triumph of Stalinism in Eastern Europe. Western Europe (with the partial exception of Spain and Portugal) was able to emerge from the 'Fascist era', but in Eastern Europe pre-war authoritarian and wartime Fascist regimes were merely swapped for the new Stalinist people's democracies. The Cold War ensured that for only half of the European Continent, the era of dictatorships ended in 1945.

Marxist–Leninist principles
The theories of revolution based on the writings of Karl Marx and Vladimir Ilyich Lenin, which foresaw the overthrow of capitalism, the creation of a workers' democracy (dictatorship of the proletariat) and the subsequent creation of a just and harmonious society in which the state would gradually 'wither away'.

To what extent did these dictatorships possess common characteristics? Their form varied from the Bolshevik regime in Russia, which was inspired by **Marxist–Leninist principles**, to the Italian Fascist and German Nazi dictatorships and the authoritarian governments of the Iberian peninsular and Eastern and South-Eastern Europe. The Bolshevik regime was the first of the new dictatorships, which based itself on a pseudo-democratic legitimacy, but it evolved and changed, and historians debate the degree of continuity between Leninism and Stalinism.

Similarly, how much in common did the Italian Fascist and the German Nazi regimes have? Was Nazism in fact a form of Fascism or was it, as some historians argue, 'altogether a unique phenomenon, emerging from the peculiar legacy of the Prussian–German authoritarian state and German ideological development, but owing its uniqueness above all to the person of Hitler.[1] On the other hand it was argued, particularly strongly at the height of the Cold War in the 1950s, that the new political movements that seized power in Italy, Russia and Germany did have much in common. Hannah Arendt and Carl Friedrich both described them as totalitarian regimes sharing the following characteristics:[2]

- an official ideology
- a political monopoly by a single mass party
- a police state
- total control over the media
- central control over the economy
- a monopoloy of armed power.

The dictatorships that sprang up in the Iberian peninsular and Central and South-Eastern Europe had little in common with the dynamic new movements of Fascism, Nazism and Communism. At most they were what one Czech historian called 'half-cock fascism'.[3] Essentially, except perhaps in Spain, these dictatorships lacked any popular backing and relied on the officer corps great landowners and the bureaucracy for support. Only in the late 1930s and early 1940s, with the apparent triumph of German Nazism and Italian Fascism in Europe, did these regimes begin to adopt increasingly Fascist tendencies.

NOTES

1   I. Kershaw, *The Nazi Dictatorship: Problems and Perspectives*, London, Edward Arnold, 3rd ed. 1993, p. 19.

2   H. Arendt, *The Origins of Totalitarianism*, New York, Harcourt, 1951; C.J. Friedrich and Z.K. Brzezinski, *Totalitarian Dictatorship and Autocracy*, Cambridge, MA., Harvard University Press, 1956.

3   J. Valenta, 'The drift to dictatorship', in *History of the 20th Century*, no. 52, London, Purnell, 1968–9, p. 1433.

PART ONE

The origins of the dictatorships

CHAPTER ONE

The years of crisis, 1890–1918

TIMELINE

1890	Julius Langbehn's *Rembrandt als Erzieher* published	
1894–9	Protocols of the Elders of Zion forged by agents of the Russian Secret Police in Paris	
1899	Houston Stewart Chamberlain's *Foundations of the Nineteenth Century* published	
	Action Française formed	
1902	Lenin's *What Is To Be Done* published	
1903	Brussels Conference and formation of the Bolshevik or majority group	
1905	Uprising in Russia	
1908	Publication of Sorel's *Réflexions sur la violence*	
1909	Futurist manifesto published	
1910	Foundation of the Italian National Association, which amalgamated with the Fascist Party in 1923	
1912	SPD emerges as largest party in the *Reichstag* elections	
	Mussolini becomes a key figure on the left-wing of the Italian Socialist Party and appointed editor of *L'Avanti*	
1912–14	Industrial and agrarian unrest in Italy	
1913	First Italian election under the new suffrage law	
1914	August	Outbreak of First World War
1915	May	Italy declares war on Austria
1916	August	Italy declares war on Germany
1917	February	Russian Revolution
	April	USA declares war on Germany
	August	Mass strike against war in Turin
	October	Bolshevik Revolution in Russia
		Italian defeat at Caporetto
1918	January	Strikes break out in Berlin
	March	Treaty of Brest–Litovsk

March–April	German offensive on the Western front
29 September	German High Command calls for an armistice
11 November	Armistice signed between Germany and Allies

INTRODUCTION

During the years 1917–45 Europe was reshaped by the revolutionary forces of Fascism, Nazism and Communism. For historians the key question is whether the triumph of these movements was caused by the cataclysm of the First World War or whether their emergence as powerful forces would have happened even without the war. In retrospect the years immediately before the outbreak of the First World War seemed to be a golden age of peace and prosperity, yet they were also a period of massive change, dislocation and political and social crisis. Accelerating industrialization led to the development of a new mass culture, large cities and the expansion of the working classes, which challenged the nineteenth-century liberal and conservative dominance of the political system. However, it is all too easy to read into these years an inevitability that did not exist. In Russia Lenin had developed his revolutionary variant of Marxism, and in Western and Central Europe there certainly was an intellectual revolt against rationalism and liberalism, and the emergence of the core ideas of what was later to be called Fascism, but without the First World War it is doubtful whether this revolt would have been sufficient to destabilize and finally to overthrow the existing political systems.

THE KEY ISSUES IN THIS CHAPTER ARE:

- The difficulty in defining Fascism.
- The intellectual backlash against liberalism and the rise of irrational ideologies.
- The fusion of nationalism and Socialism.
- The decline of Socialism as a revolutionary force and the emergence of syndicalism and Bolshevism.
- The radicalizing impact of the First World War.

PROTO-FASCISM

Before tracing the origins of Fascism it is important to define the term. It is, as the American historian Stanley Payne has observed, 'probably the vaguest of the major political terms'.[1] Apart from Italian Fascism, most of the regimes that could be regarded as Fascist in inter-war and wartime Europe never called themselves Fascist and differed significantly from each other. Consequently one of the major tasks of historians of Fascism has been to define what is meant by the term and try to identify common points in the regimes that have been described as 'Fascist'. Payne[2] has drawn up a table in which he breaks up the characteristics of political Fascism into three main sections:

1 Ideology and aims:

- An idealist or 'vitalist' philosophy (see p. 10) aiming at creating a new nationalist, authoritarian state, which would not be based on traditional conservative principles.
- Its economy would be controlled by the state, or be **'corporatist'**, and attempts made to integrate both the workers and employers into one common organization.
- The worship of force and the readiness to use it to achieve territorial expansion.

Corporatism
The attempt to defuse class hatred by giving both capital and labour a role in running industry – see pp. 109 and 110.

2 It was opposed to:

- liberalism
- Communism
- conservatism, although it might temporarily ally with the traditional Right.

3 Its style and organization:

- Creation of a party militia and mass mobilization of the population.
- The use of symbols, language and orchestrated mass meetings, which emphasized the mystical or religious side of the movement.
- Stress on male dominance and superiority over the female.
- Emphasis on the dynamism of youth and the conflict of generations.
- The creation of a charismatic authoritarian leadership.

The revolt against materialism, rationalism and liberalism

During the period 1890–1914 the cultural elite in Continental Europe, particularly Germany, Italy and France, began to reject the prevailing beliefs of liberalism and rationalism which had been accepted almost without question by the preceding generations. The attack on liberalism gathered strength, while the yearning for great men, heroism and violence grew. Typical of this new spirit was the Futurist movement in Italy, in which Filippo Marinetti played the leading role. Its art, drama and philosophy stressed the glories of war and aimed to exalt aggression and violence. After the war both Italian Fascism and Russian Communism were to draw on the ideas and imagery of the Futurist manifesto published 10 years earlier (see Document 1 and pp. 58 and 93).

In Germany the reaction against liberalism took the form of a rejection of modernity by the new *völkisch* philosophy, which by 1914 dominated nationalist and right wing thought in Germany. The *völkisch* writers, Lagarde, Langbehn and later Moeller Van der Bruck, propagated a nostalgic, anti-modernist ideology, which looked back to an idyllic Germanic pre-industrial rural society. Its message was that urbanization, industrialization and liberalism were destroying the good old pre-industrial Germany with its heroic values. Above all in this process the Jews were playing a leading role (see Document 2). These nationalist fantasies and utopias, which composed the new Germanic ideology, had an immediate resonance and were to colour the attitude of a whole generation of Germans, and make them more receptive to Nazi propaganda. Langbehn's work, ***Rembrandt als Erzieher***, for instance, was republished 39 times in two years.

Similarly, in the hands of minor intellectuals and textbook writers, the ideas of the great late-nineteenth-century philosophers and scientists, such as the German philosopher **Friedrich Nietzsche**, the French thinker **Henri Bergson** and the English biologist Charles Darwin (1808–82), were simplified and made accessible to a much wider audience. Darwinian biology, for example, gave rise to 'social Darwinism', which viewed life as a bitter struggle for the survival of the fittest and opened the way up to **eugenics** and racial engineering. The new theories of the supremacy of the Germanic races drew heavily on these ideas.

Rembrandt als Erzieher
Literally, *Rembrandt as Educator.*

Friederich Nietzsche (1844–1900)
Argued that in contemporary culture religion had been replaced by materialism and the quest for pleasure, drawing the conclusion from this that God was 'dead'. To remedy this he urged in *Thus Spake Zaruthustra* the creation of a new ruthless elite under a totally amoral leader or 'superman'.

Henri Bergson (1859–1941)
In his book *L'Evolution Creatrice* he stressed the importance of the 'vital instinct' (*élan vital*) in life which favoured the creativity of the individual as opposed to the drab conformity of society.

Houston Stewart Chamberlain, for example, in his two-volume *Foundations of the Nineteenth Century*, linked the superiority of the German race to their racial purity, and argued that the real threat to this superiority came from the Jews. The theories of Gustav Le Bon, which stressed that crowds were essentially irrational and hysterical, as well as the views of the Italian Vilfredo Pareto, that politics rested on emotion rather than reason, also created a climate in which great men, charismatic leadership and daring deeds, rather than the more prosaic virtues of liberalism and internationalism, seemed to be the requirements of the time.

The alliance of nationalism and Socialism

The years 1880–1914 were the incubation period for Fascism and National Socialism. Fuelled by France's humiliating defeat at the hands of Prussia, new radical nationalist groups, such as the League of Patriots and the *Action Française* were formed in France, while in Italy Enrico Corradini was popularizing the view that Italy was treated like a proletarian nation by the great powers. He urged a new national revolution that would create a more united and powerful state. In this context he sometimes used the term 'National Socialism'. In Germany extreme nationalism became increasingly popular with pressure groups like the Pan German League, the Navy League and the Agrarian League. In 1893 small anti-Semitic parties managed to win 16 seats in the Reichstag, although by 1912 their number had fallen to seven. In Bohemia, a province of the Austrian Empire in 1904, a German Workers' Party was set up, which increasingly became more nationalist and racist, and by 1918 called itself the German National Socialist Workers' Party.

Taken together the ideologies and policies of these groups anticipated much of the Fascist and National Socialist programmes of the 1920s:

- They all advocated an authoritarian nationalism.
- They were hostile to liberalism and the parliamentary process.
- The nation counted for far more than the individual. Thus their nationalism had a socialist dimension to it. Charles

---

Houston Stewart Chamberlain (1855–1927)
The son of an English admiral, who became a German citizen and was a great admirer of the composer, Wagner, whose daughter he married.

Gustav Le Bon (1841–1931)
One of the founders of sociology and the writer of *The Psychology* of *the Masses*.

Vilfredo Pareto (1848–1923)
An economist, whose most important book, *Mind and Society*, was written in 1916.

Eugenics
The science of improving the population by selective breeding.

Enrico Corradini (865–1931)
A journalist and nationalist politician.

Maurras, who founded *Action Française* in 1899, declared, for instance, that there existed a 'form of socialism, which, when stripped of its democratic and cosmopolitan accretions, would fit in with nationalism just as a well-made glove fits a beautiful hand'.[3]

- They advocated the doctrine of corporatism for regulating competing social and economic interests.
- They were anti-Semitic and realized that anti-Semitism could be used to integrate the workers into the national community.

How much impact, however, did these radical groups have? They influenced intellectuals and university students, and appeared to provide some answers to the problems created by accelerating industrialization and the growing power of the masses. However in 1914 the prospects of any proto-Fascist seizure of power in a European state were still inconceivable. It is true that there was a growing disillusionment with nineteenth-century liberalism and parliamentarism in both Italy and Germany, and the increasing industrial unrest and growth of socialist parties was producing a conservative backlash with demands for limiting the franchise and the creation of a more authoritarian state but, as long as there were no cataclysmic and polarizing crises, a peaceful absorption of the new mass parties on the left into democratic politics was still possible.

MARXISM AND THE REVOLUTIONARY LEFT

In Western and Central Europe

Marxism (see p. 14) was a revolutionary political theory, which provided a structure for inevitable change from **feudalism** to **capitalism** to **Socialism**. By the late nineteenth century it was the dominant revolutionary theory in Western and Central Europe, and gaining ground in Russia. In Germany the Social Democratic Party (SDP) was a Marxist party, but it was far from revolutionary. Growing prosperity had shown that Marx's prediction that industrialization would only impoverish the workers and lead to revolution was clearly inaccurate. In Germany the Social Democrat Eduard Bernstein had already drawn the conclusion

Feudalism
The social system in medieval Europe whereby land was held by a vassal from a superior in exchange for military allegiance and other duties.

Capitalism
An economic system in which the production of goods and their distribution depend on the investment of private capital (money) with a view to making a profit.

Socialism
The belief that the community as a whole, rather than individuals, should control the means of production, the exchange of goods and banking.

that Socialism could be achieved peacefully by using the democratic process. The SPD had become an uneasy alliance between moderates or 'revisionists' and radicals, who still clung to the idea of a revolutionary struggle. These two contradictory views were partly reconciled by the Erfurt Programme of 1891, which combined an orthodox Marxist criticism of society with a set of moderate demands, that did not have to be implemented by a revolution. The moderates were greatly strengthened by the trade union wing of the party, which was much more interested in using its power to achieve concrete reforms rather than indulging in what it saw as the futile gesture of a general strike. This policy became known as economism.

The decline of Socialism as a revolutionary force as a consequence of the rise of economism led to a radical revision of Marxism in both France and Italy. In France Georges Sorel (1847–1922), a retired engineer, began to develop the idea of **syndicalism**. He argued that socialism would have to be radically restructured if it were to regain its revolutionary momentum:

Syndicalism
A movement aimed at securing the ownership of industries by the workers through direct action by strikes.

- It must accept for the time being capitalism, the development of which would lead to growing tensions between the workers and employers.
- Unlike the dry 'materialism' of Marxism, it must develop a new culture and psychology that stressed the importance of idealism and myth as a way of inspiring the workers.
- Liberal democracy must be completely rejected, and direct action, such as a general strike, should be used to achieve change and revolution.
- Finally, in his seminal *Réflexions sur la violence* (1908), Sorel stressed the importance of violence in creating commitment to a cause and unity in a political movement. He regarded violence not just as an unfortunate necessity, but something that was good in itself and which would create a revolutionary consciousness.

By the early 1900s revolutionary syndicalism had begun to take root in Italy. As it became clear after the strikes of 1907–8 that the workers alone could not achieve revolution, the Italian Syndicalists began to develop the theory of revolutionary national socialism. Already by 1902 this synthesis of nationalism and socialism began to have some impact on Mussolini, who at times even called himself a Syndicalist, although he could still bitterly attack nationalism (see p. 91).

In Russia

In nineteenth-century Russia Marxism was never as influential as it was in Western and Central Europe. This was partly because of the backwardness of the economy, the repressive nature of the state and competition from the Russian Populist revolutionary tradition. Essentially the Populists hoped that the bourgeois stage of the revolution that was so essential for Karl Marx could be avoided and that Russia would develop its own form of Socialism based on the **village commune**. However, after the famine and cholera epidemic in 1891–2, which showed up with brutal clarity the inability of the tsarist state to cope with an emergency, the Marxist argument that Russia needed more of modern capitalism began to appeal strongly to the intelligentsia. Grigorii Plekhanov, a Marxist theoretician, in a series of influential books popularized a version of Marxism, and argued that the unique situation in Russia would not hasten the outbreak of revolution. Russia would first of all have to undergo, as in Germany and Britain, industrialization and a bourgeois revolution. Acting on this advice, a group of Marxist intellectuals, which included Lenin, formed the St Petersburg Union of Struggle to assist the workers in their fight against the employers and to develop an understanding of the wider class struggle. The Union of Struggle was quickly broken up by the authorities and most of its members, including Lenin, were sent to Siberia.

Village commune
Apportioned state taxes, selected the number of conscripts for the army and apportioned the land that had been made available for the peasantry when the serfs were emancipated in 1861.

Marxism

Karl Marx (1818–83) was a German philosopher of Jewish extraction. The theoretical and philosophical system he constructed was the intellectual basis of the Leninist and Stalinist ideologies (see Chapters 2 and 10). The key elements of Marxism are:

- 'Historical materialism': Marx was convinced that the economic system of a country determined its political and social structures. To him, religion simply reflected the current economic realities.

- Marx, being a student of the German philosopher, Georg Wilhelm Hegel (1770–1831), also believed in 'historical inevitability', which would eventually lead to Communism. In practice this meant that historical change was the inevitable result of economic inequalities, which produced class hatred.
- Consequently, Marx was convinced that capitalism would inevitably be overthrown by the workers or 'proletariat'. Initially they would create a 'dictatorship of the proletariat' in order to defend the revolution from a backlash from the dispossessed capitalists and bourgeoisie, but once the revolution was safe the new proletariat state would simply begin to 'wither away' and be replaced by a communist society where economic production would be subordinated to human needs. Marx idealistically believed that once this stage was achieved, crime, envy and rivalry would become things of the past. For him the 'state' was merely the means by which one dominant class suppressed the inferior classes.

Like the Syndicalists, Lenin and his colleagues were horrified by the popularity of Bernstein's revisionism and the 'economism' of the German trade unions, and were determined to prevent similar developments in the Russian labour movement. In a pamphlet, *What Is To Be Done*, Lenin urged the setting up of a centrally controlled party which would be able to stop the drift towards compromise politics (see Document 4). These ideas on party organization did not come from Marx, but from the Russian revolutionary tradition, as exemplified by **The People's Will**, which, to survive persecution, became a centrally organized party of professional revolutionaries.

The People's Will
Formed in 1879; two years later assassinated Tsar Alexander II.

In 1903 Lenin's colleagues, Plekhanov and Martov, began to see that Lenin's ideas would turn a social democratic party into an elite autocratic force, which would become a caricature of the tsarist state. When the constitution of the Russian Social Democratic Workers' Party was debated at a Congress in Brussels later that year, this issue was bitterly divisive. Initially Lenin was defeated but then, thanks to withdrawal of a small number of 'economists'and *Bund* members, he was able to claim majority support. From now on he called his group the *Bolsheviki*, or majority, while his opponents were labelled the minority, or *Menschiviki*. The Congress did, however, manage to agree on a minimum party programme:

Bund
The organization of Jewish workers.

- the abolition of the monarchy and the creation of a democratic republic
- a single chamber legislature elected on a universal franchise
- extensive local self-government and self-determination for the minority peoples
- the creation of a people's militia to replace the army
- progressive income and inheritance taxes
- complete legal equality for the peasants and the return to them of the land they had lost to the gentry at the time of the emancipation of the serfs in 1861.

Neither the Bolsheviks nor the Mensheviks played an important part in the revolts in Russia of 1905. Their rivals, the Socialist Revolutionaries, were far more successful in mobilizing the peasants by promising to socialize the land and hand it over to the peasant communes. The Tsar managed to divide his enemies with the offer of an elected *Duma*, or parliament, and restore some semblance of his authority by 1907. To escape arrest, Lenin and the leading Social Democrats and Socialist Revolutionaries had to go into exile. Significantly, for the future he also drew the conclusion that the Bolsheviks needed to appeal to the peasantry by promising to seize the land from the gentry and redistribute it to them.

On paper Lenin had created a tightly centralized party, but historians now question whether the Bolsheviks between 1905 and 1917 were really such a united group. Stephen Cohen, for instance, has argued that Bolshevism was not Leninism but a 'diverse group led by dissimilar men and women'.[4] Much to Lenin's disgust, the writings of Sorel were read by many of the Bolsheviks. Alexander Bogdanov, a contemporary and rival of Lenin, for instance, saw Socialism not so much as a product of Marxism, but as 'a useful myth that organized mass experience'.[5]

THE IMPACT OF THE FIRST WORLD WAR

Before 1914 Bolshevism was a force in Russian revolutionary politics, while the ideology of Fascism could already be discerned. It was, however, the Great War of 1914–18 that was to create the environment in which both these ideologies could flourish. The pressures each belligerent nation, particularly the less developed states of Russia, Austria Hungary and Italy, faced were enormous and potentially destabilizing:

- Heavy industry had to be rapidly expanded to provide munitions, which led to economic dislocation and in the less developed industrial states the rapid expansion of an industrial proletariat.
- The war made necessary state intervention in industry and created corporatist economies in the belligerent states.
- Financing the rapidly expanding war economy led to inflation that impoverished the middle classes.
- Each side attempted to destabilize the home fronts of its enemies by blockade. This led to increasing worries about food shortages in all the belligerent nations.
- After initial unity the war provoked bitter divisions, which in the defeated nations led to revolution.
- The war encouraged the creation of more authoritarian regimes and an aggressive nationalism.
- On the front it also produced the unique 'trench experience': in the trenches millions of men developed 'a new collective consciousness of a separate society, a warrior group partially isolated from the rest of the nation and from normal experiences'.[6]

In broad outline these factors affected all the participants in the war, but the severity of the impact varied from state to state. Ultimately it became clear that military defeat on the field of battle would lead to revolution at home. Defeat, or at least – in the case of Italy – disappointment in victory, were to be important contributory factors to the emergence of the dictatorships in inter-war Europe.

Russia

Of all the belligerent great powers Russia was the most vulnerable to the strains that total war would bring. The tsarist regime had already been deeply shaken by the revolution of 1905, and was only able to survive by making considerable political concessions, which involved the election of a *Duma* on a relatively wide franchise. Possibly, if these concessions had been granted in good faith, the regime might have survived the strains of industrialization and modernization, but Tsar Nicholas was intent on restoring his power and by 1914 there was, in Hans Rogger's words, 'remarkably wide agreement that Russia in 1914 was in the throes of an internal crisis which might assume revolutionary proportions'[7] (see Document 5).

Between 1914 and 1917 Russia was confronted with ever-deepening economic, military and political crises. Militarily, Russian attempts to advance into Germany and Hungary had met with defeat, and by 1916 Russian casualties were the highest of any of the belligerent states. Industry expanded spectacularly, but this success was achieved at a heavy financial and social cost. It was paid for by inflating the currency, which in turn ensured that prices rose over 300 per cent between August 1914 and December 1916. This hit the urban population and particularly the greatly expanded factory workforce. The economic situation was made worse by the acute grain shortage, which was caused partly by the failure of the transport system to supply both the front and the towns, and the growing unwillingness of the peasantry to sell their produce for money that was rapidly losing its value.

With competent leadership, Russia's economic and military problems might have been sorted out. In August 1915 it looked briefly as if the Tsar was about to appoint effective ministers and cooperate with the *Duma*, but over the following year it became clear that his hostility to the *Duma* was unabated. He sacked Polivanov, who was an efficient War Minister, and refused to appoint men like **Prince Lvov**, who were capable of organizing the home front. By the autumn of 1916 with the collapse of General Brussilov's offensive against Austria–Hungary, the Russian liberals and increasingly members of the court and the armed forces were convinced that the Tsar would have to abdicate and a more representative government be appointed. Within the *Duma* the socialists were openly calling for revolution.

**Prince G.E. Lvov
(1861–1925)**
Aristocrat and great landowner; was to become the first Prime Minister of the Provisional Government in March 1917.

Austria–Hungary

Austria–Hungary did not lack the industrial base to wage war, but the multinational nature of the empire, which was composed of a mosaic of ethnic groups, made it uniquely unsuitable for fighting a war that inevitably intensified nationalist passions. The Hungarian and Germans, as the two dominant races, presided over the empire's economic and military mobilization, which in turn intensified friction with the other races, such as the Czechs and South Slavs. Increasingly, too, Austria–Hungary became a German satellite, as its armies had to depend more and more on German leadership and organization. As a result of the Allied blockade of Central Europe and the poor transport system, food shortages became acute, and opposition increasingly found expression in demands by the larger ethnic groups within the empire for independence. Once they gained the support of the Western Allies, Austria–Hungary was doomed.

Germany

In Germany the growth of the Social Democratic Party, which in 1912 became the largest party in the *Reichstag*, threatened the fragile constitutional compromise that Bismarck had created in 1871 as the foundation of the new united Germany. This had managed to preserve the powers of the Prussian Crown while appeasing the Liberals with constitutional concessions and an elected parliament. The rise of the SPD met with determined opposition from the right, which was not ready to make any political concessions to the labour movement. By 1914 the deadlock between the conservative forces in Germany and Prussia, and the SPD, had created a serious political crisis, which members of the Kaiser's court believed could only be solved by a military coup against the *Reichstag* (see Document 6).

Left and right

The terms 'left' and 'right' are used frequently by historians, and are a way of describing basic attitudes and beliefs. They go back to the first session of the French Estates-General in 1789 and refer to where particular groups of representatives sat. Broadly speaking, the difference between the values of right and left can be summed up as follows:

Left-wing ideologies value:

- the slogans of the French revolution: liberty, equality and fraternity
- human rights and a general belief in reform and progress
- peace and internationalism.

Right-wing supporters, on the other hand, put more emphasis on:

- authority, social hierarchy or class, tradition and order
- duties rather than rights
- reaction or opposition to reform
- nationalism.

The weakness of German liberalism and the growing strength of nationalism and authoritarianism in Germany before 1914 has led to the argument that Germany was pursuing a *Sonderweg* or special way that would inevitably lead to Nazism. Yet in many ways Germany was an enlightened country with an exemplary welfare system, a strong economy, a large middle class and an increasingly well-educated and moderate working class. It is looking at history backwards to assume that Germany was already locked into a path that would lead inexorably to dictatorship.

However, it is true to say that the First World War did make the establishment of a liberal–democratic consensus more difficult to achieve. Wolfgang Mommsen argues, for instance, that 'the seedbed of extremist nationalism and the eventual rise to power of the National Socialists was a set of social and economic factors that had their origins in the First World War.'[8] It left behind a legacy of economic hardship and political divisions that made it almost impossible for the subsequent democratic Weimar Republic to hold the loyalties of the majority of the population. The war polarized society into winners and losers: apart from the owners of the war industries – about 120,000 people – who made immense fortunes, those who gained most were the skilled workers in the war industries, while the middle classes were the greatest losers. Civil servants, **white-collar workers**, small businessmen and craftsmen all saw their status eroded, and their savings – which many had invested in war loans – destroyed. As most of the war expenditure had been financed by loans, bonds and the printing of money, inflation gathered pace. Prices rose by 250 per cent during the war, which was only a taste of what was to come. The war bonds into which many patriotic Germans had poured their savings were to be valueless by 1923.

White-collar workers
Office workers, as contrasted to factory workers or blue-collar workers.

Military deadlock and food shortages caused by the British blockade increasingly polarized German society into those who wanted peace, and those who were determined to fight on until victory. The appointment of **Hindenburg** as Supreme Commander on the western front and **Ludendorff** as his Chief of Staff in 1916 resulted, a year later, in the creation of a puppet regime, which was to set a precedent for further intervention in German politics by the High Command. The million-strong Fatherland Party, the formation of which was inspired by Ludendorff in the autumn of 1917 to oppose the demand for a negotiated peace, had some potential Fascist traits in that it was recruited mainly from the *Mittelstand* (lower middle classes) and was an extra parliamentary movement.

Italy

In Italy the political system, the *transformismo*, which, after the completion of unification in 1870 united or transformed the leading bourgeois groups of the centre and right into a ruling coalition, was beginning to break down when confronted by the growing strength of socialism. **Giovanni Giolitti** attempted, by increasing the franchise, legalizing strikes and passing a number of social reforms to integrate the workers into the state. He met with some limited success in the north but was unable to appease the impoverished peasantry in the south. The divisions in Italian society were made worse by the outbreak of a series of bitter strikes between 1912 and 1914, both in industry and agriculture. In June 1914 these culminated in what amounted to open rebellion against the government, when large parts of central Italy were taken over by revolutionary Socialists and Syndicalists. Only the intervention of the army restored order.

Paul Corner argues that by 1914 the Italian state faced 'a crisis of legitimacy',[9] as parliamentary government was increasingly seen as corrupt and ineffectual, and incapable of unifying Italy. Italian intellectuals on both the Right and Left were convinced that the *Risorgimento*, the unification of Italy 1859–61, had been carried out by a small minority aided by the French and Prussians and had failed miserably to create a popular regime with which the Italian people could identify.

Italy joined the war only in May 1915 after the Treaty of London had been secretly negotiated with Britain and France.

Field Marshal Paul von Hindenburg (1847–1934)
Defeated the Russians at Tannenberg in 1914 and was Supreme Commander of the Western front, 1916–18. He was elected President of the Weimar Republic in 1925.

General Erich von Ludendorff (1865–1937)
Had been Hindenburg's Chief of Staff during the First World War. His organizational skills complemented Hindenburg's enormous popularity and together they were a major political force. He took part in the Munich putsch and was a Nazi *Reichstag* deputy from 1924 to 1928.

Giovanni Giolitti (1842–1928)
Formed four government before 1914 and was Prime Minister again, June 1920–June 1921.

The war was supported by an alliance of revolutionary Syndicalists, break-away Socialists led by Mussolini, Conservatives, Nationalists and left-wing Liberals. The Syndicalists and Mussolini hoped that war would lead to revolution, while the Conservatives and Liberals believed that it would create a new unity, in which class conflicts would be subordinated to the nation state. In fact the war polarized political opinion, as it did in no other allied state. Militarily the war quickly became a stalemate with ever-increasing casualties, and by 1916 there were frequent outbreaks of mutinies amongst the front-line troops. Accelerated industrialization led to a large increase in the proletariat who were subjected to semi-military discipline in the factories. Hours of work were increased and strikes made illegal. The situation was made worse by rapidly increasing inflation and severe food shortages. In Turin in August 1917 a workers' demonstration against the war and the food shortages was broken up by the army after some 50 people were killed.

In October 1917 the Italian army was routed at Caporetto by Austrian and German forces, and the front had to be stabilized with the help of British and French troops. The defeat only served to polarize the situation further: the moderates who had favoured intervention moved closer to the views of the extreme Nationalists and bitterly attacked the Socialists as traitors. In turn these attacks confirmed the Socialists' hostility to the existing state, the war coalition and big business.

ASSESSMENT

What enabled Fascism to become a mass political movement was the First World war, which George Kennan called '*the* great seminal catastrophe' of the twentieth century.[10] Economic impoverishment, a sense of betrayed nationalism and the fear of revolution created the potential for mass Fascist movements. In Italy Mussolini, the leader of the new Fascist party, was able to exploit these emotions to gain power in 1922. In Germany, where the Left and trade unions were stronger, it took a second great crisis – the World Depression – before that potential was realized.

The collapse of the Austro-Hungarian Empire, the defeat first of Russia by Germany and then of Germany by the Western

Allies, created a vacuum, which was filled by the formation of a series of small weak successor states. These for the most part still lacked an industrial infrastructure and their cohesion was threatened by ethnic rivalries. With the exception of Czechoslovakia, all of these states had became dictatorships by the 1930s. Their existence was again a direct consequence of the First World War.

In Russia, on the other hand, a revolution was already likely by 1914, but it is perhaps difficult to predict what form it would take. The 'dress rehearsal' of 1905 was certainly some guide, but it was, again, the war that acted as a catalyst to the revolutions of 1917. Without the war it seems unlikely that the Bolsheviks would have been able to seize power.

DOCUMENT 1

Futurism in Italy

The Futurist movement, which was shaped by Filippo Marienetti, broke radically with the traditional art of the past and tried to reflect the new industrial twentieth century. It welcomed the industrializing of Italy and believed that this new 'third Italy' (coming after the Roman Empire and the Renaissance) should be led by an elite of young geniuses who would carve out a new Italian empire. In 1909 the Futurist manifesto declared:

1 We want to sing the love of danger, the habit of energy and rashness.
2 The essential elements of our poetry will be courage, audacity and revolt.
3 ... we want to exalt movements of aggression, feverish sleeplessness, the forced march, the perilous leap, the slap and blow with the fist ...
9 We want to glorify war – the only cure in the world – and militarism, patriotism, the destructive gesture of the anarchists, the beautiful ideas which kill and contempt for women.
10 We want to demolish museums and libraries, fight morality, feminism and all opportunist and utilitarian cowardice.

Source: S.G. Payne, *A History of Fascism, 1914–45*, London, Routledge, 1995, p. 64.

▶

DOCUMENT 2

Julius Langbehn's anti-Semitism

In his influential book, Rembrandt als Erzieher, *Langbehn stressed that:*

The modern Jew has no religion, no character, no home, no children. He is a piece of humanity that has become sour ... The aspiration of present-day Jews for spiritual and material domination evokes a simple phrase: Germany for the Germans. A Jew can no more become a German than a plum can turn into an apple ... Now that the Jews are the oppressors and the enemies of all German being [even] **Lessing** would fight them to death.

Source: F. Stern, *The Politics of Cultural Despair: A Study in the Rise of the Germanic Ideology*, Berkeley, University of California Press, Berkeley, 1974, p. 141.

DOCUMENT 3

The limited appeal of early Fascism

The historian Zeev Sternhill observed that:

What early National–Socialism lacked was the social backdrop which would transform it into a political force; there were as yet no huge numbers of unemployed and frightened petty bourgeois, and no impoverished middle classes; it was fully possessed, however, of a framework of ideas no less developed than those of any other contemporary political movement.

Source: Z. Sternhill, 'Fascist ideology' in W. Laquer, ed., *Fascism: A Reader's Guide*, Harmondsworth, Penguin, 1979, p. 341.

DOCUMENT 4

Early Leninism

In a Letter to a Comrade *Lenin explains his plans for the creation of new revolutionary party:*

The leadership of the movement must be in the hands of a minimum number of homogeneous groups as possible, composed of tried and experienced professional revolutionaries. Participation in the movement must be extended to a maximum number of as diverse and heterogeneous groups as possible, consisting of people

Gotthold Lessing (1729–80)
German poet and playwright, who, as a man of the eighteenth-century Enlightenment, urged the toleration of other religions, particularly Judaism.

from the most varied strata of the proletariat (and of other classes).

Source: V.I. Lenin, *What Is To Be Done* (introduction by S.V. Utechin), Oxford, Oxford University Press, 1963, p. 39.

DOCUMENT 5

The dangers of war for the tsarist regime

The former Minister of the Interior, P.N. Durnovo, perceptively warned the Tsar in February 1914 of the threat that a war would present to the stability of Russia:

The trouble will start with the blaming of the Government for all disasters. In the legislative institutions a bitter campaign against the Government will begin, followed by revolutionary agitation throughout the country, with Socialist slogans, capable of arousing and rallying the masses beginning with the division of the land and succeeded by a division of all valuables and property. The defeated army, having lost its dependable men and carried away by the tide of primitive peasant desire for land, will find itself too demoralized to serve as a bulwark of law and order. The legislative institutions and the intellectual opposition parties, lacking real authority in the eyes of the people, will be powerless to stem the popular tide, aroused by themselves, and Russia will be flung into hopeless anarchy, the issue of which cannot be foreseen.

Source: O. Figes, *A People's Tragedy. The Russian Revolution, 1891–1924*, London, Pimlico, 2nd ed. 1997, p. 250.

DOCUMENT 6

The advantages of a victorious war for Germany

In 1909 the prestige of the German Emperor was at a very low ebb after the unguarded and farcical interview he gave to the Daily Telegraph. *The Russian Ambassador described the reaction of the army and the conservatives to this:*

The war party regards war as the only means to restore the prestige of the monarchical power, which has been shaken in the eyes of the masses. The mood of military circles is nourished by the conviction that the present superiority of the army promises

Germany the greatest chance of success ... a victorious war could at least for an initial period, repel the radical currents among the people pressing for a change of the Prussian as well as the Reich constitution in a more liberal direction. These are, in general outline, the symptoms of the German domestic situation which could help to explain the causes of the current military preparations.

Source: V.R. Berghahn, *Germany and the Approach of War in 1914*, London, Macmillan, 1973, p. 81.

NOTES

1 S.G. Payne, *A History of Fascism, 1914–45*, London, Routledge, 1995, p. 3.

2 Ibid., p. 7.

3 Z. Sternhill, 'Fascist ideology' in W. Laqueur, ed., *Fascism: A Reader's Guide*, Harmondsworth, Penguin, 1979, p. 340.

4 S. Cohen, quoted in R. Williams, 'The Bolsheviks' in A. Geifman, ed., *Russia under the Last Tsar*, Oxford, Blackwell, 1999, p. 38.

5 Ibid., p. 39.

6 Payne, *History of Fascism*, p. 73.

7 Hans Rogger, 'Russia in 1914', *Journal of Contemporary History*, vol. 1, no. 4, 1966, p. 95.

8 W. Mommsen, *Imperial Germany*, London, Edward Arnold, 1995, p. 232.

9 P. Corner, 'State and society, 1901–1922' in A. Lyttelton, ed., *Liberal and Fascist Italy*, Oxford, Oxford University Press, 2002, p. 29.

10 Quoted in R. Chickering, *Imperial Germany and the Great War*, Cambridge, Cambridge University Press, 1998, p. 192.

PART TWO

THE LEGACY OF WAR
AND PARTIAL
RECOVERY

CHAPTER 2

The victory of Leninism in Russia, 1917–27

TIMELINE

1917 18 February	Strike begins at the Putilov factory
23 February	Workers demonstrate in Petrograd
26 February	*Duma* dissolved, but unofficial *Duma* Committe set up
	Petrograd Soviet established
1 March	Order No. 1 issued by the Petrograd Soviet
2 March	Nicholas II abdicates and Provisional Government created
3 April	Lenin returns to Petrograd
4 April	Lenin announces April Theses
4 May	Trotsky returns to Petrograd
5 May	Formation of first coalition government
3–14 June	First All Russian Congress of Workers' and Soldiers' Soviets
18 June	The Galician offensive begins
3–5 July	The July disturbances
6 July	Lenin flees to Finland
7 July	Kerensky government formed
26–30 August	The Kornilov Affair
1 September	Republic proclaimed
9 September	Bolshevik majority in the Petrograd Soviet
15 September	Lenin's plans for an uprising rejected by Bolshevik Central Committee
7 October	Lenin returns to Petrograd in disguise
12 October	Petrograd Soviet establishes the Military Revolutionary Committee
12 November	Elections to Constituent Assembly
7 December	Establishment of *Cheka*

1918 5–6 January	Constituent Assembly meets and is dissolved by the Bolsheviks
15 January	Red Army formed
1/14 February	Adoption of the Gregorian calendar (13 days in advance of the Russian or Julian calendar)
3 March	Treaty of Brest–Litovsk
28 June	Nationalization of large industries
6 July	Rebellion by left-wing SRs
30 August	Assassination attempt on Lenin
11 November	Germans sign armistice with the Western Powers
1919 13 March	Kolchak launches offensive towards the Volga
18–23 March	Eighth Party Congress: decision to disband the *Kombedy*
19 May	Denikin launches offensive on South-Eastern front
9 June	Kolchak in full retreat: Ufa retaken by Reds
14 October	Denikin occupies Orel
20 October	Red Army retakes Orel and retreat of Denikin's forces begins
1920 27 March	Novorossisk falls to Reds
6 June	Wrangel moves into Crimea
15 August	Battle of Warsaw
14 November	Wrangel evacuates Crimea
1921 1–18 March	Kronstadt revolt
8 March	NEP introduced
1922 3 April	Stalin elected General Secretary
December	Formation of the Union of Soviet Socialist Republics (USSR)
1923 4 January	Lenin in a postscript to his Testament recommends the removal of Stalin from all positions of power
15 December	Stalin opens a campaign in *Pravda* against Trotsky
1924 21 January	Lenin dies in Gorki
1926 July	Emergence of the United Opposition – Trotsky, Kamenev and Zinoviev
1927 November	Expulsion of Trotsky, Kamenev and Zinoviev from the party

INTRODUCTION

The Russian Revolution was a product of the First World War and was one of the seismic upheavals that were to shape world history in the twentieth century. The Bolshevik regime was the first of the new twentieth-century dictatorships. Despite the Marxist belief in the relative unimportance of the individual as a factor in history, a charismatic dictatorship under Lenin emerged as early as 1918. While in practice eliminating democracy, the Bolshevik dictators claimed that they were carrying out the will of the people. Thus they set precedents, which both the German and Italian dictatorships were to follow.

THE KEY ISSUES IN THIS CHAPTER ARE:

- The outbreak of the February Revolution.
- The collapse of the Provisional Government and the takeover of power by the Bolsheviks.
- The initial survival of the Bolsheviks and the significance of the Treaty of Brest–Litovsk.
- War Communism and the social revolution.
- The NEP and its consequences.
- Stalin's emergence as Lenin's successor.
- Bolshevik Russia's survival in a hostile world.

THE FEBRUARY AND OCTOBER REVOLUTIONS

The February Revolution

The American historian, William Chamberlain, described the February Revolution as one of 'the most leaderless, spontaneous, anonymous revolutions of all time'.[1] There is some truth in this observation, as there was no dominating figure like Lenin, but there were many activists in the factories and the army. Some of these were Bolsheviks. Others, however, were, as David Longley has observed, non-party-people 'who simply rose to the occasion'.[2] The key events that were to lead to the February Revolution took place in Petrograd between 23 February and 4 March 1917:

- On 23 February a demonstration took place in **Petrograd** to celebrate International Women's Day. This was joined both by women textile workers, who had struck in protest against the lack of bread, and by employees from the militant state-owned Putilov works, where the Bolsheviks had a considerable influence. By the evening, some 100,000 workers had already come out on strike.

Petrograd
The original German name of St Petersburg was russified and changed to Petrograd in 1914. In 1924 it became Leningrad. In 1991, with the collapse of the Soviet Union, the name changed back to St Petersburg.

- Over the next two days the demonstrations escalated into a general strike and demands were made not just for food, but also for an end to the war and the overthrow of the monarchy.
- On 26 February the Tsar prorogued the *Duma*, although an unofficial committee remained illegally in session. On the streets outside a turning point was reached when troops, while trying to restore order, killed 50 demonstrators.
- By the following morning the troops of the Petrograd garrison began to mutiny and the disorders of the previous days escalated into revolution. The Petrograd Soviet was set up on the initiative of a small number of Menshevik intellectuals (see Document 1).
- On 2 March the Provisional Government, headed by Prince Lvov, was formed from the *Duma* Committee. The first decision it made concerned the future of the monarchy. The generals were adamant that Tsar Nicholas would have to abdicate. Initially, Nicholas wanted to make way for his brother, but it soon became clear that the mood of the people was hostile to the continuation of the monarchy, regardless of whoever might be the Tsar. The Provisional Government accordingly decided on a republic, although this was not officially announced until September.

The Provisional Government

The immediate consequence of the February Revolution in Petrograd was the complete collapse of the tsarist state. The Crown had been the authority, which had held together the state. Its removal led to its collapse and the creation of a vacuum, which the Provisional Government unsuccessfully struggled to fill. Throughout Russia the political structure of the tsarist state was spontaneously dismantled by the people: the police were arrested, prisoners liberated and the garrisons behind the front dismissed their officers.

The main problem now was how was this vacuum to be filled and a consensus forged that would support the institutional reconstruction of a new Russian state. Where did power now lie? There were two new institutions that could claim it: the Provisional Government, which was composed of leading members of the Liberal parties and one Democratic Socialist, **Alexander Kerensky**; and the **Petrograd Soviet**. The latter saw itself primarily as a guarantee that the Provisional Government did not betray the revolution. As early as 1 March, it had effectively gained control of the army through the announcement of Order No. 1, which set up soldiers' committees in the army with instructions to obey the Provisional Government as long as its orders did not contradict those of the Soviet.

The contradictions inherent in this situation became clear in April when it emerged that **Miliukov**, the Foreign Minister, still supported the war aims of the tsarist regime. The Soviet demanded an immediate revision of his policy, and when demonstrations again broke out in Petrograd, it vetoed an order by the military commander of the city garrison, **General Kornilov**, to defend the government. Miliukov and the **Kadet Party** responded by demanding the recognition of the government's monopoly of power and the end to 'anarchy'. Miliukov and **Guchkov**, the War Minister, were forced to resign. In an attempt to avoid a repetition of such a clash, Prince Lvov invited the leading Menshevik leaders in the Soviet to join the government. They accepted this, hoping to strengthen a moderate liberal government against the perceived danger of a right-wing backlash.

The Soviet and the Provisional Government were now yoked together, but this failed to create the basis for the democratic consolidation of the Russian state, as throughout the summer and early autumn of 1917 the economic, military and social situation steadily deteriorated.

After an unsuccessful attempt to bring about peace by summoning an international socialist conference at Stockholm, the Provisional Government agreed to launch an offensive in Galicia in June, which failed disastrously and resulted in the collapse of the Russian front, mutiny and mass desertion. As Orlando Figes observed, 'more than anything else, the summer offensive swung the soldiers to the Bolsheviks'.[3] The continuation of the war placed major strains on the economy, which brought it to a state of near collapse by October 1917. The railway system had virtually collapsed, vital raw materials were not reaching the factories and grain was not being delivered to the towns. To finance the war, money continued to be printed in ever-increasing quantities, which led to hyper-inflation and massive rises in the

Alexander Kerensky (1881–1970)
Leader of the *Trudoviki* (Democratic Socialists). He was the only political leader to be a member of both the Provisional Government and the Petrograd Soviet. He was Minister of Justice in March, Minister of War in May and Prime Minister from July to October 1917.

The Petrograd Soviet of Workers' Deputies
Set up spontaneously by factory workers. Socialist Revolutionaries, Mensheviks and Bolsheviks were all represented on it. Initially it had no ambition to act as a government but its influence grew as an increasing number of soldiers and workers acknowledged its authority and looked to it to take the initiative.

Pavel Miliukov (1859–1943)
Historian and leader of the Kadet Party. He was Foreign Minister March–May 1917 and emigrated to the West in 1921.

General Lavr Kornilov (1970–1918)
Appointed Commander-in-Chief by Kerensky in July 1917, and then was the first leader of the counter-revoltionary volunteer army against the Bolsheviks in 1918.

**Alexander Guchkov
(1862–1936)**
Leader of the moderate liberal Octobrist party, and Minister of War and Naval Affairs, March–May 1917.

Kadet Party
The Constitutional Democratic Party, formed in autumn 1905.

price of food, while workers' wages lagged far behind (see Document 5).

The land policy of the Provisional Government was 'suicidal'[4] and played into the hands of the Bolsheviks. Despite both the wishes of the Socialist Revolutionaries (SRs) and the Mensheviks, the Kadets used their majority on the Land Committee to block any immediate action. By insisting that the distribution of land to the peasantry could only be carried out once an elected constituent assembly had passed the necessary legislation, the government alienated the peasantry, who effectively seized the land themselves. As Lenin caustically observed, to the peasants, it seemed as if the government's message was: 'Wait until the Constituent Assembly. Wait until the end of the war for the Constituent Assembly. Wait until total victory for the end of the war.'[5]

The Kornilov coup

By July 1917 there was a growing power vacuum in Russia. The Provisional Government had failed to create a consensus and lay the foundations for a new state. Power had now filtered down to the peasant committees and the factory soviets, which were intent on keeping it. The fall of the Provisional Government was only a matter of time, but would it be an authoritarian government of the left or right that would replace it?

On 7 July Prince Lvov resigned and handed over power to Kerensky. The new Prime Minister had many of the qualities necessary for a revolutionary leader. He was a far better speaker than Lenin and could catch the mood of the crowds, as Hitler was able to over a decade later. Once he became War Minister in June, he dressed himself in a semi-military uniform, which was to set a precedent for Stalin later, and cultivated the Napoleonic pose. By many he was seen as the only strong personality around and many of the peasants saw him as the new Tsar. He formed what he called 'the government of salvation of the revolution', but in reality he had little scope for political manoeuvre. Accurately describing his situation, he observed: 'If I move to the left, I have an army without a general staff, and if I move to the right I have a general without an army.'[6]

The right-wing Kadets, business leaders and the officer corps, increasingly resenting the growing power of the soviets and the granting of autonomy to the nationalities within the empire, began to call for a more authoritarian regime that could restore order, even if this meant civil war. The only figure who appeared to be capable of doing this was General Kornilov, who shortly after his appointment as Commander-in-Chief of the Russian forces in July 1917 had demanded the imposition of martial law throughout Russia, the banning of strikes and workers' meetings, as well as compulsory output quotas. His supporters urged him to seize power, but, contrary to the version spread by Kerensky in his own memoirs, Kornilov was primarily aiming to save the Provisional Government by pressurizing Kerensky into creating a dictatorship in which he was ready to serve.

Kerensky initially negotiated with Kornilov, but he had no intention of sharing power with him. Then, without consulting the Cabinet, he sacked him from his position as Commander-in-Chief on 27 August. In retaliation Kornilov, convinced that the Provisional Government was under threat from the Bolsheviks, ordered his troops to occupy Petrograd. Kerensky had to depend on the military organization of the Bolsheviks, who were able to mobilize the mass of the workers and peasants in and around the city in defence of the government. The attempted 'coup' rapidly collapsed. When Kornilov's troops were reassured that the Provisional Government was in no danger, they deserted in large quantities to the Bolsheviks.

The failure of the coup left Kerensky in a situation where both Left and Right viewed him as a traitor. Kornilov and some 30 other officers were imprisoned in the Bykhov monastery, where they drew up plans for the creation of the Volunteer Army, which was to form the nucleus of the anti-Bolshevik White forces in the Civil War (see pp. 45–53). On the Left, Kerensky was equally distrusted, as many workers and soldiers were convinced that he had been deeply involved in the Kornilov incident and that neither an end to the war nor real social change could ever be achieved by cooperating with the bourgeoisie.

Kerensky created first of all a temporary five-man directory in early September, and two weeks later managed to negotiate a second coalition government with the Kadets, right-wing Mensheviks and SRs, but its decrees were ignored, and a dangerous power vacuum opened up at the centre of Russian politics. Kerensky lost all backing from Russia's Western allies, and increasingly his former supporters on the Right became resigned to a Bolshevik takeover, believing that it would be short-lived and plunge Russia into such chaos that only a military dictatorship would be able to restore order.

Lenin and the Bolshevik Party

The failure of the Provisional Government to grapple successfully with the problems facing Russia played into the hands of Lenin and the Bolsheviks. Both the Menscheviks and the SRs had compromised themselves by joining the coalition. This provided an increasingly viable opportunity for the Bolsheviks to seize power. In retrospect the Bolshevik seizure of power and dictatorship seem inevitable. It has been argued that if Lenin and the Bolsheviks had not existed, they would have had to be invented.[7] Yet was a Leninist dictatorship really the only option left for the consolidation of the Russian state?

Vladimir Ilyich Lenin (1870–1924)

Figure 2.1 Lenin
Source: Getty Images/AFP

Lenin's family name was Ulyanov. Lenin (see Figure 2.1) was born at Simbirsk as the son of a school inspector. The execution of his elder brother for his involvement in a plot to assassinate the Tsar, when Lenin was 16, had a profound influence on him. He was banned from attending St Petersburg University in person and could only gain his degree through a correspondence course. He read Marx, became involved in Social Democratic politics (see p. 15) and was arrested and sent to Siberia for three years. Between 1900 and 1905 he lived in Germany, Paris, Brussels and London. Thanks to his pamphlets and his editorship of *Ikra* ('The Spark'), he became the leader of the radical wing of the Russian Social Democrats, who in 1903, at the Second Congress of the party, became known as the Bolsheviks (see pp. 15–16). In November 1905 Lenin returned to Russia and for three months helped organize the resistance of the workers in St Petersburg. In early 1906 he once more had to go into exile and in 1914 settled in Geneva. He was only able to return to Russia in April 1917 in a sealed train, as the German General Staff felt that his presence would encourage revolution and mutinies in the Russian army.

During the war Lenin wrote *Imperialism: The Highest stage of Capitalism* in which he maintained that the First World War was essentially a fight for markets between the great powers and that it would end in revolution because the workers and peasants formed the backbone of the new mass armies and would revolt as conditions deteriorated. In November 1917 he summed up his ideas about the European war and the situation in Russia in an unfinished pamphlet, *State and Revolution*. He argued that the new workers' state – the dictatorship of the proletariat – was of necessity an instrument of power and repression, which could only wither away when all opposition had been destroyed.

After the October Revolution Lenin became the head of the Council of People's Commissars. His first policies were to nationalize the banks and carry out a major land redistribution in favour of the peasantry. To save the revolution he insisted on negotiating the Treaty of Brest–Litovsk with Germany in March 1918, which bought him the time to consolidate his party's grip on Russia. Under his leadership the Bolsheviks attempted to bring about a communist social and economic revolution, while fighting a civil war, against the Whites. Although they won the war, such was the growing opposition to War Communism that Lenin was forced to adopt the New Economic Policy in order to remain in power. He suffered from a series of strokes from May 1922 onwards and died on 21 February 1924. Until 1989–90 Marxism–Leninism remained the dominant ideology in the USSR.

Lenin arrived in Petrograd on 3 April. The next day he astonished his colleagues on the Bolshevik Central Committee when he urged the party to abandon the conventional Marxist doctrine that first of all a bourgeois revolution must take place before the socialist stage could be reached (see p. 15). Instead he announced the adoption of the programme he had set out in the April Theses (see Documents 2 and 3). This involved:

- the transfer of all power to the soviets
- the nationalization of land and banking
- the abolition of the police force, the army and bureaucracy
- the immediate end to the war.

Initially the Central Committee rejected the Theses, but three weeks later the All Russian Bolshevik Conference enthusiastically endorsed them. As revisionist historians have stressed, this 'reflected rank and file radicalism as much as Lenin's own authority'.[8] Lenin was successful because he could articulate opinions and demands, which had begun to be formed before his return, and steadily became more popular quite independently of him. The party was, therefore, hardly Lenin's poodle. Local Bolshevik leaders frequently defied him. For instance, until the Mensheviks became too closely associated with the Provisional Government in May, many Bolsheviks refused to break with them.

Neither did Lenin plan the disturbances in Petrograd on 3–5 July. It was the local Bolshevik organizations which orchestrated these demonstrations that demanded the transfer of power to the soviets. Lenin could not make up his mind whether the moment was ripe for the seizure of power, and played no role in them. When they were dispersed by loyalist troops, Lenin fled to Finland to avoid arrest, but the debacle did not permanently damage the Bolsheviks' popularity. Their very distance from the Provisional Government ensured that they were seen as the only effective defenders of the workers and peasants. Their position was further strengthened by the Kornilov incident. It had led to a dramatic deterioration in army discipline as the soldiers suspected their officers of having supported Kornilov, and in the cities the Bolsheviks were increasingly gaining control in the factories and soviets. They won, for example, a majority in the Petrograd Soviet on 9 September and in the Moscow Soviet six days later.

Democratic Conference, 27 September–5 October 1917
This failed because the right-wing Mensheviks and SRs wanted a coalition with the Kadets, the centre wanted a coalition with the bourgeoisie but excluding the Kadets, while the Left wanted a coalition based on the soviets.

The October Revolution

Fleetingly in September there seemed to be a possibility that the three major left-wing parties – the SRs, the Bolsheviks and the Mensheviks – might be able to create a socialist government based on the soviets. Lenin, too, seemed ready to consider at least a temporary left-wing coalition but when the **Democratic Conference,** which was attended by delegates of all three parties, failed to come to any conclusion. Lenin called for an immediate Bolshevik uprising. Here again, recent research has shown that Lenin had hardly turned the party into an instrument to be manipulated at will. Lenin wished to proceed independently of the soviets and seize power before the second National Congress of the Soviets met in October. In fact, his strategy was changed by Trotsky and the Military Revolutionary Committee (MRC), which had been set up by the Petrograd Soviet in the middle of October to plan the defence of the capital both against the Germans and a possible coup by the Provisional Government.

Lev Davidovich Trotsky, 1879–1940

Trotsky (see Figure 2.2) was born a Ukrainian Jew with the family name of Bronstein. In 1898 he was arrested as a revolutionary and sent to Siberia, from where he escaped and fled to join Lenin in London. He was an independent socialist who attempted to reconcile the Bolsheviks and Mensheviks. In 1905 he organized the St Petersburg Soviet. He was again arrested and sent to Siberia but escaped for a second time, and spent the period up to 1917 in exile. In February 1917 he was in New York. He rapidly became a leading figure in the Petrograd Soviet and by October 1917 was its chairman. He was the main organizer of the October Revolution. He became Commissar for War in the Civil War and created the Red Army. After Lenin's death he was excluded from office by Stalin and sent into exile in 1929. In 1940 he was murdered by a Stalinist agent in Mexico.

Figure 2.2 Trotsky
Source: Getty Images/Hulton Archive

It was clear that there was relatively little popular backing for a purely Bolshevik uprising, but that there would be massive support if Kerensky attempted to move against the soviets. Trotsky cleverly used the MRC's preparations to defend the city both against the advancing Germans and the Provisional Government as a camouflage for the Bolshevik takeover. As the

MRC had been set up by the Petrograd Soviet, it gave the Bolshevik majority a credibility, which a purely party-led coup would have lacked.

Although Lenin was insistent that the Provisional Government should be overthrown before the Soviet Congress was convened, the action would, however, only gain legitimacy if it was endorsed by the Congress. Consequently Trosky planned to overthrow the government actually while the Congress was assembling and then present it with a fait accompli for its approval. His task was made easier when on 21–2 October the MRC was able to win the loyalty of the Petrograd garrison, and control the Peter and Paul Fortress, which overlooked the Winter Palace, the seat of the Provisional Government.

Despite the visible impotence of the Provisional Government, the MRC feared a repeat of 'June days', and, as late as 24 October, Trotsky was still urging restraint. However, early the following day, partly under pressure from Lenin, the MRC acted unilaterally, and ordered military units and the Red Guards to seize key points in the city. Kerensky managed to escape by car, but his ministers in the Winter Palace were arrested.

While the Winter Palace was being bombarded, the Soviet Congress opened. The overwhelming majority favoured a government based on the parties represented in the Congress. Again it appeared briefly possible that a united left-wing democratic coalition might just be formed, but then, as Lenin had indeed hoped, in protest against the coup against the Provisional Government, the right-wing Mensheviks and SRs walked out, leaving the way clear for the creation of a Bolshevik-dominated dictatorship.

THE EARLY MONTHS AFTER THE BOLSHEVIK SEIZURE OF POWER, OCTOBER 1917–JANUARY 1918

In the immediate aftermath of the October Revolution, the Bolsheviks faced almost insurmountable problems. Their power base was a small red enclave in the midst of a vast non-Bolshevik Russian ocean. The central government had collapsed, inflation was accelerating, in the towns the revolution was in danger of degenerating into an orgy of violence, drunkenness and vandalism, while in the countryside the peasants were turning the village soviets into independent organs of self-government, which were not only repartitioning the land, but electing judges, and forming local militias. In short there was not just one revolution but several different ones running concurrently – in the cities, on the land, in the armed forces and among the ethnic populations in the borderlands.

Inflation, January 1918–January 1921

Paper roubles		Value in gold roubles
1 January 1920	225,015,000,000	93,000,000
1 January 1921	1,168,596,000,000	69,600,000

Source: W.H. Chamberlain, *The Russian Revolution, 1817–1921*, vol. 2, New York, Grosset & Dunlap, 1965, p. 103.

Looking at the initial problems faced by the Bolsheviks, foreign observers and the Russian press assumed that they would almost certainly fail to form a lasting regime. Just outside Petrograd there were 18 Cossack companies, which were still loyal to Kerensky, while in Moscow the Bolsheviks were meeting stiff opposition from those still loyal to the Provisional Government. Lenin was thus forced to bow to demands from the railway workers' union, *Vikzhel*, which alone could paralyze the rail network, to begin negotiations on forming a coalition with the SRs and Mensheviks.

The Bolshevik Party was split over the question of power sharing. A group led by Kamenev, who conducted the negotiations, welcomed a coalition, while Lenin and Trotsky were determined that the Bolshevik Party should not share power with other parties. The disintegration of Kerensky's forces, the ultimate success of the Moscow Revolution and the impossibly high demands set by the right-wing Mensheviks and SRs ensured that the talks collapsed by 6 November, although the left-wing SRs were given three seats in the cabinet. Orlando Figes argues that this failure to form a more broadly based coalition effectively 'marked the beginning of the civil war'[9] as it led to growing polarization between the Bolsheviks and the moderate Socialists (see Document 4).

Lev Kamenev (1883–1936)

Like Trotsky, Kamenev was of Jewish origin. His family name
was Rosenfeld. He joined the Russian Social Democratic Party in
1901 and from 1909 to 1914 with Lenin and Zinoviev directed
the Bolshevik Party organization from abroad. Early in 1914 he
returned to Russia to take charge of the Bolshevik parliamentary
party and *Pravda*, the party paper, but when war broke out he
was banished to Siberia. After the February Revolution he led the
Bolsheviks until Lenin's return but, unlike Lenin, advocated a
coalition of all the Socialist parties. In 1918 he was elected
Chairman of the Moscow Soviet and was at his most influential
from 1923 to 1926, when he worked with Stalin and Zinoviev to
block Trotsky's rise to power. In turn, he, too, became a critic of
Stalin's policies, and was arrested in 1935 and executed a year
later (see also p. 343).

Faced with hostility from the Russian civil service, Lenin
initially attempted to govern through the MRC, but by the middle
of November, when the Bolsheviks Commissars had gained
control of the ministries (which were now renamed People's
Commissariats), power was transferred to *Sovnarkom*, or the
Council of People's Commissars. Initially there was 'an extraordinary mishmash of competing and clashing authorities'.[10] As later
in Nazi Germany, new agencies and committees sprang out of the
ground like mushrooms (see pp. 209–12). The Executive
Committee of the Soviet was initially able to subject *Sovnarkom*
to effective scrutiny and criticism, but Lenin tripled its membership in a successful bid to paralyze its decision-making capacity
and also replaced its chairman, Kamenev, with **Yakov Sverdlov**, a
strong supporter of the Bolshevik dictatorship.

**Yakov Sverdlov
(1885–1919)**
Secretary of the Bolshevik
Party and leader of the
Ekaterinburg section of
the party. He was also one
of the organizers of the
uprising of October 1917.

The Constituent Assembly

The most immediate challenge facing the new regime was the
looming elections to the Constituent Assembly, which Lenin had
little option but to let go ahead. He was trapped by his own
propaganda, as he had sought to justify the Bolshevik seizure of
power by arguing that it guaranteed the calling of a constituent
assembly. As the Bolsheviks feared, the elections were a nasty

shock for them, since they won just 24 per cent of the total. They immediately began a campaign of intimidation. Lenin also managed to delay the calling of the Assembly until January. The Kadet Party was outlawed and its leaders arrested and incarcerated in the Peter and Paul Fortress, where they were joined by some of the SR and Menshevik leaders. By the middle of December Lenin had decided to abolish the Assembly unless it unconditionally agreed to subordinate itself to the soviets by accepting the Declaration of Rights of Working People and to endorse unconditionally all the decrees of *Sovnarkom*.

When the Assembly met on 5 January 1918, martial law was declared and a crowd of demonstrators shouting 'all power to the Constituent Assembly' was actually fired upon by Bolshevik troops, killing 10 people. A precedent was set, which was later to be followed by both Mussolini and Hitler (see pp. 102 and 103). Troops crowded into the Catherine Hall, where the delegates were gathered, and overtly sought to terrorize them. Then, when the Declaration of Rights was defeated by 237 votes to 146, Lenin ordered the **Red Guards** to close the Assembly down.

How was it that Lenin was able to use force to close down a parliament in which the Bolsheviks had no more than a quarter of the votes? Was it, as Pipes argued,[11] a result of a conspiracy by a small intellectual elite? There is no doubt that Lenin was determined to establish a Bolshevik dictatorship, but he could not have done it unless his regime was supported or at least tolerated by the great mass of the people. The initial decrees announced by *Sovnarkom*, such as instant peace, land reform, an eight-hour day and nationalization of industry, were primarily propaganda and were designed to inspire and to excite the masses. Lenin had no neatly worked out 'road map' for establishing his dictatorship, but as Figes has observed, he had 'an instinctive sense of general direction', which involved 'a two fold process of state building and destruction'.[12] On the one hand, he sought to concentrate power within the Bolshevik Party and destroy all political opposition from whatever group it came, while, on the other, he worked hard to bring about the destruction of the traditional tsarist administrative and social hierarchies by encouraging the local soviets, the factory organizations and the soldiers' committees to seize power at local level. His opponents were hampered by the lack of any armed forces and the absence of a large middle

Red Guards
Originated in March 1917 when the workers set up their own armed brigades to defend the factories.

class in Russia, which would have provided the backbone of opposition to Bolshevism. The SRs, although the largest party, were split. Their left wing had joined *Sovnarkom*, while the right wing placed its trust in the Assembly, and even when it was dissolved, believed that popular pressure would force its reinstatement. (See Documents 5 and 12.)

A powerful weapon in the hands of the Bolsheviks was the exploitation of class war and the potent cry for the annihilation of wealth and privilege. The Russian peasantry had a deep and ingrained religious belief that surplus wealth was immoral. Lenin was able to exploit these feelings to destroy the Bolsheviks' enemies. The ***Cheka,*** which later became a centralized political police force, was at first, when it was set up in December 1917, a decentralized organization which was principally driven by local hatreds against the landowners and bourgeoisie. The new People's Courts, whose task was to dispense revolutionary justice, were also inspired by class hatred. By being able to go with and at times direct this torrent of hatred, the Bolsheviks were able to tighten their grip on Russia.

Cheka
The Extraordinary Commission to Combat Counter-Revolution and Sabotage was a secret police force under Felix Dzerzhinsky. It was replaced in 1922 by the GPU (see Document 6).

ENDING THE WAR WITH GERMANY: THE TREATY OF BREST–LITOVSK

Essential to the survival of the revolution was ending the war with Germany. As there was little chance of persuading the Western Powers to negotiate a general peace, the Bolsheviks sent on 26 November a peace delegation to the German army headquarters at Brest–Litovsk. The initial intention was to play for time in the hope that the German and then the armies of the Entente would be overwhelmed by revolution. The Germans initially agreed to a four-week armistice period, and then in January 1918 presented the Soviet Delegation, which was headed by Trotsky, with demands for massive annexations involving the Baltic States, Russian Poland and eastern Galicia (see Map 1). They also occupied Ukraine and helped the Ukrainian Nationalists defeat the Bolsheviks.

The peace terms led to a bitter debate in the Central Committee. Lenin argued strongly for their acceptance. Opposed to him were the left-wing SRs and a strong group of Bolsheviks led by **Bukharin** and **Radek**. At first Lenin had to compromise by supporting Trotsky's tactics of 'neither war nor peace', which involved rejecting the German peace terms, while not actually reverting to full-scale hostilities. On 10 February Trotsky walked out of the peace conference, but a week later the Germans called the Bolsheviks' bluff and rapidly began to advance towards Petrograd. Faced with this formidable threat Lenin argued strongly that 'it is a question of signing peace terms now or signing a death sentence of the Soviet Government three weeks later',[13] and even threatened to resign if they were rejected. He managed to convince Trotsky, and on 3 March the Treaty of Brest–Litovsk was signed with Germany.

The Russians had to grant independence to Poland, Courland, Finland, Estonia and Lithuania, which were all put under German 'protection', and Soviet troops had to be evacuated from Ukraine. The new Soviet Republic thus lost 34 per cent of its population, 32 per cent of its agricultural output and 54 per cent of its industries.

The treaty enabled the Bolsheviks to consolidate their regime, but its terms split the Bolsheviks and led the Left SRs to resign from *Sovnarkom* in protest. It also isolated Russia from the West and made any idea of an international revolution much more unlikely. Although efforts to 'export' the revolution to Germany and the Western Powers were not abandoned, in reality the aim of the regime increasingly became to consolidate 'Socialism in one country' (see p. 73).

Nikolay Bukharin (1888–1938)
One of the leading theorists of the Bolshevik Party.

Karl Radek (1885–1939)
His real name was Sobelsohn; he was born in Austria–Hungary. After the February Revolution he worked as a Bolshevik agent and settled permanently in Russia in 1922.

THE CIVIL WAR

Military operations

In the Stalinist era the Civil War was interpreted as a series of conflicts masterminded by Britain and France. It is true, of course, that the Western Powers did intervene to assist the anti-Bolshevik forces, or Whites, and that Lenin was convinced that the Bolshevik revolution could only be saved by a civil war on a European scale, which would involve the proletariat of the advanced European states rising up against their ruling classes. However, Lenin was psychologically ready for a civil war in Russia. He argued that civil war had in fact already been launched by the forces of the right during the summer of 1917 and that the subsequent revolutionary seizure of power in October was just part of the armed struggle. Arguably, to quote Figes, 'all Lenin's policies from the October seizure of power' to the closure of the Constituent Assembly and the Treaty of Brest–Litovsk could be seen 'as a deliberate incitement to civil war',[14] which was bound to provoke the right-wing SRs, the Kadets and the Whites. Civil war, by eliminating the class enemy, paved the way for the social revolution. This is what Trotsky meant when he said: 'Long live the civil war! Civil war for the sake of the children, the elderly, the workers and the Red Army, civil war in the name of direct and ruthless struggle against counter-revolution.'[15] Thus the Civil War was not primarily a result of foreign intervention, but an integral part of the Bolsheviks' political programme (see Documents 5 and 7).

The creation of the Red Army

The creation of the Red Army, by Trotsky in his role as Commissar for War, was crucial for the triumph of the Bolshevik revolution. Initially in January 1918 it was set up on the basis of the worker's militia or Red Guards, but in the summer of 1918 it was expanded by the mass conscription of workers and peasants. Despite considerable opposition within the party, the Red Army was also strengthened by the conscription of former Tsarist officers, who provided the professional backbone of the army. Their obedience was assured both by Trotsky's threat to arrest their families in case they deserted and by the creation of political commissars. By 1920 the Red Army numbered 5 million men, whom the Soviet authorities struggled to feed and supply. A smaller, better trained force would have been much more effective, but, as the White forces were better trained, Trotsky sought an overwhelming superiority in numbers.

The Red Army became the school of the revolution. It provided opportunities for ambitious young peasants and workers and also provided chances for the regime to teach the soldiers to read and to write and also to instruct them in the principles of Bolshevism. During the course of the Civil War half a million Red soldiers joined the party. When they were demobilized, they emerged as 'the missionaries of the revolution'[16] because, once back in their towns and villages, they rapidly became key figures in the local bureaucracy. The Red Army with its centralized command structure became a model for the development of the Soviet governmental system, as well as shaping the attitudes of those who served in it.

To the Bolsheviks the Civil War was fought on two fronts: the civilian and military. Operations against civilians involved arrests and executions by the *Cheka* and forced requisitioning of food from the peasantry. On the military front, which is conventionally regarded as the real civil war, operations could not have been more different from those waged on the Western front in 1914–18. It was essentially a railway war in which troops moved with great rapidity along the rail roads, leaving huge unoccupied areas behind the front, over which frequently roamed marauding partisan bands. Not surprisingly, as Pipes has observed, 'Some maps of the civil war fronts resemble a Jackson Pollock painting, with white, red, green and black lines running in all directions and intersecting at random.'[17]

The Civil War of 1918–20 can be divided into four major phases (see Map 2):

1 The first campaign in the winter of 1917–18 eliminated the initial centres of anti-Bolshevik resistance in the southern Urals and the Caucasus. By February 1918 the Ukranian Nationalist government, the *Rada*, was defeated, and conservative anti-Bolshevik forces driven from Rostov.

2 At this stage Lenin was prematurely talking of the 'triumphal march of Soviet power',[18] but then the advance by the Germans in the early spring of 1918 into Estonia, Latvia, Belorussia, Ukraine and the Transcaucasus led to the overthrow of Soviet power in those regions and the formation of the Volunteer Army and the mobilization of the Don Cossacks. Despite Brest–Litovsk, Germany was determined to build its power in western Russia, where abundant raw materials and grain supplies would enable Germany to defy the British naval blockade. Germany therefore used the excuse of appeals for help from anti-Bolshevik groups to launch further invasions.

   The successes of the Central Powers also provoked intervention by the Czechoslovak Legion, which in May turned against the local soviets in Siberia. The Czech Legion was made up of some 35,000 Czech and Slovak prisoners of war who were in transit to the port of Vladivistock, where via America they would return to fight for the Entente Powers against the Central Powers. They were frequently held up by the local soviets and finally, when they were told to turn round and head for the port of Arkhangelsk, they decided to fight their way to Vladivostock. Ironically, but unknown to them, the orders to head for Arkhangelsk in fact came from the Western Allies. In the absence of any properly trained Red troops in the region, the Czech Legion became a major military force in Siberia, under the protection of which anti-Bolshevik regional power centres could develop.

At Omsk a government had been set up that rapidly fell under the influence of right-wing politicians and tsarist officers, while at Samara moderate SRs managed to form an anti-Bolshevik government (the *Komuch*). Initially the *Komuch* government enlisted the help of the Czechs, and their joint forces swept all before them, taking both Simbirsk and Kazan, but by the beginning of September the Reds were able to transfer some 70,000 troops from the west and by early October both Samara and Simbirsk were retaken. The *Komuch* collapsed and the SRs fled eastwards to Ufa.

3   The third and most decisive stage covered the period March to November 1919. The collapse of Germany in November 1918 had eased the pressure on the Bolsheviks in the west, but in the east the Whites now dominated the anti-Bolshevik movement after the White coup in Omsk had installed Admiral Kolchak as dictator. In the south General Denikin, with considerable assistance from the Don and Kuban Cossacks, was able to build up a formidable army under a unified command, the Armed Forces of Southern Russia (AFSR). In the north a small force under General Yudenich was biding its time in Estonia before striking at Petrograd. Behind both the Eastern and Southern fronts the Reds were weakened by widespread guerrilla activity carried out by the local peasantry or Greens.

If the three White armies had been able to coordinate their campaigns, the Reds would have been in serious trouble. As it was, they were able to defeat each force separately. Kolchak's was thrown back at the Volga in May 1919 and forced into a headlong retreat just at the point when AFSR broke out of the Don–Donbas region and began to advance northwards, taking both Kharkov, one of the key industrial cities in Russia, and Tsaritsyn. By November Denikin was only 400 kilometres (250 miles) from Moscow, but his forces, overstretched and outnumbered by the Red Army, were forced into retreat. In October Yudenich, with some help from British tank units, made a dash for Petrograd. Trotsky effectively mobilized the Petrograd working classes and brought up reinforcements by rail from Moscow, and the Whites were pushed back towards Estonia. By the end of the year both Deniken's and Kolchak's forces were destroyed. Kolchak had been captured and shot and the remnants of his forces retreated to the Pacific coast, while Denikin's army withdrew to the Black Sea, where some were lucky enough to be evacuated by Allied ships from the port of Novocherkassk.

4   The rump of the White forces managed to hold the Crimean peninsular. They would rapidly have been destroyed by the Red Army if it had not been distracted by the Polish invasion of Ukraine in April 1920. In retaliation, Lenin launched a full-scale attack on Poland. Soviet forces reached Warsaw, but were decisively defeated by a better trained and equipped Polish army. The subsequent Soviet–Polish armistice enabled the remaining White forces in Crimea finally to be defeated, although the survivors were evacuated to Constantinople by British and French ships.

The Greens

On the Eastern front in the spring and on the Southern front in the summer of 1919 men were deserting from the Red Army faster than they could be recruited. The Red Army commissars carried out a ruthless campaign of terror against the villages that were suspected of hiding deserters. This merely had the effect of further alienating the local peasantry, who were already suffering from the forced requisitioning of their food crops by the Bolsheviks (see p. 56). In some places the deserters formed themselves into guerrilla bands, which became known as the Greens, in an attempt to distinguish themselves from the Red and White forces. They developed their own political programmes, and claimed that they were fighting to defend the local peasant revolution from both the Whites and the Reds.

Allied intervention

Initially Allied forces intervened in Russia to encourage the anti-Bolshevik forces to build up a front against the Germans, but once the war with Germany ended they began to assist the Whites in the Civil War. In the summer of 1918 a mixed Allied force under British command landed in Archangel and the Trans-Siberian Railway to Vladivostock was guarded not only by Czechs, but also by Japanese, British, Americans, Poles, Romanians and Italians. With the collapse of Kolchak's government in the winter of 1919–20 all the interventionist forces except the Japanese left Siberia. The Japanese remained in Vladivistock and the neighbouring coastal regions until October 1922, when the Soviet government regained control. The British and French divided southern Russia into two zones of influence: the British zone was the Caucasus, Armenia, Georgia and Kurdistan, while the French zone consisted of Besserabia, Ukraine and Crimea (see Map 2). French, Greek and Polish troops landed in Odessa in December 1918, but were rapidly withdrawn when they showed signs of fraternizing with the Bolsheviks.

In 1919 Britain sent nearly 100,000 tons of arms, ammunition, equipment and clothing to Kolchak, and Denikin was also sent advisers, 30 tanks, and a large number of rifles and guns. In the north Yudenitch, too, received military equipment, and in September 1918 a flotilla of British motor boats actually attacked Kronstadt. In southern Russia the British pursued the dual but contradictory policy of helping Denikin and building up satellite states that would look to Britain rather than Moscow for protection. By the summer of 1919, however, they, too, pulled out of southern Russia.

Why was a Red rather that a White dictatorship triumphant by December 1920?

In 1918 both the Reds and Whites faced similar problems: they had to conscript unwilling peasants, requisition scarce grain and grapple with the immense task of restoring industrial production and civil administration. Both regimes also faced intense hostility from much of the local peasantry. Yet, even though the Whites could draw on the greater military experience and had the better generals, it was the Bolsheviks who enjoyed the key strategic and political advantages.

The Reds had the overwhelming strategic advantage of controlling the centre of Russia and the largest concentration of population and industry, whereas the Whites could only attack along the periphery (see Map 2). The Bolshevik regime could draw on the resources of some 70 million people, while Denikin and Kolchak controlled at the height of their power sparsely inhabited regions, which together had a population of not more than 20 million inhabitants. Thus, despite the shortcomings of War Communism (see pp. 55–6), the Bolsheviks had a much larger and firmer mobilization base than the Whites. The Red Army also had a single unified command, which took orders from a tightly organized ruling party, while the Whites forces, which were under separate commands, were unable to coordinate their strategy (see p. 48).

The Whites were also outclassed politically by the Bolsheviks. Essentially the Whites were the party of restoration (see Document 8). Even if the monarchy could not be restored, White officers made it clear that they wanted to restore as much of the *ancien régime* as was possible. Kolchak did understand the need to reassure the peasantry, but he was preoccupied by the war and lacked the political power to force his ministers to embrace social and land reforms. **General Wrangel**, too, spoke of carrying out 'leftist policies with rightist hands',[19] but in reality his land reforms were too cautious and conservative. The industrial workers in the industrial regions of the southern Russia, which were occupied by Denikin's forces in the summer of 1919, were also alienated by his orders to dissolve their trade unions, and strike action was met with ruthless reprisals. Crucial to the whole ethos of the White cause was the White's greater Russian nationalism, which prevented them from making timely concessions to win the support of the Finns, Ukranians and the many other non-Russian nationalities. The Bolsheviks, on the other hand, were sufficiently flexible to offer promises, which were later not kept, of a federal Russia in which these peoples would enjoy self-government.

The Bolsheviks were not identifed with the past, whatever cruelties they were carrying out in the present. In their propaganda campaigns they did, above all, claim to be defending the gains of

Wrangel
Replaced Denikin as commander of the White forces in April 1920.

the revolution, and to the majority of the peasantry, the workers and the non-Russian peoples they were, despite everything, the lesser of the two evils on offer. However, once the war was over, this grudging support by the peasantry rapidly turned into hostility (see p. 60). Considering both the strategic and psychological advantages which the Reds enjoyed, 'the surprising thing is not that they won the Civil War, but that it took them three years to do it.'

The defeat of the leftist opposition

The signature of the Treaty of Brest–Litovsk and the steadily worsening economic conditions in the towns led to a deepening political crisis, which could have brought about the collapse of the Bolshevik regime. The left-wing SRs resigned from the government coalition in March 1918, although their representatives still remained in the Soviet executive and *Cheka*. In the Spring of 1918 'Extraordinary Assemblies', which were grass-roots workers' protest movements, sprang up in the factories and had by June a membership of several hundred thousand members. In several of the local soviets they outnumbered the Bolsheviks, and their plans for a general strike in June forced Lenin to nationalize large-scale industry, and transfer the management of the factories to the party in an attempt to restore a more disciplined management structure. The Extraordinary Assemblies were banned and the leaders of the strike movement were arrested by the *Cheka*.

These measures merely drove opposition to Lenin underground. On 6 July Count Mirbach, the German Ambassador, was assassinated, in the hope that this would provoke a general uprising against the Bolsheviks. An even greater threat to the Bolsheviks was a conspiracy by the left-wing SRs within the *Cheka* itself. Initially they captured both the *Cheka* headquarters, the Lubianaka, and even managed to take its head, **Felix Dzerzhinsky**, prisoner.

Felix Dzerzhinsky (1877–1926)
Had been a member of the Polish, Lithuanian and Russian revolutionary movements. He helped form the Red Guards and became the first Chairman of the *Cheka*.

Although the rebels were supported by 2,000 *Cheka* combat troops, they missed the opportunity to seize power, because essentially they were more interested in persuading the Bolsheviks to change their policies than in forming a rival government. This hesitation allowed the Bolsheviks to recover and to recapture the Lubianka. There followed widespread arrests, the expulsion of the left SRs from the *Cheka* and the Soviet, and the unleashing of a new wave of terror, which also involved the murder of Tsar Nicholas and his family in the night of 16–17 July. The terror was further intensified when Lenin himself was shot, but not fatally wounded, on 30 August by Fanny Kaplan, a former anarchist, who had joined the SRs.

The murder of the Tsar and family

On the orders of the *Cheka* officer who was in charge of the prisoners, Tsar Nicholas II, his family and servants were shot in the cellars of the house in which they were detained. Originally the Bolsheviks were going to put the Tsar on trial. Why then did Lenin order this execution? One reason was that Czech troops were closing in on Ekaterinburg, where the Tzar was under house arrest, and would have liberated him. But there were also other reasons: the Bolsheviks were reluctant to put the Tsar on trial, as this, theoretically at least, presupposed the possibility that he could be innocent and might also lead to awkward questions being asked about Bolshevik atrocities. It was also a signal that in the developing Civil War the sanctity of human life counted for nothing.

The development of the *Cheka*

After the summer of 1918 the *Cheka*'s power expanded so rapidly that it increasingly became a state within a state, as the SS was later to become in Nazi Germany (see pp. 211–12). It ran its own concentration camps and employed over a quarter of a million people. Neither *Sovnarkom* nor the Commissariat of Justice was able to control it. With its remit to wage war on the 'counter-revolution', it could intervene in any aspect of Soviet life. The introduction of War Communism (see p. 55) subjected almost every aspect of Soviet life to regulations and controls and so opened up huge opportunities for the *Cheka* to hunt down the 'enemies of the revolution' (see Document 6).

Creation of a one-party dictatorship

The triple threat from foreign intervention, the Whites and the SRs helped determine the shape of the Bolshevik dictatorship.

**Nikolai Krestinsky
(1883–1938)**
In 1923–4 he supported
the left opposition, but
later became Soviet
ambassador in Berlin. In
1938 he fell victim to the
Stalin purges (see
pp. 344–6).

Zemstvos
Provincial and district
councils, which had been
set up in 1864.

**Grigory Zinoviev
(1883–1936)**
Came from a poor Jewish
family; joined the
Bolsheviks in 1903 and
worked closely with Lenin,
1906–1917. He opposed
the Bolshevik takeover in
October 1917, but was
later made Chairman of
the Comintern. He was
arrested and executed
during the Stalin purge of
1936 (see p. 343).

With the expulsion of the SRs from the Soviet in July 1918, Russia became a one-party dictatorship.

In early 1919 an effective centralized Bolshevik party apparatus began to be constructed. Crucial decisions were no longer taken by *Sovnarkom* or the All Russian Central Executive Committee but by a small sub-committee of the Bolshevik Central Committee, the Politbureau, of which Lenin, Trotsky, Stalin, Kamenev and **Krestinsky** were members. Over the course of the year a further nine party departments were formed, as well as the party Secretariat and the Organizational Bureau, to which was given the key task of organizing the party throughout the Bolshevik-controlled areas of the country. By means of this machinery the party leadership was able to bring its local organizations under strict control. In essence a system of 'democratic centralism' was created in which the chain of command went down from the top to the bottom. Local Bolshevik leaders became 'mini Lenins',[20] although this neat pattern was still, of course, subject to disruption from the ebb and flow of the Civil War.

Soviet rule witnessed a massive increase in bureaucracy, as it not only nationalized industry and banking, but it also took over the hitherto autonomous local government organizations, the *zemstvos*. The Bolshevik Party underwent a large expansion. Between 1917 and 1920 some 1.4 million people joined it, many of whom came from the peasantry. This growth offered opportunities to the ambitious and the upwardly mobile, but it also led to widespread corruption and the creation of mafia-like local cliques.

The emergence of the Lenin cult

Marxists, believing that impersonal historical and economic forces shape history, play down the role of the individual. Initially Lenin was hardly known in Russia, but his rapid recovery from the assassination attempt turned him into a mixture of a latter-day Jesus Christ and a Red Tsar. The party deliberately created this new image of Lenin. **Zinoviev**, in a pamphlet, claimed him to be the son of a peasant and 'the chosen one of millions'.[21] The new Lenin cult tapped into both the ancient practice of canonizing princes who had died in battle and into the old tradition of folklore myths, which invested leaders of popular uprisings against the Tsar with semi-divine and Christ-like powers.

War Communism

William Chamberlain[22] defined War Communism as possessing six main characteristics:

- The state controlled all means of production and wherever possible abolished private ownership.
- It also directly controlled the labour of every private citizen. Workers were mobilized and their labour allocated to where it was needed.
- The state attempted to nationalize every factory and workshop, so that it could produce everything itself.
- The control of the economy was centralized under the Supreme Economic Council (the VTsIK).
- The state sought to take control of the distribution of goods.
- An attempt was also made to abolish money as a means of exchange in favour of a system of universal rationing.

There is considerable disagreement amongst historians about the origins of War Communism. To those, such as E.H. Carr, who were sympathetic to the regime, it was essentially a pragmatic response to the challenge of the Civil War. They argue that initially Lenin had in mind creating a mixed economy along the lines of the New Economic Policy (NEP) (see p. 62), and was thrown off course by the acute emergencies created by the Civil War. The Right, however, is more sceptical. Pipes argues that the very term 'War Communism' was a 'misnomer coined to justify the disastrous consequences of economic experimentation by the alleged exigencies of the Civil War and foreign intervention'. On the contrary it was 'in fact not so much emergency responses to war conditions as an attempt as rapidly as possible to construct a communist society'.[23]

In practice, the introduction of War Communism was prompted by both ideological and practical reasons. From the very beginning the Bolsheviks – and the left SRs as well – were determined to control the market, which inevitably ensured a growing degree of coercion. On 19 January 1918 compulsory consumers' communes were set up, while a month later the local soviets and railway committees were given the power to execute on the spot black marketeers and **bagmen**, whose activities were clogging up the railways and hindering the war effort.

Bagmen
Thousands of people from the cities who travelled in the countryside regularly with bags of clothes or household goods, which they would exchange for food.

Banking was nationalized very quickly after the October Revolution, but the Bolshevik leadership was more cautious about the wide-scale nationalization of industry. Some local soviets had already seized control of factories, but it was the formation of the Extraordinary Assemblies and the growing opposition to the emerging Bolshevik dictatorship by the workers that persuaded Lenin that factory discipline could only be restored by nationalization. Finally facing the threat of a general strike, most large-scale factories were at last nationalized on 28 June 1918 (see p. 52). In November 1920 an increasingly radical Bolshevik Party forced Lenin to nationalize small-scale industry, so that even workshops employing a handful of workers became part of the centrally controlled economy.

Yet as Figes argues, 'War Communism was not just a response to the Civil War; it was also a means of making civil war',[24] particularly against the peasantry. The Bolsheviks drew heavily on the experience of the **Paris Commune** of 1871, which they believed was defeated because of a deeply hostile peasantry. Consequently they effectively waged war against the wealthier peasantry instead of following the more pragmatic approach of persuading them to sell their grain for market prices – a policy adopted later in the NEP. Food brigades were sent into the countryside to terrorize the peasantry into handing over their grain stocks. They also tried to set the poorer peasantry against the wealthier by setting up Committees of the Rural Poor (*Kombedy*), but such was village solidarity that these divisive attempts ignominiously failed.

Paris Commune

Set up in Paris in March 1871 and crushed in May. It received no assistance from the provinces and in the subsequent elections the peasantry voted heavily for Conservative parties.

Although a series of revolts against this policy in November 1918 forced Lenin to scrap the *Kombedy*, he nevertheless extended the principle of forced requisitioning to all foodstuffs, including meats. Quotas were also now set centrally rather than locally, which demanded way beyond what the peasantry was capable of producing, but this did not deter the requisitioning brigades from using the most brutal methods to force the peasants to hand over not only their very last supplies of food but also the seeds for next year's harvest. Thus the Bolsheviks were fighting not only a civil war against the Whites, but also at times against the peasantry (see p. 49).

The cultural civil war

The struggle against the tsarist regime was not just political. Tsarism also had an ideological component, and was, above all, closely associated with the Orthodox Church. The Bolsheviks, as Marxists, believed that the ruling classes inevitably shaped the culture of the times (see pp. 14–15), and were therefore determined to purge Russian culture and social customs of all traces of religious, tsarist and bourgeois influences. The independent press was liquidated by the summer of 1918, libraries were purged of 'bourgeois' or non-'politically correct' literature, and a party monopoly in publishing was effectively secured by the announcement of a state paper monopoly.

In March 1919 a textbook called the *ABC of Communism* was written by **Evegenii Preobrazhenskii** and Nikolai Bukharin in an attempt to popularize Bolshevism. Its message was that Communism would effectively create a paradise on earth: there would be no more exploitation and social divisions; criminality and poverty would disappear; while a transformed humanity would work harmoniously together. Study groups were set up in the factories so that party members could become conversant with the new ideas and pass them on. In the Red Army it was also the work of the Political Commissars (see p. 46) to educate the soldiers in the basic ideas of Communism. It was hoped that in due course the soldiers would return to their remote villages ready to spread the new gospel of Communism.

Sympathetic or 'fellow travelling' writers, playwrights, poets and artists were enlisted to make propaganda for the Soviet cause. **Marc Chagall**, for instance, was appointed Artistic Commissar in Vitabesk. In a country where the majority of the population was illiterate, theatre and cinema were vital ways of getting across Bolshevik propaganda. In August 1919 theatres and circuses were nationalized and the new **'agitprop theatre'** was devised to celebrate in pageants that employed hundreds of actors such events as the capture of the Winter Palace in October 1917. Plays and films were also a major vehicle for Soviet propaganda, and were used to instruct the peasantry on the iniquities of religion, the need for personal hygiene and above all to preach hatred for the kulaks (the richer peasants), the *ancien régime* and the Western Powers.

Evgenii Preobrazhenskii (1888–1937)
Head of the Bolshevik Party in the Urals, Secretary of the Russian Communist Party, 1920–1. He was a leading Soviet economist and a critic of Stalin, who had him executed in 1937.

Marc Chagall (1887–1985)
An artist and poet, who emigrated later to Paris.

Agitprop theatre
Sought through 'agitation and propaganda' to break down the barriers between theatre and reality by encouraging audience participation.

**Anatoliy Lunarcharsky
(1875–1933)**
Writer and journalist who
wrote for Bolshevik papers
while in exile in Geneva.
He was people's
Commissar for Education
from 1917 to 1929.

Lunarcharsky, the Commissar for Enlightenment, also used the Proletarian Cultural-Education Association, *Proletkult*, to spread the new proletarian culture amongst the workers and peasants. *Proletkult* groups saw themselves as 'laboratories of proletarian culture' where experiments in a new workers' culture could be conducted. These involved collectively written poems and literature, industrial machinery used as musical instruments, and non-competitive sports. Lenin viewed *Proletkult* with considerable suspicion, because its founder, A.A. Bogdanov (see p. 16), was adamant that the workers should be allowed to develop their own culture independently of the party, and in December 1920 Lenin put it under much tighter controls.

Proletkult poetry

In *Proletkult* poetry circles the emphasis was no longer on individual inspiration. Instead poems had to be written cooperatively, with each participant contributing an individual line. Poetry also had to reflect the new reality of proletarian life, as the classic Russian poetic form was now deemed to reflect 'gentry leisure'. According to one *Proletkult* writer, the world was about to witness 'the electrification of poetry in which the rhythm of the modern enterprise is provided by the central dynamo'.[25] In its cult of the modern, *Proletkult* had certain similarities with Futurism (see p. 10). Both enthusiastically embraced the modern mechanized world. For instance, Krillov, the *Proletkult* poet wrote:

> In the name of our tomorrow we shall burn Raphael
> Destroy the Museums and crush the flowers of art.[26]

Religion was attacked 'with a vehemence not seen since the days of the Roman Empire'.[27] As early as October 1917 Church lands were nationalized and in 1919 a further blow was delivered when the churches were not allowed to own buildings or levy money from their parishioners to pay the **stipends** of the clergy. Attacks were made on monasteries (see Figure 2.3), churches, mosques and synagogues, and in the summer of 1919 the head of the Russian Orthodox Church, Patriarch Tikron, was arrested.

Attempts were also made to bolshevize education. In May 1918 all schools were placed under the Commissariat for

Stipend
A priest's salary.

Figure 2.3 Red Army
soldiers confiscate
valuable items from the
Semenov Monastery in
Moscow, 1923
Source: Russia On-Line

Enlightenment, a uniform network of consolidated labour schools
was created, and all citizens over 16 were given the automatic
right to enter any institution of higher learning. At the universities academic self-government was abolished.

Young people between the ages of 14 and 28 were also
recruited into the *Komosol*, to fight alongside the Red Army. At
the end of the war this gradually developed into the party youth
movement, which was to provide a model for the Fascist and Nazi
regimes (see pp. 222 and 262). Young children below the age of
nine joined the Little Octobrists, they then transferred to the All

Union Lenin Pioneer Organization, before graduating to the *Komosol*.

Within the party a woman's department, the *Zhenotdel*, was set up with the mission to emancipate women. Divorce was made easier in December 1917, serial monogamy was encouraged and abortion was made legal in 1920 (see Document 11).

THE NEP

The Bolshevik regime survived the Civil War only to come to the brink of collapse in the spring of 1921. It faced formidable opposition:

Collectivization
The creation of large-scale cooperative or state-run farms producing directly for the state (see p. 335).

- In the late summer of 1920 peasant revolts spread from Tambov and soon engulfed Russia from the Black Sea to the Pacific Ocean. The peasantry protested bitterly at the continued demand for food deliveries at a time when the bad harvest of 1920 ensured that they had no surplus. Added to this was their implacable hostility to Lenin's declared aim of **collectivizing** agriculture. By 1920 some 16,000 collective and state farms had been set up, which controlled almost a million acres of land. To peasants this represented 'a restoration of the great estates under the Soviet flag'. [28]
- The Bolsheviks were also facing opposition from the industrial workers, who resented the militarization of the factories and Trotsky's attempts to destroy what was left of trade union independence. The situation was made even more acute by a cut of one-third in the bread ration in January 1921 and the closure of a large number of factories as a result of fuel shortages. Not surprisingly, the following month a wave of strikes and demonstrations swept over Russia. In Petrograd the situation was ominously reminiscent of February 1917. At the beginning of March, sailors at the Kronstadt naval base mutinied and elected a new soviet, in which the Bolsheviks represented only a minority (see Document 9).

The combination of these formidable threats had the potential to overthrow the Soviet regime. The Kronstadt revolt was quickly crushed (see Figure 2.4), and in Petrograd martial law was declared, but faced with the massive revolts in the countryside (see Figure 2.5) Lenin had to make an instant concessions to the peasantry by immediately cutting the food levies by over 50 per cent. This went far to appease the peasantry, but it was still necessary in the spring to crush the remaining pockets of opposition by sending troops into the countryside.

Initially the government had hoped that the peasantry would barter their surplus food in exchange for industrial goods, so it would still be possible to keep control of the national economy, but in practice these concessions to the peasantry had profound economic consequences and gradually forced the government 'step by step, to carry out ever more ambitious reforms that in the

Figure 2.4 The Red Army storms across the ice to assault the Kronstadt naval base
Source: RIA Novosti

Figure 2.5 Peasants attack a train of requisitioned grain, February 1921
Source: Russia On-Line

end produced the unique hybrid of socialism and capitalism known as the New Economic Policy'.[29] The main characteristics of the NEP were:

- Private trade in grain and foodstuffs was restored.
- There was a return to a conventional rouble based on gold controlled by a new central bank, the *Gosbank*.
- Small-scale private businesses and cooperatives were legalized and allowed to employ a limited number of workers.
- Middle-sized concerns were leased back to private employers, often their former owners.
- Only large-scale industries, businesses and banks, the so-called 'commanding heights' of the economy, remained in the state's hands.
- These state industries were grouped into trusts, which were free to buy raw materials on the open market.

The extent of these concessions led the Communist regime into completely new territory that could have ended in the restoration of capitalism and bourgeois democracy. Both in Russia and abroad the NEP was constantly compared to the French Revolution's 'Thermidorian phase', which in July 1794 marked the downfall of the **Jacobins** and the beginning of a more moderate period in the history of the French Revolution. In Russia this did not happen because the Bolshevik leadership was acutely aware of this danger and ready to take the necessary measures to halt any such developments.

At the Tenth Party Congress in March 1921 Lenin openly conceded that the NEP was a retreat and consequently stressed that in order to avoid it becoming a rout it was 'indispensable to punish strictly, severely, unsparingly the slightest breach of discipline'.[30] This ensured that concessions to economic liberalism would not spread to political liberalism. Mensheviks and SRs were arrested or forced to emigrate, and in 1922 14 'right-wing' SRs were condemned to death in a **show trial**. The *Cheka*, which was renamed the GPU in 1922, was also given by the state wide-ranging powers to combat 'open counter-revolutionary actions ... espionage and to carry out special assignments' (see Document 10).

The Jacobins
The most radical group in the French Revolution.

Show trials
Trials put on 'for show' or propaganda purposes, in which the guilt of the accused is taken for granted (see pp. 342–344).

The ban on factionalism

While the power of the opposition groups outside the party was broken by 1921 at the latest, there was the danger that the party itself would become fragmented through a growing diversity of opinion. Already at the Tenth Party Congress this tendency was becoming visible, when the party broke up into factions over the trade union question and, to quote Sheila Fitzpatrick, developed 'its own version of parliamentary politics, with the factions playing the role of political parties in a multi-party sytem'.[31] To halt this growing **factionalism** and the threat to Lenin's leadership it represented, Lenin introduced the resolution 'on party unity'. This banned any further factional activities within the party and even contained secret provision for expelling those guilty of factionalism.

Factionalism
The creation of rival groups or parties.

THE CREATION OF THE USSR

The recreation of the Russian Empire

Although in 1917 Moscow lost control over Finland, Poland and the Baltic states, the Soviet victory in the Civil War enabled the Bolsheviks to reassert Russian control over Ukraine, European Russia, Belarus, central Asia and Siberia. In 1921 Armenia, Georgia and Azerbaidzhan were also reintegrated into the new Soviet Russia (see Map 2). The new nationality policy of the Soviet Empire, or USSR, as it was called after 1923, was one of the successes of the NEP. While the regime made efforts to impose the new Soviet culture, it was tolerant of minorities and their languages and worked through local Bolsheviks rather than imposing an alien bureaucracy on them.

The 1924 constitution

Theoretically the USSR's constitution of 1924, reflecting its multinational nature, was federal. It possessed a **bicameral chamber**, the All Union Congress of Soviets, in which the individual states of the USSR were represented. The Central Committee represented the Congress when it was not sitting. On it sat all the most important party officials, government ministers, generals,

Bicameral chamber
A parliament with an upper and lower house.

etc. Below this were local, district, provincial and republic soviets. Only at the bottom level were the soviets elected by universal adult suffrage. The next level of soviets were elected by the members of the district soviets, and this principle system of indirect elections continued right to the top and enabled the Communist Party to ensure that only reliable candidates were selected.

Theoretically the governmental structure was headed by the Congress, whose will was implemented by the Council of People's Commissars (*Sovnarkom*), or cabinet, and the General Secretariat, or civil service. However, in reality, power rested with the party and its key executive body, the Politburo. At every level of government there were parallel party organizations. In essence a vertical system of command, or democratic centralism, was created, in which orders were communicated through the party from the top to the bottom.

LENIN'S DEATH AND THE BATTLE FOR THE SUCCESSION, 1922–8

Lenin's death

Despite the way the Lenin cult had been used in the Civil War (see p. 54), the Bolsheviks themselves were scornful about the need for a charismatic leader, and were ready to criticize Lenin to his face in a way that rarely, if at all, happened to either Hitler, Mussolini or Stalin. Yet while he was in enjoyment of good health, Lenin towered over his contemporaries, and, in the final analysis, on all key issues, such as the Treaty of Brest–Litovsk (see p. 45) or the introduction of the NEP, he could get his way. As chairman of *Sovnarkom* and the Politburo, he controlled both the party and the government.

Consequently, as long as he was in good health, Lenin had nothing to fear from his colleagues in the Politburo. Above all, he saw Stalin as a conscientious, loyal and industrious bureaucrat, who would carry out the tasks that his more brilliant colleagues considered beneath their ability. By 1922 Stalin had effectively become the man to whom Lenin turned to ensure that the policies of the Politburo and the party were carried out:

- As Commissar for Nationalities he liaised with the local Bolshevik parties in the non-Russian areas of the USSR, and was effectively responsible for reuniting Russia.
- As Commissar for *Rabkrin*, the Workers' and Peasants' Inspectorate, he set up mixed commissions of workers and peasants to check on the loyalty and efficiency of the local bureaucracy so as to ensure that it carried out party policies.
- In March 1922 Lenin also agreed to Stalin's appointment as General Secretary of the party, as he seemed the only person capable of coordinating and then enforcing party policy throughout the USSR.

Josef Stalin (1879–1953)

Stalin, whose family name was Djugashvili, was born in Georgia as the son of a cobbler. He was originally going to become a priest but was expelled from the seminary for being a revolutionary in 1899. He was twice sent to Siberia but each time managed to escape. At various times he was in exile in Paris and Vienna, and in 1912 became the Bolshevik Party's expert on racial minorities. He edited the party newspaper, *Pravda*, in 1917 and became Commissar of Nationalities in the first Soviet government. In 1922 he became General Secretary of the Bolshevik Party. By 1929 he had defeated his rivals for the control of the Bolshevik Party, and was in a position to launch the first of the Five-Year Plans involving the collectivization of agriculture and the massive expansion of heavy industry. He defended himself from the criticism that followed the ruthless implementation of these policies through purges, show trials and the Terror. In May 1941 he became Chairman of the Council of Ministers, and during the Great Patriotic War against Germany took over supreme control of the Soviet war effort. The Soviet victory in 1945 was celebrated as his supreme achievement, and enabled the USSR to control most of Eastern Europe. Until his death in 1953 Stalin's position in the USSR was unchallenged. He relied on a small committee, the Commission for Foreign Affairs, or the 'Quintet', to ensure that his policies were carried out and potential critics removed from power. (See Chapters 10, 15 and 16.)

Collectively these three posts enabled Stalin to create a formi-dable power base. His office had the personal details of all party members and officials and was able to 'recommend' candidates, who were loyal to Stalin for key appointments all over the USSR. He also emerged as the one senior Bolshevik with whom local party secretaries could identify, as he was not a cosmopolitan intellectual like Trotsky, Zinoviev or Kamenev.

From May 1922 onwards, when Lenin suffered a series of strokes, which progressively incapacitated him and raised the question of who would succeed him, he began to see Stalin's growing power in a different light. He became particularly concerned by Stalin's policy in Georgia, where officials had ruthlessly purged all opposition in the local Bolshevik party to Stalin's plans for creating a Caucasian Soviet Republic, in which Georgia would be forcibly merged with Azerbaijan and Armenia (see Map 2).

To counteract Stalin's influence, Lenin talked of a forming a 'bloc against bureaucracy', a term used to describe Stalin's increasing power over the party, and tried to persuade Trotsky to become the Deputy Chairman of *Sovnarkom*, but his efforts were severely undermined by two further strokes, which left him paralyzed and unable to talk. If it had not been for these, he would probably have been able to sack Stalin for his handling of the Georgian question.

For the last year of Lenin's life, party policy and the running of the country were determined by the triumvirate of Stalin, Zinoviev and Kamenev. Although they attempted to sideline Lenin by insisting that, in view of his health, he should neither receive visitors nor dictate for more than 10 minutes a day, he was nevertheless still able to draft memoranda on the Georgian question and put forward proposals for halting the increasing bureaucratization of the party and state; these were published in *Pravda*, the party newspaper, in January and March 1923. He also wrote his final message to the Party Congress, which became known as his 'Testament'. He was deeply concerned about the growing rivalry between Stalin and Trotsky and hoped that it could be contained by expanding the numbers of representatives on the Central Committee. He had no illusions about Stalin, whom he proposed to remove from the position of General Secretary.

Despite the attempt by the triumvirate to gag Lenin, his opinion of Stalin was no secret. How was it, then, that Stalin managed to survive as General Secretary of the party?

- He had crucial support from his two fellow Politburo members, Zinoviev and Kamenev, who feared and detested Trotsky.
- Potentially Trotsky had charisma and a reputation as a revolutionary leader second only to Lenin's, but he appeared reluctant to challenge Stalin head on. For instance, at the Twelfth Party Congress in April 1923 Trotsky did not attend the debate on the nationalities, and thus missed the chance to press home Lenin's criticism of Stalin's handling of the Georgian question.
- Ultimately Trotsky, for all his brilliance, was no match for the political machine created by Stalin, who was increasingly able to pack the Central Committee and party conferences with his own supporters. The Thirteenth party Conference of January 1924 was 'an important milestone in the history of the Russian Communist party',[32] as it was stage-managed and its key decisions were made in advance.

Although Lenin's death on 21 January 1924 removed a potential threat to Stalin's position, he still had to face the possibility that Lenin's Testament might be made public, and that he might be forced to resign. However, he was again saved by Zinoviev and Kamenev's dislike of Trosky, who feared that Stalin's dismissal would only strengthen Trotsky. The Testament was thus hushed up and not read out to the Party Congress.

The defeat of Trotsky and the United Opposition

Lenin's death did not mean an end to the leadership struggle. The Bolshevik leaders remained locked into a struggle, in the words of the London *Times*, like 'spiders in a jar'.[33] Ultimately, however, Stalin was to emerge the victor (see Figure 2.6). Firstly in 1924, to isolate Trotsky, he cooperated with Zinoviev and Kamenev. Trotsky made the mistake of underestimating Stalin, as he believed that Zinoviev and Kamenev were his real enemies, but it was Stalin who made the running in alleging that Trotsky was seeking to discredit Lenin. Stalin invented the heresy of 'Trotskyism' which branded Trotsky as a permanent rebel, whose every idea was hostile to the Soviet Union. He also managed to twist Trotsky's belief that the revolution was not secure in the

Socialism in one country
Contrary to Trotsky and Lenin, who believed that the Russian Revolution would only be safe if the rest of the developed world went Communist, Stalin argued that the revolution in Russia was self-sufficient and independent of developments in the outside world.

USSR until the rest of the developed world had also become Communist by implying that this showed a lack of confidence in the USSR's ability to develop '**socialism in one country**'. In January 1925 Trotsky was forced to resign his post as Commissar for War, but he remained a member of the Politburo.

With Trotsky weakened, Stalin, in alliance with Bukharin, who became a full member of the Politburo in 1924, begin to move against Zinoviev and Kamenev. The latter sought to defend themselves by moving to the left and attacking Stalin and Bukharin for their failure to divert more money to industrialization and for their alleged favouritism towards the richer peasants, the kulaks. At the Fourteenth Party Congress in December 1925, however, Stalin was again able to isolate his opponents and accuse them of factionalism.

Belatedly in the spring of 1926 Zinoviev, Kamenev and Trotsky began to regroup to form what in July became known as the United Opposition. Trotsky argued that Stalin was destroying the revolution. Not only was his bureaucracy stifling party democracy, but the NEP was favouring the kulaks, and abroad he was failing to use every opportunity to spread communism. Stalin and his allies on the Politburo, Bukharin, Rykov and Tomsky, retaliated by arguing that these criticisms were essentially

Figure 2.6 Lenin's successors: (from left) Stalin, Rykov, Kamenev and Zmoviev
Source: Empics

unpatriotic and revealed a lack of confidence in the Russian Revolution and the USSR's ability to catch up with the West.

In April 1926 Trotsky fought back by using the failure of Soviet policy in China (see pp. 74–5) as evidence that the United Opposition's duty was to oust Stalin and his allies. In a powerful speech in October to the Central Committee Trotsky argued that 'the rudeness and disloyalty of which Lenin wrote are no longer mere personal characteristics. They have become the fundamental character of our present leadership.'[34]

Stalin, however, having packed the Central Committee with his own supporters, was able to turn the tables on Trotsky by positively embracing his reputation of being 'rough' towards those like the United Opposition, who were splitting the party. Neither did he seek to hide that he had ordered the arrest of dissident Bolsheviks in the name of party unity. Shortly afterwards he was able to have both Trotsky and Zinoviev, as well as 1,500 rank-and-file members, expelled from the party. A year later Trotsky was sent into exile to Alma Ata on the frontier of Soviet Central Asia.

The defeat of Bukharin, Rykov and Tomsky

Once the United Opposition was crushed, Stalin was free to adopt the very policies for which he had so bitterly criticized them. He suddenly swung round to advocating the seizure of grain by force, collectivization of agriculture and a massive increase in industrialization (see pp. 333–40). In vain Bukharin, **Rykov** and **Tomsky** attempted to oppose this, but were easily outvoted by Stalin's loyalists on the Central Committee. By the end of 1928 all three had lost their positions and were forced to accept Stalin's policy.

How did Stalin achieve this success? He was, as we have seen, a consummate politician, who used his powers as General Secretary to the full. He slowly and cautiously ensured the appoinment of his supporters in the party bureaucracy, and was gradually able to pack the Party Congresses with people loyal to him. Yet he did not defeat his opponents merely because of his political skills. As Christopher Read has observed, 'behind Stalin and the rise of Stalinism were real historical forces'.[35] Stalin's policies of socialism in one country, opposition to factionalism and collectivization were all genuinely popular policies, which

Aleksey Rykov (1881–1938)
Joined the Russian Social Democrats in 1901 and later sided with the Bolshevik faction. He worked in the underground in Russia and broke with Lenin in 1910. In 1917 he advocated coalition with the Mensheviks. He was Deputy Chairman of the Council of People's Commissars, 1921–4 and Chairman 1924–30.

Mikhail Tomsky (1880–1936)
Joined the Social Democratic Party in 1903 and helped establish the Revel Union of Metal Workers. He was arrested several times and sent to Siberia. In 1920 he became General Secretary of the Red International of the Trade Unions. He became a member of the Politburo in 1922. He committed suicide in 1936 rather than face arrest and trial (see p. 343).

seemed to the younger Bolshevik Party members to offer a way forward.

THE NEP YEARS: THE ATTEMPT TO CREATE A NEW RUSSIA

The NEP era, which lasted eight years, is subject to differing and often contradictory interpretations. Some see it as a mere breathing space between the upheavals of 1917–21 and the massive changes of the 1930s, while for others it was an alternative model for Soviet society, which could have avoided the horrors of Stalinism. However, to many – probably the majority – in the Bolshevik Party, the NEP was a pragmatic but temporary concession to necessity which would be withdrawn as soon as possible. In the meantime a rigorous policy of damage limitation needed to be practised to preserve the key gains of the revolution and to prevent a counter-attack by the bourgeoisie. Not surprisingly, then, the NEP years were a period of irreconcilable contradictions. The party's vision and plans for the future clashed fundamentally with much of Russian society. On the one hand, the party longed for accelerated industrialization and the triumph of socialism, but the peasantry, on the other hand, remained a stubbornly inert conservative mass, and private trade, unemployment and profit-driven enterprises seemed to make a mockery of Bolshevik ideal.

The peasantry and the NEP

In the countryside the Soviet government and the party struggled to modernize rural society and sweep away what they regarded as obsolete traditions. Demobilized soldiers were given party posts in the villages, medical centres were set up, and traditional saints' days abolished and replaced by new revolutionary holidays. Persistent attempts were also made to discredit age-old rural superstitions and myths and encourage female emancipation, but in practice the regime made little headway in overcoming peasant separateness. One paradox of the peasant revolution of 1917–18, which had enabled many peasants to acquire smallholdings of their own (see p. 34), was that the village communes had been strengthened and were therefore more immune to Bolshevik propaganda.

The workers

By 1921 the class structure in Russia had collapsed. The aristocracy and possessing classes had either been liquidated or fled abroad and even the proletariat had dramatically declined. Many of the workers, who had made the revolution in 1917, had returned to the land, or had been absorbed by the party and become administrators and officials. Thus, to quote Sheila Fitzpatrick, 'the proletariat coach that had brought Cinderella to the revolution had turned into a pumpkin'.[36]

The NEP signalled a new period for the Soviet working class, as it entailed subjecting it to market forces. Thus when the expected demand for manufactured goods in the countryside did not materialize, the workers were confronted with redundancies, wage cuts and attempts to rationalize and speed up production. At the same time they faced competition from the mass migration of the peasantry into the cities, which provided a reservoir of cheap labour and put added pressure on housing and facilities in the cities. Women figured particularly heavily in the ranks of the unemployed and were increasingly driven to prostitution and begging (see Document 11).

Inevitably this generated resentment on the shop floor. As the workers' opposition had been crushed in 1921, it could only take the form of localized strikes and walk-outs. To counter this, the Bolshevik Party attempted with some success to launch mass campaigns aimed at recruiting younger and more skilled workers into the party. By 1927 labour disturbances were increasingly limited to the 'new' workers coming in from the countryside. The government also began an active campaign to resettle the migrating peasantry back in the countryside.

The mood of the workers, party activists and workers was turning against the peasantry. In 1927 the United Opposition (see p. 67) openly campaigned against the NEP in the countryside and began to urge collectivization, and also bitterly criticized the replacement of permanent workers by temporary migrants from the countryside. This was potentially a popular programme, which Stalin was to adopt and use to defeat his opponents and to launch the second revolution (see p. 68).

Was the NEP bound to fail?

Under the NEP Russia did achieve a remarkable economic recovery. For instance between 1921 and 1925 coal production doubled from 9 to 18 million tons and steel output rose from 183,000 to 2.1 million tons. Small traders also flourished. In Moscow in 1925 more that 50 per cent of the volume of consumer goods sold came from private merchants By 1928 pre-war levels of economic production had been reached. The question now was whether the structure of the NEP could be used to expand the economy any further (see p. 337).

Goods supplied by private traders in the NEP

	1924–25 (%)	1925–6 (%)
Hemp	45	30–50
Seeds (for oil)	20	40–60
Wool	no data	50
Hides	no data	50
Furs	60	60
Meat	no data	67
Flax	9	3
Cotton	4	3
Tobacco	21	24
Butter	64	63
Eggs	54	61

Source: A. Ball, 'Private trade and traders during NEP' in Sheila Fitzpatrick et al., eds, *Russia in the Era of the NEP*, Bloomington, Indiana University Press, 1990, p. 94.

The problem was that the NEP was drawn up as a desperate concession to save the revolution and was not really seen as a long-term way of healing the deep divisions caused by the revolution. Forced to witness the re-emergence of private trade and the private trader – the 'Nepman' – the Party was determined to keep up the pressure for a cultural revolution which would finally destroy the old world in Russia. According to Roger Pethybridge, the NEP 'was intended from its inception to be doomed. As long as it lasted, it behaved like a slaughter house animal rushing wildly at a large number of possible exits from the cage. No one, not even the practical Stalin nor the visionary Trotsky, could tell the form of the final exit'.[37]

BOLSHEVIK RUSSIA AND THE WORLD, 1918–27

Initially the leaders of the Bolshevik Revolution were convinced that revolution would sweep Europe and America. In 1917 brigades of ex-prisoners of war were formed, with the dual intention of assisting the Red war effort inside Russia and then acting as Communist spearheads in their own countries. In the winter of 1918–19 efforts were made to 'export' revolution to Finland, the Baltic republics, Germany and Austria. In January 1919 Karl Radek, **Adolf Joffe** and Nicholas Bukharin were sent to Germany to take charge of the infant German Communist Party, but with little success, as the mass of the German workers, while opposed to the war and 143 monarchy, had no desire to see a soviet Germany (see p. 143). Initially the Communists were more successful in Hungary, where Bela Kun, the commander of the Hungarian Internationalist detachment, managed briefly to build up a coalition with the Social Democrats, but in April 1919 he was defeated by the Romanians and forced to flee.

When the Polish attack on Ukraine was repulsed in June 1920 (see p. 49), and Soviet troops advanced into Poland, the Soviet leadership was convinced that the Versailles Treaty would be destroyed and Central Europe become Communist. However, the defeat of Soviet forces outside Warsaw in August destroyed this hope for a generation, and in March 1921, by the Treaty of Riga, the USSR had no option but to concede considerable areas of Belorussia and the western Ukraine to Poland (see Map 2).

Once the mirage of a world revolution vanished, the leaders of the USSR gave the interests of Soviet Russia the highest priority, for, to quote Pipes, 'Communism in Russia was a reality, whereas everywhere else it was but a hope'.[38] The defence of Soviet interests involved a dual approach. On the one hand, Moscow needed to consolidate its relations with the European Powers and the USA. On the other hand, it never renounced its ultimate intention of world revolution. Thus in 1921 the Soviet government signed trade agreements with most of the Baltic and Scandinavian states, Poland, Germany, Britain and Turkey. The USSR scored a major success when it signed the Rapallo Treaty with Germany in

Adolf Joffe (1883–1927)

Joined the Social Democratic Party in 1903 and after the 1905 Revolution moved to Berlin and Vienna where he edited *Pravda* with Trotsky. During the October Revolution he was Chairman of the Military Revolutionary Committee and then in 1918 became Commissar for Foreign Affairs. He was a loyal supporter of Trotsky and committed suicide when the latter was expelled from the Central Committee by Stalin in 1927.

1922. Both powers agreed to renounce their mutual war debts and to cooperate economically.

This did not stop, however, the Politburo and Comintern supporting subversive activities in Germany, Western Europe and the European colonial empires. With the onset of the Ruhr crisis in 1923 (see pp. 150–4), Trotsky, in his role as Commissar for the Armed Forces, actually drew up a timetable for a series of armed uprisings in Germany. Apart from a poorly planned operation in Hamburg, these operations had to be aborted because they became known to Western intelligence, and, to counter them, white émigré units along the Western frontiers of Russia were mobilized and the French garrison in the Rhineland was significantly strengthened.[39]

The Comintern

Unlike its rival the Socialist International, which was a federation of genuinely independent and democratic parties, the Comintern (the Communist International) followed the Leninist principle of democratic centralism. It was formed in 1919 and controlled from Moscow. In the words of its Chairman, Zinoviev, it was in reality a single foreign Communist Party with sections in different states. To maintain absolute control, the Russian Communist Party had five seats on the Executive, whereas the other parties had only one each.

Pan Islamism, Pan Turkism
Attempts to unite the Muslims or the Turks right across frontiers, and so create an independent Islamic or Turkish power.

Mustapha Kemal, 1880–1938
Became the ruler of Turkey in 1922.

Chiang Kai-shek (1886–1975)
Sun Yat-Sen's successor as leader of the Kuomantang. He was eventually defeated by the Communists in 1949.

In September 1920 a Congress of the Peoples of the East was held at Baku, and a jihad, or 'holy war', against imperialism and capitalism was announced. To achieve this the Soviets were initially ready to exploit **Pan Islamism**, **Pan Turkism** and even Buddhism. Again, the Soviets had only mixed success. In Turkey, for instance **Kemal** welcomed Soviet support, but he had no intention of allowing the Communists to operate on his own territory.

The Comintern was able to exploit the situation in China where it supported the Kuomintang, the Chinese Nationalist Party. This became a major issue of contention between Trotsky and Stalin. Stalin believed that General **Chiang Kai-shek**, its leader, would be an effective challenge to British power in the Far East, while Trotsky preferred to build up the small Communist Party. Stalin's advice prevailed, but in 1927 the Kuomintang attempted to liquidate the Communist Party, and so weakened it that it did not become an effective force until the 1940s (see p. 480). As with Kemal, the danger of cooperating with a Nationalist leader became evident.

ASSESSMENT

As long as the USSR existed, a balanced assessment of the Russian Revolution and the NEP was made difficult by the ideological battles between capitalism and Socialism, which were exacerbated by the Cold War. With the development of the Lenin cult, despite Marxism's belittling of the personal role in history, Lenin was seen as the real hero of the revolution by Soviet and **'fellow travelling historians'**. By the same token, the revolution was described by conservative historians in the West as a conspiracy by a tightly knit group of intellectuals backed by foreign troops – Latvians and Hungarians, the *Internationalisty* – who 'foisted and fastened an alien revolution on a hapless Russia'.[40] In 1970 Richard Pipes, a leading conservative historian of the Revolution wrote: 'The elite that rules Russia lacks a legitimate claim to authority ... Lenin, Trotsky and their associates seized power by force, overthrowing an ineffective but democratic government. The government they founded, in other words, derives from a violent act carried out by a tiny minority'[41] (see Document 12).

Fellow travelling historian
An historian who sympathized with the USSR, such as E.H. Carr.

This view both minimizes the support for the Bolsheviks from the winter of 1917–18 until the end of the Civil War and exaggerates their organizational and conspiratorial skills. To the mass of the workers and peasants they were the lesser of two evils, when contrasted with the Whites. It was only when the Whites were defeated that War Communism, forced requisitioning of grain and the threat of collectivization became unbearable.

In early 1921 Lenin, faced with mass unrest in the cities and a large-scale rural uprising, had little option but to salvage what he could by conceding the NEP. This virtually relinquished party control over the countryside, but the party was able to hang on to power until a 'second revolution', which Stalin launched in 1928, could finally eliminate peasant opposition to communism.

DOCUMENT 1

The mutiny of the Guards regiments in Petrograd, 27 February 1917

The psychological moment when the soldiers go over to the revolution is prepared by a long molecular process, which, like other processes of nature, has its point of climax. But how to determine this point? A military unit may be wholly prepared to join the people, but may not receive the needed stimulus ... the more the soldiers in their mass are convinced that the rebels are really rebelling – that this is not a demonstration, after which they have to go back to the barracks and report, that this is a struggle to the death, that the people may win if they join them, and that this winning will not only gurantee impunity but alleviate the lot of all – the more they realize this, the more willing they are to turn aside their bayonets, or go over with them to the people ...

The critical hour of contact between the pushing crowd and the soldiers who bar their way has its critical minute. That is when the gray barrier has not yet given way, still holds together shoulder to shoulder, but already wavers, and the officer, gathering his last strength of will, gives the command: 'Fire!' The cry of the crowd, the yell of terror and threat, drowns the command, but not wholly. The rifles waver. The crowd pushes. Then the officer points the barrel of his revolver at the most suspicious soldier. From the decisive minute now stands out the decisive second ... At the critical moment, when the officer is ready to pull the trigger, a shot from the crowd ... forestalls him. This decides not only the fate of the street skirmish, but perhaps the whole day, or the whole insurrection.

Source: L. Trotsky, *History of the Russian Revolution*, vol. 1, London, Sphere, 1967, pp. 127–8.

DOCUMENT 2

Lenin as a leader

Robert Service, in his biography of Lenin, made the following observation about Lenin's tactics at the Bolshevik Party Conference in April 1917:

[Lenin's] rhetoric and imposing presence had made the best of a situation in the party that was already propitious. And both he and the Conference as a whole saw that the situation in the country was also turning in favour of the far left. The difficulties facing the new government were almost intractable in current conditions. The food-supply crisis was becoming acute. On the war fronts there was no good news. The framework of state administration, already somewhat creaky, was tottering dangerously. The abolition of the monarchy had opened politics to discussion and organisation, and the workers, soldiers and peasants expected much from the provisional Government. Its ministers would find it extremely hard to satisfy them.

Source: R. Service, *Lenin. A Biography*, London, Pan, 2002, p. 269.

DOCUMENT 3
The April Theses

On 4 April 1917 Lenin published the April Theses outlining his policy for a workers' and peasants' revolution:

1 In our attitude toward the War, which on Russia's side, also under the new Government of Lvov and Co. remains a predatory imperialistic war, as a result of the capitalistic character of this Government, not the least concessions to 'revolutionary defensivism' are permissible.

   The class conscious proletariat can give its consent to revolutionary war, which would justify revolutionary defensivism only on these conditions: (a) The passing of power into the hands of the proletariat and of those poorest groups of the peasantry who side with it; (b) Renuciation of all annexations in deeds, and not in words; (c) Complete breach with all interests of capital ...

2 The peculiarity of the present period in Russia is the transition from the first stage to its second stage, which must give power into the hands of the proletariat and the poorest classes of the peasantry ...

3 No support for the Provisional Government, explanation of the compete falsity of all its promises, especially regarding the renunciations of annexations ...

4 ...While we are in a minority we carry on the work of criticism and explanation of mistakes, at the same time advocating the necessity that all state power should pass into the hands of Soviets of Workers' Deputies, so that the masses by experience should free themselves from mistakes.

5 Not a parliamentary republic – the return to this from the Soviet of Workers' Deputies would be a backward step – but a republic of workers', farmhands' and peasants' deputies in the whole country from below to above. Elimination of the police, army and bureaucracy (i.e. replacement of the regular army by a general arming of the people). Pay to all officials who are to be elected and removed at any time, not more than the pay of a good worker.

6 ... nationalization of all land in the country, management of the land by local Soviets of Farmhands' and Peasants' Deputies. Selection of Soviets of deputies from the poorest peasants. Creation out of every big estate ... of a model farm under the control of farm hands' deputies and at public expense.

7 Immediate fusion of all the banks of the country into one general national bank and the introduction of the Soviet of Workers' Deputies over this bank.

8 Not the 'introduction' of socialism as our immediate task, but the transition only to control of the Soviet of Workers' Deputies over public production and distribution of products.

9 ... (a) Immediate convocation of a Party Congress ...

10 Revival of the International.

Source: Abridged from W. H. Chamberlain, *The Russian Revolution, 1817–1921*, vol. 1, New York, Grosset & Dunlap, 1965, pp. 441–3.

DOCUMENT 4
Criticism of Lenin's divisiveness

Maksim Gorky (1868–1936), the Russian poet and writer, joined the Bolsheviks, but became increasingly critical of Lenin. After the February Revolution he organized a non-Bolshevik Social Democratic group named the New Life. He was fiercely critical of Lenin's divisive policies. On 14 June 1917 he wrote:

I have come to the end of my tether. Physically I am still holding out. But every day my anxiety grows and I think that the crazy politics of Lenin will soon lead us to civil war. He is completely isolated but his slogans are very popular among the mass of the uneducated workers and some of the soldiers.

Source: O. Figes, *A People's Tragedy*, London, Pimlico, 2nd ed. 1997, p. 404.

DOCUMENT 5

The mood in Russia in the winter of 1917–18

General Denikin, the future White commander, had to disguise himself as a Polish nobleman and travel in a third-class railway carriage on his journey to the Don:

Now I was simply a *boorzhui* [bourgeois], who was shoved and cursed, sometimes with malice, sometimes just in passing, but fortunately no one paid any attention to me. Now I saw life more clearly and was terrified. I saw a boundless hatred of ideas and of people, of everything that was socially or intellectually higher than the crowd, of everything which bore the slightest trace of abundance, even of inanimate objects, which were the signs of some culture strange or inaccessible to the crowd. This feeling accumulated over the centuries, the bitterness of three years of war, and the hysteria generated by the revolutionary leaders.

Source: Figes, *A People's Tragedy*, p. 520.

DOCUMENT 6

The setting up of the *Cheka*, December 1917

The establishment of the Extraordinary Commission to Combat Counter-Revolution was set out in the Decree of 20 December, 1917:

The Commission is to be named the All Russian Extraordinary Commission and is to be attached to the Soviet of People's Commissars ...

The duties of the Commission will be:

1 To persecute and break up all acts of counter-revolution and sabotage all over Russia, no matter what their origin.
2 To bring before the Revolutionary Tribunal all counter-revolutionists and saboteurs and to work out a plan for fighting them.
3 To make preliminary investigations only – enough to break up [the counter-revolutionary act]

The Commission ... is to watch the press, saboteurs, strikers and all the Socialist-revolutionists of the Right. Measures [to be taken against these counter-revolutionists] are confiscation, confinement, deprivation of [food] cards, publication of the enemies of the people, etc.

▶

Source: J. Bunjan and H.H. Fischer, eds, *The Bolshevik Revolution of 1917–1918: Documents and Materials*, Stanford, Stanford University Press, 1934, pp. 297–8.

DOCUMENT 7

Lenin's uncompromising view of the Civil War

It was important for Lenin to keep alive the fear of the possibility of a bourgeois restoration and to emphasize that no compromise was possible. This message was delivered on 24 August 1919:

Kolchak's victories in Siberia and the Urals have been a clear example to us all that the least disorder, the slightest laxity or negligence at once serve to strengthen the landowners and make for their victory. For the landowners and capitalists have not been destroyed and do not consider themselves vanquished; every intelligent worker and peasant sees, knows and realizes that they have only been beaten and gone into hiding, are lying low, very often disguising themselves by a 'Soviet' 'protective' colouring. Many landowners have wormed their way into state farms . . .

It is criminal to forget not only that the Kolchak movement began with trifles but also that the Mensheviks . . . and SRs assisted its birth . . . Since the Kolchak experience, can there still be peasants other than a few isolated individuals, who do not realize that a 'united front' with the Mensheviks and Social Revolutionaries means union with the abettors of Kolchak?

There is no middle course . . . either the dictatorship of the bourgeoisie . . . or the dictatorship of the proletariat. He who has not learned this from the whole history of the nineteenth century is a hopeless idiot. And we in Russia have all seen how the Mensheviks and Socialist Revolutionaries dreamed of a middle course under Kerensky and under Kolchak.

Source: V.I. Lenin, *Selected Works in Three Volumes*, Moscow, Progress Publishers, 1973, pp. 262–5.

DOCUMENT 8

The White Terror

In June 1919 General Denikin issued the following order:

According to reports which have come to me, immediately after troops enter places which have been cleared of the Bolsheviki, appear proprietors, who by force regain, often with direct support of the military units, their property rights, which have been violated at different times. In this connection they resort to activities which are characterized by the settling of personal scores and the taking of revenge. I order that such actions be severely repressed and that those who are guilty of them be held to strict responsibility.

Source: W. Chamberlain, *The Russian Revolution*, vol. 2, p. 256

DOCUMENT 9

The programmatic statement of the Revolutionary Committee of Kronstadt

On 10 March 1921 the Revolutionary Committee of Kronstadt published a programmatic statement: 'What we are fighting for':

In carrying out the October Revolution, the working class hoped to achieve its liberation. The outcome has been even greater enslavement of human beings.

Power has passed from a monarchy based on the police and *gendarmerie* into the hands of usurpers – Communists – who have given the toilers not freedom but the daily dread of ending up in the torture chambers of the *Cheka*, the horrors of which exceed many times the rule of the Tsarism's *gendarmerie*.

... the glorious emblem of the toiler's state – the hammer and sickle – Communist authority has in truth replaced with the bayonet and the iron bar, created to protect the tranquil and careless life of the new bureaucracy, the Communist commissars and functionaries.

But basest and most criminal of all is the moral slavery introduced by the Communists: they have also laid their hands on the inner world of the working people, compelling them to think only as they do.

Source: Figes, *A People's Tragedy*, pp. 763–4.

DOCUMENT 10

The NEP and political controls

At the Eleventh Party Congress in 1922 Lenin explained why the economic concessions that constituted the NEP were to be accompanied by draconian political controls. He compared the NEP to a military retreat:

Then discipline must be more conscious and is a hundred times more necessary, because, when a whole army retreats, it is not clear to it, it does not see, where it will stop, it sees only retreat; then sometimes a few panic voices are enough to start everyone running. Then the danger is immense. When such a retreat is being carried out with a real army, machine guns are brought out and, when the orderly retreat becomes disorderly, the command is given: 'Fire'. And quite right ... At such a moment it is indispensable to punish strictly, unsparingly the slightest breach in discipline.

Source: E.H. Carr, *The Bolshevik Revolution*, vol. 1, Harmondsworth, Penguin, 1966, pp. 216–17.

DOCUMENT 11

Marriage and divorce during the NEP

The Bolsheviks' concept of marriage derived from Karl Marx . They believed that under capitalism women were the property of their husbands. Under Socialism the state would take over the basic functions of the family and set up communal dining rooms, day care centres, etc. Women would be free to work as equals of men and the family would gradually 'wither away'. In practice this created severe problems, which were described by delegates when the Central Executive Committee of the Soviet met in Moscow in 1926 to ratify the new Code on Marriage, The Family and Guardianship. Vera Lebedeva, the Head of the Department for the Protection of Maternity and Infancy observed:

The weakness of the marital tie and divorce create masses of single women who carry the burden of child care alone. Imagine yourself such a woman, without support from your husband, with a child on your hands, laid off because of a reduction in staff and thrown out of the dormitory ... With no possibility to continue supporting yourself ... Where do these thousands go? ... There is one exit – the street.

Source, W.Z. Goldman, 'The withering away of the family' in S. Fitzpatrick et al., eds, *Russia in the Era of the NEP*, Bloomington, Indiana University Press, 1990, p. 132.

DOCUMENT 12

Historical debate on the Russian Revolution

In his review article, of Richard Pipe's The Russia Revolution, *Peter Kenez criticizes Pipes for attributing too much influence to Lenin and the other leaders of the Bolshevik Party:*

An approach to the history of the Revolution that sees every event as a consequence of the sinister manipulation of revolutionaries implies that there is no point in examining the views and desires of ordinary people. Indeed Pipes utterly disregards the voluminous studies by Western scholars of the working classes and soldiers of 1917. He attributes great power to propaganda; he believes that people do not want what they seemed to want, for their views and therefore their actions have been manipulated by others ...

Depicting the Bolsheviks as the villains who successfully brought down the Provisional Government may be emotionally satisfying, but it prevents Pipes from seeing what really happened. The Provisional Government failed because it attempted to administer the country on the basis of principles in which socialists and liberals genuinely believed, but which proved irrelevant at a time of crisis. The government faced irresolvable problems. The ministers wanted to continue the war because they believed in its importance and because they did not know how to get out. The workers, peasants and soldiers, on the other hand, were tired of blood letting and the government had no means to compel them to go on fighting. The ministers could not resolve the land question, not so much because they believed in the sanctity of private property, but because they rightly feared that land reform at a time of war would lead to the disintegration of the army. The government, however, lacked the strength to prevent illegal land seizures. The nationalities, aware of the vacuum at the center, demanded autonomy, but the government could neither accept these demands nor successfully resist them. Had there been no Bolsheviks, and had Lenin never returned from exile, Russia still could not have been administered on the basis of liberal and social democratic principles.

Source: P. Kenez, 'The prosecution of Soviet history: a critique of Richard Pipes' *The Russian Revolution, The Russian Review*, vol. 50, 1991, pp. 349–50.

NOTES

1 W. Chamberlain, *The Russian Revolution, 1917–21*, vol. 1, New York, Grosset & Dunlap, 1965, p. 73.

2 Quoted in T. Hasegawa, 'The February Revolution' in E. Acton et al., eds, *Critical Companion to the Russian Revolution*, London, Edward Arnold, 1997, p. 53.

3 O. Figes, *A People's Tragedy. The Russian Revolution, 1891–1924*, London, Pimlico, 2nd ed. 1997, p. 408.

4 E. Acton, *Rethinking the Russian Revolution*, London, Edward Arnold, 1990, p. 138.

5 Ibid., p. 139.

6 B.I. Kolonitski, 'Kerensky' in Acton et al., eds, *Critical Companion*, p. 146.

7 J. Frankel, '1917: the problems of alternatives' in E. and J. Frankel and B. Knei-Paz, eds, *Revolution in Russia. Reassessments of 1917*, Cambridge, Cambridge University Press, 1992, p. 8.

8 Acton, *Rethinking the Russian Revolution*, p. 196.

9 Figes, *People's Tragedy*, p. 499.

10 R. Service, 'The Soviet State' in Acton et al., eds, *Critical Companion*, p. 305.

11 R. Pipes, *The Russian Revolution 1899–1919*, New York, Alfred A. Knopf, 1994.

12 Figes, *People's Tragedy*, p. 503.

13 Ibid., p. 547.

14 Ibid., p. 616.

15 Ibid., p. 615.

16 Ibid., p. 602.

17 R. Pipes, *Russia under the Bolshevik Regime, 1919–24*, London, Harvill, 1994, p. 9.

18 E. Mawdley, ' The Civil War: The Military Campaigns' in Acton et al., eds, *Critical Companion*, p. 93.

19 Figes, *People's Tragedy*, p. 717.

20 Service, 'Soviet State', p. 309.

21 Figes, *People's Tragedy*, p. 628.

22 W. Chamberlain, *The Russian Revolution, 1917–21*, vol. 2, ch. 25, pp. 96–117.

23 Pipes, *Russia under the Bolshevik Regime*, pp. 370–1.

24 Figes, *People's Tragedy*, p. 628.

25 Pipes, *Russia under the Bolshevik Regime*, p. 290.

26 Figes, *People's Tragedy*, p. 737.

27 Pipes, *Russia under the Bolshevik Regime*. p. 337

28 E.H. Carr, *The Bolshevik Revolution*, vol. 2, Harmondsworth, Penguin, 1966, p. 169.

29 Pipes, *Russia under the Bolshevik Regime*, p. 392.

30 Carr, *Bolshevik Revolution*, vol. 1, p. 217.

31 S. Fitzpatrick, *The Russian Revolution*, Oxford, Oxford University Press, 2nd ed. 1994, p. 100

32 A. Bullock, *Hitler and Stalin Parallel Lives*, London, Fontana, 1998, p. 142.

33 R. Pethybridge, *One Step Backwards, Two Steps Forward*, Oxford, Oxford University Press, 1990, p. 228.

34 Bullock, *Hitler and Stalin*, p. 219.

35 C. Read, *The Making and Breaking of the Soviet System*, Basingstoke, Palgrave, 2001, p. 52.

36 S. Fitzpatrick, 'The problem of class identity' in S. Fitzpatrick et al., eds, *Russia in the Era of the NEP*, Bloomington, Indiana University Press, 1990, p. 13.

37 Pethybridge, *One Step Backwards*, p. 417.

38 Pipes, *Russia under the Bolshevik Regime*, p. 166.

39 See B.A. Starkov, 'Paths to world socialist revolution: West and East' in C. Brennan and M. Frame, *Russia and the Wider World in Historical Perspective*, Basingstoke, Macmillan, 2000, p. 156.

40 J. Erickson, 'Red Internationalists on the march: the military dimension, 1918–22' in Brennan and Frame, *Russia and the Wider World*, p. 145.

41 Quoted in, R.G. Sunny, 'Historiography of 1917: social history and its critics', *Russian Review*, vol. 53, April 1998, p. 168.

CHAPTER THREE

Italy: the creation of the Fascist state, 1918–29

TIMELINE

1818 October	Italian victory at Vittorio Veneto
	Occupation of Trent and Trieste
4 November	Armistice with Austria ends hostilities
1919 January	*Partito Popolare* (PPI) formed
March	Mussolini founds *Fasci di Combattimento*
June	Nitti forms government
	Peace treaty of St Germain signed with Austria
September	D'Annunzio occupies Fiume
November	First national elections held under the new proportional representation system: the *Popolari* (100) and the Socialists (156) win 50 per cent of the seats
1920 June	Giolitti forms government
September	Workers occupy factories
November	Fascists strong enough to oust the Socialist administration in Bologna
	Fascist squads (*squadrisimo*) begin offensive in the Po Valley
December	D'Annunzio's occupation of Fiume ends
1921 January	Communist Party founded after Socialist split at the Congress of Livorno
May	General election: Fascists gain 35 seats after joining national bloc
July	Ivan Bonomi forms government
August	The Fascist–Socialist Pact of Pacification
November	The Fascist movement becomes the National Fascist Party (PNF)
1922 January	Pius XI elected Pope
February	Luigi Facta forms a government

August	General strike called by Alliance of Labour smashed by the Fascists
28–9 October	Fascist 'march' on Rome
	Victor Emmanuel refuses to sign decree declaring martial law
	Mussolini appointed head of coalition government
December	Fascist Grand Council set up
1923 January	Fascist militia legalized
March	Pact of fusion between Nationalists and Fascists
August	The Corfu incident
November	Acerbo Electoral Law
1924 April	Fascist victory in the general election
June	Murder of Giacomo Matteotti and withdrawal of opposition parties from parliament (Aventine Succession)
1925 January	Mussolini defends himself in speech to parliament.
May	National Afterwork Agency (OND) set up
June	Last Fascist Party Congress held
	'Battle for grain' launched
October	Palazzo–Vidoni Pact
December	Mussolini calls himself Head of Government
1926 April	Law on the Judicial Regulation of Labour Relations
	Formation of *Opera Nazionali Balilla* (ONB)
August	'Battle for lira' begins
October	Opposition parties outlawed
1927 January	Mussolini's circular to the prefects stressing that the party is the instrument of the state's will
April	Charter of Labour
July	Revaluation of the lira
1928 May	Electoral Law: deputies to be chosen from single nationals list
December	Grand Council Law
	Land Reclamation Law
1929 February	Lateran Pacts signed

INTRODUCTION

Paul Corner observed that 'the history of Italian participation in the [Great] war is in effect the history of a gamble which did not pay off'.[1] Far from unifying Italy, it intensified the tensions in Italian society (see pp. 21–2).

Eventually Italy did achieve victory, but it brought little compensation for three years of war. There was a general expectation that the end of the war would bring about radical changes, and a growing impatience on both the Right and on the Left with the pre-war Liberal parliamentary state. The Left believed that it should be replaced with socialism, while the Right looked at the way the army, the state and the industrialists had cooperated to boost production and control labour during the war as a possible model. Much of Mussolini's success can be explained by how he was able to harness the feeling that the liberal state was a relic of history that needed to be swept away by a more dynamic regime.

THE KEY ISSUES IN THIS CHAPTER ARE:

- The decline of the liberal state, 1919–22.
- The rise of Fascism and the formation of the first Mussolini government.
- Mussolini's consolidation of power.
- The economic and social impact of Fascism on Italy, 1922–9.
- Mussolini's foreign policy.

THE POST-WAR CRISIS OF THE LIBERAL STATE, 1919–22

The end of *transformismo*

The granting of universal male suffrage in December 1918 and then proportional representation the following August destroyed the old system of *transformismo*, that is, the 'transformation' of opponents into friends by absorbing them into the government coalition through offering them various posts and privileges. Instead, a new era of mass politics began, to which the traditional politicians found it difficult to adjust. In the elections of 1919, in place of the former liberal majority of some three-fifths of the Chamber of Deputies, three large blocs emerged:

- the Liberals, with 170 seats;
- the Catholics (the *Popolari*) with 100;
- the Socialists, with 156.

A combination of any two groups would have been able to dominate parliament, but common ground was difficult to find. The *Popolari* were an uneasy coalition of right, centre and left-wing

Catholics. The *Popolari* were hostile to Liberalism and enjoyed support from the northern and central Italian peasantry, since they agitated for agrarian reform and land redistribution. The Socialists were determined to copy in Italy the successes of the Russian Bolsheviks and create through revolution a dictatorship of the proletariat. Thus just at the point when strong governments were needed to deal with the intricate problems of the post-war era, the mutual hostility of the *Popolari* and Socialists ensured that a series of weak Liberal cabinets remained in power and in the end sought salvation in an alliance with Mussolini's new Fascist Party.

The 'mutilated peace' and the Fiume incident

Italy emerged from the First World War victorious, yet it rapidly 'acquired the psychology of a defeated nation'.[2] Although its old enemy the Austrian Empire was now shattered, and Italy gained South Tyrol, Trent and Trieste (see Map 7), US President Wilson's abrupt refusal to grant Italy Dalmatia and the city of Fiume, which had a majority of ethnic Italians, was interpreted as a humiliating rebuff. **Orlando** and **Sonnino** withdrew in protest from the peace conference and President Wilson and the Allied leaders overnight became 'villains' and betrayers of the Italian cause, and their attempts to create a democratic new world order were discredited. In the eyes of the nationalists the peace was brilliantly summed up by **D'Annunzio** as 'a mutilated victory'.

In September 1919 the Nitti government's decision to withdraw the Italian garrison from Fiume led to a military coup organized by leading Nationalists and army officers, and financed by money from industry. D'Annunzio seized control of the city with 2,000 'legionaries' in September 1919. He caught the imagination of the nation, and Futurists, Nationalists, Syndicalists and adventurers rapidly joined him. D'Annunzio's regime was a living reminder of the weakness of the Liberal government in Rome.

D'Annunzio also pioneered a new type of mass politics, which Mussolini and other dictators were later to adapt. He installed a semi-Fascist government in Fiume with its own militia and constitution, which proclaimed the city a 'producer's state'. The economy was to be run by 'corporations', which would elect

Vittoria Emmananuele Orlando (1860–1952)
Italian Prime Minister, October 1917–June 1919.

Baron Sidney Sonnino (1847–1922)
Italian Foreign Minister, 1914–19.

Gabriele D'Annunzio (1863–1938)
Nationalist poet, writer and leader of the coup in Fiume.

**Nitti Francesco Nitti
(1868–1953)**
Italian Prime minister,
June 1919–June 1920.

members to the upper house of parliament. D'Annunzio managed
to defy not only his own government but international opinion
for some 15 months. **Nitti** simply ignored him, but his successor,
Giolitti (see p. 21), managed first to persuade the Yugoslav government to agree to Fiume becoming a free or independent city
and then ejected D'Annunzio by force on Christmas Day 1920.

Economic and social problems

In 1919 wartime economic controls were removed and Italian
industry had to adapt to more competitive peacetime conditions.
Heavy industry contracted and some firms went bankrupt. At the
same time millions of soldiers were demobilized and could not be
absorbed by the labour market. In November 1919 unemployment reached a peak of 2 million. Recession and industrial
dislocation was also accompanied by rocketing inflation. The
wholesale price index rose from 412.9 in 1918 to 590.7 in 1920.
As in Germany, it wiped out the savings of the middle classes, cut
the income of the **rentier class**, and eroded the wages and pen-
sions of the state employees (see p. 151).

Rentier class
People who lived from an
income drawn from rented
property and investments.

The economic crisis both helped cause, and in turn was made
worse by, the breakdown in labour discipline and the emergence
of socialist militancy. Throughout industrial Italy strikes, riots,
the occupations of factories and lock-outs by employers became
almost everyday occurences. In both 1919 and 1920, which
became known as the *bienno rosso* or the red years, more than a
million workers went on strike. In 1920 over 400,000 workers
seized control of their factories and ran them for nearly four
weeks. Elsewhere there was much talk of the coming revolution
and creating soviets. In Ferrara, for instance, Red Guards were
formed to force shopkeepers to lower their prices.

Unrest also spread to the countryside. Demobilized troops
coming home in 1919 had been promised land by the government.
When this was not forthcoming, the peasants in southern Italy
seized some million hectares of uncultivated or barren land. In the
north, where there were small tenant farmers and labourers, who
worked for large landowners or more prosperous tenant farmers,
Socialist land leagues and chambers of labour, forced the landlords
to raise wages and guarantee their tenants' holdings often by means
of campaigns of terror involving rick burning, boycotts and assaults.

Both the Socialists and their opponents were aware of the precedents created by the Russian revolution. On the one hand, local Socialists ostentatiously hung up red flags, and spoke of collectivizing agriculture and nationalizing industry, while, on the other, the middle and property-owning classes viewed with dread the prospects of an Italian Bolshevik revolution. The Prefect of Ferrara, for example was convinced that 'the tactics of the socialist party aim ... to take possession of the powers of the state'.[3] This, then, was the context in which Italian Fascism was able to grow into a strong movement, which was aided and abetted by both the state and the middle classes.

MUSSOLINI AND THE RISE OF FASCISM

Mussolini's career, 1883–1919

Benito Mussolini (1883–1945) (see Figure 3.1) was born near Forli in the Romagna. His mother was a devout Christian and headmistress of the village school, while his father, a blacksmith, was a revolutionary Socialist. For a short time Mussolini became a school teacher, but he ran away to Switzerland to escape military service. As a young teacher he already had a reputation for being a Socialist. In Switzerland he rapidly became involved in left-wing politics and gained some understanding of Syndicalism. Mussolini

Figure 3.1 Mussolini
Source: Empics

returned to Italy in 1904, completed his military training, and for a brief period was again a teacher, after which in 1908 he became the editor of a left-wing periodical. In 1911, like Lenin, he attempted to set up an independent and much more radical Socialist Party, but the Socialists reunited in protest over the Italian occupation of Libya, and in 1912 he became the editor of their leading Socialist paper, *Avanti!* Mussolini was no orthodox Socialist. His mixture of anarchism, Syndicalism, Marxism and emphasis on violence was not unlike the Russian Socialist Revolutionaries (see p. 15).

In October 1914 Mussolini completely surprised his fellow Socialists by arguing that Italy should enter the war on the side of Britain and France. Like Lenin he believed that the war might cause the very revolution he longed for. He immediately started a new pro-war paper, *Il Popolo d'Italia*, and joined one of the small revolutionary action groups, the *Fasci Di azione Rivoluzionaria*, to agitate for Italy's participation in the struggle. Once Italy declared war on Austria, Mussolini joined the army and fought until he was invalided out in February 1917. He returned to editing *Il Popolo*, and began to argue that only a dictatorship could win the war and secure the peace. At this stage his programme was effectively 'National Socialist': he advocated giving the workers a share in their company's profits, reducing their working day to eight hours and giving the landless peasants small holdings. Simultaneously he appealed to the nationalists by demanding the annexation of Trieste, Fiume and most of Dalmatia (see Map 7).

In 1919 Mussolini was the most effective right-wing demagogue in Italy. He was highly intelligent, politically ambitious, but dismissive of conventional politics. Essentially his skills as a jounalist and the editorship of the newspaper, *Il Popolo d'Italia*, which he both edited and controlled were his greatest strength, and enabled him to become the voice and leader of a very disparate Fascist movement.

Fascism
The early Fascists were members of a *fascio* (*fasci*, plural) or group, which literally means a bundle, or in a political context, a small group of people. In ancient Rome the *fasces*, an axe encased inside a bundle of rods, was carried in front of a magistrate as a symbol of authority.

Enrico Corradini (1865–1931)
Journalist and Nationalist politician.

In the early months of 1919 the problem for Mussolini was how he would find a space in the post war political world for his particular variant of **Fascism**. During the war he had been useful to the government as a 'drummer'[4] for the interventionist cause, but he was overshadowed by other Nationalist politicians – D'Annunzio and **Corradini**, for example. How could he 'connect' with the masses? After Mussolini had been invalided out of the army in 1917 he attempted through his paper, *Il Popolo d'Italia*, to project the wartime spirit of discipline, comradeship and self-sacrifice throughout Italy. Like Lenin, Mussolini's thinking about revolution evolved from the idea of 'revolution through war' to 'revolution as war'.[5] He also believed in a dynamic minority, which would in effect wage a 'permanent revolution'. What form the 'Fascist revolution' would take was by no means clear. It could mean a sort of 'National Socialism' involving economic and social reforms for the returning soldiers, or a continuing 'war' against the non-interventionists, which would involve confrontation with Socialists.

Superficially it seemed that the Italian masses were either supporters of the Socialists or the *Popolari*, However, post-war Italian Socialism could only thrive if it was accepted that the war had been a disaster, and for many patriotic Italians this was hard to swallow. Patriotism, the weakness of the traditional elite and the threat from the left all eventually led to a gap in the political scene for Mussolini, or a similar figure, to exploit.

In March 1919 an assorted group of ex-Arditti, Futurists, Syndicalists and students met in Milan to found the *Fasci di Combattimento*. The movement's programme attempted to find a 'third way' between the Right and the Left. It announced that it was both a 'national programme' and 'revolutionary' (see Document 1). It also demanded universal suffrage, an eight-hour day, social insurance legislation and a minimum wage, as well as a swingeing tax on war profits. In that sense it is possible to argue, as Nicholas Farrell does, that early Fascism was 'anything but a right-wing movement'.[6]

The Fascists of the 'first hour' were recruited mainly from ex-servicemen, especially the *Arditi*, young demobilized officers, but the movement also attracted the revolutionary Syndicalists, students and Socialists who had left the Socialist Party with Mussolini in 1914. They were united by an intense patriotism, hatred of parliamentary government and liberalism, Catholics, bureaucracy, war profiteers and Socialism, which they felt had betrayed the nation by not supporting Italy's entry into the war in 1915. During the summer of 1919 Mussolini began to build up armed groups of some 200 to 250 men who were attached to the local *fasci*.

Arditi
Commandos or elite troops.

Fascism was too divided to make much impact on the electorate in the elections of November 1919. There were 16 rival groups, all of which used the term Fascist. D'Annunzio's exploits in Fiume overshadowed Mussolini's own somewhat muddled message of National Socialism. The Socialists and the *Popolari* won more than half the seats in the Chamber, while the Fascists failed to gain a single representative. By the end of the year Fascism had been reduced to a token existence in a handful of northern towns.

The resurgence of Fascism

By the end of November 1919 membership of the Fascist party
had sunk to just 870 members, but a year later it had risen sharply
to 250,000. What accounted for this spectacular increase was the
crisis in law and order that reached its peak with the occupation
of the factories by the workers in September 1920 and the seizure
of private land and estates by the Socialist leagues in the countryside. The Socialist Party managed through wild talk of revolution
and collectivization to create a role for the Fascist squads. As the
historian Paul Corner observed, if its intention 'had been to
offend and frighten as many people as possible in as short a space
as possible, it would have been brilliant ... Democrats, Liberals
and Catholics recognizing the extreme nature of the crisis were
ready to try extreme remedies'[7] (see Document 2).

In the autumn of 1920 the Socialist leaders could have negotiated a very favourable deal with the government. After the
occupation of the factories Giolitti and even some Conservatives
believed that only concessions to the Socialists would head off
revolution, but the Socialist leadership missed the chance to
exploit this offer because it feared that its critics on the left would
accuse it of betrayal. This failure on the part of the moderate
Socialists was to enable Mussolini to pose as the defender of law
and order and the ally of the government. By December 1921
fasci had sprung up in all the major cities in northern and central
Italy and for the most part had the support of the middle classes.
Mussolini's power base was Milan, but his grip on the *fasci*
leaders, or *Ras*, as they were called in imitation of the tribal chief-
tains in Ethiopia, was very tenuous. *Ras* like **Italo Balbo** of Ferara
and Roberto Farinacci (see p. 105) in Cremona controlled
powerful local baronies. While the *fasci* were primarily anti-
Socialist and so attracted the support of industrialists and
landowners, they were initially a revolutionary force in their own
right. They appealed to the resentments of the non-unionised
white-collar workers, the peasantry and small shopkeepers.
Initially some land was handed over, yet as the struggle against the
Socialists intensified, the Fascists were driven into the arms of the
landowners, and the industrialists and became a less radical force.

The winter and spring of 1920–1 was the decisive period of
Fascist growth. Fascist squads, *squadrisimo* waged highly effec-

Italo Balbo (1896–1940)
Ras of Ferara, and one of
the four organizers of the
march on Rome. He was
later Minister of Aviation
and Governor General of
Libya.

tive campaigns of terror against the Socialists. By absorbing members from Liberal, republican and Catholic organizations without demanding that they should abandon their party loyalties, Fascism encouraged the belief that that the movement was just a temporary phenomenon that would vanish once the threat from the left had abated.

Fascism in Ferrara

Paul Corner's seminal study of Fascism in Ferrara has provided historians with an invaluable case study, which sheds considerable light on the growth of the Fascist Party in an important province in Italy. Initially in 1919 and for most of 1920 Ferrara was dominated by the Socialists. In February 1920 a general strike broke out in the countryside, which forced the employers to increase wage rates and to help the poorest labourers by employing extra workers during winter. The situation for the landowners deteriorated sharply in the summer, when the price of hemp, one of the staple crops of the area, fell sharply. It was this situation that prompted many of the landowners to give financial support to the local Fascists.

In early 1921 the Fascists were able to move on the offensive against the Socialists. Balbo's squads, which usually numbered over 100 men, systematically attacked local Socialist offices and headquarters. Their tactics were copied throughout the Po Valley, and in October Balbo was ambitiously demanding that the Fascists should 'conquer the nation'. By early summer 1921 the Socialist power base had all but collapsed and Ferrara had changed from a *provincia rossa* to *provincia fascista*.[8] This success was, however, achieved at the expense of the more left-wing Fascists like Olao Gagglio, whom Balbo excluded from influence and power.

From movement to party

Mussolini had played a key role in enabling Fascism to maintain a high profile. He had wisely distanced himself from D'Annunzio. Through the pages of *Il Popolo d'Italia* he had a very effective means of projecting his message across Italy, and his anti-Socialist and nationalist message also reached the ears of the industrialists and the governing elite. Sometimes his articles showed a sympathy for the workers, but they always ended up rejecting the ideals and actions of the Socialists.

Bologna attacks
On 21 November 1920
squadrisimo fired at the
newly elected Socialist
mayor when he appeared
on the balcony of the city
hall. This led to a series of
clashes between the
Socialists and the
squadrisimo in which a
pro-Fascist Nationalist
councillor was shot dead.

As early as October 1920 Mussolini had opened up contact
with Giolitti via the Prefect of Milan, and privately assured
Sforza, the Foreign Minister, that his support for D'Annunzio had
limits. The attack by the Fascist squads on the seat of the Socialist
government in **Bologna** in November 1920 showed the potential
for Fascism as a counter-Socialist force. Mussolini commented for
example that 'the reality is this. The Socialist party is a Russian
army encamped in Italy. Against this foreign army, Fascists have
launched a guerrilla war . . .'.[9]

Consequently it is not surprising that Giolitti thought that he
could construct a new 'national bloc' or coalition in which he
would be able to include Fascism. There was first of all an
informal agreement between Giolitti and Mussolini that Fascist
candidates should enter into an electoral alliance with pro-
government parties in the local elections of November 1920, and
then a more official agreement that the Fascists should enter the
bloco nazionale in May 1921. It was this pact that was to open
the doors of power to Fascism. Giolitti made the same mistake as
the German Nationalists were to make 10 years later with Hitler
(see pp. 185–9). He was convinced that he would be able to
manipulate the Fascists effectively and told Sforza that they were
just 'fireworks; they'll make a great deal of noise but only leave
smoke behind'.[10]

Giolitti's decision to dissolve parliament in 1921 turned out to
be 'a disastrous error'.[11] The Socialists lost relatively few seats
while the *Popolari's* vote remained stable. Mussolini won only 35
seats. Virtually half the Chamber still remained hostile, and the
parties that supported the government were too fragmented to
support a stable government. Once it became clear that he could
not keep the support of the *Popolari*, Giolitti resigned at the end
of June. His successor, Bonomi had two options for establishing
stability:

- the formation of a broadly based anti-Fascist coalition,
  which would be supported by the Socialists
- offering Mussolini a place in government provided that he
  renounced violence: this would almost certainly lead to a
  split between the moderates and hard-liners in the party.

The latter option appeared to be the more practical. The divisions
in the Fascist Party were exposed when Bonomi attempted to end

the escalating violence between the Fascists and the Socialist by promoting a Pact of Pacification. Mussolini was aware that the continued and excessive violence by the squads was beginning to alienate public opinion and might indeed result in a crackdown by the police, which could lead to a ban on Fascism. By concluding such a pact on 2 August with the parliamentary Socialist Party and the trade unions, Mussolini hoped that he would strengthen Fascism in its political and parliamentary role.

This view was not accepted by the *Ras*, who rejected it some two weeks later and continued their campaign against the Socialists. Mussolini took a considerable risk by resigning as leader or *Duce* of the Fascist movement, gambling that he would soon prove indispensable. He remained, however, the leader of the Fascist parliamentary group, and in October began the process of creating a National Fascist Party (PNF), which was aimed at recruiting respectable middle-class members.

Social or professional background of National Fascist Party members, November 1921

Background	% of PNF members
Farm workers	24.3
Urban workers	15.4
Students	13.8
Farmers and landowners	12.0
Private employees	9.8
Salesmen and artisans	9.2
Members of free professions	6.6
Manufacturers	2.8
Teachers	1.1
Seamen	1.0

Source: S.G. Payne, *A History of Fascism, 1914–45*, London, Routledge, repr. 2001, p. 103.

In November 1921, at the third Fascist National Congress in Rome, Mussolini conceded that the Pact of Pacification was a dead letter and, in the absence of any rival, won back his position after a brilliant speech. Significantly the Congress also agreed that the Fascist movement was now a 'party under the centralized control of Mussolini'. The National Fascist Party was to consist of three separate sections:

- the party membership
- the squads
- the Fascist trade unions.

The local *fasci* would still be allowed to organize their own squads and elect their own leaders, but the party would create special 'competence groups' which 'would provide advice and leadership in all important technical areas of national life'.[12]

On 1 December, in his first major speech in the Chamber, Mussolini announced that 'the Fascist programme is not a theory of dogmas about which no discussion is tolerated. Our programme is a process of continual elaboration and transformation'.[13] This pragmatic vagueness thus allowed Mussolini to move sharply to the right and embrace a laissez-faire economics that would remove subsidies, encourage free trade and reduce taxes. Significantly he also announced that the party was not necessarily opposed to the monarchy.

The 'march' on Rome

In January 1921 the Bonomi government collapsed as a result of a quarrel between the Democrats and the *Popolari* over the number of seats each had been allotted in the cabinet. There was no clear successor government in prospect, so the King interviewed each party leader in turn, including Mussolini, in an attempt to build a viable coalition of parties. In the end, after almost a month, a weak caretaker government under **Facta** was created , which had no authority and only existed because the major political forces were deadlocked.

Luigi Facta (1861–1930)
Elected deputy in 1891 and was at various times Minister of the Interior and Finance Minister before becoming Prime Minister in 1922.

In the meantime Fascist violence escalated. Mobs led by Farinacci occupied Cremona and forced its local Socialist administration to resign. Indications from both the *Popolari* and the Socialists that they would be ready to support a 'ministry of pacification' in July led to the collapse of the Facta coalition, but Giolitti's refusal to participate destroyed this initiative and led to a second weak Facta government, which moved 'the centre of gravity of the crisis to the right'.[14]

The emphasis now switched to a solution which would involve a cabinet in which Mussolini would participate. In August the Socialists played right into Mussolini's hands when they called a general strike as a protest against the government's inability to keep order. Mussolini immediately acted and announced that, as the government was unable to crush it, the squads would have to. The Fascists could thus once more claim to be the defenders of order, and at the same time break the Socialists' power. By September the *Ras* controlled most of the north Italian towns and their squads were within striking distance of Rome itself.

'Given the breadth of Fascist control of provincial Italy, ... would the seizure of national power prove "a fact before it happened", as one Fascist asked?'[15] It was now inconceivable that any government could be formed without Mussolini, and by October it was clear that the Facta Government could not last much longer.

In this developing political crisis Mussolini skilfuly kept every option open. His chances of success were increased by the divisions among the leading Liberal politicians, who all hoped that they could use Mussolini to strengthen their own position and defeat their political rivals. Giolitti, Facta, Nitti and **Salandra** were all pressing for some sort of governing coalition with him. He also attempted to reassure both the Pope and the King that he was not a revolutionary. However, he did not exclude the option of force, as he was aware that the longer he waited, the more his reputation as a man of action would suffer. On 24 October, in an effort to reassure the party militants, he told a PNF party conference assembled at Naples that 'either we are allowed to govern or we will seize power by marching on Rome.'

During the night of 27–8 October the squads began to seize government offices all over Italy. Facta requested King **Victor Emmanuel** to declare an act of emergency which would allow the army to restore order. If clear orders had been given by both the King and his government then the army would have acted, although many officers sympathized with the Fascists, but the King refused to grant the request. Why did he do this? Probably he had little trust in Facta's ability to control the mounting violence in Italy. Salandra had also advised him against signing the orders because he had hoped that this would lead to Facta's resignation and a new government headed by himself. The King was also inaccurately advised that the army would not be able to defend Rome from the Fascists. Like so many of the governing class he believed in the traditional policy of *transformismo* (see p. 88) and was

Antonio Salandra (1853–1931) Leader of the Conservatives and Prime Minister, 1914–16. He believed that an aggressive foreign policy would unify Italy. He supported the Mussolini regime until 1925.

Victor Emmanuel III King of Italy, 1900–47.

convinced that Mussolini would soon be tamed by being locked into a coalition. He first asked Salandra to form a government, but when Mussolini refused to join, he had little option but to appoint Mussolini on 29 October.

Mussolini was appointed Prime Minister constitutionally, even though the threat of violence was always in the background. Yet to save the face of the squads and the party militants, he was now anxious to give the impression that he had seized power only after 300,000 Fascists had marched on Rome. In fact this was a myth. Mussolini travelled to Rome in a railway sleeping car, while the next day 25,000 disorganized and poorly armed Fascists staggered into Rome. The 'march' on Rome, as Denis Mack Smith has observed, was really 'a comfortable train ride followed by a petty demonstration, and all in response to an express invitation from the monarch'.[16] On 31 October the King and two war heroes, General Diaz and Admiral Thaon di Revel, who were to serve in Mussolini's first cabinet, took the salute as the Fascists marched passed them. They were then sent home by train.

THE CONSOLIDATION OF POWER, 1922–5

This period was shaped, to quote Adrian Lyttelton, by the 'ambiguity of the March on Rome, a violent armed movement prepared by political intrigue and legitimized by royal investiture'.[17] Initially Mussolini had to adapt to the constitutional realities of the Italian state. Although he took over the key posts of interior and foreign affairs as well as the premiership, he still had to negotiate a coalition to give his government a sufficient majority to survive. After protracted negotiations his cabinet consisted of three Fascists, one Nationalist, one Liberal, three Democrats, two non-party military officers and, finally, thanks to Papal pressure, two *Popolari*. It was in fact more 'conservative rather than revolutionary'.[18]

When parliament met on 16 November, Mussolini aggressively demanded 'full powers because we want to assume full responsibility' (see Document 3). On 25 November the Chamber approved this demand and gave Musssolini the necessary emergency powers for one year to introduce, independently of parliamentary approval, measures to reform the economy, bureaucracy, education and the army. Why in a parliament where there were only 35 Fascist members did this happen? It was widely recognized that emergency powers were needed to reorganize the bureaucracy and reduce expenditure. Many deputies and senators were also convinced that Mussolini was the strong man that Italy temporarily needed. In the Senate the Liberal senator, Luigi Albertini, summed up the mood when he observed: 'Mussolini has given to the government freshness, youth and vigour ... he has saved Italy from the Socialist danger which has been poisoning our life for twenty years'.[19]

Mussolini made immediate use of the emergency legislation to disband D'Annunzio's paramilitary legion and to destroy the Communist Party. Over the next two years his power increased dramatically. Yet he took care not to alarm his coalition partners. There was widespread support for his programme for restoring law and order and his economic policy. Land reform was suspended, death duties reduced by half and the commission on the sale of wartime profits was dissolved. The Economics Minister, **Alberto de Stefani**, began an ambitious policy of liberating industry from controls and monopolies.

Alberto de Stefani (1879–1969)
Fascist deputy in 1921 and Finance Minister 1922–5; in 1943 he voted for Mussolini's dismissal.

To many of the *squadrisimo*, Mussolini appeared to be betraying the revolution. Both to strengthen his own position and to appease his followers Mussolini created the Fascist Grand Council as a 'parallel' Fascist cabinet. He also created the National Militia, which incorporated the Fascist squads into a national paramilitary force that replaced the state security forces set up in 1919. This was designed to place the squads firmly under his control and to create an armed force that swore an oath of loyalty to him rather than to the King.

The Acerbo Electoral Law and the election of April 1924

A major barrier to a 'constitutional' Fascist victory achieved peacefully through the ballot box was proportional representation. It was therefore vital, if Mussolini was to be sure of retaining power, that the electoral system should be reformed to ensure that the Fascists had a built-in majority. To achieve this, Giacomo Acerbo, the Fascist undersecretary in the Prime Minister's office, drew up a plan for electoral reform. It was a

mixture of majority and proportional electoral systems. The party
which gained most votes, provided they were at least 25 per cent
of the total votes cast, would be automatically allotted two-thirds
of the seats in the Chamber. If no party gained more that 25 per
cent then all the seats would be divided up according to proportional representation. Constituencies were to be abolished and
Italy divided into 16 electoral districts, in which parties would
draw up lists of candidates.

The Fascists, even after their amalgamation with the small
Nationalist Party in February 1923, had only 42 deputies in parliament. Why then did the Acerbo bill, which was a transparent
device to secure a massive Fascist majority, pass parliament so
easily? It is true that Mussolini ostentatiously crowded the gal-
leries with armed *squadrisimo*, who menacingly played with their
daggers during the debate. Certainly many deputies feared that
Mussolini might be about to launch a second revolution, but the
Liberals and Conservatives were glad to see the end of an electoral system that had so strengthened Socialism. They also hoped
that a secure party majority in parliament would normalize
Fascism and lead it to abandon violence.

This sentiment was also shared by the Pope, who was both
grateful that the Mussolini government had made religious
instruction in schools and universities compulsory and had also
saved the *Banco di Roma*, which financed the Catholic Church's
organizations in Italy, from bankruptcy. It was Papal intervention
that finally persuaded the majority of the *Popolari* to abstain
from voting against the bill, which on 10 July was accepted by the
Chamber 235 to 139, and in the Senate by 165 to 41.

In the subsequent election in April 1924 bribery and violence
were used on a large scale. Socialists were particularly singled out
for attacks and intimidation and several hundred people were
killed. However, even without the Acerbo Law Mussolini would
have achieved a majority, as indeed his enemies conceded. He
enjoyed the support of the monarchy and the papacy, and he also
fought the election as a coalition leader, who enjoyed the backing
of such eminent politicians as Salandra and Orlando. When parliament met, the government had the backing of 403 deputies, with a
further 29 giving their qualified support, while the opposition consisted of 39 *Popolari*, 25 moderate Socialists, 22 **Maximilists**, 19
Communists, one dissident Fascist and two Sardinian Nationalists.

Maximilists
Radical Socialists, who
wished to implement a
purely Socialist
programme.

The Matteotti Affair and its consequences

Even after the election Mussolini's aims were far from clear. As Richard Bosworth has observed, 'hindsight always smoothes the confusions of real life, locating patterns and inevitabilities, where they might not have existed.' Bosworth goes on to argue that it was quite possible that Mussolini, as many moderates within his own party hoped, would at last become a constitutional prime minister and absorb the Socialists into 'the big tent', as he had already done with the parliamentary centre and right[20] (see Document 4). What prevented this neat *transformismo* was the refusal of the opposition to recognize the legitimacy of the Fascist victory. Thus **Giacomo Matteotti**'s speech at the opening of parliament, criticizing the validity of the elections, was a major challenge to Mussolini (see Document 5). Matteotti's subsequent murder on 10 June by the *Ceka*, a gang of Fascist thugs, triggered a major crisis, which threatened Mussolini's position and appeared to give the Italians one last chance of ousting him. Yet this very possibility was also a moment of truth that made the King, the Vatican, the majority of the Senate and several other key institutions realize why they had supported Mussolini in the first place. They still feared above all the Left, and also were convinced that, rather than give up power quietly, Mussolini – or the *Ras* – would plunge Italy into civil war.

The King was initially reassured when Mussolini handed over the post of Ministry of the Interior to the ex-Nationalist and loyal royalist, **Luigi Federzoni**, and dismissed **Emilio de Bono**, the head of police. On 24 June the Senate gave Mussolini a massive vote of confidence, which was opposed by only 21 senators. Mussolini was also helped by the fact that the opposition parties, following the precedent set by the Aventine Succession (when the plebians of ancient Rome in 494 BC retreated to the Aventine Hill in protest against patrician rule), decided to withdraw from parliament in protest rather than stay and fight. Unfortunately this merely removed opposition from the Chamber, and enabled Mussolini's government for the rest of the session to escape from searching criticism.

The crisis did not, however, die down. In August the discovery of Matteotti's body led to a renewed outburst of criticism both in the press and in parliament, when it reconvened after the summer

Giacomo Matteotti (1885–1924)
Came from a wealthy family; first elected to parliament in 1919, he became a bitter critic of the Fascists before the march on Rome. In 1922 he joined the break-away moderate or 'minimalist' Socialist Party.

Ceka
Small squad or gang composed of about 12 violent criminals, which had been set up in early 1924 to teach the most dangerous opponents of Mussolini a lesson; it was run by Giovanni Marinelli, the Party Treasurer. It was called by Mussolini's critics in parliament the *ceka* after the much larger and more formidable Bolshevik secret police in Russia (see p. 53).

Luigi Federzoni (1878–1967)
Nationalist deputy, Colonial and Interior Minister, 1924–9 and then President of the Senate. He supported Mussolini's dismissal in July 1943.

Emilio de Bono (1866–1944)
One of the four organizers of the march on Rome in 1922, Governor of Libya in 1925 and then commander of the Italian troops in Ethiopia. He helped topple Mussolini in 1943.

recess (see Document 6). Mussolini now faced a growing challenge from two different sources:

- He was in danger of alienating the Conservatives and those Liberals who had joined the Fascist list in the elections.
- He was also facing mounting criticism from the *Ras*, who feared that he was selling out to his opponents and making too many concessions to them in his attempts to keep their support. With the dismissal of Balbo they feared, above all, that they, too, might lose their jobs in the militia.

The crisis finally came to a head when on 27 December the liberal newspaper, *Il Mondo*, published a memorandum, written a few days earlier, by the former director of Mussolini's press office, which implicated Mussolini in a long list of assaults and murders. When the cabinet met on 30 December two ministers pressed for the government's resignation, but at the same time Mussolini was given an ultimatum by 33 of the *Ras*, who informed him that he should either forcefully impose a Fascist regime on Italy or else they would act independently to save Fascism. Their message was underlined by large-scale rioting in Florence.

To remain in power Mussolini had now to seize the initiative. He declared full responsibility 'for all that had happened' and then vowed to give Italy the tranquillity it craved – 'peacefully if possible but through force if necessary'. Parliament was then adjourned. The Minister of the Interior also ordered the **prefects** to close down all organizations which threatened 'to subvert the powers of the state', even if they were only bars where 'subversives' might meet to talk politics. Parliament and the opponents of Fascism had suffered a decisive defeat (see Document 7).

Prefects
The chief administrative officers of Italian provinces.

THE GROWTH OF THE TOTALITARIAN STATE, 1925–9

After 1925 the word 'totalitarian' became one of the most popular terms used by the Fascist regime . Initially it seemed to suggest that the Fascist movement itself would be a totality 'within which all other institutions were to move',[21] but in 1925 Mussolini devised the formula 'everything within the state, nothing outside the state', which indicated that the Fascist 'revolution' would be carried out by the state aided by the party in a firmly subordinate position.

Party–state relations

In January 1925, when the Mussolini regime was saved by the intervention of the *Ras*, it seemed as if the party would regain some of the influence it had lost since October 1922. In February Mussolini appointed Farinacci, the hard-line *Ras* of Cremona, as the party's Secretary. Farinacci fanatically believed in the party's role as guardian and guarantor of the Fascist revolution and aimed to create 'the strictest dictatorship of the party in the nation' which implied that the state would be subordinated to it. He launched a campaign of terror against the regime's opponents throughout the country and attempted to replace traditional civil servants with 'men of proven Fascist faith'. The party even managed to set up its own political groups within the ministries.

Roberto Farinacci (1892–1945)

In his early years Farinacci was a rail road worker and, like Mussolini, he initially joined the Socialist Party, but became an ardent supporter of intervention in 1914. In 1919 he joined the Fascist movement and became the local *Ras* of Cremona. So strong was his position by 1922 that he was able to appoint himself the city's mayor. Farinacci was the leader of the *intransigenti*, the party's hard-liners, and accused Mussolini of being too liberal. After his year as Party Secretary, he retreated into the background, but volunteered to fight in the Ethiopian war. He became a member the Fascist Grand Council, and in 1938 joined the cabinet with a special brief to enforce the new anti-Semitic laws (see pp. 281–4). He was a great supporter of the alliance with Germany and remained loyal to Mussolini after his downfall. In 1945 he was shot by Italian partisans.

In many ways, however, these actions clashed with reality. Mussolini still needed the backing of the Crown, Church, army and industry and could not afford to allow the Fascist party to embark upon a policy of '**permanent revolution**'. Thus at the

Permanent revolution
A policy of accelerating change, which maintains the original radicalism of a revolutionary party.

Augusto Turati
(1888–1955)
Journalist and
interventionist in 1914. In
1920 he joined the Fascist
movement, and between
1926 and 1930 was the
Party Secretary. In the
early 1930s he was
expelled from the party for
criticism of Mussolini's
economic policy. In 1938
he was allowed to rejoin,
provided he worked for a
time in Ethiopia. During
the Second World war he
worked as a legal
consultant.

Party Congress in June he stressed that, although the party should aim at the 'Fascistization' of Italy, it must obey orders from above. In April 1926 Farinacci was replaced by **Augusto Turati**, whose task was to restore discipline within the party. Initially he purged the party of some 60,000 veterans, and in October 1926 its organization was transformed by a new statute agreed upon by the Grand Council. By abolishing internal party democracy and laying down that it had to accept candidates nominated by the secretariat in the name of the *Duce*, it broke the tribal system of the *Ras*.

The party was now tightly controlled from the centre and subordinated to the state. In his circular to the prefects of 5 January 1927 Mussolini stressed that 'all citizens . . . owe respect and obedience to the highest political representative of the Fascist regime' (see Document 7). The restoration of the prefects' powers had been made acceptable by the appointment of eight Fascist prefects drawn from the party. Yet this did not stop a growing rivalry between the local party leaders and the individual prefects, who had a vested interest in preserving their influence and superiority over the party.

By 1929 the Fascist Party had become largely depoliticized and bureaucratized. E.R. Tannenbaum, the American historian, argues that 'the "Fascist revolution" was merely history' by 1930.[22] The tenth anniversary exhibition devoted to the 'march' on Rome of 1922 (see pp. 98–100), for example, glorified the *squadristimo* but also made very clear that they belonged to the past. The party militia, too, was suspended in a limbo. It was neither permitted to become a real force independent of the state, nor was it integrated into the army. It was kept on as a 'living sign of the permanence of the Fascist Revolution with its militaristic overtones'.[23]

Dino Grandi
(1895–1988)
An early supporter of
Mussolini. He was elected
to parliament as a Fascist
deputy in 1921, and was
Foreign Minister, 1929–32
and then Italian
ambassador in London,
1932–9. He played a key
role in Mussolini's
downfall in July 1943 (see
pp. 439–40).

The main role of the party remained, as **Dino Grandi** observed in 1922, to educate 'the masses to a sense of national discipline'. Essentially the party was to carry out this role by orchestrating propaganda on behalf of the government, administering mass organizations like the OND and EOA (see pp. 265–7) and by taking charge of the various youth organizations (see p. 262).

The police state

With the subordination of the party to the state, the repressive role of the squads and the militia was transferred to the state police, which became the regime's main instrument of control. What still remained of the liberal state was swept away in response to three separate attempts to assassinate Mussolini. A series of emergency laws drafted by **Alfredo Rocco**, the Minister of Justice, gave the government enormous powers to eliminate the opposition:

Alfredo Rocco (1875–1935)
Rector of the University of Rome and a leading Fascist intellectual; Minister of Justice, 1925–32.

- The Law of Associations (November 1925) banned officials from joining any organization of which the state disapproved.
- In October 1926 all the opposition parties were outlawed.
- The introduction of the Public Safety Law in November 1926 swept away individual rights and restraints on the political power of the state. The police could now arrest at will and the citizen was left without any effective form of appeal.
- A special tribunal was also set up to judge crimes against the state. Political prisoners convicted by this court could be sent to penal settlements on Lipari and other remote islands off southern Italy. Between 1927 and 1929 5,046 people came up before the tribunal, of whom a fifth were convicted.
- At the end of 1927 **Arturo Bocchini**, the Chief of the Security Police, set up the OVRA. The Fascist regime never explained what these initials stood for, but it was assumed that it stood for *Organizzazione di Vigilanza Repressione dell'Antifascismo* (Organization for Vigilance against Anti-Fascism), whose task was to investigate any activity that was potentially hostile to the state. It tapped telephones, read private correspondence and 'even drew up reports on graffiti in the public urinals'.[24]

Arturo Bocchini (1880–1940)
Chief of Police and senator.

Attempts to assassinate Mussolini

- On 4 November 1925 Tito Zaniboni, a member of Matteotti's Socialist Party, was arrested with a sniper's rifle in his hand before he could take aim at Mussolini.
- The second attempt was made on 7 April 1926 by the Honourable Violet Gibson, an Anglo-Irish aristocrat, who was

> mentally ill and was intending to kill either the Pope or
> Mussolini. She would have killed Mussolini if he had not
> moved his head moments before she pulled the trigger of her
> revolver. The bullet merely grazed his nose.
> - The third unsuccessful attempt was made by an anarchist on
>   11 September 1926, who hurled a grenade at Mussolini's car.
> - The final attempt was made in Bologna by a 16-year-old boy
>   on 31 October 1936, although there are theories that dissident
>   Fascists were really behind the incident. The bullet actually
>   passed through a sash Mussolini was wearing without grazing
>   him. The unfortunate boy was lynched and his family
>   arrested.

Parallel to the increase in powers to the repressive organs of
the state went the emasculation of parliament and democratic
local government. In December 1925 Mussolini was declared
Head of Government, and was now no longer answerable to parliament. Only the King could now ask for his resignation. The
cabinet became increasingly unimportant as Mussolini was able
to make laws by decree, which would only later be rubber-
stamped by parliament. In May 1928 parliament itself was
radically transformed. Direct elections were abolished and membership of the Chamber of Deputies was made up of 400
representatives who were chosen by the Grand Council from a list
of 1,000 names put forward by the syndicates (see p. 110) and
other approved organizations such as the National Combatants'
Association. The voters could only vote or reject the whole of the
list. Parliament was dissolved without being given any chance to
debate this bill. In the subsequent election, which was more like a
plebiscite on Mussolini's record, some 90 per cent of the voters,
who were heavily influenced by the Pope's endorsement of the
regime after the successful negotiation of the Lateran Parts (see
p. 112), voted for the party list.

Democracy at local level was also abolished. Democratically
elected councils and local mayors were replaced by an official, the
podestà, selected by the local prefect. Many of these officials were
recruited from the ranks of the landowners who had controlled
local government before 1919, and were being rewarded for their
backing during the key period of 1922–5.

The development of corporatism

The guiding principle behind corporatism was that both workers and employers would be represented in the same organization – or corporation, as it was called. It was assumed that the corporations would coordinate and improve production by creating a new harmony between workers and employers. As Farrell has observed, 'the emphasis was not on nationalisation of the means of production – private property in other words – but on the nationalisation of the people – the forces of production. The aim was the abolition of class war – the creation of class collaboration'[25] (see Document 8).

The reality was to be different and in practice the new corporations favoured the employers rather than the workers. This inevitably contradicted the ambitions of **Edmondo Rossoni**, the leader of the Fascist syndicates. The weakness of the existing Fascist unions, the syndicates, was shown all too clearly when in 1924 during a strike by the metal workers in northern Italy the majority of the workers followed the leadership of the Socialist-controlled Federation of Metalworkers. The strike was only ended by party and governmental intervention.

Edmondo Rossoni (1884–1965)
Former Syndicalist and revolutionary agitator. He became the Secretary of the National Confederation of Syndical Corporations in 1921 and member of the Fascist Grand Council. In July 1943 he voted for Mussolini's removal.

Once Mussolini had purged the more militant Fascist Syndicalist leaders, he was able to impose an agreement, drafted by Alfredo Rocco, the Minister of Justice, on both the employers and the syndicates. By the Palazzo–Vidoni Pact, which became law in April 1926, the employers, organized in the *Confindustria*, the most influential employers' association, agreed that the syndicates alone would represent organized labour. The employers in their turn insisted that elected factory councils should be abolished and that the syndicates should have no authority within the workplace. The law did not deal with the two sides of industry in an even-handed way:

- unions and employers were not combined into single corporations
- the employers were still represented by the *Confindustria*
- both strikes and lock-outs were made illegal, but without strikes employers hardly needed to threaten to lock workers out of the factory
- there was an arbitration court, but it consisted of a judge and two legal advisers; no workers' representatives with experience of industrial disputes were consulted.

**Giuseppe Bottai
(1895–1959)**
A journalist who joined the
Fascist Party in 1919. He
was Minister of
Corporations, 1929–32
and of Education,
1936–43. He voted for
Mussolini's dismissal in
July 1943.

In July 1926 the Ministry of Corporations was set up nominally under Mussolini's control, although really it was run by
Giuseppe Bottai, whose ultimate aim was to create mixed organizations of both workers and employers. A year later, in an
attempt to appease the workers, who were facing the economic
consequences of the 'battle for the lira' (see p. 111), the Charter
of Labour was produced. This defined workers' rights in the area
of employment laws, social insurance and welfare provision, but
it never became more than a statement of intent and was never
given the force of law.

In 1928 the syndicates were reorganized into six workers'
associations, which were now controlled by the government. This
corresponded exactly with the number of employers' organizations and effectively weakened the power base of the syndicates.
Clearly, the corporatist ideology had been used as a front to
undermine the remaining powers of the syndicates. It was, too, a
belated response to the unrest and illegal strikes that had broken
out against the regime's attempts to lower wages (see p. 111).

Reorganization of the corporations continued until 1934 when
The employers, workers, representatives of the Fascist Party, technical experts and managerial staff were now represented in 22
'mixed corporations', which were given the power to fix wages,
settle labour disputes and advise generally on economic issues.
Most historians, however, argue that these corporations were a
façade behind which the government and the employers merely
continued to control the workforce. By 1937 the National
Council of the Corporations no longer even met, but labour continued to be subject to severe controls, whereas big business,
represented through the Italian Confederation of Employers and
Cartels, managed to retain its independence. As Roland Sarti, the
American economic historian, observed, 'corporatism was a
useful smoke screen to disguise the retention of economic power
in private hands'.[26]

The economy: the 'battles' for the lira and for grain

Mussolini did not entirely abandon his dislike of capitalism, but
in his early years of power he needed the support of Italian businessmen and bankers. His first Minister of Finance, Professor
Stefani, a strong advocate of free enterprise, set about creating a

more favourable environment for capitalism. Taxes were cut, rent controls removed, and telephones and life insurance privatized.

Initially the Italian economy benefited from the general European economic upturn, but by the end of 1925 inflation was rising steeply and the lira was falling sharply against the British pound and American dollar – in July 1926 it was worth 153 to the pound. To curb inflation and attract inward investment Mussolini launched the 'battle for the lira', which was revalued in stages until in July 1927 it was worth 92 to the pound. Mussolini proceeded against the advice of most businessmen, who argued that this was far too high a rate of exchange with sterling, but for Mussolini it became a matter of prestige, and the credibility of Fascism was seen to be at stake.

The economic and social cost of this was, however, high. Unemployment increased from 225,346 in January 1927 to 439,000 in January 1928, and the export industries were badly hit, as Italian cars, light engineering and textiles priced themselves out of the world market. This led to officially imposed wage cuts, which were only partly balanced by attempts to peg the prices of the main foodstuffs. On the other hand, the steel and chemical industries benefited from the new exchange rate, which enabled them to draw on cheaper imports. By 1929 Italy had become self-sufficient in chemicals, and steel production had increased from 982,000 tonnes in 1922 to 2,122,000 in 1929.

In an effort to make Italy self-sufficient in grain supplies Mussolini also waged a 'battle for grain'. High tariffs were imposed on imported grain, and through subsidies, compulsory marketing agencies and the encouragement of new farming techniques, the government encouraged farmers and peasants to switch over to cereal crops. If measured by the increase in wheat harvested, the government's achievement was impressive. The average harvest rose from 5.39 million tons in 1921–5 to 7.27 million tons by 1935, yet this was achieved at a considerable economic cost. In the south, olive and citrus fruit trees and vines were destroyed to make way for grain crops, and valuable export markets in olive oil, citrus fruits and wine were lost to Spain and Greece.

To make more land available for the growing of cereals, another propaganda battle was waged for land reclamation. In 1928 large amounts of money were poured into land-drainage schemes. Most of these were in the north. The Pontine marshes, near Rome, were successfully drained and populated with small farms worked by ex-soldiers, the Emilia Canal was constructed and the Volturno Valley partially colonized, but elsewhere, particularly in the south there was little success.

Church–state relations

As a Marxist before 1914, Mussolini had dismissed the Church as a tool of capitalism and the bourgeoisie, but once he was elected to parliament he began to make overtures to the Papacy. As a realist, he appreciated its influence and strength in Italy. Consequently, during his first few years in power, even though the squads attacked the *Popolari* and the Catholic trade unions, Mussolini was determined not to alienate the Papacy. He thus tolerated a return to hanging crucifixes on the walls of classrooms and other public buildings, and saved the Bank of Rome, which was the Vatican's bank, from collapse (see p. 102).

Although the Papacy pursued a policy of benevolent neutrality towards the regime during the Matteotti crisis, it was worried about the impact of the 'totalitarian state' on the independence of the Church. The Pope was particularly concerned about the impact of the *Balilla* – the Fascist Youth Movement (see p. 262), which was determined to organize and to indoctrinate the whole of Italy's youth between the ages of 8 and 17 – on Catholic Action, a network of youth clubs and professional organizations. His solution was to negotiate an agreement recognizing the Fascist state in return for securing safeguards and concessions for the Church.

Negotiations were completed with the signature of the Lateran Pacts in February 1929, which consisted of three agreements:

- A treaty: recognizing the independence of the Papacy with its own sovereign state, the Vatican City.
- A financial convention: paying financial compensation to the Papacy for the annexation of the Papal states, 1860–70.
- A concordat: confirming the teaching of Christianity in both secondary and primary schools. It also guaranteed the existence of Catholic Action's organizations 'in so far as ... they maintain their activity wholly apart from every political

party and under immediate control of the hierarchy of the Church for the diffusion and practice of Catholic principles' (see Document 9).

For Mussolini the Lateran Pacts were a great propaganda triumph. He had negotiated a settlement with the Papacy, which had eluded his predecessors and in return apparently won the Pope's support for the Fascist state. Pius XI described Mussolini as 'the man of Providence', and urged Catholics to vote for the government in the 1929 elections. On the other hand, Mussolini had to tolerate the continued existence of Catholic Action, which as Martin Clark points out, 'mocked any claim that the *Duce* was rearing a new Fascist generation'[27] (see pp. 262–3).

FOREIGN POLICY, 1922–9

The traditional interpretation of Mussolini's foreign policy stresses its opportunism and rejects any suggestion that Mussolini had long-term plans for Italian expansion. Gaetano Salvemini, for instance, argued that it was improvised daily for purely propaganda purposes, while Mack Smith dismissed Mussolini as a 'cloud-cuckoo-land amateur'.[28] Once the Italian government began to publish the relevant diplomatic documents in the 1960s and 1970s, it was possible to form a more balanced judgement. Ennio di Nolfi, for instance, argued that even though Mussolini viewed the Italian Foreign Office 'as a branch of the Ministry of Propaganda', he had 'a clear and early awareness of his objectives'.[29] What, however, were these objectives? Bosworth, echoing the **Fischer** debate on German policy, stresses the continuity with Liberal Italy.[30]

In practice, outside events and pressures imposed restraints on Mussolini and, certainly until the diplomatic revolution of the 1930s, there was a strong continuity in Italian foreign policy. Nevertheless this should not be allowed to obscure the essential differences between the Fascist regime and the professional diplomats of the Italian Foreign Office. As MacGregor Knox points out, for Mussolini and Hitler 'war was an instrument as well as a goal; an instrument not merely for external conquest but for the barbarisation of Italian and German society and the final taming or destruction of all institutions, from churches to officer corps to the Italian monarchy, that blocked the regimes' paths at home'.[31]

Fritz Fischer
German historian, whose *Germany's Aims in the First World War* (London, Chatto & Windus, 1967) traced a continuity between the foreign policy of Imperial Germany and the Third Reich.

As Italy in 1922 still lacked sufficient economic and military resources, Mussolini, like his predecessors, needed the direct backing of the Great Powers or else an opportunity skilfully to exploit international tensions and rivalries to win key concessions. However, in the 1920s, particularly after the resolution of the Ruhr crisis, the three great European powers – Britain, France and Germany – cooperated in reasonable harmony, and Italy had to remain a marginal player on the European stage.

The Corfu crisis

Briefly the potential dynamic of Fascist foreign policy was revealed in Mussolini's reaction in August 1923 to the murder of an Italian general and his staff, who were killed by bandits operating from within Greece, while they were mapping out the Greco-Albanian frontier for an international inter-Allied Commission. Mussolini seized the chance to confront Athens with a seven-point ultimatum in which he demanded a humiliating apology from Greece and a massive fine of 50 million lire. When the Greeks tried to negotiate, the Italian troops occupied Corfu. As Bosworth has observed, 'Fascist Italy was announcing itself on the international stage with what seemed a replica of the squadrist raids, so ruthlessly deployed against its socialist and other domestic enemies.'[32] In the end, however, under Anglo-French pressure Italian troops were forced to withdraw and negotiate a more modest indemnity with Athens.

Italy, Britain and France

After the Corfu incident Mussolini was forced back to following a more conventional foreign policy. Under the influence of his professional diplomats, Mussolini agreed, together with Britain in 1925, to become one of the guarantors of the **Locarno Pact**. Cooperating with Britain at Locarno opened the way up for closer relations with London. At the end of 1925 the British agreed that Italy should take over Jarabub on the Libyan–Egyptian frontier and recognized Italy's right to claim influence over a large part of Ethiopia.

Relations with France, on the other hand, were complicated by rivalry in the Balkans, the election of a left-wing government in

Locarno Pact
The agreement between France and Germany, 1925, that the Rhineland should remain permanently demilitarized and the Franco-German–Belgian frontiers made inviolable.

1924 and, after Matteotti's murder (see p. 103), by the presence of a growing number of anti-Fascist Italian exiles in France. Mussolini attempted unsuccessfully to put pressure on France by trying to draw closer to Germany. He attempted, for instance, to portray the German–Italian Arbitration Treaty of 1926, which was nothing more than a conventional statement of good will between the two powers, as an anti-French alliance.

The Balkans and the colonies

In early 1924 Italy acquired Fiume peacefully from Yugoslavia, through a treaty which pledged mutual 'support and collaboration' between the two states, but Mussolini did not abandon his attention of dismembering Yugoslavia. Briefly in 1926 he contemplated the idea of launching 20 divisions across the frontier, but in the end he settled for the more realistic policy of subsidizing the Macedonian and Croat **separatist** movements.

Separatism
A political movement that wants a region or an ethnic group to break away from a country to create its own state.

The centre of Italian influence in the Balkans lay in Albania. In 1926 Mussolini re-established Italian influence there by backing the claims to power of a local chieftain, Ahmed Zog, and by investing heavily in the Albanian economy. By 1928 Albania was, to all practical purposes, an Italian colony.

The Mussolini government also consolidated Italy's grip on the colonial territories of Libya, Somalia and Eritrea. In Somalia the northern Sultanites, which had previously been self-governing, were firmly brought under Italian colonial rule after a two-year military campaign. In Libya Mussolini vetoed the agreement of 1919, which had allowed Tripoli and Cyrennaica to govern themselves, and insisted that Italian control should become a reality. This was, however, only accomplished after a protracted and brutal colonial war.

In 1928 Mussolini concluded a treaty of friendship with Haile Selassi, the Emperor of Ethiopia, which he hoped would lead to Ethiopia becoming an Italian satellite, but the Emperor skilfully avoided this fate by negotiating similar agreements with other powers.

ASSESSMENT

By 1929 Mussolini had consolidated a dictatorship that still, to a great extent, relied on the traditional machinery of the Italian state – the civil service, the police and the army – rather than the party. While the power of the Left was broken, big business, the landowners, the Crown, the Senate and, of course, the Church had all survived. Had Mussolini then simply resided over a conservative restoration? Early, predominately left-wing observers, such as Luigi Salvatorelli and Giovanni Zibordi, saw it as a movement for the social and political aggrandizement of the middle classes in the unique context of the immediate post-war world. Zibordi was convinced that Fascism was 'the instrument of a counter- revolution'[33] against the workers. Certainly corporatism ensured that the working classes were subjected to the control of the state, but Mussolini's government was not the tool of big business or the Conservatives. Initially there were some Bolshevik observers in Moscow who believed that Fascism was predominantly a left-wing ideology, which was in fact a 'heresy from, rather than a mortal challenge to, revolutionary Marxism'.[34]

Liberals, Democratic Socialists and Conservatives in Britain were inclined to accept Fascism as a 'third way' between socialism and capitalism. (see Document 5) **George Bernard Shaw**, for instance, wrote in 1927 that 'some of the things Mussolini has done, and some that he is threatening to do, go further in the direction of Socialism than the English Labour Party could yet venture if they were in power.'[35] Mussolini accepted private property and capitalism, but it had to be subordinated to the state's overall aims, as was shown in his 'battles' for the lira and grain.

George Bernard Shaw (1856–1950)
Anglo-Irish playwright, dramatist and socialist.

The historian E.R. Tannenbaum claims, on the other hand, that Mussolini was only interested 'in personal power and in not making a revolution or otherwise'.[36] In his first seven years of power Mussolini was often forced to be pragmatic to cling onto power, but he nevertheless frequently talked of Fascism as being a 'permanent revolution', and in 1922 described his advent to power as marking 'a profound political, moral, social revolution that in all probability will leave nothing or almost nothing of the past still in existence'.[37] Obviously much of this was just rhetoric, as many continuities with the past remained during his regime. Yet by 1929 Mussolini had created a one-party state and had begun the ambitious process of attempting to create the new tough, Fascist Italian, who would be first and foremost a warrior – which is explored in Chapter 8.

Figure 3.2 Mussolini depicted in December 1936 by the cartoonist 'Kem' as the she-wolf from Rome's Capitoline Hill suckling Europe's 'infant' Fascists: (from left) Hitler, Kemal Attaturk of Turkey, Metaxas of Greece, General Franco, and (far right) Oswald Mosley, leader of the British Fascists, waiting his turn
Source: Estate of Kimon Marengo/Centre for the Study of Cartoons & Caricature, University of Kent.

DOCUMENT 1

The programme of the Fascist movement was announced on 6 June 1919. It was to be considerably changed over the next few years:

Italians!

Here is the national programme of a solidly Italian movement. Revolutionary because it is opposed to dogma and demagogy; robustly innovating because it rejects preconceived opinions. We prize above everything else the experience of revolutionary war.

Other problems – bureaucratic, administrative, legal, educational, colonial etc. – will be dealt with when we have established a ruling class.

For this WE REQUIRE:

For the political problem

a) Universal suffrage with regional *scrutin de liste*, proportional representation with votes for women and their eligibility for office.
b) Minimum age for votes lowered to 18 years; that for deputies lowered to 25 years.
c) Abolition of the Senate.
d) The summoning of a National Assembly to sit for three years, its main task being to establish the constitutional structure of the state.
e) The formation of National Technical Councils for labour, industry, transport, public health, communications etc. to be

elected by professional or trade organisations, to have legislative powers and the right to elect a Commissioner General with ministerial power.

For the social problem WE REQUIRE

a) The prompt promulgation of a state law which sanctions for all the workers the eight-hour working day.
b) Minimum pay.
c) The participation of worker' representatives in the technical management of industry.
d) Entrusting these same workers organizations (if they are morally and technically qualified) with the running of industries and public services.
e) The swift and complete reorganization of railway men and all those in the transport industry.
f) A much needed revision of the draft law on insurance for sickness and old age, lowering the present proposed age limit from 65 to 55 years.

For the military problem WE REQUIRE

a) The establishment of a National Militia with short training periods and designed exclusively for defence.
b) The nationalisation of all arms and munition factories.
c) A foreign policy aimed at enhancing Italy's position in the world through peaceful competition among civilized nations.

For the financial problem WE REQUIRE

a) A heavy, extraordinary and progressive tax on capital which would involve a meaningful PARTIAL EXPROPRIATION of all forms of wealth.
b) The confiscation of all property belonging to religious organizations ...
c) ... the confiscation of 85% of war profits.

Source: J. Whittam, *Fascist Italy*, Manchester, Manchester University Press, 1995, pp. 144–6 (translated from R. de Felice, *Mussolini il Rivoluzionario*, Turin, 1965, pp. 744–5).

DOCUMENT 2
Socialist leagues in Emilia

A. Rossi (the pen name for Angelo Tasca), who was expelled from the Communist Party in 1929, gave the following account of the growth of socialism in Emilia, 1919–21:

Out of 280 communes in Emilia 223 were in socialist hands. The landowners, living in town or country, with their sons, their friends, their contractors and their customers were impotent before the all-powerful workers' syndicates. In the country the prizes and distinctions of public life were almost entirely denied to the whole *bourgeoisie*, and also to members of the lower middle class who were not members of the socialist organizations. The country landowner, who for years had been cock of the walk, head of the commune, manager of all local and provincial bodies, was ousted from all of them. On the land he had to reckon with the 'League' and the employment office, in the market with the socialist cooperative society which fixed prices, in the commune with the red list, which won crushing majorities. Profit, position, power, were lost to him and his children. Hatred and bitterness were welling up, ready at any moment to overflow.

Source: A Rossi, *The Rise of Italian Fascism*, London, Methuen, 1938, pp. 94–5.

Document 3

Mussolini's address to parliament, 16 November 1922

When the Italian parliament met for the first time after Mussolini had been appointed Prime Minister, Mussolini addressed the deputies as follows:

I could have made of this dull and gray hall a bivouac for corpses. I could have nailed up the doors of Parliament and have established an exclusively Fascist Government. I could have done those things ... I do not want, as long as I can avoid it, to rule against the Chamber, but the Chamber must feel its own position. That position opens the possibility that it may be dissolved in two days or in two years. We ask for full powers because we want to assume full responsibility ... The country cheers us and waits. We will not give it words but facts. We formally and solemnly promise to restore the budget to health ... We want to make a foreign policy of peace, but at the same time one of dignity and steadiness ...We intend to give the nation a discipline ... Let none of our enemies of yesterday, of today, of tomorrow be illusioned in regard to our permanence of power.

Source: B. Mussolini, *My Autobiography*, London, Hutchinson, 1928, pp. 185–6.

▶

DOCUMENT 4

A British view of Mussolini, 1923

G.M. Trevelyan, a Liberal historian and a great admirer of Italy, wrote in 1923:

Let us not be impatient with Italy if she is for the moment swerving from the path of liberty in the course of a very earnest attempt to set her house in order and to cope with the evils which the friends of liberty have allowed to grow up ... Signor Mussolini is a great man and, according to his lights, a very sincere patriot. Let our prayer for him be, not that he victoriously destroy free institutions in Italy, but that he may be remembered as a man who gave his country order and discipline when she most needed them, and so enabled those free institutions to be restored in an era happier than that in which it is our present destiny to live.

Source: G.M. Trevelyan, *The Historical Causes of the Present State of Affairs in Italy*, Oxford, Oxford University Press, 1923, p. 20.

DOCUMENT 5

Matteotti's criticism of the General election of May 1924

Against the validity of this election, we present this pure and simple objection – that the ... government, nominally with a majority of over four million ... did not obtain these votes either in fact or freely ... No Italian voter was free to decide according to his own will ... The Premier had entrusted the custody of the booths to the Fascist militia men.

Source: R. Collier, *Duce!*, London, Collins, 1971, pp. 72–3.

DOCUMENT 6

Mussolini on the Matteotti crisis

In his autobiography, which was published in 1928, Mussolini wrote as follows:

The development of the Italian public life from June till December 1924 gave a spectacle absolutely unparalleled in the political struggle of any other country. It was a shame and a mark of infamy which would dishonour any political group. The press, the meetings, the subversive and anti-Fascist parties of any quality, the false intellectuals, the defeated candidates, the brain-soft cowards, the rabble, the parasites, threw themselves like ravens on a corpse. The arrest of the guilty was not enough. The discovery of the corpse and the sworn verification of surgeons, which stated that the death was not due to a crime, but was produced by trauma, was not enough.

Source: Mussolini, *My Autobiography*, 1928, p. 206.

DOCUMENT 7
Mussolini's circular to the prefects, 5 January 1927

I solemnly reaffirm that the prefect is the highest authority of the state in the province. He is the direct representative of the central executive power. All citizens, and in particular those having the great privilege and supreme honour of supporting Fascism, owe respect and obedience to the highest political representative of the Fascist regime and must work under him to make his task easier.

Whenever necessary, the prefect must stimulate and harmonize the various activities of the party ... The party and its members, from the highest to the lowest, now that the revolution is complete, are only a conscious instrument of the will of the state whether at the centre or the periphery ...

Now that the state is equipped with all its own methods of prevention and repression there are some 'residues' that must disappear. I am speaking of *squadrisimo* which in 1927 is simply anachronistic, sporadic but which reappears in an undisciplined fashion, during periods of public commotion. These illegal activities must stop ... The era of reprisals, destruction and violence is over ... the prefects must prevent this happening by using all means at their disposal, I repeat by using all means at their disposal.

Source: Whittam, *Fascist Italy*, p. 153.

DOCUMENT 8
The corporate state

In July 1926 Mussolini wrote an official press release announcing the setting up of the Ministry of Corporations:

▶

Fascists of all Italy! . . . for the first time in the history of the world a constructive revolution as ours is has achieved peacefully in the field of production and labour, the organization of all the economic and intellectual forces of the nation, so as to direct them towards a common goal. For the first time a powerful system of thirteen organizations has been created, all placed on the same level of parity, the legitimate and reconcilable interests of all recognized by the sovereign State . . . Black shirts! Raise up your banners! Celebrate, with an act of will and of faith today's date! It is among the most brilliant of our revolution.

Source: N. Farrell, *Mussolini. A New Life*, London, Weidenfeld & Nicolson, 2003, pp. 192–3.

DOCUMENT 9
The Lateran Pacts

The Lateran Pacts were signed on 11 February 1929 by Mussolini and Cardinal Gasparri. These consisted of a treaty, a financial convention and a concordat. Quoted below are extracts from the Concordat:

Article 20
All bishops, before taking possession of their diocese, will take an oath of fealty to the head of state, according to the following formula: Before God and his Holy Gospel I swear and promise as is fitting in a bishop, fealty to the Italian State. I swear and promise to respect, and to make respected by my clergy, the King and Government established according to the constitutional laws of the State . . .

Article 36
Italy considers the teaching of the Christian doctrine, in accordance with Catholic tradition, as both the basis and the crown of public education. It therefore agrees that the religious teaching now given in the public elementary schools shall be extended to the secondary schools in accordance with a programme to be drawn up by the Holy See and the State.

Article 43
The Italian state recognizes the organizations forming part of Catholic Action, in so far as, in accordance with the injunction of the Holy See, they maintain their activity wholly apart from every political party and under the immediate control of the hierarchy of the Church for the diffusion and practice of Catholic principles.

The Holy See takes the opportunity of the drawing up of the present Concordat to renew to all ecclesiatics and religious throughout Italy the prohibition to be members of, or take part in, any political party.

Source: J. Pollard, *The Vatican and Italian Fascism*, 1929–32, Cambridge, Cambridge University Press, 1985, pp. 210–15.

DOCUMENT 10

Italianization programme for the territories gained in 1919–20

The Fascist Federal Secretaries from the six frontier provinces met in Trieste on 12 June 1927 and drew up a memorandum, extracts of which are quoted below:

It is necessary to prevent the Slav lawyers, who are dangerous, from making free use of their profession for the purpose of that petty propaganda which attracts proselytes and nourishes illusions.

It is necessary to cut the Slav teachers out of the schools, the Slav priests out of the parishes. In this way Fascism will resolve fully the question of those of alien language in Italy, in the interests of the state, and also in the interests of the Slav population itself; because it does not profit the Slavs to be guided by those professional agitators who give them the appearance of rebels and anti-state persons.

Source: D. Rusinow, *Italy's Austrian Heritage, 1919–46*, Oxford, Oxford University Press, 1969, p. 20.

NOTES

1 P. Corner, 'State and liberty, 1901–1922' in A. Lyttelton, *Liberal and Fascist Italy*, Oxford, Oxford University Press, 2002, p. 32.

2 A. Lyttelton, *The Seizure of Power. Fascism in Italy 1919–1929*, London, Weidenfeld & Nicolson, 2nd ed. 1987, p. 30.

3 P. Corner, *Fascism in Ferrara, 1915–1925,* Oxford, Oxford University Press, 1975, p. 80.

4 R.J.B. Bosworth, *Mussolini*, London, Edward Arnold, 2002, p. 128.

5 Lyttelton, *The Seizure of Power*, p. 43.

6 N. Farrell, *Mussolini. A New Life*, London, Weidenfeld & Nicolson, 2003, p. 81.

7 P. Corner, *Fascism in Ferrara*, p. 105.

8 Ibid., p. 138.

9 Bosworth, *Mussolini*, p. 152.

10 Ibid., p. 156.

11 Lyttelton, *The Seizure of Power*, p. 77.

12 S.G. Payne, *A History of Fascism, 1914–45*, London, Routledge, repr. 2001, p. 102.

13 Ibid., p. 102.

14 Lyttelton, *The Seizure of Power*, p. 81.

15 Bosworth, *Mussolini*, p. 164.

16 D. Mack Smith, *Italy. A Modern History*, Ann Arbor, University of Michigan Press, 1959, p. 372.

17 Lyttelton, *The Seizure of Power*, p. 94.

18 Ibid., p. 96.

19 Quoted in Mark Smith, *Italy*, p. 374.

20 Bosworth, *Mussolini*, p. 195.

21 Lyttelton, *The Seizure of Power*, p. 269.

22 E.R. Tannenbaum, *Fascism in Italy*, Harmondsworth, Allen Lane, 1973, p. 73.

23 Ibid., p. 84.

24 Farrell, *Mussolini*, p. 184.

25 Ibid., p. 192.

26 R. Sarti, *Fascism and the Industrial Leadership in Italy, 1919–1940*, Berkeley, University of California Press, 1971, p. 101.

27 M. Clark, *Modern Italy, 1871–1982*, Harlow, Longman, 1984, p. 255.

28 Quoted in A.A. Kallis, *Fascist Ideology*, London, Routledge, 2000, p. 7.

29 Quoted in D. Williamson, *Mussolini, From Socialist to Fascist*, London, Edward Arnold, 1997, p. 113

30 R.J.B. Bosworth, *The Italian Dictatorship: Problems and Perspectives in the Interpretation of Mussolini and Fascism*, London, Edward Arnold, 1998, p. 89.

31 M. Knox, 'Expansionist zeal, fighting power, and staying power in the Italian and German dictatorships' in Richard Bessel, ed., *Fascist Italy and Nazi Germany*, Cambridge, Cambridge University Press, repr. 1997. p. 114.

32 Bosworth, *Mussolini*, p. 187.

33 F.L. Carsten, 'Interpretations of Fascism', in Walter Laqueur, ed., *Fascism: A Reader's Guide*, Harmondsworth, Penguin, 1979, p. 464.

34 Payne, *A History of Fascism*, p. 126.

35 Farrell, *Mussolini*, p. 157.

36 E.R. Tannenbaum, quoted in Williamson, *Mussolini, From Socialist to Fascist*, p. 50.

37 Ibid., p. 50.

CHAPTER FOUR

The vacuum of power and the rise of authoritarianism, 1918–29

TIMELINE

1918 31 October	Revolution breaks out in Hungary
3 November	Independent Polish Republic proclaimed
16 November	Hungarian Republic declared in Budapest
1 December	Kingdom of Serbs, Croats and Slovenes (Yugoslavia) declared
1919 10 April	Romanian troops advance into Hungary
15 May	Greek troops advance into Anatolia
1 August	Fall of Bela Kun regime in Hungary
17 August	Peasant Party wins Bulgarian election
1920 I March	Horthy becomes Hungarian Regent
June	Social Democrats resign from Austrian government
1921 1 January	New centralized constitution is proclaimed in the Kingdom of Serbs, Croats and Slovenes, setting up a central government dominated by Serbs
17 March	Polish constitution is created
1923 9 June	Stamboliski overthrown in Bulgaria
1925 16 April	Communists explode bomb in Sofia Cathedral
1926 12 May	Military coup in Poland led by Marshal Pilsudski
28 May	General Gomes de Costa seizes power in a coup d'état in Lisbon
22 August	General Panaglos overthrown in Greece
1927 July	Civil war in Vienna between Left and Right
1929 January	King Alexander of Yugoslavia suspends constitution

INTRODUCTION

The defeat of the Central Powers created a vacuum in Eastern and Southern Europe, which was filled by the successor states set up by the victorious Allies in 1919. The failure of the Red Army in Russia to link up with Communists in Germany, Vienna and Budapest ensured that the constitutions of these states would, initially, at any rate, be determined by the Western Powers, who were convinced that the principle of **national self-determination** would lead to a stable and democratic Europe. Yet this was to prove an optimistic assumption. Apart from Finland and Czechoslovakia, all the successor states in Southern and Eastern Europe had either dictatorships or semi-authoritarian regimes by 1930. The reasons for the failure of democracy to take root were economic, political and social:

National self-determination
The right of nationalities to create their own nation-states.

- The populations were overwhelmingly peasant and illiterate.
- The forces that could unite the nation were the traditionally conservative focus points of the Crown, the Church and the army. They were determined to seize control in order to block the spread of Bolshevism. Like their counterparts in Italy, and later Germany, they were ready to look to the radical Right for allies. However, in contrast to Italy and Germany, they were able to dominate these weak far-right groups, which had sprung up in imitation of Mussolini's **Black Shirts**, and establish traditional conservative dictatorships.

Black Shirts
The uniform of the Italian Fascist movement was black shirts; they were worn by the Fascist squads.

- The moderate liberal, democratic centre was weakened by the social and economic problems caused by the war.
- None of the states was a nation-state as such, and all had large ethnic minorities, yet frequently the exploitation of extreme nationalism was the means used to win the support of the majority.
- The peace settlement, particularly the Treaty of Trianon, destroyed the economic unity of Eastern Europe.

THE KEY ISSUES IN THIS CHAPTER ARE:

- The defeat of Bela Kun's Soviet republic in Hungary and the creation of a reactionary conservative regency under Admiral Horthy.
- The overthrow of the Stamboliski government in Bulgaria in June 1923 by the Military League and the Internal Macedonian Revolutionary organization.

- The role of the Crown in Romania in defeating radical governments and establishing a Conservative regime.
- The emergence of the 'Romanian variant' of Fascism.
- Was General Primo de Rivera's regime in Spain 'Fascism from above'?
- The political role of the army in Greece, Poland, Lithuania and Portugal.
- The military coup carried out in Yugoslavia by orders of the King.
- The growing influence of the Italian Fascist model in Austria.

CENTRAL, EASTERN AND SOUTHERN EUROPE

Hungary: the defeat of the Soviet dictatorship

Bela Kun, 1886-?1939
The son of a Jewish Hungarian lawyer; he was converted to Bolshevism, while a prisoner of war in Russia, and was sent back to Hungary in 1918. From 1921 he was a member of the executive of the Comintern and was reported as shot on Stalin's orders in 1939.

Hungary was the only country outside Russia to experience, even though only very briefly, a Soviet dictatorship. In October 1918 a Liberal–Social Democratic coalition under Count Karolyi was formed but, like the Provisional Government in Russia (see pp. 32–6), much of its agenda was dictated by the workers' and soldiers' councils, or soviets, which by February 1919 were already taking over the royal estates and setting up directorates to oversee the administration of many of the counties and cities. In March 1919 Karolyi resigned in protest at the Allied decision to hand over virtually half the kingdom to Romania. The Socialists then formed a coalition with the Communists and agreed to create a Soviet republic in which power resided in the Council of People's Commissars led by **Bela Kun** (see Figure 4.1). Although Kun modelled his regime on the Bolshevik pattern by declaring a class war on the wealthy bourgeoisie and the great estate owners, creating a *cheka* (see p. 53), persecuting priests and forcibly requisitioning food from the peasantry, in reality 'this supposed soviet republic', as Norman Stone observed, 'was never more than a front: nationalism was a more important element in it than anything else'.[1] Faced with the punitive demands of the Allies and the advance into Hungarian territory by Romanian troops, the Hungarians had little option but to look to the USSR for help. Their Socialism, as Kun commented, was really a form of 'national Bolshevism'.

Figure 4.1 Bela Kun, the
Hungarian Communist
leader
Source: Getty Images/
Hulton Archive

Initially it seemed as if the new regime might stem the
Romanian advance. The trade unions and workers councils mobilized a 'red army', which stopped the Romanians from crossing
the River Tisza. In June 1919 it even managed to invade Slovakia
and set up a Soviet republic there, but ultimately this was only a
temporary success because the Soviet Red Army, which had been
forced to retreat from Ukraine (see p. 49), was unable to link up
with the Hungarians. Faced with the overwhelming military superiority of the Czech and Romanian forces, morale crumbled on
the home front, and on 1 August the government resigned. Kun
fled first to Vienna and then to the USSR. In late August the

**Admiral Miklos Horthy
(1868–1957)**
A member of the
Hungarian landed gentry,
who had joined the
Austro-Hungarian navy.
He was aide-de-camp to
Emperor Francis Joseph
during the First World War
and Regent of Hungary,
1920–45. He died in exile
in Portugal in 1957.

White terror
A counter-revolutionary
terror directed at the Left.

**Gyula Gömbös
(1886–1936)**
A professional soldier,
Minister of War and Prime
Minister, 1932–6.

Romanians occupied Budapest and the more moderate regime that briefly replaced the soviet republic government was rapidly overthrown by **Admiral Horthy**.

Horthy immediately unleashed a '**white terror**' which involved purges of the army and police force and executions of Communists, Social Democrat politicians and even of working men and farm labourers. He was not, however, a revolutionary Fascist like Mussolini, but an authoritarian monarchist, who nominated himself 'Regent' until such a time as the monarchy might be restored. He established a regime that remained in power until 1944 and was, to quote Stanley Payne, a 'rarity among twentieth-century systems, a truly reactionary state which endeavoured to maintain as much as possible of the nineteenth century order'.[2] A degree of stabilization was achieved under the Prime Minister Count Stephen Bethlen, who managed to confine Hungarian politics 'within an authoritarian straitjacket' for a decade.[3] The percentage of the population entitled to vote was reduced from 50 per cent to 27 per cent in the countryside, where the gentry could influence the peasantry. The secret ballot was also abolished in favour of open voting, which did much to ensure that the government party of unity won every election until 1944. On the other hand, the Bethlen government made considerable progress in the reconstruction of the economy by checking inflation and negotiating an international loan through the League of Nations. Bethlen also extended accident and sickness insurance for the workers.

To the right of Horthy were several radical Nationalist societies, the most powerful of which was the Association of National Defence, which modelled itself on the Italian Fascists (see Figure 3.2). Its leader **Gyula Gömbös** called himself a National Socialist and had links with both Mussolini, Hitler and Ludendorff (see pp. 154–7) in Germany. By 1923 Gömbös had become disillusioned with the government and even considered a 'march on Budapest', but he lacked sufficient support to overthrow the government. Thanks to the recovery of the economy in the 1920s, Hungarian Fascism declined as a political force and Gömbös himself moved toward the centre and became Minister of War in 1929.

Bulgaria

Like Hungary and Austria, Bulgaria was on the losing side in 1918. By the Treaty of Neuilly Bulgaria was saddled with heavy reparations and lost western Thrace to Greece. Bulgaria's first post-war government was headed by **Alexander Stamboliski** and was based on the Agrarian Union Party, which drew its support from the great mass of the peasantry, who made up some 80 per cent of the population. Stamboliski became in effect a peasant dictator and imposed an unfair burden of taxation on the middle and urban working classes. He was opposed on the left by the Communists and on the right by several groups who were determined to defeat the Agrarians' monopoly of power:

Alexander Stamboliski (1879–1923)
Studied agriculture in Germany and from 1908 to 1915 became an effective spokesman for the peasantry. He played a key role in forcing King Ferdinand to abdicate in 1918.

- The White Guard, which was formed by the Conservatives.
- The army, which with the support of a large number of demobilized and unemployed officers created the Military League.
- The IMRO (Internal Macedonian Revolutionary Organization), which, strengthened by refugees from Thrace, campaigned for the integration of Macedonia in to the Bulgarian state. The IMRO was the most formidable of all these groups.

In June 1923 the Military League, the IMRO and key urban politicians with the backing of King Boris overthrew the government and murdered Stamboliski. As in Hungary, the new government under Professor Tsankov and his successor, Liapchev, was Conservative, although the real power in the cabinet was exercised by General Vulkov, the political leader of the Military League. In 1925 the explosion of a bomb placed by the Communist Party in Sofia Cathedral, which killed more than a hundred people including the Mayor of Sofia and the Chief of Police, prompted a new 'white terror' in which thousand of people were killed and tortured.

As the Right in Bulgaria had no difficulty in containing Communism and Socialism, Fascist groups enjoyed little popular support. In early 1923 the *Rodna Zashtita* (Home Defence), whose members wore a black shirt and adopted the Fascist salute, was formed, but it failed to attract a mass membership. A similar group, the National League of Fascists, was equally isolated and ineffectual.

Romania

Romania was one of the victorious powers in 1918 and managed to double its territory (see Map 1). It lacked, however, the economic resources to integrate the large Hungarian minority in the north-west and the smaller Ukrainian and Turkish minorities in the east. The first election held with universal male franchise was won by the National and Peasants' Parties, which formed a coalition government. Within months, however, it was dismissed, as its attempts at land reforms alarmed the King and the traditional elites. General Averscu, the leader of the People's Party, formed the next government, but in turn he too was dismissed when plans for a property tax fell foul of the King. In 1922 the Liberals won the election and introduced a centralized constitution, which still reserved considerable powers for the Crown. In 1928, however, the National Peasant Party won an outright majority, and for two years formed a genuinely representative government.

The ethnic, political and social tensions within Romania led, as elsewhere in the Balkans, to the emergence of right-wing Nationalist movements, many of which modelled themselves on the Italian Fascist Party. The Romanian variant of Fascism was developed by Cornelieu Codreanu in 1927 when he founded the Legion of Archangel Michael. The historian Ernst Nolte called it 'the most interesting and most complex ... movement [in Europe] because like geological formations of superimposed layers it presents at once both pre-fascist and radically fascist characteristics'.[4] Its overriding aim was to regenerate Romania along Christian lines, although it had no detailed programme.

The League of Archangel Michael was more interested in a state of mind, which demanded faith in God and the leader and loyalty to one's comrades. It identified fully with the Romanian Orthodox Church and took its name from the country's patron saint. It had a hierarchical and conspiratorial type of organization in which the basic unit was a small cell of 12 members at the maximum. At the top was the 'captain'. Its members were imbued with a deep sense of death and personal sacrifice. Its leaders tended to be young intellectuals – Codreanu himself had studied at both Romanian and German universities – while its rank and file came overwhelmingly from poor isolated regions where there was a relatively large Jewish population.

Politically Codreanu had ideas that were similar to Hitler's. For him politics was the equivalent of war, and life was an eternal **Darwinistic struggle**. The nation could be purified and redeemed only through violence and murder. He shared, too, with the Nazis the biological concept of the nation, whose strength was apparently dependent on the blood of the ethnic Romanians (see pp. 231–5 and Document 1). He was convinced that their chief enemies were the Jews.

Darwinistic struggle
A struggle for survival, which the strongest win.

SPAIN

Although Spain had been neutral in the First World War, it nevertheless faced political and social problems in 1919 as deep as any country in Eastern or Southern Europe. As in Italy, the old pre-war parliamentary system of 'elitist Liberalism' could not adapt to the new system introduced by universal franchise. There were bitter strikes in Barcelona, and the Spanish army had suffered a humiliating military disaster in 1921 in Spanish Morocco at the hands of rebel forces. In the summer of 1923 a Liberal coalition came into power with a genuine reform programme, but it was swept away in September 1923 when **General Primo de Rivera** launched a *pronciamento*, or coup, and persuaded the King to appoint him Prime Minister. He was, as Raymond Carr has observed, successful because 'he caught parliamentary rule in its transition from **oligarchy** to democracy . . . Not for the first nor for the last time had a general claimed that he was killing off a diseased body, when he in fact was strangling a new birth.'[5]

Miguel Primo de Rivera (1870–1930)
Fought in Morocco and the Philippines and was made Major-General in 1910.

Oligarchy
A government by the few, i.e. wealthy landowners, etc.

To what extent was Primo de Rivera a Fascist? He certainly admired Mussolini and some of the vocabulary and practices of Fascism were imported from Italy, but essentially he was a modernizing conservative. He launched an impressive public works programme involving road building, electrification and the construction of dams. His state labour arbitration system was partly inspired by Fascist corporatism and he summoned a corporative assembly in 1928 to debate a new constitution. He also attempted to create a large apolitical grouping in the centre, the Patriotic Union, which was a curious mix between the new and old. On the one hand, it was for 'Nation, Church and the King'. On the other hand, it was supposed to represent that 'daily plebiscite of public opinion expressed in streets and railway stations'.[6]

Primo de Rivera's new constitution, however, failed to win over any of his critics, and in January 1930 he resigned after it became clear that he had lost the support of both the Crown and the army. Primo's successor, General Berenguer, failed to establish a new consensus, and a year later – in response to sweeping Republican victories in the municipal elections – the King abdicated.

1926: THE YEAR OF THE FOUR COUPS IN GREECE, POLAND, PORTUGAL AND LITHUANIA

The fragility of democracy in post-war Europe is underlined by the four military coups that occurred in Central and Southern Europe in 1926. They were partly a reaction against weak and divisive political systems in an undeveloped societies, but also a consequence of economic instability.

Greece

Greece, for instance, had suffered a brief civil war in 1917, a disastrous defeat at the hands of the Turks and a coup in 1922, which led to the trial and execution of five former ministers. It was faced, too, with the difficult task of integrating its new northern territories into its economy and then of absorbing over a million refugees from **Smyrna**, who were expelled by the Turks. Civilian government was restored in 1924, only to be swept away again by another military coup by General Panaglos two years later. This time, however, military rule only lasted a few months and Panaglos was overthrown by his own colleagues. The parliamentary regime was restored and managed to survive until 1936 (see p. 378).

Smyrna
In 1920 Greece was awarded Smyrna, but to hold it Greece needed to defeat the Nationalist Turkish forces under Mustapha Kemal. In August 1921 Kemal defeated the Greek army, and expelled the Greek population from Smyrna.

Poland

In Poland the existence of some 26 political parties in parliament, many of which owed their existence to proportional representation, made the formation of a constitutional government strong enough to deal with the economic and fiscal problems facing the country impossible. In April 1926 the coalition government broke up when the Social Democrats refused to support expenditure cuts and heavy increases in taxation. This led in May to a military coup by **Marshal Pilsudski**, 'the first of the post war Bonapartes',[7] who was determined to create a government of national unity. Unlike his Greek counterparts, he had to fight to gain control of Warsaw, but as a member of the Polish Socialist Party he could appeal to the workers. The regime that he established has been described by Payne as a 'moderate pluralist authoritarian regime'.[8] Pilsudski himself exercised power indirectly as Minister of Defence, and his government gained the necessary support in parliament through the creation of a non-party 'Bloc for Cooperation with the Government'.

Josef Pilsudski (1867–1935)
Born in Russian Poland, and was both a Socialist and a Nationalist. In 1919 he was provisional Head of State and commander of the army. He retired in 1923, but returned to politics when he staged the 1926 coup. Until his death he was the virtual dictator of Poland.

Portugal and Lithuania

In Portugal the army also emerged as a crucial stabilizing factor. In May 1926, as in Poland, the attempt to create a stable government after several weak and divisive governments was again led by the army, and six months later a similar coup took place in Lithuania.

YUGOSLAVIA

The **Yugoslav state** was increasingly destabilized by the fierce opposition of the Croats to a centralized constitution that gave power to the Serbs. The Croat Peasant Party was adamant that that this should be replaced by a fairer federal constitution. In December 1928, when the government fell over its rejections of demands to compensate the peasants financially for the failure of their crops, the refusal of the Peasants' Party to serve in a new coalition led to a political deadlock in which the appointment of a constitutional government seemed impossible to achieve. Accordingly, the army with the support of King Alexander intervened, and imposed a dictatorship to safeguard the unity of the kingdom and Serbian hegemony. This dictatorship dissolved the existing parties, imposed restrictions on the press and gave executive powers to the Crown and General Zivkovic, a close friend of Alexander's.

Yugoslav state
The kingdom of Serbs, Croats and Slovenes officially became known as Yugoslavia on 3 October 1929.

AUSTRIA

By the end of the 1920s Austria was in a condition of suppressed civil war. From being the dominant state in a large empire, it had become in 1919 a small state with a huge capital city, Vienna, that was a legacy from the imperial past. The city was dominated by the Socialists, while the other areas of the country were clerical, conservative and above all anti-Marxist.

As in Germany (see pp. 142–5), the Social Democrats (SPD) were in 1919–20 the senior partners in the governing coalition, which drew up the constitution and made peace with the Allies. They were initially more successful than their German counter-parts in creating in Vienna a Socialist militia, the *Volkswehr*, which was able to defend the revolution, but in June 1920 they withdrew from the coalition in protest against the refusal of the Allies to permit the **Anschluss**. This was a tactical error and allowed the Right to form a government. The *Volkswehr* was then disbanded, but on the frontiers with Hungary and Yugoslavia the **Heimwehr**, a right-wing paramilitary force, fought over disputed areas and received help from similar organizations in Germany. In 1923, as a counter to this, the SPD created its own paramilitary force, the *Schutzbund*. The growing friction between the *Heimwehr* and the *Schutzbund* escalated into a major confrontation in 1927 when the former was used to smash a general strike in Vienna. This was a turning point in Austrian inter-war history. The ruling Christian Social Party now 'adopted' the *Heimwehr*.[9] Under the influence of Mussolini and Count Bethlen, the Prime Minister of Hungary (see p. 130), the *Heimwehr* evolved into a semi-Fascist party, which aimed to seize power, and replace what it saw as the Socialist Austrian constitution with an authoritarian corporative state. In September 1930 the leader of the *Heimwehr*, Prince Starhemberg, entered the government as Minister of the Interior and a year later staged an unsuccessful coup.

A rival to the *Heimwehr* was the Austrian Nazi Party. By the early 1920s it had effectively become a branch of its larger sister party in the north. It driving aim was to see Austria incorporated into a great Nazi Reich. It was, however, much smaller than the *Heimwehr* and had a membership of only 4,500 in 1928 (see Document 2).

Anschluss
The union of Austria with Germany.

Heimwehr
Literally, home guard.

ASSESSMENT

In Italy Fascism was an ally, but not a puppet, of big business and the Conservatives, as it had developed through the *squadrisimo* (see p. 93) a powerful force that could neutralize the Socialist trade unions and agrarian organizations. In the less developed states of Eastern Europe Fascism was a marginal movement, as the great landowners, the Crown and above all the army were capable of defending their own interests and intervening decisively in politics to establish authoritarian and conservative regimes. Small Fascist and Nationalist groups did exist, but unlike the Italian Fascists, they were unable to become mass movements, largely because the threat from the left had already been countered (see Document 3).

DOCUMENT 1

The Legion of Archangel Michael

Codreanu describes a speaking tour through the Romanian countryside in December 1929:

After four kilometers I came to the village of Slivna. The night had fallen. The people awaited me in the street with burning lanterns and torches. At the entrance of the village I was received by the Legionaries ... In Comanesti, too, the whole village awaited me with torches and lanterns. The young were singing ... From village to village our number grew. Soon we were twenty horsemen. We were all young, between twenty-five and thirty years old ... As we were so many, we felt that we needed a badge, a uniform. As we had no other possibility, we decorated our caps with turkey feathers. The news of our coming spread through all the villages from mouth to mouth ... The Rumanians came out of their houses full of joy. They put large buckets filled with water in our path. According to old custom this was to bring us plenty and luck. We assembled in the yard of Nicu Balan where the meeting was to take place. Now more than 3,000 people had assembled.

Source: F.L. Carsten, *The Rise of Fascism*, London, Batsford, 1967, pp. 185–6.

DOCUMENT 2

The failure of communism in Austria

Otto Bauer, the leading left-wing politician in Austria, explained to Bela Kun in 1919 why it would be impossible for a communist revolution in Austria to succeed:

German Austria is not a state but a loose bundle of provinces which have been left after the dissolution of the old empire. The provinces are totally different from Vienna, they hate Vienna and daily toy with the idea of separation from the capital on which rests the power of the proletariat and which deprives them of food. The power of the working class in the provinces, which have few towns, is far too small to overcome these centrifugal tendencies ... In these circumstances the coherence of the German Austrian lands is much too loose to be able to withstand a serious upheaval. The proclamation of the Soviet dictatorship would thus probably lead to the immediate secession of the mainly rural and therefore clerical agrarian provinces from Vienna. In Upper Austria ... the workers would be overcome by armed peasants; these lands would repudiate Vienna; the power of the proletarian government would be limited to Vienna, the Wiener Neustadt industrial area and Upper Styria; the provisioning of these districts would be absolutely impossible, and under the pressure of famine the dictatorship would collapse within a very brief time.

Source: F.L. Carsten, *Revolution in Central Europe*, London, Wildwood House, 1972, p. 237.

DOCUMENT 3

Trotsky on the new authoritarian Regimes

In May 1929 Trotsky wrote in the periodical, The New Republic, *the following:*

There is no epoch in human history so saturated with antagonisms as ours. Under too high a tension of class and international animosities, the fuses of democracy 'blow out'. Hence the short circuits of dictatorship. Naturally the weakest ' interrupters' are the first to give way. But the force of internal and world controversies does not weaken; it grows. It is doubtful if it is destined to calm down, given that the process has so far only taken hold of the periphery of the capitalist world.

Source: R. Griffin, ed., *International Fascism: Theories, Causes and the New Consensus*, London, Edward Arnold, 1998, p. 71.

NOTES

1 N. Stone, 'Bela Kun' *In the History of the 20th Century*, no. 33, London, Purnell, 1968, p. 923.

2 S.G. Payne, *A History of Fascism, 1914–45*, London, Routledge, repr. 2001, p. 132.

3 A. Palmer, *The Lands Between. A History of East-Central Europe, 1815–1968*, London, Weidenfeld & Nicolson, 1970, p. 202.

4 Quoted in Payne, *A History of Fascism*, p. 280.

5 R. Carr, *Spain, 1808–1939*, Oxford, Oxford University Press, 1966, p. 523.

6 Ibid., 576.

7 Palmer, *The Lands Between*, p. 194.

8 Payne *A History of Fascism*, 141.

9 K.R. Stadler, 'Austria' in S.J. Woolf, ed., *European Fascism*, London, Weidenfeld & Nicolson, 1968, p. 90.

CHAPTER FIVE

Weimar Germany, 1919–29: the seedbed of Nazism?

TIMELINE

1918	29 September	German High Command calls for an Armistice
	9 November	William abdicates
	10 November	Council of People's Representatives set up
	11 November	Armistice signed between Germany and Allies
	12 November	Central Working Association Agreement signed between heavy industry and trade unions
	16–20 December	Congress of Councils held in Berlin: decision taken to hold national elections
1919	1 January	KPD formed
	5–11 January	Spartacus Union uprising in Berlin
	18 January	Peace Conference opens in Paris
	19 January	Elections to National Assembly
	6 February	National Assembly opens in Weimar
	11 February	Ebert elected first Reich President
	13 February	Scheidemann cabinet based on Weimar Coalition formed (SPD, DDP and Centre)
	7 April–2 May	Soviet republic declared in Munich
	7 May	Peace terms given to German delegation at Versailles
	20 June	Scheidemann cabinet resigns
	28 June	Versailles Treaty signed
	11 August	Weimar constitution comes into operation
	18 November	Hindenburg gives evidence to Committee of Enquiry and genesis of 'stab in the back' myth
1920	10 January	Versailles Treaty comes into operation
	13–16 March	Kapp–Lüttwitz putsch
	March–April	Ruhr uprising
	19 March	US Senate rejects Versailles

6 June	*Reichstag* elections – minority government formed by Fehrenbach (Centre, DDP and DVP)
1921 27 April	German reparation total revised to 132 billion gold marks
10 May	Wirth government formed and policy of fulfilment starts
1922 24 June	Rathenau murdered
August	Inflation accelerates
14 November	Wirth's government resigns; minority government formed by Cuno
1923 11 January	Occupation of Ruhr by French and Belgian troops
13 January	Passive resistance starts
12 August	Fall of Cuno government; Grand Coalition formed by Stresemann
26 September	Passive resistance ends
October	Separatist movements in Rhineland and Palatinate
	Deutsche *Rentenmark* introduced to stabilize currency
	SPD–KPD government in Saxony deposed
3 November	SPD withdraws from Grand Coalition
8–9 November	Hitler–Ludendorff putsch
15 November	*Rentenmark* introduced at value of 1:1 billion paper marks
23 November	Fall of Stresemann cabinet, but he remains as Foreign Minister in subsequent governments up to 1929
30 November	Reparation Commission appoints international committee of exports to assess Germany's capacity to pay
1924 1 April	Hitler sentenced to five years' imprisonment
19 August	Dawes Plan approved by the *Reichstag*
20 December	Hitler released from jail
1925 26 April	Hindenburg elected President
1926 8 September	Germany joins League of Nations
1928 20 May	*Reichstag* elections
29 June	Grand Coalition formed
20 October	Hugenberg becomes leader of DNVP
1929 9 July	Nazis and DNVP jointly oppose Young Plan
3 October	Death of Stresemann
24–9 October	US stock market crashes

Introduction

Given the coming to power of the Nazis in 1933, it is tempting to see the Weimar Republic as the 'seedbed of Nazism' and to interpret the many crises and problems that confronted it as the inevitable countdown to the Third Reich. Wolfgang Mommsen argues, for instance, that the fate of the Weimar Republic was in a sense 'sealed from the start'.[1] The Republic certainly had deep structural problems, yet it was far from inevitable that it would be replaced by a Nazi dictatorship. It survived threats from both the Right and Left in its first four years It had a strong social democratic party, the SPD, and a disciplined and predominantly moderate working class that was able to prevent either a communist or an authoritarian dictatorship being created in the troubled years, 1919–23. By 1926 the Republic seemed to have turned the corner and to be on the road to recovery. In many ways, as John Hiden has observed, 'Weimar democracy was more resilient than has been acknowledged.'[2] The Republic was, however, weakened by the bitter legacy of a lost war. While it might well have survived had the economic and international climate been more benign, it is true to say that the seeds of its downfall, but not necessarily of the Nazi triumph of 1933, were present in 1918–19.

The key issues in this chapter are:

- Whether there was a German revolution, 1918–19?
- The threats to the Republic from both the Left and Right, 1919–23.
- The impact of the Ruhr occupation and hyper-inflation.
- The development of the Nazi Party, 1920–9.
- The stabilization of the Republic.
- The structural weaknesses of the Republic.

THE DEFEAT OF THE REVOLUTIONARY AND AUTHORITARIAN CHALLENGES, 1918–23

The revolution of 1918–19

For Germany the end of the First World War marked the beginning of a period of intense instability. The Admiralty's rash decision to order the German high seas fleet out to launch a suicide attack on the British fleet was the catalyst for a revolution that swept the country. In protest the sailors in Wilhelmshaven and Kiel mutinied and set up soviets or councils modelled on the Soviet pattern (see p. 33). Over the next few days soldiers and workers councils were created in all the large cities of the Reich. 'What started as a naval mutiny within a few days overthrew a mighty empire which seemed to have been built for eternity.'[3] The German emperor was forced to abdicate and then power was handed over to a new Council of People's Representatives under **Friederich Ebert**, the leader of the majority Social Democratic Party, which was formed after negotiations between the two German Socialist parties, the SPD and USPD, and confirmed in office by the Berlin soviets. To the Bolsheviks in Moscow it appeared, as E.H. Carr put it, that 'Germany had entered its Kerensky period [see pp. 34–5]. It seemed inconceivable that, under the stimulus of the Russian example and Russian encouragement, the parallel of the Russian revolution would not be followed to the end.'[4]

Yet such an assessment is misleading. Ebert in fact hated the 'revolution like sin'.[5] The leaders of the majority Socialists had already achieved their principal aims when in October the German government had already effectively introduced parliamentary government by amending the Bismarckian constitution of 1871. For them the November 'revolution' was really a distraction from the crucial priorities of demobilization, food distribution and preparing for the peace negotiations, all of which needed the help of the traditional military and bureaucratic elites.

At most, Ebert saw the Council as a caretaker government until a **constituent assembly** had been elected. Consequently he was prepared not to interfere with the internal discipline of the army as long as it supported the new government. The moderate trade union leaders were also ready to cooperate with the heavy industrialists of the Ruhr, and negotiated the Central Working Association Agreement, which granted the unions an eight-hour day and the establishment of workers' councils in all firms with a workforce larger than 50.

On the other hand, the far Left, which included the Spartacus Union, led by **Karl Liebknecht** and **Rosa Luxemburg**, and the left wing of the USPD, wanted a soviet rather than a

Friederich Ebert (1871–1925)
Co-chairman of the SPD and leader of the provisional German government, 1918–19. He was then appointed the first President of the Weimar Republic.

Constituent assembly
An elected assembly that draws up a constitution.

Karl Liebknecht (1871–1919), Rosa Luxemburg (1870–1919)
Publicly opposed the war and were jailed for anti-war activities. They were released in October 1918 and founded the Spartacus Union.

parliamentary regime in Germany, the formation of a 'red army' or workers' militia and the nationalization of all medium to large-sized farms and the key industries. They attempted to put pressure on the moderates by organizing strikes and demonstrations, which only pushed the SPD leadership further to the right and made it more determined to dampen down unrest at home. Thus, instead of creating a new workers' militia as their counterparts did in Vienna, they looked to the remnants of the imperial army reinforced by the *Freikorps* to restore order (see Document 1).

The *Freikorps*

The *Freikorps* were companies composed of young right-wing volunteers, students and ex-soldiers, particularly the men from the elite Storm Battalions, which sprang up spontaneously throughout the Reich both to combat the revolution within and to defend the eastern frontiers against the Poles and the Russians. They were anti-Semitic, despised democracy, the new Republic and the SPD. In many ways they were the German version of the Fascist squads in Italy and played the same role in crushing German communism. In 1933 Hermann Göring called them the 'first soldiers of the Third Reich'. They certainly had some of the characteristics of the later Nazi movement, yet their main loyalty was to their corps leader and their comrades rather than to a national charismatic leader.

The moderation of the majority of the German workers was shown when the first Congress of Workers' and Soldiers' Councils, which met in Berlin in December 1918, fixed the date for elections to the National Assembly for 19 January, the task of which was to devise the future constitution of the Republic. Ultimately the majority had thus signalled that they wanted a parliamentary republic, in which the bourgeois parties would play an important role. Until the elections, the SPD leaders adopted the attitude that there should be no revolutionary experiments, as the councils would inevitable be superseded by the newly elected government.

The failure to carry out any more radical reforms, such as socialization of industry or the creation of a worker's militia, led to the resignation of the Independent Socialists from the Council and the **Prussian government**. This caused a further polarization between the SPD and the Independent Socialists, which in the view of one German Socialist was 'the root of all evil', that had caused a revolutionary government to become 'dependent upon the old bureaucrats, generals and capitalists. . .'.[6]

On the far left the Spartacus Union and the Bremen left-wing radicals, who had close links with the Bolshevik Party in Russia, united to create the German Communist Party (KPD). On 5 January they staged an unsuccessful uprising in Berlin, which has been called the 'revolution's battle of the Marne',[7] which in September 1914 stopped the German advance on Paris. The uprising was ruthlessly repressed by the military (*Reichswehr*) and *Freikorps* units, and two of the KPD's most prominent members, Karl Liebknecht and Rosa Luxemburg, were murdered. During the next four months strikes and riots broke out throughout the Reich, and 'soviet republics' were declared in Munich, Bremen, Mühlheim and Halle. The army, supported by the *Freikorps*, brutally crushed the revolts, which in turn led to an increasing polarization in German society.

Prussian government
As Germany was a federal state, Prussia, like the other member states of the Empire, such as Bavaria, had its own parliament or *Landtag*.

The revolution in Munich

After the Bavarian King had abdicated on 7 November 1918, an unstable USPD–SPD coalition government was formed by **Kurt Eisner**. In response to his assassination on 12 February 1919 by the Munich university student, Graf Anton von Arco-Valley, a group of USPD members and anarchists declared a 'soviet republic'. On 13 April this was taken over by a group of far-left extremists, under the leadership of the Communist Eugen Levine, a veteran of the Russian 1905 revolution (see p. 16), who set up a dictatorship based on the Russian model. After bitter fighting, which involved atrocities on both sides, it was swept away by *Reichswehr* and *Freikorps* troops two weeks later . These traumatic events had a lasting impact on public opinion in Bavaria and help explain why Munich became such a strong centre of the radical Right (see p. 149) (see Document 2).

Kurt Eisner (1867–191)
Socialist journalist and writer. In 1917 he became the leader of the anti-war Bavarian USPD.

The Weimar constitution

When the elections took place for the national assembly on 19 January, the SPD shared power with the Centre and Democratic

Parties to form the Weimar Coalition. It was faced with the dual challenge of drawing up a constitution and negotiating a peace treaty with the Entente Powers and the USA.

The constitution that emerged and gave shape to the Weimar Republic was much criticized in the years immediately after 1945. Proportional representation, which favoured the growth of small parties, the powers of the president as defined in Article 48 (see pp. 199–200) and the legal obligation for the government to call a referendum if a tenth of the voters demanded it, were all seen as destabilizing factors that played into the hands of extremists. Like Italy and the Eastern European states, the fathers of the Weimar Republic struggled to come to terms with the sudden advent of democracy in a society in which there were still entrenched anti-democratic interests. The constitution certainly provided the context in which the political battle was fought, but it was the voters and politicians who would determine whether it would be abused or respected. These were above all influenced by the legacy of the lost war (see Figure 5.1) and the hopes and fears raised by the brief spasm of revolution in the autumn and winter of 1918–19.

Figure 5.1 An ex-officer is reduced to begging in post-war Germany
Source: Snark International.

The Treaty of Versailles

Until 1918 the hope had been that victory would enable Germany to unload its war costs on her defeated enemies, but defeat deprived Germany of this solution. The Treaty of Versailles, as the historian, Karl Erdmann wrote, was 'too severe since Germany could do no other, from the first step onwards, than to try to shake it off; too lenient because Germany was not so far weakened as to be deprived of the hope and possibility of either extricating herself from the treaty or tearing it up'.[8] Under the Treaty of Versailles:

- Upper Silesia and most of the provinces of west Prussia and Posen were ceded to Poland; only in Marienwerder was there to be a plebiscite; Danzig, linked to Poland by a 'corridor', was to become a free city, under the protection of the League of Nations.
- In the west , besides Alsace-Lorraine returning to France, Eupen and Malmedy were to be ceded to Belgium, while the Saar was placed under the administration of the League of Nations for 15 years, after which there would be a plebiscite; the Rhineland was to be occupied for a period of 15 years by Allied troops (see Map 4).
- Germany lost its colonies and foreign investments, as well as well most of its merchant navy.
- The German army was to be cut down to 100,000 men, its navy to 15,000, while the general staff was to be disbanded. Tanks, aircraft, submarines and poison gas were all forbidden.
- In April 1921 reparations were fixed at 132 billion gold marks.

Versailles, and above all the reparation question, which raised the divisive question of who would have to sacrifice the most to fund the reparation bill – the workers or the bosses – hung like an albatross around the neck of the Weimar Republic. Attempts to fulfil it led to bitter attacks by Nationalists.

Containment of the Left and re-emergence of the Right

By early 1920 the authority of the SPD was already beginning to ebb. Workers' demands for nationalization and workers' factory councils with real power had come to nothing, and, as Ernst Troeltsch observed, 'the old patriotic circles of the social order, for a long while surprised, overtaken and rendered completely helpless are emerging again'.[9] On the far right the anti-Semitic League of Protection and Defiance had a membership of over 100,000 by August 1919. In Bavaria, enflamed by the brief Munich soviet, a mass of *völkisch* (see p. 10) and extreme right-wing groups sprang into existence, amongst which was the German Worker's Party. It was in this party in the autumn of 1919 that Hitler made his first political appearance when he began to address his party on the Treaty of Versailles and the Jews (see p. 155).

Right-wing papers and pamphlets maintained a constant barrage of agitation against the Treaty of Versailles and the 'traitors' who had signed it. When Field Marshal **Hindenburg** used the term 'stab in back' to explain how the German army had been 'sabotaged' by the strikes and unrest at home, the term was seized upon as further evidence of the role of Jews and Bolsheviks in undermining Germany. Many nationalist academics, teachers, Protestant priests and members of the judiciary sympathized with these attacks, and the latter, holding posts from which they could not be constitutionally dismissed, often dispensed a highly politicized form of justice. Leading Weimar politicians, such as **Matthias Erzberger**, became the target of constant verbal abuse.

This was the atmosphere in which Ludendorff, Wolfgang Kapp (a founder member of the patriotic Fatherland Party, which had been set up to back the war effort in 1916), and General Lüttwitz (the commander of the *Reichswehr* in central and eastern Germany) formed the National Association with the aim of overthrowing the Republic. Their chance came when the Government, as a result of Allied pressure, began to disband the *Freikorps*. Exploiting the anger of the *Freikorps* members, Lüttwitz demanded on 10 March 1920 that Ebert should resign and that the *Freikorps* should be reprieved. When the govern-

Paul von Hindenburg (1847–1934)
Commanded the German armies on the Western Front, 1916–18. He was elected President in 1925 and in 1932.

Matthias Erzberger (1875–1921)
A Centre Party deputy and Finance Minister, 1919–21. He was assassinated by right-wing paramilitaries.

ment refused, one of the *Freikorps*, the *Ehrhardt Marine Brigade*, occupied Berlin and proclaimed Kapp Chancellor (see Document 3). General Reinhardt, *the Reichswehr* Commander-in-Chief, was ready to crush the putsch, but, as his generals refused to obey him, the government fled first to Dresden and then to Stuttgart. However, a nationwide general strike by the trade unions paralyzed all public services and called Kapp's bluff. On 18 March both Kapp and Lüttwitz fled to Sweden. Only in Bavaria did the putsch succeed, where the *Reichswehr* commanders forced the government to resign, and replaced it with a right-wing regime that claimed to be a 'focus of order' in a nation threatened by communism. To quote Eberhard Kolb, Bavaria rapidly became 'an Eldorado for extreme right-wing organizations and the leading personalities of militant right-wing radicalism'.[10]

The unions hoped that the defeat of the putsch would lead to a purge of hostile right-wing elements in the army and administration, an accelerated socialization programme and the formation of a new more left-wing government, but the outbreak of the Ruhr workers' uprising in March effectively prevented the regime from moving decisively against its enemies. As in the winter of 1919–20 *Reichswehr* and *Freikorps* troops, who had not yet been disbanded, were again needed to restore order and to defeat the 'red army' in the Ruhr.

Although the Kapp putsch, temporally at least, discredited a coup as a means of reasserting nationalist and extreme right-wing influence, the subsequent elections led to heavy losses for the Weimar coalition and gains for both the Independent Socialists and the Nationalists (DNVP). The conservative revival thus continued through institutional channels rather than on the streets. The new minority cabinet contained no SPD members, and was determined to drop the previous government's plans for introducing further economic and social reforms.

Until 1924 domestic politics were dominated by the problems connected with the execution of the Treaty of Versailles. The bitter wrangles with the Allies over reparation payments gave successive governments every excuse to delay stabilizing the currency. They were caught between the demands of big business and fear of social unrest. **Hugo Stinnes** and the Ruhr industrialists argued that there was no point in controlling inflation until the reparation bill

Hugo Stinnes (1870–1924)
A German industrialist with interests in coal mining, steel, iron, the press and catering.

was significantly reduced. Ending inflation would also entail a policy of financial cuts and retrenchment, which would simultaneously increase unemployment and cut welfare benefits and thus risk serious unrest in the industrial areas. The growing strength of the Communist Party, with which the left wing of the USPD had amalgamated in October 1920, was evidence that, despite the defeat of the Ruhr uprising, left-wing militancy was far from dead. In the spring of 1921 insurrections broke out in Merseburg, Halle and Mansfeld, although they were defeated within a few days by paramilitary police.

The bitter struggle with the Allies over the execution of the peace terms encouraged the growth of the radical Right. Patriotic Leagues and secret societies sprang up to replace the *Freikorps*, which were at last disbanded in 1921 under the pressure from the Entente. Some of these developed into terrorist groups, which assassinated **separatists** and informers who had helped the Allied occupying forces in the Rhineland. They also murdered prominent socialists and politicians of the Weimar Coalition, who had tried to reach a financial settlement with the Entente Powers. In the summer of 1921 both Karl Gareis, the USPD leader, and Matthias Erzberger were murdered, and a year later, **Walther Rathenau**, the Foreign Minister, was also assassinated because he was attempting to pursue a policy of cooperation, rather than confrontation, with the Entente as a means of persuading Britain and France to revise the Treaty of Versailles.

Rathenau's murder temporarily rallied support to the Republic. A Law for the Protection of the Republic was passed, despite opposition from both the Nationalists and the Communists, which enabled the government to prohibit extremist organizations, but its effectiveness was limited by both the judiciary's and the Bavarian government's reluctance to act on it.

Separatists
Those who wanted a separate Rhineland, looking to Paris rather than Berlin.

Walther Rathenau (1867–1922)
Prominent Jewish businessman, writer, philosopher, was the son of Emil, the founder of the AEG. Early in the First World War he had headed the Raw Materials Department, which played a key role in countering the British blockade.

THE RUHR OCCUPATION, 1923–4

The simmering crisis over reparations came to a head in January 1923, when in early January 1923 the **Reparation Commission** declared Germany to be in default on deliveries of timber and coal. The French seized the chance to occupy the Ruhr, despite British opposition, and on 11 January French and Belgian engi-

Reparation Commission
An inter-Allied body set up to deal with Germany's payment of reparations.

neers, protected by five French and one Belgian division, began to take control of the Ruhr industries.

For a short period after the occupation of the Ruhr the German nation achieved a fragile national unity and, briefly, the **spirit of 1914** reappeared. Reparation payments were suspended and the Ruhr workers conducted a policy of passive resistance by refusing to work for the French. In the short term these tactics worked, and deliveries to the French were reduced to a trickle, but this policy put enormous pressure on the German economy. To subsidize the strikers and make up for the lost tax revenues from the Ruhr, the government printed money, which led to accelerating hyper-inflation, and by August the mark was virtually valueless.

Spirit of 1914
The patriotism that united all the German people in 1914 at the outbreak of war.

Inflation: dollar quotations for the mark, 1914–23

July 1914	4.2
January 1919	8.9
January 1920	64.8
July 1920	39.5
January 1921	64.9
January 1922	493.2
January 1923	17,972.0
July 1923	353,412.0
August 1923	4,620,455.0
September 1923	98,860,000.0
October 1923	4,200,000,000,000.0

Source: G. Craig, *Germany, 1866–1945*, Oxford, Oxford University Press, 1978, p. 450. By permission of Oxford University Press.

This completed the impoverishment of the large number of the middle classes dependent on fixed incomes and the income from war bonds and insurance annuities. Gordon Craig, the American historian, observed that the German hyper-inflation 'created a lunatic world in which all the familiar landmarks assumed crazy new forms and all old signposts became meaningless, in which the simplest of objects were invested by alchemy with monstrous value – the penny postage stamp costing as much as a **Dahlem** villa in 1890'.[11]

Dahlem
An expensive inner suburb in Berlin.

Of course, not everybody suffered from the inflation. Industrialists, for instance, could secure credit from banks to expand their factories or buy up other plants, and then they could pay off the loan in a rapidly depreciating currency. Similarly, small speculators and many of the occupation troops in the Rhineland were able to buy up antiques and the treasured possessions of the German middle classes, who had to sell all they could on the black market to survive.

By midsummer 1923 it was clear that, although France's financial position was weakening, Germany could no longer maintain the passive resistance campaign. In July public order was threatened by strikes and rioting in the cities in unoccupied Germany, and senior civil servants were warning the government that unless inflation was halted 'the war of all against all will begin in the city . . . and the Reich will thus fall apart'.[12] When the Cuno government resigned in August, the political situation was reminiscent of October 1918, except that 'the measure of defeat was no longer the progress of the Allied armies, but the rout of the mark from 200,000 to 2 million per dollar within a fortnight'.[13] As in 1918–19, the SPD again played a pivotal role. It joined a 'Grand Coalition' of the SPD, DDP and DVP, with Gustav Stresemann as Chancellor, and supported the termination of passive resistance on 26 September.

Gustav Stresemann (1878–1929)

Stresemann was the most prominent Liberal politician in the Weimar Republic. In the war he was an extreme Nationalist. He became leader of the DVP (National Liberals) in 1919 and was hostile to Weimar, but rallied to it after Rathenaus' assassination. He was Chancellor August–November 1923, and, as Foreign Minister from August 1923 until his death in October 1929, he started the process of revising the Treaty of Versailles.

The Grand Coalition faced a period of acute crisis, which could easily have resulted in the collapse of democratic government in Germany:

- The DNVP, military circles around General von Seeckt, Chief of Staff of the *Reichswehr*, and Ruhr industrialists like Hugo

Stinnes were intriguing to set up a 'directorate cabinet' under Otto Wiedfeldt, a former Krupp director and currently Ambassador in Washington. The idea, as Count Westarp, a leading DNVP politician said, was to replace parliamentary government 'by a dictatorial authority free from the pressure of the streets, the parties and the party coalitions'.[14]

- The Communists were planning a '**German October**' and in both Saxony and Thuringia were making preparations for an uprising.

- However, the most dangerous threat came from Bavaria where the right-wing state government was under increasing pressure from patriotic, nationalist and paramilitary organizations to stage a coup against the central government.

German October
Reference to the Russian October Revolution.

The DNVP and its Nationalist allies were highly critical of the decision to terminate passive resistance. In Bavaria the state government immediately and without consulting Berlin declared a state of emergency, and appointed **von Kahr**, a leading Bavarian conservative monarchist, Commissioner with dictatorial powers. The Reich cabinet was divided on how to deal with von Kahr. The SPD wanted to take immediate action and demand Kahr's resignation, while the DVP and the right wing of the Centre Party refused to consider the use of force against Bavaria, and also urged Stresemann to break with the SPD and bring in the DNVP as a coalition partner. The DNVP, however, was not interested in joining the government, as it wished to see parliamentary rule replaced by a dictatorship.

Gustav Ritter von Kahr (1862–1934)
Murdered by Hitler in the 1934 purge (see p. 196).

On 3 October it seemed briefly that this might happen when the government's request for an Enabling Act, which would give it immediate powers to deal with the economic crisis, was rejected by the *Reichstag*. The SPD voted against it because it suspected that it would lead to an extension of the eight-hour day for the workers. This led to the temporary collapse of the Grand Coalition on 3 October and immediate talk on the right of a non-parliamentary 'government of directors', but this threat was averted when the Coalition was reconstructed three days later. The SPD was reassured that the eight-hour day would only be extended in exceptional circumstances if the economic good of the country clearly demanded it. The Enabling Act was then approved by the *Reichstag* and the necessary measures for restoring currency stability could go ahead.

Almost immediately cabinet unity was again threatened by events in Saxony and Thurigia. On 10 October a SPD–KPD coalition was formed in Saxony and the Communists began to organize for the 'revolution' by forming an armed militia. Once again the cabinet was paralyzed by a right–left split. The DVP and the *Reichswehr* wanted immediate military action against the Saxon *Land* government, while the SPD insisted that the Bavarian government should be treated similarly. As the *Reichswehr* refused to act against the Bavarian authotities, Stresemann attempted to master the crisis by showing as much concern as he could for the fears of the SPD. In practice this meant that the *Reichswehr* restored order in Saxony and Thuringia, but merely negotiated with the Bavarian government. When *Reichswehr* troops staged what seemed to the Left as a victory march through Dresden, the SPD resigned and the Grand Coalition broke up on 2 November.

According to Charles Maier, 'the week between the intervention in Saxony and Hitler's putsch represented the most critical days of German parliamentarism since 1918'.[15] Pressure grew from the army and the DNVP for a non-party directorate, and the SPD decided to push for a vote of no confidence in the way Stresemann had handled the crisis in Saxony and Thuringia, while giving Bavaria more favourable treatment. The fact that this vote, which resulted in the defeat of Stresemann, was delayed until 23 November, some two weeks after the failure of the Munich putsch, probably saved democracy in Germany for the time being.

THE GROWTH OF THE NAZI PARTY AND THE MUNICH PUTSCH

Bavaria was the one German state in which the Kapp putsch succeeded (see p. 149). In March 1920 the SPD–Catholic coalition collapsed and the conservative Catholic bureaucrat, Gustav von Kahr, became the Minister-President (prime minister). He was anxious to turn Bavaria into a 'cell of order'[16] and restore the traditional values of pre-war Germany. He was keen to rally the Nationalist Right, that is the ex-*Freikorps* members, the Bavarian *Selbstschutz* and the small *völkisch* parties, of which the Nazi Party was to become the most prominent. The reasons for the latter's success were partly the personality and skills of its leader, Adolf Hitler, who possessed a 'political genius' of a sort[17] and the fact that the party received generous financial contributions from the Bavarian *Reichswehr* and government.

Adolf Hitler's life and career up to 1923

Hitler was born in Braunau am Inn, Upper Austria in 1889. In *Mein Kampf* he stressed his poverty-stricken childhood, but in fact his father Alois, an Austrian customs official, earned a sufficient salary to keep his family. In 1905 Hitler left school without any academic qualifications, and failed to gain a place at the Academy of Fine Arts in Vienna. Up to 1914 he was unemployed, and lived an increasingly impoverished existence in Vienna and then in Munich. In the former city he acquired a superficial knowledge of contemporary Social Darwinist, *völkisch* and racist thinking (see pp. 10–11), and also observed the political tactics of the Austrian Social Democrats, the Pan German Nationalists and the Christian Social Party. He was impressed by how this last party attracted support from the **Mittelstand**, who felt their existence threatened by the forces of modernization.

In August 1914 he volunteered to join a Bavarian regiment. He fought for the next four years on the Western front with considerable personal bravery and was awarded the Iron Cross (First Class). In 1918 he was wounded in a British gas attack. He rejoined his regiment in Munich in late November and observed the dramatic events surrounding the establishment of the Munich 'Soviet republic' in April 1919. After its collapse on 3 May, Hitler was employed as a *V-Mann,* or informant, to counter the impact of Bolshevik propaganda among the troops. This brought him into touch with the German Workers' Party, which was one of the many *völkisch*-radical groups which had sprung up throughout Germany in the aftermath of the November Revolution (see p. 148). In April 1920 Hitler started working full time for the party, which in February had changed its name to the German National Socialist Workers' Party (NSDAP). Two years later he had not only established his control over it, but had begun to create an organizational structure that ensured its subordination to his leadership. The programme of the NSDAP – the Twenty-Five Points (see Document 5) – which Hitler drew up with Anton Drexler, the original founder of the DAP (German Workers' Party), was a mix of *völkisch* and National Socialist ideas, which most of the other far-right groups shared.

Mittelstand
Literally, 'middle estate'. The term embraces small-scale farmers, self-employed businessmen, artisans and white-collar workers.

Hitler's strength lay not in the originality of his ideas but in the way in which he expressed them and how he was able to exploit the fear, anger and resentment of the impoverished middle classes in the post-war period (see Document 4). National Socialism would have existed without Hitler, but it was he who turned it into a major force, first in Bavaria and then in the Reich as a whole. By the end of 1922 Hitler was increasingly being compared to Mussolini by his followers, yet at that stage Hitler probably perceived himself as 'drumming up' support for another more authoritative figure, possibly General von Ludendorff.

In 1923 the Ruhr crisis gave Hitler the chance to play a greater role in national politics. Although initially the French occupation of the Ruhr united the Reich behind the government and its campaign of passive resistance, Stresemann's decision to call off the passive resistance ignited opposition on the right. In Bavaria, however, the Right was unable to form a united front against Berlin. On the one hand, there was the Bavarian establishment, which included the army, the bureaucracy and the government, while, on the other, there were the Patriotic Associations and the Nazi Party. In February Ernst Röhm, who was both an army staff officer and a paramilitary leader (see p. 195), had persuaded these far-right groups to join the Working Community of the Patriotic Associations, where their paramilitary groups, including **the SA**, were given military training by the *Reichswehr*. Although General Ludendorff was the most influential figure on the far right, Hitler played a prominent role in the leadership of the Working Community. He was by far the most effective speaker and, as Röhm stressed, was a potentially valuable to the Nationalists and DNVP because he also aimed at attracting the workers to the national cause, and thus had the potential for creating a patriotic or National Socialist fighting front to overthrow the Weimar Republic.

Hitler's efforts, however, to forge closer links with the Bavarian authorities met with little success. Throughout the summer the Bavarian government was torn between fear of the Left and its suspicions of the intentions of the Working Community. Hitler, through rallies and propaganda, raised the expectations of his followers to fever pitch, although he had no clear idea of how to proceed. As Kershaw has observed, 'crisis was Hitler's oxygen'.[18] In early September, as passive resistance in

The SA

Sturmabteilung – Nazi storm or assault troops. The SA was founded in 1921 to protect party meetings from being disrupted by the Communists and others.

the Ruhr began to falter, the Nazi Party joined the *Kampfbund*, an association of militant groups on the far right, which was more tightly organized than the Working Community, to coordinate tactics against the Republic. The SA was integrated into the military wing of the *Bund*, while Hitler was given the political leadership of the *Bund*. Hitler was again seen as a 'drummer' whose task was to mobilize public opinion to support a putsch in Munich as a preliminary to taking Berlin by force. The new government was to be headed by Ludendorff, although Hitler would be a member.

To have any chance of success, the *Kampfbund* needed the backing of Kahr, the Bavarian State Commissioner, Seisser, the head of the Bavarian police, and General von Lossow, the commander of the Bavarian *Reichswehr*. On 3 November 1923, however, Seisser was told by General von Seeckt that it would not oppose the elected government in Berlin. The Bavarian triumvirate consequently began to have second thoughts about a putsch, which left Hitler in an exposed situation. His followers expected action, and feared that if he delayed for too long, the favourable moment would pass. Hitler therefore attempted to coerce Kahr into supporting his plans by seizing him and his colleagues while addressing a public meeting at the *Bürgerbraükeller* on the evening of 8 November. Reluctantly bowing to force, they had little option but to support him.

Hitler, who was then called away to deal with a problem involving the seizure of the Engineers' Barracks, left them in the charge of Ludendorff. The latter allowed them to leave once he received their word of honour that they would support Hitler. This promise was not kept and the following morning they ordered the police to break up the *Kampfbund's* planned march into the city centre.

A few days later Hitler was arrested. In April 1924 he was given the minimum sentence of five years' imprisonment with a virtual promise that he would be released early on probation. The publicity the putsch received and the subsequent trial turned Hitler into a national figure. He was imprisoned in the Landsberg Fortress where he dictated *Mein Kampf* as a political testament to his secretary, Rudolf Hess, who was later to become Deputy Leader of the party, and was released from prison in December 1924.

STABILIZATION, 1924–9

German economic recovery

After the failure of the Munich putsch, the wave of unrest in the Reich subsided, and it became clear that the Republic had survived. As the costs of the Ruhr occupation had caused a sharp decline in the value of the franc, Anglo-American pressure was able to force the French to agree in principle to the setting up of an experts' committee chaired by the American banker, Charles Dawes, to review the whole question of reparations. This produced the Dawes Plan in April 1924, which, while not cutting down the final total of reparations, gave the hard-pressed German economy crucial relief. It stipulated that reparations payments would start gradually and rise to their maximum total in five years and it also made provision for a loan of 800 million marks. In November 1923, to stabilize the currency, Hans Luther, the Minister of Finance, had replaced the devalued *Reichsmark* with a temporary currency, the *Rentenmark*, which was backed by mortgage bonds based on the assets of industry and agriculture. In August 1924 it was succeeded by the new *Reichsmark*.

Between 1924 and 1928 the Germany economy did stage a recovery of sorts, and by 1927 industrial production had returned to the level of 1913.

German industrial production, 1913–28 (%)

Year	%
1913	100
1919	37
1922	70
1923	46
1924	69
1927	100
1928	103.8
1929	102.8

Source: Adapted from K. Borchardt, *Perspectives on Modern German Economic History and Policy*, Cambridge, Cambridge Univeristy Press, 1991, pp. 171–72.

The peaceful erosion of the Versailles Treaty

Stresemann, as Foreign Minister from 1924 to 1930, exploited every opportunity to revise the Treaty of Versailles. He ensured that there would be no repetition of the Ruhr crisis by putting forward, with British support, plans for a guarantee by the Europen Great Powers of the Franco-Belgian–German frontier and the demilitarization of the Rhineland, which led to the Locarno Pact of 1925 (see p. 114). A year later Germany joined the League of Nations. Stresemann skilfully used the goodwill that Germany gained through this more cooperative policy to extract concessions from Britain and France. In January 1927 the Allied Disarmament Commission was withdrawn from Germany, and in August Britain, France and Belgium withdrew 10,000 troops from their garrisons in the Rhineland.

In 1928 the German government launched a major initiative to persuade Britain and France to evacuate the Rhineland, and to agree to a revision of the Dawes Plan. During the winter of 1928–9 a committee of financial experts, which was chaired by the American banker, Owen Young, considered the reparation problem. In June 1929 it recommended the reduction of the overall reparation total from 132 billion (gold) marks to 40 billion (gold) marks and the dismantling of the international controls over the German economy, which had been set up under the Dawes Plan.

At the Hague Conference in August 1929 Stresemann was able to achieve both the implementation of the Young Plan and the agreement to evacuate the Rhineland by 30 June. In December the government had to face a referendum forced upon it by the Nazi and Nationalist Parties declaring that its signature would be an act of high treason, but this was easily defeated and the Young Plan was officially implemented on 20 January 1930.

Structural problems of the Republic

Despite the partial economic recovery and the steady erosion of the Treaty of Versailles, the Republic was not popular and faced severe problems, which, to quote Detlev Peukert, were 'an outward sign of hidden weakness that might prove fatal when the structure was next subjected to severe strain':[19]

- A time bomb for the Republic was the legacy of the inflation, which had destroyed the savings and pension provisions for millions. The government's unwillingnes and indeed financial inability to compensate for more that 25 per cent of the sums lost caused deep resentment and the subsequent growth of small special interest parties, whose voters began to go over to the Nazis in 1929 (see Document 6).
- The constitution of the Weimar Republic had committed the state to developing an expensive welfare policy, which proved an increasingly expensive burden on its finances. A fair distribution of these costs and of the financial burdens imposed by the lost war between employers and employees, pensioners and the state, and town and country could only take place within the context of years of economic prosperity, but with the onset of the Great Depression in 1929 this proved impossible to achieve within a democratic context.
- Employers, particularly in the heavy industries in the Ruhr, were anxious to cut wages and to weaken the trade unions in an attempt to boost production and win exports. Increasingly they began to favour an authoritarian government that could dismantle the welfare state and discipline the unions.

Structural weaknesses also prevented the development of a stable parliamentary democracy. A strong government, which could command a majority in the *Reichstag*, needed to be based on a 'grand' coalition. Effectively there were two options: either a coalition of the SPD, Centre and Liberal parties (DDP and the DVP) or on a Centre, DVP and DNVP grouping. The problem, however, was that disagreements on economic and social questions between the SPD and the Liberal parties made the former difficult to sustain, while foreign policy differences complicated relations between the DNVP and the Centre and the DVP.

Towards the end of 1920s the Centre Party began to move to the right, which inevitably made cooperation with the SPD more difficult, while the Liberal parties suffered an increasing loss of their core support as a consequence of the rise of the special interest parties. In the 1928 election the special interest parties attracted 14 per cent of the vote, which overtook the total of the two Liberal parties combined, and nearly equalled the DNVP's share of the vote. In 1930 many of these voters were to switch to the Nazis (see p. 183).

National election results in the Weimar Republic, 1919–30 (%)

	NSDAP	DNVP	DVP	Centre/BVP	DDP	SPD	USPD	KPD	Others
19.1.19	–	10.3	4.4	19.7	18.6	37.9	7.6	–	1.5
6.6.20	–	14.9	13.9	17.6	8.3	21.6	17.9	2.1	3.7
4.5.24	6.5	19.5	9.2	16.6	5.7	20.5	1.1	12.6	8.3
7.12.24	3.0	20.5	10.1	17.3	6.3	26.0	–	9.0	7.8
20.5.28	2.6	14.2	8.7	15.2	4.9	29.8	–	10.6	14.0
14.9.30	18.3	7.0	4.9	14.8	3.8	24.5	–	13.1	13.6

Source: T. Childers 'Inflation, stabilization and political realignment in Germany, 1924–1928' in G.D. Feldman et al., eds, *The German Inflation Reconsidered*, Berlin, Walter de Gruyter, 1982, p. 430.

The unpopularity of the Republic

The Republic's opponents never allowed it to forget that its creation was consequence of a lost war, and that its government had signed the hated Treaty of Versailles. Much of the popular press, which was owned by Nationalists like Alfred Hugenberg, conducted a sustained campaign of hatred against the Republic and depicted it as morally corrupt and decadent.

The end of censorship allowed the theatre to experiment with new forms of drama, which sometimes copied the Soviet agitprop (see p. 57). Modern art and architecture flourished on a far greater scale than before the war. The radio and films also did much to promote new artistic ideas. All this inevitably attracted a backlash of criticism from both cultural and political conservatives. The film version of Erich Maria's Remarque's *All Quiet on the Western Front* stirred up a bitter campaign by the Nationalists. The new forms of poetry as practised by the Berlin **Dada** group and such *avant-garde* operas as Paul Hindemith's *News of the Day*, in which a naked woman sang an aria in a bath, were also disorientating for many Germans. Jazz, which one prominent critic called 'the most disgusting treason against all occidental civilized music'[20] also became very popular, particularly in the large number of night clubs, bars and dance halls that opened in the large cities.

There was also among many of the older generation a fear that the growth of feminism was producing a 'new' woman who was

Dadaism
Started in Zurich in 1916. It involved the visual arts, poetry and graphic design. It rejected all conventional art and literary forms.

working by day in the office and 'frittering away the night dancing the Charleston or watching Ufa and Hollywood films'.[21] Inevitably this image attracted a considerable backlash and concern about the decline in the birthrate. Some of the more conservative observers of both sexes attributed the decline in the population to 'the "boundless egoism" of women who were betraying their natural vocation and striving for greater personal freedom and independence'.[22]

HITLER AND THE NAZI PARTY, 1925–9

When Hitler was released from prison in December 1924, the lesson he drew from the failure of the Munich putsch was that the NSDAP would have to campaign constitutionally and achieve regime change through what he was later to call a 'legal revolution' (see pp. 198–9). Once the ban on the party was lifted in Bavaria in January 1925, he was able to rebuild the party (see Figure 5.2). This time Hitler was not ready to serve as a 'drummer'. He created a position for himself of absolute power as a charismatic leader, who could distance himself from the petty bickerings and disagreements within the party. This *Führer* cult was the means for integrating the multitude of often mutually hostile groups that made up the party into some sort of coherent whole. In the course of the next four years the character of the party was determined: its organization became institutionalized through party bureaucrats in Munich, such as Rudolf Hess, who, by relieving Hitler of the more routine organizational tasks, were able to protect Hitler's charismatic image without posing any threat to his power. Hitler would only intervene in an issue that involved his supreme authority.

Each level of the party was subordinated to the one above it. Nationally it was divided into 35 *Gaue*, or regions, each controlled by a *Gauleiter*. Below these were the local branches, which were run by a **cadre** of activists. However, this apparently logical pattern was undermined by the determination, which Hitler did nothing to discourage, of the organizations affiliated to the party – the SA, the Hitler Youth, the Nazi Teachers' Association, etc. – to see themselves as responsible to Hitler alone, rather than being firmly integrated into a tightly knit party hierarchy.

Cadre
A core unit, which can serve later as a basis for mass expansion.

Figure 5.2 Hitler speaking
to Nazi Party leaders,
1925
Source: Mary Evans
Picture Library

Officially Hitler never revised the party's 1920 programme,
but in practice he was forced to moderate its more socialistic
economic points to attract new supporters. *Mein Kampf*, where
page after page reveals his obsession with the Jewish threat, is a
better guide to Hitler's first principles. His identification of the
Jews with Russian Bolshevism, while far from original, had, to
quote Ernst Nolte, an 'explosive political effect',[23] and made it
possible for his ideas to reach out to a wider middle-class public,
which was terrified by the prospect of a communist coup in
Germany. Hitler's whole programme for the future regeneration
of Germany depended on creating a racially pure state, which
would be demographically strengthened by the German colonization of western Russia – in other words the creation of
Lebensraum or 'living space'.

Until 1927 the Nazi Party followed the example of Italian
Fascism, and tried to seize control of the cities by appealing to the
workers, but potentially the party's core supporters were the
Mittelstand (see p. 155), which had been impoverished by the war
and the inflation of 1918–23 . However, in the winter of 1927–8,
which saw the start of the agricultural depression, Hitler abandoned the Urban Plan, toned down the party's emphasis on land

confiscation, and the Nazis started to campaign more effectively in the countryside (see Document 7). Although this did not help the Nazi Party much in the 1928 elections, its potential for the future was shown by the fact that in some rural areas in north-west Germany, such as Schleswig-Holstein, the Nazis won over 10 per cent of the vote.

ASSESSMENT

Despite the strains imposed by a lost war, democracy in Germany did survive the first 10 years of peace. The strength of the unions and the labour movement had defeated the Kapp putsch, and the Nazi Party had yet to become a mass movement.

Yet the political stabilization of the Republic, to quote Kolb, was at best 'fragile and superficial'.[24] The war, the inflation and then the agricultural crisis had impoverished the *Mittelstand* and created demands for financial compensation, which the state could not meet. The employers, faced with intense international competition in the global export markets, were ready to welcome a more authoritarian government that would control the unions and enable them to push through wage cuts.

The war, and the upheavals that it caused, also quickened the pace of change and the 'modernization' of German society. Even in times of prosperity and peace this is often painful and disorientating for a society, but in the aftermath of a lost war and in the midst of deep-seated economic and political crises the accelerating modernization of German society fuelled a demand for the restoration of traditional family and cultural values, and for a strong, authoritarian leader, who could 'clean up' Germany.

DOCUMENT 1

SPD criticism of the Spartacists, January 1919

The SPD paper Vorwärts *bitterly attacked the Spartacists when they launched their revolution on 6 January 1919:*

The despicable actions of Liebknecht and Rosa Luxemburg soil the revolution and endanger all its achievements. The masses must not sit quietly by for one minute longer while these brutal beasts and their followers paralyze the activities of the governmental offices, incite the people more and more to civil war and strangle with their dirty fists the right of free expression.

Source: R.M. Watt, *The Kings Depart*, London, Weidenfeld & Nicolson, 1968, p. 254.

DOCUMENT 2
The Munich soviet, May 1919

As the Freikorps *were assembling to attack Communist-controlled Munich, Rudolf Engelhofer, the organizer of the Bavarian Red Army, issued a plea to the Munich workers:*

Workers! Soldiers of the Red Army! The enemy is at the gates of Munich. The officers, students, sons of the bourgeoisie, and White Guard mercenaries are already in Schleissheim. There is not an hour to be lost . . . Everything is at stake! At Starnberg the White Guard dogs murdered our hospital attendants . . . Forward into combat for the proletarian cause!

Source: Watt, *The Kings Depart*, p. 335.

DOCUMENT 3
The Kapp putsch, March 1920

Lord Kilmarnock, the British Chargé d'Affaires (representative) in Berlin, wrote to Lord Curzon, the Foreign Minister, on 15 March 1920:

As far as it is possible to judge the present situation Kapp sees the game is up and is trying to save his skin if not his face. His Govt. has existed by lies and will vanish in ignominy. He is trying to make terms with the legal government but may have to surrender without conditions. It is doubtful whether the Ebert government will negotiate or will stand out for unconditional surrender . . . The really disturbing factor is the attitude of the Independent Socialists who hope by prolonging the strike to produce chaos and get power into their own hands. This danger may induce the Ebert Govt. to compromise but they may feel themselves strong enough to combat the strike.

Source: *Documents on British Foreign Policy, 1919–1939*, First Series, vol. 9, London, HMSO, 1960, pp. 148–9.

DOCUMENT 4

Hitler's skills as a political speaker, Munich 1920

Hans Frank, who later became Governor-General of German-occupied Poland in 1939, recalled first hearing Hitler speak in January 1920 in Munich:

I was strongly impressed straight away. It was totally different from what was otherwise to be heard in meetings. His method was completely clear and simple. He took the overwhelmingly dominant topic of the day, the Versailles *Diktat*, and posed the question of all questions: What now German people? What's the true situation? What alone is now possible? He spoke for over two-and-a half hours, often interrupted by frenetic torrents of applause – and one could have listened to him for much, much longer. Everything came from the heart, and he struck a chord with all of us ... he uttered what was in the consciousness of all those present and linked general experiences to clear understanding and the common wishes of those who were suffering and hoping for a programme. In the matter itself he was certainly not original ... but he was the one called to act as spokesman of the people ... he concealed nothing ... of the horror, the distress, the despair facing Germany. But not only that. He showed a way, the only way left to ruined people in history, that of the grim new beginning from the most profound depths through courage, faith, readiness for action, hard work, and devotion to a great, shining, common goal ... he placed before the Almighty in the most serious and solemn exhortation the salvation of the honour of the German soldier and worker as his life task ... When he finished, the applause would not die down ... From this evening onwards ... I was convinced that if one man could do it, Hitler alone would be capable of mastering Germany's fate.

Source: I. Kershaw, *Hitler*, vol. 1., *1889–1936 Hubris*, London, Allen Lane, 1998, pp. 148–9.

DOCUMENT 5

The party programme

The party programme of the German Workers' Party (later the National Socialist German Worker's Party – NSDAP) was announced at a public meeting in the Hofbräuhaus in Munich on 24 February 1920. It was written mainly by Hitler and Drexler:

The Programme of the German Workers' Party is designed to be of limited duration. The leaders have no intention, once the aims announced in it have been achieved, of establishing fresh ones, merely in order to increase, artificially the discontent of the masses and so ensure the continued existence of the Party.

1 We demand the union of all Germans in a Greater Germany on the basis of the right of national self-determination.

2 We demand equality of rights for the German people in its dealings with other nations, and the revocation of the Peace Treaties of Versailles and St-Germain.

3 We demand land and territory (colonies) to feed our people and to settle our surplus population.

4 Only members of the nation may be citizens of the state. Only those of German blood, whatever their creed, may be members of the nation. Accordingly no Jew may be a member of the nation.

5 Non-citizens may live in Germany only as guests and must be subject to laws for aliens.

6 The right to vote on the state's government and legislation shall be enjoyed by the citizens of the state alone . . .

7 We demand that the state shall make it its primary duty to provide a livelihood for its citizens. If it should prove impossible to feed the entire population, foreign nationals (non-citizens) must be deported from the Reich.

8 All non-German immigration must be prevented. We demand that all non-Germans who entered Germany after 2 August 1914 shall be required to leave the Reich forthwith.

9 All citizens shall have equal rights and duties.

10 It must be the first duty of every citizen to perform physical or mental work. The activities of the individual must not clash with the general interest, but must proceed within the framework of the community and be for the general good. *We demand therefore*:

11 The abolition of incomes unearned by work. *The breaking of slavery of interest.*

12 In view of the enormous sacrifices of life and property demanded of a nation by any war, personal enrichment from war must be regarded as a crime against the nation. We demand therefore the ruthless confiscation of war profits.

▶

13 We demand the nationalisation of all businesses which have been formed into corporations (trusts).

14 We demand profit-sharing in large industrial enterprises.

15 We demand the extensive development of insurance for old age.

16 We demand the creation and maintenance of a healthy middle class, the immediate communalising of department stores, and their lease at a cheap rate to small traders, and that the utmost consideration shall be shown to all small traders in the placing of state and municipal orders.

17 We demand land reform suitable to our national requirements, the passing of a law for the expropriation of land for communal purposes without compensation, the abolition of ground rent, and the prohibition of all speculation in land.

18 We demand the ruthless prosecution of those whose activities are injurious to the common interest. Common criminals, usurers, profiteers, etc., must be punished with death, whatever their creed or race.

19 We demand that Roman Law, which serves a materialistic world order, be replaced by a German common law.

20 The state must consider a thorough reconstruction of our national system of education (with the aim of opening up to every able and hard working German the possibility of higher education and of thus obtaining advancement). The curricula of all educational establishments must be brought into line with the requirements of practical life ...

21 The state must ensure that the nation's health standards are raised by protecting mothers and infants, by prohibiting child labour, by promoting physical strength through legislation providing for compulsory gymnastics and sports, and by the extensive support of clubs engaged in the physical training of youth.

22 We demand the abolition of the mercenary [i.e. professional] army and the formation of a people's army.

23 We demand legal warfare on deliberate political mendacity and its dissemination in the press. To facilitate the creation of a German national press we demand:

(a) that all editors of, and contributors to newspapers appearing in the German language must be members of the nation ...

...We demand the legal prosecution of all those tendencies in art and literature which corrupt our national life, and the suppression of cultural events which violate this demand.

24 We demand freedom for all religious denominations in the
state, provided they do not threaten its existence nor offend
the moral feelings of the German race.

   The Party as such stands for positive Christianity, but does not
   commit itself to any particular denomination. It combats the
   Jewish-materialist spirit within and without us on the basis of
   the principle: the common interest before self-interest.

25 To put the whole of this programme into effect, we demand
the creation of a strong central state power for the Reich; the
unconditional authority of the political central Parliament over
the entire Reich and its organisations; and the formation of
Corporations based on estate and occupation for the purpose
of carrying out the general legislation passed by the Reich in
the various German states.

The leaders of the Party promise to work ruthlessly – if need be to
sacrifice their lives – to translate this programme into action.

Source: J. Noakes and G. Pridham, eds, *Nazism, 1919–45*, vol. 1, *The
Rise to Power, 1919–34*, Exeter, Exeter University Press, 2nd ed. 1998,
pp. 14–16.

DOCUMENT 6

The special interest parties and the fragmentation of the Bourgeois parties, 1924–30

The historian Thomas Childers wrote:

In the extensive historical literature devoted to the interaction of
economics and politics in the Weimar Republic, the principal
thematic emphasis has traditionally been placed on the
disintegration of the democratic party system during the Great
Depression. More specifically, analysts from a variety of
disciplines have probed the complex relationship between the
severe economic dislocations of the depression years – particularly
unemployment – and the meteoric rise of Hitler's NSDAP. Yet, the
destabilization of the Weimar Party system did not originate
during the Great Depression and was already far advanced when
the National Socialists began their dramatic march from obscurity
to the forefront of German electoral politics. A symptomatic and
portentous erosion of traditional voter loyalties, especially within
the middle class electorate, had in fact, been underway since
1924. The two national elections of that year, held in the

aftermath of the hyper inflation of 1923 and in the midst of the
extensive programme of economic stabilization marked the onset
of a profound, if subtle, realignment of electoral sympathies ...
Indeed the sudden emergence and surprisingly strong performance
of special interest parties in 1924 provided the first glimpse of
what within the next four years would become a fundamental
breakdown of voter identification with the established parties of
both the bourgeois centre and right. Significantly, that breakdown
was not impeded by the return of political and monetary stability
between 1924 and 1928. Instead the disintegration of traditional
bourgeois electoral loyalties continued unabated, seriously
undermining the sociopolitical foundations of the Weimar party
system well before the effects of the Great Depression were felt in
Germany.

Source: T. Childers, 'Inflation, stabilization and political realignment in
Germany, 1924–1928' in G.D. Feldman et al., eds, *The German Inflation
Reconsidered*, Berlin, Walter de Gruyter, 1982, pp. 404–5.

Document 7
The NSDAP and the rural vote

After the May 1928 election the Nazi newspaper, the Völkischer
Beobachter, *stressed that the party could learn the following
lessons from the results:*

The election results from the rural areas in particular proved that
with a smaller expenditure of energy, money and time, better
results can be achieved there than in the big cities. In small towns
and villages mass meetings with good speakers are events and are
often talked about for weeks, while in the big cities the effects of
meetings with even three or four thousand people soon disappear.
Local successes in which the National Socialists are running first
or second are, surprisingly, almost invariably the result of the
activity of the branch leader or of a few energetic members.

Source: J. Noakes and G. Pridham, eds, *Nazism, 1919–45*, vol. 1, *The
Rise to Power, 1919–34*, Exeter, Exeter University Press, 2nd ed. 1998,
pp. 63–4.

NOTES

1 W. Mommsen, *Imperial Germany, 1867–1918*, London, Edward Arnold, 1995, p. 231

2 J. Hiden, *Republican and Fascist Germany*, Harlow, Longman, 1996, p. 43.

3 F.L. Carsten, *Revolution in Central Europe*, London, Wildwood House, 1972, p. 323.

4 E.H. Carr, *The Bolshevik Revolution*, vol. 3., Harmondsworth, Penguin, 1966, p. 105.

5 General Groener; quoted in Carsten, *Revolution*, p. 324.

6 Ibid., p. 141.

7 E. Kolb, *The Weimar Republic*, London, Routledge, 1988, p. 16.

8 Quoted in ibid., p. 33.

9 C.S. Maier, *Recasting Bourgeois Europe*, Princeton, Princeton University Press, repr. 1988, p. 165.

10 Kolb, *Weimar Republic*, p. 38.

11 G. Craig, *Germany, 1866–1945*, Oxford, Oxford University Press, 1978, p. 451,

12 Maier, *Recasting*, p. 372.

13 Ibid., p. 373.

14 Ibid., p. 382.

15 Ibid., p. 384.

16 I. Kershaw, *Hitler*, vol. 1, *1889–1936 Hubris* London, Allen Lane, 1998, p. 159.

17 Craig, *Germany*, p. 544.

18 Kershaw, *Hitler*, vol. 1, p. 200.

19 D.A. Peukert, *The Weimar Republic: The Crisis of Classical Modernity*, London, Allen Lane, 1991, p. 178.

20 R.J. Evans, *The Coming of the Third Reich*, London, Penguin, 2004, p. 125.

21 Peukert, *The Weimar Republic*, p. 99.

22 U. Frevert, *Women in German History*, Oxford, Berg, 1989, p. 186.

23 E. Nolte, *Three Faces of Fascism*, New York, Mentor, 1969, p. 419.

24 Kolb, *Weimar Republic*, p. 66.

PART THREE

THE 1930s: THE IMPACT OF THE GREAT DEPRESSION

CHAPTER SIX

The collapse of Weimar and the triumph of National Socialism, 1930–4

TIMELINE

1930	29 March	Brüning becomes Reich Chancellor
	16 July	*Reichstag* votes against government finance decree and is dissolved
	14 September	*Reichstag* elections; NSDAP gains 107 seats
1931	February	Unemployment total approaches 5 million
	March	Customs union plan announced – later vetoed by France
	July	Failure of Austrian *Kreditanstalt*
	6 July	Hoover moratorium
	13 July	Failure of *Darmstädter und Nationalbank*
	11 October	Harzburg Front formed
1932	March–April	Presidential elections: Hindenburg re-elected
	13 April	Prohibition of SA and SS
	30 May	Papen becomes Chancellor
	20 July	Prussian government suspended
	31 July	*Reichstag* elections: NSDAP becomes the largest party, with 230 seats
	13 August	Hindenburg refuses to appoint Hitler Chancellor
	6 November	*Reichstag* elections: NSDAP loses 34 seats
	2 December	General von Schleicher becomes Chancellor
1933	4 January	Papen–Hitler meeting
	30 January	Hitler appointed Chancellor
	1 February	Dissolution of the *Reichstag*
	27 February	*Reichstag* fire
	28 February	The Decree for the Protection of People and State
	5 March	*Reichstag* elections; NSDAP wins 288 seats
	23 March	Enabling Act passed

REDCAR & CLEVELAND COLLEGE LIBRARY

	31 March	First Law for the Coordination of the Federal States
	April	Gestapo created
	7 April	Law for the Restoration of a Professional Civil Service
	2 May	Trade unions dissolved
	6 May	Creation of German Labour Front announced
	14 July	NSDAP declared only legal political party
	20 July	Concordat with Catholic Church
	13 September	Reich Food Estate set up
	29 September	Reich Entailed Farm Law
	1 December	Law to Ensure Unity of Party and State
1934	20 April	Himmler appointed 'Inspector of the Gestapo'
	30 June	Night of the Long Knives; Röhm murdered
	20 July	SS established as an independent force under Himmler
	2 August	Death of Hindenburg; Hitler becomes President as well as Chancellor; Schacht made Economics Minister

INTRODUCTION

In view of the destruction and suffering that Hitler's rise to power was to bring, Karl-Dietrich Erdmann's observation made in 1955 that 'all research into the history of the Weimar Republic is necessarily governed, whether expressly or otherwise, by the question as to the causes of its collapse'[1] is still valid today. The collapse of the Weimar Republic and the formation of the Third Reich was not just a change of regime but a revolution that was to destroy Germany and much of Europe, open the door to the creation of Communist regimes in Eastern Europe and terminally damage both the French and British empires. While Hitler's rise to power was by no means inevitable and events right up to January 1933 could have taken a different course, his eventual success, nevertheless, has to be explained within the context of a complex range of causes:

- The Weimar constitution through proportional representation encouraged a multi-party system that could rarely deliver a strong government; it also gave strong emergency powers to the presidency, which could all too easily be abused (see Document 3).

- Except briefly in 1928–9 the German economy failed to deliver prosperity. This prevented the Republic from effectively compensating those who had suffered most in the war and in the hyper-inflation of 1923. It was a saddled with a welfare state, which it was increasingly unable to support financially.
- The elite in the bureaucracy, judiciary, big business and the officer corps longed to turn the clock back to 1914 and hated the Weimar Republic.
- The devastating impact of the war and inflation on the middle classes, combined with the decline of the Liberal parties and the rise of the *Interessenparteien*, the single-issue parties, which were composed of those who had lost out in the inflation, created a large reservoir of potential voters for the NSPD (see pp. 169–70).
- Nationalism and the hatred of the Treaty of Versailles.
- The charismatic appeal and political skills of Hitler.
- The impact of the world Depression of 1930–3.

This was the context that made Hitler's takeover of power possible, but it was still individual decisions and miscalculations by key figures like Hindenburg, Brüning, Schleicher and Papen that turned this possibility into a reality.

THE KEY ISSUES IN THIS CHAPTER ARE:

- The impact of the Great Depression on Germany
- The break-up of the Grand Coalition in March 1930.
- Did Brüning destroy Weimar, or were his governments its last chance of survival?
- Brüning's dismissal in May 1932.
- The failure of Papen and Schleicher to stabilize the situation in Germany in 1932.
- Whether Hitler's appointment as Chancellor was inevitable.
- The failure of the Nationalists–Conservative elite to restrain Hitler, January 1933–August 1934.
- Hitler's consolidation of power and prevention of a 'second revolution', March 1933–August 1934.

THE IMPACT OF THE GREAT DEPRESSION

The Wall Street Crash, followed by the Great Depression, which Robert Boyce has aptly called 'the third global catastrophe of the century'[2] (along with the two world wars) was a turning point in international history. Between 1929 and 1932 the volume of world trade fell by 70 per cent. Unemployment rose to 13 million in the USA, to 6 million in Germany and to 3 million in Britain.

Already by the autumn of 1928 there were signs of a global recession. American investment began to fall and German production was stagnant. By the spring of 1929 unemployment had already climbed to 2.5 million. On 29 October 1929, 'Black Tuesday', the dramatic collapse in the value of American shares on the New York stock exchange caused 10 billion dollars to be wiped off the value of major American companies, and marked the start of a major economic depression. As American companies went bankrupt, the banks had no alternative but to call in the short-term loans upon which most of German industry was dependent. This hit the German economy just at the point when it needed the injection of further money to revive. Deprived of investment, German factories began to cut back on production or even close down completely.

The massive collapse in production and withdrawal of foreign investments also threatened the German banks, which since the inflation of 1923 had only small capital reserves. In July 1931 the whole German banking system was plunged into crisis when the Austrian bank, the *Kreditanstalt*, in Vienna collapsed. This immediately triggered a large-scale withdrawal of deposits from the German banks by their customers, who feared a similar collapse. On 13 July the *Darmstädter und Nationalbank* (DANAT) stopped all payments, and two days later it was joined by the other German banks. A banking crash was only prevented by the government's immediate investment of 1 billion marks by allowing the mark to float free from the gold standard.

In human terms the Depression had a devastating impact on Germany. By 1932 almost one worker in three was officially registered as unemployed, and in such industrial areas as the Ruhr and Silesia the proportion was even higher. Industrial workers suffered the most but white-collar workers were also hit badly – by 1932 more than half a million white-collar workers were out of work. By January 1932 the unemployed together with their dependent families altogether made up a fifth of the total German population – almost 13 million people. Many skilled workers were forced to accept wage cuts, unskilled work or part-time work merely to survive. The unemployed were eligible for financial relief, but the length of the Depression steadily eroded the benefits and by 1932 large numbers received nothing at all.

It was not surprising that many of the younger unemployed tried to escape from the tedium and frustration of unemployment by joining the paramilitary organizations of either the right or the left – the SA, or the KPD's *Rotfront* (see Document 2).

German unemployment, 1928–33 (in millions)

Year	January	July
1928	1.862	1.012
1929	2.850	1.251
1930	3.218	2.765
1931	4.887	3.990
1932	6.042	5.392
1933	6.014	4.464

Source: Adapted from B. Gebhardt, *Handbuch der Deutschen Geschichte*, vol. 4, ed. K.D. Erdmann, Stuttgart, Union Verlag, 1959.

THE FALL OF THE GRAND COALITION

The onset of the Depression acted, to quote Detlev Peukert, 'as a trigger to the abandonment of a political system which had already lost its legitimacy'.[3] Once the Young Plan referendum (see p. 159) had been won, the divisions in the cabinet over financing unemployment benefits, which the Depression was making ever more expensive, came to a head. The SPD rejected any attempts to economize on benefits, while the DVP, backed by the heavy industrialists, pressed for drastic cuts. A compromise was offered by the Centre Party, which would have delayed a decision on the crucial issue of reform until the autumn. This involved a further grant of money from the government, and, if this was not enough, it would be topped up by an increase of 0.025 per cent from both employers' and workers' contributions. Chancellor Müller was ready to accept this but when, under the influence of the trade unions, his party, the SPD, rejected it, he resigned on 27 March 1930, and the Grand Coalition disintegrated. Later Rudolf Hilferding, the left-wing SPD deputy, bitterly criticized the trade unions and SPD backbenchers for being 'ready to let German democracy and the German Republic go to the devil ... over the question of thirty pfennigs for the unemployed'.[4] Historians have generally accepted this view, as the demise of the Grand Coalition fatally weakened German democracy, but Hitler's success in the election of September 1930 could not necessarily be foreseen, and at stake was not just the question of unemployment benefits but the future of the whole welfare state, which the DVP was increasingly wanting to scale down or even abolish on the grounds that the German economy could not afford it.

As Müller's successor, President Hindenburg appointed Heinrich Brüning, the leader of the Centre Party in the *Reichstag*. Hindenburg and his advisers, particularly General Schleicher (see p. 185), had been planning to replace the coalition with a more authoritarian and 'anti-Marxist' chancellor. In January 1930 Hindenburg had already raised with Count Westarp, the chairman of the DNVP parliamentary party, the possibility of appointing a presidential cabinet, which would be largely independent of the *Reichstag*.

BRÜNING, THE 'HUNGER CHANCELLOR', MARCH 1930–MAY 1932

Heinrich Brüning, 1885–1970

After serving in the First World War, Brüning was elected as a Centre Party deputy to the *Reichstag* in 1924 and in 1929 became the party's parliamentary leader. By inclination he was a monarchist and somewhat sceptical of parliamentary democracy. He lacked any charisma or ability to make rousing speeches, and was hardly the ideal statesman to win the trust of the electorate during the acute economic and social crisis of the Depression.

Brüning's responsibility for the downfall of the Republic is much debated. Amongst his contemporaries the historian, Arthur Rosenberg, for instance, argued that his chancellorship brought about the 'death of the Weimar Republic'.[5] On the other hand, it has been argued, particularly by his recent biographer William Patch, that he was aiming to strengthen the executive by creating a presidential constitution in response to the problems caused by the collapse of coalition politics, and that only *after* his dismissal did, to use **Friedrich Meinecke**'s words, 'the path to the abyss' open up.[6] In his posthumous autobiography[7] Brüning claimed that his main aim was to end reparation payments, achieve military equality with Britain and France and restore the monarchy. This, however, may well have represented a later rationalization of what seemed to contemporaries an increasingly confused set of policies.

In 1934 Brüning emigrated, first to Britain and then to the USA, where he taught at Harvard University. He was briefly considered as a possible leader of the West German Christian Democrat Party in 1949 (see Documents 5 and 6).

Friedrich Meinecke (1862–1954)
German historian, professor of history at Berlin and editor of the *Historische Zeitscrift*, from which he was dismissed by the Nazis.

Brüning's government was formed on 29 March 1930 and was supported by the Centre and Liberal Parties. He announced that if it was defeated by a vote of no confidence, he would request a dissolution of the *Reichstag* and govern with emergency decrees. His first finance bill was passed by a small majority, but the second one, which announced increased taxation, cuts in welfare expenditure and 'an emergency contribution' from those on fixed incomes, was thrown out in July.

The election of September 1930

When Brüning's attempts to implement these measures with the help of Article 48 of the constitution were declared unconstitutional, the *Reichstag* was dissolved and a general election was held on 14 September. Given the uncertainties of the political situation, it can be argued that this was a decision of 'breathtaking irresponsibility',[8] which enabled the Nazi Party to become a major political force. During the electoral campaign, which was masterminded by Goebbels, the Nazi Party played on the growing insecurity and fears of the voters with great skill. From the party propaganda office in Munich Goebbels sent out instructions to the local and regional party offices. His main message was that only Hitler could unite the German people – whom parliamentary democracy had demoralized and split into competing interest groups – into a new national community. Whole regions were saturated with Nazi canvassers and electoral meetings, while Hitler himself addressed political rallies in the large cities. Campaigners were carefully coached by the Nazi propaganda apparatus to appeal to different sections of the population. The party had also organized a series of subdivisions, which targeted the pressure groups and sectional interests, which increasingly dominated German politics.

Paul Joseph Goebbels (1897–1945)

Goebbels studied at Bonn and Heidelberg universities. As a result of his club foot he was unable to fight in the First World War. Like the young Hitler, he was a Bohemian who spent much of his time dreaming of an artistic career. He joined the NSDAP in 1924 and became *Gauleiter* of Berlin in 1926 and Reich Director of Propaganda in 1929. He was given the key post of Minister of Popular Enlightenment and Propaganda in 1933 and managed to build up a highly effective system for controlling the mass media and cultural life of the German state. In 1944 he was made Plenipotentiary for Total War. On 2 May 1945 he first killed his wife and family and then committed suicide.

The results on 14 September were no less than 'a political earthquake':[9] the NSDAP increased its seats from 12 to 107, and became the second largest Party in the *Reichstag*. In 1930 6.5 million or 18.3 per cent of the electorate voted for the Nazis and this increased to 37.3 per cent in July 1932. Where did these votes come from?

- Many young people were attracted to the dynamism of the Nazi Party and the 'glamour' of the SA. Consequently the large number of first-time voters, who came on to the electoral roll between May 1928 and July 1932, benefited the Nazis (see Document 2).
- They also profited from the sharp increase in the electoral turnout in 1930 and 1932 when many, who normally could not be bothered to vote, this time round voted for the Nazis.
- Although the SPD and the Communist Parties were relatively successful in fending off the Nazi challenge, Hitler's pledges

to create work did attract working-class voters from the young and unemployed, as well non-unionized workers in small firms and employees in the state sector – the railways and postal service. Jürgen Falter has estimated that roughly 40 per cent of the Nazi votes came from the working class.[10] In many ways the NSDAP, by promising work-creation schemes and a new classless community, contrasted favourably to the SPD, which became increasingly identified with Brüning's deflationary policy.

- By 1930 the NSDAP had built up separate sections, which targeted, for instance, doctors, lawyers, teachers, civil servants, war pensioners, farmers and artisans and retail traders. These encouraged middle-class voters to quit the interest parties that had proliferated in the late 1920s (see p. 160).

- Statistics show that the NSDAP did best in the Protestant and rural districts of northern Germany, and was not as effective in the Catholic areas and cities, but that is not to say that it did not attract votes from all sections of society.

Election results, 1930–3

	NSDAP	DNVP	DVP	Centre/BVP	DDP	SPD	KPD	Others
14.9.30	18.3	7.0	4.9	14.8	3.8	24.5	13.1	13.6
31.7.32	37.3	5.9	1.2	15.7	1.0	21.6	14.3	3.0
6.11.32	33.1	6.5	1.8	15.0	1.0	20.4	16.9	5.3
5.3.33	43.9	8.0	1.1	13.7	0.9	18.3	12.3	1.08

Brüning's second government, September 1930–May 1932

Despite having no majority in the *Reichstag*, Hindenburg refused to dismiss Brüning. For a majority in the *Reichstag*, Brüning initially looked to the NSDAP and the DNVP, and proposed to Hitler that 'in all *Land* parliaments where it was arithmetically possible, the NSDAP and the Centre might combine to form a government',[11] but Hitler rejected this on the grounds that Brüning was not prepared immediately to cancel reparation payments. Brüning was equally unsuccessful with the DNVP, but in the end the SPD came to his rescue, and agreed to 'tolerate' his government, rather than run the risk of Hitler gaining power (see Document 6).

Confident now that the SPD would not vote against him and, enjoying the support of Hindenburg, Brüning began to lay the foundations for a more authoritarian regime. Over the next two years parliamentary democracy in Germany was progressively weakened. The government increasingly bypassed the *Reichstag* by using Article 48, which gave the President in times of crisis sweeping powers to enact emergency legislation. The number of emergency decrees rose from 5 in 1930 to 66 in 1932. The *Reichstag* was also marginalized either by direct negotiations with party and pressure group leaders or by using the *Reichsrat*, the upper house, as a substitute for the legislature.

Brüning hoped to exploit the misery of the Depression both to persuade Britain and France to end reparations and to lay the foundations for economic recovery by cutting back on welfare costs. To appeal to the Nationalist Right he supported the plan for a customs union with Austria, which would be the first step towards a union between the two states. The French government was hostile to this idea from the start, and when Germany was plunged into a major banking crisis in July 1931 (see p. 178), the French blocked every proposal for emergency loans until Germany not only gave up plans for the customs union but also for seeking a revision of reparations payments for a period of at least five years. However, the severity of the banking crisis moved President Hoover, the US President, to intervene and persuade the French to agree a year's moratorium on reparation payments.

Brüning, at great financial and human cost, had now come near to achieving his key aim of eliminating reparations. He managed to convince the committee of international financial experts, which was monitoring the reparation problem, that Germany would not be in a position to make any payments even when the Hoover moratorium had expired. The committee's proposal that both reparations and inter-Allied debts should be cancelled, was adopted at the Lausanne Conference in June 1932.

Ironically, Brüning was not able to exploit this breakthrough, as he was dismissed from office by Hindenburg on 29 May 1932, just as he was 'within a hundred yards short of the goal'.[12] Why, when he was nearly successful, was he so abruptly removed from power?

- The severity of the Depression did great damage to the Brüning government. His deflationary policies, which involved cutting the salaries of state employees, wage freezes and making unemployment payments ever more difficult to secure, inevitably angered both the *Mittelstand* and the workers, and were so unpopular that Brüning became known as the 'Hunger Chancellor'. Once the Mark had left the gold standard in July 1931 (see p. 178), Bruning could have risked reflating the economy, but he was frightened that if he did this, inflation would return. He also wanted to use the Depression as a chance to dismantle the welfare system, and once and for all weaken organized labour.

- He failed to gain the support of either the DNVP or the Nazis. On 11 October they organized a joint rally at Bad Harzburg to demonstrate their hostility to the government. They were highly suspicious of his dependence on the SPD and his failure to break decisively with the Weimar constitution (see Documents 4 and 6). The dependence of the Brüning government on the SPD also lost the support of the Ruhr industrialists, who in January 1932 invited Hitler to speak to their representatives at the Industry Club in Düsseldorf.

- Brüning's survival was guaranteed as long as Hindenburg supported him, but by the spring of 1932 this, too, was beginning to be eroded. Hindenburg never forgave Brüning when he failed to win a majority in the *Reichstag* for a constitutional amendment, which would have prolonged his term in office without a **presidential election**. By the spring of 1932 Hindenburg was advised by General **Schleicher** to dismiss Brüning, since his dependence on the SPD offended big business, industry and the Nationalist Right, which his administration was supposed to protect, while his foreign policy had failed.

The immediate causes of Brüning's dismissal were the ban on the SA of 13 April 1932, which was made necessary by the mounting evidence that it was planning a putsch, and his government's proposals for dividing up the bankrupt estates into small farms. These were immediately characterized by the East Elbian landowners as 'agrarian Bolshevism'. Schleicher played a key role

Presidential election, March 1932
Hindenburg stood as the candidate of the constitutional parties; in the second ballot his main opponent was Hitler, who gained 36.8 per cent of the vote.

Kurt von Schleicher (1882–1934)
Served on the General Staff during the First World War and was political adviser to General Groener during the revolution of 1918. He then worked under General von Seeckt at the Ministry of Defence, where he played a leading role in planning German rearmament. By 1929, as a result of his close friendship with Hindenburg, he became a powerful figure behind the scenes in the Republic. He was Chancellor, December 1932–January 1933 and was murdered by Hitler in the Night of the Long Knives (see p. 196).

in bringing about Brüning's downfall. He attacked the SA ban on the grounds that it would deprive the *Reichswehr* of a vital military reserve in case of war, but in reality his intention was to engineer the formation of a Nationalist coalition with the Nazis, which would be led by Franz von Papen, and would replace the Republic with an authoritarian regime. It would be given the necessary popular backing by including Hitler in the new cabinet (see Document 4).

Hitler, however, was convinced that the Nazis were capable of winning an overall majority in an election and consequently responded to these overtures with caution, as he was determined not to enter a coalition in a subordinate position. Nevertheless he agreed to tolerate the Papen government, provided that the SA ban was lifted and a general election was held within weeks. Hindenburg and Schleicher accepted these conditions and on 30 May 1932 Papen replaced Schleicher as Chancellor.

Franz von Papen (1879–1969)

Papen was a career officer, who joined the General Staff in 1911 and then became a military attaché in Washington. He was recalled from this post because the US government suspected him of having contacts with German spies. In 1919 he was elected to the Prussian *Landtag* and represented the right wing of the Centre Party. He also owned the majority of shares in the Catholic paper, the *Germania*. After serving as Chancellor, May–November 1932 and then Vice Chancellor under Hitler, 1933–34, Papen was German Ambassador in Austria, 1934–38 and then in Turkey, 1939–44. He was acquitted by the Nuremburg War Crimes Tribunal in 1946, but sentenced to eight years' imprisonment by a German de-Nazification court, although he was released in 1949.

THE PAPEN AND SCHLEICHER CABINETS, JUNE 1932–JANUARY 1933

The coup against Prussia

On 20 July Papen eliminated the last bastion of SDP support when he deposed the SPD–Centre government in Prussia. He argued that its failure to prevent the Altona riots indicated that it was no longer capable of maintaining law and order within

Prussia. He immediately took the post of Minister-President (prime minister) himself, while a Reich Commissioner was appointed Minister of the Interior with direct control over the Prussian police. The willingness of both the *Reichswehr* and the SA to intervene ensured that there was no effective opposition from the *Reichsbanner*, the SPD's own paramilitary force. The consequence of the coup was that the SPD now lost its influence in German politics and became marginalized (see Document 7).

The elections of 31 July and 6th November

In the election of 31 July the Nazi Party won 230 seats, but still could not command an overall majority, even though it was the largest party in the *Reichstag*, while Papen could only rely on the 37 DNVP members. Hitler nevertheless insisted that he had sufficient backing to form a new government. Hindenburg, however, was only ready to offer him the post of vice-chancellorship in Papen's cabinet, which Hitler rejected, as he was not prepared to serve in a subordinate position in a coalition.

Initially, Papen hoped that he would be able survive without Hitler. He had already deposed the Prussian government in July, and had plans for dissolving the *Reichstag* and delaying elections until he had drawn up a new constitution in which a restricted franchise and a non-elected upper chamber would drastically reduce parliament's powers. However, the timing of his plans went wrong, when he was compelled on 12 September to dissolve the *Reichstag* prematurely after an overwhelming vote of no confidence in his government. At first he still hoped that he could draft the new constitution before the election, but when the Centre and the NSDAP threatened to use Article 59 of the constitution to indict him for violating the constitution, he had to abandon that plan.

In the elections of 6 November the growing public disenchantment with the Nazis was beginning to make itself felt. They lost 2 million votes and number of their seats in the *Reichstag* declined to 196. Yet Hitler still refused to serve in a Papen cabinet. Papen was ready to persevere with his plans for a new constitution and use the army to dissolve the newly elected *Reichstag*, but he was opposed by Schleicher, now Minister of Defence, who feared that this could lead to civil war. Instead,

**Gregor Strasser
(1892–1934)**
A Bavarian, he joined the
NSDAP in 1922; he
believed passionately in a
'German' or National
Socialism. In 1928 he
played a key role in
improving the party's
organization. He was
murdered in the Night of
the Long Knives (see
p. 196).

Schleicher optimistically believed that he could win over Hitler, or
at very least persuade **Gregor Strasser** and a group of some some
60 Nazi deputies to support the government. Hindenburg had
been quite ready to back Papen, but once Schleicher made it clear
to him that the *Reichswehr* had withdrawn its support from him,
Hindenburg dismissed Papen and appointed Shleicher Chancellor
on 2 December.

The Schleicher government, 4 December 1932–30 January 1933

The following day the Nazi Party was faced with a severe crisis
when Schleicher offered Gregor Strasser the positions of Vice-
Chancellor and Minister President of Prussia. When Hitler
refused to allow Strasser to join the new government, he resigned
from the party in protest. Only by appealing successfully to the
loyalty of the *Reichstag* deputies, *Gauleiter* and Regional
Inspectors to their *Führer*, was Hitler able to prevent a damaging
split in the party. Schleicher's attempts to win over the SPD and
the trade unions through a package of economic reforms and
work creation projects not only failed, but had also alarmed both
the industrialists and the east Elbian landowners. In their determination to deny power to the moderate Left, they were ready to
consider an alliance with the Nazis.

By January 1933 the Nazis appeared to be on their way to 'the
rubbish pile of history'.[13] It is true they had managed to win 39.5
per cent of the vote in the state election of Lippe, but it had a electorate of only 100,000. Other indicators were not so optimistic:
their share in the student union elections at the universities had
declined by 5 per cent. More ominously for the Nazis as a party
of protest, the Depression was bottoming out and Schleicher was
planning a massive job-creation programme, which Germany's
departure from the gold standard in July 1931 had made possible.
The SA was also becoming increasingly restless at Hitler's failure
to gain power.

Angry at being outmanoeuvred by Schleicher, Papen had been
considering doing a deal with the NSDAP. In early December, he
had contacted Hitler via the Cologne banker, Kurt von Schröder,
who on 4 January 1933 had arranged a meeting between them. At
first it seemed that Hitler would be ready to accept office in a

Papen cabinet, provided that the NSDAP controlled the Defence and Interior Ministries. In mid January Hindenburg instructed Papen 'personally and in strict confidence'[14] to explore the possibility of forming a governing coalition with the Nazis.

On 28 January Schleicher had little option but to resign, after Hindenburg refused both to dissolve the *Reichstag* and to grant him wide-ranging emergency powers. Hitler was now in a strong position to demand the Chancellorship for himself and the Ministries of the Interior of both the Reich and Prussia for Dr Wilhelm Frick (see p. 210) and Hermann Göring respectively. Papen reassured Hindenburg that by appointing reliable Conservative figures to the other nine posts, he would be able to minimize Nazi influence on the government. Schleicher himself remarked that 'if Hitler wants to establish a dictatorship in the Reich, then the army will be the dictatorship within the dictatorship'.[15] On the evening of 28 January Hindenburg agreed and the new Hitler cabinet was sworn in on 30 January.

Herman Göring (1893–1946)

In the First World War Göring joined the air force and commanded the famous *Richthofen* squadron in 1918. He joined the Nazi Party and became head of the SA in 1923. He was elected as a Nazi *Reichstag* deputy in 1928, and in 1932 became the President (speaker) of the *Reichstag*. In 1933, as Prussian Minister of the Interior in Hitler's cabinet in 1933, he set up the **Gestapo** and the first concentration camps. He was appointed Minister of Aviation and later Commander-in-Chief of the *Luftwaffe*. In 1936 he was put in charge of the Four-Year Plan. As a result of defeat in the Battle of Britain, his influence declined after 1940. He was sentenced to death as a war criminal at Nuremberg, but managed to commit suicide before his execution.

Gestapo
The state secret police.

THE FAILURE TO CONTAIN HITLER

In retrospect it seems to later generations that the German Nationalists, Hindenburg and the *Reichswehr* were naïve to believe that Hitler could be controlled. Could they not grasp the revolutionary nature of the Nazi movement? Papen's notorious boast that within two months 'we will have pushed Hitler so far

into a corner that he'll squeak'[16] was revealed to be a misjudge-
ment of epic proportions: How did this occur? To answer this we
need to remember Martin Broszat's advice that we should not
always study history backwards.[17] The aims of both the German
elites and a great majority of the German people overlapped with
the initial stages of Nazi policy. Hitler's determination to destroy
the Versailles Treaty and restore the economy were aims that had
universal backing. It is also true, as Papen wrote his memoirs in
the early 1950s, that his 'own and Schleicher's Cabinets and
Hitler's Government were only part of a logical sequence of
events'.[18] Hitler inherited a situation where rule by decree was the
norm and a coup against the Weimar Republic had been considered by both the Papen and Schleicher governments. Their
mistake, which many others were to make, was to ignore the revolutionary dynamism of the Nazi movement and Hitler's own
determination to outflank his Conservative 'minders' (see
Documents 7 and 8).

The election of 5 March 1933

Hitler's intention to eliminate the remaining powers of the
Reichstag was shared by his nationalist colleagues. He rejected
the offer of an agreement with the Centre Party, which would
have given him a working majority in parliament, and decided on
an immediate dissolution of the *Reichstag* followed by a general
election. The only dissenting voice in the cabinet was Alfred
Hugenberg, the Economics Minister, who feared the increased
power that a victorious election would give Hitler.

Hitler fought an effective election campaign. On the one hand,
he stressed the total failure of the '**November parties**' and by
implication cleverly managed to associate his allies in the cabinet
with them. On the other hand, he sought to dispel the apprehen-
sions of those who feared the revolutionary potential of Nazism
by pledging to protect 'Christianity as the basis of our morality
and the family as the nucleus of our nation and state'. He also
promised a programme to help agriculture and to launch 'a
massive and comprehensive attack on unemployment'.[19]

By exploiting Article 48 (see Document 3) the government was
able to ban political meetings and opposition newspapers. Thanks
to Papen's abolition of the Prussian government in June 1932 (see

November parties
The parties that were held
responsible for the
November armistice, the
creation of the Weimar
Republic and the
acceptance of the Treaty
of Versailles.

p. 186), Hermann Göring, as Prussian Minister of the Interior, was able to control the Prussian police and reinforce them with SA men as auxiliaries. The *Reichstag* fire on 27 February 1933 was used as a justification to impose the draconian 'Decree for the Protection of People and State, which not only gave the central government the powers arbitrarily to order the arrest of individuals, censor the post and have private houses searched, but also to dismiss *Land* governments if they refused to implement the necessary 'measures for the restoration of public security'. This decree was 'a kind of *coup d'état*',[20] but nevertheless on 5 March 1933 the NSDAP only won 43.9 per cent of the votes. The coalition could only claim a majority on the strength of the 8 per cent won by the Nationalist Party.

Reichstag fire

The fire was so opportune that contemporaries were convinced that the Nazis started it, but in fact it was the work of an unemployed Dutch building labourer, Marinus van der Lubbe. He had been a member of the Communist Party, but disliking its discipline had joined a radical anarcho-syndicalist organization. He had attempted already to burn down prominent public buildings in Berlin, and was convinced that this would spur the unemployed on to spontaneous mass action. He managed to force his way into the *Reichstag* at night and start a fire in the debating chamber.

Alerted by Goebbels, Hitler insisted on attending van der Lubbe's interrogation and decided to have the Communists and their sympathizers in Berlin arrested. It was Göring's adviser who suggested that an emergency decree would provide the necessary legal cover for the arrests.

The Enabling Act

The Reichstag fire and the subsequent election results unleashed what amounted to a '**revolution from below**'. The SA not only destroyed the Communists, but also began to beat up and imprison in unofficial concentration camps other opponents of the Hitler government. The wave of initially uncontrollable violence that swept through Germany threatened to alienate both the NSDAP's coalition partners and the Reich President, whose

Revolution from below
A revolution that is driven by the grass-roots of the party rather than being dictated from above.

support at this stage was still essential. To bring an end to the violence, and particularly the 'obstruction or disturbance of business life' that this caused,[21] Hitler made repeated appeals to the SA. On 21 March in an effort to reassure his coalition partners Hitler organized an impressive ceremony at the **Garnisonskirche** in Potsdam, to which he invited the Crown Prince and the generals and the President (see Figure 6.1), where he pledged allegiance to the military traditions of Prussian Germany and deliberately reawakened memories of national unity in August 1914.

Two days later the delegates of the newly elected *Reichstag* were summoned to the Kroll Opera House to debate the Enabling Bill, the aim of which was to transfer full legislative and executive powers to the Chancellor for a four-year period. As it involved a change in the constitution, the government had first to secure a two-thirds majority, if the fiction of the legal revolution was to be continued (see Document 1). Although the majority of the KPD deputies and several SPD members had already been arrested, the necessary majority was only made possible when the Centre Party decided to vote for the bill. Its support was secured by Hitler's promises to protect the rights and privileges of the Catholic Church. It naïvely assumed that by cooperating with the govern-

Garnisonskirche
The military or garrison chapel in Potsdam.

Figure 6.1 Hitler greeting President von Hindenburg on Potsdam Day, 21 March 1933.
Source: Getty Images/ Hulton Archive

ment, it would be able to influence it from the inside, as it had every Weimar government since 1919 (see Document 9). Hitler reassured the bourgeois parties that the *Reichstag* and *Reichsrat*, the Presidency and the *states* would not be permanently weakened, but like Mussolini in 1922 (see p. 119), he threatened that if he did not gain the necessary majority he was 'prepared to go ahead in face of the refusal and the hostilities which will result from that refusal'.[22] To show that this was not an empty threat the opera house was surrounded by the SS (see p. 211), and inside SA men openly intimidated the deputies. The bill was passed by 444 votes to 94, with only the SPD voting against it. By preserving the façade of the legal revolution, the Enabling Act played a vital role in removing any doubts the civil service or the judiciary had as to the legality of the Nazi takeover.

Gleichschaltung and the creation of the one-party state

By ensuring that the President's counter-signature was no longer a legal requirement before decrees and emergency legislation could come into force, the Enabling Act immensely strengthened Hitler's position as Chancellor. In April, Joseph Goebbels, Minister for Popular Enlightenment and Propaganda (see p. 182), observed that 'the *Führer*'s authority in the Cabinet is absolute'.[23] Empowered by the Enabling Act, assisted by the ultimate threat of violence from the SA and enjoying considerable backing from the public, through the process of coordination or **Gleichschaltung**, Hitler was able to create a one-party centralized Reich far more quickly that Mussolini had been able to in Italy (see pp. 107–8). The key stages in this process were:

Gleichschaltung
Originally an electrical term, meaning synchronization.

- Through a mixture of revolutionary pressure from below by the SA, and action from above by the government, the states were coordinated. This process went through a number of stages:
  - in the states that the Nazis did not yet control, the local police forces were taken over by Nazi commissioners
  - then the state parliaments were dissolved and reconstituted to reflect the ratio of the parties in the *Reichstag*
  - Reich governors, who were usually the local *Gauleiter*, were appointed, with full powers to enforce coordination

in the Prussian provinces *Gauleiter* were also appointed to the post of *Oberpräsident* (senior administrative official) – the state parliaments were dissolved in January 1934, and their governments were subordinated to the Reich government.

- During the summer of 1933 all parties, associations and private armies were either abolished or taken over by the Nazis. On 2 May the SA and SS occupied trade union offices throughout Germany. The trade unions were dissolved and the workers were enrolled in the new German Labour Front (DAF). On 22 June the SPD was banned, and on 14 July the Law against the New Formation of Parties made the Nazi Party the only legal party in Germany. Although employers' associations' had to join the Reich Chamber of German Industry, businessmen were allowed to manage their own affairs and were able to protect themselves from interference from party fanatics, who wanted the complete takeover of business and industry.

- Education, the media and culture were quickly brought under Nazi control. Broadcasting and news coverage in the press were the responsibility of the Ministry of Propaganda. In September 1933 the Reich Chamber of Culture was formed, which all 'intellectual workers' were forced to join. Teaching organizations also were affiliated to the National Socialist Teachers' Organization.

THE DEFEAT OF THE 'SECOND REVOLUTION'

By July 1933, far from being pushed into a corner, as Papen had predicted, Hitler had created a one-party state and a dictatorship, but even so his dicatatorship was not complete. Papen and Hindenburg were still in office, and the 'conservative bearers of state',[24] the bureaucratic, military and big business elites, still exerted considerable influence, as Hitler was dependent on their help to revive the economy and rearm Germany (see p. 217). Their influence, however, was resented by both the SA and the radical wing of the party, which had assumed that the seizure of power would entail a clean break with the *ancien régime*. Hitler's most dangerous critic was Ernst Röhm, the Chief of Staff of the

SA, who controlled a potentially revolutionary force of some 2.3 million men (see Document 10).

Ernst Röhm (1887–1934)

Röhm, the son of a Bavarian civil servant, had a distinguished war record. In the immediate post-war period he remained an army staff officer, and played an important part in liaising with the Bavarian paramilitary groups, especially the Nazis, which he joined in 1923. He was involved in the abortive Munich putsch (see pp. 156–7). In 1928 he emigrated to Bolivia as a military instructor, but was called back by Hitler in 1930 to become Chief of Staff of the SA.

In July 1933, to reassure the army and big business, Hitler declared an end to the 'legal revolution'. Röhm, on the other hand, still hoped for a second and much more radical Nazi revolution, which would achieve the more socialist aspects of the Nazi programme. As a guarantee of this, he hoped that the SA would form the basis of a new mass Nazi army. This ambition inevitably threatened the *Reichswehr* and led to its growing rivalry with the SA.

In January 1934 Hitler had already indicated that he would retain the *Reichswehr* when he decided in principle on the reintroduction of traditional military conscription. However, this had failed to calm the increasingly bitter dispute between Röhm and the army, which suspected that he might either stage a coup or force Hitler to change his mind. By the spring of 1934 Hindenburg's ill health and great age made a solution to the problem increasingly urgent. It was possible that the generals, backed by the whole of the Conservative elite, might even attempt to block Hitler's own ambitions to succeed Hindenburg if they perceived the SA was a threat to their role in rebuilding Germany's armed forces. For Hitler there was a real danger that the army and the Conservative elites after Hindenburg's death might press for a monarchist restoration, which would act as a most unwelcome restraint on a Nazi government. Regrets were already surfacing in Nationalist–Conservative circles about having helped bring Hitler to power. Edgar Jung, a leading right-wing intellectual and Papen's speech writer, observed, for instance, that 'We are partly responsible that this fellow has come to power [and] we must get rid of him again'.[25] However, provided Hitler controlled the SA, the *Reichswehr* would not support a restoration, since both **General Blomberg**, the Defence Minister, and **General Fritsch**, the new Commander-in-Chief of the army, as well as many junior officers, believed that Hitler was the right man to rearm Germany.

From March 1934 onwards Hitler, encouraged by Göring, Himmler (see p. 212) and Hess, who all saw Röhm as a dangerous rival to their own ambitions within the party, 'moved erratically and with spells of doubt and indecision towards a show-down with the SA'.[26] On 17 June Papen, in a sensational speech at Marburg University, warned against the consequences of a second revolution and even criticized the growing *Führer* cult. 'Never again in the Third Reich', as Ian Kershaw has written, 'was such striking criticism at the heart of the regime to come from such a prominent figure'.[27] When Hitler visited the President at his estate at Neudeck, on 21 June, he was informed by Blomberg that if he failed effectively to control the SA, Hindenburg would hand over power to the army.

Consequently, if his regime were to survive unchallenged, Hitler had no alternative but to destroy Röhm, but at the same time he seized the opportunity to eliminate many of his leading critics on the right as well. In the subsequent 'Night of the Long Knives', 30 June/1 July, Röhm the SA leaders, the two Conservative monarchists in Papen's office (Herbert von Bose and Edgar Jung), Schleicher and Gregor Strasser were all murdered. According to police records at least 85 people were liquidated, while the 'white book', which was published in Paris by German émigrés, claimed that it was 401.

Röhm's murder removed the last barriers to Hitler's consolidation of power (see Figure 6.2). Papen was dismissed and was lucky to escape with his life. When Hindenburg died on 2 August, there was no opposition from the *Reichswehr* to Hitler holding both the offices of Chancellor and President – a step which was confirmed by plebiscite on 19 August. As head of state, Hitler became the supreme commander of the armed forces, which now swore an oath of loyalty personally to him. Hitler had survived a crisis which could have led to the collapse of the Nazi regime, and had eliminated the threat from the SA without becoming the prisoner of the Conservative elites.

General Werner von Blomberg (1878–1946)
Minister of Defence (1933–5) and War Minister (1935–8); he was dismissed in February 1938 after he married Eva Gruhn, a former prostitute.

General Werner Freiherr von Fritsch (1880–1939)
Commander-in-Chief of the *Wehrmacht*. He was critical of the risks Hitler ran in his foreign policy and was forced to resign in February 1938 as a result of being falsely accused of homosexuality. He was killed in the Polish campaign in 1939.

Figure 6.2 Hitler laughing and joking with Göring and Himmler just after the Röhm purge, 1934.
Source: Corbis/Bettmann

ASSESSMENT

The decline of the Weimar Republic and Hitler's appointment as Chancellor are two related but distinct historical problems. The Weimar Republic, faced with deep-seated structural political and economic problems, was already losing its political legitimacy in the eyes of a large number of Germans by late 1929. Hindenburg and his advisers, particularly General Schleicher, were considering the possibility of strengthening the executive and returning to a more authoritarian constitution, comparable to the one Bismarck created in 1871. In that sense it was possible that the Weimar

Republic would, anyway, have been replaced with a more authoritarian regime. The Great Depression and the emergence of the
Nazi Party as a mass movement of protest in September 1930,
however, made the dissolution of the Republic much more likely,
as it held out the prospect to the Nationalist–Conservative Right
of mass backing for their plans for an authoritarian presidential
regime.

Over the period 1930–2 a de facto presidential regime was
formed and the Prussian government destroyed, yet the traditional elites still needed to harness the mass support given to
Hitler if they were to be successful in creating a new anti-democratic authoritarian regime. Paradoxically the electoral reverses
that the NSDAP had suffered in November 1932 encouraged
them to hope that the Nazis could be more easily exploited as
lobby fodder, and led to Papen confidently predicting that Hitler
would be easily contained within the Conservative–Nationalist-
dominated cabinet. The mistake of the Nationalists and the old
elites was not so much to ignore the revolutionary dynamism of
the NSDAP but to underrate Hitler's political skills and determination to eliminate all opposition.

Big business and industry were able to block the threat from the
Nazi rank and file for the abolition of department stores and control
of the big cartels. In the summer of 1934 the *Reichswehr* and Papen
also successfully put pressure on Hitler to eliminate Röhm, but only
at the cost of increasing Hitler's own power. Ultimately Hitler was
to use this power to subvert what remained of the German
Rechtstaat and to introduce a chaotic programme of creeping
Nazification that did amount to a second revolution.

Rechtstaat
A state based on the rule
of law.

DOCUMENT 1

Working within the constitution

*In September 1930 three young officers stationed in Ulm were
accused of working for the Nazi Party within the army. The three
were put on trial before the Supreme Court at Leipzig. Hitler was
called as a witness, and in his statement he stressed how he aimed
to achieve a 'legal' revolution:*

The National Socialist movement will try to achieve its aim with
constitutional means in the state. The constitution prescribes my

methods, not the aim. In this constitutional way we shall try to gain decisive majorities in the legislative bodies so that the moment we succeed we can give the state the form that corresponds to our ideas.

Source: J. Noakes and G. Pridham, eds, *Nazism, 1919–45*, vol. 1, *The Rise to Power, 1919–34*, Exeter, Exeter University Press, 1998, p. 62.

DOCUMENT 2
An SA Convert

A British tourist, Patrick Leigh Fermor, met a young German worker who had just left the KPD for the NSDAP:

[The walls of his room] were covered with flags, posters, slogans and emblems. His SA uniform hung neatly ironed on a hanger. He explained these cult objects with a fetishist zest, saving up till the last centrepiece of his collection. It was an automatic pistol . . . When I said that it must be rather claustrophobic with all that stuff on the walls, he laughed and sat down on the bed, and said: '*Mensch!* You should have seen it last year! You would have laughed! Then it was all red flags, stars, hammers and sickles, pictures of Lenin and Stalin and Workers of the World Unite! I used to punch the heads of anyone singing the Horst Wessel Lied! . . . Then suddenly, when Hitler came to power, I understood it was all nonsense and lies. I realized Adolf was the man for me, All of a sudden!' Had a lot of people done the same, then? [Fermor asked] 'Millions! I tell you, I was astonished how easily they all changed sides!'

Source: P.L. Fermor, *A Time of Gifts*, London, John Murray, 1977, p. 130.

DOCUMENT 3
Article 48

The key emergency powers, which enabled the issue of legislation by Presidential decree, were contained in paragraph 2 of the Weimar Constitution:

II   If a *Land* does not fulfil the responsibilities assigned to it under the constitution or laws of the *Reich*, the *Reich* President can take the appropriate measures to restore law and order with the assistance of the armed forces. In the event of a serious disturbance or threat to law and order, the *Reich* President may take the necessary measures for restoring law and order, intervening if necessary with armed forces. To achieve this he may temporarily suspend either completely or partially the basic rights in Articles 114, 115, 117, 118, 123, 124 and 153.

III The *Reich* President is bound to report immediately to the *Reichstag* all measures taken under paragraphs 1 and 2 of this article. The measures are to be rescinded on the request of the *Reichstag*.

Source: W. Michalka and G. Niedhart, *Die Ungeliebte Republik, Dokumente zur Innen-und Aussenpolitik Weimars 1918–1933*, Munich, DTV, Deutsche Taschenbuch, 1980, p. 62 (translated by the author).

DOCUMENT 4
The debate about the cooperation of the NSDAP with the Nationalists

The following is an extract from a conversation between President Hindenburg and the Nationalists' leader, Hugenburg, on 1 August 1931:

The Reich President referred to the cooperation of the German Nationalists with the National Socialists, who, he feared, were more socialist than nationalist and whose behaviour in the country he could not approve ... He did not regard them as a reliable national party.

To this Privy Councillor Dr Hugenberg replied that it was for this very reason – to bind the National Socialists to the national side and prevent their slipping towards socialism or Communism – that he had decided to work with the Nazis over the past one-and-a-half years and he took credit for this. He believed that the National Socialists had been politically educated thereby.

Source: Noakes, J. and Pridham, G. (eds) (1998) *Nazism 1919–1945. Volume 1: The Rise to Power 1919–1934*, pub University of Exter Press, p. 96.

DOCUMENT 5
Brüning and German nationalism

Brüning was bitterly critical of the way the NSDAP attempted to claim that they were the only patriotic German party. He told the Nazi deputies in the Reichstag:

You are always talking about the 'system'. Sometimes you call it the Brüning system, sometimes the system of 9th November ... gentlemen, don't you dare to connect me in any way with 9th November! ... Where was I on 9th November? ... Gentlemen, on 9th November I belonged to the army unit formed from the spearhead of the Winterfelde Group for the suppression of the revolution.

Source: M. Burleigh, *The Third Reich*, Basingstoke, Macmillan, p. 137.

DOCUMENT 6
The SPD tolerates Brüning

A Conservative member of Brüning's cabinet recalled in his memoirs that:

No party was called upon to make greater sacrifices in the interests of the whole than the Social-Democratic party, and no class was called upon to make greater economic sacrifices than the working class ... I remember one of the famous night sessions – it was probably in May 1932 – when the government was represented by Brüning, Stegewald and me, whilst opposite us sat workers' representatives of all shades. Once again the topic of discussion was the government's demand that social expenditure be cut. An almost fierce discussion proceeded for several hours, and the dawn was actually breaking when the Social-Democrat trade-union chairman, Leipart, said finally: 'Well, if there's no other way to do it ...'.

Source: H. Schlange-Schoeningen, *The Morning After* (translated by Edward Fitgerald), London, V. Gollancz, 1948, p. 48.

DOCUMENT 7
Papen on Hitler's appointment as Chancellor

In his memoirs, Papen wrote as follows:

When Hitler became Chancellor on January 30 1933, he had been brought to power by the normal interplay of democratic processes. It must be realized that neither he nor his movement had acquired the character or perpetrated the atrocities for which they were to be execrated fifteen years later. His character doubtless had acquired all those traits which have now become familiar, but they were not yet developed in the form in which we

▶

Potempa

Five SA men had kicked to death a Communist miner in Potempa, a village in Silesia, on 9 August 1932. Hitler sent the men responsible, who had been arrested and sentenced to death, a telegram that gave them his complete support.

know them. **Potempa** had provided a warning, but it still seemed reasonable to suppose that a responsible head of government would adopt a different attitude from that he had shown as an irresponsible party chief ... Those who now declare that they knew exactly how things were going to develop are merely wise after the event. If they had really been so far-sighted, many of the events I have now to describe would have turned out very differently.

Source: F. von Papen, *Memoirs*, London, André Deutsch, 1952, pp. 250–1.

DOCUMENT 8
The revolutionary essence of Nazism

As a former Nazi and President of the Danzig Senate, who fled to Switzerland in 1935, Rauschning sought in his perceptive book, Germany's Revolution of Destruction, *to inform the world of what he perceived to be the true nature of National Socialism:*

What then, are the aims of National Socialism which are being achieved one after another? Certainly not the various points of its programme: even if some of these are carried out, that is not the thing that matters. The aim of National Socialism is the complete revolutionizing of technique of government, and complete dominance over the country by the leaders of the movement. The two things are inseparably connected: the revolution cannot be carried out without an elite ruling with absolute power, and this elite can maintain itself in power only through a process of continual intensification of revolutionary disintegration. National Socialism is an unquestionably genuine revolutionary movement in the sense of a final achievement on a vaster scale of 'the mass rising' dreamed of by Anarchists and Communists. But modern revolutions do not take place through fighting across improvised barricades, but in disciplined acts of destruction. They follow irrational impulses, but they remain under rational guidance.

Source: H. Rauschning, *Germany's Revolution of Destruction*, London, Heinemann, 1939, p. 20.

DOCUMENT 9
The Centre Party and the Enabling Bill

Carl Bachem, who was the historian of the Centre Party, reflects on whether the Centre Party should have voted for the Enabling Bill:

If the Centre had voted against it, it would, given the current mood of the National Socialists, probably have been smashed at once just like the Social Democratic Party. All civil servants belonging to the Centre would probably have been dismissed. There would have been a great fracas in the *Reichstag*, and the Centrists would probably have been beaten up and thrown out. The parliamentary group would probably have made an heroic exit, but with no benefit to the Catholic cause or to the cause of the Centre Party. The links between the Centre and National Socialism would have been completely cut, all collaboration with the National Socialists and every possibility of influencing their policy would have been out of the question. Perhaps, then, it was right to make the attempt to come to an understanding and cooperate with the National Socialists, in order to be able to participate in a practical way in the reshaping of the future ...

In any case: as in 1919 we climbed calmly and deliberately into the Social Democrat boat, so in the same way, we were able to enter the boat of the National Socialists in 1933 and try to lend a hand with the steering. Between 1919 and 1933 this proved quite satisfactory: the Social Democrats, since they were not able to govern without the Centre, were unable to do anything particularly antireligious or dubiously socialistic. Will it be possible to exercise a similarly sobering influence on the National Socialists now?

Source: Noakes, J. and Pridham, G. (eds) (1998) *Nazism 1919–1945. Volume 1: The Rise to Power 1919–1934*, pub University of Exeter Press, pp. 157–8.

DOCUMENT 10
The clash between Hitler and Röhm

(a) Röhm wrote in a newspaper article in June 1933:

Already here and there philistines and grumblers are daring to ask in astonishment what the SA and SS are still there for, since Hitler is now in power. We are after all, they point out, nationalist again. Swastika flags fly over the streets. There is law and order everywhere. And if it is disturbed, the police will take care that it is restored as quickly as possible.

Source: Noakes, J. and Pridham, G. (eds) (1998) *Nazism 1919–1945. Volume 1: The Rise to Power 1919–1934*, pub University of Exeter Press, p. 168.

(b) Hitler's speech to the Reich Governors, 6 July 1933:

More revolutions have succeeded in their first assault than, once successful, have been brought to a standstill and held there. Revolution is not a permament state, it must not develop into a lasting state. The full spate of revolution must be guided into the secure bed of evolution ... A businessman must not therefore be dismissed if he is a good businessman even if he is not yet a good National Socialist; especially not if the National Socialist put in his place knows nothing about business.

Source: Noakes, J. and Pridham, G. (eds) (1998) *Nazism 1919–1945. Volume 1: The Rise to Power 1919–1934*, pub University of Exeter Press, pp. 170–1.

NOTES

1 Quoted in E. Kolb, *The Weimar Republic*, London, Routledge. 1988, p. 129.

2 R. Boyce ' World War, World Depression: some economic origins of the Second World War' in R. Boyce and E.M. Robertson, eds, *Paths to War: New Essays on the Origins of the Second World War*, London, Macmillan, 1989, p. 55.

3 D.A. Peuckert, *The Weimar Republic: The Crisis of Classical Modernity*, London, Allen Lane, 1991, p. 249.

4 G. Craig, *Germany; 1866–1945*, Oxford, Oxford University Press, 1978, pp. 532–3.

5 A. Rosenberg, *History of the German Republic,* London, Methuen, 1936, p. 306.

6 W. Patch, *Heinrich Brüning, and the Dissolution of the Weimar Republic*, Cambridge, Cambridge University Press, 1998; F. Meinecke, *The German Catastrophe*, Cambridge, MA, Harvard University Press, 1950, p. 70.

7 Quoted in Kolb, *Weimar Republic*, p. 114.

8 I. Kershaw, *Hitler*, vol. 1, *1889–1936 Hubris*, London, Allen Lane, 1998, p. 324.

9 Ibid., p. 333.

10 J. Falter, 'Die Wähler der NSDAP 1928–1933: Sozialstruktur und parteipolitische Herkunft' in W. Michalka, ed., *Die nationalsozialistische Machtergreifung*, Padeborn/Munich, Schöning, 1984, pp. 47–59.

11 Kolb, *Weimar Republic*, p. 113.

12 Kolb, *Weimar Republic*, p. 118.

13 D. Orlow, *The History of the Nazi Party*, vol. 1, *1919–33*, Newton Abbot, David & Charles, 1971, p. 308.

14 Kolb, *Weimar Republic*, p. 124.

15 R. Evans, *The Coming of the Third Reich*, London, Penguin, 2004, p. 307.

16 Quoted in K. Bracher, *The German Dictatorship*, Harmondsworth, Penguin, 1973, p. 248.

17 M. Broszat, 'A plea for the historisation of National Socialism' in P. Baldwin, ed., *Reworking the Past*, Boston, Beacon Press, 1990.

18 F. von Papen, *Memoirs*, London, André Deutsch, 1952, p. 251.

19 Quoted in J. Noakes and G. Pridham, eds, *Nazism 1919–45*, vol. 1, *The Rise to Power, 1919–34*, Exeter, Exeter University Press, 2nd ed. 1998, p. 132.

20 Ibid., p. 142.

21 Ibid., p. 150.

22 Quoted in A. Bullock, *Hitler. A Study in Tyranny*, Harmondsworth, Penguin, 1962, p. 269.

23 M. Broszat, *The Hitler State*, London, Longman, 1981, p. 281.

24 Ibid. p. 262.

25 Kershaw, *Hitler*, vol. 1, p. 508.

26 Craig, *Germany*, p. 588.

27 Kershaw, *Hitler*, vol. 1, p. 510.

CHAPTER SEVEN

The Third Reich, 1933–9

TIMELINE

1933	October	Germany withdraws from the Disarmament Conference and the League of Nations
1934	July	Abortive coup in Vienna
1935	15 September	Nuremberg Laws
1936	7 March	Military reoccupation of the Rhineland
	17 June	Himmler appointed Head of German Police
	July	Start of Spanish Civil War
	October	Rome–Berlin Axis
	November	Anti-Comintern Pact
	18 October	Decree on the Execution of the Four-Year Plan
1937	30 January	*Reichstag* prolongs Enabling Act for a further four years
	14 March	Papal Encyclical, *Mit brennender Sorge*, published
	5 November	Meeting at Reich Chancellery recorded by Colonel Hossbach
	26 November	Schacht resigns as Economics Minister
1938	February	Weakening of Conservative elite is accomplished by appointment of Ribbentrop as Foreign Minister, dismissal of Fritsch as Commander-in-Chief of the army, and Hitler's takeover of the command of the armed forces
	5 February	Last meeting of the Reich Cabinet
	March	*Anschluss* of Austria
	1–10 October	Occupation of the Sudetenland
	7–8 December	*Reichskristallnacht*
1939	21 January	Schacht dismissed from Presidency of the *Reichsbank*

15 March	Occupation of Bohemia
25 March	Hitler Youth membership compulsory for all Germans between 10 and 18
27 August	Food rationing starts
1 September	Invasion of Poland
3 September	Britain and France declare war on Germany

INTRODUCTION

The Third Reich is one of the most thoroughly researched periods in modern history, with an academic literature 'beyond the scope even of specialists'.[1] At first contemporaries perceived Nazism to be a development of Fascism. Marxist thinkers interpreted it as a mass movement primarily manipulated by industrialists and financiers to defend capitalism from socialism, while to many Conservatives Hitler was not a demonic figure but, like Mussolini, a great patriot. Churchill, for instance, in 1935 observed that Hitler might well one day be seen as one of those 'great figures whose lives have enriched the story of mankind'.[2]

The Second World War inevitably encouraged a more simplistic approach to the interpretation of Nazism. Historians and propagandists, like Rohan Butler, Sir Robert Vansittart and Edmond Vermeille, attempted to identify lines of continuity in German history, which allegedly stretched 'from Luther to Hitler'. In the early years of the Cold War political scientists such as Hannah Arendt and Carl Friedrich interpreted Nazism as a variant of totalitarianism, which had more in common with Soviet Russia than Mussolini's Italy (see pp. 257–8 and 354–6).[3] In the 1960s and 1970s an increasing number of specialized studies on all aspects of the Third Reich began to show that the concept of totalitarianism did not do justice to an understanding of the structure of the Third Reich and the role of Hitler. Hans Mommsen and Martin Broszat challenged the orthodox view that Hitler was an all-powerful dictator and argued that he was, on the contrary, a prisoner of forces and structures within the Third Reich, which he could not control. Inevitably this emphasis on **structural determinants** rather than the individual in history is fiercely criticized by the more traditional historians, such as Andreas Hillgruber and Klaus Hildebrand, who insist that Hitler is the key to the study of the Third Reich (see Document 1).

Structural determinants
Political or social structures in a state and society that determine the behaviour of politicians.

Many historians see Nazism as essentially reactionary, as it destroyed the German labour movement, reversed female emancipation, and favoured the inefficient small businessman and farmer at the expense of the modern economy. Other historians argue that the 'dysfuncionality' and chaotic nature of the regime drove Hitler into a premature war, which ultimately destroyed the whole Reich. Yet more recent research had shown that Nazism did have a more modern and efficient side to it as well. The Nazi regime presided over an impressive economic recovery, a massive rearmament programme and, far from dismantling the welfare state, in many areas was planning to expand it. Rainer Zeitelmann and Michael Prinz, for instance, have argued that the Nazi Labour Front (see p. 225) not only began to bring about 'the modernisation of leisure'[4] through the introduction of mass tourism for the German workers, but in the early 1940s drafted ambitious plans for a comprehensive post-war welfare state.

It does nevertheless remain difficult to reconcile this enlightened or 'modern' aspect of the Nazi regime with its barbaric racial policies. Mark Roseman has argued that 'untangling the relationship between the barbaric and the modern lies at the very heart of understanding National Socialism'.[5] On the other hand, **modernization**, of course, does not always have to be equated with the development of pluralism and democracy. As Detlev Peukert has reminded us, the paradoxical association of the concepts of 'normality and modernity' with 'fascist barbarism' in the Third Reich raises fundamental questions about the 'pathologies and seismic fractures within modernity itself, and about the implicit destructive tendencies of industrial class society'.[6]

Modernization
Much used by modern historians to describe the process of building a modern state with a constitutional government; an industrial, capitalist economy; and an efficient bureaucracy.

THE KEY ISSUES IN THIS CHAPTER ARE:

- The government of Nazi Germany and the nature of Hitler's dictatorship.
- The creation of full employment and the degree to which the German economy was prepared for war.
- The nature of the *Volksgemeinschaft*.
- The racial policies of the Third Reich.
- The aims of German foreign policy.

THE POLITICAL STRUCTURE OF THE THIRD REICH

The Third Reich was characterized by rival hierarchies and lacked a clear command structure. There were four rival centres of power:

- the central government, with its traditional ministries and civil service
- the Nazi Party
- Himmler's SS state
- the charismatic dictatorship of Hitler.

Central government

When Hitler came to power he had no constitutional blueprint for a Nazi state. Although the Reich cabinet became increasingly less relevant after the passing of the Enabling Act, Hitler strengthened the central ministries at the expense of the state governments. As late as the winter 1937–8 seven key ministries of state were still occupied by Nationalists rather than Nazis. The traditional bureaucracy survived virtually intact, although by the Law for the Restoration of a Professional Civil Service in April 1933, it was purged of known opponents of the regime and of Jews, unless they had fought in the war. It was not until February 1939 that party membership become an essential condition for any new entrant to the civil service.

Alongside the traditional ministries, there grew up numerous 'hybrid' Reich organizations, which combined both party and state responsibilities. These were headed by prominent Nazis, who were responsible directly to Hitler. As Inspector General for German Roads, **Fritz Todt**, for example, was given the necessary power to carry out the *Autobahn* programme. His office formed 'an element of direct *Führer* authority',[7] parallel to the normal state government and administration.

Another characteristic of the Nazi government was the tendency for individual Nazi leaders to control a whole string of ministries and governmental posts. In 1936, for instance, Göring was put in charge of the Four-Year Plan (see p. 218) but still retained his posts of Prussian Minister-President and Minister of the Interior, as well as Reich Aviation Minister.

Fritz Todt (1891–1942)
An SS colonel; he was appointed Armaments Minister in 1940, but was killed in an air crash in January 1942.

The Nazi Party

Once the Enabling Act had been passed, the role of the NSDAP (the Nazi Party) in the new Nazi Germany was far from clear. Hitler's determination to prevent a second revolution deprived the party of a revolutionary role in the new Germany. Whether the NSDAP should become a cadre party, which would train the future leaders of the regime, or merely a large depoliticized mass movement, which could be used for propaganda and the mobilization of the masses, was a matter of debate. In the summer of 1933 Hitler had briefly considered creating a National Socialist Senate comparable to the Fascist Grand Council in Italy (see p. 101), but he dropped the idea for fear that it might undermine his own position. In July 1933 he observed that the 'party had now become the state' and that all power lay with the Reich government,[8] but he was less cryptic when he told the *Gauleiters* in February 1934 that through propaganda and indoctrination the party was 'to support the Government in every way'.[9] In Nuremberg in September 1935 he announced that 'whatever can be solved by the state will be solved through the state, but any problem which the state through its essential character is unable to solve will be solved by means of the movement'.[10]

Until 1938 ministers and civil servants were usually successful in resisting party influence within the government. Paradoxically it was often the ministries, which were headed by senior Nazis, like **Wilhelm Frick**, the Minister of the Interior, where the most vigorous attempts were made to block party interference. As long as the wishes of the *Führer*, as far as they could be understood, were not ignored, it was relatively easy to contain the Party's meddling, and civil servants were quick to learn that the party was 'a rival but not necessarily an invincible one'.[11]

However, in the winter of 1937–8 Nazi influence within the government did began to grow:

- The new foreign minister, **Ribbentrop**, was appointed specifically to counter the influence of the career diplomats.
- In February 1938 the army lost much of its independence when Hitler dismissed both General Fritsch, the Commander-in Chief, for allegations that he was a homosexual, and the Defence Minister, Blomberg, for marrying a former

**Wilhelm Frick
(1877–1946)**
Worked in the Munich police offices from 1904–1924, when he was elected to the *Reichstag* representing the Nazi Party. In 1930 he became Minister of Interior in Thuringia, and in January 1933 was promoted to Reich Minister of the Interior. In 1943 he was replaced by Himmler and given the post of Protector of Bohemia and Moravia. In 1946 he was hanged at Nuremberg.

**Joachim von Ribbentrop
(1893–1946)**
Nazi Foreign Minister, 1938–45. He was hanged at Nuremberg.

prostitute. Hitler seized the chance to replace the Defence Ministry with the High Command of German Armed Forces (OKW), which was directly responsible to him.

- The *Anschluss* with Austria and then the annexation of the Sudetenland and Bohemia (see pp. 238–41) further strengthened the party's influence, as the newly appointed commissioners and officials were free to carry out Nazi policy without any of the restraints from the judiciary or the bureaucracy that still existed in the old Reich.

The SS state

The SS had been formed in 1925, as a small force to protect the leading Nazis. Under Himmler, who became its head in 1929, it took over the NSDAP intelligence and espionage section (the SD). In 1934 it was made independent of the SA and given responsibility for running the concentration camps, for which task the notorious Death's Head Units (*Totenkopfverbände*) were formed as a reward for loyalty to Hitler in 1934 during the confrontation with Röhm (see pp. 194–6). Despite strong opposition from Frick, the Minister of the Interior, Himmler was put in charge of the **Gestapo** in February 1936, and was able to amalgamate it with the SD. In 1936 he was appointed Chief of the German police forces, and the potential of the SS was further increased by the formation of a small number of armed regiments based on the SS squads, which had operated together with the SA as a 'revolutionary strike force' in the early months of the takeover of power.

By 1939 the SS had been built up by Heinrich Himmler into the most important of the Supreme Reich authorities. Like so many National Socialist organizations, it 'tended', to quote Martin Broszat, 'repeatedly to generate new positions having a "direct" relationship with Hitler and to encourage these in turn to strive for a separate existence, like some permanent process of cell division'.[12] The legal structure of the SS presented 'in miniature' the same picture as the Third Reich of 'subsidiary offices, ancillary organizations and leader authorities, which could only be held together with difficulty at the top'.[13] Like the SA, the SS was a revolutionary fighting organization whose character was formed before 1933. Unlike the SA, however, it avoided any

Gestapo
Geheime Staatspolizei (secret state police). During the Weimar Republic, Department 1a of the Berlin Police Praesidium ran the Prussian political police. In April 1933 Göring, as acting Prussian Interior Minister, set up a new secret state police office (*Gestapa*). To strengthen it, he appointed Himmler as 'Inspector of the Gestapo' a year later. Its task was to maintain discipline in the factories and keep political and ideological opponents of the regime under surveillance.

lessening of its powers, and thanks to Himmler'control of the Gestapo and the state police apparatus, its revolutionary dynamism became entrenched in the state bureaucracy. Above all the SS was now in a position to implement what it perceived to be Nazi racial policy by setting up special offices, which were run by officials determined to carry out Hitler's and Himmler's will. In October 1939 Himmler was made Reich Commissar for the Protection of the German People, which empowered him to 'eliminate the harmful influences of such alien parts of the population as constitute a danger to the Reich and German community'[14] (see Document 11).

Heinrich Himmler (1900–45)

Himmler, the son of a Bavarian secondary school teacher, studied agriculture in Munich. He immersed himself in anti-Semitic literature, and become a fanatical believer in German racial superiority. He was involved in the Munich putsch (see pp. 156–7) and joined the Nazi Party in 1926. In 1929 he was put in charge of the SS, and in 1933 appointed Chief of the Police in Bavaria. By 1936 he was effectively in charge of the whole police apparatus in Germany. In 1939 Hitler made him Commissar for the Consolidation of German Nationhood (RKFDV), which enabled him to control Nazi racial and settlement policy in the occupied areas. In 1943 he became Minister of the Interior, but his attempt to end the war in April 1945 by using secret contacts in Stockholm led to Hitler ordering his arrest. In May he was captured by British troops, but committed suicide before he could be tried for war crimes.

The role of Hitler

As *Führer* of the German Reich, Hitler (see Figure 7.1) was not only 'supreme legislator, supreme administrator and supreme judge' but also 'the leader of the Party, the Army and the People'.[15] Cabinet meetings were rarely held after 1934, and the *Reichstag* was reduced to a rubber stamp. As Hitler had combined the presidency with the chancellorship in August 1934 (see p. 196), unlike Fascist Italy where the king still remained on the throne, there was no symbolic figure of authority independent of the *Führer*. Paradoxically, despite possessing these enormous powers, Hitler played little part in the actual day-to-day running of the government. One historian, E.N. Peterson, has described him as a 'remote umpire handing down decisions from on high',[16] but even this exaggerates his actual role in government. Hitler seldom made decisions and usually preferred to let events take their course rather than intervene, although in the key areas of foreign policy, rearmament and military planning he could act rapidly and ensure that his wishes were carried out. Normally, however, he would limit himself to vague declarations of intent that did not translate into clear instructions. For months on end his ministers would have no communication with him at all, especially when he was away from Berlin in his chalet in the Berghof in Bavaria. Consequently, both ministers and officials had to interpret Hitler's intentions themselves, often drawing contradictory conclusions from them. Werner Willikens, the State Secretary in the Prussian Agriculture Ministry, character-ized this process as 'working towards the *Führer*' (see Documents 1, 2 and 3).

Although historians agree that the Third Reich was chaotically administered and riven by personal and institutional rivalries, the reasons why this was so are still sharply debated. The intention-alists, argue that Hitler intentionally resorted to a policy of divide and rule to defend his own position as *Führer*, while the struc-turalists insist that, far from being intended, this was the result of Hitler's unstable, charismatic rule. The structuralist analysis raises the question whether this chaos at the centre of the Nazi regime meant that Hitler was in reality a 'weak dictator'. Hans Mommsen summed up this argument when he observed that Hitler was 'reluctant to take decisions, often uncertain, concerned only to maintain his own prestige and personal authority, and strongly subject to the influence of his environment – in fact, in many ways, a weak dictator'.[17] Is this an accurate picture of Hitler? As Kershaw has pointed out, there is little evidence that Hitler ever wanted a more efficient system. On the contrary, his charisma could only survive if he avoided becoming involved in the day-to-day decisions of government.[18]

However, Hitler was not immune to the pressure of events. Some of these pressures came from the party, which wanted him to step up the persecution of the Jews (see p. 233), while others came from events beyond his control. He had no magic wand to solve, for example, the intractable economic problems, which

Figure 7.1 Hitler
Source: Corbis/Bettmann

were caused by the breakneck speed of his rearmament programme (see p. 219). Nevertheless, by 1938 he had broken most
potential centres of opposition to his regime, and had effectively
destroyed the Versailles system. These very successes brought him
widespread popularity. Arguably his 'weakness', if that is the
really the right word, lay in the fundamental instability of the
regime he had created.

THE ECONOMY, 1933–9

In January 1933 the incoming Nazi government faced formidable economic problems: the unemployment rate was well over 6 million and industrial production had declined to the levels of the 1890s, while the volume of German trade had sunk by 50 per cent. Hitler had no detailed plans for dealing with the economic crisis, but, if the Nazi regime was to survive, he had to engineer a rapid recovery.

Kick-starting the economy

Rearmament alone was not the magic key to 'kick-starting' the German recovery. The Nazi government had also to apply, in the words of one Ministry of Labour official, 'a multitude of inter-related measures':[19]

- Several thousand young people were removed from the labour market and were employed temporarily by such organizations as the Voluntary Labour Service or the Land Service. In 1935 the reintroduction of conscription ensured that 1 million young men were annually absorbed for a period of two years by the *Reichswehr*.
- The length of the working week was cut, and many young, single women were persuaded to leave the labour market by the offer of a marriage loan, which was only available to newly married couples on condition that the wife stayed at home.
- A billion *Reichsmarks* were pumped into public works, such as road and canal building, by the Law for Reducing Unemployment. Government grants were also made available for house construction.
- Tax concessions helped the revival of the car and components industries.

Thanks to these measures, as well as the gathering pace of rearmament, unemployment fell to 1.7 million in the summer of 1935. By 1938 full employment had effectively been achieved.

Hitler also reassured businessmen and industrialists that there would be no 'wild experiments'[20] in the economy. The lowering of industry's costs, the dissolution of the trade unions and the fixing

Unemployment, 1934–9 (in millions)

Year	January	July
1934	3.773	2.426
1935	2.974	1.754
1936	2.520	1.170
1937	1.853	0.563
1938	1.052	0.218
1939	0.302	0.038

Source: Adapted from B. Gebhardt, *Handbuch der Deutschen Geschichte*, vol. 4, ed. K.D. Erdmann, Stuttgart, Union Verlag, 1959, p. 352.

of wage rates at 1932 levels effectively prevented a rise in inflation. While employers' associations were subject to state control, businessmen were nevertheless allowed to manage their own businesses.

Mittelstand ideology
The aim of dismantling big business in the interests of the small-scale industries.

Hitler had little interest in implementing the radical **Mittelstand ideology** of the party programme, as he needed the expertise of big business and the bankers to plan rearmament and to help bring down unemployment. Nevertheless, he did make some token concessions, such as the Law for the Protection of the Retail Trade in May 1933, which banned the extension of the department stores. Yet he had no intention of closing these stores down. On the contrary, in July 1933 the government actually invested over 14 million *Reichmarks* in the Jewish-owned Hertie stores in a successful attempt to prevent their collapse, which would then have thrown thousands out of work. To reassure big business and industry, the *Mittelstand* pressure group, the 'fighting organizations of the industrial middle classes', was dissolved and their members absorbed into the newly created Estate for Handicraft and Trade, which rapidly sank 'to the status of a mere organization under the control of big business'.[21] Also in complete contradiction to the original Nazi programme (see pp. 166–9), the years 1933–6 witnessed an increase in the number of **cartels** created, and the growing influence of big business over the economy.

Cartels
Manufacturers' groups set up to control and regulate production and prices. Between July 1933 and December 1936 over 1,600 new cartel arrangements were signed.

Agriculture

In early 1933 agriculture was in an even worse state than industry: it was burdened with debt and uncompetitive internationally. The Reich Food Estate was formed in the summer of 1933, to assume responsibility for the whole process of food production and marketing. At first higher tariffs, tax cuts and guaranteed prices for the farmers helped boost the agrarian economy. In 1938–9 productivity was 25 per cent higher than 10 years earlier, and Germany was 83 per cent self-sufficient. However in 1935 price controls on food prices were imposed in an attempt to stop a rise in the cost of living, which prevented farmers from profiting from the growing demand for foodstuffs. This ensured that the profit margins of agriculture remained relatively low, and rural labourers continued to migrate to the towns for higher wages (see p. 223).

Rearmament and the Four-Year Plan, 1933–6

To finance rearmament, while large-scale work creation projects were simultaneously in progress, Schacht, the President of the Reichsbank, introduced in the summer of 1933 an ingenious methods for paying firms in *Mefo* bills or credit notes. These were issued by four large private companies and two government ministries under the name of the *Metall-Forschungs AG* (Metal Research Company – abbreviated to *Mefo*). On receipt of the *Mefo* bills the *Reichsbank* paid cash, and so ensured that companies were promptly reimbursed, but, as the bills were valid for a five-year period, the government also raised large sums of money by offering them at 4 per cent per annum on the money market and by also forcing banks to invest 30 per cent of their deposits in them.

As the economy recovered, it sucked in a growing volume of imports that caused a recurring **balance of payments crises**, which threatened the pace of rearmament. In an attempt to prevent unnecessary imports Schacht, who had became Economics Minister in September 1934, introduced the New Plan, which controlled imports and currency exchange.

To give German exports a boost, Schacht negotiated a series of bilateral trade agreements with several Balkan and South American states. German purchases of raw materials in those countries would be paid for in *Reichsmarks*, which would be used both to finance the purchase of further German imports and to invest in the construction of plants, which would later produce

Balance of payments crisis
Crisis caused by the increase of imports, which were not balanced by an equivalent increase in exports.

goods required for the German war economy. Schacht's efforts
however, failed to cut down the ever-growing volume of imports.
By December the situation had so deteoriated that when the
Defence Ministry requested the doubling of copper imports,
Schacht argued that Germany just did not have sufficient foreign
exchange to pay for this and that there was no alternative to
financing rearmament out of increased exports.

The German economy, as Richard Overy has stressed, now
'stood at the crossroads': either Germany could pursue policies
that led through the revival of the export trade and domestic con-
sumerism to its reintegration into the world economy, or else
follow the road of autarky. The latter involved self-sufficiency
and controlled trade, tariffs, military production and state
control, and ultimately the building of a 'large economic region
dominated by Germany and seized by military force if
necessary'.[22] Like Stalin and Mussolini (see pp. 276 and 337–40)
Hitler decisively favoured autarky. In April 1936 he appointed
Göring Commissioner of Raw Materials and Currency, and in
August, in a memorandum that is 'one of the basic documents of
the Third Reich',[23] announced the Four-Year Plan, for which
Göring was made responsible (see Document 4). Its aim was to
make Germany as independent as possible of imports through
increasing production and encouraging the use of substitutes for
imported raw materials, so that it would be in a position to wage
war by 1940. Richard Overy argues that it marked 'the point at
which the armed forces' conception of recovery of defensive
strength gave way to Hitler's conception of large-scale preparations for aggressive imperialism over which the armed forces were
to have less and less say'.[24] During the winter of 1936–7 Göring
effectively took over responsibility for rearmament from the
Ministries of Economics and Defence, and forced Schacht to
resign in November.

In 1938 the Plan's offices took over the major Austrian iron,
steel and machinery companies, and, six months later, the Škoda
works in the Sudetenland. Impressive increases in production
were achieved, but the Plan did not meet its targets, particularly
in synthetic fuel, and consequently imports continued to be a
drain on Germany's currency reserves.

Was Hitler now preparing the economy for total war? In 1959
the American economic historian, Burton Klein argued that,

despite the Four-Year Plan, the 'scale of Germany's economic mobilization for war was quite modest'.[25] He based his arguments on statistics that seemed to indicate that consumer goods output had increased by over 30 per cent between 1936 and 1939. A.J.P. Taylor drew on this information to argue that Hitler had no plans for a major war (see p. 235), while Alan Milward insisted that he envisaged only a series of brief *Blitzkriege* that would not over-strain the German economy.[26] The Klein–Milward thesis became something of a '**new orthodoxy**' in the 1960s and 1970s, and fitted in with the structuralists' 'weak dictator thesis'.

New orthodoxy
A revisionist theory that has become universally accepted.

Some 20 years later Richard Overy effectively demolished these arguments, and showed that the Four-Year Plan really was 'a decisive step towards preparing Germany for total mobiliza-tion', which created the economic base for the later expansion of the armaments industries. Overy argued that the production of consumer goods as a share of national income far from rising in fact declined from 71 per cent in 1928 to 58 per cent in 1938, and that between 1936 and 1939 armaments and preparations for war absorbed over 60 per cent of all capital investments made. This does not, of course, imply that Hitler would not have welcomed a short war, but in May 1939 he specifically warned his generals, ' the government must ... also prepare for a war of from ten to fifteen years duration'.[27]

Was there a growing economic crisis by 1939?

The sheer pace of German rearmament created economic prob-lems. There were production bottlenecks and inter-service rivalry for scarce resources, as well as growing labour shortages and insufficient reserves of foreign exchange to pay for imports. There was also an increasing inflationary threat as the number of bank notes in circulation trebled between 1933 and 1939. Full employ-ment, which Franz Neumann called Hitler's 'sole gift to the masses',[28] also gave the workers a growing economic power, which they were beginning to exploit, to raise their wages. In 1936 absenteeism, go-slows and unofficial strikes increased. Tim Mason has argued that 'acute social and political tension'[29] forced Hitler into war in 1939. Yet there is no direct evidence of this. The regime moved quickly to introduce laws to control the labour situation:

- Workers who broke their contracts with their employers to move on to better paid jobs ran the risk of having their 'work books', which contained the records of their past employment, confiscated, without which they could not be employed.
- In June 1938, to stop employers from bribing workers from other factories to work for them by offering higher wage rates, the Trustees of Labour were given the power to fix uniform wage levels in key industries.
- Labour conscription was also introduced, which could channel workers towards particular industries. Labour shortages were being met increasingly by foreign workers from Southern and Central Europe. Industrial retraining programmes were also creating more skilled workers.
- Uncooperative workers could also be sent by the Gestapo to 'the camps of education for work', which were almost as brutal as the concentration camps.

To finance industrial expansion without running the risk of rising inflation, Schacht's successor, Walther Funk, launched the New Finance Plan, by which industries with state armaments contracts would receive 40 per cent of their payments in tax certificates, a certain proportion of which could only be cashed in after a period of three years. By 1939 the German economy was second only to the American and far less vulnerable to global pressures than either the British or the French. Not surprisingly Overy insists that '"crisis" is an inappropriate characterization of the German economy in the months before the war.'[30]

THE *VOLKSGEMEINSCHAFT*

The roots of the *Volksgemeinschaft*, or 'people's community', go back to the early days of the First World War when the 'spirit of 1914' temporarily united Germans of all classes and parties. The deep divisions of the Weimar Rebublic led to a longing for unity, which Hitler in the electoral campaigns of 1930–3 skilfully exploited by promising a new *Volksgemeinschaft*, which would reunite a bitterly divided Germany (see pp. 181–2). The aim of the Nazi *Volksgemeinschaft* was to integrate all classes of German people into a new racial community and ultimately mobilize the population for war. It has been characterized by Michael Prinz as an 'attempt to re-enact the First World War but with a thoroughly revised script, and one in particular that corrected the mistakes of domestic and social policy'.[31]

The concept of the *Volksgemeinschaft* involved appealing to the different sections of the German community with differentiated and often conflicting policies. On the one hand, Nazi ideology with its emphasis on land settlement, the peasant, the artisan and the family, gave an old fashioned anti-modernist message, which suggested that the Nazis wished to turn the clock back to pre-industrial times. On the other hand, there was also stress on the rationalization of production, mass mobilization of the population, the removal of class barriers and the science of race, or **eugenics**.

Eugenics
The science of improving the population by controlled breeding based on what are judged to be favourable inherited characteristics.

Influencing a new Nazi generation: education and youth movements

Although Hitler had to compromise temporarily in the summer of 1933 and leave many of the old elites still in position of power and influence, in the longer term he hoped that the education system and the mass mobilization of young people in youth movements would ultimately produce a new dynamic race-conscious generation of Germans. Hitler was later to boast that he had 'sown seeds that have sunk deep',[32] but was this in fact so?. The regime attempted to influence youth on three levels:

- The penetration of the existing education system with Nazi values. Here the regime was helped by the fact that many of the teachers were already Nazis. In 1934, for instance, over a quarter of the total number of teachers in the schools were members of the party. In the universities there was also a strong Conservative–Nationalist culture, even though some 15 per cent of the teaching staff had to be purged. Outwardly the traditional structure of the German educational system remained in place, but educational syllabuses were revised in light of Nazi ideology. More time was made available for the teaching of history, biology and German, since these were the three subjects best suited to exploitation by Nazi propaganda, and in September 1933 a new subject, 'racial science', was introduced as a compulsory element in the timetable.

- The Nazis also set up a number of elite schools and institutions, which were entrusted with the task of producing the future party leaders of Germany. These consisted of the *Napolas* (National Political Educational Establishments), the Adolf Hitler Schools, and the *Ordensburgen*, which were intended to be the finishing schools for the future Nazi elite. The *Napolas* attracted very few members from the professional classes, who continued to send their children to the grammar schools and universities.

- The most effective way, however, for indoctrinating the nation's youth was through the Hitler Youth (HJ), to which by 1936 some 60 per cent of all young people in Germany belonged. In 1939 membership became compulsory and the Catholic Church was forced to dissolve its own youth organizations. Boys joined the the *Deutsches Jungvolk* at 10, and the HJ at 14, where for the next four years their time was taken up by a mixture of sport, war games and propaganda. The parallel organization for girls was the *Jungmädel* and the *Bund Deutscher Mädchen* (German Girls' League), where the emphasis was on phsyical fitness and the teaching of traditional female domestic skills. Undoubtedly the HJ had the potential for attracting many young people, as it offered a sense of belonging and adventure. Christa Wolff, who was later one of East Germany's leading authors, recalled in her memoirs how at first it seemed to offer 'the promise of a loftier life'.[33] By the late 1930s it had developed into a large bureaucratic organisation run by middle-aged leaders.

However, compulsory membership of the HJ also meant that a considerable number of bored and resentful teenagers were forced to join, who increasingly began to reject its message and form their own groups outside the HJ. Two youth movements in particular emerged, which were hostile to the ethos of the HJ Youth: the Swing Movement and the Edelweiss Pirates. The former was mainly composed of university students who loved jazz, which the Nazis dismissed as *Negermusik* – 'nigger music', and American dances like the 'jitterbug'. They also cultivated British and

American fashions and refused to reject Jews. This defiance of the social norms of the *Volksgemeinschaft* led Himmler to threaten their 'ringleaders' with imprisonment in the concentrations camps.[34] The Edelweiss Pirate groups, on the other hand, were composed of young teenage workers, for the most part in the Ruhr and Rhineland cities, which began to emerge at the end of the 1930s as a reaction against regimentation in the Hitler Youth and the factories (see pp. 420–2).

The peasantry

David Schoenbaum has argued that support for the peasantry was 'one of the few consistent premises of Nazi life'.[35] The *Volksgemeinschaft* certainly paid lip service to the supposed superiority of rural life over the cities, and lost no opportunity to describe the peasantry as 'responsible carriers of German society renewing its strength from blood and soil',[36] but the reality was rather different. Rainier Zitelman has shown that Hitler was in fact not a backward-looking 'archaic-romantic', but somebody who positively 'welcomed and accepted industrial society'.[37]

Initially the Reich Entailed Farm Law of September 1933 guaranteed the small farmer's **security of tenure** by declaring that farms between 7.5 and 125 hectares (18 and 309 acres) were to remain the permanent property of the original peasant owners, but once the economy started to expand, the government made clear that its priority was rearmament, industrial expansion and efficiency. Agricultural subsidies were kept down, and the big estates in the east were not broken up for settlement as they were more efficient units for food production. Young people consequently continued to turn their back on the countryside and migrate to the cities where they could earn more, and, despite Nazi rhetoric about the idyllic rural life, Germany increasingly continued to develop into an advanced industrial society.

Security of tenure
The tenant is secure from eviction.

Women and the family

To quote Gabriele Czarnowski, 'women were of political interest, both negatively and positively'. They were the 'mothers of the race'[38] (see Document 7). Fit, healthy, German women were to be encouraged to have children, while those who suffered from hereditary diseases or were Jewish, for instance, were if possible to be prevented from doing so.

To train women for the responsibilities of motherhood and marriage the regime set up the National Socialist Womanhood (NSF) and the German Women's Enterprise (DFW). Initially attempts were made to bribe young women to leave work by offering loans, tax-relief schemes and family allowances (see p. 215). However, the Nazi regime did accept that women would continue to work in industry once the economy recovered, and took steps to ensure that racial policy did not clash with the needs of industrial policy. Gisela Bock has shown that in fact women were forced out in only relatively small numbers – a far smaller percentage than in the USA.[39]

A Women's Section was formed within the German Labour Front in July 1934 under Gertrud Scholtz-Klinik, and women were recruited to work in the new plants, which were built under the Four-Year Plan (see p. 218). By May 1939 12.7 million women were in employment and constituted 37 per cent of the German workforce. Although in 1933 many women were dismissed from the higher ranks of the civil service and the medical and legal professions, by the mid-1930s they had begun to rejoin these professions in greater numbers. The total of female doctors, for example, increased from 5 per cent in 1930 to 7.6 per cent in 1939. The *Völkischer Beobachter* conceded in 1937 that 'today we can no longer do without the woman doctor, lawyer, economist and teacher in our professional life'.[40]

Nazi policy was not simply to encourage the full-time housewife and mother. Certainly the family was the 'germ cell'[41] of the nation, but nevertheless, as a small oasis of privacy, it was distrusted by the regime. Parental control over their children was threatened by the government's racial laws and eugenic policies (see pp. 231–5) and by the growing pressure for children to join the Hitler Youth. Claudia Koonz has observed that Nazi family policy was in fact 'deeply revolutionary because it aimed at the creation of a family unit that was not a defence against public invasion as much as the gateway to intervention'.[42] For the Nazis the key priority was not the family but the birth of healthy 'Aryan' children. Hitler himself observed that 'it must be considered reprehensible conduct to refrain from giving healthy children to the nation'.[43] This attitude led to a ban on abortion in

May 1933, and to a greater toleration of the status of unmarried mothers, even though public opinion and the party had reservations on this issue.

The unmarried mother's greatest defender was Himmler, who argued that she should be 'raised to her proper place in the community, since she is during and after her pregnancy, not a married or an unmarried woman but a mother'.[44] As long as single-parent children were 'racially and hereditarily valuable', Himmler was ready to protect them through a 'legal guardianship'. He opened the *Lebensborn* homes for pregnant and nursing mothers whose children had been fathered by SS men and 'other racially valuable Germans'.[45]

Lebensborn
Spring of life.

The workers and the *Volksgemeinschaft*

The *Volksgemeinschaft* was supposed to be a national community of 'racial equals'. Central to this were Nazi claims that the Nazis had liberated the workers from their corrupt, Marxist, union and party bosses, and had for the first time integrated them into the community. Hitler claimed to have 'broken with a world of prejudices' and created equality between the 'workers of the brain and fist' (see Document 6).

Was this claim just propaganda? Tim Mason, in his monumental work on the German workers in the Third Reich, argued that the Third Reich was far from being a classless society and that the Nazis never trusted the workers.[46] There is certainly much evidence to support this view. The workers were corralled into the Labour Front, and their employers were officially called 'plant leaders', who could call on the Gestapo for support, if necessary, against their own workers. It is true that elected Councils of Trust were set up in all factories where there were more than 20 workers, but once these showed signs of independence there were no more elections. An employer could be taken to the Court of Social Honour by his works council, but only so long as it had the support of the local Labour Trustee, an official appointed by the Ministry of Labour. This effectively ensured that this procedure was only very rarely followed – between 1934 and 1936 there were, for example, only 616 cases out of a workforce of well over 20 million. Robert Ley, the Leader of the Labour Front, firmly insisted that there should be equality in leisure time and not at the workplace.

Like its counterpart in Italy, the OND (see pp. 265–7), the Labour Front also sought to control the workers' leisure to create 'if not social and industrial peace, then at least a social and industrial truce'.[47] To achieve this, it created two organizations, which owed much to the experiments in **welfare capitalism** in the 1920s:

Welfare capitalism
Schemes carried out by big firms to look after their workers so that they would be happier and therefore more productive.

- The 'Beauty of Labour' scheme, headed by Albert Speer, attempted to persuade employers to make their factories a more humane environment by improving the lighting and installing swimming baths, showers and canteens. By 1939 nearly 70,000 companies had agreed to implement these improvements.
- 'Strength Through Joy' (KDF), the Labour Front's leisure organization, aranged concerts and plays for the workers and arranged a number of subsidized cruises or holidays in the German countryside.

The *Volkswagen*, the people's car

One of the most popular policies of the KDF was the *Volkswagen* (VW) project. Work started on building the VW in the summer of 1938. The workers were offered a savings scheme, which in theory would eventually enable them to purchase the car. However, unlike conventional hire-purchase agreements, the VW would only be delivered after the final payment had been made. By 1940 300,000 people had already signed up, although the war halted production, and the cars were never produced.

How integrated were the workers into the *Volksgemeinschaft*? Did they feel themselves to be in 'a great convict prison',[48] to quote Wilhelm Leuschner, the former SPD trade union leader, or did they feel themselves to be part of the *Volksgemeinschaft*? While a working-class culture did continue to exist in the Third Reich, Kershaw nevertheless argues that there was 'some penetration of Nazi values'.[49] The Hitler Youth and the Adolf Hitler Schools provided opportunities for young working-class men. It was the younger workers, too, who took advantage of retraining possibilities and transferred to more skilled jobs. Material benefits like longer holidays and low heating and lighting costs also appeased the workers, while admiration of Hitler's foreign policy successes cut across class barriers. As oral history projects have showed, in the grim years immediately after 1945 many workers looked back nostalgically to the years 1934–9 as a period of 'work, adequate nourishment, KDF and the absence of disarray'[50] (see Document 5).

The workers' underground

As the Nazis had dissolved both the political parties and the trade unions, political opposition could only operate from underground. The left-wing opposition consisted of three main groups:

- From its party headquarters first in Prague and then in Paris, the SPD was able to smuggle in illegal pamphlets and monitor the attitude of the workers towards the Nazis.
- The Communists, directed from Moscow, where many of the KPD leaders fled in 1933, built up a more effective underground movement, which the Gestapo was never able totally to destroy.
- Two smaller groups, the *Roter Stosstrupp* and *Neu Beginnen*, aimed to unify the Left in Germany and avoid the divisions of the Weimar years, but neither could overcome the mistrust between the SPD and KPD.

The left-wing opposition was hindered by the deep divisions between the KPD and SPD. Even though in 1935 Stalin ordered the KPD to negotiate a united front with the SPD against Fascism, years of mistrust and hostility between the two parties was impossible to overcome. With the signature of the Nazi–Soviet Pact in August 1939 (see p. 241), the KPD was given the contradictory instructions of backing Hitler's foreign policy, while opposing his domestic policy.

Selling the *Volksgemeinschaft*: the Reich Ministry of Popular Enlightenment and Propaganda

Upon the Propaganda Ministry under Goebbels, which was formed on 13 March 1933, fell the task of selling the sometimes contradictory policies of the *Volksgemeinschaft*. Goebbels told a meeting in May that 'our historic mission' is 'to transform the very spirit itself to the extent that people and things are brought into a new relationship with one another'.[51] Goebbels set up departments responsible for propaganda, film, theatre, the press and 'popular enlightenment'. The radio and the press were vital instruments for influencing and shaping public opinion (see Figure 7.2). Regional radio stations, which previously had been under control of the local state governments, were formed into the Reich Radio Company, whose director cooperated closely with Goebbels. Cheap radios were mass produced and great efforts were made by the government through local radio wardens to encourage the Germans to buy them and to tune in to the programmes.

Figure 7.2 An advertisement for the *Volksempfänger* (the people's radio receiver). The German translates as: 'All Germany listens to the *Führer* on the *Volksempfänger*'

Similar control was exercised over the press by the Reich Press Chamber directed by the Nazi publisher, Max Amman. By the 'Editors' Law' of October 1933 it was declared that the task of the editor was merely to record the views and opinions of the regime in his newspapers, and two years later papers were forbidden to appeal to any 'confessional, vocational or special interest groups'.[52]

Strict guidelines were laid down for all the arts to ensure that the public was provided with a suitable cultural programme which conformed to Nazi ideology; experiments in modern art forms were especially condemned. Hitler as a failed art student was particularly interested in painting. To him modern art was 'degenerate', and he favoured, instead, conventional pastoral scenes or else paintings of battles and heroic warriors According to the Theatre Law of 15 May 1934, the production of plays was a 'public exercise' subject to 'police supervision' and state guidance.[53] There was even an attempt to create a new Nazi art form, the *Thingspiel*, which Richard Grünberger described as 'open-air medleys of "Nazi agit-prop", military tattoo, pagan oratorio and circus performance.[54] Books and films were encouraged on such topics as war, the early history of the Nazi movement, Germany's historic mission in the East and similar topics. On the other hand, provided that they contained no hostile political message, Goebbels also realized that there was a place for light music, comedies and romances.

The churches and Volksgemeinschaft

Roland Freislar, the President of the Nazi People's Court, remarked that Christianity and Nazism had one thing in common: 'We claim the whole man.'[55] The reality, however, was rather more complicated than that. Although a determined break-away group of Protestant priests defeated attempts by the Nazi regime to create a Nazi *Reichskirche* under Bishop Müller in 1933 by setting up the Confessional Church, most priests were not ready to oppose Hitler politically, as long as he conceded their church's independence.

The Pope, too, sought to protect the Catholic Church from the totalitarian claims of the *Volksgemeinschaft* and to preserve its right to manage its own affairs by negotiating the Concordat with

Hitler in July 1933. The Concordat reconciled the vast majority of Catholics in Germany to the new regime. Only if its independence was challenged did the Catholic Church confront the Nazis, as when it attempted unsuccessfully to prevent the absorption of Catholic youth groups into the Hitler Youth. The attitude of both the German Protestant and Roman Catholic Churches to the Nazi regime was compromised by their support for some of Hitler's policies, particularly his foreign policy, anti-Bolshevism and in some circles even anti-Semitism. Catholic Churches, for instance, celebrated the annexation of the Sudetenland in October 1938 with a 'festive peal of bells'.[56]

Policing the *Volksgemeinschaft*

Policing the *Volksgemeinschaft* was not simply a matter of keeping the peace and enforcing certain specific laws. In 1937 Hitler made it quite clear that the role of the justice system was 'to contribute to the preservation and the securing of the *Volk* in face of certain elements who, as **asocials**, strive to avoid common duties or who sin against those common interests'. He stressed that the '*Volk* takes precedence over persons and property'.[57]

Asocial
A category of people considered by the Nazis to be 'biologically criminal'.

The defence of the *Volksgemeinschaft* was in the hands of the political police, the Gestapo; the special branch or detective force, the *Kripo*; and the uniformed police. Together the Gestapo and *Kripo* waged 'war' against both the political and asocial enemies of the state. Legal niceties were not allowed to stand in the way. Special courts were set up to speed up justice, and in 1936 the Gestapo was allowed to operate outside the law. Any action it chose to take was not subject to review by the courts. In the words of Werner Best, the legal expert at the Gestapo headquarters, the task of the police was watch over 'the health of the German body politic', to recognize 'every system of sickness' and destroy all 'destructive cells'.[58] The role of the police as the defenders of the *Volksgemeinschaft* was given prominence in the local press and considerable efforts were made to link in the public's mind the Jews with Communism, embezzling, swindling smuggling, etc. (see Documents 8 and 11).

RACE AND EUGENICS

The *Volksgemeinschaft* was first and foremost a racial community whose health and racial purity were to be protected at all costs (see Document 9). Consequently those Germans who were judged to be of 'lesser racial value' were increasingly discriminated against. They could not receive, for instance, any of the financial privileges normally given to those with large families. In January 1934, by the Law for the Prevention of Hereditarily Diseased Progeny, alcoholics and those with hereditary diseases were liable on medical advice to be sterilized. Increasingly criminals, 'asocials' and sexual deviants, by which was usually meant **homosexuals**, were also sterilized on the grounds that their behaviour was determined by genetic factors.

Homosexuals
Between 1937 and 1939 some 25,000 homosexuals were arrested and about 15,000 sent to concentration camps.

Euthanasia was a logical development of this policy. Initially in the winter of 1938–9, it was carried out on children with 'congenital deformities' and then extended to adults. When news of it leaked out to the public, it caused widespread revulsion and was publicly condemned by the Bishop of Münster in August 1941. Hitler was forced temporarily to suspend the programme, but it soon recommenced and new extermination centres were opened where foreign workers judged to be suffering from incurable physical illnesses, racially 'inferior' babies of Eastern European women working in the Reich, terminally sick inmates from the German prisons and sometimes *Wehrmacht* soldiers suffering from incurable shellshock were murdered.

Wehrmacht
The *Reichswehr* changed its name to the *Wehrmacht* in 1935.

The non-Jewish racial minorities

The sterilization laws were also extended to cover the small number of mixed-race children fathered by French African soldiers during the **Rhineland occupation**. The Nazi regime, like the Weimar Republic, also discriminated against the Sinti and Roma (gypsies). In 1935 a research unit financed by the SS in the Reich Ministry of Health decided that as 90 per cent of the Sinti and Roma were of 'mixed race', and were likely therefore to be of a criminal and 'asocial' predisposition, they should consequently be sterilized. In September 1939 Himmler, in his role as Commissar for the Consolidation of German Nationhood (RKVD) (see p. 395), ordered the forced removal of the 30,000 gypsies in the

Rhineland occupation
French troops were in the Rhineland 1919–30.

Reich to occupied Poland. The programme was halted in the summer of 1940 to give priority to the Jews, but resumed again in 1942, when Himmler ordered their transportation straight to Auschwitz (see p. 399).

The Third Reich also viewed its Slav minorities as inferior racial aliens, but initially the Nazis had little option but to adopt a relatively tolerant policy towards the **Sorbs** for fear of retaliation against the German minorities in Poland and Czechoslovakia. Once Czechoslovakia was dismembered and Poland occupied in 1939, this toleration rapidly ended and the leaders of the Sorb and Polish communities were sent to concentration camps. Himmler originally intended to transport the Sorbs to occupied Poland, since the Nazis perceived them to be 'the same racial and human type'[59] as the Poles, but they escaped this fate as Himmler's energies were absorbed by dealing with the far larger number of Jews.

Sorbs
A distinct racial group living in south-eastern Germany in an area originally called Lusatia. In 2000 there were still some 80,000 Sorb speakers.

The Jews

Although the great majority of the 500,000 Jews in Germany in 1933 were well integrated in German society and were in fact 'Germans of Jewish faith', Jews in general were seen by the Nazis to be the very embodiment of evil, the power behind Russian Bolshevism, the cause of Germany's defeat in 1918 and the major threat to the racial community. As Noakes and Pridham observed, they 'formed a propaganda stereotype, a collection of negative attributes representing the antithesis of a true German'.[60] However, once Hitler came in power his policy towards the Jews was frequently hesitant and contradictory, and no clear guidelines on the Jewish question were issued.

In March 1933 increasingly violent attacks by the SA on individual Jews and their property, which threatened to damage Hitler's government's reputation and alienate the Conservative-Nationalist elite, forced Hitler to attempt to channel the violence into a boycott of Jewish shops. This began on 1 April, but was rapidly called off, when it was sharply criticized both at home and abroad. Hitler then tried to appease the party's expectation of action by purging the civil service, the universities and the media of Jews.

Over the next two years, in an attempt to avoid a global boycott of German trade, the Nazi government discouraged overt racial violence against the Jewish community and even allowed, for example, Jewish textile firms to bid for military contracts. Confronted by further pressure from party activists, Hitler attempted to placate them when he announced at Nuremberg in September 1935 the Law for the Protection of German Blood, which forbade marriage or sexual intercourse between Jews and German gentiles, and the Reich Citizenship Law, which deprived Jews of their German citizenship. Both these Laws, however, fell far short of what the Nazi activists wanted.

By the spring of 1938 Göring, as Commissioner of the Four-Year Plan (see p. 218), was demanding the rapid economic expropriation of all German Jews. The *Anschluss* (annexation) of Austria and the growing threat of war with the Britain and France over Czechoslovakia also whipped up further demands for punitive measures and led to a series of decrees, which ranged from compelling Jews to adopt specifically Jewish forenames to having their wealth and property registered as a preliminary for expropriation by the state.

The turning point in the treatment of the Jews was the *Reichskristallnacht* riots of 7–8 November 1938. These were ostensibly caused by the assassination of Ernst von Rath, a junior diplomat in the German Embassy in Paris, by Herschl Grynszpan, a 17-year-old student, whose parents, together with 17,000 other Jews of Polish descent, had recently been expelled from Germany. As the Polish government refused to admit them, they were forced to camp on the no-man's land between the Polish and German frontiers. Goebbels, apparently with the tacit approval of Hitler, organised 'spontaneous' attacks on synagogues and Jewish-owned businesses. Some 25 million marks' worth of damage was done and nearly 100 Jews were killed, while nearly 30,000 were put into concentration camps.

After the riots Göring initially coordinated all initiatives on the Jewish question. The Jewish community was first of all forced to pay a collective fine of 1.25 billion marks, and then in April 1939 their remaining wealth was seized. Jews were excluded from jobs in the retail trade, skilled labour and management, and banned from public places, such as theatres and beaches. The small number of Jewish children who were still pupils in state schools were also expelled.

In January 1939 the influence of the SS on formulating Nazi Jewish policy was strengthened when **Reinhard Heydrich**, the

Reinhard Heydrich (1904–42)
Became Himmler's deputy in 1933. In January 1939 he was appointed head of the Reich Central Office for Jewish Emigration, and in September the head of the Reich Security Head Office. He organized the deportation of the Jews to occupied Poland. He was appointed Reich Protector of Bohemia and Moravia 1941, and was assassinated by the Czech underground in 1942.

**Adolf Eichmann
(1906–62)**
Joined the SD in 1934. In
1935 he was appointed
head of the 'Office for
Jewish Emigration', and in
1938–9 dealt with the
expulsion of the Jews from
Austria and Bohemia. In
1942, as a consequence of
the decisions taken at the
Wannsee Conference (see
p. 398), he was given
responsibility for carrying
out the 'final solution'. In
1945 he fled to Argentina,
but was kidnapped by the
Israelis and executed in
1962.

Chief of the Security Police and the SD, was given responsibility for organizing the emigration of the remaining 214,000 Jews in Germany. To achieve this he set up an organization modelled on the Central Office, which **Eichmann** had already established in Vienna. Paradoxically, however, Göring's ruthless expropriation policies had made Jewish emigration more difficult to achieve, since foreign states were unwilling to accept refugees without any financial means of support.

Hitler's role in the formulation of anti-Semitic policy: the structuralist–intentionalist debate

Intentionalist historians, such as Lucy Dawidowicz, Klaus Hildebrand and Karl Dietrich Bracher, argue that Hitler from the very beginning intended the mass murder of the Jews, even though he could not implement this straight away. Structuralists, however, like Martin Broszat, Hans Mommsen and Karl Schleunes, certainly do not dispute Hitler's anti-Semitism, but locate the ultimate cause of the Holocaust in the disjointed and chaotic way in which Nazi Germany was governed rather than in the consistency of Hitler's planning. They argue that the bureaucracy and Nazi leaders attempted 'to work towards the *Führer*' (see Document 2), and competed with each another in formulating anti-Semitic policies, which led to ever more radical policies being implemented. Intentionalists are critical of structural interpretations, which they believe depersonalize the responsibility of what ultimately led to the Holocaust. Dawidowicz has even described such an approach as initiating a new 'cycle of apologetics' in German history.[61]

There is ample evidence of Hitler's anti-Semitism in *Mein Kampf* (see Document 9), but can Hitler be described as the driving force behind Nazi policy towards the Jews from 1933 to 1939? Although on 12 November 1938 Göring claimed that Hitler had made clear both through his Chief of Staff and by phone that 'the Jewish question [should] be now once and for all co-ordinated and solved one way or another',[62] Hitler made no public announcement on the anti-Semitic policies, which were initiated in the aftermath of *Kristallnacht*. On the other hand, in January 1939 he was apparently unambiguous about the ultimate fate of the Jews. He told the Czech Foreign Minister that he intended to 'destroy the Jews',[63] and then a few days later announced in the *Reichstag* that the outbreak of war would lead to the 'annihilation of the Jewish race in Europe' (see Document 10).

The intentionalists view this as evidence of Hitler's ultimate aims, but the structuralists are still sceptical and warn historians against interpreting Hitler's words too literally. Hans Mommsen, for example, argues that Hitler 'considered the "Jewish question" from a visionary political perspective that did not reflect the real situation',[64] and believes that Hitler was invoking a ritual hatred of the Jews, rather than spelling out precise plans for their murder. These horrific threats were not of course a blueprint for the Holocaust, but it is difficult not to see them as expressions of intention to eliminate the Jews in Europe in one way or another. As Lucy Dawidowicz remarked about earlier speeches by Hitler, 'in the post-Auschwitz world' his words carry a 'staggering freight'.[65]

FOREIGN POLICY

The historical debate on Hitler's foreign policy

Whether Hitler's foreign policy was planned or merely a response to favourable opportunities is the subject of intense historical debate. A.J.P. Taylor argued that Hitler simply pursued a pragmatic policy of making Germany 'the greatest power in Europe from her natural weight'.[66] Hans Mommsen, too, is sceptical as to whether Hitler's foreign policy really consisted of unchanging priorities, and suggests that, like his anti-Semitic policy, it was determined more by economic pressures, opportunism and expectations from within the Nazi Party. Inevitably these interpretations, which play down Hitler's intentions, are strongly opposed by intentionalists of the Programme School, such as Andreas Hillgruber and Klaus Hildebrand, who argue that Hitler formulated his foreign policy in the mid-1920s . This consisted of two distinct periods – the continental phase, which involved the defeat of France and the USSR, and then a global phase involving war with the USA and the British Empire and the eventual establishment of global German hegemony.[67] Nazi foreign policy generates such controversy because Hitler's actions were often contradictory and opportunist. However, his obsession with the need for *Lebensraum* in western Russia is a persistent thread that runs through his speeches to generals, officials, businessmen and journalists. Hitler combined, as Alan Bullock has argued, 'consistency of aim with complete opportunism in methods and tactics'.[68]

The first three years

During his first three years in power Hitler could not afford an aggressive foreign policy because Germany was still militarily inferior to France. Nevertheless, he did take several initiatives during the period 1933–5, which began to undermine the Versailles system:

- In October 1933 Germany ceased to be a member of the League of Nations.
- In January 1934, against the advice of his own Foreign Minister, Hitler signed a 10-year non-aggression pact with Poland, which breached the French alliance system in Eastern Europe.
- He also gave secret backing to an unsuccessful coup by Austrian Nazis in Vienna in July 1934 (see p. 377).
- In March 1935 he announced the introduction of conscription.

The introduction of conscription led to a meeting of the British, Italian and French heads of government at Stresa, who issued a joint statement stressing their determination to maintain the peace settlements. When Hitler responded by offering to conclude bilateral disarmament agreements with the three powers, Britain, without consulting either Italy or France, accepted his offer of a naval pact, which limited the German navy to 35 per cent of the British Royal Navy. This broke up the unity of the Stresa front and, in Karl Bracher's words 'set in motion the momentous chain of events that prevented a possible anti-Hitler coalition and freed the Third Reich from the threat of isolation'.[69]

Mussolini's attack on Ethiopia in October 1935 (see pp. 281–4) and the belated Anglo-French decision to impose sanctions on Italy gave Hitler the opportunity to remilitarize the **Rhineland**. To escape isolation Mussolini turned to Germany.

Rhineland
The Rhineland was demilitarized according to the Treaty of Versailles and the Locarno Pact. This meant that German troops could not be stationed there.

Hitler was able to exploit Mussolini's predicament to extract promises from him that he would not oppose the remilitarization of the
Rhineland. Despite the reservations of his generals and diplomats,
and using the ratification of the **Franco-Soviet Pact** of 27 February
1936 as a justification, Hitler reoccupied the Rhineland on 7 March
with a weak military force without any opposition from either
France of Britain. This deprived France of its main strategic advantage over Germany – a demilitarized Rhineland – and showed that
neither Britain nor France was ready to defend the Locarno Pact
(see pp. 114 and 159) and the Versailles Treaty.

Franco-Soviet Pact
The rise of Hitler had led
to a *rapprochement*
between France and the
USSR. The introduction of
conscription led to the
signature of the Franco-
Soviet Pact in May 1935.

Although Germany's military weakness ruled out any major
initiatives for the next two years, Hitler was quick to overrule the
objections of the professional diplomats and sent a small force of
6,500 troops with air support in July 1936 to help General
Franco, the Spanish Nationalist leader, in his rebellion against the
left-wing Republican government (see p. 315). Hitler feared that
a Republican victory would result in a Communist takeover in
Spain, which would then influence the political situation in
France where a left-wing Popular Front government had just been
formed. The Civil War in Spain would also divert the attention of
the Great Powers from Germany's rearmament programme and
its ambitions in Central Europe, while a Nationalist victory
would have the added bonus of giving Germany access to Spain's
valuable tungsten and iron ore deposits.

The German–Italian **October Protocols**, and the **Anti-
Comintern Pact** of November 1936 with Japan, which Italy joined
a year later, were two further propaganda coups. Although these
agreements lacked any substance for the time being, they pointed
in the direction of a new global alliance, which threatened the
democracies in Europe, the Mediterranean and the Far East.

October Protocols
Called the Rome–Berlin
Axis by Mussolini in a
speech in Milan on 1
November 1936. They
were only a loosely
worded understanding for
collaboration.

By December 1937 Germany's military and diplomatic position was
much stronger, and rearmament was progressing rapidly (see p. 219).
On 5 November 1937 at a conference in the Reich Chancellery, which
was attended by his military chiefs, Hermann Göring, and Constantin
von Neurath, the Foreign Minister, Hitler reviewed Germany's foreign
policy options for the next seven years. Hitler's views, minuted in the
Hossbach Memorandum, were that Germany's 'problem of space' had
to be solved by 1943–5, but that if the right opportunities, such as a political crisis in France or a Franco-Italian war, occurred, Austria could be
annexed and Czechoslovakia destroyed as early as 1938.

Anti-Comintern Pact
Aimed against the
Comintern – the
Communist International
set up by Lenin in 1919.

Historians and the Hossbach Memorandum

The memorandum was used by the prosecution during the Nuremberg War Crimes Trials in 1946 to show that Hitler had a precise blueprint for war. A.J.P. Taylor, however, in 1961 showed that not only was it written some five days after the meeting, by Hitler's adjutant Colonel Hossbach, but that it is a fragment of a copy that has disappeared. He argued that it was essentially concerned with the allocation of raw materials rather than foreign policy and that Hitler's exposition was for the most part 'day dreaming unrelated to what followed in real life'. While historians agree that the memorandum was hardly a blueprint for action, the consensus of research still favours W. Carr's views that Hitler was warning his generals that 'a more adventurous and dangerous policy was imminent'.[70] (See Document 12 and Map 4.)

The *Anschluss*

The opportunities to annex Austria and then to destroy Czechoslovakia did in fact occur in 1938, but in a different form from that foreseen by Hitler on 5 November. Schuschnigg, the Austrian Chancellor, was the unwitting catalyst for the *Anschluss*. In July 1936 he had negotiated an agreement with Hitler whereby Germany recognized Austrian independence, while in return Vienna promised to pursue a German-orientated foreign policy and appoint two pro-German Conservatives to the cabinet. In practice Nazi agitation continued. Consequently Schuschnigg sought an interview with Hitler in the hope of reaching some agreement that would have controlled the activities of the Austrian Nazis. This provided Hitler with an opportunity to dictate a series of conditions that would have effectively turned Austria into a German satellite.

Schuschnigg then had second thoughts about the agreement and on 9 March 1938 attempted to regain a measure of independence by asking his countrymen to vote in a referendum for a 'free and German, independent and social, Christian and united Austria'. This challenge persuaded Hitler three days later to invade Austria. Faced with an enthusiastic reception from the crowd at Linz, he quickly abandoned his original idea of appointing a satellite government under Seyss-Inquart and instead incorporated Austria into the Reich.

The *Anschluss*, as Ian Kershaw has observed, was a 'watershed for Hitler and the Third Reich'.[71] French and British failure to intervene convinced Hitler that his ambitions for creating a Greater German Reich were now possible, but, before he could do that, he still had to liquidate Czechoslovakia, whose strategic position, modern army and efficient armaments industry made it a real threat to Germany's southern flank. Czechoslovakia's potential strength, however, was undermined by ethnic tensions between the Czechs and Slovaks and the existence of 3 million Sudeten Germans who wished to follow the example of Austria and join the Reich.

The Sudeten crisis and the destruction of Czechoslovakia, March 1938–April 1939

On 28 March 1938 Hitler instructed Henlein, the Sudeten German leader, to draw up a formula for Sudeten self-government, which in fact could only be realized by breaking up the Czech state. In May the Czech government, mistakenly believing that German manoeuvres near the borders were for preparations for an invasion, mobilized its army. When Britain, France and the USSR made it clear that they would intervene, Hitler was quick to protest his innocence, but the whole incident confirmed his suspicions that Czechoslovakia was a strategic threat to Germany, and persuaded him to set 1 October as the deadline for 'smashing' it. In the meantime Hitler continued to encourage Sudeten separatism, and stir up similar demands among the Hungarian and Polish minorities in Czechoslovakia so that Poland and Hungary would support the planned destruction of the Czech state.

On 12 September the campaign entered a new stage, when Hitler at the Nuremberg Rally demanded immediate self-determination for the Sudetens. This caused escalating unrest in the Sudetenland and prompted the intervention of Neville Chamberlain, the British Prime Minister, who flew over to Germany to have three separate meetings with Hitler between 15 and 29 September:

• At Berchtesgaden on 15 September Hitler initially agreed to Chamberlain's proposals that, subject to agreement with the

French and the Czechs, all those regions in the Sudetenland where the German population was in a majority would eventually be ceded to Germany.

- Chamberlain returned to Bad Godesberg on 22 September for a second meeting. Anglo-French pressure had forced the Czechs to agree to the handover of the Sudetenland, subject to the new border being mapped out by an international boundary commission and a Czech–German non-aggression pact. Hitler rejected these proposals and demanded instead the immediate German occupation of the Sudetenland. Consequently the conference broke up without agreement. The weight of evidence undoubtedly suggests that Hitler was ready for war. He calculated that the Czechs would reject his terms and be abandoned by the Western Powers, who would turn a blind eye to the destruction of Czecholsovakia. But in the face of partial British and French mobilization and the lack of enthusiasm of his generals and Mussolini for war, 'the unthinkable happened'.[72]

- Hitler accepted Mussolini's offer of mediation and on 29 September Chamberlain, Mussolini, Daladier, the French Prime Minister, and Hitler met at the Munich, where Hitler agreed to an international guarantee of rump Czechoslovakia, while German forces would be allowed to occupy the Sudetenland in stages between 1 and 10 October 1938 (see Map 4).

Even though Germany had gained the Sudetenland without war, Hitler nevertheless viewed the Munich settlement as a diplomatic defeat. The compromise deprived him of the chance to destroy Czechoslovakia and also showed that Britain, despite its willing- ness to appease, would not allow Germany a completely free hand in Eastern Europe. Consequently on 21 October 1938 he again ordered the army to draw up new plans for the invasion of Czechoslovakia. His opportunity came when the tensions between the Czechs the Slovaks, which he had done so much to provoke, erupted in March 1939. Like Schuschnigg before him, Hacha, the Czech President, went to Berlin in an attempt to nego- tiate with Hitler, but was ruthlessly bullied into agreeing to the German occupation of Prague and the creation of an independent Slovakia, which became a German protectorate.

The attack on Poland and the Anglo-French declaration of war

The occupation of Prague was followed on 23 March 1939 by the annexation of Memel. The British and French governments responded by guaranteeing the independence of Poland. As German diplomatic initiatives in the course of the winter had failed to persuade Poland to agree to the restoration of Danzig and the 'corridor' (see p. 147) to Germany in return for eventual gains in Ukraine, the Anglo-French guarantee now convinced Hitler that he would have to destroy Poland, if he were ever to achieve his aim of winning *Lebensraum* in Eastern Europe. As early as 3 April orders were therefore issued to the army to prepare for an invasion of Poland by 1 September at the latest.

Both the Western Powers and Germany, recognizing that the key to the coming conflict over Poland lay in Moscow, began negotiations with Stalin (see pp. 360–1). To many Nazis, an agreement with Bolshevik Russia was a bitter pill to swallow, but as Ribbentrop, the Nazi Foreign Minister, explained to Mussolini, Poland was the 'immediate enemy' and Britain and France, who might assist Poland, were 'intermediate enemies', so it made good strategic sense to seek an alignment with the USSR, which was a 'later enemy'.[73] The subsequent Nazi–Soviet Non-Aggression Treaty of 23 August was an major triumph for Hitler, since it secured Stalin's benevolent neutrality in return for territorial concessions in Eastern Europe, and deprived Britain and France of the only alliance that could have averted Poland's defeat.

Hitler was now convinced that the Western Powers would not intervene, but on 25 August they unexpectedly responded by ratifying their treaties of guarantee with Poland. Hitler postponed the attack on Poland for a week and made several unsuccessful attempts to separate Britain and Poland by offering Britain an alliance and a guarantee of her empire. Once these attempts failed, Hitler gave the order for war on 31 August. Taylor argues that that the war began because Hitler launched 'on 29 August a diplomatic manoeuvre aimed at persuading the British to force the Poles to make concessions, which he ought to have launched on 28 August'.[74] Perhaps given more time, Hitler might have separated Britain and Poland, but he did not want a compromise settlement with the Poles. At most he was hoping to manoeuvre them into a position where their 'stubbornness' could be blamed for causing the war.

When German troops crossed the Polish frontier at 4.45 a.m. on 1 September 1939 Hitler did not abandon his attempts to keep Britain out of the war. Birger Dahlerus, the Swedish industrialist and friend of Göring, flew to London for unofficial talks, while Chamberlain's adviser, Sir Horace Wilson, was invited to Berlin, but the British insisted that a precondition for talks was the withdrawal of all German troops from Poland. As Hitler contemptuously rejected this, Britain and France had little option but to declare war on Germany on 3 September.

ASSESSMENT

Hitler's government in January 1933 was seen by many Germans, as inevitable, or, as Golo Mann has remarked, 'historically right'.[75] Its brutalities and illegalities, which most Germans assumed would only be temporary, were tolerated in the hope that Hitler would create a more united and prosperous Germany, which would be able to reassert its power in Europe.

The Nazi regime had created a political structure that was characterized by the creation of rival hierarchies and a lack of a clear command structure, and was essentially kept together by the **Führerprinzip**. Nevertheless its achievements in 1939 appeared to be formidable. Unemployment had virtually ceased to exist. Hitler's foreign policy had completed the destruction of Versailles, and brought Austria and the Sudetenland into the Reich. The *Volksgemeinschaft*, where membership was defined by race rather than class, claimed to be inclusive. Yet despite Nazi propaganda on the social, and indeed racial equality, of all 'Aryan' Germans, Germany in many ways remained a class society, as big business, the **Junkers** and the bourgeoisie still survived, but these facts were skillfuly disguised by a 'verbal revolution',[76] which created the illusion of social unity (see Document 6).

Führerprinzip
The principle of absolute obedience to the *Führer*.

Junkers
The term 'Junker' comes from the German *Jungherr*, which applied to sons of the Prussian landed gentry serving as officer cadets. Later the term came to describe the Prussian landowners with large estates east of the Elbe.

DOCUMENT 1

Hans Mommsen on Hitler's style of government

As Chancellor ... Hitler personified the specific political style which ensured the movement's success. One aspect of this was the postponement of decisions on political priorities for the sake tactical flexibility: even after 1933, Hitler did his utmost to avoid hard and fast political rulings wherever possible. A side effect of this tendency was to obscure the real intentions of the National Socialist leadership, however often they might be displayed in all their ambiguity. As dictator, Hitler still obeyed the maxims of the successful publicity man: to concentrate on the aims of the moment, to profess unshakable determination to achieve them, and to use parallel strategies, heedless of the political consequences resulting from the inevitable inter-institutional friction entailed.

Source: H. Mommsen, 'National Socialism: continuity and change' in W. Laqueur, ed., *Fascism: A Reader's Guide*, Harmondsworth, Penguin, 1976, pp. 175–6.

DOCUMENT 2

'Working towards the Führer'

The State Secretary in the Prussian Agricultural Ministry, Werner Willikens, in a speech on 21 February 1934 to representatives from the agricultural ministries of the other German states, gave his advice on how to interpret the will of the Führer, when no precise instructions were given by him:

Everyone with opportunity to observe it knows that the *Führer* can only with great difficulty order from above everything that he intends to carry out sooner or later. On the contrary, until now everyone has best worked in his place in the new Germany, if, so to speak, he works towards the *Führer* ...

Very often, and in many places, it has been the case that individuals, already in previous years, have waited for commands and orders. Unfortunately, that will probably also be so in the future. Rather, however, it is the duty of every single person to attempt, in the spirit of the *Führer*, to work towards him. Anyone making mistakes, will come to notice it soon enough. But the one who works correctly towards the *Führer* along his lines and towards his aim will in future as previously have the finest reward of one day suddenly attaining legal confirmation of his work.

Source: Noakes, J. and Pridham, eds, *Nazism 1919–1945*, vol. 2, *State, Economy and Society, 1933–1939*, Exeter, University of Exeter Press, 2000.

DOCUMENT 3
Hitler's policy of divide and rule

The classic analysis of Hitler's calculated attempt to divide and rule is given by Otto Dietrich, Hitler's former press chief, in his memoirs written in 1955:

In the twelve years of his rule in Germany Hitler produced the biggest confusion in government that has ever existed in a civilized state. During his period of government he removed from the organization of the state all clarity of leadership and produced an opaque network of competencies. It was not laxness or an excessive degree of tolerance which led the otherwise so energetic and forceful Hitler to tolerate this real witch's cauldron of struggles for position and conflicts over competence. It was intentional. With this technique he systematically disorganized the upper echelons of the Reich leadership in order to develop and further the authority of his own will until it became a despotic tyranny.

Source: J. Noakes and G. Pridham, eds, *Nazism, 1919–45*, vol. 2, *State, Economy and Society, 1933–39*, Exeter, University of Exeter Press, 1984, p. 205.

DOCUMENT 4
The Four-Year Plan

Hitler's memorandum of August 1936 was aimed at silencing economic objections, but it was also a clear statement of his basic philosophy and foreign and economic policy intentions.

Since the outbreak of the French Revolution, the world has been moving with ever increasing speed towards a new conflict, the most extreme solution of which is called Bolshevism and the essence and goal of Bolshevism, is the elimination of those strata of mankind which have hitherto provided the leadership and their replacement by world-wide Jewry ...

Germany will, as always, have to be regarded as the focus of the Western world against the attacks of Bolshevism ...

Germany's economic situation

Just as the political movement among our people knows only one goal, the preservation of our existence, that is to say, the securing of all the spiritual and other prerequisites of our existence for the self-assertion of our nation, so neither has the economy any other goal than this. The nation does not live for the economy, for economic leaders or for economic or financial theories; on the contrary, it is finance and the economy, economic leaders and theories, which all owe unqualified service in this struggle for self-assertion ...

It is not sufficient merely to establish from time to time raw material or foreign exchange balances or to talk about the preparation of a war economy in time of peace; on the contrary, it is essential to ensure all the food supplies required in peacetime and, above all, those means for the conduct of a war which can be secured by human energy and activity. I therefore draw up the following programme for a final provision of our vital needs:

I   Parallel with the military and political rearmament and mobilization of our nation must go its economic rearmament and mobilization, and this must be effected in the same tempo, with the same determination, and if need be with the same ruthlessness as well. In future the interests of individual gentlemen can no longer play any part in these matters. There is only one interest, the interest of the nation: only one view, the bringing of Germany to the point of political and economic self sufficiency.

II For this purpose, foreign exchange must be saved in all those areas where our needs can be satisfied by German production, in order that it may be used for those requirements, which can under no circumstances be fulfilled except by import.

III Accordingly fuel production must be now stepped up with the utmost speed and brought to final completion within eighteen months ...

IV The mass production of synthetic rubber must also be organized and achieved with the same urgency.

V   The question of cost of producing these raw materials is also quite irrelevant.... There has been time enough in four years to find out what we cannot do. Now we have to carry out what we can do.

I thus set the following tasks:

▶

I   The German armed forces must be operational within four
    years.
II The German economy must be fit for war within four years.

Source: Noakes, J. and Pridham, G. (eds) *Nazism 1919–1945, Volume 2, State, Economy and Society, 1933–1939*, pub University of Exeter Press, pp. 281–7.

DOCUMENT 5

A police report of 1934 on the attitude of mine workers in Aachen

The mine worker is vacillating in his criticism and far from constant. His opinion is influenced mainly by particular economic events. When on the one hand, the Labour Front sees to it that he receives additional vacation money, he unreservedly praises the new state and all its institutions; but soon afterwards, when he comes home and his wife complains that potatoes have become scarce, he goes to the other extreme of being critical.

Source: T. Siegel, 'The attitude of German workers' in R. Bessel, ed., *Fascist Italy and Nazi Germany*, Cambridge, Cambridge University Press, repr. 1997, p. 71.

DOCUMENT 6

Social equality in the *Volksgemeinschaft*

In a speech made in Berlin on 1 May 1937 Hitler claimed to have created a new equality in Germany:

We in Germany have really broken with a world of prejudices. I leave myself out of account. I, too, am a child of the people; I do not trace my line from any castle: I come from the workshop. Neither was I a general: I was simply a soldier, as were millions of others. It is something wonderful that amongst us an unknown from the army of the millions of German people – of workers and of soldiers – could rise to be head of the Reich and of the nation. By my side stand Germans from all walks of life who today are amongst the leaders of the nation: men who once were workers on the land are now governing German states in the name of the Reich ... It is true that men who came from the bourgeoisie and former aristocrats have their place in this Movement. But to us it matters nothing whence they come if only they can work to the profit of our people. That is the decisive test. We have not broken down classes in order to set new ones in their place: we have broken down classes to make way for the German people as a whole.

Source: N. Baynes, ed., *Hitler's Speeches*, vol. 1, Oxford, Oxford University Press, 1942, pp. 620–1.

DOCUMENT 7

Women's place in the Nazi state

In his address to the National Socialist Women's Section on 8 September 1934, Hitler summed up the Nazi view of the woman's position in society:

If one says that man's world is the State, his struggle, his readiness to devote his powers to the service of the community, one might be tempted to say that the world of woman is a smaller world. For her world is her husband, her family, her children and her house. But where would the greater world be if there were no one to care for the small world? . . . Providence has entrusted to women the cares of that world which is peculiarly her own . . . Every child that a woman brings into the world is a battle, a battle waged for the existence of her people.

Source: Baynes, *Hitler's Speeches*, vol. 1, pp. 528–9.

DOCUMENT 8

The mission of the Gestapo

Werner Best, the legal expert at the Gestapo headquarters, summed up the mission of the Gestapo as follows:

The preventive police mission of a political police is to search out the enemies of the state, to watch them and at the right moment to destroy them. In order to fulfil this mission the political police must be free to use every means required to achieve the necessary goal. In the National Socialist leader state it is the case, that those institutions called upon to protect state and people to carry out the will of the state, possess as of right the complete authority required to fulfil their task, an authority that derives solely from the new conception of the state and one that requires no special legitimization.

Source: Quoted in R. Gellately, *Backing Hitler*, Oxford, Oxford University Press, 2001, p. 41.

DOCUMENT 9

Hitler on the racial state

In Mein Kampf *Hitler clearly described his intention to create the racial state where eugenics would strengthen the race and the 'physically and mentally unhealthy and unworthy' would be sterilized:*

The Folkish [*völkisch*] state must ... set race in the centre of all life. It must take care to keep it pure. It must declare the child to be the most precious treasure of the people. It must see to it that only the healthy beget the children; but there is only one disgrace: despite one's own sickness and deficiencies, to bring children into the world, and one's highest honour: to renounce doing so. And conversely it must be considered reprehensible: to withhold healthy children from the nation. Here the state must act as a guardian of a millennial future in the face of which the wishes and the selfishness of the individual must appear as nothing and submit. It must put the most modern medical means in the service of this knowledge. It must declare unfit for propagation all who are in any way visibly sick or who have inherited a disease and can therefore pass it on, and put this into actual practice. Conversely, it must take care that the fertility of the healthy woman is not limited by the financial irresponsibility of a state regime which turns the blessing of children into a curse for the parents. It must put an end to that lazy, nay criminal indifference, with which the social premises for a fecund family are treated today, and must instead feel itself to be the higher guardian of this most precious blessing of a people. Its concern belongs more to the child than to the adult.

Source: A. Hitler, *Mein Kampf* (introduction by D.C. Watt), London, Hutchinson, 1969, pp. 367–78.

DOCUMENT 10

Hitler and the Jews

In a speech delivered to the Reichstag on 30 January 1939, Hitler specifically warned the Jews of their fate should war break out:

Today I will once more be a prophet: If the international Jewish financiers in and outside Europe should succeed in plunging the nations into a world war, then the result will not be bolshevization of the earth and thus the victory of Jewry, but the annihilation of the Jewish race in Europe!

Source: Baynes, *Hitler's Speeches*, vol, 1 p. 741.

DOCUMENT 11

The SS and the Racial State

Martin Broszat explains how the SS were able to implement their racial theories:

It was the state police apparatus which first provided the SS with an instrument for translating National Socialism's propaganda picture of the enemy, as stereotyped as it was vague, into the bloody reality of a bureaucratically planned and organized campaign against opponents. Only after the fusion with the police were slogans like the 'Jewish question', the 'freemason problem' and other hostile figures in the National Socialists' ideological rhetoric 'taken literally', as it were, bureaucratically systematized, allotted to departments and made a basis of a branch of zealously refined Criminal Police science and technique. Before 1933 the notion that the 'Jewish question' would have to have some sort of final 'solution' was common to the radical anti-Semites of all the regions, as bombastic as it was imprecise. The fact, however, that this slogan (final solution of the Jewish problem) could become the ultimate goal of a secret operation of the Security Police, planned as if by the General Staff and perfectly organized, was the result of the bureaucratization of the National Socialist ideology in the context of the merger between the SS and the Police.

Source: M. Broszat, *The Hitler State*, London, Longman, 1981, p. 277.

DOCUMENT 12

The Hossbach Memorandum

Hitler summoned a meeting of his key ministers and service chiefs on 5 November 1937. Five days later minutes of the meeting were compiled by Hitler's adjutant, Colonel Hossbach. In 1946 what survived from these minutes was accepted by the Nuremberg Tribunal as a 'blueprint' of Hitler's intentions to wage war:

The aim of German policy was to make secure and to preserve the racial community and to enlarge it. It was therefore a question of space [*Lebensraum*] ... The question for Germany was: Where

▶

could she achieve the greatest gain at the lowest cost? German policy had to reckon with two hate inspired antagonists, Britain and France, to whom a German colossus in the centre of Europe was a thorn in the flesh ... Germany's problem could only be solved by the use of force ... If the resort to force with its attendant risks is accepted ... there then remains still to be answered the questions 'When?' and 'How?' In this matter there were three contingencies to be dealt with.

Contingency 1: Period 1943–5

After that date only a change for the worse, from our point of view, could be expected ... Our relative strength would decrease in relation to the rearmament which would then have been carried out by the rest of the world. If we did not act by 1943–5 any year could, owing to lack of reserves, produce the food crisis ... and this must be regarded as a 'waning point of the regime' ... If the *Führer* was still living, it was his unalterable determination to solve Germany's problem of space by 1943-5 at the latest ...

Contingency 2

If internal strife in France should develop into such a domestic crisis as to absorb the French army completely and render it incapable of use for war against Germany, then the time for acting against the Czechs would have come.

Contingency 3

If France should be so embroiled in war with another state that she could not 'proceed' against Germany. For the improvement of our politico-military position our first objective, in the event of our being embroiled in war, must be to overthrow Czechoslovakia and Austria simultaneously in order to remove the threat to our flank in any possible operation against the West.

Source: *Documents on German Foreign Policy, Series D*, vol.1, London, HMSO, 1957–66, pp. 29–38.

NOTES

1 K. Hildebrand, *The Third Reich*, Routledge, London, 1991, p. 101.

2 Quoted in K. Hildebrand, 'Hitlers Ort in der Geschichte des preussisch-deutschen Nationalstaates', *Historische Zeitschrift*, vol. 217, 1974, p. 602.

3 C.J. Friedrich and Z.K. Brzezinski, *Totalitarian Dictatorship and Autocracy*, Cambridge, MA., Harvard University Press, 1956, p. 294.

4 See the discussion in M. Roseman, 'National Socialism and modernization', in R. Bessel, ed., *Fascist Italy and Nazi Germany*, Cambridge, Cambridge University Press, repr. 1997, pp. 209–11.

5 Ibid., p. 198.

6 D. Peukert, *Inside Nazi Germany*, Harmondsworth, Penguin, 1989, p. 16.

7. M. Broszat, *The Hitler State*, London, Longman, 1981, p. 266.

8 J. Noakes and G. Pridham, eds, *Nazism, 1919–45*, vol. 2, *State, Economy and Society 1933–39*, Exeter, Exeter University Press, 1984, p. 171.

9 Ibid., p. 234.

10 Ibid., p. 237.

11 D. Orlow, *The History of the Nazi Party*, vol. 2, Newton Abbot, David & Charles, 1973, pp. 135 and 193.

12 Broszat, *Hitler State*, p. 276.

13 Ibid., p. 277.

14 Ibid., p. 319.

15 F. Neumann, *Behemoth: The Structure and Practice of National Socialism*, London, Frank Cass, repr. 1967, p. 74.

16 E. Petersen, *The Limits of Hitler's Power*, Oxford, Oxford University Press, 1969, p. 4.

17 Quoted in Hildebrand, *Third Reich*, p. 137.

18 For a full discussion of this, see I. Kershaw, *The Nazi Dictatorship: Problems and Perspectives*, London, Edward Arnold, 3rd ed. 1993, pp. 60–7.

19 Quoted in R. Overy, *War and Economy in the Third Reich*, Oxford, Oxford University Press, 1995, p. 5.

20 Ibid., p.56.

21 S. Schweitzer, *Big Business in the Third Reich*, London, Eyre & Spottiswoode, 1964, p. 146.

22 Overy, *War and Economy*, p. 15.

23 Noakes and Pridham, *Nazism* vol. 2, p. 280.

24 Overy, *War and Economy*, p. 186.

25 B.H. Klein, *Germany's Economic Preparations for War*, Cambridge, MA., Harvard University Press, 1959, p. 78.

26 A.J.P. Taylor, *The Origins of the Second World War*, London, Hamish Hamilton, 1961; and A. Milward, *The German Economy at War*, London, Athlone Press, 1965.

27 Overy, *War and Economy*, pp. 185, 192 and 190.

28 Neumann, *Behemoth*, p. 431.

29 T. Mason, 'Intention and explanation: a current controversy about the interpretation of National Socialism' in G. Hirschfield and L. Kettenacker, eds, *The Führer State, Myths and Realites*, Kletta Cotta, Stuttgart, 1981, p. 29.

30 Overy, *War and Economy*, p. 223.

31 Quoted in Roseman, 'National Socialism' p. 212.

32 N. Baynes, ed., *Hitler's Speeches, 1922–39*, vol. 1, Oxford, Oxford University Press, 1942, p. 616.

33 C. Koonz, *Mothers in the Fatherland*, London, Jonathan Cape, 1987, p. 193.

34 Peukert, *Inside Nazi Germany*, p. 168.

35 D. Schoenbaum, *Hitler's Social Revolution*, London, Weidenfeld & Nicolson, 1967, p. 161.

36 J.E. Farquharson, *The Plough and the Swastika. The NSDAP and Agriculture in Germany, 1928–45*, London, Sage Publications, 1976, p. 212.

37 Quoted in Roseman, 'National Socialism' p. 209.

38 G. Czarnowski, ' The value of marriage for the *Volksgemeinscaft*' in Bessel, ed., *Fascist Italy and Nazi Germany*, p. 95.

39 Roseman, 'National Socialism', p. 208.

40 J.S. Stephenson, *Women in Nazi Society*, London, Croom Helm, 1975, p. 172.

41 Koonz, *Mothers*, p. 178.

42 Ibid., p. 180.

43 Stephenson, *Women in Nazi Society*, p. 61.

44 Ibid., p. 64.

45 R. Grünberger, *A Social History of the Third Reich*, Harmondsworth, Penguin, 1974, p. 314.

46 T.W. Mason, *Arbeiterklasse und Volksgemeinschaft. Dokumente und Materialien zur deutschen Arbeiterpolitik, 1936–1939*, Opladen, Westdeutscher Verlag, 1975. See discussion in T. Siegal, 'The attitude of the German workers' in Bessel, ed., *Fascist Italy and Nazi Germany*, pages 63–7.

47 Ibid., p. 67.

48 Quoted in Overy, *War and the Economy*, p. 224.

49 Kershaw, *Nazi Dictatorship*, p. 145.

50 Ulrich Herbert, 'Good times, bad times; memories of the Third Reich' in R. Bessel, ed., *Life in the Third Reich*, Oxford, Oxford University Press, 1987, p. 97.

51 Quoted in Noakes and Pridham, *Nazism*, vol. 2, p. 397.

52 Ibid., p. 391.

53 Ibid., p. 397.

54 Grünberger, *Social History*, p. 459.

55 J.S. Conway, *The Nazi Persecution of the Churches, 1933–45*, London, Weidenfeld & Nicolson, 1968, p. 289.

56 Ibid., p. 84.

57 R. Gellately, *Backing Hitler*, Oxford, Oxford University Press, 2001, p. 38.

58 Ibid., p. 41.

59 M. Burleigh and W. Wippermann, *The Racial State in Germany 1933–45*, Cambridge, Cambridge University Press, 1991, p. 135.

60 Noakes and Pridham, *Nazism*, vol. 2, p. 521.

61 L. Dawidowicz, *The War Against the Jews, 1933–45*, Harmondsworth, Penguin, 1986, p. xxvi; Hildebrand, *Third Reich*; K. Bracher, *The German Dictatorship* Harmondsworth, Penguin, 1973; M. Broszat, 'Hitler and the genesis of the final solution' in H.W. Koch, ed., *Aspects of the Third Reich*, London, Macmillan, 1985, pp. 390–429; H. Mommsen, 'The realization of the unthinkable: the "final solution" of the Jewish question in the Third Reich' in G. Hirschfeld, ed. *The Policies of Genocide*, London, Allen & Unwin, 1986, pp. 97–144; K.A. Schleunes *The Twisted Road to Auschwitz*, London, Deutsch, 1972.

62 Quoted in Noakes and Pridham, *Nazism*, vol. 2, p. 588.

63 Dawidowicz, *The War Against the Jews*, p. 142.

64 Mommsen, 'Realization of the unthinkable', p. 112.

65 Dawidowicz, *The War Against the Jews*, p. 43.

66 Taylor, *Origins*, p. 68.

67 H. Mommsen, 'National Socialism: continuity and change' in W. Laqueur, ed., *Fascism: A Reader's Guide*, Harmondsworth, Penguin, 1979, pp. 151–92; K. Hildebrand, *The Foreign Policy of the Third Reich*, London, Batsford, 1973; A. Hillgruber, *Hitlers Strategie, Politik und Kriegsführung, 1940–41*, Frankfurt am Main, Bernard & Graefe, 1965.

68 A. Bullock, 'Hitler and the origins of the Second Word War' in E.M. Robertson, ed., *The Origins of the Second World War*, London, Macmillan, 1971, p. 193.

69 Bracher, *The German Dictatorship*, p. 369.

70 Taylor, *Origins*, p. 132; W. Carr, *Arms, Autarky and Aggression*, London, Edward Arnold, 2nd ed. 1979, p. 128.

71 Kershaw, *Hitler*, vol. 2, *1936–45 Nemesis*, London, Allen Lane, 2000, p. 83.

72 Ibid., p. 119.

73 G.L. Weinberg, *The Foreign Policy of Hitler's Germany*, vol. 2, *Starting World War II, 1937–39*, Chicago, University of Chicago Press, 1970–80, p. 567.

74 Taylor, *Origins*, p. 278.

75 Quoted in Gellately, *Backing Hitler*, p. 12.

76 Schoenbaum, *Hitler's Social Revolution*, p. 52.

CHAPTER EIGHT

The development of Italian Fascism, 1929–39

TIMELINE

1929–33		Impact of the Great Depression
1930		Party urged 'to go resolutely to the people'
1931		OND membership charge reduced by 50 per cent
		IMI set up
1933	January	Hitler comes to power
		IRI set up
1934–8		Expenditure on rearmament doubles
1934	August	Dollfuss murdered
1935	January	Rome Agreements
	Octobter	Start of Ethiopian War
1936	March	Rhineland remilitarized
	July	Spanish Civil War starts
	October	Rome–Berlin Axis
1937		Ballila and Young Fascists form Italian Youth of the Lictors (GIL)
	December	Italy withdraws from the League of Nations
1938–9		Reform of Custom
1938	March	The *Anschluss*
	September	The Munich crisis
	July	Race manifesto published
1939	January	Chamber of *Fasces* and Corporations set up
	April	Italian occupation of Albania
	May	Pact of Steel
	September	Britain and France declare war on Germany
1940	June	Italy declares war on Britain and France

INTRODUCTION

After the Lateran Pacts were signed in 1929 (see p. 112) the Fascist regime enjoyed a period of genuine popularity, which was significantly boosted by the Ethiopian war . With both party and state under control, Mussolini appeared to be effortlessly in command of Italy. Yet was this merely a façade? Could Mussolini in any way be described as a 'weak dictator'? Had, as Richard Bosworth asks, Mussolini in fact 'mastered Italy ... or had Italy mastered him'?[1]

THE KEY ISSUES IN THIS CHAPTER ARE:

- How Italy was governed in the 1930s.
- The role of the party in spreading the message of Fascism and controlling the population.
- The impact on Italian society of the Mussolini regime.
- The Fascist 'cultural revolution'.
- The development of the economy.
- Mussolini's foreign policy.
- The strength of the Fascist regime in 1939.

THE *DUCE* AND HIS GOVERNMENT

By 1929 Mussolini was politically the single most powerful force in Italy, but he ruled through the state rather than the party. He was sufficiently secure to hand over the eight ministries, which he nominally supervised, to the Undersecretaries, who in reality had always done all the work, and retained only the key positions of *Capo del Governo* (Head of Government). Nevertheless he took the precaution of eliminating from the government and leading party positions such strong personalities as Rocco, Federzoni and Rossoni (see pp. 103, 107 and 109). In the early 1930s the cabinet still met frequently, but by 1936 Mussolini, boosted by success in Ethiopia, increasingly governed by personal decree (see Document 7).

Unlike Hitler, Mussolini did work reasonably hard (see p. 213) and read most of the documents put in front of him by his civil servants (see Figure 8.1), but in many areas of policy he had no strong preferences. In the economy, for instance, he set the tone and let the experts get on with the details. Although he sometimes criticized the Italian bureaucracy, he rejected attempts to reform it. The number of agencies, quangos and semi-official bodies, like the IRI, the Institute for Industrial Reconstruction, multiplied during the 1930s, and the civil service steadily expanded. Increasingly his regime, like the Nazi government in Germany, spawned 'a proliferation of rival administrative structures',[2] which often pursued contradictory policies.

The development of totalitarianism

In 1932 in an article written under his name for him by the former Education Minister, Professor Giovanni Gentile, Mussolini stressed that 'for the Fascist, everything is in the state, and nothing human or spiritual exists, much less has value outside the state. In this sense Fascism is totalitarian'.[3] The accuracy of this has been the matter of constant debate amongst historians. The essential elements of totalitarianism (see p. 2) are:

- a dominant ideology
- a single mass party
- supreme power, with political decision making concentrated in a single leader or a small group.

Figure 8.1 Mussolini at his desk
Source: Getty Images/ Time and Life Pictures

Italian Fascism certainly possessed some of these characteristics, and the two dominating historians of contemporary Italian historiography, De Felici and Emilio Gentile, both agree that the Fascist regime was moving towards totalitarianism in 1930s. Gentile, for instance argues that the PNF, the Italian Fascist party, was 'the first experience for the Italian people of mass organization conducted through rigid centralized and totalitarian principles'.[4] The problem about Fascist 'totalitarianism' is that the Fascist party, unlike the Russian Bolsheviks, never managed to destroy the original pre-Fascist power structure or even dominate it, as Hitler was eventually able to do. It was the state not the party that ran Italy, and the Church, the monarchy and the army all remained major stumbling blocks for Fascist control.

In 1939 the Chamber of Deputies was abolished and replaced by the Chamber of *Fasces* and Corporations, but significantly the Senate remained unreformed. Momentarily it looked, too, as if the monarchy might be swept away when Mussolini appointed himself the First Marshal of the Empire. This gave him, rather than the King, control over the armed forces in war, but then, once again, Mussolini withdrew from actually deposing the monarch. Italian Fascism arguably provided the first and most coherent rationale for totalitarianism in the twentieth century, but in reality its system was far from totalitarian. Juan Linz has argued that a 'limited **pluralism**' existed within the Fascist system, and has consequently characterized the Fascist regime as 'pre-totalitarian'.[5] (see Document 1).

Pluralism
A situation in which different groups in society maintain their independence.

PROPAGANDA

The key message that had to be put across by propaganda was the concept of an imperial Italy, or 'Greater Italy', and the mobilization of every aspect of national life to achieve this. The leader of the Fascist 'revolution', the *Duce*, would embody personally the national ideal, and a new national consciousness would replace class, regional, sectarian and organizational divisions. A modern Italy populated with new Italians, who would 'speak little, gesticulate less and seem driven by a single will' was to be created.[6] The Fascist message was shot through with the concept of *bonifica* and involved launching a series of campaigns to 'combat degener-

Bonifica
The reclamation of the race as well as, more literally, reclamation of marshes and agricultural land.

ation and radically renew Italian society by "pulling up the bad weeds and cleaning the soil"'.[7]

To emphasize its monopoly of patriotism and consequently its right to exercise a monopoly on power, Fascism also increasingly attempted to develop a religious dimension. The philosopher of Fascism **Giovanni Gentile**, argued that the totalitarian character of Fascism derived from its religious nature. Fascism consequently developed many of the attributes of a religion; it had its martyrs, myths, festivals, quasi-religious art, and its new party headquarters were even built complete with bell towers and inner sanctuaries, as if they were churches.

Giovanni Gentile (1875–1944)
An early supporter of Fascism and the leading intellectual within the party. He was Education Minister, 1922–4.

With the institutionalization of the new Fascist 'religion', the link between the *Duce* and his followers, the Fascists was transformed 'into a charismatic relationship in which the latter gave him dedication and obedience based on faith and on his historic mission as founder and chief interpreter of Fascism'.[8] The *Duce* became a god-like being for whom no task was too great. It was even claimed that his heroic will power had halted the flow of lava on Mount Etna before it had engulfed a village. Mussolini did everything he could do to nurture this image among the Italian people. In a way that no politician had done before, he established direct contact with the masses. He frequently toured Italy, and his picture frequently appeared on public buildings. He was regularly compared favourably with the geniuses of world history. Turati, the Party Secretary, declared that he was the leader 'the revolution wanted between 1914 and 1922. In October he brought it about, and ever since he has guided it. One leader, the only leader, from whom all power flows. One Steersman, whose place no below decks rabble can take.'[9]

At local level propaganda was entirely in the hands of the party, which organized lectures and rallies and special ceremonies for honouring long-serving workers and other deserving employees with diplomas and financial rewards. On a national level the main means of spreading the Fascist message to the people were the press, film and the radio, which became a major media force in the 1930s. Fascist Italy was the first state in Western Europe effectively to exploit the mass media for the purpose of controlling the population. By 1938 over a million families possessed a radio set. To run public broadcasting, a public corporation was set up, which was controlled by the state, while the party was allowed to run the *Ente Radio Rurale*. Special efforts were made to appeal to children through such radio programmes as 'The *Balilla*'s Friend' (see p. 262).

The press was freer and of better quality than in Nazi Germany, yet it was still subjected to censorship by Mussolini's press office. Newspapers were regularly sent notices about what they should print or not print. The sheer scale of the economic Depression of 1929–33, for example, was not allowed to be commented upon until late 1932. Carrying out the censorship orders was usually left to the newspaper editors, although sometimes the prefects would intervene if an editor ignored them.

The Italian film industry was reconstructed in 1936 with the help of the IRI (see p. 275). The regime also set up an Experimental Centre of Cinematography, which trained 100 students a year to a high standard. Although, as in Germany, the majority of the films were sentimental and escapist and consisted mainly of costume epics and romances, there was also a series of films glorifying Fascism, and at every film performance, official newsreels, which were little more than propaganda, had by law to be shown.

Sport was also used to unify the country. Prominence was given to it in the newsreels and the press. At the Los Angeles Olympics, Italians won 12 gold medals and were immediately know as 'Mussolini's boys'. In 1934 when Italy both hosted and won the World Cup in soccer, the regime won a major propaganda triumph, which boosted its image significantly among the population. Mussolini took care to attend the Final and to be seen on the newsreels handing out medals to the Italian victors. The Italians also went on to win the Olympic Football Championship in 1936 and the World Cup for a second time in 1938.

THE IMPACT OF FASCISM ON THE EDUCATIONAL SYSTEM

Initially under Giovanni Gentile, Mussolini's first Education Minister, Fascist educational policy had been primarily concerned with creating an academic elite. It was not until 1925 that a determined effort was made to make education an instrument for propagating Fascism. In December 1925 Mussolini announced that 'the Government demands that the schools should be inspired by the ideals of Fascism'.[10] All teachers and lecturers had to swear an oath of loyalty to Mussolini, and many non-Fascist teachers were purged from the schools. For inspectors, school heads and rectors of universities, political correctness, which in this context meant loyalty to Mussolini's interpretation of Fascism, rather than ability, became the key to promotion. In 1928 the curriculum began to be revised to ensure that more time could be given to political indoctrination. At primary school level this was the easiest to introduce, while in secondary schools and universities the regime had to be more cautious. Traditional subjects were subtly modified to emphasize nationalism, and courses were given on Fascist culture and corporatism.

In 1933 new recruits to teaching at all levels from primary school to university were compelled to join the party. The Ministry of Public Instruction also changed its name to the Ministry of National Education, a change which signified that it was interested in the 'total upbringing of the child'[11] and took control of the ONB (see p. 262). New text books with a specific 'Fascist' content also began to be published.

The Fascistization of education accelerated under **Vecchi**, who was Education Minister in 1935–6 and his successor, Giuseppe Bottai (see p. 110). Both attempted to eliminate from the educational system what the former described as 'the individualistic and decentralizing attitude which is least compatible with the ethics and doctrine of the Fascist state'.[12] The universities lost their autonomy and, wherever possible, private schools and colleges were brought under state control. Vecchi also introduced a programme for military instruction in the high schools, which was taught by retired army officers. Paradoxically, however, the government strengthened the teaching of religion in schools, even permitting its instruction by Roman Catholic priests in the secondary schools (see Document 5).

In 1939 the school system was reorganized in an attempt to bring secondary education nearer to the world of work. Bottai's aims were threefold: study, physical fitness and manual work. Manual labour was introduced into the curriculum of the last two years of primary school, the technical schools were restored, and a single junior secondary school system for all children from 11

Count di Val Cismon de Vecchi
One of the key organizers of the 'march on Rome' in 1922, then Commander of the Fascist militia, Governor of Somaliland and Education Minister, 1935–6.

to 14 was formed (see Document 2). Possibly if these reforms had not been interrupted by the war, they would in time have had considerable impact. However their influence was limited. Illiteracy slowly declined and the number of pupils in secondary education increased, but Bottai's attempts to build up the vocational and scientific schools failed. As in Germany (see p. 222), the middle classes continued to send their children to the traditional grammar schools, where the classics were still the premier subject.

Fascist youth groups

The Fascist youth groups also played an important role in indoctrinating boys and girls in the ideology of the regime (see Figure 8.2). The various Fascist youth groups were united into the *Balilla* (*Opera Nazionale Balilla* – ONB) in 1926. This comprised:

- Children of the She Wolf for both boys and girls aged 6–8
- the *Balilla* for boys aged 8–15
- the *Avanguardisti* for boys aged 15–18
- the *Picole Italiane* for girls aged 8-12
- the *Giovanni Italiane* for girls aged 13-18.

In 1928 Mussolini ordered the dissolution of all non-Fascist youth movements, although he was forced to compromise with

Figure 8.2 Children saluting the *Duce*
Source: Getty Images/ Hulton Archive

the Church over this (see p. 112). Party organizations played a key part in the attempted Fascistization of Italian youth. The ONB was increasingly given responsibility for the teaching of physical education, pre-military training and organized leisure.

In 1930 the Young Fascist organization (*Fasci Giovanile*), which concentrated so much on military training that Mussolini feared that Starace, the Party Secretary, was reviving the defunct squads, was set up to fill a gap in provisions for young people between 18 and 21, who were already at work. Their motto, 'Believe, obey, fight' was the watchword of the new Fascist man, whom Mussolini wished to create. In 1937 the *Balilla* and the Young Fascists were combined into a single youth movement, the *Gioventu Italiana del Littorio* (**GIL**), and placed under the direct control of party, which enabled it to increase its influence in the schools.

In the universities, except for the extra-curricular activities of the **GUF**, the party had little influence. The majority of students did, however, at least nominally belong to the GUF, which was directly controlled by the party. Its aim was to create a new Fascist elite, which was given relative freedom to debate issues, publish newspapers and to make films. Through the student games or *Littoriali*, competitions were held that involved debates and presentations in all disciplines. The debates, according to Tannenbaum, 'were the freest forum in Fascist Italy, the only place where serious criticism of any aspect of the regime was possible'.[13]

To what extent did the party through these youth groups manage to forge a generation of Fascists? Certainly a new generation of Fascist youth leaders emerged and virtually all school children were brought into contact with the new Fascist ethos, but the extent to which this actually had an impact is more difficult to assess. In 1934, for instance, the Party Secretary in Savona observed that 'the Young Fascists were a joke from all points of view ... Discipline did not exist and I was forced to resort to ... severe punishments to get them to show up at meetings'.[14]

GIL
The Italian Youth of the Lictors. In ancient Rome the *Lictores* were the executioners of justice and public servants.

GUF
Gioventù Universitaria Fascista, the University Students' Fascist Organization, which comprised students between 18 and 25 years old.

FASCISM AND THE ITALIAN PEOPLE

The workers

The attitude of the workers to Fascism is 'an historiographical minefield'.[15] Felice argues that the regime did establish a consensus with the working classes during the period 1929–35, but this argument is by no means accepted by many other historians. Felici's arguments are closely linked with the debate about living standards in Italy in the 1930s. Paul Corner, however, has shown 'beyond reasonable doubt'[16] that the decline in living standards began before the Depression and recovered only very slowly in the later 1930s, as the table shows.

The standard of living, 1929–39

This tables shows the nominal index of the 'real wages' of industrial workers and the cost of living (1928 = 100). During the Fascist period a complicated system of payment by bonuses, family allowances and severance pay acted as a substitute for wages. Hence the 'real wages' were often different from the official hourly or monthly rates.

	Real wages	Cost of living
1929	101.6	99.0
1930	98.4	97.4
1931	88.9	98.7
1932	84.9	100.0
1933	81.4	105.1
1934	77.2	106.1
1935	78.3	95.1
1936	84.2	92.7
1937	92.2	98.7
1938	99.3	95.8
1939	103.7	100.8

Source: E.R. Tannenbaum, *Fascism in Italy*, Harmondsworth, Allen Lane, 1973, Table 1, p. 116, The *Fascist Experience: Society and Culture 1922–1945*, Basic Books 1972

Mussolini in the 1920s called the workers 'a generation of irreconcilables' and initially all he expected from industrial workers was 'a silent industriousness and acquiescence to pay reductions and speed ups in the tempo of their work'.[17] Nevertheless, he did attempt to integrate the working class into the Fascist state. The institutions for achieving this were the OND (see below) and the Fascist unions. Although the unions had little power and the workers compared them negatively to the defunct Socialist unions, during the 1930s their membership expanded sharply. In the province of Milan, Pietro Capoferri, a former Syndicalist, managed even in the depths of the Depression to negotiate reasonably favourable contracts for the workers, and in 1939 succeeded in getting shop stewards reinstalled. Tannenbaum has argued that 'despite all these specific complaints about the inadequacies of the Fascist unions, these unions did help to break down the workers' feeling of social and cultural isolation and to give them a sense of belonging to a national comunity.'[18] The unions also had considerable welfare responsibilities: they handled social security payments and claims for severance pay, and also operated as labour exchanges. All in all, together with the OND, to which nearly 40 per cent of the industrial workforce joined it can be argued that they 'brought the workers into the mainstream of Italy's emerging mass society'.[19]

The task of the OND, or *Opera Nazionale Dopolavaro*, which was set up in 1925, was to run the various workers' leisure clubs originally run by the Socialist unions or the Fascist syndicates. Initially, however, it appealed more to the white-collar workers as it offered opportunities for educational improvement rather than sport, but in the 1930s it became more popular when sport was allowed to play a greater part in its programmes.

From 1927 onwards the OND was run by the Fascist Party. In 1931 membership charges were reduced by 50 per cent and the state increasingly subsidized it, while insisting that firms should pay for their own local branches. By the late 1930s most towns and villages throughout Italy, including the south, had an OND clubhouse with a sports field, a small library and a radio. The OND also organized ambitious programmes involving holiday camps and skiing in the Alps.

The OND was the regime's largest adult organization. Its membership increased from 1,771,000 in 1931 to 3,831,331 in 1939, and 40 per cent of all industrial workers, and over 80 per cent of all state and private salaried employees, were members. However these statistics do not necessarily prove that Fascism was tightening its grip on the Italian people. Essentially the OND in the 1930s set out to provide entertainment rather that instruction in Fascist ideology, but this did not trouble Mussolini, for whom the important thing was that 'people are able to meet in places where we can control them'.[20] Only through the censorship of the books and films available at the local OND centres was the Fascist Party able to exert any control over what the OND membership thought or read.

Membership of the OND, 1926-36

Year	Salaried employees	Manual workers	Total
1926	164,000	116,000	280,000
1927	289,000	248,000	537,000
1928	437,000	445,000	882,000
1929	524,000	921,000	1,445,000
1930	528,000	1,093,000	1,621,000
1931	674,000	1,097,000	1,771,000
1932	675,000	1,099,000	1,774,000
1933	725,000	1,201,000	1,926,000
1934	795,000	1,312,000	2,107,000
1935	805,000	1,571,000	2,376,000
1936	864,000	1,921,000	2,785,000

The peasantry

The Fascist regime was less successful in reaching out to the peasantry. The economic backwardness of the countryside ensured that apart from a few communal radio sets, the revolution in the mass media passed the peasantry by. The farmers and agricultural union enjoyed little support, while the youth organizations and the OND had relatively little impact on them. Fascist propaganda had hardly any affect on the southern peasantry. One historian has observed that 'Even when they were forced to listen to Mussolini on the radio in the village square, his words went over their heads, leaving no trace.'[21]

The Depression had hit Italian agriculture particularly hard because it was already so backward and vulnerable. Mussolini's plans – which might well have won over the peasantry – for creating a large number of compact and economically viable small farms were hardly realized. Most of the small landowners continued to hold their land in uneconomic separate plots and the lot of the agricultural day labourer worsened. It was no wonder that migration into the cities continued and that Mussolini was viewed with indifference by the peasantry. **Carlo Levi**, who was banished to the bleak and impoverished southern Italian village of Eboli by OVRA (the Italian secret police), later recalled that the only pictures he saw on the walls of the peasants cottages were of the **black Madonna of Viggiano** and of President Franklin D. Roosevelt, the American President (see Document 9).

Welfare

Welfare policies were, in the first instance, attempts to win political support amongst the workers and peasants for the regime. Although most of these policies were developments of those already in place before 1922, the Fascist regime claimed that every measure was inspired by the Fascist ideology. In 1927 the regime issued the Charter of Labour, which committed the Fascist state to creating an ambitious welfare state. What was actually achieved was in fact more modest:

- In 1934 a system of family allowances were introduced to compensate workers for reduced wages.
- After 1928 sickness insurance was included in most labour contracts, but until 1939 it compensated a worker for only 50 per cent of their wage.
- The unemployment insurance system was left unchanged and the system of retirement insurance was only marginally changed.

The Great Depression of 1929–33 enabled the party to strengthen its influence by launching a major welfare programme in the cities. Employers and workers' syndicates, as well as the banks, were forced by party pressure to donate a percentage of their profits to agencies for welfare activities (EOAs), which coordinated the distribution of financial relief for the unemployed throughout Italy. Each province was subdivided into small units, sometimes consisting of individual streets. The distribution of food was often labelled as the 'Gift from the *Duce*'. In the winter of 1934–5 about 3 million Italians were in receipt of regular daily welfare from the EOA. Felice argues that these programmes of relief earned Mussolini and the Fascist regime genuine popularity.

Carlo Levi (1902–75)
A member of the social reform movement, Justice and Liberty, who was banished in 1936–7 for his anti-Fascist activities. He described his experiences in a bestseller, *Christ Stopped at Eboli*, which was published in 1945.

Black Madonna of Viggiano
An ancient statue of the Virgin Mary, which is kept in a sanctuary near Viggiano.

Women

Although the party did create a mass organization for women, the *Fasci Femminili*, which provided some outlet for the energies and ambitions of middle-class women, in the warrior state that Mussolini envisaged, women of necessity were relegated to second-class citizens whose main duty was to give birth, rear children and look after their husbands. Mussolini pronounced, for instance, that 'war is to man what motherhood is to woman'. His target was to increase the population of Italy from 40 million to 60 million by 1950 in order for there to be sufficient soldiers for the future and enough Italians to settle in the colonies. Consequently in 1927 he launched the 'battle for births' to increase the birthrate and to encourage women to stay at home and be mothers and housewives. A new tax was to be levied on bachelors, divorce made impossible and the contraction of syphilis was made a criminal offence, as it destroyed the fertility of both men and women. Lower wages were established for women as a deliberate attempt to discourage them from working, but this merely had the effect of persuading employers to recruit more women, since they were cheaper than men. The National Foundation for the protection of Maternity and Infancy (ONMI), which was founded in 1925, also made available health care to many women and children, although it made little impact in the rural south.

The Depression and the subsequent near collapse of the Italian economy strengthened the determination of the regime to stop women competing with men for scarce jobs. In 1935 female members of GUF were specifically told that their goals were not to be 'the displacement of men from professions or employment', but rather, as 'educated women to prepare for their roles as mothers and wives'.[22] In September 1938 a decree limited to 10 per cent the number of women who could occupy posts in public, professional and managerial positions.

Within the party women played a minor role. Although the girls' section of the GIL was well financed, the adult female organizations within the party were kept short of funds. The *Fasci Femminale* was little more than a traditional do-gooding middle-class wives' organization. The party did attempt to reach out to peasant women through the rural housewives' organization, the

Massaie Rurali, but it had only moderate success in the north, and in the south it proved impossible to break the taboo on women appearing in public. In the workplace the syndicates did try to help women. In Milan, for instance, they managed to negotiate contracts in the dyeing and printing plants, as well as in book-keeping, which gave women equal pay with the men.

At the same time the Mussolini government also intensified the 'battle for births'. It tried to encourage earlier marriages through loans to married couples under 26. It also awarded mothers with large families much publicized prizes and medals, and young women not yet encumbered with their own families were encouraged to do voluntary work with various organizations involved in public hygiene in order to improve their overall awareness of health issues. As in Nazi Germany, a crackdown on abortions went hand in hand with attempts to modernize and improve maternity practices and child care (see pp. 224–5).

How much impact did these measures in reality have on women? Victoria de Grazia has argued that 'the one real moment of involvement in the mass politics of Fascism, the first and last for a majority of females', was through the after school youth groups, the *Picole Italiane* and the **Giovanni Italiane**.[23]

Giovanni Italiane
The Fascist girls' movement for 13–18 year olds.

THE CATHOLIC CHURCH AND THE FASCIST REGIME

The attitude of the Catholic Church to Fascism was a matter of the greatest political importance to Mussolini. Italy had the highest proportion of priests of any Christian state. There were, too, over a million children in Catholic schools and in 1938 another million young people in *Azione Cattolica* (Catholic Action). Some 25 per cent of the population were practising Catholics, while at least another 30 per cent, even if they did not go often to church, still called themselves good Catholics. Inevitably the attitude of individual priests differed. Some openly identified with the regime, while others ignored it (see Documents 4 (a) and (b)).

As a general rule it can be argued that the majority of Catholics accepted Mussolini's dictatorship, but reacted unfavourably when the regime threatened the Church and its organizations. The

Risorgimento
The unification of Italy, 1859–70, which the papacy had opposed. After unification the Church was seen as a hostile oganization by the government, and a completely secular education system was set up.

Re-clericalization
A programme to regain the Church's influence and privileges within the state.

Encyclical
Papal letter sent to all bishops of the Roman Catholic Church.

Concordat of 1929, which effectively made Italy into a confessional state, undid much of the work of the *Risorgimento* by allowing the teaching of religion in schools. The Pope indeed saw it as a step towards 'the **re-clericalization** of Italy'[24] (see Document 5), thereby ensuring that there would always be an element of tension between the papacy and the regime.

A key provision of the Concordat was Article 43, which recognized the existence of Catholic Action as long as it did not indulge in any political activities. This ensured that one carefully defined area of national life would be immune from Fascist pressure and coercion. In 1931 Mussolini, acting under the influence of the Fascist anti-clericals led by the Party Secretary, Giovanni Giurati, who were jealous of the Catholics' labour and youth activities and feared that these might lead to a relaunching of the Catholic party, the *Populari*, had all the local centres of Catholic Action shut down. The Pope retaliated by issuing his **encyclical**, 'Non abbiamo bisogno', in which he condemned the principle of the totalitarian state.

The Pope infuriated Mussolini by saying that those who had to swear allegiance to Mussolini for career reasons should make the mental reservation that this oath could only be respected 'within the laws of God and the church'.[25] However, in September 1931 a compromise was negotiated which, as in 1929 (see p. 112) allowed Catholic Action to continue with its activities as long as they were not political. It was not to rival the *Balilla* by sponsoring sports of any kind.

Richard Webster has described the years 1931–8 as the 'idyllic years'[26] for cooperation between the Church and the regime. There were certainly many points of mutual support and contact between the two:

- state assistance for missionaries in Africa
- Black Shirt and Fascist youth chaplaincies
- the support of the Catholic Church for corporatism
- the conquest of Ethiopia, which the Church hoped would strengthen Catholicism in eastern Africa (see Document 4(a))
- the war against the Spanish Republic (see pp. 284–5)
- the hope that Fascist foreign policy might develop a Catholic alliance stretching from Lisbon to Budapest which would shut out Communism and block German expansionism.

However by 1938 Mussolini's growing closeness to Nazi Germany and the introduction of anti-Semitic legislation led to a cooling off between the regime and the Vatican. Yet there was no evidence that the mass of the clergy or laity were anti-Fascist in principle. They appeared to accept the legitimacy of the regime and only complained when its policies irritated them.

The leaders of the *Popolari* Party were in exile in London, New York and Brussels, but others like the writer, Giulio Giordani and Alcide de Gasperi, the post-war Italian Prime Minister, found protection by working in the Vatican. Gasperi was able to develop a programme for a post-Fascist **Christian Democratic Party**. Another source of opposition was the Catholic University Students' Federation, which was part of Catholic Action. Its young president Igino Righetti attempted with considerable success to turn the Federation into 'an incubation ground for Catholic leaders'.[27] It was, however, in Milan that the most overt anti-Fascist group existed, although it had to operate clandestinely. It published a series of anti-Fascist leaflets and manifestos, which eventually led to the arrest and imprisonment of its leaders, and only in 1938 after their release did it begin to revive (see Document 4(b)).

Christian Democrat Party
A democratic party based on specifically Christian values.

Historians and Catholic–Fascist relations

D.A. Binchy argues that although many bishops approved of most of the actions taken by the Fascist regime, the Roman Catholic Church in Italy always retained its independence, and many of the lower clergy were sceptical of Fascism.[28] This view is modified by Italian historians like A. Ricardi, who have produced plenty of evidence to show that a large number of priests viewed Mussolini for all his failings as 'one of their favourite sons'.[29] Nevertheless historians do agree that Mussolini's relations with the Church were subject to considerable tension. Richard Webster and J.E. Pollard have shown that even after the Lateran Pacts and Concordat, Church–state relations were frequently very tense. This was not always the result of Fascist aggression, as the Church, too, was actively building up an elite and even hoping to reverse the secular reforms of the nineteenth century.[30]

FASCISM ACCELERATES, 1936–9: THE FASCIST CULTURAL REVOLUTION

Ruth Ben-Ghiat has observed that 'the invasion of Ethiopia constituted a watershed in the history of the Italian regime.'[31] The regime not only reached new levels of popularity but it also exploited the successful war to further the Fascist dream of 'national regeneration' and of creating a 'new type of humanity'. Young Fascist intellectuals joined the Universitarians, the student battalion, to fight in Ethiopia, and were convinced that Fascism could turn Ethiopia into a model colony run on modernizing Fascist lines, which would actually benefit the native Ethiopians. Once the war was won, the emphasis was on colonial settlement and the remaking of Italians as colonial rulers. Various laws were passed for the protection of racial prestige, which banned any social or sexual contact with the Ethiopian peoples.

The war also marked the beginning of a new era in propaganda control. The Ministry of Press and Propaganda was renamed the Ministry of Popular Culture in May 1937, and clearly had ambitions to create a popular Fascist culture. Under its new minister, **Dino Alfieri**, five General Directorates were set up covering press, propaganda, cinema, tourism and theatre. Particular attention was paid to film as a means of shaping a new imperial and racial consciousness.

Building the new imperial Italian led to an ambitious master plan which involved:

- the anti-bourgeois campaign
- the reform of custom
- racial legislation directed at both Jews and Africans.

The thinking behind these measures was aimed at to eradicating 'attitudes and behaviors that in the past had relegated Italy to the rank of secondary power'[32] (see Document 3).

The anti-bourgeois campaign

This new wave of Fascism was reminiscent of the attitude of the more revolutionary members of the squads in 1920–2 (see p. 95). Mussolini was increasingly critical of the prosperous bourgeoisie, whose lack of enthusiasm for empire and war clearly did not fit

Dino Alfieri (1886–1966)
Later became Italian ambassador in Berlin.

in with the image of the new Italian warrior. In an unguarded moment, Mussolini once remarked that 80 per cent of that class would have to be eliminated. Foreign observers were convinced that he was moving back to the left and some businessmen as a precaution were beginning to move money into Swiss bank accounts. In reality, however, his campaign was directed, more generally, against 'the bourgeois mentality' – allegedly defeatist, pacifist, cosmopolitan and unpatriotic – rather than property or big business.

The reform of custom

Desultory attempts were also made to change the lifestyle of Italians. In 1938 the PNF banned the use within its own organizations of the impersonal form of address *lei*, and insisted on the use of the more classless *voi*. This was extended to all those in state employment by June 1939. The abolition of *lei* was supposed to be a sign of the end of Italian servility to foreign social customs. Similarly, the traditional handshake was officially banned in place of the Fascist salute, and all state officials were made to wear uniform, while the goosestep was introduced as the marching step within the army and militia in an effort to build up their physical endurance. Even the design of clothes and bathing suits was subject to political control.

Anti-Semitism

The Jews in Italy

The Jews made up less that 1 per cent of the Italian population. They were enthusiastic supporters of Italian unification, as only then did they gain full civil rights. They rapidly integrated with the Italian population. By the 1930s very few could speak Yiddish or Hebrew. Mixed marriages were increasingly common: according to the 1938 census 43.7 of all marriages involving Jewish people were with a partner who was not Jewish. The Jews played a role in all parts of national life and many joined the Fascist Party. Although the numbers of Jews in business and commerce was way beyond their proportion to the population, unlike in the rest of Europe this caused little resentment. There was, to quote Jonathan Steinberg 'no Jewish problem as such in Italy'.[33]

Before 1938 anti-Semitism had played no role in Fascist doctrine, even though there were anti-Semites within the Fascist Party. Indeed in 1933–4 Mussolini had even attacked Nazi racism as utopian and impractical. He had, after all, a Jewish mistress. It is arguable that his attitude towards the Jews was pragmatic. He was quite ready to tolerate them when they were useful to the regime, but once they became an obstacle to the Axis alliance he was ready to attack them. Certainly only two months after the Rome–Berlin Axis the *Duce* began to criticize the Jews, but it was not until 1938–9 that a series of race laws were enacted:

- Jews were banned from teaching or attending schools or universities and expelled from academies and institutions
- intermarriage between Jews and Italians was banned
- Jews were also excluded from the PNF and its affiliates, public employment and the armed forces.

To contemporaries, including the Pope, these laws appeared to be motivated entirely by the need to draw nearer to Nazi Germany. Yet although they were modelled on the Nazi Nuremberg Laws, they were also a response to specifically Italian national issues and traditions. As Ruth Ben-Ghiat stresses:[34]

- They need to be seen within the context of the policies already mentioned to 'create a race of hardy conquerors and child bearers'.
- They were a product of Fascist attempts to create a modernity that would also protect Italy's own native traditions.
- They were also attempts to cure the national 'weaknesses' that had apparently led to Italian backwardness and lack of national unity. 'The Jew emerged after 1938 as a primary symbol of the forces that had consigned Italy to a position on the margins of modernity'[35] (see Document 8).

THE ECONOMY, 1930–9

The impact of the Depression

The economic crisis of 1929–34 was a watershed in Fascist economic policy. It enabled the government to intervene much more decisively in both banking and industry, but 'from the beginning to the end this intervention took place outside the apparatus of corporatism.'[36] Italian exports declined by nearly two-thirds between 1929 and 1935, because of newly introduced protectionist measures by other countries and the government's continued refusal to devalue the lira in line with the devaluation of the pound sterling in 1931 and the dollar in 1933. In an attempt to defend the lira's exchange rate, Italy's gold reserves were drained away. National bankruptcy was only avoided by the sharp decline in imports caused by the slump. Between 1929 and 1934 car production fell by 50 per cent and the output of steel fell from 2,122,000 to 1,396,000 tons.

In 1931 the government was faced by a major banking crisis. Three of the big banks, *Credito Romano*, the *Banca Commerciala* and the *Banca di Roma*, were in immediate danger of collapse, as they had made loans to companies on the security of their shares, which now, as a result of the Depression, had become valueless. The government intervened immediately and set up the *Instituto Mobiliare Italiano* (IMI) with an endowment of 500 million lira to buy up these shares to give the banks sufficient liquid capital to keep them afloat. When this was not enough, it created in January 1933 the IRI (*Instituto per la Ricostruzione*) to distribute further funds. The IRI also encouraged technical and organizational changes in the firms involved so that the government could recoup its costs by restoring the industries to profitability. Through the IRI the Italian state acquired an increasingly large stake in the economy. By 1939 it controlled several steel works and shipping lines, as well as most of the Italian electrical and telephone systems.

Mussolini, as ever pragmatic, avoided antagonizing the business community by appointing to the IRI 'capable technicians of no noticeable political color'.[37] Albert Beneduce, its director, had been a minister under Bonomi in 1921–2. The significance of the IRI has been the subject of considerable discussion by economists. Champions of laissez-faire like Stefani (see p. 101) initially argued that it merely used tax payers' money to help inefficient banks and businesses, but the economic historian Roland Sarti has come to the conclusion that the IRI 'represents the closest that Fascism ever came to creating the post-capitalist economic order that it promised to achieve through its syndical and corporative reforms'.[38] It is true that, while the IRI represented no immediate threat to private industry, it nevertheless gave the government a control over the economy that was unequalled outside the Soviet Union.

The government also launched an ambitious programme of public works projects, which by 1935 employed some 500,000 people. These involved hydro-electrical projects, electrifying some 5,000 kilometres (3,100 miles) of track and building modern motorways, the *autostrade*, between the main towns in northern Italy and the tourists areas.

Autarky

The collapse of Italian export markets as a result of the over-valued lira and then the impact of the Depression both played a role in Mussolini's attempts to create an autarkic, or self-sufficient, economy. In February 1935 imports were subjected to a system of licensing, and consequently the more difficult it became for Italian firms to obtain industrial supplies from abroad, the more they had to rely on domestic substitutes or low-grade iron ores. This resulted in the drawing together of the industrial and agricultural sectors and the creating of mixed cartels. Yet, arguably, it was political rather than financial factors that pushed the Italian economy into a policy of fully fledged autarky. Only after the League of Nations had imposed economic sanctions (see p. 282) did Mussolini declare that autarky was officially one of his aims. In the heightened patriotic fervour of the Ethiopian War, the reservations and criticism of the industrialists were easily overridden.

Lanital
A wool substitute produced from milk proteins.

Rayon
Textile fabrics or fibres made from cellulose.

Although considerable ingenuity was devoted to developing *Ersatz*, or substitute, goods such as **lanital** and **rayon,** the administration of the autarkic economy was chaotic. Initially attempts were made to administer it through the 22 corporations and the several hundred cartels. When this did not work, Mussolini merely superimposed new agencies on the existing chaotic structure. 'The resulting maze of intersecting bureaucratic channels and the overlapping jurisdictions'[39] enabled businessmen to evade effective control by the state over production.

Preparing the economy for war

As a result of Italy's isolation during the Ethiopian War, its foreign trade shifted away from Britain, Western Europe and the USA towards Germany, the Balkan states and the Italian colonies. By 1939 Germany was Italy's major trading partner. Germany supplied Italy with coal, steel, machine tools and chemicals, while Italy exported food, wines, silk, cotton and hemp to Germany. Reflecting the growing diplomatic closeness of the two countries, the Italian and German economies were becoming increasingly integrated. In February 1939 Mussolini bound Italy still more tightly to Germany when he signed a new commercial treaty with Hitler. One of its most significant clauses was agreement for transferring Italian migrant workers to Germany.

Government expenditure on armaments doubled between 1934 and 1938. The extra expenditure was to a certain extent met by increased taxation, but nevertheless the states's financial deficit rose from 2 billion lira in 1934–5 to 28 billion in 1938–9.

Was Fascism economically a failure?

Tannenbaum declared categorically that 'economically Fascism was a failure'[40] and marshalled some impressive evidence to support that statement:

- The corporative state did very little to reduce the antagonisms between management and labour. Employers frequently abused the contracts with their workers. The large companies, like Fiat, Ansaldo and Montecatini, did not hesitate to settle disputes in an arbitrary way and to sack workers who protested too vigorously.
- Economic growth was modest. From 1922 to 1929 industrial growth grew from a base of 100 to 204, but from 1929 until 1934 there was a sharp decline and by 1938 it had only increased to 216.5.
- As in Britain and France, the 1930s was a decade of unemployment. Although the figures were doctored by the government, unemployment remained high until 1939.
- The north–south divide intensified. The low price of food in the inter-war period and the emphasis on growing grain at the expense of fruit, vegetables and wine ensured that in

practice the number of small farmers declined from 3.4 to
slightly less than 3 million in 1931. The Depression hit
hardest in the south, both in terms of unemployment and
increased poverty. The south's problem's were made worse
when the American government cut down the number of
immigrants that it was ready to admit into the USA.
Tannenbaum argues that the southern peasantry were
effectively second-class citizens, 'much like the blacks in the
American south'.[41]

On the other hand A.J. Gregor argued that Fascism like Bolshevism
in Russia was essentially a 'modernizing movement',[42] which set
out to modernize and industrialize a relatively primitive industrial
and economic system:

Liquidity crisis
A crisis caused by there
not being enough
available money to finance
a project.

- Thanks to the intervention of the IRI in the economy, there
  were no more **liquidity crises** to disrupt economic growth
  and impede the construction of the industrial and transport
  infrastructure of Italy.
- An ambitious programme of hydro-electric power was
  completed, and by 1937 most of Italy's electricity came from
  water power.
- The iron and steel industry expanded and a state-owned oil
  corporation (the AGIP) was set up. Also progress was made
  in developing new chemical and artificial fibre industries.

However these real successes (see Document 6) were undermined
by the escalating costs of rearmament and imperial expansion,
which by the late 1930s accounted for over a third of public
spending. National finances were further burdened by a sharp rise
in welfare spending, which by 1940 swallowed up 20. 6 per cent
of all state and local tax receipts.

FOREIGN POLICY, 1933–9

The historians and Fascist foreign policy in the 1930s

One of the key questions about Mussolini's foreign policy is
whether it was intentionalist, that is the result of his own actions
and planning, or structuralist in that it was determined by Italian
traditions and Fascist domestic policies and assumptions.

Certainly Fascist propaganda and many of Mussolini's speeches would indicate that war was the *raison d'être* of the regime. Achille Starace, the Party Secretary, 1931–9, observed, for instance, that war was as simple and natural a matter as eating a dish of macoroni.[43] The cultural historian, S. Falasca-Zamponi, has no doubts that it was Fascism's 'original totalitarian culture' that drove Mussolini to invade Ethiopia.[44] R.J.B. Bosworth, on the other hand, stresses the continuities between the foreign policy of Liberal and Fascist Italy. After all, before 1914 the Italians were seeking to expand into Ethiopia, Albania and Asia Minor. Bosworth compares the conquest of Ethiopia to Giolitti's occupation of **Libya** in 1912, and poses the question whether there are 'structural explanations, which made it difficult for any Italian statesman from 1860 to 1945 to go beyond the expected behaviour of the least of the Great Powers? And rather than Mussolini's personality or the ideology of Fascism, was the real key to inter-war Italian policy the nation's position among the powers?'[45]

The more conventional view, however, is the intentionalist interpretation, which sees Mussolini as the main force behind Italian foreign policy. To Salvemini it seemed that Mussolini 'did his wicked utmost to follow Hitler's footsteps, his evil doing being limited solely by his inability to do worse',[46] and nearly 30 years later the American historian, Macgregor Knox, stressed that 'Mussolini made policy, and, from 1934–5 on, lightheartedly risked state bankruptcy in pursuit of empire'.[47]

Revisionist historians question the post-war interpretation put forward by Salvemini, Wiskemann and Mack Smith that Mussolini was essentially an ineffective, albeit evil buffoon, who did not know what he was doing. Rosaria Quartarraro argues that Mussolini followed a logical, realistic policy, which aimed to strengthen Italy in Europe and build up a colonial empire. Far from being a rogue statesman, she insists that it was the British who eventually triggered the Second World War, in order to defend their decaying empire. Mussolini's negotiations with Nazi Germany were only 'a mechanism for pressuring England towards a general accord'.[48]

Libya
Nominally part of the Ottoman Empire. The Giolitti government declared war in September 1911, and by May 1912 the Turks were ready to recognize the Italians as de facto rulers, provided they paid off much of the Turkish national debt.

Revisionist historians
Historians who question the accepted interpretations of events.

Mussolini and Germany, 1933–5

Hitler's rise to power introduced a new and incalculable factor into European diplomacy and directly affected Italy's position in Europe. On the one hand, a strong Germany might enable Italy to become the 'determinant weight' between the Entente Powers and Nazi Germany. On the other hand, a new powerful Germany would exert a pull over Austria and attract ethnic German support in the Tyrol.

In June 1933 Mussolini seized the initiative with a proposal for a four-power pact to be signed between Britain, France, Italy and Germany, which would lead to a peaceful revision of the Treaty of Versailles and the setting up of a new framework for cooperation over European and colonial problems. Mussolini hoped that Italy would be the decisive weight in this new arrangement and consequently be able to increase both Italian power and influence. In reality, as a result of the reservations of the other three powers, only a very watered-down version was ever signed, and even this was never ratified by the French parliament.

Austria, however, was the major issue that had the potential to divide Rome and Berlin. Mussolini supported the authoritarian regime of Dollfuss, the Austrian Chancellor (see p. 377), who had promised him that he would gradually move towards Fascism. In August 1933 Mussolini met Dollfuss at Rimini and, although Mussolini advised him to seek a *modus vivendi* with Germany, he promised that if Germany actually threatened Austria he would move troops up to the frontier.

This did indeed happen when the Austrian Nazis, with financial and propaganda backing from Berlin, staged an attempted coup in July 1934, which was crushed, but only after Dollfuss had been murdered. A direct consequence of the coup was increasing cooperation between Italy and France, which resulted in 1935 in the Rome Agreements. These resolved long-running differences in Tunisia, allowed Italy to extend the Libyan border southwards, and, if Germany broke any more of the limitations imposed upon it by Versailles, both states agreed to consult on what policy they should adopt.

The Ethiopian War

The historical debate on the Ethiopian War

The debate on the causes of the Ethiopian War is crucial to an understanding of Mussolini's Italy. Some historians see it essentially as an anachronistic colonial war made possible by Germany's recovery and the subsequent new balance of power in Europe. Bosworth has observed that 'to a large degree, Mussolini in east Africa was still seeking "glory, God and Gold", just as his predecessors in other European countries had done in the world beyond their continent during earlier centuries'.[49] Other historians, such as Enzo Santarelli, stress that the war was primarily a response to the Depression.[50] Certainly, Italian imperialism predated Mussolini, and the Depression did provide Mussolini with arguments for war, as Ethiopia was believed to be rich in raw materials, which would strengthen Italy's economy. Yet there are also strong arguments that the war was neither solely an old-fashioned colonial campaign nor the result of the Depression. Macgregor Knox, for instance, stresses that Mussolini really did intend 'to remake the Italian state and people through war'.[51] De Felice has argued that victory turned the war into what he called 'Mussolini's political masterpiece',[52] as it brought the regime to a new high in popularity. The war did indeed increase the regimes's popularity and quicken the pace of Fascistization (see p. 272).

In 1932, after Mussolini took over direct responsibility for running the Foreign Office from Dino Grandi, preparations for war against Ethiopia were started. In November 1934 Italian–Ethiopian relations were enflamed by an incident at the Wal Wal Oasis, which lay some 80 kilometres (50 miles) inside the Ethiopian frontier. A sharp clash occurred between Ethiopian and Italian troops, who had been illegally occupying it, which prompted Haile Selassi, the Emperor of Ethiopia, to appeal to the League of Nations. On 30 December Mussolini, in a secret memorandum, informed the Italian Foreign Office that 'it is imperative that the problem be resolved as soon as possible . . . the objective can be no other than the destruction of the Abyssinian [sic] armed forces and the total conquest of Ethiopia.'[53]

**League of Nations
Union**
Established in June 1918
to win support for the
League of Nations.

For the next six months Mussolini attempted to get the agreement of the British and French. He had little trouble with the French, but the British were more enigmatic. Mussolini still believed, in the words of Lowe and Mazari, that 'if London would not close both eyes as Paris had done, it would at least close one',[54] but over the summer of 1935 opposition in London stiffened. This was largely the result of public opinion and the coming general election. In June the **League of Nations Union** had organized an unofficial peace ballot in which 10 out of 11 million replies had backed the use of economic sanctions by the League in case of aggression. By September Mussolini had amassed an army of nearly a quarter of a million men in Italian East Africa, which was accompanied by a massive propaganda programme in Italy. It seemed that Mussolini had locked himself into a position from which he could not retreat without an enormous loss of prestige.

On 3 October 1935 Mussolini gave the signal for the invasion to start (see Figure 8.3). Yet he had not quite given up the possibility of finding a compromise. To quote Bosworth, 'for all the fascist tirades which issued from one side of his mouth (including, for example, unlikely threats to take on the British navy in the Mediterranean), from the other he had never ceased to suggest that Italy was the natural associate of Britain and France in Europe, committed to blocking any convulsion from Berlin.'[55] Acting on these hints, the British and French governments drew up a compromise, the Hoare–Laval Plan, which would have ceded considerable areas of northern and eastern Ethiopia to Italy and given Italy exclusive economic influence in the south of the country. On 18 December Mussolini and the Fascist Grand Council accepted the plan 'as a possible basis for discussion', but then it was leaked to the French press and an explosion of rage among the supporters of the League forced both Hoare and Laval's resignations and the subsequent dropping of the plan. The League then imposed sanctions on Italy, but these, as a result of American pressure, stopped short of an oil embargo, and Britain refused to close the Suez Canal in case it led to war with Italy.

On 5 May 1936 Italian forces entered Addis Ababa and Mussolini claimed that he had won 'the greatest colonial war known to history'. Three days later the Italian Empire was declared. Not only had Mussolini defied Britain, France and the

Figure 8.3 The *Domenica del Corriere*, the weekend supplement of the Italian newspaper *Corriere della Sera*, showing Black Shirts in action against Ethiopian troops

League of Nations, but he had also united Italian public opinion behind him. Yet the triumph was in reality somewhat hollow:

- Ethiopia was to become a heavy drain on Italy's finances.
- The war did not really end in 1936: two-thirds of Ethiopia had still to be pacified and unrest continued up to its liberation by British Commonwealth forces in 1941.

The war also played into Hitler's hands. To escape isolation Mussolini agreed to the German remilitarization of the Rhineland (see p. 237) and he also had to make concessions over Austria. While he was still anxious to delay a formal *Anschluss*, he nevertheless urged the Austrians to negotiate a settlement with Berlin. This resulted in the 11 July 'gentleman's agreement' whereby Austria harmonized its foreign policy with Germany's, while still retaining its independence. It was becoming increasingly obvious that Mussolini had gained a colonial empire in East Africa at the cost of his position in Central Europe. Mack Smith argues that these inconvenient facts make the Italian victory look more like 'a propaganda stunt'.[56]

**Rodolfo Graziani
(1882–1955)**
Governor of Italian Somaliland in 1935 and Viceroy of Ethiopia, 1936–7. In 1939 he was appointed Chief of Staff of the Italian army and then Minister of Defence in the Salò Republic (see p. 440).

The Italians in Ethiopia, 1936–41

In July 1936 Mussolini had ordered Marshal **Graziani**, the Viceroy of Ethiopia, to conduct a policy of 'systematic ... terror and extermination against rebels and any in the population who favour them'.[57] However, this was not effective. In February 1937 the rebels were able to launch an attack on the Viceroy and his entourage, which wounded 30 Italians, including Graziani himself. In reply the local Fascist authorities conducted a campaign of terror that cost anything from 3,000 to 30,000 deaths. Only about 3,000 Italians settled in Ethiopia and the colony never made a profit for the Italian state.

The Spanish Civil War

The Spanish Civil War, which broke out in July 1936, aligned Fascist Italy more firmly with Germany and complicated its relations with Britain and France at a time when both these powers were attempting to minimize the damage caused by the Ethiopian crisis. Mussolini had given some limited financial support to the Spanish Right during the years 1931–6, and was approached on 19 July 1936 by an agent from General Franco, the Nationalist leader (see p. 310), with a request to supply aircraft and airlift Spanish Moroccan troops to the mainland. This was granted seven days later. Bosworth has argued that the decision 'is a case study in accident and in the limitations of charismatic decision making',[58] and most historians agree that Mussolini stumbled into the war both in response to information that the French were allowing the export of arms to the Spanish Republicans and out of a desire to prevent the growth of Soviet

influence in Spain. However, the potential rewards were considerable – the creation of a semi-Fascist satellite Spain, which would
grant Italy economic concessions and perhaps even a naval base
on the Balearic islands. It would also serve as a means for tough-
ening up the Italian character through war.

Mussolini assumed that the Civil War would end in a swift
victory for Franco, but it dragged on until the spring of 1939 (see
Chapter 9). By January 1937 nearly 50,000 Italian 'volunteers' –
Black Shirts and troops – were in Spain. After their defeat at
Guadalajara in March 1937 (see p. 311), the very prestige of the
regime was at stake, and Mussolini was trapped into pouring in
reinforcements, which he could not afford to withdraw until
Franco had won.

The struggle became increasingly ideological and aligned Italy with
Nazi Germany in a struggle against the Republic, which was supplied
with equipment and 'advisers' from the USSR (see p. 311). The British
and French, in an attempt to stop the war from spreading proposed a
non-intervention agreement, which Mussolini and Hitler both signed,
but in practice ignored. Attacks by Italian submarines on British and
French shipping in the Mediterranean caused further deterioration in
relations between the Western democracies and Rome.

The historical debate on Mussolini's foreign policy, 1936–9

Historians disagree as to whether there was an inevitable
sequence of events leading from the Ethiopian War to the Pact of
Steel, the Italian–German alliance of May 1939. Felice, for
instance, argued that Mussolini at times attempted to exploit
Britain's fear of Germany to extract concessions on the colonies
from Britain. He was in effect attempting to follow a 'pendulum
policy' – the oscillation between Germany and Britain – the so-
called policy of 'determinant weight'.[59] On the other hand,
historians such as Philip Morgan, Felix Gilbert, Manfred Funke
and Macgregor Knox argue that the Axis agreement in October
1936 marked a fundamental turning point in Italian foreign
policy, which was as significant as May 1915, the date of Italy's
entry into the world war as an ally of the Entente (see p. 21), and
marked a realignment of Italian foreign policy with Germany.

The German alliance

Gian Ciano (1903–43)
Mussolini's son-in-law and from 1936 to 1943 Italian Foreign Minister. In 1944 he was executed by Mussolini for his opposition to the war.

Axis
An imaginary line around which bodies or planets rotate.

Over the course of the period 1936–9 Mussolini increasingly moved closer to Berlin. In October 1936 Mussolini's son-in law, **Ciano,** the Italian Foreign Minister (see Figure 8.4), visited Berlin and signed the October Protocols, which Mussolini described as forging a new '**Axis**' between Berlin and Rome, after wide-ranging talks with Hitler and his opposite number in Germany, Constantin von Neurath. Italy conceded German predominance in Austria, while Hitler recognized the Italian empire in East Africa. Both governments agreed on the threat from Communism, the need to stop British attempts to contain the two Axis powers, and to cooperate closely in Spain.

The Axis agreement was not a treaty and did not commit Italy to a formal alliance with Germany. Historians are divided as to whether closer links with Germany were the first stage in his

Figure 8.4 Galeazzo Ciano, the Italian Foreign Minister
Source: Corbis

attempt to 'smash the European balance' and so constituted 'an Italo-German revolutionary alliance against the West',[60] or whether Mussolini was playing the blackmailer's card in order to frighten the British into making concessions, as D.C. Watt has argued.[61] Mussolini celebrated it as 'an axis', around which all European states with 'a will to colloboration' could revolve, but beneath this pro German propaganda 'oscillations continued'.[62] Links with Britain were renewed in the summer of 1937, and Mussolini even conceded that the two states were not on course for collision in the Mediterranean or elsewhere.

In September 1937 Mussolini visited Germany. After witnessing army manoeuvres, inspecting Krupp's armament factories in Essen and addressing a mass meeting in Berlin, he appeared, on the surface, to be convinced that the Nazi regime was the major force in Europe and that Italy had inevitably to ally itself with Germany. Lowe and Mazari called this visit 'one of the crucial events in the pre-war period',[63] and argue that it finally persuaded Mussolini to back Hitler. It certainly led to Italy joining the **Anti-Comintern Pact** in November 1937, which was, however, an agreement that was of more symbolic than practical importance aimed at the Communist International or Comintern, but otherwise Mussolini made no long-term commitments to the Germans.

Mussolini's attitude to German policy in Austria also remained ambiguous. He accepted that the *Anschluss* was inevitable but he nevertheless hoped that it would be long delayed. His lack of influence in Vienna was underlined when Schuschnigg, the Austrian Chancellor, went to Berlin in February 1938 in an attempt to negotiate an agreement with Hitler without consulting Mussolini. Hitler presented Schuschnigg with a ten-point ultimatum that would have reduced Austria to satellite status. In the ensuing crisis, triggered by Schuschnigg's attempt to reject the ultimatum, (see p. 238) Mussolini was powerless to support him, and, on hearing from Hitler's special messenger, the Prince of Hess, on 12 March that German troops were about to invade Austria, Mussolini had little option but to consent. Years later one of Mussolini's officials argued that in March 1938 Italy lost its independence to Germany and that consequently the existence of 'real' independent Fascism came to an end at that date.[64]

In the summer of 1938, when the crisis with Czechoslovakia was growing, Mussolini rashly stated that he would enter any

Anti-Comintern Pact
Aimed at countering the subversive influence of the Comintern, which was theoretically an international Communist body independent of the Soviet government, rather than being an alliance against the USSR (see p. 74).

conflict 'at once on the side of the Germans'. In reality Mussolini realized that Italy was not prepared for war and he readily responded to appeals from Chamberlain, the British Prime Minister, to mediate (see p. 240), and he managed to persuade Hitler to delay the occupation of the Sudetenland until 10 October. His triumph cast him in the role of a global statesman, who had saved the peace of the world, and he was praised in Italy as 'the Saviour of Europe'.

Throughout the winter of 1938–9 Hitler continued to press Mussolini to conclude a military alliance with Germany, but Mussolini remained unwilling to commit himself. Ciano advised him that Italy should continue to 'keep both doors open' and maintain close contacts with Britain and France. In January 1939 the British Foreign Secretary, Lord Halifax, and Neville Chamberlain visited Rome (see Figure 8.5), but the British had little to offer in the way of concessions, and Mussolini, as Chamberlain observed, 'remained throughout absolutely loyal to Hitler'.[65]

In February Mussolini bound Italy still more tightly to Germany, when he signed a new commercial treaty with Hitler, one of the clauses of which agreed to the dispatch of Italian migrant workers to Germany (see p. 220). Bosworth pertinently asks, 'could the Fascist regime, which typically sent the workers off with great fanfare, hereafter contemplate a U-turn on this matter, or indeed on any aspect of Axis policy'? [66] Bowing to this logic, Mussolini at last agreed to an Italian–German alliance and signed the Pact of Steel with Hitler on 22 May 1939. Optimistically Mussolini believed that he had gained two important advantages: an alliance with the most powerful state in Europe and a breathing space of several years before war broke out. Although the treaty committed Mussolini to assisting Germany in the event of war, Hitler had assured him that he had no intention of unleashing war for at least three years.

The occupation of Albania

On 7 April 1939 Italian troops invaded Albania with Hitler's blessing. Was this the fruit of Mussolini's ever closer relations with Germany? Paradoxically it can be argued that the occupation was in fact a defensive act aimed at blocking German expansion into the Balkans. The Nazi occupation of Prague on 15

March 1939 (see p. 241) had destroyed the Munich settlement, of which Mussolini had claimed to be the proud architect, and significantly strengthened Germany's position in South-Eastern Europe. The British and French were informed that 'the Italian action is designed to block German expansion in the Balkans'.[67] The message reassured neither power and led rapidly to the Anglo-French guarantees of Greece and Romania.

Italian neutrality, September 1939–June 1940

In August 1939, when Hitler was preparing for war against Poland, Mussolini was convinced both by Ciano and the obvious inadequacies of the Italian war machine that Italy could not honour its commitment to go to war. He informed Hitler that Italy could only fight if the Germans gave it the necessary equipment, but he took care to make the list so long that even the German war machine could not meet his requests. On 29 August Mussolini tried to repeat his success at Munich by proposing a four-power conference to meet on 5 September, but this was rejected by Hitler, who then proceeded to attack Poland on 1 September. Britain and France then declared war on Germany two days later, but Italy remained neutral.

What influenced Italian policy over the next nine months? Was it essentially structural reasons comparable to those in 1914 that determined first Italy's neutrality and then its coming into the war

Figure 8.5 Mussolini shows off his arms collection to Neville Chamberlain, the British Prime Minister
Source: Getty Images/ Time and Life Pictures

on the German side in June 1940, or did Mussolini finally align with Nazi Germany as a result of a common ideological fanaticism and passion for war? Mussolini had three options. He could:

- intervene, at the right moment, on the German – or even Allied – side
- remain neutral
- create a third force of neutral countries under Italian leadership.

In the course of the winter of 1939–40 Mussolini rejected overtures from Britain and France and dropped the idea of creating a neutral bloc composed of Spain and the Balkan states. Although Mussolini remained loyal to the German alliance, he remained unsure of how and when he should enter the war on Germany's side. In the end it was the string of German victories, starting with the occupation of Norway in April 1940 and ending with the fall of France in June, that at last convinced him to intervene on 10 June. He assumed that Britain would rapidly negotiate a peace with Hitler and he wanted above all to share in the great redistribution of territory and colonies that he would follow. Like his predecessors in 1915, he expected a short war, but unlike them he took Italy in on the side that was eventually to lose.

ASSESSMENT

De Felici argues that Fascism after the Abyssinian War, which was Mussolini's 'political masterpiece and greatest success', gained a 'special vitality',[68] and that the masses were at last being nationalized through the Fascist mass organizations. He stresses that there was no sign of any collapse in the support of Fascism by 1939 and that it was only the Second World War that led to its destruction.

Fascism may well not have been on the brink of collapse by 1939 but, despite the attempted cultural revolution, the regime was becoming increasingly ossified. Internal reports were describing party activity in the provinces as 'aimless' and there was increasing evidence of 'rampant corruption'.[69] The OND had certainly expanded greatly but was Fascist 'only in name'.[70] Working-class disillusionment with the party was widespread and led to increasing rivalry between the PNF and the Fascist unions, the syndicates. There was also a fundamental contradiction between 'the static acceptance of the regime fostered by the OND's politically insipid policies'[71] and the compromises that Fascism had to make with both the Church and the state, on the one side, and, on the other, the regime's dynamic and expansionist policies, which were both attempts to mobilize the population and use war as a means to further the Fascist revolution.

The regime, however, was not directly under threat. At one level it had 'disorganized' the workers and thus destroyed much of their potential for resistance. It had, too, through the syndicates and the OND swept away the old '**messianic**' **socialism** and 'changed the very terms in which workers conceived of their relations to the state and the prospects for any fundamental change within it'.[72] There was certainly discontent and grumbling, but nevertheless a broad acceptance of the Fascist welfare state.

Messianic socialism
An almost religious belief in a socialist revolution, which would create heaven on earth.

DOCUMENT 1
The difference between Nazism and Fascism

George Mosse, who came from a distinguished German–Jewish publishing family, and who fled Nazism to become an emigré in the USA, recalled the following incident in his memoirs:

If there really was a difference [between Fascism and Nazism] it was perhaps of national character. Let me tell you a story which perhaps better illustrates it than any great historical analysis. I remember in 1936 riding a train from Florence to Rome and every train had a *carabiniere* on it with a machine gun. The people in my compartment were telling anti-Mussolini jokes. The *carabiniere* of course walked up and down the train corridor and I, coming from a German ambiance, was terrified. But what happened in the end was that the *carabiniere* came into the compartment, not to arrest us but to tell other Mussolini jokes . . . Such an episode could never have happened in Germany.

Source: G. Mosse, *Nazism; A Historical and Comparative Analysis of National Socialism* New Brunswick, Transaction Books, 1978, pp. 104–5.

▶

DOCUMENT 2

Education

In February 1939 the Minister of Education Bottai announced a series of radical reforms in his Schools Charter. Its credo or basic message was:

To all, the effective possibility of enrolling in school and following a course of study, but to each one, the duty of fulfilling his scholastic obligation in the interests of the State, that is according to his truest aptitudes, committing all his faculties and his entire responsibility in such a way that the schools may be the reserve from which the State continually draws all the fresh energy it needs and not simply the agency in which thoughtless bourgeois vanity looks for seals and diplomas for its sterile ambitions.

Source: E.R. Tannenbaum, *Fascism in Italy*, Harmondsworth, Allen Lane, 1973, p. 188.

DOCUMENT 3

Teaching the imperial mission in schools

The following extract is an example of how the first anniversary of the conquest of Ethiopia was celebrated in schools throughout Italy:

One year has passed since 18 November 1935; we have shown the world that we are the strong ones, the just ones, the best ones. The fifty-two sanctionist nations denied us bread, iron, coal and cloth; we found it all anyway: bread from the fields of Italy. Iron from the houses of Italy. Gold from the women of Italy. White coal from the water of Italy. Black coal from the mines and forests of Italy. They wanted to humiliate us, but our victory and sacrifice has raised us above them.

Source: Tannebaum *Fascism in Italy*, p. 202.

DOCUMENT 4

Opposing views on the Fascist regime from within the Catholic Church

(a) The Jesuit, Father Messineo, was an enthusiastic supporter of Mussolini's Ethiopian policy, and gives this 'clerico-Fascist' view on the colonization of Ethiopia:

We may now legitimately conclude that a state, under the pressure of vital necessity because of the narrowness of its own territories and the deficiency of the means indispensable to individual and collective life, has the faculty of a appropriating a part of the earth possessed by others, in the measure required by its necessity. The power becomes even more evident if the material means necessary for freeing oneself from these straits lie inactive, in the possession of a people that does not use them, exploit them, and increase their value ... Vital necessity can legitimize the occupation of a part of colonial territory, in order to satisfy the needs of individual and social life.

Source: R.A. Webster, *The Cross and the Fasces*, Stanford, Stanford University Press, 1960, p. 123.

b) A manifesto of the Guelf Movement in Milan, 1931, directed to a meeting of Christian Democrats in the Vatican on the fortieth anniversary of the Rerum Novarum, the Papal encyclical summed up the social teaching of the Papacy on the social question:

The direct representatives of the Italian Catholic laborers are not among you. The political tyranny, notwithstanding all the good will of the Vatican, is holding far away from your sessions even those few that prison or exile have spared. Those few, with heartfelt passion, freely and boldly, want to tell you that you are not walking only among tombs; that the people is keeping its lamps lit; that the Italians are worthy of their past and of themselves. You will feel us among you in spirit, you will hear the beating of our hearts when you make of your breasts a crown for the Holy Father.

Source: Webster, *The Cross and the Fasces*, p. 149.

DOCUMENT 5
Church involvement in the *Balilla*

A Vatican assessment of the Church's prospects in the Ballila:

[The *Balilla*] is a mighty army, which in July of this year touched the numerical level of 4, 327,000 members ... It is an immense unbounded diocese with 1,425 priests and a bishop of its own. A magnificent field of modern apostolate, which can put the priests in contact with vast zones of souls, ordinarily unapproachable. Let us not forget the specific mark of this movement, as it concerns us; all of its members are obliged to attend religious instruction.

Source: Webster, *The Cross and the Fasces*, p 153

DOCUMENT 6

A Marxist interpretation of Fascism as a modernizing force

In 1972 the Hungarian Marxist, Mihaly Vajda, argued that Fascism was effectively the only solution after World War I to modernizing Italy economically:

The alliance with Mussolini, on the other hand, meant that the haute bourgeoise renounced political power, but would become able to vigorously increase its economic power: a path to capital accumulation ... Under Fascist rule, Italy underwent rapid capitalist development with electrification of the whole country, the blossoming of automobile and silk industries, the creation of an up to date bank system, the prospering of agriculture, the reclaiming of substantial agricultural areas through the draining of marshlands, the construction of a considerable network of highways, etc. Italy's rapid progress after World War II and the fact that today it is clearly moving towards intensive capitalist development would have been unimaginable without the social process begun during the Fascist period.

Source: M. Vajda, 'Crisis and the way out: the rise of Fascism in Italy and Germany', *Telos*, vol. 12, 1972, pp. 12 ff.

DOCUMENT 7

Mussolini on the burdens of office

In April 1932 Mussolini told an admirer:

One must accept solitude ... A chief cannot have equals. Nor friends. The humble solace gained from exchanging confidences is denied him. He cannot open his heart. Never.

Source: R.J.B. Bosworth, *Mussolini*, London, Arnold, 2002, p. 243.

DOCUMENT 8

Mussolini's defence of his racist policy

In a speech on 18 September 1938 Mussolini gave his support to the publication of the Manifesto of Racist Scientists, which had appeared the previous July, and also criticized Pope Pius XI's assertion that the regime was merely imitating Nazi Germany:

With respect to domestic affairs, the burning question of the moment is the racial problem ... Those who try to make out that we have simply imitated, or worse, that we have been obedient to suggestions, are poor fools whom we do not know whether to pity or despise. The racial problem has not broken out suddenly ... It is related to our conquest of our Empire; for history teaches that empires are won by arms but held by prestige, which is based not only on difference but on the most definite superiority. The Jewish problem is thus merely one aspect of this phenomenon ... In spite of our policy, world Jewry for the last sixteen years has been an irreconcilable enemy of fascism ... nevertheless, Jews possessing Italian citizenship who have attained indisputable military or civil merits ... will find understanding and justice. As for the others, a policy of segregation will be followed. In the end perhaps the world will be more astonished by our generosity than by our rigour.

Source: J. Whittam, *Fascist Italy*, Manchester, Manchester University Press, 1995, pp. 1163-4.

DOCUMENT 9

The desolation of southern Italy

The Italian writer, Carlo Levi, who was exiled for a year to two isolated villages in the province of Luciana, described his experiences in a bestseller, Christ Stopped at Eboli, *which was first published in 1945:*

Christ did stop at Eboli, where the road and the railway leave the Costa for Salerno and turn into the desolate reaches of Lucania. Christ never came this far, nor did time, nor the individual soul, nor hope, nor the relation of cause to effect, nor reason nor history. Christ never came, just as the Romans never came, content to garrison the highways without penetrating the mountains and forests, not the Greeks, who flourished beside the Gulf of Taranto. None of the pioneers of western civilization brought here his sense of the passage of time, his deification of the state or that ceaseless activity which feeds upon itself. None has come to this land except as an enemy, a conqueror, or a visitor devoid of understanding.

Source: Carlo Levi, *Christ Stopped at Eboli: The Story of a Year*, London, Penguin, 2000.

NOTES

1 R.J.B. Bosworth, *Mussolini*, London, Edward Arnold, 2002, p. 245.

2 E.R. Tannenbaum, *Facism in Italy*, Harmondsworth, Allen Lane, 1973, p. 74.

3 Quoted in D. Williamson, *Mussolini From Socialist to Fascist*, London, Edward Arnold, 1997, p. 39.

4 Quoted in R.J.B. Bosworth, *The Italian Dictatorship*, London, Edward Arnold, 1998, p. 128.

5 See J. Linz, *Totalitarian and Authoritarian Regimes*, Boulder, CO, Lynne Rienner, 2000.

6 Quoted in R. Ben-Ghiat, *Fascist Modernities. Italy 1922–1945*, Berkeley, University of California Press, 2001, p. 4.

7 Ibid., p. 4.

8 Emilio Gentile (translated by Keith Botsford), *The Sacrilization of Politics in Fascist Italy*, Cambridge, MA., Harvard University Press, 1996, p. 136.

9 Ibid., p. 136.

10 A. Lyttelton, *The Seizure of Power*, London, Weidenfeld & Nicolson, 2nd ed. 1987, p. 408.

11 Tannenbaum, *Fascism in Italy*, p. 184.

12 Ibid., p. 185.

13 Ibid., p. 150.

14 Quoted in D. Thompson, *State Control in Fascist Italy*, Manchester, Manchester University Press, 1991, p. 116.

15 Tobias Abse, 'Italian workers and Italian Fascism' in R. Bessel, *Fascist Italy and Nazi Germany*, Cambridge, Cambridge University Press, 1996, p. 45.

16 Quoted in ibid., p. 45.

17 V. De Grazia, *The Culture of Consent*, Cambridge, Cambridge University Press, 1981, p. 4.

18 Tannenbaum, *Fascism in Italy*, p. 125.

19 Ibid., p. 125.

20 Quoted in Williamson, *Mussolini*, p. 55.

21 Tannenbaum, *Fascism in Italy*, p. 247.

22 A.J. Gregor, *Italian Fascism and Developmental Dictatorship*, Princeton, Princeton University Press, 1979, p. 286.

23 V. de Grazia, *How Fascism Ruled Women, 1922–1945*, Berkeley, University of California Press, 1992, p. 158.

24 Tannenbaum, *Fascism in Italy*, p. 229.

25 Ibid., p. 225.

26 R.A. Webster, *The Cross and the Fasces*, Stanford, Stanford University Press, 1960, p. 112.

27 Ibid., p. 137.

28 D.A. Binchy *Church and State in Fascist Italy*, Oxford, Oxford University Press, 1970.

29 Bosworth, *Italian Dictatorship*, p. 145.

30 Webster, *The Cross* and J.E. Pollard, *The Vatican and Italian Fascism, 1929–32: A Study in Conflict*, Cambridge, Cambridge University Press, 1985.

31 Ben-Ghiat, *Fascist Modernities*, p. 123.

32 Ibid., p. 157.

33 J. Steinberg, *All or Nothing: The Axis and the Holocaust, 1941–43*, London, Routledge, 1990, p. 224.

34 Ben-Ghiat, *Fascist Modernities*, p. 149.

35 Ibid., p. 149.

36 Tannenbaum, *Fascism in Italy*, p. 111.

37 R. Sarti, *Fascism and the Industrial Leadership in Italy*, Berkeley, University of California Press, p. 119.

38 Ibid., p. 124.

39 Ibid., p. 107.

40 Tannenbaum, *Fascism in Italy*, p. 128.

41 Ibid., 247.

42 Gregor, *Italian Fascism*, p. 317.

43 Quoted in Bosworth, *Italian Dictatorship*, p. 84.

44 Quoted in Bosworth, *Mussolini*, p. 295.

45 Bosworth, *Italian Dictatorship*, p. 100.

46 Quoted in ibid., p. 85.

47 Ibid., p. 101.

48 Ibid., p. 95.

49 Bosworth, *Mussolini*, p. 297.

50 See Robert Boyce, 'World War, World Depression: some economic origins of the Second World War' in R. Boyce and E. Robertson eds, *Paths to War*, London, Macmillan, 1989 p. 84, and E. Santarelli, 'The economic and political background of Fascist imperialism' in R. Sarti, ed., *The Ax Within: Italian Fascism in Action*, New York, Modern Viewpoints, 1974, pp. 167–8.

51 M. Knox, 'Fascism: ideology, foreign policy and war' in A. Lyttelton, ed., *Liberal Italy and Fascist Italy*, Oxford, Oxford University Press, 2002, p. 138.

52 Quoted in Williamson, *Mussolini*, p. 84.

53 C.J. Lowe and F. Mazari, *Italian Foreign Policy, 1870–1940*, London, Routledge, 1975, p. 254.

54 Ibid., p. 264.

55 Bosworth, *Mussolini*, pp. 305–6.

56 Quoted in Williamson, *Mussolini*, p. 84.

57 Bosworth, *Mussolini*, p. 320.

58 Ibid., p. 315.

59 S.C. Azzi, 'The historiography of Fascist foreign policy', *Historial Journal*, vol. 36, 1993, p. 201.

60 M. Knox quoted in Bosworth, *Mussolini*, p. 327.

61 Quoted in Williamson, *Mussolini*, p. 389.

62 Bosworth, *Mussolini*, p. 328.

63 Quoted in Williamson, *Mussolini*, p. 89.

64 Quoted in Bosworth, *Mussolini*, p. 331.

65 Quoted in ibid., p. 350.

66 Ibid., p. 351.

67 Quoted in Lowe and Mazari, *Italian Foreign Policy*, p. 328.

68 Quoted in Bosworth, *Italian Dictatorship*, pp. 121–2.

69 De Grazia, *The Culture of Consent*, p. 225.

70 Ibid., p. 229.

71 Ibid., p. 226.

72 Ibid., p. 229.

The Spanish Civil War and the beginning of the Franco regime

TIMELINE

1931	14 April	Proclamation of Second Republic
	June	Elections to the Constituent *Cortes*
	October	Zamora resigns and Azaña becomes Prime Minister
1932	August	General Sanjurjo's attempted coup
1933	January	CNT calls for general strike
		Cassas Viejas incident
	February	CEDA founded
	November	Centre Right wins general election
	December	CNT uprising – four days of fighting in Zaragoza
1934	September	CEDA demands seats in the cabinet; in response UGT call general strike
	October	Asturian uprising
1936	16 February	Popular Front wins the election
	April	Stabilization attempt by Azaña and Prieto fails
		Quiroga becomes Prime Minister
	17–18 July	Beginning of military insurrection and civil war
	30 July	Mussolini sends bombers to assist Nationalists in Morocco
	14 August	Badajoz falls to Army of Africa
	4 September	Popular Front government set up under Largo Caballero
	5 September	Irun falls to Nationalists
	9 September	Non-intervention committee meets in London
	29 September	Franco becomes head of Nationalist Spain

	7–23 November	Battle for Madrid
	18 November	Germany and Italy recognize the Nationalist government
	22 December	Italian troops arrive in Spain
1937	7 February	Malaga taken by Nationalists and Italians
	19 April	*Falange* and Carlists united into a single party under Franco
	26 April	Guernica bombed
	3–8 May	May Days in Barcelona
	17 May	Negrín becomes Prime Minister of Republican Spain
	16 June	POUM dissolved
	19 June	Bilbao falls to Nationalists
	October	War in the north ends with Nationalist victory
1938	30 January	*Junta Técnica del Estado* becomes the government of Nationalist-dominated Spain
	14 April	Nationalist army reaches the Mediterranean
	24 July	Ebro offensive
	September	International Brigades withdrawn from Spain
1939	26 January	Barcelona falls to the Nationalists
	9 February	Law of Political Responsibilities
	27 February	France and Britain recognize Franco government
	27 March	Fall of Madrid
	1 April	Franco announces victory

INTRODUCTION

The Spanish Civil War was seen by many foreigners as a straight clash between international Fascism and the forces of the left – a dress rehearsal, perhaps, for the coming world war. The involvement of German and Italian forces on the Nationalist side and Soviet advisers on the Republican side lent credence to this interpretation. It was, of course, a struggle influenced by contemporary events, yet General Franco, the Nationalist leader, was not a Spanish Mussolini. He did not come to power with the help of a mass Fascist party. On the contrary, his power rested on support from the Church and, above all, on the army. He was in many ways a traditional Spanish Conservative. Like the papacy itself, he was sympathetic to much of the ideology of Fascism, such as corporatism, and his political techniques and propaganda were influenced by it. He cultivated the role of charismatic leader and created a 'movement' or party to indoctrinate the country with the ideals of the regime.

On the Republican side the initial outburst of revolutionary enthusiasm for land seizures and control of the factories by the workers echoed the chaotic early period of the Russian Revolution. As the struggle dragged on, there were also parallels with the Russian Civil War in that the discipline and centralization necessary to wage a successful struggle meant that the initial revolutionary excesses of the Republic's most enthusiastic supporters needed to be curbed. However, the tactics of the Spanish Communist Party, increasingly dictated from Moscow, markedly differed from those used by Lenin in the Russian Civil War (see pp. 44–60). Rather than seeking an immediate dictatorship, the Spanish Communist Party sought to support the centre–left coalition as the best way of maximizing support against Franco.

THE KEY ISSUES IN THIS CHAPTER ARE:

- The failure of the Republican Socialist coalition, 1931–3, to establish a consensus.
- The revival of the Right, and the *bienio negro*, or the two black years, of 1933–5.
- The electoral victory of the Popular Front and its failure to create a strong government.
- The military coup of 18 July 1936 and the course of the civil war up to March 1939.
- The impact of foreign intervention.
- The extent to which there was a social and economic revolution in Republican Spain.
- Politics and organization of the war on the Republican side and the key role of the Spanish Communist Party.
- The domination by Franco of the nationalists and the creation of the Franco government.
- The politics of the French government and ideological similarities with Fascism.

THE SECOND REPUBLIC

The Republican Socialist coalition, 1931–3

The fall of General Miguel Primo de Rivera's dictatorship (see p. 134) in January 1930 and the subsequent collapse of the monarchy appeared to defy the trends elsewhere in Europe towards authoritarian and Fascist regimes. A provisional government consisting of representatives of the moderate Socialist Party, the PSOE, and the Republican Liberal parties was formed in April 1931, and two months later elections were held for the **constituent** *Cortes*. The elections resulted in an impressive victory for the Socialists and Republican Left. Out of the 457 deputies elected, the Left won 251 seats, while the Liberals 155 and the Conservatives only 41. These election results were greeted with enormous enthusiasm by the workers, peasants and middle-class Republicans, but once this great 'popular fiesta' ended, problems were to multiply 'by the score'.[1]

Essentially, given the widespread expectations of its supporters, the regime had little option but to embark on social reforms, but these would in turn provoke social conflict. The economic, social and political problems facing the coalition were daunting:

- Spain, like the rest of Europe, was hit by the Depression. Industrial production had declined and unemployment had risen. Rural labourers were particularly badly hit and their suffering was increased by droughts and the failure of the olive harvests in 1931, which combined to create a poverty virtually unknown elsewhere in Western Europe, except perhaps in Sicily.

- There were also long-term structural problems, such as the unfair distribution of wealth and land, which generated bitter conflicts especially in the countryside, and the deeply rooted power of the Church and the army.

- Politically, the unity of the coalition was fragile. The Spanish Republican Left was divided into several different groups. The Socialists had only agreed with some reluctance to join the coalition, and once the initial honeymoon period was over, they faced fierce opposition from their own members and, further to the left, the Communists and the

Constituent *Cortes*
A parliament elected to draw up a constitution.

Anarcho-Syndicalist trade union, the CNT (*Confederacion Nacional del Trabajo*).

- Although the Right was temporarily disorganized and lacked any effective political party, the opposition of the Church, the army and the great landowners was implacably opposed to any root-and-branch reforms, which would destroy their influence.

The government aimed ambitiously to create a new Spain by destroying the influence of the Church and army, granting greater autonomy to the **Catalans** and the **Basques** and by breaking up the great estates. Its reforms, however, failed to win the support of the mass of the rural and urban workers, while alienating powerful conservative forces. Its constitution, which defined Spain as 'a republic of workers of all classes', appeared to guarantee a sweeping social revolution. It contained clauses for devolving power to the regions, while also baldly stating in Article 44 that the wealth of the country was subordinate to national needs and that property could be expropriated without compensation if necessary. In Article 26 it also ended the privileged position of the Church and prohibited church schools and charities. These measures, which were largely the work of the Prime Minister, the left Republican leader, **Manuel Azaña**, infuriated the Right and led to an increasing political polarization. They alienated above all the moderate conservatives in the Catholic middle classes, whose support the Republic needed if it were to unite the divisions in Spain.

This would not have been so politically damaging if the government had been able to hang on to the support of the Left. In reality, however, it quickly showed that it was more interested in reforming institutions than in introducing Socialism. If it was to keep the Socialists in the government and weaken the CNT, it had to alleviate the conditions of the peasantry, particularly the landless labourers. While measures were passed enforcing an eight-hour day and protecting tenants from expulsion by their landlords, the government was slow to grapple with agrarian reform, as it would involve handing a third of the cultivated land in Spain to the peasantry.

It was only as a reaction to the failed **monarchist-military revolt** in August 1932 that the government decided to press on

Anarcho-syndicalism
The belief that the state should be replaced by the trade unions and other collective organizations that would negotiate directly with each other and exchange all the necessary goods and services to meet the needs of the population.

Catalans and Basques
The population of Basque Country and Catalonia, where there were strong separatist traditions.

Manuel Azaña (1880–1940)
Prime minister 1931–3 and again briefly in 1936. From 1936 to 1939 he was President of the Republic.

Monarchist-military revolt
In August 1932 General Sanjurjo led an abortive coup in Seville, which was defeated by a general strike.

with the reform. However, when the bill at last became law, it was a compromise that pleased neither the Right nor the Left. Only limited funds were provided for compensation, and the great majority of landholders, who were liable to have their land confiscated, were the small and medium-sized holders in the north and the centre of Spain. Even when the bill was passed, the government did not hurry to carry it out and seemed more interested in reforming the army, anti-clerical legislation and in balancing the budget.

Consequently on the left the anger with the government grew. In January 1933 the CNT called for a nationwide strike. This was swiftly defeated by the Civil Guards and troops, but one incident in the village of Cassas Viejas, in the province of Cadiz, where 24 impoverished workers were killed while attempting to form an Anarchist commune, created martyrs, and made the rank-and-file Socialists increasingly critical of the participation of their party in the coalition. The Anarchists intensified their terrorist activities and a wave of strikes, bomb attacks and assassinations spread throughout Spain. Paul Preston argues that the incident 'heralded the death of the coalition symbolizing as it did the government's failure to resolve the agrarian problem'.[2] Not only did the incident alienate the workers and peasants but it also provided ammunition for the Right to smear the Republic as 'corrupt, incapable of preserving public order, yet violent'.[3]

In the summer of 1933 the coalition government began to fall apart. The Radicals, the largest middle-class party on the left, demanded that the Socialists should either resign or control the anti-government activities of the Socialist trade union, the UGT. By the autumn the Socialists had withdrawn from the coalition and new elections were called in November.

The revival of the Right

Through lack of organization the Right had done badly in the elections of 1931, but the coalition's policies and the mounting unrest in the country had revived its fortunes. Like the Left, the rightist opposition was composed of several different groups:

- Anger at the anti-clerical measures taken against the Catholic Church led to the emergence of a mass Catholic political party, the *Confederación Española de Derechas Autónomas*, or CEDA, which was led by **Gil Robles**. It was ready to work within the constitution to reverse the policies of the government (see Document 3).

- To the right of CEDA was *Acción Española*, whose political leader was **José Calvo Sotelo**. Although the movement took its name from a radical right-wing journal, it was really modelled on the *Action française* (see p. 11). In 1934 Calvo founded a broader movement of the Radical Right, the *Bloque National*. At times, he called himself a Fascist and believed in some aspects of the corporate state, but essentially he was a monarchist and traditionalist, whose ideas were to be a considerable source of influence on Franco's Spain.

- Ever since the nineteenth century the traditional radical right-wing monarchist movement in Spain was Carlism. In reaction to the policies of the Republican government Carlism was reorganized by the lawyer, Manuel Fal Conde. Like *Acción Española* it was corporatist (see p. 109) and inevitably in the climate of the times it, too, acquired a Fascist colouring. Yet it was also traditionalist, ultra-Catholic and monarchist – and so comparable with Fascism or Nazism.

- The first Fascist party in Spain, *Juntas de Ofensiva Nacional-Sindicalista* or JONS, was founded by the intellectual Ramiro Ledesma Ramos. In early 1934 it merged with the Spanish Phalanx or *Falange*, which was founded in October 1933 by **José Antonio Primo de Rivera**, the oldest son of the former dictator. The *Falange* had much in common with Italian Fascism. Its official programme, the Twenty-Seven Points, exhibited all the main points of Fascist doctrine; it drew on syndicalism and corporatism and believed that Spaniards could only be united through 'the eternal metaphysic of Spain'[4] or, in more prosaic language, through Spanish nationalism.

Bitter enemies of the Republic were also to be found in the Church and the army. The Church was alienated by the Republic's anti-Catholicism, while the special position of the army within Spanish society was also threatened by Azaña's cuts in the officer corps, and the removal of many of its privileges.

Gil Robles (1901-80)
Appointed Minister of War in 1935, but was criticized by the right for not using the army to crush worker unrest. Although he supported the military uprising in 1936, he was distrusted by Franco and had to flee into exile.

José Calvo Sotelo (1893–1936)
Served in Primo de Rivera's government, was exiled in 1931, but was pardoned and returned to Spain in 1934. By 1936 he was the most significant right-wing opposition figure in Spain. His murder on 13 July 1936 triggered the military revolt.

José Antonio Primo de Rivera (1903–36)
Elected to the *Cortes* in 1933. The street violence of the *Falange* led to his arrest in 1936, and he was executed in November. He was later turned into a martyr by Franco.

The *bienio negro* or 'two black years'

The elections of November 1933 were a disaster for the Left, which was deeply divided. The Socialists refused to fight on a joint platform with the Left Republicans, while the Syndicalists in protest abstained from voting. The Right on the other hand was united and formed, as it proclaimed, an 'anti-Marxist counter-revolutionary front'. Not surprisingly it won 212 seats, while the Left won 98 and the Radicals 102.

Distrusting CEDA's close links with the Church, the President initially entrusted **Alejandro Lerroux** of the Radical Republican Party to form a minority government. Lerroux hoped eventually to form a coalition with CEDA, on whose votes in the *Cortes* he was dependent. The Left viewed Lerroux as a mere puppet of the CEDA. Within weeks the CNT launched an uprising in the Anarchist strongholds of Aragon, Rioja and Catalonia. It was easily crushed, but the harshness of the government's counter-offensive awoke a bitter hatred and desire for revenge. The extreme Right, contemptuous of the moderate Lerroux government, worked on plans for a violent takeover of power. In northern Spain Carlists began to form a paramilitary force, and funds from Mussolini enabled them to carry out manoeuvres in Libya. In December 1934 the Radical Right was strengthened when Calvo Sotelo created the *Bloque Nacional*. The growing polarization of Europe between Fascism and communism further fuelled political tensions in Spain. As Preston has written, 'The left saw fascism in every action of the right; the right smelt revolution in every left-wing move.'[5]

In September 1934 a major crisis was triggered when Lerroux gave CEDA three ministries in the cabinet. The Socialists, hoping to persuade the President to call an election, retaliated by calling a general strike, while Catalonia declared itself an independent state 'within the Federal Republic of Spain'. Order was quickly restored in Barcelona, but it was a different story in the mining area of the Asturias, which was controlled for two weeks by the local workers' committees of the Socialists' Republic and the 'Red Army militia'. The uprising in the Asturias was in many ways a dress rehearsal for the Civil War. It was defeated with great brutality by Spanish Moroccan troops at the cost of some 4,000 casualties.

Alejandro Lerroux (1864–1949)
First elected to the *Cortes* in 1901 and led several governments between 1933 and 1935. He supported Franco in the Civil War, but was forced into exile until 1947.

The slide to civil war, February–May 1936

From October 1935 to February 1936 Spain continued to be governed by a series of short-lived Radical–CEDA coalition ministries. At the end of 1935 Lerroux was forced to resign as a result of financial scandals. Since the President still mistrusted the ultimate ambitions of Robles and refused to appoint him Prime Minister, no ministry could be formed and elections were held on 16 February 1936.

The Left, learning from its defeat, fought the election as a united bloc. Azaña had managed to reunite the shattered Republican Party and the Socialists, Communists and Anarchists all responded to the call for working-class unity. The Right, on the other hand, was divided. Calvo Sotelo was bitterly critical of the failure of Robles' decision to join the coalition, while the Centre Right had disintegrated. The Popular Front gained a conclusive victory by winning 271 seats as compared to 137 by the Right. Yet the Spanish voting system obscured the underlying strength of the Right. Spain in reality remained fairly equally divided between the two blocs and the Right still dominated Leon, Castile and Navarre (see Map 3), which were to be the heartlands of Nationalist Spain in the Civil War.

The initial reaction of the Right was to refuse to accept the election results. The industrialists and the great landowners adopted an aggressive attitude towards their workers, while the working class retaliated by strikes, demonstrations and arson attacks, and were determined to exact vengeance for the wage cuts and repression during the *bienio negro*. The *Falange* also began to grow, as disaffected young Catholics deserted CEDA (see Document 4).

To avoid civil war, Spain desperately needed a firm government, but the alliance that had won the election did not stand firm behind the new government: the Socialists refused to join the coalition. Consequently, until the revolt in July 1936, Spain was ruled by a minority Republican government first under Azaña and then under Casares Quiroga.

The military coup of 18 July 1936

On the extreme right numerous plots to overthrow the government had been planned, but without military backing none of

**Emilio Mola
(1887–1937)**
Served in Morocco and
was the key planner of the
military uprising in 1936.
He commanded the Army
of the North but was killed
in a plane crash in 1937.

**José Sanjurjo
(1887–1937)**
Made his reputation in
Morocco. He organized
the unsuccessful military
coup in 1932 and was
sentenced to death, but
he was given an amnesty
and exiled to Portugal. He
died while attempting to
return to Spain.

them had any chance of success. The army was united in its desire
to get rid of the Republic, but there was no consensus on what
sort of regime should replace it. Some of the junior officers were
beginning to draw near to the *Falange*. The most influential generals, Manuel Goded, Francisco Franco and **Emilio Mola**, wanted
above all a regime of order, whether it was Republican or monarchist, and in the early spring of 1936 they began to draw up plans
for a military takeover. In each provincial capital the military
commander was to declare martial law and takeover power. The
coup would be backed by the army in Morocco. The future head
of state was to be **General Sanjurjo**, while Mola would play a key
role in organizing the new regime. Franco would have responsibility only for Morocco. The plans were backed both by José
Antonio Primo de Rivera and by Calvo Sotelo.

It was, however, the murder of Calvo Sotelo on 13 July 1936
by Republican Assault Guards in response to the murder of one
of their officers by the extreme right-wing *Unión Militar
Española* that finally prompted the army to revolt. The murder
reinforced the generals' message that Spain needed the army to
intervene to restore order, and even won over Franco, who was
still undecided about joining the revolt. On 18 July the African
army under Franco's command was firmly in control of Morocco
and the revolt had spread to the garrison towns of Spain by the
afternoon of the following day.

Francisco Franco (1892–1975)

Franco (see Figure 9.1) wished
originally to follow the family
tradition of joining the navy,
but as a result of cutbacks in the
fleet he joined the army in 1907.
In June 1910 he was sent to
Morocco, where he rapidly
earned a reputation of being a
brave and resourceful officer,
and in 1920 was appointed
second in command of the
Spanish foreign legion. Franco
fully shared the assumption of
his fellow officers that victory

Figure 2.1 Franco
Source: Corbis/Bettmann

could only be achieved through the most brutal terrorizing of the civilian population. In 1928 he was appointed director of the Spanish General Military Academy, but when it was closed down he was demoted to command an infantry brigade. Only with the victory of the Right in 1933 did his career begin to prosper again, and he was offered the post of War Minister, which he turned down. He played a key role in the defeat of the Asturia uprising (see p. 306), using Moroccan troops and practising the terror tactics regularly used in colonial wars. For this service he was appointed to the position of the Chief of General Staff, but in February 1936 the new National Front government transferred him to the post of Commanding Officer of the Canary Islands. Over the next few months his attitude was ambiguous. He remained in touch with the military conspirators against the Republican regime, but as late as 23 June he wrote 'an extraordinary letter'[6] to the Prime Minister warning him that he had alienated the army but that it was not too late to undo some of the damage. It is possible, as several historians argue, that he was in fact offering himself as War Minister to the Republican government. Only with the murder of Calvo Sotelo on 13 July 1936 did Franco finally commit himself to the uprising.

What sort of man was Franco? He remains, as Paul Preston has observed, 'the least known of the great dictators of the twentieth century'.[7] This is partly because during his long period in power a 'smoke screen was created by his hagiographers and propagandists',[8] who compared him to the great heroes of Spanish history. Franco contributed to this by regularly rewriting his own life story. On the left the opposite view is, of course, taken. Franco is seen as an evil but unintelligent dictator who gained power with the help of Hitler and Mussolini, and then, after 1945, was tolerated only as a result of the Cold War. His most authoritative but highly critical biographer, Paul Preston, concedes that this 'view is nearer the truth than the wild panegyrics of the Falangist press, but it explains equally little. Franco may not have been **El Cid**, but neither was he so untalented nor so lucky as his enemies suggest'.[9] In many ways Franco still remains an enigma (see Document 5).

El Cid
A Castilian knight and a Spanish national hero, who fought against the Moorish occupation in the eleventh century.

THE CIVIL WAR

The outline of events

The rebels had hoped that they would seize power through a sudden coup, but initially, except in Morocco, they encountered strong opposition in the main cities and industrial areas and some two-thirds of the population were hostile to them. The prospects of the rebels, however, were decisively helped by the decision of Hitler and Mussolini to provide ships and planes to transport loyal troops from Spanish Morocco.

By early August 1936 the bulk of the Moroccan army had been landed in Spain and was able to seize the Republican-held town of Badajoz. The road to Madrid now lay open and, if Franco had acted quickly, he could have brought the Civil War to an early conclusion. Instead he delayed for six valuable weeks besieging the Republican fortress of Alcazar in Toledo (see Map 3). This delay enabled the Spanish Communist Party, in the absence of the Republican government (which had fled to Barcelona) to strengthen the city's defences. Its task was made easier by the supply of Soviet planes and tanks and the arrival of the first international volunteers – the International Brigades. By 22 November the Nationalists were compelled to retreat. Franco then attempted to cut off Madrid from its Republican hinterland, but this too failed when a Nationalist force, reinforced by Italian troops, was heavily defeated at Guadaljara in March 1937.

Figure 9.2 A group of Republican soldiers talk to journalists during the Spanish Civil War, including the American novelist Ernest Hemingway (seen with his back to the camera), who served as a war correspondant.
Source: Corbis/Hulton-Deutsch Archive

The International Brigades

In the first week of the Spanish Civil War a small number of foreign anarchists joined the CNT militia, but the decision to recruit an international volunteer force for the Republican side was taken by the Comintern in Prague on 26 July 1936.

Figure 9.3 Members of the International Brigades
Source: Getty Images/Roger Viollet

Volunteers, who were mainly recruited by the Communist Party, came from all over the world, although the largest single contingent was French. Their mission was to fight what they thought was Fascism. Initially the International Brigades (see Figure 9.3) were not fully integrated into the People's Republican Army. They had their own training schools and general staff. At their height, the International Brigades numbered about 35,000.

Apart from the Moroccan battalions, the German special units and the Italian corps, there were also foreign volunteers serving with the Nationalists. The French Jeanne d'Arc Battalion, for instance, was full of French right-wing volunteers, while 700 Irish Blue Shirts under the Fascist General Eoin O'Duffy joined to fight what amounted to a religious crusade against the Republic.

By the spring of 1937 the future patterns of the war had been set. Spain was effectively cut into two zones (see Map 3). Both sides were being supplied by foreign powers – the Nationalists by Germany and Italy, largely through Portugal, and the Republicans by Soviet Russia. When the French, in an attempt to limit the conflict, closed their frontiers with Spain, the Republic could only be supplied by sea.

Franco took a key decision when he launched a major offensive in northern Spain and occupied the important industrial areas. He was greatly helped by the Salazar regime in Portugal, which opened up the Portuguese frontier and so allowed him to receive the necessary ammunition and equipment for his operations. In the spring of 1937 this, together with German air power, enabled Franco to launch another offensive in the north. For the first time large-scale air raids were launched by the German Condor Legion against the cities of Durango and Guernica, which were razed to the ground. Bilbao fell on 19 June and two months later the Italians took Santander. In October the vital mining region of the Asturias was overrun and occupied, which gave the Nationalists control of north-west Spain and blocked Republican access to the Atlantic ports. The Republicans were now limited to eastern Spain and dependent on supplies from the Mediterranean, which was vulnerable to pressure from the increasingly effective Nationalist navy, assisted by Italian air and naval power. By the end of 1937 the Republic had lost 36 per cent of its industrial production, 60 per cent of its coal output and most of its steel production.

Guernica

As a result of incendiary bombs in April 1937 some 70 per cent of the town of Guernica was destroyed and several hundred of its population were killed. The bombing led to a very effective propaganda campaign by the Republicans, which was aimed at a global audience. Picasso's famous painting, *Guernica*, 'contributed more than any factor in making the incident world famous'.[10] Up to a point the city was a fair military target as it contained military barracks, a communications centre and some small-arms factories. However, Franco played into the hands of the Republicans by totally denying responsibility for the bombing and alleging that the burning of the city was a result of arson by the Left.

The Nationalists broke through to the Mediterranean in April 1938, but Franco again missed a chance of an easy victory. Instead of moving against Barcelona, which was defenceless, he attempted unsuccessfully to take Valencia. With the help of Soviet weapons, and even a temporary flow of supplies from France, Republican forces in Catalonia managed for a short time to recover, and in July 1938 they launched an attack aimed at breaking the Nationalist blockade of Catalonia. After impressive initial successes the struggle became a battle of attrition, which the superior Nationalist military machine inevitably won. Catalonia was occupied and Barcelona itself fell on 26 January 1939.

The Civil War was now virtually won by the Nationalists, but Negrín, the Republican Prime Minister, attempted to fight on in the hope that the outbreak of a general war in Europe would bring the Republicans some allies, while Franco was determined on unconditional surrender. This came only when Madrid surrendered on 27 March 1939.

Historians and the coming of the Civil War

As Stanley Payne has observed, 'the political history of the Second Spanish Republic is one of the most controversial and mythified [sic] in twentieth century Europe'.[11] During the Franco dictatorship a bitter propaganda war was waged between the Madrid regime, on the one side, and Spanish Republican exiles and Western European and American historians, on the other. The Franco regime attempted to present the Civil War as a crusade against the godless and Marxist workers.

Because of the strict censorship in Franco's Spain, the first analytical studies of the war and its causes were written abroad. The initial assumption was that the war had been a straight clash between Fascism and communism, but as early as 1943 Gerald Brennan's *Spanish Labrynth* argued that the Spanish Civil War was a consequence of Spanish history and largely a result of the tensions in the countryside caused by the abject poverty of the landless peasants and the refusal of the great landowners to agree to agrarian reform.[12] Then Raymond Carr in two major studies *The Spanish Tragedy* and *Spain 1808–1939* argued that the roots of the Civil war lay in the failure of the Liberals to force the landed elite to accept political and economic reforms that would modernize the country. [13] Hugh Thomas's book, *The Spanish Civil War*, which was first published in 1961, was also very influential. It is a well-written and objective study of the war, particularly in its international context, and it rapidly became 'the bible of the Spanish left'[14] as thousands of copies were smuggled into Spain.

With Franco's death in 1975 and the emergence of a democratic Spain, the Spanish archives gradually became accessible to scholars. Since the early 1980s an increasing number of detailed studies by historians like Martin Blinkhorn, Shlomo Ben-Ami and above all by Paul Preston have illuminated the interactions between religious, regional and social confrontations and shown how the Spanish civil war was in fact composed of many separate wars.[15] Preston, with his massive biography of Franco, his book, *The Coming of The Spanish Civil War* and

numerous articles on the agrarian question, dominates Civil War
studies in Britain. He is fiercely critical of the great landowners
and the industrialists, whom he argues 'wanted the Republic
destroyed because its moderate reform could not be carried out
without some redistribution of wealth'.[16] His trenchant arguments
do, however, need to be balanced by the views put forward by
more conservative historians. Stanley Payne, for instance, in *The
Spanish Revolution*, firmly attributes the blame for the outbreak
of the war to the intransigence of the Left, while Richard
Robinson's *The Origin's of Franco's Spain* rehabilitates Gil Robles
and CEDA and argues that CEDA was essentially a moderate
Christian Democratic Party, which only moved to the extreme
right in response to activities of the extreme left.[17]

The Great Powers and Spain, 1936–9

Essentially the Great Powers determined the course of the conflict. The Republicans were gravely weakened by the
non-intervention policy pursued by Britain and France, which
ensured that both sides were treated equally and that the legal
government was denied the right to buy armaments and weapons
from the Western democracies. This initially deprived the
Republican government of weapons, which would have helped it
not only to restore order internally within its own zone, but also
to strike more effectively against the rebels. Britain and France
were determined to isolate the Spanish conflict and seek to stop it
from escalating into a European conflict.

The only power to assist the Republicans was the USSR. In
September 1936 it began to deliver cargoes of foodstuffs, and
then, during the autumn and winter it followed this up with the
delivery of military equipment, arms and ammunition. The
Comintern also trained and organized the International Brigades
of volunteers, who played a key role in the defence of Madrid.
Support from the USSR, however, came at a price. The Spanish
Communist Party (PCE) was taken over by Soviet officials and
waged a civil war within a civil war with the POUM, the revolutionary Marxist party with its base in Catalonia, whose leaders
were judged to be Trotskyites (see pp. 67–8). (see Document
8(a)).

For the Nationalists, foreign help was also crucial. The Germans and Italians helped airlift the Army of Africa from Morocco to the mainland, establish Nationalist control over the Mediterranean and sink the Republican fleet. The Germans also sent the Condor Legion, which was composed of 5,000 troops, backed up by air force and specialist units, while the Italians committed a larger force of 70,000 soldiers.

THE REPUBLIC AND THE CIVIL WAR, 1936–9

The social and economic revolution

When the Republican government failed to negotiate a compromise with the rebels, it took the fateful step of arming the people, which effectively ensured that it armed its most bitter critics. The authority of the Madrid government was ignored, and in each region of the Republican-controlled areas power was initially wielded by committees of CNT or POUM militants. Even though the national leadership of the CNT urged moderation and cooperation with the Popular Front parties, local militants rushed to exploit the power vacuum and to realize the revolution. Within a few days, for example, the Barcelona Committee of Anti-Fascist Militias took control of the city. Large and small enterprises, public transport and even cinemas and greyhound tracks were taken over and run by the workers. In cities that were controlled by Anarcho-Syndicalists, dress fashions and speech were proletarianized. Ties and hats, for instance were banned and restaurants were turned into canteens run by the unions.

In the countryside left-wing militants also formed committees to administer the local towns and villages and forcibly set up collective farms. In Aragon, for instance, three-quarters of the land was collectivized. Frequently, as in Soviet Russia in 1929–30 (see pp. 333–7), collectivization was forced on the small landowning peasantry by armed columns of urban workers. By mid-1938 confiscations of land amounted to slightly more than one-third of the arable land in the Republican zone.

The military revolt and the fear that it would be successful 'opened a valve of destructive fury among the revolutionary groups, which surprised and horrified some of the latter's own leaders'.[18] Armed squads formed by the revolutionary parties

REDCAR & CLEVELAND COLLEGE LIBRARY

roamed the countryside, both settling old scores and murdering anybody associated with Conservative or right-wing organizations, such as landowners, Falangists, army officers and policemen. Many church buildings were destroyed and nearly 7,000 priests, monks and nuns were murdered, which was, as Filipo Ribeiro de Meneses has observed, 'the worst massacre of Catholic clergy in history'.[19]

The restoration of discipline

Largo Caballero (1869–1946)
Labour minister, 1931–3; he headed the Popular Front government, September 1936–May 1937. He was exiled to France and later sent by the Nazis to Dachau.

This outburst of uncoordinated revolutionary activity seriously harmed the Republic's ability effectively to wage war. To survive, the Republic needed to gear itself for total war on both the military and home fronts. In late July 1936 the first steps were taken in setting up a Republican army when a voluntary force was formed. It was, however, not until the formation of the **Cabellero** government in September 1936 that the authority of the state and its capacity to wage war began to revive. This government, which contained Liberals, Socialists and Communists, and was even unofficially backed by the CNT, was a conscious resurrection of the Popular Front (see p. 307), as it was hoped that it would rally all the Republican elements against the Nationalists. Over the next six months the foundations of the Republican war effort were laid:

- On 11 September 1936 Largo Caballero appointed an overall military Commander-in-Chief and a General Staff. Gradually, too, the militia was brought under control and placed under a single command and conscription was introduced.

Juan Negrín (1889–1956)
Socialist and Professor of Physiology at the University of Madrid. He was finance minister, September 1936–May 1937, and then Prime Minister until the defeat of the Republic.

- The finance minister, Professor **Juan Negrín**, created the necessary legal and operational infrastructure for the Republican war economy. The Bank of Spain's gold reserves were first transported to the Republican naval base at Cartegena and then handed over to Moscow to pay for military equipment.
- To strengthen the central government, pressure was brought to bear on the CNT to join the government in November 1936 and share in the responsibility for reining in the revolution.
- Efforts were also made to control collectivized agriculture and industry, and eventually the Catalan war industries were put under the control of the War Ministry.

The role of the Communists

The Spanish Communist Party (PCE) rapidly emerged as the dominant force in Republican Spain. Its leadership had grasped that Spain faced a long exhausting civil war and that only a strong central government could organize an effective war effort. To achieve this, it needed to secure the widest possible alliances with the Spanish middle-class parties, as well as with the Western bourgeois democracies, Britain and France. Thus it was crucial that the wild libertarianism of the anarchists should be controlled, as it only frightened off the very forces that the Republic needed to conciliate. To the cries from POUM and the CNT that the Civil War could only be won in defence of a revolution that had already been carried out, the PCE argued that revolution could only be achieved once the Civil War had been won. In the fertile district of Valencia, for instance, the Communists used their influence to block any further collectivization, and actively encouraged the Provincial Peasants Federation to defend the landowning rights of their members. The Russian military experts, who began to arrive in October 1936 and worked with the PCE, also played a key role in training and building up the Republican People's Army (see Document 2).

The Communists had no wish for a formal takeover of the Republican government, but, as their influence within the Popular Army grew and under camouflage of the united front, they intensified their pressure on the regime to follow their policies and eliminate their political rivals on the left, the Anarcho-Syndicalists, POUM and Left-Socialists, who had rival concepts of revolution. This sectarian policy finally erupted in May 1937 into street fighting in Barcelona, where the Communists defeated the CNT and POUM.

With the defeat of the CNT and its allies, the Communists demanded that the government should dissolve POUM and arrest its leaders. When Largo refused, they forced his resignation and replaced him with Juan Negrín. POUM was ruthlessly purged and its leader, **Andrés Nin**, killed.

Did the crucial role of the PCE in the Spanish Civil War prove counter-productive? Conservative historians argue that it alienated both the Western democracies and many Spaniards, but, as Preston stresses, the 'Communist Party for all its crimes and

Andrés Ninn (1892–1937)
A Spanish Communist who broke with Stalin and formed his own Marxist party, the POUM. He was seized after the May Days in Barcelona and sent to a Soviet-run prison camp, where he was tortured to death.

errors, played a major role in keeping Republican resistance as long as it did'[20] (see Documents 1, 6 and 8).

Attempted consolidation: the Negrín ministry, 1937–9

Negrín came to power in the most unpromising of conditions. He had little option but to work closely with the Communists, even though their ruthless liquidation of dissidents created a bad impression among the Western democracies. He had, too, to wage a war in which accumulating military defeats led to mounting economic and social crises on the home front. Nevertheless, through a policy of economic and political reform, the Republic managed to fight on under adverse conditions for almost two more years. It managed to boost food production by some 6 per cent, through encouraging private property cooperatives among smallholders, and in the factories drastically reducing worker control. In the early summer of 1938 the People's Army in Catalonia was reconstituted, which 'ranks as one of the major achievements of the Republicans war effort'.[21] Increasingly the key Catalan war industries were also subjected to government controls. Negrín in alliance with the Communists in effect liquidated the revolution.

THE NATIONALISTS AND THE CIVIL WAR

The Nationalists won the Civil War for two main reasons:

- Foreign intervention, including the 'neutrality' of Britain and France, gave the Nationalists a material and military edge over the Republicans.
- Franco was able to forge an effective united front at an early stage in the war.

In July 1936 this unity was not by any means a foregone conclusion. Individual generals had their own ideas for the future, while there was tension between the *Falange*, the Carlists and the Alfonsist monarchists. Nevertheless, Franco proved to be a remarkably adroit politician, who exercised power 'with the skill and arbitrariness of a Borgia'.[22]

Forging a united Nationalist regime

Initially on 23 July 1936 a seven-member military junta was set up by Mola, and it was only on 3 August that Franco became a member. Franco by that date had already emerged as the strongest of the generals. Not only did he command the key 'Army of Africa', but from the very beginning of the Civil War he had exercised strong leadership and had taken the initiative in contacting the Germans and Italians. In early September, as the Nationalist forces were converging on Madrid from the south, Franco proposed to the junta that there should be a unity of command, and it was agreed initially on 21 September that he should be the Commander-in-Chief. A week later he was also appointed 'Chief of State so long as the war may last'.

Franco's most immediate tasks were to unify the Nationalists and to prepare for a long and bitter war. He replaced the military junta with a new 'Technical Council' made up of seven commissions to supervise the state administration. The Nationalist media were instructed to orchestrate a massive personality cult to emphasize the unique qualities of Franco as the *Caudillo* or 'Leader'. This would not, of course, have succeeded if genuine mass support for the Nationalists had been lacking. The outburst of mass violence in the Republican zone, with the burning of churches and massacre of priests and nuns, had rallied the more conservative half of the country to the Nationalist cause. Drawing on these strong wells of support, Franco was able convert the revolt into what amounted to a crusade.

Initially, as in the Republican zone, there was an outbreak of terror and mass executions by the Nationalist militias. Both in Seville and later in Malaga they were on such a large scale that the Italians were appalled and complained directly to Franco. This persuaded Franco to centralize the process of repression and insist that all death sentences should be approved first by the military judicial section at his headquarters and then by himself. Terror and executions, aimed at ridding Spain of any potential left-wing leadership, did, however, remain a central policy of the Nationalist regime. The exact number of executions during the Civil War is debated, but the number could be as high as 200,000.

Franco rewarded the Church for its support by restoring saints' days and its influence in schools. In July 1937, with only three exceptions, the Spanish bishops signed a long and detailed letter of support urging the population to support Franco's 'civic-military movement'. Franco, however, took good care not to be swallowed up by the Church. As Payne observed, 'he administered a primarily but not totally clerical regime and he wanted to reserve other non clerical cards to play, though his public posture of total piety could never admit it'.[23] His new regime also gradually absorbed the existing Catholic political and social organizations such as the Catholic Trade Union Federation and the Catholic University Student Group.

In December 1936 all the various right-wing militias were united and subject to military orders. In April 1937 Franco was then able to group together the *Falange*, the Carlists and the Alphonsine monarchists into a united movement, the FET, which was subservient to the military regime. This essentially laid the foundation of a one-party system, which remained unaltered until the death of Franco in 1975 (see Document 7).

The FET's structure was similar to the pre-war *Falange* (see p. 305): its charismatic leader was Franco, it had an executive committee, and a consultative body of delegates – the National Council – and a party uniform. It also adopted the *Falange* salute and party symbol. When the Civil War ended in April 1939 the Falangist doctrine was declared to be 'the programmatic norm of the new state'. In January 1938 Franco replaced his temporary wartime administration with a more conventional cabinet, which was a good example of his ability to balance between the key forces in Nationalist Spain and to give representation to all the main political groups. The vice presidency went to a moderate monarchist, Lieutenant Gen Gómez Jordana; the Ministry of Justice to the Carlist Conde de Rodezno; and the Ministry of Finance to a former colleague of Calvo Sotelo; while a member of the FET was appointed Minister of Agriculture and another made responsible for forming the new labour syndicates or unions. Sheelagh Ellwood argues that the role of the two FET ministers was of considerable significance, as the Civil War had, to a large extent, 'been provoked by the issues of the distribution of land and power of an organized working class'.[24] Nevertheless, no faction was able effectively to overshadow Franco, whose leadership dominated the Nationalist forces.

Policies of Franco's wartime regime

Much of the domestic policy of Franco's cabinet was a cross between Social Catholicism and Italian Fascism:

- The Charter of Labour was approved on 9 March 1938, which announced an 'economic middle way' between 'Liberal capitalism and Marxist materialism'. Workers were promised social security, holidays and a limited working day, while each peasant family was promised a small parcel of land.
- A Ministry of National Syndical Action and Organization was set up on 30 January 1938, with branches in each province.
- In agriculture the Republican land reforms of 1936 were reversed and no changes were to be introduced for the duration of hostilities.
- The FET also set up its women's section, which by the end of the Civil War consisted of some 580,000 women, who worked in hospitals and staffed canteens for the troops. It also developed a welfare programme, which in late 1937 was made the official social assistance agency of the regime.
- As in Fascist Italy and Nazi Germany, efforts were made to create a 'pure' Spanish culture. For instance, in May 1938 children could only be christened with traditional Spanish names.

Did Franco establish a Fascist state in 1939?

Once the Civil War ended in March 1939, with a complete victory for the Nationalists, Franco was able to consolidate his position. A decree announced on 9 August declared that Franco had full governmental powers and in times of crisis had no legal need to consult his cabinet. Although Spain was not a totalitarian state, theoretically his government was 'a more direct dictatorship than those of the Soviet, Union, Italy or Germany'.[25] The regime was also the most centralized in Spanish history. Catalonia and the Basque provinces lost their regional autonomy and the official use of their languages was banned.

Given the growing dominance of Italy and Germany, Franco's Spain took on a Fascist colouring. In the spring of 1939, for instance, Franco made a tour of Spain and in each city large crowds, often composed of the FET and members of the labour syndicates, chanted 'Franco, Franco, Franco'. As a concession to the new Fascistic era that seemed to be dawning in Europe, five cabinet posts were given to Falangists, but this was balanced by an equal number given to the military. Some observers believed that this was a Falangist government, but in reality Franco was again craftily balancing the various forces friendly to his regime.

The membership of the FET steadily increased until it reached its peak in 1942 at slightly short of one million. Essentially, however, this was 'a little mobilized and basically passive membership'.[26] Its main task was to carry out the political indoctrination of the population. In the larger cities it supplied a network of *jefes de bloque*, or block chiefs, in imitation of the USSR and Nazi Germany. It did too have a youth division, but it was a pale copy of its counterparts in Italy and Germany. An attempt by a fanatical university student, Enrique Sotomayor, to create a semi-autonomous Fascist student organization, which aimed to push for a national Fascist revolution, was rapidly brought under control by Franco. The youth movement, as a whole, never attracted more than 13 per cent of the total male population and 7 per cent of the female between the ages of 7 and 18.

This stifling of Falangist ambitions was to be the pattern right across the board. Encouraged by the Minister of the Interior, Serrano Súñer, the political council of the FET produced a draft constitution for what amounted to a corporative state (see p. 109). Franco, the army and the Conservatives were worried by Article 28, which stated that 'the *Junta politica* is the supreme political council of the regime and the collegiate organ of coordination between state and movement'. Faced with these claims Franco rapidly vetoed the whole project. He also took care that the new syndical system, which Salvador Merino, a radical Falangist veteran of the FET, was charged with creating, had no real power. By January 1940 a new syndical structure had been created to which all private economic organizations except for the liberal professions and the chambers of commerce had to belong. By the end of the year national syndicates had been organized in ten sectors of the economy, and a National Agrarian Council had been set up. Yet, as in Italy, it was in reality a paper tiger, and real economic authority lay with the government ministries.

It was becoming increasingly clear that Franco's regime was essentially a right-wing authoritarian regime 'flavored with Fascist rhetoric but little more'.[27] This inevitably led to tension with the veteran Falangists, who, encouraged by the growing power of Germany, especially after the fall of France in 1940 (see pp. 392–3), attempted to intrigue against Franco. In December 1940 a group of conspirators tried to obtain German backing against Franco, and even considered assassinating him, but in end they decided that he was irreplaceable and that Falangism was in reality dependent upon his survival. In May 1940 the Navy Minister, Salvador Merino, discussed with Goebbels a possible scenario for German support for a Falangist takeover, but in July he was dismissed from his post and sent to the Balearic Islands.

Economic policy

Franco's economic policy was a combination of ultra-conservativism with ambitious attempts to develop Spanish industry as quickly as possible. Although the Civil War was less destructive than the Second World War, it had seriously disrupted the Spanish economy. In 1939 industrial output had declined by 35 per cent compared to 1935, while agricultural production had fallen by 21 per cent. The states' pre-war gold reserves had also been used by the Republic to finance the war.

Franco's solution to these problems was to develop an autarkic economy (see p. 276). In October 1939 this policy was set out in a 10-year plan aimed at economic modernization, self-sufficiency and a reduction in imports, while simultaneously increasing exports. Copying the Italian IRI (see p. 275), a state investment and holding company, the *Institutio Nacional de Industria*, was set up with the intention of assisting the development of key industries such as shipbuilding, steel and chemical production.

Foreign policy

Not surprisingly, given the assistance from Rome and Berlin, Spanish policy in the few months before the outbreak of the Second World war was orientated towards the Axis Powers, but Franco was nevertheless determined that Spain should not become a satellite of Nazi Germany. He signed a treaty of friendship with

Germany in March 1939, joined the Anti-Comintern Pact (see p. 287) and withdrew from the League of Nations, but he signalled his independence by signing a 10-year pact with Portugal and negotiating commercial agreements with Britain and France. He also signed a 25-year debt repayment agreement with Italy, but managed carefully to block any further German economic penetration. When war broke out in September 1939 Franco followed a policy of what he called 'adroit prudence'. He offered to mediate between Germany and Poland, and declared Spain's neutrality.

ASSESSMENT

Compared to the two world wars, the Spanish Civil War was a minor conflict, yet it was seen both at the time and since as a dress rehearsal for the coming clash between Fascism and the Left. On both sides there was a degree of crusading spirit. On the one side, the International Brigades contributed invaluable assistance to the Republic, while on the other, a smaller number of passionate Roman Catholics and anti-Communists, particularly from the Irish Free State, rallied to the defence of Nationalist Spain and the Church. The Civil War played a key part in forming political attitudes and determining later military strategies and tactics. The books and poetry written about the Civil War by some of the intellectuals who joined the International Brigades played an important role in spreading these attitudes, and certainly in Britain strengthened the willingness of the Left to fight Fascism.

What sort of conflict, however, was it? It was not a straight conflict between Communism and Fascism, or even between Western democracy and Fascism. The two great Western European democracies, Britain and France, desperately wanted to stay out of the conflict, while the USSR only reluctantly became involved because it wished to preserve the European balance of power and stop Spain from becoming Fascist. Neither was the Civil War a struggle between revolution and reaction. On the Republican side there was an 'undeclared civil war'[28] between the Communists and the moderate Socialist and Republican leaders on the one side, and the Anarchists on the other. The Right, too, although united by Franco, was not a monolithic bloc and was subject to considerable internal tensions. Nor was it entirely a Spanish Civil War, as Germany, Italy, the USSR and thousands of volunteers from all over Europe and the Americas were involved. In that sense the Spanish Civil War was 'an episode in a greater European civil war that ended in 1945'.[29]

DOCUMENT 1

The problem of popular mobilization

The Spanish Socialist Party (PSOE) failed to understand the need for inspiring the population to fight and tended to see the efforts of the Communists as opportunistic. The following is an extract from a letter of complaint from the provincial leadership in Almeira sent to the national executive of the PSOE in March 1938:

The [Socialist] Party, somewhat startled by Communist methods – so given to excessive publicity and dramatic gestures, to vulgar and ornate ritual . . . – had become even more sparing in its public declarations, which were always austere and dignified. But what we disdain in terms of methods employed, we cannot ignore in terms of effects produced. The people here are uneducated and impressionable. Until very recently they were in thrall to a religious mysticism – which for all that it was distorted, met a certain need in them. Communist propaganda, full of puerile, rhetorical flourishes, peppered with clichés and accompanied by impressive gestures, has filled a void in these simple people.

Source: H. Graham, 'War, modernity and reform: the premiership of Juan Negrín' in P. Preston and A. Mackenzie, eds, *The Republic Besieged. Civil War in Spain, 1936–39*, Edinburgh, Edinburgh University Press, 1996, p. 187.

DOCUMENT 2

Comparisons with the NEP

Ruiz Ponseti, the Communist Undersecretary of the Catalonian Generalidad Council of the Economy, compares the experience in Catalonia with the New Economic Policy, which was announced by Lenin in 1921 (see pp. 60–62):

When we want to establish the initial parallel between the transformation carried out in the Union of Soviet Socialist Republics and the transformation carried out in out land, we can say that the beginning of the transformation was about the same;

▶

the first steps were quite similar. There the evolution has been long and painful and has presented great difficulties at certain times. In our country we have tried to carry out the transformation in the most rapid way possible. It would be senseless not to try to profit by the experience of others ... And so, since our Russian comrades after long years of war communism followed by misery and hunger finally arrived at the beginning of the NEP ... here we have tried to avoid that painful experience ... and leap in a single jump ... from the primitive war communism that we experienced to the period of subsistence ... to good comradeship of socialized property side by side with private property.

Source: S.G. Payne, *The Spanish Revolution*, London, Weidenfeld & Nicolson, 1970, p. 309.

DOCUMENT 3

The foundation of CEDA, February 1933

A Congress of the various groups affiliated to the Acción Popular met in Madrid at the end of February 1933, where Gil Robles announced the formation of a new party:

When the Social order is threatened, Catholics should unite to defend it and safeguard the principles of Christian civilization ... We will go united into struggle, no matter what it costs ... We are faced with a social revolution. In the political panorama of Europe I can see only the formation of Marxists and anti-Marxist groups. This is what is happening to Germany and in Spain also. This is the great battle which we must fight this year.

Source: P. Preston, *The Coming of the Spanish Civil War*, London, Routledge, 2nd ed. 1994, p. 65.

DOCUMENT 4

The Eve of Civil War

The reaction of Calvo Sotelo, the political leader of the monarchist opposition during the Second Republic, when Azaña presented his government's programme in March 1936 in the Cortes:

Half the nation will not resign itself to die. If it cannot defend itself by one path, it will defend itself by another ... Civil war is being brought by those who seek the revolutionary conquest of power and it is being sustained and weaned by the apathy of a government which does not turn on its supporters ... when civil war beaks out in Spain, let it be known that the weapons have been loaded by the negligence of a government which has not been able to fulfil its duty towards groups which have stayed within the strictest legality.

Source: Preston, *The Coming of the Spanish Civil War*, p. 254.

DOCUMENT 5
Franco's character

Colonel Valentin Galarza, who was one of the leading figures in the abortive coup of 1932, described the enigmatic Franco as follows:

Franco is a man who declares himself, and then retracts; draws near, and then steps back; vanishes or slides away; always vague, never clear and categorical. He had seemed to be the most monarchist of the young Spanish generals, and had presented himself as such before the King who firmly believed in him ... On the other hand, in spite of the fact that his participation in the coup had for some time been considered certain, shortly before the day appointed for its execution, he excused himself from all obligations and counseled various officers to do likewise

His constant declarations of loyalty to the Republican regime ... won him the confidence of successive Republican cabinets.

Source: S.G. Payne, *Politics and the Military in Modern Spain*, Stanford, CA, Stanford University Press, 1967, p. 290.

DOCUMENT 6
The long shadow of the Russian Revolution

Martinez Barrio, who worked closely with Azaña after the Popular Front's victory in February 1936, complained that:

Certain Socialists and all the Communists were suffering from the mirage of the Russian revolution of 1917, and handed us the dismal role of Kerensky. According to them our mission was limited to smoothing their road to power, since the possibilities of the democratic revolution in the history of the Republic had been exhausted.

Source: Payne, *The Spanish Revolution*, p. 179.

▶

DOCUMENT 7

Franco and the one-party state

On 19 April 1937 Franco announced the dissolution of all parties. Sheelagh M. Ellwood has called the preamble to the decree 'a subtle mixture of Franco's long term vision of political organization and veiled threat for those who might disagree with it':

Efficient governmental action, such as must be that of the new Spanish State, born, moreover under the sign of unity and the greatness of the Fatherland, demands that the individual and collective action of all Spaniards be subjugated to its common destiny. This truth ... is incompatible with the struggle of parties and political organizations which waste their best energies in the struggle for predominance of their particular styles or, what is worse, on questions of a personal nature, which give rise to petty discords within the organizations, resuscitating old political intrigues and threatening with disintegration organizations and forces whose masses are moved by the impulse of the purest of ideals.

Source: S.M. Ellwood, *'Falange Española*, 1933–9: from Fascism to Francoism' in M. Blinkhorn, ed., *Spain in Conflict*, London, Sage Publications, 1986, p. 220.

DOCUMENT 8

Criticisms of Communist tactics in Spain

(a) A junior Left-Socialist member of the government complained that the Communist Party:

... tried to absorb, monopolize everything, acting with the wildest sectarianism. Instead of unity, there was the opposite. The war was being fought for the freedom of Spain, not to win a victory which would hand the country over to the Communists who in turn, served the interests of another nation. But from the propaganda, and the large posters of Stalin, etc., the impression was gained that Spain was in the Soviets' hands. That only alienated large sectors of the population on our side and helped the enemy.

Source: R. Fraser, 'The popular experience of war and revolution, 1936–39' in P. Preston, ed., *Revolution and War in Spain, 1931–39*, London, Methuen, 1984, p. 233.

(b) The view of Timoteao Ruiz, a member of one of the militias:

A great mistake was being made in thinking that the war could be waged with classic strategies. This wasn't a traditional war – it was a civil war, a political war. A war between democracy and fascism, certainly – but a popular war. Yet all the creative possibilities and instincts of the people in revolution were not allowed to develop.

Source: Fraser, 'The popular experience', p. 233.

(c) An officer in the Communist Lister's division agreed with Ruiz:

If we hadn't been convinced that the democratic countries would come to our aid, different forms of struggle would have developed. It was as though we had to be ashamed of revolution, as though we were frightened they would get wind of it abroad. If we had realized from the start that we were alone – even opposed to the bourgeois parties which were boycotting us – it would have become a popular revolutionary war.

Source: Ibid., pp. 233–4.

NOTES

1 S. Julia, 'Economic crisis, social conflict and the Popular Front: Madrid, 1931–1936' in P. Preston, ed., *Revolution and War in Spain*, London, Methuen, 1984, p. 139.

2 P. Preston, 'The agrarian war in the south', in P. Preston, ed., *Revolution*, p. 172.

3 R. Carr, *Spain, 1808–1939*, Oxford, Oxford University Press, 1966, p. 625.

4 S.G. Payne, *The Franco Regime, 1936–1975*, London, Phoenix Press, 2nd ed. 2000, p. 58.

5 P. Preston, *The Spanish Civil War*, London, Fontana Press, 1996, p. 36.

6 F. Meneses, *Franco and the Spanish Civil War*, London, Routledge, 2001, p. 32.

7 P. Preston, *Franco: A Biography*, London, Fontana, 1995, p. xvii.

8 Ibid., p. xvii.

9 Ibid. p. xviii.

10 Payne, *The Franco Regime,* p. 139.

11 Ibid., p. 34.

12 G. Brennan, *The Spanish Labyrinth*, Cambridge, Cambridge University Press, repr. 1993.

13 Carr, *Spain and The Spanish Tragedy: The Civil War in Perspective*, London, Weidenfield and Nicolson, 1977.

14 P. Preston, 'Introduction', in Preston, ed. *Revolution*, p. 4; H. Thomas, *The Spanish Civil War*, Harmondsworth, Penguin, 3rd ed. 1977.

15 See the essays in M. Blinkhorn, ed., *Spain in Conflict, 1931–1939: Democracy and its Enemies*, London, Sage Publications, 1986, and in Preston, ed., *Revolution*.

16 Preston, ed., *Revolution* p. 2.

17 S.G. Payne, *The Spanish Revolution*, London, Weidenfeld & Nicolson, 1970, and R. Robinson, *The Origins of Franco's Spain*, Newton Abbot, David Charles, 1970.

18 Payne, *The Spanish Revolution*, p. 224.

19 Meneses, *Franco*, p. 64.

20 Preston, *Spanish Civil War*, p. 190.

21 Payne, *The Franco Regime*, p. 149.

22 Preston, *Franco*, 1995, p. 198.

23 Payne, *The Franco Regime*, p. 207.

24 S.M. Ellwood, '*Falange Española*, 1933–39: from Fascism to Francoism' in Blinkhorn, ed., *Spain in Conflict*, London, Sage Publications, 1986, p. 221.

25 Payne, *The Franco Regime*, p. 234.

26 Ibid., p. 239.

27 Ibid., p. 260.

28 P. Preston and A.L. Mackenzie, eds, *The Republic Besieged*, Edinburgh, Edinburgh University Press, 1996, p. xii.

29 Ibid., p. viii.

CHAPTER TEN

Stalin and the second revolution, 1927–41

TIMELINE

1927	December	Collectivization agreed on at the Fifteenth Party Congress
1928	January	Stalin visits Siberia and orders grain requisitioning
1929	January	Trotsky expelled from the USSR
	September	Collectivization policy begins
	November	Bukharin expelled from the Politburo
		Stalin announces mass collectivization and liquidation of the kulaks
1930	March	Stalin's 'Dizzy with success' article
1933	September	Second Five-Year Plan
1934	January–February	Seventeenth Party Congress
	July	OGPU reorganized as NKVD
	September	USSR joins the League of Nations
	December	Assassination of Kirov and start of the Terror
1935	January	Kamenev, Zinoviev and 17 others arrested
	July–August	Popular Front policy announced
1936	August	USSR becomes involved in the Spanish Civil War
		Show trial of Kamenev Zinoviev, and 14 others
	September	Yezhov appointed Head of the NKVD and launches the Great Purges
	December	New constitution accepted
1937	May	Purge of Red Army begins
1938	March	Bukharin, Rykov, Yagoda and others tried and shot
	September	Munich Agreement

	December	Beria appointed Head of NKVD
		Third Five-Year Plan announced
1939	August	Nazi–Soviet Pact
	1 September	German invasion of Poland
1940	June	USSR occupies Baltic states
1941	22 June	Germany invades USSR

Introduction

There is no doubt that Stalin was a cunning and able politician, who had used his position as Head of the Orgburo (Organizational Bureau) and as General Secretary to build up a network of supporters. He was also able to use the Leninist ban on party faction (see p. 63) to isolate his opponents and eventually remove them from the Politburo (see p. 69). Building on Lenin's elimination of political opposition, Stalin arguably created a tighter dictatorship in the 1930s than either Hitler or Mussolini. He certainly used terror on a far greater scale and carried out far more drastic purges than either of them.

Yet Stalinism was not just the construction of one man; it was shaped both by the unfinished revolution of the 1920s and by the challenges facing the USSR in the 1930s. Stalin's policies of collectivization and forced industrialization, for all their brutality, were, at least with the younger and more dynamic members of the party, genuinely popular. Even the Terror directed against the bureaucrats and middle management had some popular backing.

The key issues in this chapter are:

- The impact and consequences of collectivization.
- The achievements of the Five-Year Plan.
- The causes and degree of support for the purges and the Terror.
- The impact of the Stalinist revolution on the Russian people.
- The creation of the Stalinist system and the extent to which it was totalitarian.
- The aims of Soviet foreign policy.

COLLECTIVIZATION AND THE END OF THE NEP

The impact of the October Revolution on agriculture was 'profoundly reactionary'.[1] The large estates, which had produced grain for the market, were broken up and given to the peasantry, the majority of whom produced primarily for their own consumption. With the introduction of the NEP in March 1921, attempts to collectivize agriculture were abandoned. This inevitably led to a decline in the amount of grain that was sold to the towns and available for export. The Soviet government attempted to overcome this in the short term by manipulating the grain prices. In 1925 price increases temporarily produced more grain for the urban population, but at the cost of industrial crops such as cotton and flax. In the following year the Soviet government reversed this policy and reduced the price of grain by nearly 25 per cent, but also, in an attempt to make available consumer goods to the peasantry, it reduced retail prices by 10 per cent in February 1927. This was a disastrous combination. Scarce commodities such as soap, candles, matches, shoes, etc., were immediately bought up by urban buyers, leaving nothing for the peasantry, who responded by hoarding their grain as there seemed to be no point in selling it, since there was nothing their money could buy.

By December 1927 grain purchases made by the state agencies had dropped by 50 per cent compared to 1926, which not only threatened the towns with hunger but also the Soviet industrialization programme. The crisis occurred at a time when there was mounting pressure within the Bolshevik Party to increase the pace of industrialization. This seemed all the more urgent as Britain's decision to break off **diplomatic relations** with the USSR in May 1927, together with deteriorating relations with France and Poland, revived the fears in Moscow that the Western Powers might again attempt to invade the USSR.

At the Fifteenth Party Congress in 1927 Stalin called for the peasants – voluntarily at this stage still – to pool their land, implements and animals and form collective farms. In January 1928 he himself visited Siberia and instructed the local party officials to concentrate on extracting grain from the **kulaks** at the low prices set by the government. He hoped that they would, as in the Civil

Diplomatic relations
Britain broke off diplomatic relations in 1927 in protest at anti-British speeches in the USSR and at the activities of Comintern agents.

Kulaks
Slightly better off than the average peasants, who were sometimes able to employ one or two landless peasants to work on their land.

War, be able to mobilize pressure within the villages against the kulaks. Local officials thus began to seize grain, close down markets and fix tight price controls on the grain produced by each village – a process that became known as the 'Ural–Siberian method', and provoked unrest and desperate attempts by the peasants to hold back reserves until the price rose again. In the cities bread shortages intensified and rationing had to be introduced (see Document 1).

The Politburo was divided as to how to react to this. Bukharin urged an increase in grain prices, which he believed would persuade the peasantry to grow and sell more grain. His colleagues, Stalin, Kuibyshev and Kaganovich, however, argued strongly that the power of the kulaks to hoard grain needed to be broken, and a clear priority given to industrialization. In December 1928 the situation was made worse when the scale of the harvest failures in central and south-eastern Russia became clear. In response, the Ural–Siberian methods were again ruthlessly used to extract grain and Bukharin supporters steadily lost influence. In November 1929 Stalin openly came out for collectivization and the liquidation of the kulaks, and Bukharin was sacked from the Politiburo.

In January 1930 an accelerated collectivization programme began:

- As a first step the Politburo declared that 25 per cent of the land cultivated in the main corn-growing regions of the Soviet Union would be collectivized by the spring, and the other areas would follow by the autumn of 1931.
- By the decree of 1 February 1930 the kulaks were excluded from the collective farms and divided into three categories:
  - the 'counter-revolutionaries', who were to be shot or sent to labour camps
  - the 'exploiters or active opponents of collectivization', who were to be deported to remote regions, such as Siberia
  - a third category, which could remain in their local districts, but would be excluded from the new collectives.

OGPU
United State Political Administration, or the Soviet secret police, 1923–34. It was renamed the NKVD in 1934.

To implement this policy, troops, **OGPU** units and a specially raised volunteer force of about 25,000 workers, who were organized into 'collectivization brigades', were employed. While the original Ural–Siberian methods had enjoyed some backing from the poorer peasantry, the wholesale and indiscriminating violence which these forces used to ensure collectivization drove the peasantry into a desperate resistance (see Figure 10.1) and forced Stalin on 2 March 1930 temporarily to call a halt. 'With monumental insincerity',[2] he then criticized the collectivization brigades in an article in *Pravda* ('Dizzy with success') and urged a return to the voluntary principle, but when the Sixteenth Party Congress met in June, Stalin reverted to the call for a 'mass' collectivization offensive. By 1937 almost all the cultivated land in the USSR had been collectivized (see Documents 1 and 2).

The collective farm system

Stalin's preferred model was the *Sovkoz*. These were state-run farms, which were increasingly mechanized and concentrated on one main crop. They were run by local authority officials and the peasants, who, like urban workers, were paid a set wage. However, Stalin accepted that the majority of peasants were reluctant to work as wage labourers as they wished to cling on to their independence. Hence the majority of collective farms were *kolkhozy*. These were based on the cooperative principle: the peasants elected their own chairmen, and after they had met their production targets, surplus produce would be divided amongst the members according to the number of days they had worked. They were also allowed their own smallholdings, the produce of which they were permitted in 1935 to sell in the towns. By 1940 these plots were producing 43 per cent of all marketed wool, 52 per cent of vegetables and 70 per cent of meat.

The consequences

Between November 1929 and December 1932 the way of life of the majority of the people in the USSR had been destroyed. Essentially Stalin had 'captured the countryside for the state' and 'eradicated its capacity to influence the pace and duration of the economic development of the country'.[3] Agricultural experts, who had been trying to work with the peasants were dismissed, while the task of running the new collectives devolved upon party officials and collectivization brigades. Robert Service calculates that about 4–5 million people perished in the collectivization process[4] (see Document 2).

Figure 10.1 *Kolkhozy* workers discover grain hidden from state requisition by a kulak *Source*: RIA Novosti.

In protest against forcible collectivization, the peasants killed their livestock to prevent their being corralled into the collective. As there were now too few horses left to pull the ploughs, and sufficient tractors had not yet been produced, much of the land lay untilled and became choked with weeds. Inevitably this had terrible consequences when the 1931 harvest was hit by drought. Famine appeared first in Ukraine and then spread to the north Caucasus, Kazakhstan and the middle and lower Volga. Historians cannot agree on an exact total, but probably about 7 million died.

The output of Soviet agriculture did not recover until the mid-1950s. In 1935 the grain harvest did exceed pre-collectivization levels for the first time (75 million tons), only to decline sharply to 56.1 million tons in 1936. Bread rationing was ended in 1935, but the following year harvest failures caused renewed shortages, as they were to again in 1939–40 (see Document 4).

Conventionally collectivization is usually seen as a policy unleashed by Stalin and the Politburo dominated by Stalinists, yet such a revolution could not have been sustained if there had not been considerable party and grass-roots support for it. There was a widespread popular desire in the country to break out of the straitjacket which the NEP had imposed on the economy. Inevitably, emphasis on participation from below by revisionist historians has, to quote Catherine Merridale, led to accusations of 'whitewashing the Stalinist terror' and of exonerating its leaders of the 'responsibility for mass murder'.[5] Clearly Stalin did give orders or at the least massive hints to the local officials to liquidate the kulaks, and consequently 'it would be fanciful to assume that the excesses of the collectivization campaign were somehow mainly the fault of the local officials and activists',[6] but 'history from below' does indicate that there was a considerable body of support for the goals, if not always the methods, of Stalinist policy.

Peasant holdings collectivized in the USSR, 1930–1 (%)

1930	1931	1932	1933	1934	1935	1936	1941
23.6	52.7	61.5	66.4	71.4	83.2	89.6	98.0

Source: M. Lynch, *Stalin and Khruschev*, London, Hodder, 1990, p. 32.

INDUSTRIALIZATION AND THE FIVE-YEAR PLANS, 1928–41

Formulating the first Five-Year Plan

There was general agreement within the Bolshevik Party that the USSR needed to become a modern industrial state, but there was no consensus on how to achieve this aim. The 'Right' (see pp. 68–9) believed that industrialization could only be achieved within the context of the NEP and by creating a prosperous peasantry, whose demands for consumer goods and machinery would ultimately encourage the growth of Soviet industry. Trotsky and the Left opposition (see p. 69), on the other hand, believed that agriculture should be made to finance industrialization more directly. The economist Evgenii Preobrazhensky, whose ideas Trotsky supported, argued that the government, to raise the necessary funds for industrialization, should buy grain cheaply from the countryside and sell it dearly in the cities. Stalin, publicly at least, adopted a neutral position between these two arguments until 1927.

As early as 1926 work began on drawing up possible options for a Five-Year Plan, and over the next year opinion in the party began to shift toward a programme of rapid industrialization. The reasons for this were that:

- Manufacturing had recovered to its 1913 level and consequently it seemed that any further advance could only be carried out by building new factories.
- Activists were looking forward to a new period of 'socialist construction', which would break away from the restraints of the NEP.
- It appeared that the agricultural sector was capable of providing the funds for future industrial investment, provided grain output was increased.
- The defeat of the Left opposition' (see p. 69) allowed Stalin to appropriate their economic thinking without fear of criticism.
- The 'war scare' triggered by Britain breaking off diplomatic relations with the USSR (see p. 333) also encouraged Stalin to consider quickening the pace of industrialization.

Competing agencies within the party vied with each other by proposing ever more ambitious plans. At the Fifteenth Party Congress in December 1927 several draft plans were debated without result, and it was not until April 1929 that the Plan was presented to the Sixteenth Party Congress, but, even then, there were still two versions. The aims of one of these were to:

- generate sufficient electricity to power the entire economy
- increase production of pig iron from 3.3 to 10 million tons
- increase the production of coal from 35.4 to 75 million tons
- increase the production of iron ore from 5.7 to 19 million tons
- expand light industry by 70 per cent
- increase agricultural production by 55 per cent
- increase total productivity by 110 per cent.

Over the next four years these targets were constantly revised upwards.

Implementing the Five-Year Plans, 1929–41

The first year of the Five-Year Plan witnessed an initial period of explosive growth, which then encouraged what Naum Jasny called a period of 'Bacchanalian planning'.[7] Targets were raised to totally impractical levels, graduate training was speeded up far too quickly in technical subjects and, as in the period of War Communism, activists were convinced that the promised land of Socialism would be realized in a year or two. Industrialization was assisted by the labour of the 3 million kulaks, 'criminals' and 'industrial wreckers', who were employed in mines, on construction sites and in the forests felling timber.

The completion of the first Five-Year Plan was announced as early as December 1932. While none of the major targets had been reached, much had nevertheless been achieved. In these four years the Soviet economy was fundamentally transformed. More than 50 per cent of the machine tools in the USSR in 1932 had, for instance been made or installed since 1928, and hundreds of factories had sprung up in the Urals, the Kuzbass, the Volga district and Ukraine (see Figure 10.2). Massive plants like the Magnitogorsk iron and steel combine were built. Yet the very speed of this industrialization caused chaos and dislocation. There were production bottlenecks, the cities expanded on average by about 50,000 people a week, and costs far outran what **Gosplan** had calculated, as the world Depression turned the terms of global trade against the USSR (see p. 357).

Gosplan
The Central State Planning Commission in Moscow.

The Second Five-Year Plan (1933–7) was launched in the midst of famine and in the middle of a transport crisis, and had

Figure 10.2 Tractors lined up at the Chelyabinsk tractor factory, 1935
Source: RIA Novosti

to be redrafted in 1934. Its aims were to consolidate the achievements of the first Five-Year Plan. Many of the massive projects launched in the first Five-Year Plan, such as the Magnitogorsk and the Azovstal combines, were completed. Labour productivity increased and by the mid-1930s food supplies were increasing, but in 1937 the economic situation began to deteriorate for a number of reasons:

- as a result of the international situation (see pp. 357–8), large sums of money were poured into the defence industries at the cost of the consumer industries
- the winter of 1937–8 was exceptionally cold and disrupted the train services and caused fuel shortages
- as a result of Stalin's attacks on 'wreckers' thousands of managers, engineers and functionaries were shot or vanished into the Gulags (labour camps – see p. 47).

This purge of managers and specialized personnel inevitably slowed up the drafting of the third Five-Year Plan, which was not formalized until 1938, and only approved in March 1939. It envisaged industrial production rising by 92 per cent, not so much by building more giant industrial complexes but by improving skills and productivity. The Plan was only in operation for three and half years until the Nazi invasion of the USSR in June 1941 (see p. 449).

Productivity targets, 1927–32 (million tons)

Product	1927–8 1st plan	1932–3 optimal	1932 amended	1932 actual
Coal	35.00	75.00	95–105	64.00
Oil	11.7	21.7	40–55	21.4
Iron ore	6.7	20.2	24–32	12.1
Pig iron	3.2	10.0	15–16	6.2

Source: M. Lynch, *Stalin and Khruschev*, London, Hodder, 1990, p. 37.

THE PURGES, SHOW TRIALS AND THE TERROR

The show trials and the Terror have to be seen against the background of the growing opposition to Stalin and the mounting problems caused by collectivization and the Five-Year Plans. In 1928 55 people at the Shakhty mines in the Donbass was charged with treason and sabotage. This was the first of the show trials, and was designed to provide an excuse for the failure of Stalin's industrial projects. Only four of the accused were acquitted.

By 1929 Stalin was still not yet totally dominant. Rykov, Tomsky, Bukharin and **Uglanov**, who were prominent members of the rightist opposition, had been elected to the Central Committee. The ruthless speed of collectivization, and the bottlenecks and chaos of the first Five-Year Plan also met with considerable criticism from a number of those who had previously supported Stalin. Within the Politburo Stalin probably enjoyed the absolute support only of **Kaganovich** and **Molotov**.

In 1933 Riutin, the Party Secretary for a Moscow district until 1932, circulated a long memorandum in which he called for Stalin's dismissal and the end of forced collectivization. At the Seventeenth Party Congress in 1934 it was clear that Stalin was losing support. Kirov, the popular Party Secretary in Leningrad, received an ovation that rivalled Stalin's, and in the elections to the Central Committee out of 1,225 delegates to the Party Congress only three voted against Kirov, while almost a quarter rejected Stalin. According to **Mikoyan**, a **candidate member** of the Politburo, a group of **old Bolsheviks** actually urged Kirov to stand against Stalin as General Secretary, a story which Dmitri Volkogonov, the Russian military historian, believes 'has a considerable ring of plausibility'.[8] Stalin defused the criticisms against him by allowing the Congress to abolish the post of General Secretary, and henceforth he was referred to merely as Secretary.

The Kirov assassination

On 1 December 1934 the assassination of Kirov by Leonid Nikolayev, a mentally unstable member of the Workers' and Peasants' Inspection Bureau, provided Stalin with the excuse to unleash the NKVD, the secret police, against his enemies in the party. There is a considerable debate as to whether Stalin was involved in the assassination. J. Arch Getty argues that 'neither the sources, circumstances, nor consequences of the crime suggest Stalin's complicity'.[9] It is possible that the assassination was the

N. Uglanov (1886–1937)
Formerly a metal worker, who joined the Russian Social Democrat Party in 1907.

L. Kaganovich (1893–1991)
Party leader in Moscow in 1930.

V. Molotov (1890–1986)
Started working as a colleague of Stalin's in 1922, and was Chairman of the Council of People's Commissars, 1930–41. In May 1939 he was appointed Commissar for Foreign Affairs.

A. Mikoyan (1895–1978)
Joined the Bolsheviks in 1915, fought in the Civil War, and, as a supporter of Stalin, became Commissar for Trade in 1926. In 1935 he was elected to the Politburo and during the Second World War served on the State Defence Committee.

Candidate member
A candidate awaiting election to the Politburo.

Old Bolsheviks
Those who had joined the party before 1917 and fought in the Civil War.

work of the NKVD, which hoped that the reaction to the murder would enable it to strengthen its position within the state. Yet Kirov was a potential rival to Stalin and his death would undoubtedly ease the pressure on him. Robert Conquest and Dmitri Volkogonov argue strongly that, while there is no unambiguous proof that Stalin was involved, there is strong circumstantial evidence that he ordered the assassination.[10]

As a consequence of the assassination, the NKVD were given special powers by a new decree, which speeded up the trials and subsequent executions of so-called terrorists. At the very least Kirov's murder provided an excuse for arresting Stalin's critics. In January 1935 Kamenev, Zinoviev and 17 others were arrested, charged with responsibility for the murder and given long prison terms. There was a wave of arrests in Moscow and Leningrad and in the summer the Society of Old Bolsheviks, which had enjoyed some freedom to criticize the party line, was dissolved and its papers seized.

The show trials

Getty argues that these arrests were 'knee jerk responses'[11] and were not part of a carefully thought out plan to exploit Kirov's assassination. In the mid-summer of 1935 there was certainly a brief pause in the tempo of arrests, yet this was deceptive. A number of forces were converging, which were to prompt Stalin into further action:

- Andrei Zhadanov, the Central Committee Secretary and Kirov's successor in Leningrad, was attempting to assert the party's control over the commissariats (ministries) and was pushing for the local party committees to reassert their role in propagating Marxism–Leninism, mobilizing the people, and selecting elites for public office. As the party was regaining more influence, it was thus important to purge it of any 'unreliable elements'.
- There were ongoing disputes in the Politburo about the wisdom of industrializing so rapidly. The Stakhanovite movement (see p. 351) was exploited to exert pressure on managers to increase the pace of production, although sceptics in the Politburo stressed that Stakhanov could only

achieve his miracles of production at the expense of other workers, who had to sacrifice their own output by helping him achieve his targets. Clearly a campaign against wreckers would silence such opposition.

- There was also evidence in possession of the NKVD that Trotsky, through 'clandestine groups of supporters' in the USSR, was in touch with circles close to Bukharin, Kamanev and Zinoviev.

This last factor may well have been the catalyst that prompted Stalin to move against his leading critics, who were arrested and then judged publicly in three great show trials:

- In August 1936 the first of the great show trials opened in Moscow. Sixteen defendants, including Kamanev and Zinoviev, were accused of plotting to kill Stalin and other leading members of the Politburo and of forming an opposition bloc with Trotsky. Confessions extracted under torture from Kamanev and Zinoviev implicated Bukharin, Rykov and Tomsky, the last of whom committed suicide. Ezhov was appointed NKVD's Commissar with the express remit to make up for lost time in 'exposing the Trotskyite–Zinovievite bloc'.[12]
- In January 1937 a second show trial, 'the trial of the seventeen' opened in Moscow. The principle defendants were Piatkov (Ordzonikidze's deputy at the Commissariat for Heavy Industry), Radek (see p. 45) and Sokolnikov (the former Commissar for Finance), all of whom were accused of being Trotskyites, traitors and wreckers. Thirteen of the defendants were sentenced to death. Ordzhonikidze pleaded in vain with Stalin to save Piatkov, but the day after his interview he shot himself, although officially Stalin insisted that he had died from a coronary attack.
- On 13 March 1937 Bukharin, Rykov and posthumously Tomsky were accused of being Trotskyists, and a year later a third show trial was held, the 'trial of the twenty-one'. The principle defendants in this were Bukharin, Rykov, Iagoda and the veteran Bolsheviks, Krestinskii and C. G. Rakovsky. The charges were 'nothing if not comprehensive'.[13] The defendants were accused of everything from plotting the break-up of the USSR to spying on behalf

of Britain, Japan, Germany and Poland and attempting to reintroduce capitalism. All were found guilty and sentenced to death, with the exception of Rakovskii and two others.

The *Ezhovshchina* or the Great Purges

Under both Lenin and Stalin there had been successive waves of terror, but the *Ezhovshchina* or Great Purges were, to quote Sheila Fitzpatrick 'the quintessential episode of Stalinist terror, a historical moment that crystallized and at the same time reconfigured the accumulated experience of terror over the past two decades'.[14] Previously it had been class enemies that had been purged, but the Great Purges introduced the new and more elastic term of 'enemies of the people'. These were no longer just class enemies or '**former people**', but anyone anywhere could be unmasked as an enemy, however long he or she had been a Bolshevik. Historians disagree on the exact beginning of the *Ezhovshchina*. Some argue that it started as early as July 1936, but there is agreement that it peaked in late 1937 and then eased up at the end of 1938.

Many of the initial victims were senior regional party bureaucrats. For instance, apart from Zhdanov, almost all of the Leningrad Central Committee was purged, while in Ukraine, the members of the regional Secretariat, Politburo and Orgburo were arrested. In Armenia, Turkestan, Georgia, Uzbekistan and many other of the Soviet republics there was a vicious cull of high-ranking officials. The Great Purge also played havoc in the **armed forces** and by December 1938 had removed well over 50 per cent of the officer corps.

It was not just the Soviet elite that suffered from the *Ezhovshchina*. The publicity given to the show trials and the emphasis on wreckers and the way that 'Judas Trotsky' was apparently weaving, with the help of British, German and Japanese agents, a vast conspiracy to destroy Soviet Russia was reported fully in the local papers, and local party officials were constantly exhorted to play their part in rooting out such 'enemies of the people'. The Terror was spread through both denunciation and association. Those arrested were forced to reveal the names of their associates, while the newspapers and the show trials whipped up a spy hysteria. The process was given

Former people
The middle and upper classes who were influential in tsarist Russia before 1917.

Armed forces
In the army the following were purged: three out of five marshals, nearly all the commanders, two-thirds of the corps commanders, 60 per cent of the divisional commanders and 50 per cent of the brigade commanders. Both the navy and air force also lost many of their key officers.

further impetus by the fact that NKVD officers were given arrest quotas that they had to fulfil.

Plague bearers

These were people, who as suspects 'for one reason or another infected all around them'.[15] A typical example was Pavel Postyshev, the Ukranian Party leader. In early 1937 he was demoted and transferred to a job on the Volga, where in an effort to deflect suspicion from himself he had 66 district officials arrested as 'enemies of the people' before he was himself in due course arrested.

The purges decimated both the party and the industrial management, and consequently as early as January 1938 Stalin began to signal that he wished them to ease up. In August 1938 **Ezhov** was replaced by **Beria**, and at the Eighteenth Party Congress 'mass cleansings' were announced to be at an end.

What was the human cost of these purges? Estimates vary widely and historians disagree on the totals. Robert Conquest has calculated that in 1937–8 about 7 million people were arrested, of which 1 million were executed and 2 million died in the camps[16] (see Document 3).

Assessment of the purges

Stephen Cohen remarked that the Terror must be seen as 'a central feature of the social history of Stalinism not because it was more important than anything else but because it was an essential part of everything else'.[17] Its origins and the role of Stalin in it are therefore a matter of considerable historical debate. In the 1950s, when the Soviet system was lumped together with the Third Reich and Fascist Italy as totalitarian, the Great Purges were seen as primarily as a consequence of Bolshevism and Stalin's will (p. 2). That view is still strongly represented by Robert Conquest, who wrote in 1990 that 'the totalitarian machinery, already in existence, was the fulcrum without which the world could not be moved. But the revolution of the purges still remain, however we judge it, above all Stalin's personal achievement'.[18] Yet this view is challenged by the revisionist historians: J. Arch Getty, Gabor

N. Ezhov (1895–1940)
Joined the Bolsheviks in 1917 and became a military commissar in the Civil War. He was Head of the NKVD, 1936–8, and was executed by Beria in 1940.

L. Beria (1899–1953)
Joined the Bolsheviks in 1917 and worked for the Cheka. He was Head of the Commissariat for Internal Affairs in Georgia, and from 1938 became Head of the NKVD. In 1941 he also became Deputy Prime Minister. He was executed in December 1953.

Rittersporn and Roberta Manning.[19] Essentially, the revisionists take issue with the totalitarian approach by arguing that:

- the regime 'had less actual control over society than it claimed, that its actions were often improvized rather than part of a grand design'
- 'the implementation of its radical policies often diverged from the policy makers intention'
- the regime responded to 'social pressures and grievances' and was liable to be modified in practice through processes 'of informal social negotiation'.[20]

The revisionists stress that 'no political regime, including Stalin's' functions in a social vacuum'.[21] The purges and courtroom dramas were all part of '"a conspiracy tapestry" that grew in length over time and was woven by many hands.'[22] They were fuelled by a strong sense of anti-elitism and resentment of management; a populism that approved of seeing local 'bigwigs' on trial and denunciations from people who wished to pay off old scores. They were, too, partly the product of a primitive pre-industrial tradition that attributed misfortune to the work of evil spirits and devils, who lurked everywhere from the party and factory management to the Central Committee and who needed to be unmasked. On the other hand, it would be a mistake to see Stalin as virtually a passive spectator in all this. There is plenty of evidence that he approved of the purges and encouraged them:

- he played a key role in editing the indictments for the show trials in Moscow

G. Iagoda (1891–1938)
Joined the Bolshevik Party in 1907, and worked in the *Cheka* after the Civil War. He was executed in 1938.

- it was he who replaced **Iagoda** by Ezhov and told him that the NKVD had to make good four years of neglect
- he also summoned all NKVD regional commanders to Moscow and told them that anyone who dared to question the new course would be accused of being a wrecker and arrested immediately.

For Stalin the show trials and the purges served as 'lightning conductors'[23] that shifted the blame for the economic and social crises facing the USSR to the enemy within and without. They made impossible the discussion of any alternative strategies. The purges also had a pre-emptive dimension in that they were aimed against minorities, foreigners and potential critics, who in the event of war could prove a threat to the regime.

LIFE IN STALINIST RUSSIA, 1929–41

These years were a period of sustained social and economic crisis. At least 3–4 million peasants perished in the famine of 1932–3, while in Moscow the consumption of bread sank to less than half of what it had been at the beginning of the century. Although food supplies improved, acute shortages in both food and consumer goods occurred frequently for the rest of the decade. Peasants were uprooted from the soil by the collectivization process, families were divided and children abandoned. The cities, swollen by the influx of the peasantry and the accelerated industrialization of the Five-Year Plans, expanded so rapidly that most of their population lived in cramped and inadequate accommodation.

The cultural revolution

To historians of the totalitarian school (see p. 2) the years 1929–34 were the period of the second great 'socialist offensive' launched from above (the first being 1917–21). Revisionists, however, compare the three years from the Shakhty trials (see p. 341) to June 1931, when Stalin halted the attacks on senior management and technical officials, to the cultural revolution, which took place in China in the late 1960s. Sheila Fitzpatrick, for example, does not dispute that Stalin launched the collectivization programme and the First-Year Plan, but she stresses that the attack on the rightist opposition, the bourgeois economic specialists and the bureaucrats was popular with the rank and file of the party and was to some extent driven by them.[24] The cultural revolution also gave visionaries and fanatics opportunities to further their agendas. Its activities affected virtually every aspect of life in Soviet Russia:

- The party launched a recruitment campaign to bring in more industrial workers and also encouraged thousands of workers to gain qualifications as 'red technicians'.
- In the schools and universities students forced their teachers to stand for 're-election' and demanded that their courses should be somehow linked to the 'real world' of socialism.
- Under the new Commissar for Education, Andrei Bubnov, schools were attached to collective farms or factories and

their pupils' energy harnessed to fulfilling the Five-Year Plan rather than theoretical study.

- Attacks on religion were renewed and the Orthodox Church was driven to the margin of society.
- Ethnic consciousness in the republics was also attacked and measures were taken to ensure that the party apparatus was dominated by reliable Russian Communists.
- Plans proliferated for building communal housing where families would live together, and also for creating a new Soviet legal system, which would eliminate any traces of **'bourgeois' law** (see Document 7).
- In literature, science and the arts 'social realism' again became the new orthodoxy, whereby artists and writers would have to celebrate the work of the ordinary Russian peasant or factory worker.

Bourgeois law
Law as practised in the Western capitalist societies.

The cultural revolution ground to a halt in 1931 and gradually a more conventional and conservative ethos established itself. In schools and universities the emphasis was once again on learning, while the attack on managers, for the time being, was called off. There was also 'a move away from the ascetic Puritanism characteristic of the Cultural Revolution towards a new tolerance of people enjoying themselves'.[25] Titles, ranks and uniforms were all reinstated for the armed forces and many government agencies. There was even discussion of introducing school uniforms.

In 1946 these measures were called 'the Great Retreat' in a seminal book by an American sociologist, Nicholas Timasheff,[26] while Moshe Lewin described them as 'a set of classical measures of social conservatism, law and order strategies, complete with a nationalist revival and efforts to instill values of discipline, patriotism, conformism, authority and orderly careerism'.[27] All this certainly reveals a new element of 'embourgeoisement' in the Soviet regime, but Fitpatrick stresses that contemporaries saw it differently. To them it was a symbol that 'the revolution had finally triumphed'[28] (see Document 10).

The urban revolution

Between 1926 and 1933 the urban population increased by 15 million, or nearly 60 per cent, and in the next six years there was a further increase of 16 million. What this meant in practice was that the population of Leningrad and Moscow each grew by about 1.5 million, while some cities, like Sverdlovsk in the Urals, Stalingrad and Novosibirsk, grew from about 150,000 to nearly half a million. Then there were the new towns like Magnitogorsk, the metallurgical centre in the southern Urals, and Karaganda, a new mining centre that expanded from zero population in 1926 to well over 100,000 in 1939.

The massive increase in the urban population was not, however, reflected in an increase in accommodation. Only a small privileged caste of managers had separate flats. The great majority of city inhabitants had to live in communal apartments, in which only one room was allotted to each family. Some people could only live in corridors or cubby-holes under the stairs. In Moscow the average living space was only 5.5 square metres (6½ square yards) in 1930, while in both Magnitogosk and Irkutsk it was under 4 square metres (5 square yards).

The infrastructure of the towns, with the partial exception of Moscow, also suffered under the impact of mass urban immigration and the large-scale construction of factories. In Moscow there was a public transport system and over two-thirds of its living accommodation was actually connected to the sewage system. Elsewhere life was a lot grimmer. As one American engineer in the USSR in the early 1930s observed, ' the physical aspect of the cities is dreadful. Stench, filth, dilapidation batter the senses at every turn'.[29] Dnepropetrovsk, for instance, which was an industrial city in Ukraine with a population of nearly half a million, had no sewage system in 1933, no paved streets, public transport, electric light or running water. Inevitably, too, Soviet cities were dangerous places. 'Here drink, the congregation of restless single men, inadequate policing, bad living conditions, and unpaved and unlighted streets all contributed to a lawless, frontier atmosphere.'[30]

For the urban population life was made even more difficult by the acute shortage of food, clothes and all other consumer goods. Thus shopping became 'a survival skill'.[31] There were recurring shortages in all basic foodstuffs, clothes and consumer goods, and what was available was usually of very poor quality. 'Handles fell off pots, matches refused to strike, and foreign objects were baked into bread made from adulterated flour.'[32] The government attempted to deal with scarcity by rationing and a system of 'closed distribution', which involved the selling of goods through closed stores that were only open to the personnel of particular factories or offices. In practice, a two-tier economy developed: the formal state-run system of rationing and supply and a 'second economy', which made goods produced by state-run factories available on the black market. To achieve anything but the barest subsistence Russians had to have what was called *blat* or 'pull'. In other words you needed to have contacts that would bypass state agencies and provide you with the vital goods either for a price or out of friendship (see Document 5).

The new working class

Until recently the Russian working class has not been the subject of much analysis. Soviet historians assumed that orders issued by Stalin and the Politburo were carried out and effectively enforced, while Western historians at the height of the Cold War saw the Soviet working class as little more than slaves or victims of a brutal dictatorship . In fact, however, more recent or 'revisionist' history, which tends to view history from the bottom upwards, has shown that the Russian workers were not just rubber stamps.

Between 1928 and 1932 the number of people employed in industry nearly doubled from 3.1 million to 6 million. In the construction sector the increase was even more dramatic, as the total number of workers leapt from 630,000 to 2.5 million. For the most part the new workers were drawn from the countryside, which helped destroy the cohesion of the older working class.

When the first Five-Year Plan was launched, the regime had initially attempted to mobilize the workers behind it by encouraging the most zealous to organize themselves into shock brigades composed of groups of about 12 people. Their task was to compete against each other and create new production records and to keep watch on potentially unreliable managers. In 1930 some 65 per cent of the workers were organized in these groups. However, the majority of the rank-and-file workers became increasingly resentful of the ever-accelerating tempo of work, and this at times led to brief stoppages and demonstrations, particularly in the Donbass coalfields and the Putilov works in Leningrad.

Stalin himself became concerned that the shock brigades were undermining the managers in the factories and were dictating working conditions and rates of pay. In an attempt to control the situation, in 1931 he attacked 'egalitarianism' and called for increased wage differentiation through the introduction of piece-work, which entailed each worker being paid solely for what they produced. The shock brigades were progressively replaced by 'cost-accounting brigades', which played a key role in introducing the new piece rates. In 1935 a fresh attempt was made with the Stakhanovite campaign to impose a more efficient system from above. The hope was that a series of dramatic production achievements by individuals could be used to set examples, which would lead to improvements in organization and increases in production right across the board.

The Stakhanovite movement

In the night of 30–1 August 1935 Alesei Stakhanov (see Figure 10.3) cut 102 tons of coal at the mine in the Don River basin (Donbass). This was 14 times the prescribed norm. This achievement rapidly snowballed into the Stakhanovite movement, which spread right across the USSR. Eventually the movement even included postmen and waiters. Stakhanovites, as representatives of the ordinary people, were given privileges – extra rations, consumer goods, better housing and sometimes even cars. Consequently they often aroused the anger and envy of their fellow workers. It is also argued that Stakkhanovism led to greater disruption than it alleviated,

Figure 10.3 Alesei Stakhanov (front) with his fellow miners in the Donbass, 1935.
Source: RIA Novosti.

as the efforts of the record-creating minority created bottlenecks by disrupting the smooth flow of production and exacerbating the abuse of equipment.[33]

The workers continued, however, to exploit mistakes in the system, such as the delivery of faulty equipment and breakdowns in machinery, to avoid meeting their prescribed work targets. They also exploited the acute shortage of labour to negotiate unofficial agreements and pay rates with the management. In practice workers were able to criticize their managers, and arguably had a greater degree of independence than many American workers, who were still struggling for union independence. The historian, R.W. Thurston, for example, shows that at Leningrad factory meetings in 1937, 1938 and 1939 workers were outspoken about problems ranging from low pay to poor supply of materials and unjust dismissals[34] (see Document 8).

Women and the family in the USSR

Although the Bolshevik Party had paid lip service to women's liberation, and early Soviet legislation had undermined the family, in practice equality of the sexes was not a priority for either Lenin or Stalin. To use Ina Merkel's phrase about women in post-war Communist East Germany, they suffered under 'the bondage of a double burden'.[35] Women certainly gained plenty of opportunities to work in the new factories and some 3.5 million of them entered the labour force, but they still had to play the main role in running the family and looking after their husbands, children and dependent relatives.

The massive upheavals of collectivization and accelerated industrialization broke up families and caused a spectacular rise in juvenile crime, abandoned children and broken marriages, as well as a decline in the birthrate. Given that there was a limit to the welfare measures that the state could finance, it was no wonder then that in this 'quicksand society'[36] the Soviet authorities fell back on the traditional family as the best way to restore social stability (see p. 82). Consequently in May 1936 the Soviet government produced a draft law covering abortion, divorce, child support and some form of financial encouragement for mothers of large families. The provisions were discussed in specially convened meetings in factories, offices and collective farms, and eventually resulted in the following legislation in 1936:

- abortion was banned except where it was proved that a birth would threaten a woman's life (see Document 6)

- divorce was made more difficult and maintenance fees for the men more expensive
- to encourage large families, relatively generous financial benefits were made available to mothers with six or more children.

An indication of the restoration of more conservative values was the creation of the 'Wives' Movement'. In the first decade and a half or so after the Revolution, educated women had gone out of their way not to define themselves as wives, but in 1936 first the wives of managers and engineers in heavy industry, and then the wives of army officers and rail road managers formed 'movements' dedicated to carrying out charitable activities that would assist their husbands' workplaces. It was, however, emphasized that carrying out these good works should not stop these women from being 'good wives and mothers'.

'A voice noticeably muted, if not silent, in the 1930s was that of educated women with a profession, a job and an ideology of women's emancipation, who did not define themselves as wives.'[37] Women occupied only about 10 per cent of senior administrative posts and 15 per cent of the party membership. This did not represent active discrimination against women by the regime, but rather reflected the reality of everyday life, where the sheer hard grind of work and family usually prevented women from rising to the top of their professions (see Documents 6 and 7).

THE CREATION OF THE STALINIST POLITICAL SYSTEM

The roots of Stalinism lie deep in the autocratic traditions of both tsarist Russia and the centralized one-party system created by Lenin and the Bolshevik Party 1917–22 (see Chapter 2). After the unsatisfactory compromise of the NEP, Stalin embarked on a series of major measures, which effectively recast the Soviet state:

- collectivization
- the accelerated rate of industrialization
- the establishment by the party and government of complete dominance over the entire economy

- the elimination of the 'old Bolsheviks' and the generation that dominated the party and bureaucracy from 1917 to 1937, through the purges and the Terror, and their replacement by the Stalin generation – predominantly younger men in their mid-thirties.

Paradoxically, as Roberts Service has observed, 'while emasculating much of Lenin's "legacy" ... Stalin was [striving] to energize and stabilize the whole Soviet order.'[38]

From oligarch to dictator: the evolution of Stalin's power

In 1929 Stalin (see Figure 10.4) emerged as the leader of the dominant faction in the party (see p. 69), and was able to launch both the collectivization campaign and the Five-Year Plan. This was achieved by a strategy of control from above and mass mobilization from below. The details of the policy and the 'establishment of administrative control' were organized through the experts in **Vesenkha** and Gosplan (see p. 339), the Central Control Commission (*Rabkrin*), the Party Secretariat and the OGPU.

Vesenkha
Supreme Council of the National Economy.

The autonomy of the republics and regional administrations was irreparably weakened by the transfer of power over agriculture, industry and finance to the central government. Yet despite the strengthening of the state and party organs, the famine and excesses of collectivization called Stalin's authority into question, and, even if there was a not a plot at the Seventeenth Party Congress to remove him from power (see pp. 341–2), the potential for an anti-Stalinist bloc did exist. Stalin survived by unloading the responsibility for the famine on to local officials, and by easing the pace of economic and social change. He also established a more hierarchical line of command with administrative agencies, which were granted greater freedom from supervision by the control agencies. This in turn laid up fresh problems for the future by entrenching local interests and creating further friction between the centre and the periphery. Ultimately this was broken by the purges, the growth of the Stakhanovite movement and the Terror during the years 1936–8. The Politburo and the Central Committee were also emasculated, and the power of the NKVD enormously strengthened.

Figure 10.4 Stalin
Source: Mary Evans
Picture Library.

   This marked the final establishment of the Stalinist dictatorship. At the Eighteenth Party Congress in March 1939 Stalin went
out of his way to stress that the state could not be allowed to
wither away while there was still the danger of capitalist encir-
clement. The main constitutional features of the Stalinist
dictatorship were:

- there was an enormous increase in bureaucracy and
  centralization – a result of central economic planning

- the party was increasingly an instrument of government
- the Politburo was firmly subordinated to Stalin.

The Stalin cult

The cult of the *Vozhd* or leader developed from relatively modest beginnings in 1929 to 'gigantic proportions'[39] by the late 1940s. Stalin's fiftieth birthday in December 1929 was marked with massive praise. The main characteristics of the Stalin cult emerged during the 1930s:

- Stalin was closely linked with Lenin and seen as one of the key figures of the revolution.
- His achievements were constantly stressed and he was frequently described as 'creator of our happiness'.
- He was portrayed as a great writer and political theorist – in this respect he was grouped together with Marx and Lenin.
- He was also given the image of a simple leader, who could communicate with the people and who cared about their concerns.
- The media became saturated with articles on 'the great leader', 'father of the people' or 'genius of our epoch'.
- He was given virtually a god-like status and invested with superhuman qualities of love and care for his people.

Historians working from the totalitarian model see the Stalin cult as something imposed on the people from on high. The revisionist or structuralist historians – Lewin, Rittersporn and Stites – on the other hand, argue that 'a reciprocity existed between official and traditional or popular values'.[40] For instance, many Stakhanovites, soldiers and even intellectuals who had benefited from Stalin were ready to see Stalin as the architect of the achievements of the USSR. For the great mass of the ordinary people Stalin was often seen as the person who could intercede on their behalf and help them in their daily struggle with petty bureaucracy and peremptory local officials. Drawing on Christian traditions Stalin was iconized and projected as a semi-divine leader. Yet there was also a 'grass roots input into the iconization of the leader'.[41] Some Russians, for instance, put pictures of Stalin in icon frames and prayed and crossed themselves in front of him (see Documents 9 (a) and (b)).

FOREIGN POLICY

Stalin's main preoccupation was with 'the awesome task of recasting Russia as a modern industrialized power'.[42] Consequently he delegated a large share of the responsibility for foreign affairs to the officials of *Nakromindel* (the Commissariat for Foreign Affairs). In really important questions he would, of course, intervene, but he usually preferred to let things drift. This left a vacuum in which contradictory policies could sometimes be pursued by officials at *Nakromindel*, and ensured, as Jonathan Haslam has observed, that 'Soviet foreign policy was anything but monolithic'.[43] Stalinist foreign policy was further complicated by the rivalry between the Comintern and *Nakromindel*. The latter by and large attempted to deal with the world as it was, while the task of the former was to stir up revolution and back local Communist parties. In 1930, for instance, while *Nakromindel* was attempting to pursue a policy of peaceful co-existence with France, the Comintern was supporting Communist revolutionaries in French Indo-China.

The devastating impact of the Great Depression on the Western Powers contrasted with the apparent impressive success of the first Five-Year Plan (see p. 340). To many Communists this seemed evidence that capitalism was at last collapsing, and the Comintern rejoiced at the possibility of exploiting the economic misery to bring about revolution. Yet 'it would be wrong to see the Russians smugly sheltered from the raging storm outside',[44] as the global impact of the Depression confronted the USSR with fresh challenges:

- The Soviet leadership feared that the West would not just stand by while the USSR strengthened its economy. Stalin suspected that it might launch a pre-emptive strike.
- The Depression led to an outcry against Soviet **dumping** and the imposition of tough trade restrictions on Soviet exports by the USA, Canada the Scandinavian counties and France. This was accompanied by a fierce anti-Soviet campaign in the Western press.
- The collapse of the German economy led to fears in Moscow that a hostile France would dominate Europe.
- The Depression also acted as a catalyst for Japanese aggression against China in 1931. The Soviets feared that

Dumping
Exporting cheap goods, which undermine local industries.

after the occupation of Manchuria the Japanese might ally with the Western Powers to destroy the USSR.

To deal with these perceived threats, the USSR sought to neutralize the French by supporting the proposals for disarmament at the League of Nation's Disarmament Conference at Geneva in 1933. It also attempted to draw closer to Italy and gain Italian backing for Soviet entry into the League of Nations, which was achieved in 1934. Initially Stalin also welcomed the rise of the Nazi Party in Germany on the grounds that German Nationalism would weaken the French.

The rise of Hitler

Stalin's response to the Nazi seizure of power in January–March 1933 is the subject of considerable historical debate, of which four main strands can be identified:

- A.J.P. Taylor in his *Origins of the Second World War* argues that Stalin was primarily aiming at an Anglo-French alliance against Nazi Germany and only when this was not forthcoming did he sign the Nazi–Soviet non-aggression pact of 23 August 1939.
- This view is rejected by the so-called German school, which is represented by the Western scholars Nikolai Tolstoy and Robert Tucker and the Soviet historian Mikhail Semiriaga. They argue that Stalin was not interested in collective security but in continuing the **Rapallo policy** of the 1920s and negotiating an alliance with Germany.
- The third group, in which Jonathan Haslam and Caroline Kennedy-Pipe are the key representatives, takes the line that Soviet policy was ambivalent and contradictory because it was influenced by an internal political struggle between the pro-Western Foreign Minister **Maxim Litvinov** and his rivals in Moscow and Berlin, who wanted closer relations with Germany.
- This last argument is modified by G. Roberts, who argues that the splits in Soviet policy were not caused so much by a 'fundamental split over western security but in the realm of tactical and political calculation'. He stresses that Soviet foreign policy was really a response to a complex situation

Rapallo policy
In defiance of the Western Powers, in 1922 Germany negotiated the Rapallo Treaty with the USSR. Both renounced any reparation claims on each other and agreed to normalize diplomatic relations.

Maxim Litvinov (1876–1951)
Soviet Foreign Minister, 1930–9.

and consisted of 'patterns and trends flowing from overall ideology and strategy combined with the specific reactions, calculations and decisions resulting from the assessment of particular situations'.[45]

However, once Hitler was in power, Stalin and the Politburo did begin to perceive that Nazi Germany was a potential threat to the USSR. Stalin was not concerned by Hitler's domestic policies but by the fear that ultimately Hitler might launch a war against the USSR. Initially The main thrust of Soviet foreign policy was to build up a defensive alliance against Germany. By joining the League of Nations Stalin hoped that he could turn it into a more effective instrument of collective security, and he also aimed to build, with French cooperation, a regional Eastern European defence agreement modelled on the Locarno Pact of 1925 (see p. 114). He also pursued a policy of founding popular fronts, which were often groups of disparate parties bound together only by their hatred of Fascism. These decisions marked a radical break in Soviet foreign policy and led in 1935 to a pact with France and Czechoslovakia, which was not, however, backed up by any military agreements.

German and Italian intervention in the Spanish Civil War (see p. 315) confirmed Stalin's fear of Nazi expansionism. Initially the USSR was ready to support the Non-intervention Committee set up by Britain and France, but when it became obvious that it was both unable and unwilling to stop Germany and Italy supplying Franco with arms, Stalin took the decision in October 1936 to send arms to the Republican government (see p. 310).

Yet the USSR did not abandon its attempts to come to terms with Hitler. From 1935 to 1937 there were a series of ultimately inconclusive discussions in Berlin in which David Kandelaki, the Soviet trade representative, played a key part. Although Litvinov was determined to subordinate everything to a long-term policy of containment, Stalin wished to explore the possibility of improving relations with Germany, particularly as the League had failed to deter aggression in Ethiopia (see pp. 281-4) and the French were still refusing to ratify the Franco-Soviet Pact of 1935.

The Sudeten crisis, 1938

It was Hitler's attempt to destroy Czechoslovakia in 1938 (see pp. 239–40) that finally persuaded Stalin to follow a policy of collective resistance to Nazi Germany. The USSR was directly involved in the crisis as a result of the treaty signed with Czechoslovakia in 1935. Military assistance to the Czechs was, however, dependent on France also fulfilling its military obligations under the 1924 treaty with Czechoslovakia.

When the Sudeten crisis broke on 12 September, the USSR immediately stressed its determination to honour the Czech treaty of 1935, provided France, too, guaranteed military support, but Hitler's surprising acceptance of Mussolini's compromise proposal at the Munich Conference of 29–30 September, to which the USSR was not invited, ensured that Soviet assistance was not in the end needed.

'One of the most tantalising, unanswered questions of the Munich crisis is what the Soviet Union would have done if Czechoslovakia had decided to stand and fight alone'.[46] On 24 September 1938 Beneš, the Czech Prime Minister, actually asked whether the USSR would intervene, if Czechoslovakia decided to fight Germany without France, but before Stalin could frame an answer, Benes cancelled the request. Soviet historians always argued that the USSR was ready to go it alone, but while the USSR was ready to move against Germany provided that both Britain and France did, there was no offer of unilateral help from Stalin. Moscow was wary of being trapped into a war without allies. Besides fighting alone, it also faced considerable obstacles in that it had no common frontier with Germany (see Map 4).

The Nazi–Soviet Pact

Until the diplomatic archives in Moscow were opened, it was difficult to pinpoint when exactly the Soviet government decided to abandon the strategy of collective security. The documents released now show that until mid-August 1939 Moscow was on balance convinced that Soviet security would be best provided for by an alliance with Britain and France against Nazi Germany, rather than by an accommodation with Hitler.

In April 1939 the British and French belatedly began negotiations with Moscow for a defensive alliance against Germany.
They were protracted and bedevilled by mutual mistrust. Stalin's
demand that the USSR should have the right to intervene in the
affairs of the small states on its Western borders if they were
threatened with internal subversion by the Nazis, as Austria and
Czechoslovakia had been in 1938, was rejected outright by the
British. London feared that the USSR would exploit this as an
excuse to seize the territories for themselves. Stalin, on the other
hand, was similarly suspicious that the Western democracies were
manoeuvring the Russians into a position where they would have
to do most of the fighting against Germany, should war break
out.

The evidence in the Soviet archives shows that as late as 12
August 1939, when negotiations opened between Britain, France
and the USSR on the military aspects of the security pact, the
USSR still hoped for a successful conclusion, provided that agreement could be 'watertight leaving no room for manoeuvres by
appeasers in London and Paris'.[47] When the talks broke down on
17 August over the question of securing Polish and Romanian
agreement to the passage of the Red Army through their territory,
Stalin was ready to explore the German proposals for a pact and
on 23 August he at last agreed that Ribbentrop (see p. 241), the
German Foreign Minister, should fly to Moscow and begin talks.

The Soviet–Nazi pact was signed in the early hours of 24
August. Not only did it commit both powers to benevolent neu-
trality towards each other, but in a secret protocol it outlined the
German and Russian spheres of interest in Eastern Europe: the
Baltic states and Bessarabia in Romania fell within the Russian
sphere, while Poland was to be divided between the two Powers.

Once Poland was defeated, the Red Army moved in on 17
September and occupied eastern Poland, and two weeks later Germany
and the USSR agreed on a new demarcation line between ethnic
Poland, which was occupied by the Germans, and the areas which were
mainly settled by Ukrainians that were to be ceded to the Russians.

The outbreak of war with Nazi Germany

Until June 1941 Stalin pursued a double policy of territorial
expansion in Eastern Europe aimed at defending the USSR against

aggression from Nazi Germany, while at the same time cultivating the *détente* with Germany. He signed mutual assistance pacts with Estonia and Latvia in October 1939, and the Lithuanians were pressurized into agreeing to the establishment of Soviet bases in their territory.

When the Finns refused to agree to transfer the Port of Hango to the USSR as a naval base, the Red Army invaded Finland on 30 November 1939. Far from gaining a quick victory, the Finns held out until March 1940 and inflicted some 200,000 casualties on the Russians. The war also threatened to drag the USSR into the wider European conflict. The USSR was expelled from the League of Nations, and the USA placed an embargo on the export of war-related goods to the USSR. The French and British even began to draw up plans for sending an expeditionary force to help the Finns and bomb the Baku oilfields. Had the war not ended in March 1940 when the Finns ceded Hango, its consequences would have had a dramatic impact of the course of events.

Stalin's reaction to the fall of France in June 1940 was to absorb the three Baltic states, Estonia, Latvia and Lithuania, and annex Besserabia and northern Bukovina from Romania. Soviet proposals to negotiate the division of spheres of interest in the Balkans were rejected by Italy and Germany, and in November 1940 negotiations over the USSR joining the Tripartite Pact broke down, essentially because the Germans demanded Russian acceptance of German hegemony in Europe. The adherence of Bulgaria to the Tripartite Pact in February 1941 and the German occupation of Yugoslavia and Greece in the spring of 1941 were further blows to Stalin's policy of *détente* with Germany.

In only one area did Stalin achieve diplomatic success. In April 1941 the USSR managed to negotiate a pact of neutrality with the Japanese, which freed it from the danger of war on two fronts – a simultaneous German–Japanese attack.

By the early summer of 1941 it was clear that a Nazi–Soviet war was becoming daily more of a certainty. Yet despite frequent warnings, both from Soviet agents inside Germany and the British government, Stalin did not believe that war was imminent. He was convinced that Hitler first wanted to defeat the British and that Germany would then only attack after the breakdown of further bouts of Nazi–Soviet negotiations. Naturally the longer he could delay the outbreak of hostilities, the stronger the USSR would be. This consequently made him even more ready to cling to his increasingly threadbare strategy of *détente* with Nazi Germany, which was finally proved to be an illusion when German troops crossed the frontier on 22 June 1941.

ASSESSMENT

Like the Third Reich, Stalinism has been the subject of intense debate amongst historians. At the height of the Cold War the dominant school of historiography in the West characterized it as a totalitarian system. Conservative historians, such as Richard Pipes, argue that Stalinism was Lenin's legacy, but historians on the left, like Isaac Deutscher and E.H. Carr, insisted that Bolshevism was not predetermined to become totalitarian and could have developed very differently. They emphasized party politics, the disruptive impact of modernization and the international isolation of the USSR as factors that helped produce Stalinism.

Both these interpretations, however, see Stalinism as a monolithic force that imposed a system of totalitarianism from above. The revisionists, with their view of 'history from below', seek to re-interpret the convulsions of the Stalinist era from a very different vantage point. Sheila Fitzpatrick[48] attacks the conventional political approach of totalitarianism on three levels of interpretation:

- the state had less control over society than the totalitarian school implied, and its actions were often reactive rather than planned
- the state did have to respond to definite social pressures in drafting its policies
- it also often had to act in response to political pressures from below.

Revisionism has opened up the discussion on Stalinism and shown that Stalin enjoyed significant support in the USSR by appealing to patriotism, ambition and young people's sense of adventure and idealism in building socialism. Stephen Kotkin, in his seminal book *Magnetic Mountain: Stalinism as a Civilization*, argues that Stalinism should not be dismissed as just a barbaric and backward tyranny. On the contrary, if judged by the standards of the time, it can be seen as an example of 'progressive modernity' in the key areas of economic planning and state welfare. Although the actual sums paid in benefits remained modest, Kotkin insists that 'there was no denying that the Soviet state had embraced a broad conception of social welfare – extending from employment and income to affordable housing, health care and organized leisure.'[49]

Inevitably in time revisionism was pushed too far, and its emphasis on social history and concentration on everyday life not only left out the politics but tended to 'normalize' the Stalinist system. In 1986 Geoff Eley argued that the term 'totalitarianism' still possessed some validity for Stalin's Russia, as it did for Nazi Germany, since it captured 'a definite aspect of Stalinist reality, namely the "total claim" of the regime on its population, sanctioned by coercive forms of rule and accompanied by a distinctive repertoire of political demands'.[50] Essentially, of course, no one historical approach has the monopoly of validity. Post-revisionists, helped by the opening of the Soviet archives, are adopting a more complex approach to show how decisions were taken and how a whole complex range of factors influenced developments in Stalinist Russia in the 1930s.

Document 1
Stalin and the kulaks

In 1928 Stalin visited Siberia. This is an extract of what he told the local party administrators:

Your grain surpluses are bigger than ever before. Yet the plan for grain procurements is not being fulfilled. Why? What is the reason? . . . Look at the kulak farms; their barns and sheds are crammed with grain . . .

You say the kulaks are unwilling to deliver grain, that they are waiting for prices to rise and prefer to engage in unbridled speculation. That is true. But the kulaks . . . are demanding an increase in prices to three times those fixed by the government.

But there is no guarantee that the kulaks will not again sabotage the grain procurements next year. More, it may be said with certainty that so long as there are kulaks, so long will there be sabotage of grain procurements.

Source: J.V. Stalin, *Works*, vol. 11, London, Lawrence & Wishart, 1955, pp. 3–9.

DOCUMENT 2

The anti-kulak campaign

Abdurman Avtorkhanov, a graduate history student at the Institute of Red Professors, stopped at a station of a small town during his rail journey from Grozny to Moscow in 1930. He later recalled what he saw:

Endless fields of people – women, old people – and universal wailing. They were being loaded on to cattle trucks to be sent off to Siberia. I was there for fifteen minutes and I asked the station master . . . 'What's this? What's happening here?' and he said, 'What's up with you? Have you just landed from the moon or maybe you have arrived from Persia? This is collectivization and the elimination of the kulaks as a class.' And it turned out, there were so many people, and not enough trains, that with the cold weather, people were literally dying there.

Source: J. Lewis and P. Whitehead, *Stalin: A Time For Judgement*, London, Mandarin, 1992, p. 46.

DOCUMENT 3

Mass operations of the NKVD, 1937

Victims were shot at night either in prisons, the cellars of the State Security Office or in some clearing in a forest. The following is an order issued to Captain Korobitsin of the NKVD in Ulianovsk in the Omsk region on 4 August 1937 by Grigorii Gorbach, the NKVD Chairman in Omsk:

1 Adapt immediately an area in a building of the NKVD, preferably in a cellar, suitable as a special cell for carrying out death sentences . . .
3 The death sentences are to be carried out at night. Before the sentences are executed the exact identity of the prisoner is to be established by checking carefully with the *troika* verdict.
4 After the executions the bodies are to be laid in a pit dug beforehand, then carefully buried and the pit is to be camouflaged . . .

7   Immediately on receipt of this order you are to present a list of NKVD staff permitted to participate in executions. Red Army soldiers or *militsionery* [militia] are not to be employed. All persons involved in the work of transporting the bodies and excavating or filling in the pits have to sign a document certifying that they are sworn to secrecy.

Source: B. McLoughlin, 'Mass operations of the NKVD, 1937–38' in B. McLoughlin and K. McDermott, eds, *Stalin's Terror High Politics and Mass Repression in the Soviet Union*, Basingstoke, Palgrave, 2003, p. 130–1.

DOCUMENT 4

Shortages

In August 1930 Pravda, *the official Soviet newspaper, prepared a summary of readers' letters for the party leadership:*

What are people discontented about? In the first place, that the worker is hungry, he has no fats, the bread is *ersatz* [artificial substitute], which is impossible to eat ... it's a common thing that the wife of a worker stands the whole day in line, her husband comes home from work, and dinner is not prepared, and everyone curses Soviet power. In the lines there is noise, shouting and fights, curses at the expense of Soviet power.

Source: S. Fitzpatrick, *Everyday Stalinism*, Oxford, Oxford University Press, 2000, p. 42.

DOCUMENT 5

The importance of *blat*

In 1940 Petr Gattsuk, a citizen of Novgorod, wrote to Andrei Vyshinsky, the Deputy Chairman of the Council of Ministers, and complained about the all-prevailing phenomenon of blat:

The word had appeared in the lexicon of the Russian language. I cannot literally translate that for you, since perhaps it comes from some kind of foreign word. But still in Russian I understand it well and can give you an exact literal translation. In translation into the Russian language the word *blat* means swindling, cheating, stealing, speculation, slipshod practices, and so on. And what does it mean if we meet the expression: 'I have *blat*'[?] It means that I have a close connection with a swindler, speculator, thief, cheat, toady and similar ... If you need to buy something in a shop – you need *blat*. If it's difficult or impossible to get a railroad ticket, then it is simple and easy *po blatu*. If you live without an apartment, don't ever go to the housing administration ... but just a little *blat* and you will at once get your apartment.

Source: Fitzpatrick, *Everyday Stalinism*, p. 62.

DOCUMENT 6

The abortion debate

The virtual abolition of abortion in 1936 met with considerable criticism. A young female engineer expressed her objections in a letter to the authorities:

The prohibition of abortion means the compulsory birth of a child to a woman who does not want children ... The birth of a child ties married people to each other ... Where a child comes into the family against the will of the parents, a grim personal drama will be enacted which will undoubtedly lower the social value of the parents and leave its mark on the child. A categorical prohibition of abortion will confront young people with a dilemma: either complete sexual abstinence or the risk of jeopardizing their studies and disrupting their life.

Source: G. Lapidus, 'Women in Soviet society' in D.L. Hoffmann, ed., *Stalinism*, Oxford, Blackwell, 2003, p. 229.

DOCUMENT 7

Socialist utopianism, or how to save labour by communal living

S.G. Strumlin, an official who played a key role in drawing up the first Five-Year Plan, wrote in 1926:

Every day 36 million hours are expended in the RSFR [Russian Soviet Federated Socialist Republic] for cooking alone. This means that on the basis of the eight-hour working day, four and one-half million workers or double the number that are employed in heavy industry are occupied in cooking. At the same time, collective cooking of the same amount of food would require one-sixth of this time, and would release over four million housewives for productive labour.

Source: Lapidus, 'Women in Soviet society', p. 221.

DOCUMENT 8

The limits of criticism in the USSR

After the war an émigré building engineer told his American interviewers that:

The Soviet system is a dictatorship, but on the other side you must recognize that there exists a big criticism of the small and responsible workers excluding criticism of the regime, the party or the Politburo. No doubt in their authority can be expressed, and a word against the regime, the Politburo or the party and that is the end of you. You can criticize the secretary of a *raikom* [district party committee] but it is fairly dangerous. Also you can criticize comrade Ivanov [the equivalent of Mr Smith] who works as a [second or lower] secretary of the *raikom*. If you criticize him nothing will come of you.

Source: Quoted in R.W. Thurston, 'Reassessing the history of Soviet workers: opportunities to criticize and participate in decision making, 1935–41' in Stephen White, ed., *New Directions in Soviet History*, Cambridge, Cambridge University Press, 1992, p. 161.

DOCUMENT 9

The Stalin cult

(a) In December 1937 the godlike all-knowing qualities of Stalin were celebrated in a poem by Lebedev-Kumach. The poem was printed in Pravda, *5 December 1937:*

And so – everywhere. In the workshops, in the mines
In the Red Army, the Kindergarten
He is watching . . .
You look at his portrait and it's as if he knows
Your work – and weighs it.
You worked badly – his brows lower
But when good, he smiles in his moustache.

Source: S. Davies, 'Propaganda and its reception in Stalin's Russia' in J. Channon, ed., *Politics, Society and Stalinism in the USSR*, Basingstoke, Macmillan, 1998, p. 121.

(b) In 1988 the writer Konstantin Simonov recalled the 1930s:

What good things were associated with the name of Stalin in those years for us, and for me in particular? Very much, practically everything, if only because at that time in our imagination almost everything came from him and was shrouded

in his name. The general line of the industrialization of the
country which he carried out explained everything that was
happening in that sphere. And of course many wonderful things
happened. They changed before my eyes ... Sweeping everything
from the path to industrialization, Stalin carried it out with an
iron hand. He spoke little, did a lot, met people on business a lot,
rarely gave interviews, rarely made speeches and managed to get
his every word considered and valued not only here, but in the
whole world.

Source: Davies, 'Propaganda', p. 124

DOCUMENT 10
Fascism and communism

*In 1934 Mirko Ardemagni, a Fascist theoretician, drew attention
to the parallels between Fascism and Bolshevism:*

In the course of the Russian revolution ... there has been a
surreptitious adoption of some of the fundamental political
principles that characterize Fascism ... Fascism, however one
chooses to name it, has made its appearance in Russia ... [The
Bolsheviks] have lit fires of a patriotism that was unknown in the
time of the Czars ... They have embraced a conception of
nationalism that has more affinities with the political thought of a
Mussolini than anything imagined by Lenin ... Aping the Fascist
example the Bolsheviks no longer address themselves to the 'class
struggle', but discipline the working masses to the purpose of the
community.

Source: M. Ardemagni, 'Deviazzioni russe verso il fascismo', *Gerarchia*,
vol. 14, no. 7, July 1934, pp. 571–3. Quoted in A.J. Gregor, *Italian
Fascism and Development Dictatorship*, Princeton, Princeton University
Press, 1979, pp. 211–12.

NOTES

1 A. Nove in J.R. Miller (S.J. Linz, ed.), *The Soviet Economic
Experiment*, Urbana/Chicago, University of Illinois Press, 1990,
p. 74.

2 R. Service, *A History of Modern Russia*, Harmondsworth, Penguin,
1997, p. 180.

3 J. Hughes, *Stalinism in a Russian Province. Collectivization and
Dekulakization in Siberia*, London, Macmillan, 1996, p. 213.

4 Service, *Modern Russia*, p. 181.

5 C. Merridale, ' The Moscow party and the Socialist offensive: activists and workers, 1928–31' in Stephen White, ed., *New Directions in Soviet Policy*, Cambridge, Cambridge University Press, 1992, p. 137.

6 Ibid., p. 137.

7 N. Jasny, *Soviet Industrialization, 1928–1952*, Chicago, University of Chicago Press, 1961, pp. 73–80.

8 D. Volkogonov, *Stalin, Triumph and Tragedy*, London, Phoenix Press, 2000, p. 200.

9 J. Arch Getty, *Origins of the Great Purges*, Cambridge, Cambridge University Press, 1985, p. 210.

10 Volkogonov, *Stalin*, p. 208 and R. Conquest, *Stalin and the Kirov Murder*, London, Hutchinson, 1989, p. 134.

11 Getty, *Origins*, p. 209.

12 C. Ward, *Stalin's Russia*, London, Edward Arnold, 2nd ed. 1993, p. 113.

13 Ibid., p. 115.

14 S. Fitzpatrick, *Everyday Stalinism*, Oxford, Oxford University Press, 2000, p. 191.

15 Ibid., p. 205.

16 R. Conquest, *The Great Terror. A Reassessment*, London, Hutchinson, 1990, p. 485.

17 S.F. Cohen, 'Stalin's terror as social history', *The Russian Review*, vol. 45, 1986, pp. 383–4.

18 Conquest, *The Great Terror*, p. 70.

19 Getty, *Origins*, and R. Manning quoted in S. Fitzpatrick, 'New perspectives on Stalinism', *Russian Reviw*, vol. 45, 1986, p. 369.

20 Ibid., p. 368.

21 Ibid., p. 372.

22 W. Hedeler, 'Ezhov's scenario for the Great Terror and the falsified record of the third Moscow show trial' in B. McLoughlin and K. McDermott, eds, *Stalin's Terror High Politics and Mass Repression in the Soviet Union*, Basingstoke, Palgrave, 2003, p. 50.

23 Ibid., p. 36.

24 See S. Fitzpatrick, *Cultural Revolution in Russia, 1928–31*, Bloomington, Indiana University Press, 1978.

25 Fitzpatrick, *Everyday Stalinism*, p. 90.

26 N.S. Timasheff, *The Great Retreat: The Growth and Decline of Communism in Russia*, New York, Dutton, 1946.

27 Quoted in Ward, *Stalin's Russia*, p. 247.

28 Fitzpatrick, *Everyday Stalinism*, p. 107.

29 Ibid., p. 51.

30 bid., p. 52.

31 Ibid., p. 54.

32 Ibid., p. 44.

33 D. Filzer, *Soviet Workers and Stalinist Industrialization: The Formation of Modern Soviet Production Relations, 1928–1941*, London, Pluto Press, 1986, pp. 179–207.

34 R.W. Thurston, 'Reassessing the history of Soviet workers' in S. White, ed. *New Directions in Soviet History*, Cambridge, CUP.

35 Quoted in D.G. Williamson, *Germany from Defeat to Partition*, Harlow, Pearson, 2001, p. 105.

36 Moshe Lewin quoted in G. Lapidus, 'Women in Soviet society: equality, development and social change' in D.L. Hoffman, ed., *Stalinism*, Oxford, Blackwell, 2003, p. 217.

37 Fitzpatrick, *Everyday Stalinism*. p. 162.

38 R. Service, 'Stalinism and the Soviet state order' in H. Shukman, ed., *Redefining Stalinism*, London, Frank Cass, 2003, p. 10.

39 S. Davies, 'The leader cult: propaganda and its reception in Stalin's Russia' in J. Channon, ed., *Politics, Society and Stalinism in the USSR*, Basingstoke, Macmillan. 1998, p. 117.

40 Ibid., p. 116.

41 Ibid., p. 129.

42 J. Haslam, *Soviet Foreign Policy, 1930–33*, London, Macmillan, 1983, p. 10.

43 Ibid., p. 20.

44 Ibid., p. 1.

45 G. Roberts, *The Soviet Union and the Origins of the Second World War: Russo-German Relations and the Road to War, 1933–41*, London, Macmillan, 1995, pp. 6 and 8.

46 Roberts, *The Soviet Union and the Origins of the Second World War*, p. 59.

47 Roberts, *The Soviet Union and the Origins of the Second World War*, p. 85.

48 Fitzpatrick, 'New perspectives on Stalinism', pp. 357–73.

49 Extract from S. Kotkin, 'Magnetic mountain: Stalinism as a civilization, Berkeley, University of California Press, 1995, in D.L. Hoffman, ed., *Stalinism*,' p. 122.

50 G. Eley, 'History with the politics left out – again?', *The Russian Review*, vol. 45, 1986, p. 390.

CHAPTER ELEVEN

Institutionalized authoritarianism

Timeline

1929	5 January	In Yugoslavia King Alexander proclaims a dictatorship
1932	4 October	Gyula Gömbös appointed Hungarian Prime Minister
1933	31 January	Hitler appointed German Chancellor
1934	25 July	The Austrian Chancellor, Dolfuss, assassinated
1935	12 May	Death of General Pilsudski
1937	16 October	Hungarian National Socialist Party (Arrow Cross) founded
1938	10 March	Austrian *Anschluss*
	30 November	Codreanu killed in jail in Romania
1939	7 April	Italy invades Albania
	1 September	Germany invades Poland

Introduction

By 1939 the Balkan and Eastern European states, as well as Portugal and Spain, had authoritarian governments. Each regime was different, but they did have the following characteristics in common:

- Under the impact of Germany and Italy they had taken on a Fascist colouring. Their rulers talked of corporatism and formed youth movements and militias based on the Italian and German models.
- Yet these authoritarian – and essentially conservative – regimes in reality blocked the development of genuine Fascist

movements either by absorbing them into the system, and so subjecting them to control, or else by outlawing them.

- As was shown in Italy and Germany, to seize power Fascism needed the freedom to mobilize and to campaign for public support. In Central and South-Eastern Europe it was only able to triumph as a result of foreign intervention by Germany.

THE KEY ISSUES IN THIS CHAPTER ARE:

- The consolidation of authoritarian regimes throughout Eastern and Southern Europe in the 1930s.
- The degree to which they were influenced by Fascist Italy and Nazi Germany.
- Why these regimes were authoritarian rather than Fascist.

POLAND AND THE BALTIC STATES

The general tendency in Poland, Lithuania and Latvia was for the government to become increasingly more authoritarian. In Poland a new constitution in 1935 gave greater powers to the presidency, while diminishing those of parliament. After the death of Pilsudski in 1935 (see p. 135) the government, which was dominated by the army, was convinced that Liberalism was doomed and that the powers of the state needed to be greatly strengthened. Attempts were made to build up a state party, the Camp of National Unity (OZN), which began to develop blueprints for a new corporative authoritarian system. For a time the OZN fell under the influence of the Polish proto-Fascist party, the *Falanga*, but in early 1938 this link was broken, although this did not mean that it abandoned its authoritarian and centralizing policies.

In neighbouring Lithuania and Latvia the clash between authoritarian governments and proto-Fascist organizations was more pronounced. Both responded to challenges from these movements by outlawing them and creating authoritarian regimes. These followed the pattern set in Spain, Portugal and elsewhere by paying lip service to corporatism (p. 109) and creating a one party state. In Estonia essentially the same path was followed. After the popular Nationalist party, the EVL, did well in the 1934 election, the President declared a state of emergency and created the usual one-party state complete with corporatist institutions, but in contrast to the neighbouring states the powers of the presidency were actually reduced in 1938.

Proto-Fascist and Nationalist movements in Poland and the Baltic states

With the exception of Estonia the radical movements in these states were initially influenced by Italian Fascism and then increasingly with the rise of Nazism they looked to Berlin. In Poland, for instance the Camp of Great Poland, which was founded by the Polish National Democrats, was strongly nationalist and talked much about a 'march on Warsaw'. After it was dissolved, the Camp of National Radicalism emerged. This was more inspired by the Nazi model, but when it, too, was banned, it transmuted itself into the *Falanga*, which was 'probably the only clear-cut fascist organization of any significance in Poland',[1] yet unlike Italian Fascism or German Nazism, it was strongly Catholic and argued that 'God is the highest end of man'.

In Lithuania the proto-Fascist organization was the Iron Wolf Association, which aimed at territorial expansion and the repression of the Jewish, Russian and Polish minorities, while in Latvia a similar movement was the Thunder Cross. The exception was again Estonia, where the key Nationalist force was the Estonian War of Independence Veterans League (EVL), which was a paramilitary force based on those who had fought the Russians and Communists in 1917–18. Its aims were simply a more nationalist and authoritarian regime – it had no links with any foreign Fascist party.

HUNGARY AND AUSTRIA: THE SUCCESSOR STATES

As the two greatest components of the Austro-Hungarian Empire, Hungary and Austria had suffered immense territorial losses in 1919. Both were governed by right-wing authoritarian regimes and increasingly Fascist or Nazi-inspired movements gained support in the 1930s. In Hungary, however, as in the Balkan states and Spain, Fascism's bid for power was blocked by an authoritarian regime. In Austria the same pattern would have most likely developed had it not been for the German occupation and the *Anschluss*.

Hungary

In Hungary the moderate right-wing authoritarianism of the Horthy regime discriminated against the Left and thus left the field open for the radical parties of the right to campaign for support. In the early 1930s the Right was composed of four main groups:

- the traditional Conservatives who had governed Hungary under Count Bethlen
- the new right-wing Radicals led by Major Gyula Gömbös (see p. 130), whose movement was influenced by Fascism, but in reality advocated an authoritarian system based on the bureaucracy and army, with a single-state party
- the small National Socialist parties, who imitated the Nazis
- Ferenc Szálasi's Arrow Cross movement.

In response to the impact of the Depression on Hungary, Admiral Horthy dismissed the conservatives and turned to Gömbös. Almost immediately the new premier made a 'pilgrimage' to Rome, but his regime developed only some superficial similarities to Italian Fascism. Gömbös transformed the government party into the party of National Unity, consolidated its grip on the state and also created a youth movement and a political militia, the Advance Guards, with some 60,000 members. He reinforced his position by appointing his nominees to the army commands and key ministries. Once Hitler came to power he moved closer to Germany and in 1935 he informed Göring that within three years Hungary would become a National Socialist state, but before this could be realized, if indeed he ever intended it, he died in December 1936.

Ferenc Szálasi and the Arrow Cross

In many ways the Arrow Cross was a unique movement, although it clearly had many Fascist characteristics (see p. 9). Szalasi (1897–1946), a former staff officer in the Hungarian army, was

not an impressive orator or really a man of action like Mussolini.
Payne describes him as a 'virtual sleepwalker and intense
ideologue for whom a rather mystical ideology was at least as
important as it was for Hitler'.[2]

Szálasi developed a concept of 'Hungarism', which aimed at
creating a greater Hungary – the 'Carpathian–Danubian Great
Fatherland' which along with Germany and Italy would become
one of the three great powers of Europe. The real role for
Hungary was to mediate between the Christian Balkans and the
Islamic Middle East. Szálasi claimed that 'Hungarism', together
with Christianity and Marxism, was one of the three great
ideologies of the twentieth century. His economic policy was
corporative, and he envisaged that industry would be divided into
corporative institutions, embracing employers, the state and the
workers.

His successor, Kalman Daranyi, faced the beginnings of a con-
certed challenge from Szálasi, who in October 1937 managed to
amalgamate nine smaller parties into a new Hungarian National
Socialist Party or the Arrow Cross. In response the regime, on the
one hand, followed its Balkan neighbours in the direction of a
moderate right-wing authoritarian system by strengthening
Horthy's powers. On the other hand, Daranyi took a leaf out of
Papen's book and attempted to bring Szalasi into the coalition
(see p. 186). This was vetoed by Horthy, who then appointed the
Economics Minister, Bela Imready, as his successor. However, he,
in turn, alarmed the Regent in his attempts to outflank the Arrow
Cross by launching an anti-Semitic campaign and by proposing a
radical plan for land reform. Horthy consequently moved back to
the centre and appointed the moderate Conservative Pal Teleki
Prime Minister.

The elections of 1939 showed that the Arrow Cross had a
genuinely popular base. Despite young men under 26 and women
under 30, who represented the age group most drawn to Fascism,
being excluded from the franchise, and also hostile government
interference, the Arrow Cross gained nearly 25 per cent of the
popular vote. Yet the Teleki government was implacably opposed
to making any concessions. The Senate was given extra powers to
override the lower house and so counteract the influence of the
Arrow Cross. Szálasi, who had been arrested in 1938, was kept in

jail. Thus the road to power was firmly blocked by a semi-authoritarian government, even though the Arrow Cross was proportionately as strong as the German Nazi Party in 1932.

Austria

In Austria, as in Hungary the authoritarian right was divided into three main groups:

- the moderate Christian Social Party
- the more extreme *Heimwehr* (see p. 136)
- the Austrian Nazis.

The Christian Social Party had dominated Austrian politics in the 1920s, but with the Depression the Nazis began to pick up support and in the local elections of the spring of 1932 they gained 16.4 per cent of the vote. The response by the Christian Social-dominated coalition under **Dollfuss** was to set up a dictatorship. Dollfuss then dissolved the existing parties and formed a new political organization, the Fatherland Front, which had a nominal leadership of 3 million.

Dollfuss looked to Italy for protection (see p. 280), and introduced a genuine corporatist constitution, which replaced parliament with four advisory councils. He distanced himself from the German Nazis and gave up the idea of an *Anschluss* so long as Hitler was in power. Like Franco in Spain (see p. 280), his authoritarianism had Catholic rather than Fascist roots. He contrasted the Catholic and traditional Western values of Austria with the new pagan brutality of Nazi Germany.

Not surprisingly the main opponents to Dollfuss were the Nazis, who attempted with German backing to overthrow his regime in July 1934. Although Dollfuss was murdered, the coup was easily crushed and here, as in other eastern European states, a right-wing authoritarian regime under the new Chancellor, **Kurt von Schuschnigg**, blocked the way to power of a more revolutionary Fascist movement. Again, this did not stop the governing party from 'acquiring some of the outer trappings of Fascism common to most other dictatorships in the 1930s'.[3] The *Heimwehr* was replaced by a militia; an elite force, the *Sturmkorps,* was organized; and a youth movement and various 'national social organizations' were set up. Yet the model was the

Engelbert Dollfuss (1892–1934)
A devout Catholic and agricultural expert. His first cabinet post was as Minister for Agriculture and Forestry. In 1932 he became Chancellor. He was murdered by the Nazis in 1934.

Kurt von Schuschnigg (1897–1977)
A lawyer and member of the Christian Social Party. After the *Anschluss* in 1938 (see pp. 238–9) he was imprisoned by Hitler and only released in 1945.

authoritarian, Catholic corporative system rather than German Nazism or Italian Fascism.

It was external rather than internal pressure that destroyed the Schuschnigg regime. As a result of Hitler's support for Mussolini during the Abyssinian crisis and the subsequent Berlin–Rome Axis (see p. 286), Mussolini recognized Austria as a German sphere of influence and in the 'gentleman's agreement' between Vienna and Berlin Schuschnigg agreed to raise the ban on the Austrian Nazi party. Yet it was to take outside intervention and annexation by Germany in March 1938 for the Nazis to triumph (see pp. 238–9).

ROMANIA AND THE BALKAN STATES

To a certain extent Romania, Bulgaria, Yugoslavia and Greece all followed 'the standard Balkan model of a rightist authoritarian regime',[4] which was able effectively to block the road to power of proto-Fascist parties. After the assassination of King Alexander in 1934, the Yugoslavia Prime Minister, Milan Stojadinović introduced the familiar form of a controlled system of parliamentary government supported by a state-sponsored mass movement, the Yugoslav Radical Union, which had some of the characteristics of Fascism – its members, for instance, all wore green shirts and greeted the Prime Minister as 'leader'.

In Greece General Metaxas, with the agreement of the King, set up a dictatorship in 1936 and two years later declared himself 'dictator for life'. He announced the creation of a 'New State' complete with a corporative framework. Political parties were dissolved and the great majority of Greek youth was mobilized in the EON, the National Youth Organization.

In Bulgaria in 1935 King Boris swept away an incompetent military regime and replaced it with a 'controlled' parliamentary regime, which survived until 1943. In Romania King Carol, who returned from exile in 1930, played a major role in destabilizing successive governments, until in 1938 he finally carried out a royal coup, which effectively concentrated power in his hands.

Yugoslavia, Greece and Bulgaria all had small proto-Fascist parties, which were easily contained. In Romania, however, a mass Fascist movement, the Legion of the Archangel Michael did develop (see pp. 132–3). Initially it was a small struggling fringe group. In 1930 it formed a party militia, the Iron Guard, which eventually gave its name to the movement. In January 1931 its leader, Codreanu was arrested and the Legion and the Iron Guard were dissolved, but the movement continued under another name (see Document 1).

When the Legion was once again permitted to function legally in 1933, it made an electoral breakthrough, and in the elections of December 1933 became the third largest force in the country. Its main basis of support came from the peasantry in the poorest areas of the country, where trade and moneylending were to a great extent dominated by the Jews. Like the Nazis, the Legion appealed to the peasantry by stressing their 'unspoilt soul'.[5] Members of the Legion were sent out to help the peasants in their work, and were therefore able to find a receptive audience for their propaganda. Codreanu also set up special work colonies, which helped villagers build dams, irrigate their fields and build bridges and churches. The Legion also drew support from the lower middle classes and increasingly from the skilled workers in the industrial areas. In the election of December 1937 it probably gained some 25 per cent of the vote, although the results were manipulated by the government to obscure that fact.

King Carol played with the idea of bringing Codrianu into a coalition, but in the end he accepted the advice of his Minister of the Interior that Codrianu and several thousand of his followers should be arrested. The Legion retaliated by a campaign of bombing and violence. In response, the government in the 'night of the vampires', 30 November 1938, murdered Codrianu and 13 other key figures in the Legion. Plans for an uprising in January 1939 foundered on the army's refusal to assist. As in Austria and Hungary, a rightist regime had crushed a popular Fascist movement.

PORTUGAL

In 1932 Salazar became Prime Minister and began to create a dictatorship or system of 'institutionalized moderate authoritarianism'. Two years later he introduced a new corporative constitution and a state party, the National Union, but elections continued to be held. Inevitably this was seen as a compromise by the more extremist groups, the *Liga Nacional* and the National Syndicalists. Salazar had little trouble in dealing with *Liga Nacional* and amalgamating it with the National Union. The National Syndicalists were to prove more difficult to deal with, but in July 1934 he was able to dissolve the organization. He specifically rejected their Fascistic 'exaltation of youth, the cult of force through so-called direct action, the principle of the superiority of state political power in social life, the propensity for organizing masses behind a single leader'.[6]

The Spanish Civil War radicalized the political situation in the Iberian peninsular (see Chapter 9), and led Salazar to create a youth movement and a paramilitary force which used the Fascist salute. Nevertheless the Portuguese regime, like the Austrian regime of Dollfuss, remained essentially a Catholic corporatist, authoritarian regime (see Document 2).

ASSESSMENT

In the 1930s democracy was on the defensive and Fascism and National Socialism were in the ascendant. Consequently the traditional right-wing regimes that gained power adopted some of the distinctive features of Fascism, but essentially were not Fascist regimes themselves. They also took decisive steps to ensure that no local Fascist leader had a chance of emulating Mussolini or Hitler.

DOCUMENT 1

The popularity of the Legion of Archangel Michael in the Romanian countryside

Codreanu described a tour Besserabia in January 1930:

On Monday morning I sent Potelea with fifty legionaries to Kahul ... At 10 o'clock we formed a marching column and marched across the Prut into Kahul. In front about a hundred Legionaries were riding in green shirts. They carried our flag. On our caps the turkey feathers waved and on our breasts the white linen crosses glowed. We looked like crusaders. And crusaders we wanted to be, knights who in the name of the cross were fighting the godless

Jewish powers to liberate Rumania ... I only spoke briefly and said 'We shall not leave you! We shall never forget in what oppressive Jewish slavery you are languishing. You will become free! You will become masters of the work of your hands, of your harvest and of your land!

Source: F.L. Carsten, *The Rise of Fascism*, London, Batsford, 1967, p. 186.

Document 2

Corporatism in Portugal

The following is an extract from the political constitution of the Portuguese people:

Art. 102   There shall be a Corporative Chamber, equal in length of term with the National Assembly, composed of representatives of local autonomous bodies and social interests, the latter being those of an administrative, moral, cultural and economic order; the law shall designate those bodies on which such representation falls, the manner of their selection and the duration of their mandate ...

Art. 103   It is the duty of the Corporative Chamber to report and give its opinions on all proposals or draft bills and on all international conventions or treaties submitted to the National Assembly, before discussion thereof is commenced by the latter.

Source: C. Delzell, ed., *Mediterranean Fascism, 1919–1945*, London, Macmillan, 1971, p. 345.

NOTES

1   S. Payne, *A History of Fascism, 1914–45*, London, Routledge, 1995, p. 321.

2   Ibid., p. 271.

3   Ibid., p. 250.

4   Ibid., p. 327.

5   Source: F.L. Carsten, *The Rise of Fascism*, London, Batsford, 1967, p. 186.

6   Payne, *Fascism*, p. 315.

PART FOUR

The dictators and the Second World War

CHAPTER TWELVE

Europe under German domination

TIMELINE

1939	1 September	German Invasion of Poland
	3 September	Britain and France declare war on Germany
1940	9 April	Invasion of Denmark and Norway
	10 May	Offensive against the West begins
	10 June	Italy declares war on France and Britain
	22 June	Franco-German armistice
1941	6 February	German troops sent to North Africa
	22 June	Operation Barbarossa
	2 October–5 December	Battle for Moscow
	7 December	Pearl Harbour
	11 December	Germany and Italy declare war on America
1942	20 January	Wannsee Conference
	August	Over 200,000 Jews gassed in Chelmno, Treblinka and Belzec
1943	January	Casablanca Conference: Britain and USA demand unconditional surrender
	31 January	Germans surrender at Stalingrad
	July	Mussolini forced to resign by Fascist Grand Council
	8 September	German troops occupy northern Italy
1944	27 January	Soviet forces retake Leningrad
	6 June	'D-Day' landings
1945	25 April	American and Soviet troops meet on the Elbe
	30 April	Hitler's suicide

7–8 May	Unconditional surrender of the German armed forces

INTRODUCTION

Through a series of spectacular victories between 1939 and 1942 Hitler briefly had the chance to create a new Europe. Yet, as Hans Umbreit observed, 'one gets the impression that it was easier to bring about a German empire across the Continent than it was to rule it.'[1] German rule took a number of different forms, varying from direct control to the creation of a series of conservative, authoritarian governments, which could reliably carry out its wishes. In Eastern Europe a radical and brutal new order was created based on ethnic cleansing and German resettlement. Vital to this new order was the murder of the Jews.

THE KEY ISSUES IN THIS CHAPTER ARE:

- The Nazi invasion of Russia and the creation of the 'new European order'.
- The creation of the Vichy regime in France.
- How this new order was administered and exploited by Nazi Germany.
- The resettlement policy in the east and the Holocaust.
- The reaction of the Franco regime in Spain to Hitler's triumphs.

THE GERMAN OCCUPATION OF WESTERN EUROPE AND THE INVASION OF RUSSIA, JUNE 1940–JUNE 1941

In the summer of 1940 Hitler seemed invincible. He had occupied Poland, Norway, Denmark, Belgium and Holland and had defeated France and driven British troops from the Continent. Through the Nazi–Soviet Pact Germany was protected from the worst consequences of the British naval blockade, since the USSR was ready to supply Germany with vital raw materials. Initially Hitler was convinced that Britain would terminate hostilities. When this did not happen, he half-heartedly pursued a number of options, ranging from a possible invasion of southern England to military collaboration with Italy, Nationalist Spain and Vichy France against the British Empire. Germany, however, lacked the naval power to launch a successful invasion, and a military alliance with Italy, Spain and Vichy France was impossible to negotiate as each state had conflicting **territorial demands**.

Territorial demands
Vichy wished to retain the French colonial empire, while Italy and Spain hoped for huge gains at France's expense.

Hitler's real priority, however, was the destruction of the USSR. On 18 December 1940 Hitler finally made the decision to attack Russia in the spring of 1941. Although Hitler tried to convince his generals that the defeat of the Soviet Union would also lead to the defeat of Britain, the decision to attack Russia at that juncture can only be understood within the context of Nazi ideology. The mission to destroy Bolshevism and to provide *Lebensraum* for German settlement was the real reason for the invasion. Hitler planned the operation carefully, and, to quote Allan Bullock, 'of all decisions it is the one which most clearly bears his own personal stamp, the culmination (as he saw it) of his career'.[2] The attack was launched on 22 June 1941 after German forces had first pushed the British out of Greece and overthrown the Anglophile administration in Yugoslavia (see Map 6).

EUROPE UNDER GERMAN DOMINATION, 1939–44

By the summer of 1942, apart from a few neutral enclaves, the Nazi empire stretched from the Pyrenees to the Caucasus (see Map 6). Although Hitler did not want to take any final decisions until the 'final victory', he told Otto Abetz, his Ambassador to France, that 'the new Greater German Reich will include 135 million people and rule 150 million more'.[3] It was clear that it was to be constructed on racist principles, and would be economically self-sufficient, held together by force. All the bitter rivalries and the administrative chaos, which were the features of Nazi rule in Germany, were exported to the occupied territories. As Hans Umbreit observed, 'a picture of German occupation rule cannot help but show yet again how little that was rational there was about this exercise of power'.[4] In the short term, however, the main purpose of the occupied territories was to provide labour, food and industrial materials for the German war effort.

The Nazi New European order

1 Direct territorial annexations:
   Austria, the Sudetenland, Danzig, Polish West Prussia, Posen and Silesia, Luxemburg, Eupen and Malmedy, Alsace and the Moselle, Nothern Slovenia, Yugoslav Banat.
2 Direct German administration:
   • *Under civil government*: Polish Government General, Ostland (Baltic territories), Ukraine, Norway, Holland.
   • *Under military government*: Belgium, northern France, forward military areas in the USSR.
3 Puppet regimes:
   The Protectorate of Bohemia–Moravia, Croatia, Serbia–Montenegro, Greece, Italian Social Republic 1943–5 (see p. 440).
4 Satellite regimes:
   Denmark, Finland, Hungary, Romania, Slovakia, Bulgaria, Vichy France.
5 Neutrals:
   • *Friendly*: Spain, Switzerland, Sweden.
   • '*Distant*': Portugal, Ireland, Turkey.

Source: S. G. Payne, *A History of Fascism, 1914–45*, London, Routledge, 1995, p. 376.

Western Europe

In Norway, Holland and Denmark the Germans attempted to rule through the existing administrative machinery. The Norwegian and Dutch monarchs fled to London, and Hitler had to appoint *Reichskommissaren*, who were able to rely on the existing civil service and needed only a small number of German officials to help them. For a time Denmark was the 'showpiece of Nazi Europe'.[5] Parliament and the government appeared to operate independently of the Nazis and there was even a general election in March 1943. However, when this produced a big majority against collaboration with the Nazis, the German authorities declared martial law. Northern France and Belgium were run by German military governments, as they were in the front line in the war against Britain, while the rest of France was administered by its own government under the 84-year old General **Pétain**, which was based at Vichy. Ultimately Hitler intended to turn the Scandinavian states, Holland and Belgium into German provinces, and convince their population of the benefits that their 'Germanic future' would bring them.

Vichy France and the 'national revolution'

Vichy France had the distinction of being the only state in German-dominated Europe that was allowed to maintain formal diplomatic relations with Berlin. Hitler also permitted it to retain control of the large French colonial empire, as well as of any warships which had escaped destruction by the British at Mers el Kebir on 3 July 1940, but its army was limited to a mere 75,000 men. Pétain, and his Chief Minister, **Pierre Laval**, were ready to collaborate with the Nazis and would have liked a real political and economic partnership with Berlin, but Hitler saw Vichy as only a temporary concession until final victory would enable him to demand more from the French state.

To what extent was Vichy France a Fascist state? There were certainly some similarities with the Nazi and Fascist regimes in Germany and Italy:

- it emphasized national unity
- it limited and controlled public debate and political criticism
- it banned hostile political parties, employers' associations and trade unions
- it had an officially controlled news agency
- there was no freely elected legislature
- it attempted to mobilize people, especially youth, in paramilitary organizations, the most prominent of which was the *Legion française des combattants* (the French Legion of Warriors)
- it was anti-Semitic and vigorously pursued a persecution of the Jews in France.

Yet Vichy's real similarities lay with the regimes in Spain and Portugal. Pétain was a father figure rather than a dynamic charismatic figure. Ideologically the strongest force in Vichy was Catholicism. In June 1940 Pétain launched the 'national revolution'. This sought to project the image of a new socially united

**Philippe Pétain
(1856–1951)**
Became a Marshal of France for his defence of Verdun in 1916. He was Minister of War in 1934 and Ambassador in Spain in 1939. In 1945 he was sentenced to death, but this was commuted to life imprisonment.

**Pierre Laval
(1883–1945)**
A former Socialist and Prime Minister 1931–2 and in 1936. He was forced to resign over the Hoare–Laval Plan (see p. 382). He was executed for treason in 1945.

**Jean Darlan
(1881–1942)**
Served Vichy France as
Minister of the Marine and
then Chief Minister,
1941–2. He was
assassinated in Algeria in
1942.

Prefects
High-ranking officials in
charge of a French
département.

**Jacques Doriot
(1898–1945)**
Initially a Communist, but
in the 1930s he became
an admirer of Mussolini.
He was killed in Germany
when his car was machine-
gunned by an Allied plane.

**Marcel Déat
(1894–1955)**
Originally a Socialist but
came out in support of
Pétain in 1940. He was
appointed Minister of
Labour in March 1944 and
fled to Germany a few
months later. He was
sentenced to death by a
French court, but found
refuge in an Italian
monastery, where he died
in 1955.

and regenerated France where the family and society as a whole
was more important than individualism. In short 'the French revolutionary triad of Liberté, Egalité, Fraternité was replaced by
Travail, Famille, Patrie.'[6]

Over the next two years Vichy became increasingly authoritarian. Laval's successor, Admiral **Darlan**, attempted to strengthen
the regime's control over the municipal police forces, local government and the dissemination of propaganda. The **prefects** were
given the power to chose the mayors for all towns between 2,000
and 10,000 people. 'Exceptional tribunals' were also set up to
deal with political opponents.

For both practical and ideological reasons the Vichy regime
collaborated closely with the Germans. Apart from the relatively
small number of French Fascists, who were based mainly in occupied France, in the eyes of many in Vichy collaboration was based
on the assumption that Germany would win the war and that, in
a new German-dominated Europe, France would be able to play
a key role. Germany would provide the peaceful and secure
setting, allowing Vichy to usher in its 'national revolution'. In
essence, as Michael Curtis stresses, 'collaboration was a French
invention, not a German demand'.[7] This can certainly be seen in
the enthusiastic way the Vichy regime hunted down and handed
over its Jewish population to the Germans. Between October
1940 and December 1941 109 anti-Jewish laws were promulgated
by the Vichy regime and the Jews were systematically removed
from the professions and discriminated against. By 1942 the hunt
for Jews had become as much a routine operation as an obsession.
Overall, by 1944 some 77,000 Jews had been murdered or shot.

The French Fascist parties initially played a marginal role in
both Vichy and occupied France. *The Partie Populaire Français*
(PPF) under the ex-Communist **Jacques Doriot** drew subsidies
from both the Germans and Vichy. Doriot was of direct help to
the Germans, as he helped raise a unit of French volunteers (see
Figure 12.1) to fight on the eastern front – *La Légion des
Voluntaires Françaises* – and from November 1942 to May 1943
he was allowed to take over the civil government of Tunisia in
support of the *Wehrmacht*. While the PPF attempted to model
itself on the Nazi Party, the other major French Fascist party, the
Rassemblement National Populaire (RNP), under **Marcel Déat**
was more left wing and drew on the heritage of the French

Revolution. Déat refused subsidies from big business and never entirely lost his internationalism. The Germans tolerated the RNP because they hoped it would persuade some of the French left to support the Third Reich. Both of these parties were, however, very small. The PPF only numbered about 30,000 members, while the RNP only had about 20,000.

Figure 12.1 A poster appealing for volunteers for the French division of the SS
Source: Private Collection/The Bridgeman Art Library.

When the Allies landed in North Africa in November 1942, the Germans occupied Vichy France and Pétain increasingly became a mere German puppet. In January 1944 two Fascists were brought into the government and Déat became Minister of Labour in March. Once the Allies liberated France in the summer of 1944, the Vichy government and key collaborationists fled to southern Germany.

Spain

There was no doubt that Franco sumpathized with the Axis Powers, but the economic and military exhaustion of Spain ensured that he could only enter the war once it was absolutely obvious that Nazi Germany was going to win. After the fall of France, Franco changed Spain's position from neutrality to 'non-belligerence', and he made it clear to Hitler that he would enter the war if Germany guaranteed him military and economic assistance on a large scale and gave Spain much of France's north African empire. Hitler was unable to do this because he wished to keep the support of Vichy and not alienate Mussolini, who also had claims on the same territory. Consequently 'the decision that Spain would not enter the war was thus in a sense made by Hitler rather than Franco'.[8]

The German invasion of the USSR renewed Franco's enthusiam for the Axis cause, as it seemed to echo the Civil War between the authoritarian Right and revolutionary Left on a much larger scale, and he send the 'Blue Division' of 20,000 volunteers to fight on the eastern front. However, with the fall of Mussolini in July 1943 (see p. 439) Franco gradually disassociated himself from the Nazi regime and resumed a position of official neutrality. At one stage Hitler even played with the idea of having Franco removed in favour of a Falangist government (see p. 323).

The Franco regime remained 'an eclectic mixture' of a right-wing military elite, a Fascist state party (the *Falange*, or FET) and various groups of Conservatives and monarchists, all buttressed by the strong support of a revitalized, neo-traditional Catholicism – 'a unique blend without an exact parallel in any other country'.[9] The key to Franco remaining in power was to contain and manage these three pillars of his regime. Under the impact of

German victories the Falangists became increasingly assertive, but Franco skilfully managed a balance between them and the army. In May 1941, for instance, he reorganized his cabinet and made a number of secondary appointments so that he managed to meet the minimum demands of the army, while conciliating their FET rivals. This did not, however, prevent other and more serious clashes between the party on the one side and the army and the Carlists on the other, which led the Italian government to doubt the stability of the Franco regime. These rivalries came to a climax in August 1942 when a small group of Falangists threw a bomb at a Carlist crowd in the outskirts of Bilbao. Franco again responded by a careful reorganization of the cabinet, which attempted to perfect the pragmatic equilibrium first attempted by the reorganization of the preceding year.

Once it was clear that Germany would lose the war, Franco began to defascistize the Spanish regime. This accelerated after 1945, when it was made illegal to make comparisons between Spain and Mussolini's Italy and Hitler's Germany. The Fascist salute was outlawed and the FET was renamed the National Movement.

South-Eastern Europe

In South-Eastern Europe Hitler had few territorial ambitions. At the height of German power Romania, Bulgaria and Hungary had little option but to cooperate closely with Germany, but they were still governed by their own right-wing Nationalist regimes.

In Romania General **Ion Antonescu** forced King Carol to abdicate in September 1940, and created a dictatorship on the model of Franco's Spain. He hoped to combine the parties in one major political union, but in face of opposition from the Peasants' Party he had to rely on the Legion of Archangel Michael (see pp. 378–9), which shared his pro-German orientation. Its leader, Horia Sima, became Prime Minister and Legionnaires held key cabinet posts. Like the Fascists and the Nazis the Legion had come to power constitutionally, but in February 1941 Antonescu, was able to crush it with German backing. For the next three years Antonescu ruled as a military-Nationalist dictator. Romanian troops joined the Germans in the invasion of the USSR. In the territories awarded to Romania by Hitler –

Ion Antonescu (1882–1946) Romanian Minister of Defence in 1937, Prime Minister 1940–4. He was executed in 1946.

Bukovina, Besserabia and the south-western corner of Ukraine – Romanian troops carried out their own holocaust, killing over 200,000 Jews (see Map 6).

Neither in Bulgaria nor Hungary did the war bring any immediate changes. King Boris (see p. 378) continued to preside in Bulgaria over a right-wing authoritarian system in which the parliamentary parties were still allowed to function. The country was inevitably drawn into the German sphere of influence, but managed to avoid declaring war on the USSR on the grounds that the Bulgarians were a Slavonic people. In Hungary Admiral Horthy remained in power and was even able to bring back his troops from the eastern front in the winter of 1941–2. When Soviet troops moved into Hungary in 1944, Horthy secretly began to negotiate an armistice, but Hitler had him replaced by the Arrow Cross leader, Ferenc Szalasi (see p. 376), and German troops occupied the western part of the country. In his rapidly shrinking domain Szalasi attempted to reorganize the Hungarian economy along corporate lines and create a Hungarian version of the SS, but in the spring of 1945, with the complete occupation of the country by Soviet troops, he had no option but to flee to Germany.

In the spring of 1941 Germany invaded Yugloslavia to remove a potentially dangerous pro-British government, and then Greece, where Mussolini's disastrous invasion was facing imminent defeat (see p. 434). Basically, for Hitler, the Balkans were within the Italian sphere of interest. He therefore annexed only the former Austrian territories in Slovenia, and Yugoslavia was broken up into three small countries: Croatia, Serbia and Montenegro.

Weak anti-Communist, ultra-Conservative collaborationist governments under German military supervision were set up in Serbia and also in Greece. In Croatia, however, the Axis Powers were unable to find any reliable right-wing figures to front a satellite regime and had no option but to appoint as head of government the leader of the Croatians Nationalists (*Ustashi*), Dr **Ante Pavelić**. Once in power, Pavlić began to pursue the familiar programme of corporatism, but his government's most striking characteristic was its extreme ethnic nationalism and violent programmes for ethnic cleansing. It murdered hundreds and thousands of Serbians and massacred virtually all the Jews in Croatia.

Ante Pavelić (1889–1959)

Croatian Nationalist and founder of the *Ustashi*. From 1932 to 1941 he was a refugee in Italy, but with the German occupation of Yugoslavia he returned to Croatia, where he was appointed head of government. In 1945 he fled first to Italy and then to Argentina. He died following an assassination attempt in Madrid in 1959.

Eastern Europe

In Eastern Europe German plans were far more ambitious. Not only was the territory, which had been lost in 1919 by the Treaty of Versailles, re-annexed, but what was left of Poland was placed under German administration (the Government General). Following the invasion of the USSR, three large new territories – Bialystok, Ostland and Ukraine – were created and also placed under German control.

In both Poland and western Russia the German administration was virtually paralyzed by vicious 'turf wars' with the SS and the other Reich authorities. In occupied Poland there was constant rivalry between the *Wehrmacht*, Göring in his role as Plenipotentiary of the Four-Year Plan, and Himmler, who as Reich Commissariat for the Consolidation of German Nationhood (RKFDV) was responsible for implementing resettlement policies. The same pattern occurred in Ukraine and Ostland.

Much of the chaos that marked German rule in the Soviet Union arose because there was a basic contradiction between the Reich's long-range objectives and immediate demands. For instance, there was complete disagreement over labour policy 'at the very moment when some pressed for the utmost use of labour in eastern agriculture, others forcibly transported farm hands to work in the Reich. While the Army sought to enrol Soviet prisoners as troops, German factories pressed for their use in labour.'[10]

In Poland both local businesses and a considerable amount of land and private property were confiscated by the Central Trustee Agency, which then granted licences to German companies. In Russia the main economic aim was to extract the maximum amount of food and raw materials from the occupied areas. In February 1942 the New Agrarian Order was introduced, which turned the Soviet collective farms into communal farms owned by the peasants themselves, and in June 1943 further concessions consolidated the peasants' legal rights to any lands they had gained since 1941 The growing demand for munitions also persuaded Hitler to abandon his original policy of de-industrializing the Soviet Union. By July 1942 belated steps were taken to rebuild industry in the Donets Basin, although little progress was made before the Red Army recaptured the area.

Hitler's primary aim was to build up a German population of 250 millions in Poland and western Russia in the course of about 80 years. Eventually this would entail the 'ethnic cleansing' of the existing population. A start was made in Poland by either shooting or sending the Polish elites to concentration camps. In the areas annexed by the Germany, roughly a million Germans and Jews were expelled and some 629,000 ethnic Germans were resettled there from the USSR, Banat, France and Romania. In the Government General Himmler began to clear the Zamosac region near Lublin of Poles in November 1941. Some 8,000 ethnic Germans from Bosnia and elsewhere were brought in and given the task of developing a model agricultural district made up of several large farms, which had previously been part of Polish-owned local estates (see Document 1).

For Russia Hitler had immensely ambitious but vague plans. In the future – after, of course, Russia had been defeated – German peasants would live in specially constructed villages. Motorways would link the new settlements to the Reich, and the Black Sea would become a German holiday resort. The Russians, deprived of their Soviet elites, would become an exploited under-class, which would gradually die out. As Hitler remarked in February 1942 'no vaccinations for the Russians, and no soap to get the dirt off them. But let them have all the spirits and tobacco they want.'[11]

The elimination of the Soviet elite was to start straight away. Army commanders were ordered in June 1941 to shoot any Soviet political commissar, who were taken prisoner, while four SS *Einsatzgruppen*, each composed of between 500 and 1,000 men were formed for special security duties, which in reality meant, as one of their commanders later testified at Nuremberg, 'putting to death all racially and politically undesirable elements among the prisoners'[12] – Soviet officials, gypsies, Jews and the so-called 'second class Asiatics' (see Document 2).

In August 1942 Hitler approved the General Plan East, which had been drawn up by the RKFDV. It covered all the German-occupied areas that were ultimately intended for annexation by the Reich. The main priority was the Germanization of the Baltic states and Poland, but in the course of 25 years Ukraine and the Volga regions would also be covered with a network of settle-ments. In the summer of 1942 Himmler concentrated some

10,000 Ukranian Germans around his headquarters at 'Hegewald' in Ukraine, but the defeat at Stalingrad put a stop to any further settlements.

THE HOLOCAUST

Historians and the Holocaust

Historical debate about the horrors of the Holocaust is dominated by the arguments between the structuralists and intentionalists (see p. 213). In essence the structuralist argue that the Holocaust was the result of muddle, improvization and pressure from below, while the intentionalists insist that it was all along the intention and overriding aim of Adolf Hitler, Himmler and the Nazi party as a whole (see Document 3). Intentionalist historians argue that the decision to murder the Jews was made once war broke out in September 1939, but the structuralists remain sceptical, and point out how 'evolutionary' or 'improvized' Nazi anti-Semitic policy was in reality.[13]

The structuralists argue that it was the successful Red Army counter-attack in December 1941 that was the crucial factor leading to the Holocaust.[14] By prolonging the war in the east, it created severe logistical problems in Poland and occupied Russia, which would only be made worse by bringing more Jews into the area. This is why, Broszat argues, that the Holocaust was a '"way out" of a blind alley into which the National Socialists had manoeuvred themselves'.[15] The intentionalists respond that such arguments reduce the Holocaust merely to an accidental consequence of the military situation in Eastern Europe. Dawidowicz, for example, argues that Hitler 'implemented his plan in stages, seizing whatever opportunities offered themselves to advance its execution.[16] Certainly the structuralist approach, as Burleigh and Wippermann stress, focuses 'to such a degree upon the contingent and chaotic details of the regimes administrative details that one loses sight of the motive force and consensual climate, which informed these decisions'.[17] By late 1941 there were so many Nazi plans for the eventual extermination of the Jews that it is highly likely that 'a green light was coming from the highest level'.[18] At the very least, it must have been obvious to Hitler's followers and officials that he favoured such policies. Arguably, this was sufficient

to guarantee that they would 'work towards the *Führer*' (see p. 243
to ensure that his wishes would be carried (see Document 4).

The road to the extermination camps

The resettlement of millions of people, the systematic attempts to
eliminate the Russian and Polish elites and the conquest of
Lebensraum in Soviet territory was the context in which the elimination of the Jewish population took place. The occupation of
Poland put over 2 million Jews in German hands. A further 3
million Jews lived in western Russia and half a million in occupied territory in Western Europe.

Initially in the autumn of 1939 Polish Jews were driven into
ghettos in the cities, but ultimately a large 'reservation' was to be
created near Lublin, where both the Jews from Poland and
Germany itself were to be concentrated. However, the enormous
administrative difficulties caused by transporting hundreds of
thousands of people to Poland forced Göring, who had overall
responsibility for the Jewish question, to halt the resettlement
programme. With the fall of France in June 1940 it momentarily
seemed possible that virtually the whole Jewish population in
Europe could be resettled in the French colony of Madagascar,
but the plan had to be shelved once it was clear that Britain would
not make peace, and that the British navy for the foreseeable
future would continue to dominate the Indian Ocean.

The invasion of Soviet Russia in June 1941 marked a major
escalation in Nazi policy towards the Jews. It was primarily a
genocidal war fought against 'Jewish Bolshevism'. By the end of
1941 hundreds of thousands of Jews and Russian Communists
had died in mass executions carried out by the SS and the
Einsatzgruppen. Beginning in the autumn of 1941, extermination
camps at Belzec, Sobibor and Treblinka were set up in the
Government General, and gas was first used in the Chelmo concentration camp in the autumn of 1941. The 'final solution' was
already being put into operation. At the Wannsee Conference in
January 1942 in Berlin details were drawn up for the mass conscription of Jews into labour gangs in Eastern Europe, where it
was assumed that 'a large number will drop out through natural
wastage'. The remainder would then be 'dealt with accordingly'
(see Document 4). In 1943 two more death camps were opened at

Maydanek and Auschwitz, to the latter of which were deported most of the Jews of Western Europe (see Figure 12.2). Altogether by 1945 nearly 6 million Jews had been murdered.

Italian Fascism and the Holocaust

In the areas occupied by Italian troops a much more flexible policy towards the Jews was pursued by the Italian military government than by the Germans. While Mussolini appeared to agree with Hitler that the Jews should be murdered, his commands were frequently contradictory and not obeyed by his officials in the areas of occupation. On 21 August 1942, for instance, he had initially decreed that the Jews should be handed over to the Croatians, who would almost certainly have killed them, but in the end he conceded that they should be interned. In practice this and similar decisions, according to Jonathan Steinberg, set Italy on the path 'to obstruct the final solution in Europe'.[19] Why were the Italians so much less brutal towards the Jews than the Germans? Hannah Arendt calls it 'the outcome of the almost automatic general humanity of an old and civilized people'.[20] It is certainly true that what Steinberg calls 'the vices of Italian public life made the virtues of humanity easier to practise'.[21] Unlike the Germans, the Italians were used to disobeying orders, and 'habitual disobedience' was almost a way of life. Other historians are critical of this interpretation. Bosworth, for instance, is rather sceptical about this emphasis on Italian 'niceness', while Knox does not hesitate to place Mussolini among the 'wicked men of the twentieth century'. Contemporary Italian historians, such as Angelo Del Boca and Luigi Goglia, also stress that Italian racism was a reality and that anti-Semitism did exist in Italy.[22] In practice Italian policy was influenced by a complex mixture of factors: common humanity was certainly one factor, but so was the desire to distance themselves from the Germans, and latterly the need to convince the Allies of their more compassionate attitude towards the Jews was also an important factor (see Document 5).

ASSESSMENT

Under the impact of German power a new configuration of states came into being on the European continent. However no uniform 'Fascist pattern' was established. Fascist Italy and Nazi Germany

Figure 12.2 A group of
European Jews waiting to
be sorted out into those
who would go straight to
the gas chambers and
those who would be left
for labour
Source: Getty Images/
Hulton Archive

provided the momentum for the 'new Europe', but with the
exception of the puppet Fascist regimes in Croatia and Hungary,
after the fall of Horthy, the majority of the satellite states were, in
reality, essentially conservative authoritarian regimes.

In 1940–1 the Germans talked much about a ' new European
order' where there would be, in the words of Otto Dietrich,
Germany's press chief, 'equal chances for all'.[23] The meeting of
the leaders of the Anti-Comintern Pact in Berlin in 1941 was
described as 'the first European Congress', and even a 'Song of
Europe' was written to celebrate it. Yet in reality this new order
masked massive ethnic cleansing in Eastern Europe and the creation of an economic system designed to favour Germany.
Together with the plundering of foreign economies went an
ambitious programme for integrating their businesses into the
German economy.

How much did the Nazi, Fascist and authoritarian regimes
have in common? Was there any potential for a new order? There
was certainly some common ground of shared fears, prejudices
and hatreds:

- Hitler's allies and sympathizers from Madrid to Budapest
  welcomed the attack on the USSR and initially allowed
  volunteer units to join the *Wehrmacht* and SS troops in
  Russia. Himmler also recruited a 'Black International',[24]

Occupied territories' share in German armament production in 1943 (%)

	Weapons	Ammunition	Vehicles	Shipbuilding	Aircraft
France	1.5	1.4	11.9	6.4	6.5
Belgium/Northern France	0.8	0.7	1.3	11.9	0.1
Government General	0.1	0.1	0.8	14.0	1.1
Denmark	0.3	–	0.3	1.5	0.1
Norway	0.3	0.3	0.7	1.9	–
Serbia	–	–	–	–	8.9

Source: D. Eichholtz, *Geschichte der deutschen Kriegswirtschaft, 1939–1945*, vol. 2, Berlin, Akademie Verlag, 1985, p. 508.

drawn from a wide range of European peoples, to guard the concentration camps.

- Nazi anti-Semitism was shared by many of the satellite and puppet states – Romania, Vichy France, Croatia and the Szalasi dictatorship in Hungary, for example. Apart from Spain, which refused to turn back any Jewish refugee crossing its frontiers, and possibly Italy, the new Europe was united in its anti-Semitism.

- The authoritarian but essentially non-Fascist regimes, such as Spain, Vichy and Horthy's Hungary, all played lip service to the ideology of corporatism.

In the autumn of 1940 Hitler could have won over a considerable body of European opinion for a united Europe under the leadership of Germany, had he been prepared to make any concessions, but his actions made it brutally clear that he was only interested in 'the defences and security of [Germany's] life interests'.[25] By 1943, at the latest, the Germans had lost the propaganda battle for Europe: the European peoples were aware that the new Europe was simply a euphemism for a German policy of control. Increasingly, from France to Ukraine and the Balkans, the Germans were encountering resistance from the partisans and the underground movements.

DOCUMENT 1

German settlement in Poland

Hans Frank, the Governor General of occupied Poland, told a meeting of high-ranking German officials in the Government General:

Above all we must bear the following in mind: after the re-germanization of the eastern territories of the Reich, this territory of the General Government will be the next to be totally germanized. We will build the great Reich autobahns, which will go straight across our country. Great settlements will grow up alongside these points, around which German life will gradually develop over a broad zone. Since we will then all have the opportunity to transfer any unwanted aliens to the east, it will not be an insuperable task to ensure that the German ethnic element puts down deep roots while the ethnically alien element is progressively squeezed out.

Source: J. Noakes and G. Pridham, eds, *Nazism, 1919–45*, vol. 3, *Foreign Policy, War and Racial Extermination*, Exeter, Exeter University Press, 1991, p. 966.

DOCUMENT 2

Die Einsatzgruppen

The Einsatzgruppen, *or mobile task forces, moved into the USSR behind the front-line German troops on 23 June 1941. Heydrich issued the following orders to their commanders:*

All of the following are to be executed:
Officials of the Comintern . . . top and medium-level officials and radical lower-level officials of the Party, Central Committee, and district and sub-district committees.
People's Commissars.
Jews in Party and state employment, and other radical elements (saboteurs, propagandists, snipers, assassins, inciters, etc.)

Source: M. Burleigh, *The Third Reich*, London, Macmillan, 2000, p. 602.

Document 3

The structuralist view of the road to the Holocaust

Martin Broszat explains the genesis of the Holocaust:

The situation into which the National Socialist leadership had manoeuvered itself in the planning of large scale deportations of Jews becomes sufficiently clear through the documents already cited. As is clear from Hitler's declarations, Hitler, Himmler and Heydrich launched preparations for the wholesale deportation of Jews as a matter of ideology to be pursued with fanatical eagerness. They made this principle clear in their contacts with the cities with overwhelmingly large Jewish populations ... Hitler obviously had no intention of halting the plan for the massive evacuation of the Jews even when the military situation in the east proved more difficult than had been assumed in the summer of 1941. It was for this reason that the original plans for deportation were curtailed on the one hand, while on the other decisions were made aimed at eventually removing at least part of the evacuated Jews by other means, i.e. planned killing operations.

It thus seems that the liquidation of the Jews began not solely as a result of an ostensible will for extermination but also as a 'way out' of a blind ally into which the National Socialists had manoeuvred themselves. The practice of liquidation, once initiated and established, gained predominance and evolved in the end into a comprehensive programme.

Source: M. Broszat, 'Hitler and the genesis of the Final Solution: an assessment of David Irving's theses' in H.W. Koch, ed., *Aspects of the Third Reich*, London, Macmillan, 1985, pp. 404–5.

Document 4

The Wannsee Conference

On 20 January 1942 key officials met secretly to discuss the matter of the Jews in a lakeside villa in the Berlin suburb of Wannsee. The following is an extract from the minutes prepared by Adolf Eichmann (see p. 234):

In pursuance of the final solution, the Jews will be conscripted for labour in the east under appropriate supervision. Large labour gangs will be formed from those fit for work, with the sexes separated, which will be sent to those areas for road construction and undoubtedly a large number of them will drop out through natural wastage. The remainder who survive – and they will certainly be those who have the greatest powers of endurance – will have to be dealt with accordingly. For if released, they would, as a natural selection of the fittest, form a germ cell from which the Jewish race could regenerate itself. (That is the lesson of history.)

In the process of carrying out the final solution, Europe will be combed through and through from west to east ... The evacuated Jews will be initially brought in stages to so-called transit ghettos in order to be transported there further east.

Source: Noakes, J. and Pridham, G. (eds) (2001) *Nazism 1919–1945. Volume 3: Foreign Policy, War and Racial Extermination*, pub University of Exeter Press, p. 1131.

Document 5
Italy and the Jews

Jonathan Steinberg shows how complex a task it is to unravel the background to Italian policy towards the Jews:

Italian [policy] towards the Jews emerged out of the murky atmosphere of Rome in the autumn of 1942, an atmosphere full of tension, rumour, intrigue and fear. It was one of many policies and decisions which the historian cannot follow as it disappears into the darker corners of a collapsing regime. A few figures stand out in the gloom by their frankness. There is no doubt where Count Pietromarchi [a senior Foreign Office official] or General Roatta [the Chief of Staff of the Italian army] stood because they said what they thought and left evidence of it in writing. What [Marshal] Cavallero thought, what Ciano thought, indeed what Mussolini himself thought about the Jewish question, can only be guessed. My hunch is that they tolerated the subversion of orders because saving the Jews came to seem a rational policy as the war began to go badly. If Rome had to seek a separate peace with the Allies, it would be a good idea not to have helped the Germans murder the Jews. It was perhaps not an ace up the sleeve but might be a joker.

Source: J. Steinberg, *All or Nothing The Axis and the Holocaust, 1941–43*, London, Routledge, 1990, p. 6.

NOTES

1 H. Umbreit, 'German rule in the occupied territories, 1942–45' in Research Institute for Military History, ed., *Germany and the Second World War*, vol. 5, Part 2, Oxford, Clarendon Press, 2003, p. 7.

2 A. Bullock, 'Hitler and the origins of the Second World War' in E.M. Robertson, ed., *The Origins of the Second World War*, London, Macmillan, 1971, p. 218.

3 Umbreit, *German rule*, p. 9

4 Ibid., p. 7.

5 D.G. Williamson, *The Third Reich*, Harlow, Longman, 3rd ed. 2002, p. 90.

6 M. Curtis, *Verdict on Vichy. Power and Prejudice in the Vichy France Regime*, London, Weidenfeld & Nicolson, 2002, p. 93.

7 Ibid., p. 255.

8 S.G. Payne, *A History of Fascism, 1914–45*, London, Routledge, 1995, p. 432.

9 Ibid., p. 431.

10 A. Dallin, *German Rule in Russia, 1941–45*, London, Macmillan, 1957, p. 664.

11 M. Burleigh, *The Third Reich*, London, Macmillan, 2000, p. 531.

12 H. Buchheim, M. Broszat, H.A. Jacobsen and H. Krausnick, *Anatomy of the SS State*, London, Collins, 1968, p. 62.

13 M.R. Marrus, 'The history of the Holocaust', *Journal of Modern History*, vol. 59, no. 1, 1987, p. 125

14 M. Broszat, 'Hitler and the genesis of the Final Solution' in H.W. Koch, ed., *Aspects of the Third Reich*, London, Macmillan, 1985, pp. 390–429; L. Kettenacker, 'Hitler's Final Solution and its rationalization' in G. Hirschfeld, ed., *The Policies of Genocide*, London, Allen & Unwin, 1986, pp. 73-95; H. Mommsen, 'The realization of the unthinkable' in Hirschfield, ed., *The Policies of Genocide*, pp. 97–144.

15 Broszat, 'Hitler and the genesis', p. 405.

16 L.S. Dawidowicz, *The War against the Jews, 1933–1945*, Harmondsworth, Penguin, 1986, p. xxxi.

17 M. Burleigh and W. Wippermann, *The Racial State: Germany, 1933–45*, Cambridge, Cambridge University Press, 1991, p. 98.

18 J. Noakes and G. Pridham, eds, *Nazism, 1919–45*, vol. 3, *Foreign Policy, War and Racial Extermination*, Exeter, Exeter University Press, 1998, p 1136.

19 J. Sternberg, *All or Nothing. The Axis and the Holocaust, 1941–43*, London, Routledge, p. 170.

20 Quoted in ibid., p. 170.

21 Ibid., p. 170.

22 See the debate in R.J.B. Bosworth, *The Italian Dictatorship*, London, Arnold 1998, pp. 99–105.

23 Quoted in G. Wright, *The Ordeal of Total War*, New York, Harper & Row, 1968, p. 140.

24 H. Rothfels, *The German Opposition to Hitler*, London, Oswald Wolff, 1970, p. 19.

25 Quoted in Wright, *The Ordeal of Total War*, p. 141.

CHAPTER THIRTEEN

Nazi Germany: the home front

TIMELINE

1939	30 August	Ministerial Council for the Defence of the Reich set up
	27 September	Amalgamation of Security Police and the office of *Reichsführer* SS to form the *Reichssicherheitshauptamt* (RSHA)
	7 October	Himmler appointed Commissioner for Consolidating German Nationhood
1940	22 June	Franco-German armistice; French prisoners of war drafted into German industry and agriculture
1941	22 June	Operation Barbarossa
	2 October–5 December	Battle for Moscow
1942	20 January	Wannsee Conference
	8 February	Speer becomes Armaments Minister
	26–7 March	First Jewish emigrants from Western Europe deported to Auschwitz
	28 March	RAF heavily damages Lübeck
	April	*Reichstag* resolution gives Hitler complete power to remove judges from office
		Central Planning Board established to allocate raw materials and energy supplies
	August	Otto Thierack appointed Minister of Justice
1943	14–24 January	Casablanca Conference: Britain and USA insist on unconditional surrender

	27 January	Decree concerning the Registration of Men and Women for Reich Defence Tasks
	31 January	German Sixth Army surrenders at Stalingrad
	18 February	Goebbel's 'total war speech' in Berlin White Rose Group arrested by Gestapo
	12 May	Axis armies surrender in Tunisia
	10 July	Western Allies land in Sicily
	24–30 July	Allied air attack on Hamburg kills 30,000 people
	20 August	Himmler replaces Frick as Interior Minister
1944	January	Gestapo breaks up the Kreisau Circle
	27 January	Soviet forces relieve Leningrad
	6 June	D-Day landings
	13 June	V-1 flying bomb campaign begins
	20 July	The abortive bomb plot to assassinate Hitler
	30 August	Soviet forces enter Bucharest
	21 October	Aachen falls to American troops
1945	30 January	Hitler's last radio speech
	25 April	American and Soviet troops meet on the Elbe
	30 April	Hitler's suicide; Doenitz becomes Chancellor
	7–8 May	Surrender of Germany
	23 May	Dissolution of Doenitz regime by Allies

INTRODUCTION

The Second World War was an ideological turning point in the history of Nazi Germany. In Poland and Russia it witnessed the beginning of the systematic ethnic cleansing of the Jews. At home it also marked 'a new chapter in Hitler's dictatorship'.[1] To protect the home front against the 'enemy within' the courts and the police began to act much more severely against dissidents and even common criminals, whose activities could weaken the war effort. Also the longer the war lasted, the more the influence of the Nazi Party increased to the detriment of what remained of orderly and legal government within the Reich. The party's

activists began to embark on a programme for radically trans-
forming the values and lifestyle of the German people.

The war also transformed Germany. The old Prussian officer
class was destroyed on the Eastern front and the estates of its
members seized by the Russians, as they advanced into Germany.
Ultimately the war turned Germany into a 'kicked-in anthill'.[2]
East Germans fleeing the Red Army trekked west, while urban
northerners were evacuated to the rural south to escape the Allied
bombing raids, and by 1945 not only was much of the physical
infrastructure of Germany destroyed, but so, too, was what
remained of Germany's traditional social system and **regional particularism.**

Regional particularism
Local culture and
traditions of self-
government, dating from
before Germany was
united in 1866–71.

THE KEY ISSUES IN THIS CHAPTER ARE:

* The inability of the Nazi state to devise effective
  administrative and governmental structures for waging war.
* The impact of the war on the party and the SS.
* The effectiveness of the German war economy and the
  importance of foreign labour to its functioning.
* The impact of the war on the *Volksgemeinshaft*.
* The difference between *resistenz* and resistance to the Nazi
  regime.

FÜHRER, GOVERNMENT AND PARTY

The *Führer* state

Hitler was absent from Berlin for most of the time from June
1941 until November 1944, overseeing military operations from
his headquarters in the Wolfschanze in East Prussia. In December
1941 he took over the supreme command of the army, which gave
him responsibility for both strategy and detailed military tactics.
Despite these immense responsibilities and his absence from the
seat of government, Hitler still insisted, as *Führer*, on his right to
be the only effective coordinator of national policy. The problem
remained, as in peacetime, that there was neither an effective
coordinating body, nor was Hitler himself in reality ready to fill
the vacuum left by its absence. Hitler's decisions were 'frequently
arbitrary, contradictory and followed no coherent plan'.[3]

Government officials and leading Nazis made repeated but unsuccessful efforts to remedy the problem. Hitler, however, consistently opposed the emergence of any committee with real executive powers, which could eventually be used to overrule him. As a result of an initiative by Göring, the Ministerial Council for the Defence of the Reich was set up in August 1939, but after November 1939 it ceased to meet. Hitler also vetoed attempts by Heinrich Lammers, the Head of the Reich Chancellery, to reintroduce regular cabinet meetings, and was deeply suspicious of ministers meeting unofficially.

Decisions could still be achieved only by going straight to Hitler, but increasingly access was controlled by **Martin Bormann**. To weaken Bormann's grip, Lammers suggested in early 1943 the formation of a small committee composed of himself, Keitel (the Chief of High Command) and Bormann, which would ensure that policy decisions were carried out. This 'committee of three' actually met 11 times before it withered away in the autumn of 1943.

Goebbels, concerned by Hitler's lack of leadership, absence from Berlin and the dominating role of Bormann, spoke openly of a 'leader crisis'. With Speer (see p. 415) he attempted to resurrect the Ministerial Council, but whenever they tried to confront Hitler with their proposals, their courage failed. In reality the regime was not reformable as it 'was both the inexorable product of Hitler's personalized rule and the guarantee of his power'.[4]

For the first three years of the war Hitler's image survived intact, as he could draw on the popular memory of his pre-war successes and had come to symbolize German greatness. In 1940, with the defeat of France, his popularity reached a new peak, but after the German defeat at Stalingrad in January 1943 it inevitably began to decline. By 1944 army censors found that there was little evidence of support for Hitler among the soldiers on the Eastern front. At home, however, his authority was still unshaken and most of the criticism was aimed at his subordinates. A panel of distinguished German historians even goes as far as to argue that the 'public would probably have followed the dictator even without the growing terror against "dissidents" and without the intensifying propaganda. It was only too eager to grasp at every straw'[5] (see Document 6).

Martin Bormann (1900–1945)

Joined the Party in 1925 and became Hess's Chief of Staff and Secretary in 1933. In 1941, after Hess's flight to Scotland, Bormann was appointed Head of the Party Chancellery, and then in 1943 Hitler's Secretary. He probably died whilst escaping from Hitler's bunker on 2 May 1945.

Policing the home front

In September 1939, shortly before he departed to his headquarters on the Polish front, Hitler told Himmler to keep order on the home front 'with all means'. In response to this Himmler consolidated the SD, the Gestapo and the Reich Criminal Police Department into one agency – the Reich Security Head Office (RSHA). The Ordinance against 'Parasites on the Body Politic' and the War Penal Code gave the Gestapo wide-ranging powers to arrest not only criminals but those who dared voice doubts about the war or who listened secretly to the BBC's foreign broadcasts (see Document 1).

The last vestiges of the independence of the judiciary were also destroyed. Increasingly the Gestapo acted unilaterally and executed so-called criminals before they had received sentences in the courts. In April 1942 a *Reichstag* resolution gave Hitler the power to dismiss 'judges who clearly fail to recognize the mood of the hour'.[6] In August 1942 Hitler appointed **Otto Thierack**, who was an SA *Gruppenführer* and President of the People's Court, Minister of Justice, while the top officials at the Ministry were replaced by more 'reliable' personnel. From now on it became the norm for the public prosecutors to tell judges before a trial what their verdicts should be.

Otto Thierack (1889–1946)
Joined the Nazi Party in 1932 and committed suicide in 1946.

The SS

On the first day of the war **Theodor Eicke**, who was responsible for the concentration camps, stressed that 'the main task of the SS in this war is to protect the state of Adolf Hitler's from every danger above all on the home front.'[7] It was above all through its administration of the concentration camps that the SS 'protected' Germany. The camp system consisted of a series of main camps, which were situated in strategic areas of the Reich. Each had its own network of subcamps. In September 1942 prisoners from the regular prisons in Germany were transferred to them, and increasingly foreign workers in Germany, who were guilty of even the most minor crime, were also dispatched there.

The control and administration of the concentration camps both in Germany and the occupied territories gave the SS access to a large pool of labour, which could be used exclusively in its

Theodor Eicke (1892–1943)
Joined the Nazi Party in 1928 and the SS in 1930. As a reward for his 'execution' of Ernst Röhm (see p. 196), he was made Inspector of the Concentration Camps. He was killed when his plane was shot down by the Russians in 1943.

industrial undertakings. By 1944 the economic empire of the SS comprised about 150 firms organized together into one large trust, the *Deutsche Wirtschaftsbetriebe GmbH*, the activities of which ranged from quarrying, mining and the production of foodstuffs and mineral waters to the manufacture of armaments and textiles.

During the war Himmler and the SS assumed enormous powers, which amounted to what Joachim Fest has described as a 'collateral state':[8]

- As Commissioner for Consolidating German Nationhood (RKFDV), Himmler was given responsibility for the resettlement of ethnic Germans and eliminating 'the harmful influences of such alien parts of the population as constitute a danger to the Reich and the German community'[9] in the occupied and incorporated territories (see p. 388).
- By 1944 the *Waffen*-SS (the militarized or armed SS) could also deploy a considerable military force consisting of 35 divisions.
- Himmler was also appointed Reich Minister of the Interior in 1943, Commander of the Reserve Army in 1944, and then Commander-in-Chief of the Rhine Army Group in December 1944 and of the Vistula Army Group in January 1945.

Yet paradoxically, while Himmler amassed these formidable powers, his direct influence on Hitler continued to be undermined by Bormann at the *Führer* headquarters (see p. 410).

The party

At the start of the war the Nazi Party was assigned the task of maintaining the morale of the civilian population. It was made responsible for administering the National Socialist welfare organizations and it also acted as the eyes and ears of the Gestapo by reporting on black-market dealing, defeatist talk or listening to enemy radio stations (see Document 1).

Senior *Gauleiter* (regional party leaders) were appointed Reich Defence Commissioners in the 13 military districts of Germany, and they, instead of the army, were given the task of coordinating the civil defence measures. Once the big air raids began in 1942, they had responsibility for protecting the population from their destructive impact. When Hitler created the *Volkssturm* in September 1944, which was in effect a party-controlled citizen militia, it was organized on the territorial basis of the *Gaue*. The *Gauleiter* were also made responsible for weeding out manpower from factories and offices for the army and closing down businesses that were not essential for the war.

Gaue
The area that a *Gauleiter* administered.

The war also sharpened the party's ambition to achieve the social and racial revolution that had been denied it in the 1930s. New rituals, and even 'an official calendar of celebrations'[10] were introduced in an effort to replace the traditional Christian rituals. In June 1941 Bormann, in a letter to the *Gauleiter*, stated that Christianity was incompatible with National Socialism and called upon the party to root it out. A campaign was then waged by the NSDAP against the churches: Christian publications were seized, the welfare activities of the Catholic nuns were now to be carried out by 'the brown sisters', a Nazi organization, and Christian feast days, which were traditionally kept as holidays, were moved to the nearest Sunday, so as to avoid any interruption in the war effort. Confronted by popular opposition, particularly from the Catholics, Hitler was forced to call a halt to the campaign within the boundaries of the old Reich, but in the territories that had been annexed from Poland in 1939 it continued unchecked. In the *Reichsgau* Wartheland, for example, 94 per cent of the churches in the dioceses of Posen–Gnesen were closed and 11 per cent of the clergy murdered. As Ian Kershaw has aptly observed, this 'clearly showed the face of the future',[11] should Germany win the war.

***Reichsgau* Wartheland**
The newly incorporated area of the west Prussian province of Posen.

In many other spheres the war also enabled the party to extend its social, cultural and political influence. Nearly 2 million children were evacuated from the cities to the countryside. There they were taught by their teachers for six hours a day, and for the rest of the time they were in the hands of the Hitler Youth leaders, who inevitably gave greater priority to military rather than academic disciplines.

After the **Battle of Stalingrad** the army, too, was increasingly permeated by the party. By the end of 1943 party officials participated in the selection and training of new officers, and after the 20 July plot in 1944 (see pp. 423–4) the traditional military salute was replaced by the Nazi salute. Goebbels also encouraged soldiers to inform on their officers if they appeared to be sceptical about the new Nazi education programmes.

Battle of Stalingrad
At Stalingrad, August 1942–January 1943, the German Sixth Army was surrounded and destroyed by the Russians.

In the newly incorporated territories the party was able to assert its authority without any challenge from the traditional bureaucracy, which still existed in the old Reich. The new Reich Commissioners were both state officials and party functionaries, whose task was not really to create an orderly administration but rather to carry out the ideological and racial policy of the Nazi movement. This was to be seen in their war against the churches (see above) and deportation of Poles and Jews (see pp. 396–401).

THE WAR ECONOMY

When the Allied experts analysed the German war economy at the end of the Second World War, they came to the conclusion that only in 1942 was the German economy mobilized for a total war. The argument was then developed by Klein, Milward and Mason that Hitler deliberately planned for a series of *Blitzkriege* or very brief wars, but as Richard Overy has shown, this underestimates the extent of Germany's economic mobilization In the first two years of the war German military spending rose considerably, with a corresponding fall in consumer goods production. Nevertheless, the actual production of weapons remained disappointing. In 1940, for example, Germany spent about $6,000 million on armaments, while Britain spent only $3,500 million, yet the latter produced over 50 per cent more aircraft, 100 per cent more vehicles and nearly as many tanks as did Germany.[12] These disappointing German production figures were the consequence of structural and economic factors:

- The war had broken out earlier than Hitler intended.
- Much of the initial spending had gone into military infrastructure, such as barracks, rather than weapons.
- Many of the smaller and medium-sized armament firms were also incompetent and reluctant to introduce modern mass-production techniques.
- The armed forces insisted on quality rather than quantity of armaments, and kept changing their demands. This prevented the factories from implementing long production runs of any one weapon and so inevitably slowed up production.

Comparison between the British and German war economies

	1939	1940	1941	1942	1943	1944
Index of consumer expenditure (per capita: 1938 = 100)						
Germany	95.0	88.4	81.9	75.3	75.3	70.0
Britain	97.2	89.7	87.1	86.6	85.5	88.2
Percentage of industrial workforce working on war orders						
Germany	21.9	50.2	54.5	56.1	61.0	–
Britain	18.6	–	50.9	–	–	–
Percentage of women in the native workforce						
Germany	37.3	41.4	42.6	46.0	48.8	51.0
Britain	26.4	29.8	33.2	34.8	36.4	36.2
War expenditure as a percentage of national income						
Germany	32.2	48.8	56.0	65.6	71.3	–
Britain	15.0	43.0	52.0	52.0	55.0	54.0

Source: R.J. Overy, *War and Economy in the Third Reich*, Oxford, Oxford University Press, 1995, p. 312. By permission of Oxford University Press.

The impact of Albert Speer

By December 1941 the German war economy was in a state of deep crisis. The armed forces and Hitler were multiplying demands for complex new weapons, while conscription had removed another 6 million young males from the labour market, for which the increasing use of female, foreign and prisoner of war labour could not compensate. The German failure to defeat the USSR by the end of 1941 and the coming of the USA into the war had created a potentially stronger Allied military and economic alliance, which could win a war of attrition. It was agreed by both industrialists and the armed forces that the key to overcoming these problems lay in economic rationalization. On 3 December 1940 Hitler issued his *Führer* command on 'Simplification and Increased Efficiency in Armaments Production', and appointed Fritz Todt Armaments Minister. By the time he died in an air crash in February 1942 he had set up a series of main committees, each one of which was given responsibility for producing a particular class of weapon or equipment. He was succeeded by 'Hitler's surprise candidate',[13] **Albert Speer,** who not only enjoyed the direct political support of Hitler, but was unassociated with the bitter rivalries of the Nazi leaders. He

Albert Speer (1905–81)
Studied architecture and joined the Nazi party in 1931. He stage-managed the great rallies at Nuremberg and designed the new Reich Chancellery and Party Headquarters in Munich. In January 1942 he was appointed Armaments Minister and did much to increase and rationalize production. He was sentenced to 20 years' imprisonment at Nuremberg.

was, as the German economic historian, Rolf-Dieter Müller, has observed, able to create 'the psychology of change' and an atmosphere of confidence[14] (see Document 2).

Over the next two years Speer was to achieve a 'production miracle'.[15] In April 1942 he successfully persuaded Hitler to create the Central Planning Board, which organized the allocation of raw materials to each sector of the economy, and he was also ultimately successful in wresting from the army and navy their jealously guarded right of designing their own weapons. He won the cooperation of the industrialists by promising them regular long-term armaments orders and protection from interference from the party. They were also encouraged to use new scientific management techniques to rationalize production, maximize their plant capacities and standardize designs. Initially, too, in the atmosphere of hope and enthusiasm, which Speer inspired, the consumer goods industries were ready to accept restrictions and closures. The large-scale use of foreign workers and prisoners of war (POWs) made rationalization easier, as they were subject to harsh discipline and could offer no latent hostility to the new production methods, as some German workers were still able to do.

Speer's efforts were rewarded by a steady increase in armaments production which, despite heavy Allied bombing, reached its peak in 1943–4. Much of his success can be attributed to his good relations with Hitler, which 'enabled him to chop into tiny pieces the red tape'[16] – the bureaucracy that had hindered the development of German rearmament before 1942. However, for all his successes, Speer's efforts were in the final analysis undermined by both the autonomy of the *Gauleiter*, who at times, particulary towards the end of the war, hoarded labour and economic resources so that they could keep industry in their own *Gaue* functioning, and the independence of the SS, whose considerable economic resources were beyond his grasp. In the end, of course, the German failure to 'open up the treasure-chest in the east',[17] and the Allied strategic bombing campaign, set a limit to Speer's achievements by interrupting supplies, forcing factories to evacuate and demoralizing their workers.

The labour problem

Women were an obvious source of labour for the war industries, and in September 1939 they already composed 37.4 per cent of the total German labour force, which was a considerably higher proportion than in Britain. In the spring of 1940 the Reich Labour Ministry saw no alternative to the introduction of comprehensive female conscription, but the unpopularity of this measure both at home and with married soldiers on the front caused Hitler for the time being to delay the introduction of conscription. Instead the government utilized Polish and French POW labour. The invasion of the USSR gave the Nazi regime access to an enormous pool of labour, but so sure was it of victory that there was at first little opposition from the industrialists to the policy of mass extermination through malnutrition of the Russian POWs. Only after December 1941 did the industrialists begin to press for their deportation to Germany (see Figure 13.1). This was initially opposed by many Nazis, including Himmler, for both racial and security reasons, but Speer – with the support of Hitler, the army and the industrialists – was able to overcome these objections. The party was reassured by the appointment in March 1942 of **Fritz Sauckel** (see Figure 13.2) to the post of Plenipotentiary for Labour Mobilization. He was, to quote Ulrich Herbert, 'a kind of link man between the technocratic and ideological aspects of National Socialism'.[18] In other words, as a hard-line Nazi, he was supposed to be a guarantee that the presence of a large number of foreigners in Germany would be neither a racial nor security threat. By the end of 1944 there were over 7 million foreign workers in Germany.

Fritz Sauckel (1894–1946)
Joined the Nazi Party in 1923 and was appointed a *Gauleiter* in 1927. He was sentenced to death at Nuremberg.

Figure 13.1 Ukrainian peasant women boarding goods trucks en route for Germany to work as forced labourers
Source: Getty Images/ Hulton Archive

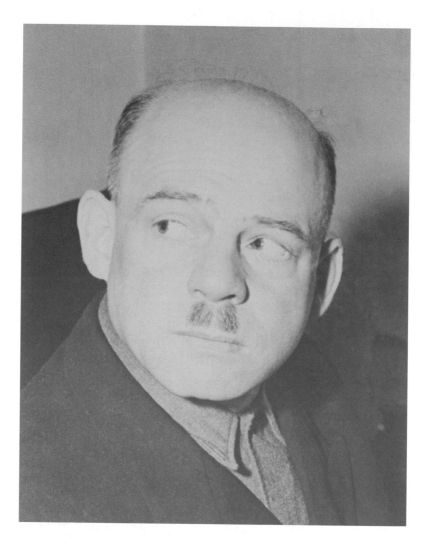

Figure 13.2 Fritz Sauckel
Source: Corbis/Bettmann

Even this number, however, was not sufficient. In response to the voracious demands for manpower by the army, Hitler announced at the end of January 1943 that all males between 16 and 65, who were not in the armed forces, and all females between 17 and 45 were to register for war work. As Hitler exempted mothers with young children, and wives of the self-employed, raised the age for women from 16 to 17 and lowered it at the top end from 50 to 45, only about 900,000 women were actually called up. The employers of the large armament industries viewed these measures with some scepticism, since they preferred foreign workers, whom they could discipline and often ruthlessly exploit, to German men and women from small unmechanized workshops and plants, who were unaccustomed to modern mass production techniques (see Document 3).

THE *VOLKSGEMEINSCHAFT* AT WAR

The essence of the *Volksgemeinchaft* was the preparation of the population for war. Although there was little enthusiasm for war when it came in September 1939, the rapid defeat of Poland and victory after victory until December 1941 soon mollified public opinion. The American journalist Wilhelm Shirer observed, 'as long as the Germans are successful and do not have to pull their belts in too much, this will not be an unpopular war'.[19] However in the winter of 1941–2 the *Volksgemeinschaft* was plunged into a total war from which there was no escape.

Women and the family

Hitler sought to shield married women from the impact of total war. Soldiers' families, who had suffered particularly in the First World War, were given special ration coupons for food and rent. Nevertheless, the longer the war lasted the greater the pressure on the home front. Total war revolutionized the life of both families and individuals . Despite Hitler's reservations, many more women had to work – in 1942 52 per cent of the German labour force was female. Evacuation split families up and removed urban mothers and children to remote urban areas. On farms and in small businesses it was often women who had to play the key role if their husbands and sons were called up. In 1942 a German soldier observed that 'a peasant wife whose husband is at the front . . . has not a single quiet minute from 4 in the morning until 9 at night'[20] (see Document 4).

From June 1942 onwards girls in the Reich Labour Service were liable to be called up for service as auxiliaries in the armed forces. Although initially both the army and Hitler were reluctant to allow women to assume combat roles, by 1944 they were replacing men in operating searchlights and anti-aircraft batteries.

Food consumption in Germany, 1939–45

This table shows fats and meat rations as a percentage of basic foodstuffs.

Period		Meat*	%	Fats*	%
September–October	1939	2,000	12.0	1,080.0	6.5
September–October	1940	2,000	12.5	1,077.5	6.7
September–October	1941	1,6600	8.4	1,077.5	5.7
September	1943	1,200	5.7	875.0	3.4
September	1944	1,400	7.1	750.0	3.8
April	1945	150	0.9	325.0	1.9

*in grams

Source: Redrawn from R.-D. Müller, 'Albert Speer and armaments policy in total war' in Research Institute for Military History, ed., *Germany and the Second World War*, vol 5, part 2, Oxford, Clarendon Press, 2003, p. 527. By permission of Oxford University Press.

Youth and the war

With the outbreak of war the demands of the Hitler Youth on both boys and girls intensified. In 1942, for example, 600,000 boys and 1,400,000 girls helped with the harvest. Increasingly, for boys, the Hitler Youth was used as a preliminary to military training. Efforts were also made to boost its prestige by introducing an induction ceremony, which would rival the Christian confirmation or first communion ceremonies. How effective these were in increasing the commitment of teenagers to Nazism is hard to say.

Inevitably there was some hostile reactions to the demands of the Nazi regime. The Swing Movement, which was popular among students, was essentially apolitical but the fact that its members liked jazz, danced the 'jitterbug', wore British fashions and above all refused to be anti-Semitic, led Himmler to threaten their ringleaders with incarceration in the concentration camps. The Edelweiss Pirate groups of young teenage workers (see p. 422) were initially located in the Ruhr and Rhineland cities, but by 1943 had spread to other conurbations throughout Germany. Their activities were at first limited to boycotting Hitler Youth activities, but some groups did go further and physically attack Hitler Youth patrols, hand out Communist leaflets or Allied propaganda sheets, which had been dropped from planes on the countryside. In Cologne–Ehrenfeld in 1944 hostility to the regime escalated to outright opposition when an *Edelweiss* Pirates gang cooperated with an underground group, which assisted *Wehrmacht* deserters, escaped POWs and foreign workers. It also attacked military installations and even managed to kill the head of the Cologne Gestapo before it was broken up.

The workers

For those workers who were able to escape conscription, the home front presented both opportunities and intense frustration. After 1942 the workers in the armaments industries had to adapt to the new mass production work practices introduced by Speer, and, often, to the evacuation of their factories out of range from Allied bombers. Understandably the dread of being sent to the Eastern front and the dependence on employers for extra rations also ensured for the most part that the discipline of the German workforce remained good, despite the abolition of overtime payments and the extension of the working week to 60 hours in 1944. The large-scale influx of inexperienced workers and foreign labour also provided new opportunities for many of the original workforce, who were promoted to supervisors and foremen.

How did the workers respond to the huge influx of foreign labour? In the factories they were inevitably drawn into the apparatus of surveillance and repression. There were both examples of brutality and 'reprisals' – especially after air raids, but equally there were cases of decency and humanity. On balance, however, it is probably true to say that the majority of German workers were immersed in their own problems, and were oblivious to the fate of the foreign workers. As Ulrich Herbert has written: 'the foreigners were simply there, as much part of wartime life as ration cards or air raid shelters ... Their own privileged position as Germans vis à vis these workers was likewise nothing exceptional, certainly no cause for misgiving.'[21]

SUPPORT, *RESISTENZ* AND OPPOSITION

Opposition was not easy in the Third Reich during the war years. Firstly, Hitler, because of the earlier diplomatic and economic achievements of his regime, was genuinely popular in the Third

Reich. Initial reservations about the war were swept away by the great series of victories in 1940 and 1941. The Ministry of Popular Enlightenment was also skilled at 'positive spin'[22] and able to stress how the Gestapo was defending the home front from traitors. As the tide of war turned, the apparatus of terror was strengthened. Right up to the end of the war Himmler was capable of ruthlessly destroying any opposition. It was no wonder, then, that the majority of the population followed the line of discretion rather than valour. One worker expressed this mood when he said. 'Rather than let them string me up I'll be glad to believe in victory.'[23] However, as in Stalinist Russia, it is a mistake to believe that the population was a passively cowed mass. On the contrary, as Robert Gellately has shown,[24] the Gestapo was dependent on information and denunciations of Germans about their fellow Germans. Many of these denunciations were the result of the desire to harm rivals at work or to get back at awkward neighbours, but the majority were probably made out of patriotic motives (see Document 6).

Inevitably this willingness to inform discouraged resistance. The opposition did not have the 'social and cultural space' to meet and mobilize for action. Consequently 'those who still wanted to say "no" had to swim against the tide, and were driven to individual acts of defiance that were important to them as moral individuals, but in the short run not threatening to the dictatorship.'[25] These acts might include joining the *Edelweiss* Pirates, refusing to use the *Heil* Hitler salute, or hanging out a church banner rather than a swastika flag. To describe such acts, historians have used the word *Resistenz*, which is a medical term and essentially means immunity to Nazi ideology. The term helps us understand that grey area between resistance to and acceptance of the regime.

However, despite the enormous dangers of opposition, there were men and women of immense bravery, who were ready to plot the overthrow of the Nazi regime (see Document 5):

- There were individuals, like the priests Dietrich Bonhoeffer and Alfred Delp, who refused to be constrained by the cautious policies of their churches, and the carpenter Georg Elser, who nearly managed to kill Hitler when he succeeded in concealing a bomb in a pillar in the Burgerbrau beer cellar where Hitler was due to speak. Hitler was only saved because bad weather conditions forced him to leave early to catch the train rather than a plane to Berlin.

- Among the students there was the White Rose Group, which was based at Munich, which was led by Professor Kurt Huber. In 1942–3 it managed to distribute a series of cyclostyled anti-Nazi leaflets in Munich. In February 1943, however, its members were arrested by the Gestapo and executed.

- On the left the Communists were initially more successful than the Social Democrats in maintaining opposition groups within Germany, but in 1942–3 a wave of arrests severely damaged them, leaving only small uncoordinated groups in the large industrial centres.

- Within the army and the bureaucracy there were also cells of opposition composed of conservative Nationalists such as Carl Goerdeler (who had been Price Commissioner 1934–5 and Lord Mayor of Leipzig 1930–7) and General Beck (Army Chief of Staff until 1938). They had at first supported Hitler, but the Sudeten crisis (see pp. 239–40) convinced them that Hitler would plunge Germany into a disastrous war.

- During 1942–3 a diverse group of resisters, led by Count Helmut von Moltke and Count Peter Yorck von Wartenburg, met in Moltke's country house in Kreisau, Upper Silesia. The Kreisau Circle, as the Gestapo called it, became a forum where Social Democrats, both Protestant and Catholic priests, civil servants and *Wehrmacht* officers could meet and discuss the shape of a post-Hitler Germany. Essentially it became the 'think tank'[26] of the non-Communist opposition, until it was broken up by the Gestapo in January 1944.

The plot of 20 July 1944

The *Reichswehr* was best placed to overthrow the Nazi regime. In 1943 opposition groups in the Army Group Centre on the Russian Front and in **General Olbricht**'s headquarters in Berlin planned a series of assassination attempts against Hitler, but, 'as a consequence of 'a barely credible succession of trivial incidents',[27] they all failed. On 13 March 1943, for instance, a bomb had been set to go off in Hitler's plane, but failed to explode.

General Olbricht
Chief of the OKW (High Command of the Armed forces).

Claus Schenk von Stauffenberg (1907–44) Wounded in Africa and appointed Staff Officer in Berlin in 1943. He was executed within hours of the failure of the 20 July plot.

In early 1944 a plan, code-named Operation Valkyrie, to assassinate Hitler and to use the reserve army to topple the Nazi regime was drawn up by Colonel **Claus Schenk von Stauffenberg**. As soon as Hitler was dead, Germany would be placed under martial law; a provisional government, which would include representatives from all groups except the Communists, would be formed; and peace negotiations would be immediately opened with the Western Allies. As Chief of Staff to General Fromm, the Commander-in-Chief of the Home Army, Stauffenberg had entry to Hitler's headquarters, where on the 20 July 1944 he was able to place a bomb in Hitler's briefcase under the conference table and withdraw. However, when the bomb exploded its impact was lessened by the fact that somebody had moved it to behind the massive oak table leg. While several people were killed, Hitler escaped with minor injuries.

Hitler's survival was a major blow to the plotters, but they had also left 'too many loose ends ... dangling':[28] they had not destroyed the communications centre at the *Führer* headquarters or seized the radio stations in Berlin and arrested party and SS leaders. Consequently, once it became known that Hitler had survived, Operation Valkyrie was doomed, and the armies both in Germany and France refused to cooperate. The plot's failure virtually crippled the German opposition and led to the arrest of more than 7,000 people, 5,000 of whom were executed by April 1945.

THE END OF THE THIRD REICH

Karl Doenitz (1891–1980) Commander-in-Chief of the German navy, 1943–5. He showed great loyalty to Hitler in the aftermath of the bomb plot in July 1944.

By the autumn of 1944 oil supplies had been severely cut and transport facilities disrupted throughout the Reich by Allied bombing raids (see Figure 13.3). Once the Red Army occupied the industrial areas of Silesia in January 1945, and British troops the Ruhr in April 1945, the German war economy collapsed. Hitler committed suicide on 30 April 1945 in his bunker in Berlin, after appointing Admiral **Doenitz** President of the Reich, with Goebbels as his Chancellor and Bormann as Party Minister. Failing to negotiate a ceasefire with the Soviets, Goebbels and his wife committed suicide on 1 May after first killing their children, while Bormann died trying to escape from Berlin. The Doenitz government managed to survive briefly in Schleswig-Holstein, until it was dissolved by the British on 23 May 1945.

ASSESSMENT

War was the ultimate aim of the Nazi regime. War was the instrument to remake society along racial lines, sweep away the last class barriers, give Germany access to new lands for settlement in the east and create German hegemony in Europe. In a sense, the mobilization of German society for war was a way of unifying Germany. The *Volksgemeinschaft* was a substitute for the democratic politics of debate, and war undoubtedly cemented it. Initially the great victories in France and at first Russia 'dazzled the nation'.[29] It is true that there was little support for the war in September 1939, but what initially so many of the population dreaded was another defeat, as in 1918. The principle of the war to make Germany the dominant power in Europe and beyond was essentially supported by the majority of the population. What the Germans hoped was that victory in war would create a better life for them, as well as making Germany a respected and great country.

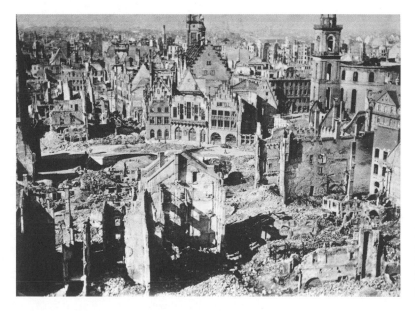

Figure 13.3 The aftermath of bombing raids in Frankfurt am Main, 1945
Source: Bundesbildstelle, Bonn. Bild Nr. 47293

When the tide turned against Germany in the winter of 1942–2, the German people threw their energies into waging a total war. Up to a point it is true they had little option, as the Allies were intent on forcing the Germany into unconditional surrender, and there was, of course, an increase in the terror carried out by the Gestapo at home and by drumhead court martials in the army, but on balance public opinion supported this too, until almost the end of the war.

The Nazis managed to harness a popular egalitarianism and meritocracy. In the army and industry the old elites were swept away and new opportunities were opened up. What mattered was success, not class. Michael Geyer argues that the regime did manage to activate 'large segments of society ... into participation' and released individual ambition from the constraints of professions, class, religion and gender – from the constraints of old society'.[30]

DOCUMENT 1

The ban on listening to foreign radio stations, 1 September 1939

The decree banning listening to foreign radios was justified in the German press in the following release:

At a time in which the German people stand unanimously behind their *Führer*, only one thing is valid for Germany: the word of the *Führer*. In the [last] World War, the enemies of Germany worked with the base weapon of incitement, with poison of the lie and with the seditious provocation – with methods that led to 9th November 1918. The speeches of enemy statesmen, without being censored or commented upon, appeared – even in the year 1918 – in the German press ... Questions only began to be raised when it was already too late.

Source: R. Gellately, *Backing Hitler*, Oxford, Oxford University Press, 2001, p. 185.

DOCUMENT 2

The war economy

Albert Speer describes his first conference after being appointed Armaments Minister:

The large conference hall of the Air Ministry was filled. There were thirty persons present ... Milch [State Secretary in the Air Ministry] took the chair. He asked Funk [Economics Minister] to sit at his right and me at his left. In a terse introductory address he explained the difficulties that had arisen in armaments production due to the conflicting demands of the three services. Vögler [head of] the United Steel Works followed with some highly intelligent explanations of how orders and counter orders, disputes over priority levels, and shifting of priorities interfered with industrial production. There were still unused reserves available, he said, but because of the tugging and hauling these did not come to light. Thus it was high time to establish clear relationships. There must be one man able to make all decisions. Industry did not care who it was.

Source: A. Speer, *Inside the New Reich*, London, Weidenfeld & Nicolson, 1970, pp. 200–1.

DOCUMENT 3
The labour problem

Fritz Sauckel, the Plenipotentiary General for Labour, issued the following programme on 20 April 1942:

All prisoners of war actually in Germany, from the territories of the west as well as of the east, must be completely incorporated into German armaments and munitions industries. Their productivity must be raised to the highest possible level. It must be emphasized, however, that a tremendous additional quantity of foreign labour must be found for the Reich.

Source: J. Noakes, ed, *Nazism, 1919–45*, vol. 4, *The German Home Front in World War II*, Exeter, Exeter University Press, 1998, pp. 241–2.

DOCUMENT 4
The impact of the war on the family

By the autumn of 1943 bombing, evacuation and the heavy fighting in Russia were all taking their toll on family life, as the following extracts from an SD report of 18 November 1943 show:

Many women are also concerned that the stability of their marriages and the mutual understanding of their partners is beginning to suffer from the lengthy war. The separation which, with short breaks, has now been going on for years, the transformation in their circumstances through total war and in addition the heavy demands which are nowadays made on every individual are changing people and filling their lives. When on leave, the front-line soldier often no longer shows any understanding for his family's domestic circumstances, which are governed by the war, and remains indifferent to the many daily cares of the home front. This often produces an increasing *distance between the married couple*. Thus wives often point out that having looked forward to being together again during their husband's leave, the occasion is spoilt by frequent rows caused by mutual tensions. That even happens in marriages which were previously models of harmony ...

The *splitting up of families* without the possibility of making visits with all the accompanying problems is in the long run felt to be an intolerable burden both by men but in particular by women ... Above all, the married men say that their family is the only compensation they have for their heavy work load. One shouldn't take away from them the only thing that makes life worth living. But the wives are no less subjected to a heavy mental burden because they want to live in their own homes, to look after them and to care for their husbands and children ...

... the majority of the evacuated women and children are accommodated in small villages and rural parishes under the most primitive conditions. They have to cook in the same kitchens with their hosts, which often give cause for conflict, since people look into each other's pots and get jealous if the other family has something better to eat. In a number of cases there can be no question of family life since sometimes not all children can be accommodated with their mother in the same house, and furthermore often the only living room that is available has to be shared with the host family.

Source: Noakes, J. (ed) (1998) *Nazism 1919–1945. Volume 4: The German Home Front in World War II*, pub University of Exeter Press, pp. 360–2

Document 5
Resistance

After the war Fabian von Schlabrendorff, a young officer during the war, recalled his last words with General von Treskow on the Russian front on 21 July, after news of the failure of Operation

Valkyrie had just been received. Shortly after this Treskow committed suicide. Treskow told Schlabrendorff:

The whole world will vilify us now. But I am still firmly convinced that that we did the right thing. I consider Hitler to be the arch enemy not only of Germany but of the world. When in a few hours I appear before the judgment seat of god, in order to give an account of what I have done and left undone, I believe I can with good conscience justify what I did in the fight against Hitler. If God promised Abraham that he would not destroy Sodom if only ten righteous men could be found there, then I hope for our sakes God will not destroy Germany. None of us can complain about our own deaths. Everyone who joined our circle put on the robe of Nessus to die for his convictions.

Source: Noakes, J. (ed) (1998) *Nazism 1919–1945. Volume 4: The German Home Front in World War II*, pub University of Exeter Press, p. 618.

DOCUMENT 6
Support for the regime

The historian Robert Gellately wrote:

Until recently historians frequently emphasized the passivity of German citizens in the Third Reich, and wrote about the Nazi police state as if it were so invasive as to leave little room for citizen initiative beyond mere ceremonials and rituals. We know now that even if all citizens did not agree with everything, including certain aspects of the persecution of the Jews and foreign workers inside Germany, the regime had no difficulty in obtaining denunciations from the population about suspected breaches of the racist system. Providing information to the police or the Party was one of the most important contributions of citizen involvement in the Third Reich.

Source: R. Gellately, *The Gestapo and German Society*, Oxford, Oxford University Press, 1990, p. 261

NOTES

1 Quoted in R. Gellately, *Backing Hitler*, Oxford, Oxford University Press, 2001, p. 77.

2 P. Ayçoberry, *The Social History of the Third Reich*, New York, New Press, 1999, p. 210.

3 J. Noakes ed, *Nazism, 1919–1945*, vol. 4, *The German Home Front in World War II, 1939–45*, Exeter, Exeter University Press, 1998, p. 9.

4 I. Kershaw, *Hitler*, vol. 2, *1936–45 Nemisis*, London, Allen Lane, 2000, p. 573.

5 B. Koerner, R-D. Müller and H. Umbreit, 'Conclusion' in Research Institute for Military History, ed., *Germany and the Second World War*, vol. 5, part 2, Oxford, Clarendon Press, p. 1072.

6 Quoted in M. Broszat, *The Hitler State. The Foundation and Development of the Internal Structure of the Third Reich*, London, Longman, 1981, p. 341.

7 Gellately, *Backing Hitler*, p. 204 .

8 J.C. Fest, *The Face of the Third Reich*, Harmondsworth, Penguin, p. 180.

9 Broszat, *The Hitler State*, p. 319.

10 Noakes, ed, *Nazism*, vol. 4, p. 106.

11 Kershaw, *Hitler*, vol. 2, p. 428.

12 R.J. Overy, *War and Economy in the Third Reich*, Oxford, Oxford University Press, 1995, p. 251.

13 R.D. Müller, 'Albert Speer and armaments policy in total war', in Research Institute for Military History, ed., *Germany and the Second World War*, vol. 5, part 2, Oxford, Clarendon Press, p. 295.

14 Ibid., 296

15 Overy, *War and Economy,* p. 343 .

16 A.S. Milward, *The German Economy at War*, London, Athlone Press 1965, p. 86.

17 Müller, 'Albert Speer and armaments policy', p. 299.

18 U. Herbert, *Hitler's Foreign Workers*, Cambridge, Cambridge University Press, 1997, p. 162.

19 Quoted in Gellately, *Backing Hitler*, p. 71.

20 Overy, *War and Economy*, p. 307.

21 Herbert, *Hitler's Foreign Workers*, p. 396.

22 Gellately, *Backing Hitler*, p. 259.

23 Quoted in Noakes, ed, *Nazism*, vol. 4, p. 638.

24 See Gellately, *Backing Hitler*, p. 259.

25 Ibid., p. 262.

26 D.G. Williamson, *Germany Since 1815*, Basingstoke, Palgrave, 2005, p. 267.

27 H. Rothfels, *The German Opposition to Hitler*, London, Oswald Wolff, 1970, p. 70.

28 Kershaw, *Hitler*, vol. 2, p. 677.

29 M. Geyer, 'Restorative, German society and the pursuit of war', in R. Bessel, ed., *Fascist Italy and Nazi Germany*, Cambridge, Cambridge University Press, 1997.

30 Ibid., p. 160.

CHAPTER FOURTEEN

Fascist Italy at war

TIMELINE

1940	June	Italy declares war on Britain and France
	September	Italian troops invade Egypt
	October	Invasion of Greece begins
1941	February	Hitler sends troops to North Africa
	May	British and Commonwealth troops seize Ethiopia
		Germans occupy Greece
1942	October	Axis troops pushed back at El Alamain
1943	January	Party of Action set up
	March	Industrial unrest in Turin
	July	Allied troops land in Sicily
		Mussolini forced to resign by Fascist Grand Council
	September	Armistice signed with Allies
		Mussolini 'rescued' by Germans
		Italian Social Republic (Salò Republic) set up
	November	Verona Congress
1944	June	Rome occupied by Allies
1945	April	Mussolini shot by partisans

INTRODUCTION

In retrospect, Italy's declaration of war on Britain and France in June 1940 was disastrous, and led to the fall of Mussolini and then a bitter conflict in the Italian peninsular not only between the Allies and the Germans but also between the partisans and the Fascists. Despite his extravagant boasting that he could mobilize an army of '8 million bayonets' and an air force that could 'blot out the sun', Mussolini had done little to modernize the armed forces. Mechanization remained low down on the army's scale of priorities, and Mussolini had also failed to build an efficient centralized administrative system, which could plan and control the production of weapons and the war economy. The weakness of the armed forces was also made worse by the deep divisions in Italian society between the north and the south; an ill-educated population, of which perhaps some two-fifths were illiterate or semi-illiterate; and Italy's lack of a large industrial base.

Mussolini, however, went to war in 1940 not just because he was an opportunist. In many ways abstention was, as the Italian historian Carlo Gambino observed, 'a greater risk than war',[1] and would have led to Italy's marginalization in Europe as a triumphant Nazi Germany dominated the Continent. A short victorious war, which Mussolini assumed he would wage, would also have the advantage of consolidating Fascist power at home and of moulding 'the Italians into a people "worthy" of the imperial mission Mussolini claimed for them'.[2] The war was therefore fought not just for foreign conquest but ultimately for the revolutionary aim of completing the Fascist revolution in Italy. Like Hitler in Russia, Mussolini was aiming to forge a *spazio vitale* – or living space – in the Mediterranean and the Middle East and to make Italy at long last a great power. Yet this parallel should not be pushed too far, as Hitler was aiming for a biological world revolution (see p. 221), while Mussolini merely sought a greater 'Italian nationalist utopia'[3] (see Documents 1 and 2).

THE KEY ISSUES IN THIS CHAPTER ARE:

- The reasons for the disastrous course of the war, 1940–3.
- The impact of this on public opinion at home, and the decline of the party.
- Economic problems and growing industrial unrest.
- Italy and the Holocaust.
- The reasons for the collapse of Fascist Italy in 1943.
- The development of Italian Fascism during the Salò Republic, 1943–4.
- The collapse of the Republic in 1945.

ITALY AT WAR, 1940–1

When Mussolini declared war on Britain and France in June 1940 he hoped to wage a parallel war alongside Germany to gain control of the Mediterranean and the Middle East. Anxious to be at the conference table when the new Fascist Europe would be hammered out, Mussolini offered troops to take part in Operation Sea Lion, the invasion of southern Britain. Initially the Italian programme envisaged the following gains:

- the annexation of Savoy (up to the River Var), Corsica and Tunisia from France
- Malta and British Somaliland from Britain, while Aden would be ceded to the Yemen and Cyprus to Greece
- the Anglo-Egyptian Sudan would become the Italian-Egyptian Sudan and the mandates of **Syria, Palestine and the Lebanon** would become effectively satellite Italian states
- Switzerland would be partitioned along the great central Alpine range and Italy would annex the Valais, the Ticino and the Grisons.

Syria, Palestine and the Lebanon
Made mandates under the League of Nations in 1919 and administered by Britain (Palestine) and France (Syria and the Lebanon)

Events were to prove that this programme was both premature and ambitious. Britain continued to fight, while Hitler hesitated to alienate the new Vichy regime by tolerating Mussolini's expansionary plans in North Africa (see p. 387).

The first and almost only Italian success was the occupation of British Somaliland in August 1940. In September Italian troops moved into Egypt. Strategically Mussolini would have been advised to concentrate his military efforts on the Egyptian campaign, but at the end of October he pursued the high-risk strategy of launching an invasion of Greece from Albania (see Map 7). It is arguable that this was as much aimed at the Germans as the British, as Mussolini was alarmed that the dispatch of German troops to guard the Romanian oil wells signalled a growing German interests in the Balkans, which he regarded as an Italian sphere of interest.

In both Greece and North Africa Mussolini's parallel war rapidly stalled. In Egypt Italian forces were forced back into Libya with the loss of 380 tanks and the surrender of 130,000 troops, while in May 1941 British Commonwealth forces advancing from Kenya had seized the entire Italian East African empire, including its jewel, Ethiopia. In the Balkans the Greeks managed not only to defeat the Italians at the beginning of the campaign but also to invade Albania.

On 18 November 1940, at the Berghof Conference, the real balance of power between Italy and Germany was revealed when Ciano, Mussolini's Foreign Minister (see p. 286) met Hitler. Hitler was highly critical of Italian tactics in Egypt and even more so of the invasion of Greece, which he feared would lead to the setting up of British air bases in the northern part of the country. Mussolini later observed that Hitler had given Ciano ' the ruler across the knuckles'.[4]

By the spring of 1941 the Italian position in both theatres was near to collapse, which led to a major domestic crisis. The British were already encouraging the Italians to drop Mussolini and make peace, but the Germans were still the stronger 'and could bolster Mussolini faster than the British could destroy him'.[5] (see Document 2).

In February 1941 Hitler decided to send a Panzer division to North Africa and began to draw up plans to help Mussolini win his parallel war in Greece, but even at this late stage Mussolini ineffectually struggled to maintain his independence. He attempted to negotiate an Italian–Yugoslav alliance which he hoped would push the Greeks into making peace, but Ribbentrop, the German Foreign Minister, insisted on a 'unified approach'. Then in response to a pro-British military coup in Belgrade, the Germans invaded both Yugoslavia and Greece in massive and sudden force. As MacGregor Knox observed, 'Italy's own war was over. Nothing remained but to follow where Hitler led, until German war culminated in German victory or engulfed the Fascist regime and Italy itself in ruin.'[6]

Initially it looked in the spring of 1941 as if the Germans would save Mussolini. The Greeks and Yugoslavs were rapidly defeated and the Italians were given Dalmatia, most of Slovenia, Croatia and Montenegro. In Greece the Germans retained a few strategically important areas such as Crete and Salonika, but left the rest of the country to the Italians. Yet in reality the Germans played the predominant role. In North Africa the Germans also brilliantly reversed British successes and advanced right up to the Egyptian frontier. To quote Richard Bosworth, Italian fortunes went though a 'feeble insurrection'.[7]

In June 1941 when Hitler invaded the USSR, Mussolini immediately offered Hitler 62,000 troops, and in early December, once the German advance had stalled, he trebled that number. His hope was that Italy could maintain its independence if closely associated with German military success. Yet he also feared the consequences of a German victory, as it might reduce Italy to the position of a vassal state (see Document 4).

THE HOME FRONT

The economy

Despite the progress made in the inter-war period, by 1938 the Italian economy had a potential capacity of only about a one-fifth of Germany and one-half of Japan. The economy was dependent on imports, but the British control of Suez and Gibraltar stopped at least two-fifths of vitally needed imports reaching Italy. It was these supply problems that contributed to Italy's eventual defeat. Italy was only permitted to import 1.5 million tonnes of oil from Romania, which was well below 50 per cent of Italian peacetime consumption. Italy was also totally dependent on German coal, but could only import just under a million tonnes of it a month. This in turn hit Italian steel production, which fell from 2.3 million tonnes to 1.9 million in 1942. The longer the war lasted the more the whole economy suffered from shortages. In the winter of 1942–3 there was virtually no fuel in the big cities in the north, shoe leather ran out, and soap and coffee were unobtainable except on the black market. Food production was also hit by the conscription of peasants into the army and the impossibility of importing animal feed and fertilizers. Rationing had to be introduced at the barely adequate level of 1,000 calories per day.

Neither was the war economy helped by the regime's inability to raise sufficient sums to finance it. As early as the winter of 1939–40 gold and currency reserves ran out, and raising of foreign loans in wartime on Wall Street or the City of London was impossible. Unlike Germany or the Japan, Italy failed to conquer and loot wealthy territories, which could have helped the economy. Tax yields actually decreased by 20 per cent between 1939–40. Wealthy businessmen with contacts with the government were able to evade taxation almost completely, while the government hesitated to squeeze the small savers even more. The failure to tax effectively ensured that the Fascist government was unable to spend more than 20 per cent of its gross domestic product per year on war production.

The government also failed to force big business to toe the line. Although the state, thanks to its policy during the Depression (see p. 275), controlled more of the heavy industrial sector than any other Western nation, in practice these state-owned industries acted as 'independent fiefdoms whose only connection to the state resided in the immunity from bankruptcy that it offered'.[8] The state was unable to galvanize industry through competition or find alternative sources of production.

By the end of 1942 the Italian economy was seriously weakened by Allied bombing raids. Martin Clark has observed that 'Northern Italy was one of the few places where mass aerial bombing proved effective in the second world war'.[9] Not only did it disrupt factory production but it weakened morale and drove thousands of people from the cities. It also provoked in March 1943 the first serious labour troubles for 18 years, when 100,000 workers struck over the government's attempt to control the payment of evacuation allowances.

The crisis of 'disappointed expectation', December 1940–March 1941

In the winter of 1940–1 the Fascist regime came near to total collapse. The military disasters in Albania and North Africa coincided with the introduction of a new and unpopular system of rationing in oil, pasta, flour and rice, which limited food consumption to a mere 400 grams per day, and also rising inflation.

Mussolini initially attempted to deflect criticism on to the army for the military disasters by dismissing the Chief of Staff, Marshal Badoglio, in December 1940, but this merely enraged the army and led to rumours of a military putsch. A well-organized coup might at this juncture have unseated Mussolini, but the party leaders were divided and the main thrust of the opposition was against Ciano rather than Mussolini. Badoglio, despite his appalling military leadership, also become something of a popular hero, as the public recognized that Mussolini was using him as a scapegoat.

This was a situation that the British immediately attempted to exploit, and on 17 December 1940 Churchill, the British Prime Minister, delivered his famous speech in which he pinned responsibility for the Italian defeats on 'one man alone' – Mussolini – and invited the Italian establishment to overthrow him. Mussolini ineffectively tried to restore trust in his regime by sending his ministers and the members of the Chamber of *Fasci* and Corporations to serve on the Albanian front. The hope was that this would recapture the atmosphere of the heady days of the Ethiopian War, when senior party figures briefly served as junior officers, to symbolize the unity between party and country. It was, however, only the German *Blitzkrieg* in the Balkans and Rommel's success in defeating the British in Cyrenaica in 1941 that dispelled the immediate crisis in morale.

The decline of the PNF

On the outbreak of war, the Fascist Party (PNF), as in the years of the Depression (see p. 267), was mobilized to assist the people in the far greater emergency of the war. As all servicemen were allowed to join the party, membership rose to 4.75 million by 1942. The PNF was responsible for civil defence and the welfare of both combatants and their families, as well as evacuees from the towns. It was also supposed to supervize rationing and control the prices of foodstuffs and basic consumer goods. Its primary role, however, remained the indoctrination of the people and maintaining their flagging support for the war. For the more committed young Fascists and intellectuals, the war was a revolutionary war which would destroy the bourgeois way of life. They fully shared Mussolini's belief that it was a struggle against 'a grim coalition of demoplutocrats, Masons and Jews',[10] and that, in the words of the Minister of Education, Giuseppi Bottai, war should become 'a way of life for the whole nation'.[11] In an attempt to reinforce this message Mussolini banned the press from mentioning the word 'Christmas' in December 1941 and replaced as Party Secretary the colourless bureaucrat Ettori Mutti with the 28-year-old Aldo Vidussoni, an action which was supposed to suggest that Fascism was still young and dynamic. Vidussoni proved a disaster. He was dismissed by the older Fascists as a 'cretin' and 'imbecile' and in February 1943 a police report assessing his term of office observed that 'his lack of organizing ability ... drains away still further the essence of the party' (see Document 3).

MUSSOLINI'S OVERTHROW

By May 1943 overt opposition to Fascist rule was growing. In March 1943 over 100,000 industrial workers struck in Turin and industrial unrest rapidly spread throughout most of northern Italy. An anti-Fascist coalition also began to emerge: remnants of pre-Fascist Republicans, Radicals and Left Liberals began to set up a Party of Action in January 1943, while the Communists and Socialists also began to rebuild their local organizations, and the Catholic opposition (see p. 271) founded the Christian Democratic Party. These groups were not yet able to overthrow the regime. For that to happen the King, the army and opposition within the Fascist Party itself was still needed.

Mussolini had created a strong dissident group within the party when he purged half the cabinet in February 1943, among whom were the key figures of Grandi, Ciano and Bottai. Their desire for revenge was fuelled by the accumulating evidence that Italy was losing the war and that the regime was in the process of collapsing. By June 1943 the Axis forces had been driven out of North Africa and the Allies were poised to invade Sicily. Although the Allies refused to negotiate directly with Mussolini, unofficial contacts with the Americans through the papacy made it clear that Washington would be ready to negotiate with an Italian military government nominated by the King. Once the Allies invaded Sicily in July and started bombing Rome, Mussolini's removal from power became a priority, if an armistice was to be negotiated, that would terminate the war with Britain and America.

The Fascist Grand Council met on 24–25 July 1943, and in a lengthy session lasting nearly 10 hours it decided by 19 votes to 7 to ask the King to resume command of the armed forces and 'that supreme initiative of decision making which our institutions attribute to him'. Essentially this was a vote to have Mussolini replaced (see Document 5). The following day, however, Mussolini began to have second thoughts and to talk about punishing the 'traitors', but when he visited the King that afternoon, he was told that Marshal Badoglio, the former Chief of Staff, would take over and was arrested on leaving the palace. He was first sent to the penal settlement on the island of Ponza and then later moved to a hotel in the isolated Apennine skiing resort of Gran Sasso.

THE SALÒ REPUBLIC

On 3 September General Castellano, Badoglio's special envoy in Lisbon, arranged a secret armistice with the Allies. American and British Commonwealth troops then landed on the toe of Italy. The Germans immediately responded by occupying Rome, and the King and the Badoglio government fled southwards to the protection of the Allies. The Germans also managed to rescue Mussolini, and restore him as the head of the so-called Italian Social Republic, which in the autumn of 1943 still controlled central and northern Italy. It rapidly became known as the Republic of Salò, where its Ministry of Popular Culture and Propaganda had its offices on the banks of Lake Garda.

Mussolini's rescue

Under the terms of the Armistice signed with the Allies on 3 September 1943 Marshal Badoglio had agreed to hand over Mussolini to the Allies, but in the panic caused by the German occupation of Rome no instructions were left as to what to do with the prisoner. Mussolini was under house arrest at Gran Sasso in the Abruzzi mountains. On 12 September 12 German gliders with 100 German commandos and an Italian general, Fernando Soleti, towed by a single-engine Stork reconnaissance plane, landed in the meadow in front of the former hotel where Mussolini was interned. The 25 *caribiniere* troops guarding Mussolini were confused by Soleti's order not to shoot. Mussolini was crammed into the Stork, which had difficulty in taking off from the rocky meadow and nearly plunged into the abyss before straightening up and flying back to Rome, from where on the next day Mussolini was flown out to Vienna. Hitler saw the 'liberation' of the *Duce* as a great moral triumph, but in reality 'Hitler had not so much liberated Mussolini as he had captured him.'[12]

To the *squadrisimo*, who had been marginalized by Mussolini nearly 20 years earlier (see p. 106), the Salò Republic appeared initially to offer the chance of a Fascist renaissance and a clean break with the compromises of the past. Mussolini immediately announced a radical programme, which aimed to :

- rebuild the Fascist party
- refound the Fascist state, starting from the bottom upwards, and return to the early spirit of corporatism (see pp. 109–10)
- summon a constitutional convention, which would announce the creation of the new republican state
- regroup the Italian armed forces.

At the end of September the Senate was abolished and the Fascist syndical organizations (see p. 110) were reorganized. **Alessandro Pavolini**, in his role as the new Party Secretary, had the task of refounding the party. As the collapse of July 1943 had effectively destroyed official Fascism, the new party had to go back to its roots in the northern cities. Any attempts to form a common front with non-Fascists were quickly stamped upon, as the more extreme leaders, who had been schooled in the Fascist squads in the early 1920s, refused to consider any collaboration with moderate elements. The old slogans of the early 1920s reappeared and attracted both ex-Socialist militants of the left and the extreme Fascists on the right.

In November delegates of the Fascist federations of syndicates met at Verona to discuss the new party manifesto. Mussolini and his advisers hoped, to quote F.W. Deakin, to 'appeal to a long suppressed desire for social justice without conceding any democratic control by the masses in any real sense or weakening the political monopoly of the neo-Fascist party'.[13] The key points of the new manifesto were:

- The head of the new 'social state' would be elected and then reappointed every five years by 'the citizens'.
- No citizen could be held under arrests for longer than seven days without judicial approval.
- The religion of the Republic was the Roman Catholic Church. Jews were regarded as belonging to the 'enemy nationality'.
- The foreign policy aims were: 'the integral unity and the independence of the fatherland and the recognition of the

Alessandro Pavolini (1903–45) Minister of Popular Culture, 1939–43. In January 1945 he was executed by Italian partisans.

necessity of vital living space for forty-five million inhabitants'.

- A European community was also to be set up, aimed at removing British influence from the Continent and also at exploiting the natural resources of Africa 'for the benefit of the European and native peoples'.
- As far as social policy went, private property was to be guaranteed by the state, but 'public services, and, as a rule, war industries must be run by the state'.[14]

The dominant mood of the Verona Congress supported this attempt to resurrect the ideology of early Fascism. The programme was approved, as was Pavolini's resurrection of the Fascist squads. The squads' attempts to consolidate the grip of the Fascist Party on the Salò Republic led to a chain reaction of assassinations and counter-assassinations, which marked the beginning of the Italian Civil War. In January 1944 a special tribunal was set up by Mussolini to try those '**traitors of 25 July**', who had fallen into the hand of the new Fascist regime.

Traitors of 25 July
Those who had voted for Mussolini's resignation at the Fascist Grand Council Meeting, July 1943.

Crucial to attempts by Mussolini to relaunch Fascism was his socialization policy. In February a new law was announced in which all companies employing more than 50 people were to reconstitute their board of directors so that half of them represented the workforce. All firms were also to have advisory councils on which both manual, clerical and technical workers would sit, to protect the interests of their employees. Potentially this won some support from the workers but it was quickly lost when a powerful combination of the Germans, Italian industrialists and Swiss investors managed to veto its effective application.

THE COLLAPSE OF THE REPUBLIC, 1944–5

The Salò Republic was in reality a German satellite state. Every key area of policy was effectively controlled by the Germans. To the Germans the main importance of Italy was as a reserve of labour for the Reich's war industries. Nearly half a million Italian troops, who had fallen into German hands in late 1943, were employed as forced labour, and in the spring of 1944 the Salò government agreed that men born between 1920 and 1921 should be called up to work in Germany.

Inevitably the failure of Mussolini to launch a new appealing brand of Fascism, the ceaseless demands by the Germans for labour and the slow but steady progress of the Allies up the Italian peninsular caused support for the Salò regime to haemorrhage. In the autumn of 1943 small bands of partisans began to form, and by early 1944 they were operating in force in Piedmont, the Alpine valleys and the Apennines. By the summer of 1944 Mussolini controlled only the plane bordering both banks of the River Po. In the large cities Communist-led underground committees were successfully staging ever-larger strikes. Mussolini also had no effective forces to restore order. The Italian army was under German control and its most reliable units were still being trained in Germany. The National Republican Guard, the successor to the party militia, proved a broken reed and its members increasingly deserted to the partisans.

In April 1945 the British and Americans at last reached Bologna. Mussolini meanwhile attempted in vain to open negotiations with both the Allies and the partisans. He also thought of escaping to Spain or Argentina, but he had left it too late. In the end he joined a group of German soldiers who were trying to get through partisan lines to Austria. Despite disguising himself as a German, he was recognized and seized by the partisans and shot. His body, together with those of several other leading Fascists and his mistress, was thrown on to a lorry, driven to Milan and hanged upside down, at the filling station in Piazzale Loreto, where in August 1944 15 Italian hostages had been executed by the Fascists (see Document 2).

ASSESSMENT

In 1939 the Fascist regime in Italy seemed totally secure. Initially, when war broke out in September 1939, Mussolini was wise enough to hedge his bets and wait. In June 1940 his decision to enter the war was backed by the Italian people, as it seemed that Britain was beaten and that the British empire would be up for grabs. Yet in retrospect this decision was to prove disastrous. The defeats administered by the Greeks and the British to Italian forces did irreparable harm to Mussolini's prestige. Fascist Italy was unable to fight a parallel war independent of Hitler, and was only saved from defeat in 1941–2 by the intervention of German forces. A German victory would still have preserved Mussolini's regime, but it would essentially have been a satellite regime in a German-dominated Europe.

However, once Rommel was defeated in Africa, and the British and Americans had landed in Sicily, Mussolini could no longer survive. In contrast to the refusal of the Western Allies to negotiate with any German resistance group, Britain and America were ready to negotiate with an alternative Italian government. It was this that led the Fascist Grand Council on 25 July 1943 to hand back power to the King, so that he could remove Mussolini from power.

If Mussolini had not been rescued by German commanders, he would have been handed over to the Allies. This epic rescue, however, merely emphasized his dependence on Germany. The Salò Republic hardly differed from Vichy or even Croatia as an artificial satellite state created merely to serve the German war effort. It is true that Mussolini set up various ministries, but these were mere camouflage for German control, as real power was exercised by German officials and agencies behind the scenes. An attempt was made to revert to the revolutionary Fascism of 1920–1, but far from rallying the population behind Mussolini this merely fanned the flames of a bitter internal conflict that was both a class war, a struggle for national regeneration and a civil war. The Salò Republic survived until the Germans were finally defeated in April 1945, and Mussolini was hanged by partisans.

DOCUMENT I
Mussolini's declaration of war

On 10 June 1940 Mussolini announced Italy's declaration of war from the balcony of the Palazzo Venezia in Rome. The speech was broadcast by radio and relayed to the piazzas in towns and villages throughout Italy:

The hour marked out by destiny beats in the sky over our *patria*; the hour of irrevocable decisions ... we depart on our campaign against the plutocratic and reactionary democracies of the west, who have always placed obstacles in the way of the march, and often threatened the very existence of the Italian people ... we take up arms to resolve, after the resolution of the problem of our continental frontiers, the problem of our maritime frontiers. We want to break the territorial and military chains which hold us asphyxiated in our sea, for a people of 45 million souls is only truly free if it has at its disposal free access to the Ocean.

Source: N. Farrell, *Mussolini*, London, Weidenfeld & Nicolson, 2003, pp. 333–4.

DOCUMENT 2
Churchill's assessment of Mussolini

Churchill, the British Prime Minister, summed up Mussolini's career as follows in his post-war memoirs:

So ended the twenty-one years of dictatorship of Mussolini in Italy, during which he had saved the Italian people from Bolshevism, into which it could have sunk in 1919, to carry it to a position in Europe which Italy had never had before. A new impulse was given to national life. The Italian Empire in North Africa was founded. Many important public works were completed in Italy ... his regime was too expensive, without doubt for the Italian people, but it is undeniable that it attracted in its period of success, a very large number of Italians ... The fatal error of Mussolini was the declaration of war against France and Great Britain after the victories of Hitler in June 1940. If he had not done it, he could have easily have kept Italy in a position of equilibrium, courted and recompensed by both sides, gaining unaccustomed wealth and prosperity from the struggle of other countries. Even when the outcome of the war appeared clear, Mussolini would have been well received by the Allies ... He could have chosen with ability and intelligence the right moment in which to declare war on Hitler. Instead he took the wrong road.

Source: W.S. Churchill, *The Second World War*, vol. 5, *Closing the Ring*, London, Cassell, 1950, p. 66.

DOCUMENT 3
Growing disillusionment with Fascism and the war

The Italian Jewish writer Primo Levi describes the feelings of a young lieutenant in his twenties in the winter of 1942–43:

One could see that he wore his uniform with some disgust ... He spoke of Fascism and of the war with reticence and with a sinister gaiety that was not hard to interpret. It was the ironic gaiety of an entire generation of Italians who were intelligent and honest enough to reject Fascism, but too skeptical to actively oppose it and despair about the future; I myself would have been part of this generation, had the racial laws not intervened to mature me and guide me towards choice.

Source: R. Ben-Ghiat, *Fascist Modernities, Italy 1922–1945*, Berkeley, University of California Press, 2001, p. 200.

DOCUMENT 4
A comparison between the military strength of the Nazi and Fascist regimes

MacGregor Knox compares the dynamism of the two regimes:

Between 1922 and 1943, and 1933 and 1945, these three layers of factors and forces combined to produce the wide difference in lust for expansion and in *Leistung* that distinguished the two regimes. The Fascist regime lacked the ideological coherence and conviction needed to generate fanaticism. It lacked the courage to delegate authority and the political freedom of action to exploit the population's thirst for careers open to talent. Italy's lower levels of literacy, economic development, and national integration, its less virulent national mythology, and the pervasive influence of the church also meant a shortage of talent for such careers, a lowered receptiveness to Fascist appeals, and a wide gulf in most Italian units between officers and men. In Germany, racist fanaticism, 'political free enterprise', and careers for masses eager to trample flat the remaining barriers of *Stand* drove Nazism forward against both internal and external foes.

Source: M. Knox, 'Expansionist zeal, fighting power and staying power in the Italian and German dictatorships' in R. Bessell, ed., *Fascist Italy and Nazi Germany*, Cambridge, Cambridge University Press, 1996, p. 130.

DOCUMENT 5
The Grand Council meeting, 24–5 July 1943

Three different motions were presented by Grandi, Farinacci and Scorza at the Grand Council meeting. The first was read out by Grandi:

Leistung
Achievement.

Stand
Class.

The Grand Council declares ... the immediate restoration of all state functions, allotting to the King, the Grand Council, the Government, parliament and the Corporations the tasks and responsibilities laid down by our statutory and constitutional laws.

It invites the Head of Government to request His Majesty the King – towards whom the heart of all the nation turns with faith and confidence – that he may be pleased, for the honour and salvation of the nation, to assume together with effective command of the Armed Forces on land, sea and in the air, according to article 5 of the statute of the Realm, that supreme initiative of decision which our institutions attribute to him and which, in all our national history, has always been the glorious heritage of our August dynasty of Savoy.

Source: F.W. Deakin, *The Brutal Friendship. Mussolini, Hitler and the Fall of Italian Fascism*, London, Weidenfeld & Nicolson, 1962, pp. 442–3.

NOTES

1 Quoted in M. Knox, *Mussolini Unleashed*, Cambridge, Cambridge University Press, 1982, p. 291.

2 Ibid., p. 286.

3 Ibid., p. 290.

4 Ibid., p. 243.

5 Ibid., p. 279.

6 Ibid., p. 285.

7 R. Bosworth, *Mussolini*, Edward Arnold, London, 2002, p. 382.

8 M. Knox, *Hitler's Italian Allies*, Cambridge, Cambridge University Press, 2000, p. 40.

9 M. Clark, *Modern Italy, 1871–1982*, Harlow, Longman, 1984, p. 289.

10 R. Ben-Ghiat, *Fascist Modernities. Italy 1922–1945*, Berkeley, University of California Press, 2001, p. 173.

11 Bosworth, *Mussolini*, p. 377.

12 N. Farrell, *Mussolini. A New Life*, London, Weidenfeld & Nicolson, 2003, p. 429.

13 F.W. Deakin, *The Brutal Friendship. Mussolini, Hitler and the Fall of Italian Fascism*, London, Weidenfeld & Nicolson, 1962, p. 627.

14 Ibid., p. 628.

CHAPTER FIFTEEN

Stalinism and the Great Patriotic War

TIMELINE

1941	June	Hitler launches invasion of the USSR
		Stalin nominates himself Chairman of the State Committee of Defence
	December	Germans halted outside Moscow
1942	August	Churchill and Stalin meet in Moscow
	November	Soviet forces encircle Stalingrad
1943	January	Germans surrender in Stalingrad
	July	Germany forced to abandon Kursk offensive
	March	Stalin becomes Marshal of the Soviet Union
	April	USSR breaks off diplomatic relations with Polish government in exile
	May	Comintern dissolved
	November	Soviet forces retake Kiev
1944	January	Soviet forces relieve Leningrad
	July	Soviet-controlled Polish government set up in Lublin
	August	Warsaw uprising
		Soviet troops enter Bucharest
1945	January	Soviet forces occupy Budapest and Warsaw
	April	Soviet and American troops meet on the Elbe
	May	Germany surrenders

INTRODUCTION

Ultimately victory appeared to vindicate Stalinism, yet Stalin himself had done much to make the USSR vulnerable to a German attack. Even though his suspicions of Britain and France after Munich (see p. 240) had been justified, the Nazi–Soviet Pact had enabled Hitler to defeat Poland and France and to build up a position of enormous strength in Western and Central Europe. Stalin's refusal to listen to warnings about an imminent Nazi attack in the first part of 1941 brought the USSR perilously near to losing the war when that attack was finally launched on 22 June. The German invasion reduced Stalin to such despair that he is reported to have observed that 'Lenin left us a great inheritance and we, his heirs, have fucked it all up.'[1] Such, however, was the brutality of the Nazi invaders (see p. 398) that the desire to beat them had a unifying effect. The hatred and fear caused by collectivization and the Terror could, at least to some extent, be overcome (see Document 4). Gradually, as the tide turned against the Germans in 1943, Stalin was able to claim credit for the victories.

THE KEY ISSUES IN THIS CHAPTER ARE:

- The initial impact of the German invasion.
- Stalin as a war leader.
- The role of the State Defence Committee.
- Patriotism and defeatism.
- The effectiveness of the war economy.
- The impact of the Great Patriotic War on the Soviet people.
- Stalin's foreign policy and the significance of Poland.

MILITARY EVENTS, JUNE 1941–MAY 1945

The scale of the Nazi attack on the USSR was unprecedented. It was composed of 5.5 million troops backed up by nearly 3,000 tanks, 5,000 aircraft and 47,000 pieces of artillery. The initial successes were staggering. By 10 July 1941 Soviet troops had already retreated 500 kilometres (300 miles) and at least 30 of their divisions had been annihilated. Leningrad was cut off and besieged in September and in October Moscow itself was threatened. By December 1941 3 million Soviet soldiers had been captured by the Germans and nearly 40 per cent of the Soviet population of 1941 and half of the USSR's economic resources were already under control of the Germans (see Map 5).

The Russian fightback started with the battle for Moscow. By bringing well-trained troops under the command of General

**Georgy Zhukov
(1896–1978)**
Served in both the Tsarist
army and then the Red
Army in the Civil War. He
became an expert in
armoured warfare and was
appointed Chief of Staff in
1940.

Zhukov from the Far Eastern provinces, where they had been
used as a deterrent against the Japanese, the Germans were surprised and forced to retreat. The second decisive Soviet victory
was achieved at Stalingrad, where at the end of January 1943
Soviet troops managed to encircle and then defeat the German
Sixth Army. Its surrender forced Hitler to pull back his forces
from southern Russia. Then in 1944 came the campaigns of the
'Ten Stalinist blows' which resulted in the liberation of Leningrad,
and the occupation of Romania, Belorussia and Lithuania. By
January 1945 the Red Army had crossed the River Oder and was
advancing on Berlin, which fell after large-scale fighting on 21
April. The *Wehrmacht* surrendered first to the Anglo-American
command on 7 May and then to the Russians the following day.
The victory, despite its horrendous cost, turned the USSR into a
great world power.

THE IMPACT OF THE WAR ON STALIN AND THE COMMUNIST PARTY

Stalin

The German invasion of June 1941 was a massive blow to
Stalin, as it proved his calculations that Germans would not
attack without warning to be disastrously incorrect. Similarly,
the initial devastating victories of the German troops again
showed up the weakness of the Soviet army, which was to a
great extent the consequences of Stalin's purge of the officer
corps in 1937. Neither had Stalin drawn up plans for a war
cabinet or committee, which could provide strategic leadership
in the war. Nor were there any contingency plans for feeding and
protecting the civil population. It was thus no wonder that
initially Stalin, between 28 and 30 June, went into deep psychological shock and virtually ceased to be leader. A general
headquarters (*Stavka*) was rapidly set up on 23 June, and it fell
to Molotov (see p. 341) to take the initiative in proposing a State
Defence Committee (GKO). Yet such was Stalin's authority that
it was agreed by the Politburo (see p. 64) that Stalin would be
head.

Stalin rapidly amassed enormous power, as he occupied all the
key posts of the command structure:

- Chairman of the GKO and the *Stavka*
- Commissar of Defence
- Supreme Commander
- General Secretary of the Communist Party
- Prime Minister (Chairman of *Sovnarkom*).

This accumulation of major posts, together with the immense prestige that the Red Army victories eventually brought him, made him even more powerful during the war than before it. He did not, of course control everything. While he concentrated on military matters, supervision of governmental business was left to the Deputy Chairmen of *Sovnarkom* (see p. 64). Stalin was particularly dependent on Beria, the head of the NKVD (see p. 345), to report on the progress of his generals. Beria was his 'inquisitor, his right hand man and his spy'[2] (see Documents 2 and 3).

Once his nerve steadied by the beginning of July 1941, Stalin cast himself as the leader of a national and popular resistance against the invading German forces. In his broadcast to the Russian people on 3 July he appealed to simple patriotism rather than Marxism–Leninism. He understood only to well, as he told the American ambassador, Averell Harriman, that the Russians were fighting 'for their homeland, not for us'[3] (see Document 1).

The party

Paradoxically, while the party expanded greatly, it lost its key role as the real political force in the USSR. The Politiburo was subordinated to the GKO and in the army the role of political commissars was downgraded. The party was further hit by the massive casualties sustained by its members in 1941 and the collapse of its cadre training schools. Some 70 per cent of the party's branch secretaries gave up their work to serve at the front. Ideologically, too, its influence declined as the class war was replaced by the patriotic war, in which the USSR was allied with Britain and America against the Germans, and criticism of capitalism had of necessity to be muted. The Politiburo met infrequently and the Central Committee only conferred once during the entire war. As in the Civil War, it was the army that became the main point of contact between the leadership and the Russian people. On the other hand, the party for the first time in its history actually became a mass movement, but its role, like the Fascist Party in Italy, was to assist the state rather than to implement revolution.

A new structure of government emerges

The immediate all-consuming need was to mobilize Russian strength to combat the German invasion. The lynchpin of the new wartime government was the GKO, which exercised enormous power:

- Its decisions had the force of law, and were binding on all party, *Komsomol* (see pp. 59–60), soviet, government and military organizations, as well as on all individual citizens.
- Its activities ranged from military strategy and administration of the armed forces to overseeing economic production and the supply of labour, materials and energy.
- It was also responsible for state security and public order, propaganda and foreign policy.

In short, as Stalin said 'all power and authority of the state were invested in it'.[4] Its membership consisted of only five people: Stalin, Beria, **Malenkov**, Molotov and **Voroshilov**, although specialists, commissars and regional party secretaries were co-opted when necessary.

Georgi Malenkov (1902–88)
In 1946 became Deputy Premier and succeeded Stalin as Premier in 1953.

Kliment Vorosholiv (1881–1969)
Defence Minister (1925–34), Chairman of the Presidium of the Supreme Soviet, 1953.

There is no doubt that the GKO was a powerful source of authority, but it could not always eliminate the clash of departmental rivalries or make its will prevail at local level. The sheer scale of the mobilization of the economy for war and evacuating factories from the war zone ensured that, despite the issuing of instructions from the centre, in reality the local factory managers, party officials or bureaucrats often took the key decisions. In that sense William O. McCagg correctly refers to 'Stalin's lessened control'.[5]

PROPAGANDA AND CONTROL

The brutality of the Germans was a main factor in uniting the Russians. The crucial message of Russian propaganda was the simple but overriding message: 'defence of the motherland'. It maximized support for the war against Germany:

- there was a conspicuous return to themes of the Russian past, particularly the war of 1812–14 against Napoleon
- the Church was rehabilitated and its influence enlisted against the enemy
- journalists stressed individual suffering and agony of families torn apart, in contrast to the disregard of the individual in the 1920s and 1930s
- above all, the media preached an undiluted message of hatred toward the German enemy.

However, this attempt to unify the Russian peoples by appealing to patriotism was not necessarily in itself sufficient. In the border-lands the Germans had initially been welcomed as liberators, while even in the interior, once the scale of the defeats inflicted on the Russians became clear, discontent, criticism and fear amongst the population surfaced. To quote John Barber, 'the collective psy-chology displayed no guarantee of unwavering support for the government. On the contrary it had the potential under extreme pressure for producing a collapse in legitimacy, resistance to the authorities, failure of social control, breakdown of law and order, and even collaboration with the enemy.'[6] Consequently the auth-orities adopted ruthless policies towards defeatism. In his speech on 3 July 1941 Stalin called for a fight against 'all disorganizers of the rear, deserters, panic-mongers, rumour mongers', but it took the defeat of the Germans outside Moscow in December 1941 and the revelation of the German atrocities in the occupied areas (see Figure 15.1) to swing the population behind Stalin.

THE ECONOMY

After the Second World War, the successful mobilization of the Soviet economy to repel the German attack was claimed by the Stalinist regime to be proof that the Soviet system actually worked, yet the history of the USSR's economic mobilization was not an unqualified success, even though by 1943 it was outpro-ducing the German economy in the production of tanks and planes.

Figure 15.1 Civilians
hanged by Germans in the
USSR, December 1941
Source: RIA Novosti.

The evacuation of plant

As early as 23 June 1941 Stalin ordered the start of the evacuation
of key factories to the Urals and set up a central Council for
Evacuation. In contrast to the appalling military defeats, evacuation
was a morale-boosting success. By the end of 1941 1,523 large-
scale plants had been moved. There is little doubt that the
evacuation was vital to the success of the Soviet war effort. It effectively preserved the country's means of survival through the winter
of 1941–2, and was an essential precondition for ultimate Soviet
victory. Yet inevitably it was often a rushed and bungled process,
impeded by lack of sufficient transport and bureaucratic delays. The
Council for Evacuation was supposed to decide on priorities and
attempted to enforce its authority through inspectors, but in reality
much of the responsibility for the evacuation depended on local initiatives, as did the reassembling of plant in the Urals. This was a
striking example of what William McCagg calls 'the no longer total
control system' over which Stalin presided during the war.[7]

War production: crisis and recovery, 1942–5

The basis of the Russian war economy was the Stalinist Five-Year
Plans of the 1930s. The expansion of heavy industry and invest-

ment in scientific and technical research created a large potential for the production of arms and ammunition, which Stalin was able to realize. Individually factories speedily converted to war production, but there was no overall plan for coordinating production right across the Soviet Union. The armaments and weapons industries expanded enormously, but in 1942 this very success created problems. The different branches of war production were not coordinated; for instance more artillery than ammunition was initially produced. The expansion of war production was also completely out of kilter with developments elsewhere in the economy. Because investment was poured almost exclusively into armaments and munitions, the production of coal, steel, electric power and industrial machinery declined sharply.

During 1942 the civilian economy nearly collapsed as a result of continuing German advances and lack of investment. The production of electricity, steel and coal were, respectively, no more than one-half, two-fifths and one-third of the levels achieved in 1941. To remedy these shortfalls, a series of emergency decrees, crash programmes and panic measures were launched, but as each bottleneck and problem was overcome, new ones opened up. To survive, factories had to be resourceful and produce their own components, or even find their own raw materials supplies.

In 1943 increased investment was made available to the civilian economy, and the competing needs of the war industries were better coordinated. At the end of 1942 a new powerful GKO Operations Bureau was formed to impose centralized controls on industry and transport. The slow retreat of the Germans after Stalingrad also made available more resources, while aid from the USA, which began to pour into Russia, accounted for as much as one-fifth of the Soviet gross domestic product.

The mobilization of labour

Although in comparison with Germany the Soviet population appeared to be limitless, in practice by 1942 the USSR had no more labour reserves. With 10 million men called up to fight, the search for alternative sources of labour for the factories became a priority. Labour shortages were made acute by the decline in the working population from 85 million to 53 million, as a result of the German occupation of the Western territories. Senior school students, pensioners, farm workers, women and Gulag prisoners (see p. 471) were all mobilized and the existing working day was lengthened. However, the Soviet government, despite the existence of a centrally planned economy, had no organization in place for classifying jobs by priority or for mediating between the rival demands of army, industry and agriculture. It was only in the winter of 1941–2 that machinery for this task began to emerge. First, in December 1941, munition workers were put under military discipline, which meant that they could not move from their work or be called up by the army. Then in February 1942 compulsory labour conscription was introduced under the Labour Committee, which progressively assumed more powers.

Once labour had been mobilized, productivity was raised by coercion and encouragement through extra privileges such as better food rations or cash incentives. There were also attempts to improve morale with a new type of Stakhanovite movement (see p. 351) – the 'two hundreders', which aimed to increase their output by 200 per cent. ***Komsomol*** youth brigades were also set up in an attempt to spur the younger workers into action. Such, however, were the disruptions to Soviet life during the war that apart from the munitions industry, where output doubled per worker, elsewhere output per worker declined by 10 per cent, before picking up again in 1944.

Komsomol
Young Communist League.

The workers, like all the Soviet population, experienced a sharp decline in their living standards during the war: they had to work a longer working day, accept compulsory overtime, forgo holidays and endure a constant shortage of food and basic necessities. Yet in some ways they were a privileged class. Their rations, such as they were, were higher than white-collar workers, while peasants on the collective farms could draw no rations at all.

Agriculture

Russian agriculture suffered enormous losses in the first two years of the war:

* Two-fifths of the grain production and two-thirds of the potato crop were lost to the Germans in the autumn of 1941 and in 1942, when Ukraine and the Black Soil regions were occupied.

- Soviet farms also lost most of their horses, which were commandeered by the army or else did not survive the evacuation. The supply of tractors and machinery also ceased as the factories switched over to the production of tanks.
- As a result of military and labour conscription, the rural workforce was also diluted by women, children, pensioners and evacuees. Output per worker fell by one-third.

The peasantry had the vital task of feeding the Red Army and the urban population. The quotas of grain and potatoes that they had to deliver to the cities increased, but they received no rations and had to live off the produce of their private plots. Disaster was only averted by the government tolerating the revival of private trade for the first time since the NEP (see pp. 60–62).

In general, the Soviet government treated the peasantry more harshly than the Tsarist government had in the First World War. Why, then, were there no peasant uprisings as in 1917 and 1921? Soviet historians have argued that the absence of this showed that the peasantry supported the Communist regime, but it is more likely that many peasants hoped that the war would end in decollectivization, and initially welcomed or looked forward to the arrival of the German army. Stalin was saved by the German decision not to dissolve the collective farms and by their barbaric treatment of the Russian people. The ability of the Soviet state to maintain order behind the front and to defeat the Germans in the Battle of Moscow in December 1941 also gave the regime a strength and legitimacy that the peasantry could not ignore.

THE SOVIET PEOPLE AND THE WAR

A society in convulsion

The war years were the third major convulsion that Soviet society had suffered since 1917 (the other two being the Revolution of 1917–20 and the implementation of Collectivization and the Five-Year Plans). Apart from the hunger and suffering, the years 1941–5 were characterized by the movement of millions of people. Evacuees fled eastwards away from the Germans, while millions of workers and peasants, who were conscripted into the

The Soviet war economy (1940 = 100)

	1941	1942	1943	1944	1945
National income produced	92	66	74	88	83
Productive fixed assets (excluding livestock)	72	68	76	84	88
Industrial production (gross value)	98	77	90	103	91
Industrial production of armaments and munitions	111	119	142	158	129
Agricultural production	62	38	37	54	60
Capital investment	84	52	57	79	92
Freight turnover of all modes of transport	92	53	61	71	76
Employment in the public sector (annual average)	88	59	62	76	87
Retail turnover of state and cooperative trade	84	34	32	37	43

Source: J. Barber and M. Harrison, The Soviet Home Front, London, Longman, 1991, p. 218.

armed forces, moved westwards. Urban inhabitants were driven out by hunger into the countryside to find food, or else evacuated there to help with the harvests, and young peasant males were mobilized to fight or work in factories. The Soviet industrial workforce, which had been transformed in the 1930s, was once again changed in its composition and was flooded with new recruits from the countryside. The move eastwards of so much industry also ensured that the majority of new workers were recruited from the eastern rather than the western territories.

The war witnessed an enormous exodus from the countryside. At least 60 per cent of the Soviet armed forces was composed of the peasantry, while a large number of young men of pre-military age were conscripted into the war industries, transport and construction. They were replaced by women, ex-servicemen, pensioners, teenagers and even young children, who had the daunting task of growing the food for the armed forces and the urban population.

The mobilization of women

There were over 800,000 women fighting in the front line, while behind the front they worked as nurses, in industry and farming, and also in the white-collar jobs in offices and schools. In the first part of the war a popular government slogan was: 'Men to the front, women to the factories.' Women, unless they had a young family, were conscripted into the labour force. By 1943–4 they made up 53 per cent of the industrial workforce. In 1942 they comprised over 25 per cent of the workers in the coalmining industry. The closer to the front line industry was, the greater the proportion of women in the workforce. In Leningrad at the Kirov works, for example, women made up two-thirds of the workforce by January 1943.

'A breath of fresh air'

During the war the intellectuals, a class that included scientists, writers and artists, played a key role. The scientists and technical specialists worked on the development of weapons, industrial technology and medicines, etc., while writers, artists and journalists attempted to focus the public's attention on the nature of the war and the German threat to Russian culture and civilization. To do this effectively, the government had to concede them a greater degree of freedom and tolerance than they had enjoyed at any time since the 1920s. As the writer and poet Pasternak later wrote, the war came as 'a breath of fresh air, an omen of deliverance, a purifying storm'[8] (see Document 4).

Government officials also enjoyed more independence, despite the enormous demands the war made on them. The need for immediate responses to problems and the lack of control from the centre often allowed them to take decisions themselves. Their ultimate success strengthened their position in Soviet society, and for years, even decades after the war, the generation of officials that had governed Soviet society in wartime remained in positions of influence, enjoying the fruits of victory.

The nationalities

Wartime propaganda encouraged Soviet citizens of all nationalities to fight for 'the motherland', which was not just Russia but the whole of the USSR. Some attempt was made to widen Russian nationalism to include the lesser nationalities in the USSR. Up to a point this was sucessful, but it did not actually create a 'Soviet people' as such. Local nationalisms remained strong and Stalins's pre-war policies were not forgotten – it was just that hatred for Hitler was the more powerful influence.

Even though the Soviet nationalities made major contributions to the war effort, the USSR's multinational character was nevertheless a potential source of weakness. From the western border territories of Soviet Russia right through to the Caucasus, local nationalists regarded the Germans as potential liberators. By not exploiting this sufficiently, the Germans contributed greatly to their eventual defeat in Russia. Even so, in Ukraine and elsewhere hundreds of thousand of people were involved in collaborating with the Germans in one way or another. When, for instance, the Germans occupied the Caucasus in the summer of 1942, the German army rather than the SS remained in charge of the occupied areas and granted both religious and cultural freedom as well as beginning a decollectivization programme. The popular support for the occupation showed what the Germans could have achieved elsewhere, had they been more pragmatic and less ideological.

However, once the victorious Red Army reoccupied the areas, retribution was brutal. Collaborators were shot or sent to the Gulags and whole nationalities were found 'guilty by association' and were deported to Kazakhstan and Central Asia (see Document 3). As early as the autumn of 1941 the 400,000-strong German population in the Volga had been deported to Siberia and Central Asia and over 50 per cent were condemned to the Gulags. In 1944–5 a considerable numbers of Balts, Georgians and Ukranians were sent into forced exile, as well as Armenians, Bulgars, Greeks from the Crimea and Turks from southern Georgia.

FOREIGN POLICY

The guiding spirit behind Soviet foreign policy was self-preservation and, if at all possible, the determination to hang on to the territory acquired in 1939–40 (see pp. 361–2). Hitler's invasion of the USSR forced Stalin to make allies first of Britain and then of the USA, but this was, to quote William McCagg 'a reluctant, unnatural, forced union'.[9] Stalin still deeply mistrusted the West and feared that it was intending to let the USSR and Nazi Germany mutually exhaust each other. Consequently he continued to explore the possibility of negotiating a peace with Germany, which would remove German troops from the USSR and give the USSR a breathing space to recover from the German ravages.

In 1942 the British conceded that the Baltic states were within the Soviet sphere of interest, and as early as December 1941 Stalin sent Comintern agents to Warsaw to strengthen the Polish Communist party. His relations with his Western allies were problematical. The failure of the Western Powers to establish a second front in 1942 certainly fed into Stalin's suspicions. Even though he imposed an 'anti-sectarian campaign', which banned any criticism of the Western democracies, the press was still allowed to stress that in comparison with the assistance being offered to the Allies by the Soviets, Allied aid to the USSR was not very effective.

Even after the victory at Stalingrad Stalin fitfully kept open links with the Germans on the grounds that:

- The USSR was not ready to fight 'one minute longer than necessary, certainly not for the interests of Britain and the USA'.[10]
- Germany would be defeated but the process would exhaust the USSR and leave it confronting a strong and virtually unharmed USA.
- The Western Allies were proving untrustworthy. Britain was pressing for a second front in the Balkans, which was an area of particular interest to the USSR.

These contacts continued in a desultory manner until the summer of 1944, but the growing strength of the USSR and the increasingly favourable response of the Allies to Soviet requests began to convince Stalin that he could, through the Western Alliance, secure the essential demands of the USSR. At the Tehran Conference in 1943 it was agreed that the USSR would be ceded eastern Poland and that the Poles would be compensated at the expense of German territory in the west. In the following October Stalin and Churchill also came to an unofficial agreement about spheres of interest in the Balkans, and at the Yalta Conference in February 1945 the Russians were included in plans for the post-war control of Germany.

Poland and Eastern Europe

As the end of the war loomed, what were Stalin's intentions? The early Cold War historians and more recently R.C. Raack argue that

'Stalin was effectively a Trotskyite running grand scale schemes, having world wide dimensions'.[11] Yet initially Stalin saw the post-war world in terms of cooperation between the 'Big Three' – Britain, the USA and the USSR. In his speech on the anniversary of the October Revolution in 1944 he appealed, for example, for continued Great Power cooperation (see Document 5). To facilitate this, he had in May 1943 already dissolved the Comintern (see p. 74) and in 1944 instructed Communist parties to form 'new types of governments', which in effect meant joining coalitions with Social Democratic and bourgeois parties. Stalin was a pragmatist, and at this stage probably believed that each state would find its way to socialism in its own time. In the West, where France and Italy were liberated by the Western powers, he realized that the Communists would be excluded from any influence unless they joined democratic coalition governments. Up to a point he pursued a similar policy in Eastern Europe, in order not to alienate the Western governments while Germany remained undefeated and to win their backing to his plans in Poland. Consequently:

- In Romania the Communists joined a coalition government, although in March 1945 Stalin did follow the precedent set by the British in Greece and sanctioned a coup which led to the setting up of the Communist-dominated National Democratic Front government.
- In Bulgaria, Hungary and Czechoslovakia coalition policies were followed, even though the local Communists resented them and did not understand why they were being restrained from seizing power.
- In Finland there was only one Communist in the cabinet.
- In Yugoslavia Stalin was already confronted by **Josip Tito**, who, independently of him, had set up a Communist dictatorship, but Stalin nevertheless kept a firm rein on him and stopped him from helping the Greek Communists seize power after the withdrawal of German forces in 1944 (see Map 1).

Josip Tito (1892–1980)
Leader of the Yugoslav Communist Party.

Poland, however, was an exception to this pragmatic policy. The Polish question was one of the most complex problems facing the Allies. Britain and France had gone to war in the first instance to preserve Polish independence, while the USSR in 1939 had profited from the German rape of Poland to annex its eastern territories. Stalin was determined not only to regain these territories, but also to ensure that there was a friendly government in Warsaw. After the advance of the Red Army into Poland in early January 1944, Stalin did not allow the Polish Communists to seize power straight away, in case that antagonized Britain and the USA, but his real policy was revealed when he refused to help the underground Polish Home Army when it rose up in revolt against the Germans in **Warsaw** in August 1944. He preferred to see it destroyed by the Germans rather than emerge as a strong anti-Communist force in the new Poland.

As Britain and the USA were still anxious to preserve Great Power unity and were hoping that a compromise could be achieved in Poland, Stalin was able formally to recognize the Communist-dominated Committee for National Liberation as the provisional government of Poland in January 1945.

ASSESSMENT

It is indisputable that the defeat inflicted by the Red Army on the *Wehrmacht* was total. Yet historians are divided whether the reason for this stunning victory was the superiority of the Soviet system or the grievous errors made by the Germans. Alec Nove summed up two views: 'On the one hand a veteran German Communist argued that "the result of the battle of Stalingrad proves the basic correctness of Stalin's policies", on the other hand a Soviet citizen retorted that "if it were not for Stalin's policies, the Germans would not have got as far as Stalingrad".'[12] Clearly, Stalin did make very serious errors. At the very least he should have responded positively to the numerous intelligence reports in the spring of 1941 that an German invasion of the USSR was imminent (see p. 362).

Stalin claimed that the 'Great Patriotic War' provided 'an all-round test' of the USSR's 'material and spiritual forces'. The Soviet economy certainly passed the test. Compared to the First World War the Soviet Union's economic record was a brilliant success. Thanks to, admittedly, very sparing rations, riots in the cities were avoided and collectivization ensured that the peasantry could not withhold grain supplies. The record of the armament industries, which by 1943 were outproducing Germany, was also

Warsaw uprising
Although Soviet troops penetrated to within 19 kilometres (12 miles) of Warsaw, the Polish insurgents were given no assistance. Stalin vetoed American requests for permission to land and refuel planes, which were carrying supplies for the rebels, until mid-September 1944. By this time it was too late to make any difference and the Germans were able to crush the revolt by late September.

a brilliant success. The Five-Year Plans helped ensure the successful mobilization of the Russian economy and the Russian people, yet this does not mean that everything worked like clockwork. As a result of production imbalances, the economy nearly collapsed in 1942, 'civilians were fed not because of the system but in spite of it',[13] and the mass programme for evacuating both workers and factories was often saved from disaster by local improvization.

The ferocity of the German attack also forged a new unity between the people and the government, which had not existed before. There was no resistance to conscription, and the burdens of war, unlike in 1914–17, were, theoretically, at least, shared equally. However, this degree of unity can be exaggerated. Had the Germans exploited the hatred for Stalin in the border lands and in the countryside, they might well have toppled the regime. Vladimir A. Kozlov stresses that during the war years 'the legitimacy of the Communist regime rested on a system of traditional Russian values only lightly swathed in the clothing of socialist ideology.'[14]

DOCUMENT 1
Stalin as war leader

In the 1980s the American Ambassador Averell Harriman was interviewed by the historian G.R. Urban, and made the following comment on Stalin:

It is a travesty of the facts to call Stalin a mere bureaucrat. He had an enormous ability to absorb detail and to act on detail. He was very much alert to the needs of his whole war machine. He had his finger on the pulse of the country. He was not just sitting in the Kremlin glorying in his power.

In our negotiations with him we usually found him extremely well informed. He had a masterly knowledge of the sort of equipment that was important to him. He knew the calibre of the guns he wanted, the weight of tanks his roads and bridges would take, and the details of the type of metal he needed to build aircraft. These were not characteristics of a bureaucrat, but rather those of an extremely able and vigorous war leader.

Source: W.A. Harriman, 'Stalin at war' in G.R. Urban, ed., *Stalinism. Its Impact on Russia and the World*, Cambridge, MA, Harvard University Press, 1986, p. 43.

DOCUMENT 2
Order No. 227

On the evening of 28 July 1942 Stalin signed Order No. 227
issued by the USSR Defence Commissariat. Stalin had made many
changes to it with his own hand. It was issued at a time when the
Germans were advancing deep into the Caucasus:

Not one more step backwards! that has to be our main slogan
from now on. We will no longer tolerate officers and commissars,
political personnel, units and detachments abandoning their battle
positions of their own free will. We will no longer tolerate
officers, commissars and political personnel allowing a few panic-
mongers to determine the position on the field of battle and to
induce other fighters to retreat and open the front to the enemy.
Panic-mongers and cowards must be destroyed on the spot.

a) The retreat mentality must be decisively eliminated.
b) Army commanders who have allowed voluntary abandonment
   of positions must be removed and sent to staff HQ for
   immediate trial by military tribunal.
c) One to three punitive battalions (of 800 men each) should be
   formed within the limits of the front to which middle ranking
   and senior officers and political officers of corresponding rank
   are to be sent ... they must be made to shoot the panic-
   mongers and cowards on the spot in the event of panic and
   disorderly retreat.

Source: D.Volkogonov, *Stalin, Triumph and Tragedy*, London, Phoenix
Press, 2000, p. 460.

DOCUMENT 3
The Role of the NKVD

Beria informed Stalin that:

In 1943 the troops of the NKVD who are responsible for security in
the rear of the Active Red Army, in the process of cleaning up territory
liberated from the enemy, arrested 931,549 people for checking. Of
these 582,515 were servicemen and 3,49,034 were civilians.

Of the total number, 80,296 have been unmasked and
detained (as spies, traitors, members of punitive squads, deserters
and similar criminal elements).

Source: Volkogonov, *Stalin*, p. 446.

DOCUMENT 4

Optimism about the post-war world

The journalist Ilya Ehrenburg recalled later:

When I recall conversations at the front and at the rear, when I re-read letters, it is clear that everybody expected that once victory had been won, people would know real happiness. We realized, of course, that the country had been devastated, impoverished, that we would have to work hard and we did not have fantasies about mountains of gold. But we believed that victory would bring justice, that human dignity would triumph.

Source: J. Barber and M. Harrison, *The Soviet Home Front*, London, Longman, 1991, p. 218.

DOCUMENT 5

Stalin's and Russian post-war foreign policy

On 6 November 1944 Stalin delivered the annual oration commemorating the Bolshevik Revolution, of which the following is a key extract:

The year just over ... was a year of consolidation of the unity and coordinated operations of the three main powers against Hitler's Germany.

There is talk of differences between the three powers on some questions of security. There are differences of course ... Differences occur among people in one and the same political party. All the more must they occur among the representatives of different parties ... it is known that these differences were resolved ultimately in a spirit of complete agreement ... This means that the foundation of the alliance between the USSR, Great Britain and the USA lies not in chance and passing considerations but in vitally important and long-term interests.

Source: in W.O. McCagg, *Stalin Embattled*, Detroit, Wayne State University Press, 1978, p. 63.

NOTES

1 Quoted in C. Read, *The Making and Breaking of the Soviet System: An Interpretation*, Basingstoke, Palgrave, 2001, p. 121.

2 D. Volkogonov, *Stalin, Triumph and Tragedy*, London, Phoenix Press, 2000, p. 480.

3 J. Barber and M. Harrison, *The Soviet Home Front, 1941–1945*, London, Longman, 1991, pp. 69–70.

4 Ibid., pp. 46–7.

5 W.O. McCagg, *Stalin Embattled, 1943–8*, Detroit, Wayne State University Press, 1978, p. 22.

6 J. Barber, 'Popular reactions in Moscow to the German invasion of June 22 1941', in R.G. Suny, ed., *The Structure of Soviet History. Essays and Documents*, Oxford, Oxford University Press, 2003, p. 272.

7 McGagg, *Stalin Embattled*, p. 23.

8 Quoted in Barber and Harrison, *The Soviet Home Front*, p. 105.

9 McCagg, *Stalin Embattled*, p. 39.

10 H.W. Koch, 'The spectre of a separate peace in the East', *Journal of Contemporary History*, vol. 9, no. 1, 1974, p. 534.

11 R.C. Raack, *Stalin's Drive to the West, 1938–45*, Stanford, Stanford University Press, 1995, p. 103.

12 Quoted in Read, *The Making and Breaking of the Soviet System*, p. 129.

13 W. Moskoff, *The Bread of Affliction*, Cambridge, Cambridge University Press, 1990, p. 238.

14 V.A. Kozlov, 'Denunciation and its functions in Soviet governance, 1944–53' in S. Fitzpatrick, ed., *Stalinism: New Directions*, London, Routledge, 2000, p. 133.

CHAPTER SIXTEEN

The survivors: the USSR, Spain and Portugal

TIMELINE

1945	July–August	Potsdam Conference
		New and more liberal Spanish legal code issued
	December	First post-war meeting of the Politburo
		Commission of Foreign Affairs set up
1946	21 April	Fourth Five-Year Plan launched
		Social Unity Party (SED) formed in Germany
1947	1 January	Anglo-UK Bizone formed
	10 February	Peace treaties signed with Italy, Romania, Bulgaria, Finland and Hungary
	12 March	Truman Doctrine announced
	May	Communists excluded from government in France and Italy
	5 June	Marshall Plan announced
	5 October	Cominform founded
1948	22 February	Communist coup in Czechoslovakia
	24 June	Start of Berlin Blockade
1949	February	Gosplan and Leningrad Affairs
	March	Voznesenskii removed from Council of Ministers and Politburo
	4 April	North Atlantic Treaty Organization (NATO) set up
		Portugal joins NATO
	12 May	Berlin Blockade ended
	23 May	Constitution of new West German state approved by Western Allies
	12 October	German Democratic Republic (GDR) set up
1950	March	Agreement to pay prisoners wages in correctional labour camps and colonies of the MVD

	25 June	Outbreak of Korean War
	October	United Nations revokes boycott of Spain
1952	10 March	Stalin's note, proposing a neutral united Germany
1953	January	Doctors' Plot
	5 March	Death of Stalin
	September	Spanish–US agreement on US bases in Spain
1969	July	Franco recognizes Prince Juan Carlos as his successor
1970	July	Death of Salazar
1975	April	Free elections in Portugal
	November	Death of Franco

INTRODUCTION

The Allied victory in 1945 did not create a new democratic order throughout Europe. Unlike Fascist Italy and Nazi Germany, the Stalinist dictatorship survived and was strengthened by victory. With the exception of Yugoslavia, the governments of Eastern Europe as a consequence of Soviet occupation also formed Stalinist-style dictatorships (see Map 8).

The only conservative authoritarian regimes to survive in Europe were Spain and Portugal. Franco rapidly divested his regime of the trappings of Fascism, which it had assumed during the height of German and Italian influence in Europe, and as the Cold War gathered pace he increasingly became accepted by the West as a valuable ally against Communism.

THE KEY ISSUES IN THIS CHAPTER ARE:

- The emergence of late Stalinism.
- The economy recovery of the USSR.
- The exploitation of the Cold War to strengthen Stalin's power.
- The Stalinist alliance with the new professioinal middle classes – the 'Big Deal'.
- Stalin's role in the outbreak of the Cold War.
- The survival in modified form of the Franco and Salazar dictatorships.

THE USSR

Economic reconstruction

Although the Great Patriotic War had ended in absolute victory, it was achieved at a terrible cost:

- Over 26 million Russians had died.
- The physical damage was immense: 1,710 towns and villages were destroyed and 70,000 villages obliterated from the map, while some 32,000 factories had been either bombed or blown up.
- The country teemed with invalids, orphans and widows – by the end of the Second World War at least 2 million invalids had been demobilized from the armed forces.
- Some 25 million people were homeless and reduced to living in ruined buildings or even dug-outs.
- The country had lost some 30 per cent of its national wealth.

Industrial recovery

In 1946 industrial output in the USSR was just 76 per cent of its pre-war level, but by 1948 output had recovered, and two years later it was officially announced that it had increased 73 per cent above the 1940 level. Even if these figures were massaged, this was nevertheless an impressive achievement. Yet this success was achieved in spite of rather than because of the fourth Five-Year Plan, which was launched in 1946, and it also 'hid serious disproportions between sectors, regions and old and new industries, as well as long-term problems of administration and efficiency'.[1] Originally the Plan foresaw an expansion in the consumer and light industries of some 17 per cent per annum, but local branch ministries tended to favour heavy industry at the expense of light industry and divert scarce resources to it. To counter this 'ministerial sabotage',[2] the government intervened and actually reallocated resources away from the heavy industrial sector to light industry, but the onset of the Cold War (see p. 479) persuaded the Soviet leadership to concentrate, as in 1940–1, on heavy industry and rearmament. The new industries, such as the chemical industries, were consequently neglected, while the infant computer industry was completely ignored. The main reason for this was that scientists did not dare to become involved in an area that was dominated by Western researchers: **Lysenko**, with his successful campaign against 'Western genetics', which was backed by Stalin, had shown the dangers of such an association.

The Soviet economy remained highly centralized. In 1948 the Head of Gosplan, **Voznesensky**, made some efforts to make state enterprises more self-reliant financially, but in the following year this was reversed when he was purged (see p. 474). Thus the rigid system of industrial centralization, which was developed in the 1930s, was never radically changed, even though its failings were becoming increasingly obvious.

T.D. Lysenko (1898–1976)
Rejected the chromosome theory of heredity in plant raising and insisted that changes could be speedily produced by environmental influences. This corresponded to Marxist thinking, and he was made President of the Academy of Agricultural sciences. Those scientists who did not agree with him were dismissed and sent to the Gulag.

N.A. Voznesensky (1903–50)
Joined the party in 1919, and became Head of Gosplan in 1938.

The role of the Gulags in the economy

Detention and transit camps as well as prisons were administered by the NKVD (later the MVD). Although many of the inmates were criminals, this Gulag system became known for its internment of political prisoners and opponents of Stalin and the party. The name 'Gulag' became familiar in the West only with the publication of Solzhenitsyn's *Gulag Archipelago*, which compared the scattered camps to a chain of islands. The Gulag prisoners had an important economic role to play in the USSR's post-war industrial recovery. They could be forced to work anywhere at any time for long hours. Gulag labour had built the massive hydro-electric plants on the Volga. On 1 January 1953 there were 2.5 million prisoners in the camps and prison colonies, 150,000 in the prisons and another 2.75 million in special settlements. The MVD found it increasingly difficult to produce enough prisoners to satisfy the requests from the other ministries for labour. It was, too, becoming clear that Gulag prisoners were costing the state more that free workers. The cost of housing, feeding and guarding a single Gulag worker came to 470 roubles a month, while a free workers' salary would amount to only 388 roubles a month Thus slowly and cautiously the MVD leadership began to modify the principle that Gulag labour should at all times be free to the state. On 13 March 1950 the government agreed to the payment of all prisoners in the correctional labour camps and colonies of the MVD.

Agriculture

Soviet agriculture had suffered even more than industry during the war. Over 7 million horses were killed and at least 26 per cent of tractors destroyed. The fighting had also devastated the rich agricultural areas of Ukraine and the northern Caucasus. Consequently it is not surprising that agricultural output in 1945 was at least one-fifth down on pre-war levels, and output was further hit by drought in 1946. Dimitri Vologonov argues that 'neither agriculture nor consumer goods were of any consequence in Stalin's reckoning',[3] but money was in fact pumped into agriculture. It went, however, to the state farms and machine tractor stations, rather than the *kolkhozy* (collective farms in which produce was divided between the peasants after they had delivered their quotas to the state – see p. 335). The peasants in the *kolkhozy* were again subjected to tight control after the relative freedom they had had during the war (see p. 457).

Late Stalinism

In May 1945 Stalin's reputation was 'virtually that of a living icon'[4] (see Figure 16.1) yet the strains of the war had aged him and 'decrepitude'[5] visibly marked the last years of his life. Some historians, like W.O. McCagg, argue that he was no longer able to able to control the powerful Malenkov–Beria faction within the Politburo.[6] Timothy Dunmore, too, talks of Stalin's 'relative weakness' as a result of the 'entrenched position' of many of his colleagues.[7] Yet recent archival research by Yoram Gorlizki and Oleg Khlevniuk shows that Stalin was far from being a prisoner of his colleagues.[8]

The emergence of the Quintet

Stalin's immediate objective was to return to the leadership system that he had set up in the aftermath of the Great Terror (see p. 450). The State Defence Committee (see pp. 353–6) was dissolved in 1945 and the first formal meeting of the Politburo in the post-war period took place in December. Stalin also took the parallel step of consolidating his inner council of advisers by creating a a sub-committee of the Politburo, the so-called Commission for

Figure 16.1 A bas relief at Taganskaya station in Moscow, showing Stalin surrounded by adoring citizens
Source: Society for Cooperation in Russian and Soviet Studies.

Foreign Affairs in December 1945. Rapidly this Commission, or 'Quintet' as Stalin described it, became the real centre of government in the USSR. Years later **Khrushchev** observed that while 'neither the Central Committee nor the Politburo ... worked regularly, Stalin's regular sessions with his inner circle went along like clockwork'.[9] Through this Commission Stalin ruled Russia in a remarkably informal manner. Milovan Djilas, the Yugoslav envoy, wrote that 'Unofficially and in actual fact a significant part of Soviet policy was shaped at these dinners ... It all resembled a partriarchical family with a crotchety head who made his kin's folk apprehensive.'[10]

This highly personalized or 'patrimonial' style of leadership contrasted with the formal bureaucratic functioning of the Council of Ministers. With advancing age and infirmity Stalin withdrew from active intervention in routine government decisions, which were carried out by the Council of Ministers, but he could still intervene with devastating consequences if he perceived any threat to his position. He relied upon the Quintet to act as 'his eyes and ears and even his brain'.[11]

Nikita Khrushchev (1894–1971)
Rose to prominence as Head of the Ukrainian Communist Party. In 1939 he joined the Politburo and between 1941 and 1945 served as Political Commissar on various fronts, including Stalingrad. In 1950 he was in charge of Soviet agriculture. After Stalin's death he was elected First Secretary of the Party, and in 1958 became Soviet Prime Minister. In 1956, at the Twentieth Party Conference, he denounced the Stalinist regime.

The Leningrad and Gosplan Affairs and the Doctors' Plot

Essentially the one 'crime' that provoked an instant reaction from Stalin was independent thinking. It was this that lay behind both the Leningrad and Gosplan Affairs.

The immediate trigger for the Leningrad Affair was the events surrounding the organizing of an all-Russian wholesale fair in Leningrad in January 1949. What made Stalin suspicious was that the decision to hold the fair was taken by the Leningrad party leadership rather than by the Council of Ministers. Stalin linked this independence of mind with attempts by the Leningrad leaders to carry out underhand plots, which were compared to Zinoviev's activities in the 1920s, when he had turned the Leningrad Party organization into a bastion of opposition to Stalin (see pp. 67–9). On 22 February 1949 Rodionov, the Chairman of the Council of Ministers of the Russian Federation, Popkov, the First Secretary of the Leningrad Regional and City Party Committee and Kuznetsov, the Secretary of the Central Committee, were all charged with belonging to an 'anti-party group'.

The Gosplan Affair was similarly a consequence of Stalin's will being flouted. Stalin had insisted that the plan for the rate of industrial growth for 1948 should be increased by avoiding the downturn in production that regularly occurred in the first quarter of each year as a result of the weather. Accordingly, the Politburo laid down a target of 5 per cent. Voznesenskii, the Chairman of Gosplan, who had already come under a shadow as a result of the Leningrad Affair, duly ordered the targets to be increased, but in reality the order was ignored. When Stalin learnt of this by accident, Voznesenskii was dismissed and Gosplan was purged. In October 1949 Voznesenskii was arrested and executed a year later on the charge of having lost some secret documents.

These purges emphasized that Stalin still had both the power and will, well over a decade after the Great Terror, to have senior political leaders and officials liquidated. They also acted as a warning to leaders in the satellite states in Eastern Europe not to disregard Stalin's instructions.

Increasingly during the last three years in power (1950–3) Stalin was in the south in his holiday *dacha* in the Caucasus. The everyday running of the country was effectively in the hands of the Quintet. Arguably, a low-key collective leadership emerged, but although its members took great care not to arouse the suspicions of Stalin, this did not prevent 'the unfurling of a complex net of crosscutting purges'.[12] The most notorious of these was the **Doctors' Plot**, the rationale behind which was to maintain Stalin's grip over the Security Services and to weaken Beria's power base. It was also possibly a prelude to removing either Malenkov or Beria or both. They were, however, saved by Stalin's death on 5 March 1953 (see Document 2).

Doctors' Plot
On 13 January 1953 *Pravda* revealed that a 'doctors' plot' had been discovered in the Kremlin medical centre. Most of those involved were Jewish medical specialists, whom it was alleged were linked with an American organization. They were accused of planning to murder the top Soviet leadership, and arrested.

The Communist Party, 1945–53

In 1945 the Party was 'a weak reed'.[13] During the Second World War millions of new recruits had joined the party without being properly screened. Many of these were soldiers who had also seen in their advance across Europe freer and more prosperous societies. Consequently the demobilization of these soldiers and their integration into party cells in the factories and machine tractor stations inevitably threatened to dilute ideological purity. Under Zhdanov attempts were made to restore the party's morale and return it the path of ideological orthodoxy by reinforcing the party's traditional controlling and propaganda roles.

The Russian peoples and the post-war period

With Stalin's prestige at an all-time high and the general conviction that the war had shown the strengths of the Soviet system, there was no prospect of an open revolt after the war, but, nevertheless, there were expectations and longings for change amongst the intelligentsia, the workers, the peasantry and particularly the returning soldiers, whom the historian Elena Zubkova perceives to be 'one of the principal moving forces of a future process of reform'.[14] Many veterans remained in contact with each other in the post-war period by meeting in the 'Blue Danube' bars that were opened in the ruins of the towns and the battle-scarred countryside. There, despite informers, they felt free to discuss and talk openly, and the bars 'came to embody by force of circumstance the last refuge of the spirit of freedom brought from the front'.[15]

Atomization
The destruction of all groups of potential opposition and the prevention of the formation of such groups. Hence people felt isolated or atomized.

Stalin reacted to these pressures through a mixture of repression, '**atomization**' and attempts to secure the support of the managerial classes. Immediately after the defeat of Germany official propaganda began to stress how the victory was a consequence of Stalin's own genius and planning. In his famous speech at the victory parade in May 1945, Stalin sounded an ambiguous note. On the one hand, he proposed a toast to the people 'who may be considered the screws on the great machine of state, without whom, we the marshals and commanders of the front armies are not worth a farthing', but, he on the other hand, made clear that it was these people who formed the base of society and thus he appeared to establish a hierarchical pattern where the people were just little cogs. Similarly, he seemed to conjure up the people as a force against their superiors. In many ways he sought to secure his position by dividing Soviet society and reinforcing his position as leader.

Andrei Zhdanov
(1896–1948)
Joined the Politburo in 1939, and led the defence of Leningrad, 1941–4.

The attack against the intellectuals was spearheaded by **Andrei Zhdanov**. In August 1946 a campaign against writers began when the journal *Leningrad* was closed down on the grounds that it was 'permeated with the spirit of servility towards everything foreign'.[16] Similar attacks were made on the theatre and the cinema and in the sciences. What was at stake was the attempt to control intellectuals by creating a climate of fear. Stalin achieved the same effect in the sciences by backing Lysenko's violent anti-Western campaign, which branded Western science as 'reactionary', 'foreign' and 'unpatriotic' (see p. 471).

Stalin also used the onset of the Cold War to create what Volkogonov has called 'a state of potential civil war, or more accurately a permanent struggle with "enemies of the people", spies, doubters, cosmopolitans, degenerates [and] wreckers', to produce 'an atmosphere in which his injunction to be vigilant fell on fertile soil'.[17] Mass repression was carried on a large scale:

- In the western regions of Ukraine, Belorussia and the Baltic republics mass deportations and arrests took place of those opposed to integration with the USSR (see Map 8).
- Labour discipline was also reinforced by a strict penal policy, which usually led to conviction and imprisonment.
- Soviet soldiers who had been in German prison camps were usually sent straight to the Gulags after they had arrived

home, as Stalin distrusted their loyalty after surrendering to the Germans.

Coercion was, however, only a short-term measure. The regime had also to drum up support for itself and find some new and reliable allies among the Soviet peoples. 'Even in Stalin's worst times ... the regime was supported by more than simple terror.'[18] While the most brutal terror was being practised, accommodation and settlement were also being pursued. Whereas the regime in its early days had relied on the workers, it now looked primarily to the new middle classes. To quote Vera Dunham, 'The middle class had the great advantage of being "our own people": totally Stalinist, born out of Stalin's push for the industrialization, re-education and bureaucratization of the country, flesh of the flesh of Stalin's revolutions from above in the thirties and ready to fill the vacuum created by Stalin's Great Purge and by the liquidation of the Leninist generation of activists'.[19] Dunham describes this as the 'Big Deal' and argues that it was a natural convergence of interests, although in the past the regime had preached hatred towards the middle classes. In fact the regime needed loyalty, hard work and professionalism, while in return the new middle class wanted secure careers, good housing, consumer goods and more leisure. Neither the regime nor the middle classes were any longer interested in ideology or further revolutionary upheavals.

LATE STALINIST FOREIGN POLICY

With the partial opening of the Soviet archives, it is now beginning to be possible for historians to understand more effectively the motives behind Stalin's foreign policy. The picture that emerges from the work of such historians as Willy Loth, Michael MccGwire and Norman Naimark is essentially that Stalin was a cautious yet clumsy pragmatist who had limited aims, which were dictated above all by security.[20]

Iran and Turkey

In 1946 the Iranian and Turkish crises brought the Cold War to the Middle East. In Iran Stalin attempted to annex Iranian

Azerbaijan, while in Turkey he demanded naval bases in the Dardanelles. In both countries his demands were rejected and led to the strengthening of Western influence. In both crises, to quote John Lewis Gaddis, 'Soviet behaviour exhibited the same combination of defensive and offensive impulsives exhibited in eastern Europe and Northeast Asia. Stalin wanted secure boundaries, but also secure spheres of influence beyond them.'[21]

Europe

Up to the spring of 1947 'diversity rather than uniformity'[22] still characterized Stalin's politics in Eastern Europe. Yugoslavia and Albania had Communist governments, which had seized power without assistance from the USSR. In January 1947 elections in Poland, in which widespread terror and intimidation had been practised, had put in power a Communist-dominated electoral bloc. There were also Communist-dominated governments in Bulgaria and Romania. In Hungary, Czechoslovakia and Finland Stalin was, for the time being, at least, ready to share power with non-Communist parties (see Document 1).

Initially Stalin was ready to cooperate with the Western Powers in Germany to create a democratic state, in which the Communist Party, as in France and Italy, would play an important though not dominating role. In June 1945 the USSR was the first occupying Power to license democratic parties in its zone. The USSR was also a more cooperative partner on the Control Council – the inter–Allied body that governed Germany – than France. Why, then, was this cooperation not maintained and Germany eventually divided? The historian Willy Loth argues that Stalin 'really only ended up with a separate socialist state as a result of incompetence of the Communists to play the democratic game'.[23] The heavy-handedness of Soviet tactics can be seen in the forced amalgamation in the Soviet zone of the German Social Democratic (SPD) and Communist Parties (KPD). In an effort to win over the SPD, the Soviets did force the German Communists to make considerable concessions, but the threats and violence used by the Soviet military alienated both the Germans and the Western Powers.

The unstable economic and political conditions in Central Europe and the lack of agreement between the wartime Allies about German reparations also helped create the conditions for the Cold War. On the one hand the USSR was determined to extract as rapidly as possible some 10 billion dollars' worth of reparations from Germany, while Britain and the USA were more interested in rebuilding the German economy up to the level where Germany could be self-supporting. This difference led to the creation of the **Anglo-American Bizone**, which was in fact the 'germ cell' of the later West Germany.[24]

Ultimately the economic weakness of Europe led to the American offer of aid, the Marshall Plan, in June 1947. Stalin certainly wanted financial credits from the USA but without any conditions attached. When the British and French insisted that a joint European programme should be drawn up rather than each individual state sending in a separate list of requests, Stalin suspected that it would merely enable American economic power to undermine Soviet influence in Eastern Europe.

Stalin's decision to veto the acceptance of Marshall Aid by the Eastern European states marked the end of his attempts to cooperate with the USA and maintain the Grand Alliance. In September cooperation with the Western Powers was formally dropped when Zhdanov announced that the world was now divided into two hostile camps: the imperialist bloc led by the USA, aiming at 'the enslavement of Europe', and the 'anti-imperialist and democratic camp', led by the USSR.

The Communist takeover in Prague in February 1948 accelerated plans for Western rearmament and the creation of West Germany. The introduction of the new Deutschmark currency into West Germany and west Berlin by the Western Allies in June 1949 led to the blockade of west Berlin by the Soviet occupying forces (see Figure 16.2). Stalin hoped that this would force the Western Allies to the conference table, but the blockade was broken by the Anglo-American airlift, and failed to halt the creation of West Germany or NATO. Stalin had little alternative but to respond by setting up the German Democratic Republic in October 1949.

Anglo-American Bizone
The economic amalgamation of the US and British zones on 1 January 1947.

The Far East

Up to 1950 the centre of gravity of the Cold War was in Europe. Stalin had relatively little interest in the Africa and believed that

Figure 16.2 Berlin in 1946
Source: Bundesbildstelle, Bonn. Bild Nr. 29.156

Atom bomb

The dropping of nuclear bombs on Hiroshima and Nagasaki in August 1945 persuaded the Japanese to surrender. Initially Roosevelt, facing the prospect of a costly invasion of Japan, had been anxious for Soviet military assistance.

Kim Il-sung (1912–94)

A young Russian-trained Communist who had fought the Japanese alongside the Chinese Communists. He was selected by the Far Eastern Command of the NKVD to take charge of a provisional government in North Korea.

decolonization was largely a sham. However, in northern China and Manchuria the USSR did have strategic interests, and despite the dropping of the **atom bomb** on Hiroshima and America's obvious cooling off towards the idea of Soviet participation, Stalin entered the war against Japan to ensure that he could gain the concessions that Roosevelt, the US President, had offered him – control of the ports and the railways in Manchuria and annexation of the southern half of Sakhalin and of the Kurile Isles.

Stalin also decided to back Chiang Kai-shek (see p. 74) rather than the Communists in the Chinese Civil War, as he calculated that the Nationalists would be more willing to make concessions to the USSR and perhaps also act as a buffer against the growing influence of the USA. Nevertheless, once the Communists had won the Civil War in 1949, Stalin was pleasantly surprised and convinced that Communism was now immune to subversion from the West. Mao's victory made him optimistic about the eventual success of Communism on a global scale and he readily agreed to sign the Sino-Soviet Treaty of 1950, which Mao hoped would deter an American assault.

This belated 'ideological euphoria'[25] lessened the caution with which Stalin had dealt with the USA and allowed him to be talked into giving the go-ahead to **Kim Il-sung**'s plans for the invasion of South Korea by North Korean forces, but there were also strategic reasons for this decision. A communist Korea would provide a useful military presence for the USSR, which would go some way to balance American military bases in Japan. Stalin was also convinced that the Americans would not defend South Korea.

Once, however, the North Koreans invaded South Korea in June 1950 and so caused the conflict that became **the Korean War,** Stalin was taken aback by the rapidity of the American response. When in late September the Americans appeared on the verge of total victory in Korea, the USSR did give some limited assistance to the Chinese, but Stalin took care to avoid a direct military clash. Soviet aircraft carried North Korean markings and their pilots were supposed to communicate with each other only in Korean. [26]

The Korean War, 1950–53
The war was prolonged by Chinese intervention in November 1950. By the summer of 1951 it had settled down into a stalemate and a ceasefire was signed in July 1953.

SPAIN AND PORTUGAL

The Franco regime

Unlike the USSR, the Franco dictatorship had not won a major victory that saw its prestige rise to unprecedented heights. The Franco regime, more by luck than skill, had survived, but it now faced universal hostility in Europe and North America. Initially Spain's only diplomatic support came from Latin America, particularly Argentina. It was only the onset of the Cold War that enabled Franco to escape this global ostracism. The establishment of Communist dictatorships in Eastern Europe, and US support for the anti-Communist forces threw the Franco regime a lifeline. When the Korean War broke out Franco rapidly offered the USA military assistance, although it was not taken up. In early 1951 Washington and Madrid exchanged ambassadors and Spain began to become integrated into various world organizations such as the World Health Organization, Unesco and the International Labour Organization. By the Pact of Madrid in 1953 the Americans set up three air and one naval base in Spain. Six years later President Eisenhower paid a brief state visit to Madrid. His tour of the capital marked 'the international apotheosis of Franco's career'.[27]

Domestically in 1945 the surest way to escape the Fascist legacy was to draw still closer to the Church and to endorse the principle of dynastic legitimacy. Thus in March 1947 the new Law of Succession announced that Spain was a 'Catholic, social and representative state which in keeping with her tradition, declares herself constituted into a kingdom'. The head of state was Franco, and Spain was declared a monarchy, which Franco would govern until his death or incapacity. He would have the right to choose his royal successor. By 1950 the Franco regime was secure. The Catholic identity of the regime had been 're-empahized' and the *Falange* had become 'a tame bureaucratic organization'.[28]

Franco was also helped enormously by the great economic boom of 1950–73, in which the Spanish economy grew at a rate second only to Japan's. Although opposition to the regime increased in the 1960s, his position was never seriously challenged, and he was able to prepare for the restoration of the monarchy on his death. On July 21 1969 he formally designated Juan Carlos as his heir, who ascended the throne on his death in November 1975.

Portugal: Salazar survives

In Portugal the Salazar regime also survived in essentials right up to the military coup of 1974. Salazar's opportune agreement with the Western Allies to allow them to occupy the Azores in October 1943 ensured that he was not viewed with the same hostility as Franco was in 1945. Indeed in 1949 Portugal was a founder member of NATO. Nevertheless there was a slight 'thaw' in the dictatorship. After 1945 opposition candidates were allowed to stand against the government in elections, but Salazar's policies still continued to be authoritarian and conservative. Nominally at least the economy remained corporate; the paramilitary organization, the *Legiao Portuguesa*, was not dissolved; and the political police still enjoyed a wide range of powers.

ASSESSMENT

Although both Fascist Italy and Nazi Germany were defeated in the Second World War, only in Western Europe was there a return to liberal democracy. Fascism and Nazism were only defeated in alliance with the Marxist–Leninist/Stalinist dictatorship. Paradoxically, while defeat shattered and totally discredited the

Fascist dictatorships, victory strengthened Stalinism, and appeared to vindicate Stalin's policies of the 1930s. The 'late Stalinism' of the period 1945–53 was in essence a period of restoration. The window of freedom that was opened in the Second World War was firmly closed again, and in both its economic and social policies the USSR returned to the spirit of the 1930s. Even in the sphere of foreign policy Stalin retreated back into the policy of socialism in one state, except, that, unlike the inter-war period, the USSR now controlled Eastern and Central Europe right up to the Elbe. Here the authoritarian but essentially conservative states that had either become allies of Nazi Germany or been occupied by German troops during the war became satellites of the USSR. Their governments, economies and social systems were all copies of those developed in the USSR. In Eastern Europe the 'the age of dictators' did not end until 1989–90.

In the Iberian peninsular both the Salazar and Franco regimes were able not only to survive but to prosper. They divested themselves of their Fascist colouring but remained essentially conservative authoritarian regimes, which were seen to have a valuable strategic role to play in the Cold War.

DOCUMENT I
The reaction of Hungarian Communists to 'the new type of government'

The Communists in the newly liberated territories were disillusioned by Stalin's apparent moderation in the new territories, as this recollection by a Hungarian Communist shows:

The greater part of those comrades who were not acquainted with . . . our strategic plan devised during the war were surprised in 1944–45 at such a broad coalition . . . and treated it with antagonism.

How often during the weeks were we reproached by good comrades: 'This is not what we expected of you.' And they told us what they wanted: 'In 1919', they said, 'the imperialists used arms to destroy the Hungarian Soviet Republic and reinstated the dictatorship of the great landowners and capitalists. Now the Red Army has liberated us. Let us profit by this opportunity to restore the proletarian dictatorship.' At the time of the liberation, we did not explain this problem soon enough to the broad masses of the party. In 1945 it was tackled only in intimate circles of the Party because even a theoretical suggestion of a goal of proletarian dictatorship would have created upheaval in the ranks of our coalition partners.

Source: W.O. McCagg, *Stalin Embattled*, Detroit, Wayne State University Press, 1978, pp. 35–6.

DOCUMENT 2

Stalin's power in his old age

In March 1951 Khrushchev dared write an article in Pravda *on how to improve agriculture in the USSR. Stalin disliked it and reprimanded him. On 6 March Khruschev immediately sent him a letter of repentance:*

Following your instructions, I have tried to dwell on the matter more deeply. Having thought it over, I now understand that my speech [on which the article was based] was, in essence flawed. In having this speech published, I have committed a profound mistake and brought great harm to the party ... I am deeply upset by this blunder and am wondering how best to make amends. I have decided to ask you to allow me to correct my mistake myself. I am quite ready to appear in print again to criticize my article.

Source: V. Gorlizki and O. Khlevniuk, *Cold Peace*, Oxford, Oxford University Press, 2004, pp. 108–9.

NOTES

1 T. Dunmore, *Soviet Politics, 1945–53*, London, Macmillan, 1984, p. 73.

2 Ibid., p. 64.

3 D. Volkogonov, *Stalin, Triumph and Tragedy*, London, Phoenix Press, 2000, p. 517.

4 E. Zubkova, 'The postwar years' in D.L. Hoffmann, ed., *Stalinism*, Oxford, Blackwell, 2003, p. 293.

5 Roy Medvedev, the former Soviet dissident historian; quoted in Dunmore, *Soviet Politics*, p. 14.

6 See W.O. McCagg, *Stalin Embattled, 1943–1948*, Detroit, Wayne State University Press, 1978, ch. 14.

7 Dunmore, *Soviet Politics*, p 16.

8 Y. Gorlizki and O. Khlevniuk, *Cold Peace, Stalin and the Soviet Ruling Circle 1945–53*, Oxford, Oxford University Press, 2004.

9 Quoted in ibid., p. 47.

10 Quoted in ibid., p. 59.

11 Dunmore, *Soviet Politics*, p. 18.

12 Gorlizki and Khlevniuk, *Cold Peace*, p. 153.

13 Dunmore, *Soviet Politics*, p. 30.

14 Zubkova, 'The postwar years', pp. 287–8.

15 Ibid., p. 289.

16 Quoted in M. McCauley, *Stalin and Stalinism*, Harlow, Longman, 3rd ed. 2003, p. 76.

17 Volkogonov, *Stalin*, p. 510.

18 V.S. Dunham, *In Stalin's Time. Middle Class Values in Soviet Fiction*, Cambridge, Cambridge University Press, 1976, p. 13.

19 Ibid., p. 13.

20 See M. MccGWire, 'National security and Soviet foreign policy' in M. Leffler and S. Painter, eds, *Origins of the Cold War*, London, Routledge, 1994; W. Loth, *Stalin's Unwanted Child: The German Question and the Founding of the GDR*, Basingstoke, Macmillan, 1998; N.M. Naimark and L. Gibianskii, *The Establishment of Communist Regimes in Eastern Europe, 1944–49*, Boulder, CO, Westview Press, 1997.

21 J. Gaddis, *We Now Know*, Oxford, Oxford University Press, 1997, p. 164.

22 G. Swain and N. Swain, *Eastern Europe since 1945*, London, St Martin's Press, 2nd ed. 1998, p. 48.

23 Loth, *Stalin's Unwanted Child*, p. 24.

24 T. Eschenburg, *Jahre der Besatzung (1945–49)*, vol. 1, *Geschichte der Bundesrepublik Deutschlands*, Stuttgart/Wiesbaden, Deutsche Verlags-Anstalt/Brockhaus, 1983, p. 419.

25 Gaddis, *We Now Know*, p. 83.

26 See K. Weathersby, 'New evidence on the Korean War', *Cold War International History Project Bulletin*, vol. 14/15, 2003–4.

27 S.G. Payne, *The Franco Regime, 1936–1975*, London, Phoenix Press, 2nd ed. 2000, p. 458.

28 Ibid., p. 434.

PART FIVE

Assessment

CHAPTER SEVENTEEN

The dual triumph of Western democracy and Marxism–Leninism

In the years 1917–45 the dictatorships in the USSR, Italy and Germany played a key role in Europe. In 1917–21 the USSR emerged, and was followed by Fascist Italy and Nazi Germany. In the inter-war years authoritarian but essentially conservative regimes increasingly began to adopt aspects of Fascism, such as corporatism and paramilitary party militias. In 1945, while the Italian and German dictatorships were destroyed, the Soviet dictatorship achieved a new lease of life, and was able to form a series of satellite states in Eastern Europe, which survived until 1989.

The rise to power of these dictatorships was determined primarily by the great European crisis caused by the First World War. The ideology of Fascism, National Socialism and Marxism-Leninism was in place well before 1919, but it took the traumatic shocks administered to the system by total war to make these ideologies capable of attracting mass support. In Russia Lenin effectively mobilized the mass of the population against the landowners and the middle classes, while in Italy Fascism could only attract mass support through nationalism, the promise of opportunities to the new upwardly mobile middle classes and the defence of property. In Germany Nazism developed later than Italian Fascism, and was as much the consequence of the Great Depression as of the Great War. It was essentially a variant of Fascism, but of course in details differed from the Italian model. It was influenced by its German context, and, as it could harness the industrial strength of Germany, it was potentially far more dynamic than Italian Fascism.

Although the Left has traditionally argued that Fascism and Communism are totally different ideologies, there were marked similarities in the way the dictatorships in Italy, Germany and the USSR developed:

- Italy, Germany and the USSR were all to some degree totalitarian, although the Bolshevik, Fascist and Nazi regimes were in reality unable to exert complete control over their states and societies. This was particularly true in Italy, where the Catholic Church still possessed considerable power.
- All three systems invested power in a charismatic leader.
- All used force and terror to break opposition.
- They also introduced a new element into government – that of the party. It was originally a creation of Lenin, but copied by both Mussolini and Hitler. These parties were not comparable to the mass parties in a democracy, but rather, as Pipes calls them, 'brotherhoods' or 'oligarchical fraternities of the elect'.[1]
- These three regimes were also opposed to 'bourgeois democracy' and the rule of law.

The dictatorships were products of different societies and therefore in practice developed differently, although all used the same political techniques. The Bolshevik dictatorship developed in an essentially undeveloped and predominantly rural society, where the middle classes were in a minority, while Nazism and Italian Fascism had to operate in more modern societies with a larger urban middle class. Theoretically Bolshevism, based as it was on Marxism, was international in outlook and class orientated, and was working for world revolution, while Italian Fascism was shaped more by Italian imperialism and nationalism. The driving force behind Nazism was race and anti-Semitism. German nationalism would only triumph as long as the race was pure. Yet over time the aims of the dictatorships seemed to converge. Stalin was a great advocate of Socialism in one state and national Bolshevism. He increasingly encouraged Great Russian nationalism and anti-Semitism, particularly after 1945. Mussolini, both as a result of Hitler's influence and as a consequence of the conquest of Ethiopia, began to stress the importance of race and to discriminate against the Jews.

In 1939 the two great Fascist dictatorships of Germany and Italy seemed secure, while the Western democracies of Britain and

France seemed doomed to decline. Authoritarian rulers in Spain, Portugal and the Balkans looked to Berlin and Rome rather than London and Paris. Yet by 1945 both the Italian Fascist and the Nazi German regimes had been swept away. Would they have collapsed anyway in time without war? The divisions and internal rivalries in Nazi Germany were debilitating, and the Fascist regime in Italy was incompetent and in need of a new dynamic, but neither Hitler nor Mussolini was unpopular or hated by significant sections of their population, as Stalin was by the Russian peasantry. The inner logic of Fascism and Nazism was war, which would shape society, and in the end both regimes perished through war.

War was also an important dynamic in Soviet Russia. In both the Civil War and the Great Patriotic War the Red Army had been the principal link between the government and the people. There was also an important strand in Bolshevism that was ready to fight a world crusade to establish Communism and defeat capitalism, but in reality both Lenin and Stalin were forced by events after 1921 to retreat into 'socialism in one country'.

The horrors associated with Fascism and above all Nazi Germany are 'the kind of historical experience that shapes the political consciousness of several generations'.[2] Historians have had great difficulty in putting 'the age of the dictators' into historical context. Auschwitz and ethnic cleansing in Eastern Europe does create, to quote Dan Diner, 'a no man's land of understanding',[3] which inhibits attempts to study Hitler's legacy to post-war Germany. On the one hand, it was total defeat, occupation by the four victorious powers and its division into two mutually hostile states in the subsequent Cold War. Yet the modernizing policies of Nazism – the modernization of leisure and equality of opportunity, for example – also left Western Germany with a legacy that was developed in a more liberal spirit in later decades.

In Italy, too, a veil was thrown over the Fascist era. The immediate legacy was negative and destructive. The country had become a battlefield and lost its overseas empire. However, as with National Socialism, in certain defined financial and economic areas the legacy was positive. The IRI, which Mussolini had set up in 1933, for instance, played an important part in the Italian economic miracle in the 1950s.

In the final analysis both the Italian and German people learnt from the failures of Fascism and Nazism. Martin Clark's observation about Italy could also apply to Western German – and now to united Germany: 'Post-Fascist Italy was set up as the regime's inverted image: a peace-loving, democratic, decentralized republic, guaranteeing civil liberties and run by men with impeccable anti-Fascist credentials.'[4]

Victory in 1945 was to give the Bolshevik regime a new lease of life and the dictatorship established by Lenin and consolidated by Stalin was given, despite the alarms and excursions of the Cold War, time to develop and to adapt, but ultimately its economic and social structure failed to meet the problems of the late twentieth century. Stalin failed, despite his genuine popularity in the immediate aftermath of 1945, to turn the Soviet dictatorship into a more flexible and democratic regime that could have survived in the long term.

NOTES

1 R. Pipes, *Russia under the Bolshevik Regime, 1919–24*, London, Harvill 1994, p. 264.

2 D. Prowe, 'Fascism, neo-fascism, new radical right' in R. Griffin, ed., *International Fascism: Theories, Causes and New Consensus*, London, Arnold, 1998, p. 306.

3 Quoted in I. Kershaw, *The Nazi Dictatorship: Problems and Perspectives*, London, Edward Arnold, 3rd ed. 1993, p. 214.

4 M. Clark, *Modern Italy, 1871–1982*, Harlow, Longman, 1984 p. 299.

Further reading

THE USSR

Edward Acton, Vladimir Cherniaev and William Rosenberg, eds, *Critical Companion to the Russian Revolution*, London, Edward Arnold, 1997, and E. and J. Frankel and B. Knei-Paz, eds, *Revolution in Russia. Reassessments of 1917*, Cambridge, Cambridge University Press, 1992, have a series of articles which form an excellent introduction to new ideas and research on all aspects of the Revolution. Robert Service, *A History of Modern Russia From Nicholas II to Putin*, Harmondsworth, Penguin, 1997, and Christopher Read, *The Making and Break*ing of The Soviet System. An Interpretation, Basingstoke, Palgrave, 2001, have good chapters on the Revolution and the NEP.

There are a large number of studies of the Revolution, 1917–21. The classic studies are still William Henry Chamberlin, *The Russian Revolution. 1917–1921*, 2 vols, New York, Macmillan, 1935 (republished in paperback, New York, Grosset & Dunap, 1965), and E.H. Carr, *The Bolshevik Revolution*, 3 vols, London, Macmillan, 1950–3 (in paperback, Harmondsworth, Penguin, 1966). Three compact and up-to-date studies are Edward Acton, *Rethinking the Russian Revolution*, London, Edward Arnold,1990; Sheila Fitzpatrick, *The Russian Revolution*, Oxford, Oxford University Press, 1994; and David R. Marples, *Lenin's Revolution*, Harlow, Pearson, 2000. A brilliant but hostile study is Richard Pipes, *The Russian Revolution*, New York, Alfred A. Knopf, 1990, as is his *Russia Under the Bolshevik Regime, 1919–24*, London, Harvill, 1994. The most readable and comprehensive recent study is Orlando Figes, *A People's Tragedy, The Russian Revolution, 1891–1924*, London, Pimlico, 2nd ed. 1997. For the 'view from below', which deals with the grass-roots of the Revolution rather than the leaders, Christopher Read, *From Tsar to Soviets: The Russian People and Their Revolution, 1917–1921*, New York, Oxford University Press, 1996, provides a good introduction.

W. Bruce Lincoln, *Red Victory: A History of the Russian Civil War*, New York, Simon & Schuster, and E. Mawdsley, *The Russian Civil War*, London, Allen & Unwin, 1987, are concise and reliable studies of the Civil War.

The best recent biography on Lenin is Robert Service, *Lenin. A Political Life*, 3 vols, Bloomington, Indiana University Press, 1985–95 – a shortened one-volume edition of this is *Lenin. A Biography*, London, Pan, 2002. A good introductory study is Beryl Williams, *Lenin*, Harlow, Longman, 2000. The classic biography on Trotsky is still Isaac Deutscher, *The Prophet Armed, 1879–1921*, and *The Prophet Unarmed, 1921–29*, Oxford, Oxford University Press, 1970.

For the NEP, Roger Pethybridge, *One Step Backwards, Two Steps Forwards*, Oxford, Oxford University Press, 1990, provides a good study of the economic aspects of the Plan, while Sheila Fitzpatrick, Alexander Rabinowitch and Richard Stites, eds, *Russia in the Era of the NEP*, Bloomington, Indiana University Press, 1990, contains some excellent essays on social and labour history in contemporary Russia.

STALIN, 1928–53

Lionel Kochan and Richard Abraham, *The Making of Modern Russia*, Harmondsworth, Penguin, 1962 has a useful section on Stalinism, and Robert Service, *A History of Modern Russia from Nicholas II to Putin*, Harmondsworth, Penguin, 1997, and Christopher Read, *The Making and Breaking of The Soviet System. An Interpretation*, Basingstoke, Palgrave, 2001, also contain chapters which provide the reader with a precise and accessible overview of the period. A good introduction to Stalinism is Martin McCauley, *Stalin and Stalinism*, Harlow, Longman, 3rd ed. 2003.

There are several biographies of Stalin. Isaac Deutscher, *Stalin, a Political Biography*, Oxford, Oxford University Press, 1949, although very dated is a classic that is worth reading. A more recent biography, based on archive research, is Dmitri Volkogonov, *Stalin, Triumph and Tragedy*, London, Phoenix Press, 2000. Alan Bullock's *Hitler and Stalin. Parallel Lives*, London, Fontana, rev. ed. 1998, is an interesting comparative study of Stalin and Hitler.

Over the last 20 years there has been much new research on Stalinism and the USSR under Stalin. An essential guide to recent research and historical debate are Stephen White, *New Directions in Soviet Policy*, Cambridge, Cambridge University Press, 1992; C. Ward, *Stalin's Russia*, London, Edward Arnold, 1993; D.L. Hoffman, ed., *Stalinism*, Oxford, Blackwell, 2003; and Harold Shukman, ed., *Redefining Stalinism*, London, Frank Cass, 2003. These contain collections of essays which, for the most part, are based on recent archival research, and explore aspects of domestic policies in Stalinist Russia. Sheila Fitzpatrick, 'New perspectives on Stalinism' in *The Russian Review*, vol. 45, 1986, pp. 357–73, and G. Eley's reply in the same volume: 'History with the politics left out – again?', pp. 385–94, also form an important introduction to the debate on the nature of Stalinism.

There is a growing literature on industrialization and collectivization. A concise and comprehensive analysis of the Soviet economy can be found in R.W. Davies, 'Economic and social policy in the USSR, 1917–1941, in P. Mathias and S. Pollard, eds, *The Cambridge Economic History of Europe*, vol. 8, Cambridge, Cambridge University Press, 1989, and in N. Jasny, *Soviet Industrialization, 1928–1952*, Chicago, University of Chicago Press, 1961. A. Ehrlich, *The Soviet Industrialization Debate, 1924–1928*, Cambridge, MA, Harvard University Press, 1960, is still the best guide to the debates within the party on industrialization. Much research has been done on the impact of industrialization on the Soviet people. H. Kuromiya, *Stalin's Industrial Revolution: Politics and Workers, 1928–1932*, Cambridge, Cambridge University Press, 1988, and D. Filzer, *Soviet Workers and Stalinist Industrialization: The Formation of Modern Soviet Production Relations*, London, Pluto Press, 1986, provide comprehensive accounts, while S. Kotkin, *Magnetic Mountain. Stalinism as a Civilization*, Berkeley, University of

California Press, 1995, gives a detailed account of the construction of the Magnitogosk complex and its social impact.

On collectivization, the classic study is R.W. Davies, *Industrialization of Soviet Russia*, vol.1: *The Socialist Offensive: The Collectivization of Soviet Agriculture, 1929–30*, and vol. 2, *The Soviet Collective Farm, 1929–30*, London, Macmillan, 1980–1. J.R. Millar (S.J. Linz, ed.) *The Soviet Economic Experiment*, Urbana and Chicago, University of Illinois Press, 1990, contains much useful material, including the Millar–Nove debate on collectivization. J. Hughes, *Stalinism in a Russian Province. Collectivization and Dekulakization in Siberia*, London, Macmillan, 1996, and C. Merridale, 'The Moscow party and the Socialist offensive: activists and workers, 1928–31' in Stephen White, ed., *New Directions in Soviet Policy*, Cambridge, Cambridge University Press, 1992, give good accounts based on local history of the collectivization process, while S. Fitzpatrick, Stalin's *Peasants, Resistance and Survival in the Russian Village after Collectivization*, Oxford, Oxford University Press, 1994, deals with the whole history of collectivization. Important revisionist studies of the Terror and the purges are J. Arch Getty, *Origins of the Great Purges*, Cambridge, Cambridge University Press, 1985, and J. Arch Getty and R.T. Manning, eds, *Stalinist Terror: New Perspectives*, Cambridge, Cambridge University Press, 1993. The traditional argument that emphasizes Stalin's role in the Terror is Robert Conquest, *The Great Terror. A Reassessment*, London, Hutchinson, 1990. A good article on the social dimension of the Terror is Stephen F. Cohen, 'Stalin's Terror as social history' in *The Russian Review*, vol. 45, 1986, pp. 375–83. An excellent overall study of everday life in Stalinist Russia of the 1930s is Sheila Fitzpatrick, *Everyday Stalinism*, Oxford, Oxford University Press, 2000.

On Stalin's foreign policy the standard works are the studies by J. Haslam: *The Soviet Union and the Struggle for Collective Security*, London, Macmillan, 1984, and G. Roberts, *The Soviet Union and the Origins of the Second World War: Russo–German Relations and the Road to War, 1933–1941*, London, Macmillan, 1995.

The best study of the USSR in the Second World War is J. Barber and M. Harrison, *The Soviet Home Front, 1941–1945*, London, Longman, 1991. Catherine Merridale, *Ivan's War,*

1939–1945, London, Faber & Faber, 2005, is a a first-class study of the Soviet army during the conflict. W. Moskoff, *The Bread of Affliction*, Cambridge, Cambridge University Press, 1990, is an excellent study of the food situation. For the late Stalinist period T. Dunmore, *Soviet Politics, 1945–53*, London, Macmillan, 1984, is the standard work, but a more recent study is Y. Gorlizki and O. Khlevniuk, *Cold Peace*, Oxford, Oxford University Press, 2004, which is based on archival research and is an important analysis of post-war Soviet government. Vera S. Dunham, *In Stalin's Time. Middle Class Values in Soviet Fiction*, Cambridge, Cambridge University Press, 1976, is a specialized study of how the Stalinist regime cultivated the new managerial class in the USSR. A useful essay on the post-war mood in the USSR is in E. Zubkova, 'The postwar years' in D.L. Hoffmann, ed., *Stalinism*, Oxford, Blackwell, 2003, pp. 280–300.

There is a considerable literature on Stalin's foreign policy and the Cold War. W.O. McCagg, *Stalin Embattled, 1943–1948*, Detroit, Wayne State University Press, 1978, is a study of the links between foreign and domestic policy, while R.C. Raack, *Stalin's Drive to the West, 1938–1945*, Stanford, Stanford University Press, 1995, is a post-revisionist text, which argues that Stalin did indeed intend to dominate the West.

HITLER'S RISE TO POWER AND NAZI GERMANY

The Weimar Republic

J. Hiden, *Republican and Fascist Germany*, Harlow, Longman, 1996, approaches the whole period from historiographic and thematic angles. It also has an excellent bibliography. The four-volume document collection by J. Noakes and G. Pridham, eds, *Nazism, 1919–45* (vol. 1, *The Rise to Power, 1919–34*; vol. 2, *State, Economy and Society, 1933–39*; vol. 3, *Foreign Policy, War and Racial Extermination*; vol. 4, *The German Home Front in World War II*) Exeter, Exeter University Press, 1983–8, is an essential companion to students studying this period. For a survey of the Weimar Republic and its collapse, concise studies are J. Hiden, *The Weimar Republic*, Harlow, Longman, 1974; E.J. Feuchtwanger, *From Weimar to Hitler, 1918–33*, London,

Macmillan, 1993; and A.J. Nicholls, *Weimar and the Rise of Hitler*, Macmillan, 1968. The best of the short overall studies is E. Kolb, *The Weimar Republic*, London, Routledge, 1988. C.S. Maier, *Recasting Bourgeois Europe: Stabilization in France, Germany and Italy in the Decade after World War I*, Princeton, Princeton University Press, 1976, is an interesting study of the German reparation and economic crisis 1919–23 and the partial stabilization after 1924. The impact of hyper-inflation is covered by E.E. Rowley, *Hyperinflation in Germany*, Aldershot, Scholar Press, 1994. T. Childers, 'Inflation, stabilization, and political realignment in Germany, 1924–28' in G.D. Feldman, C.F. Holtferich, G.A. Ritter, P.C. Witts, eds, *The German Inflation Reconsidered: A Preliminary Balance*, Berlin, de Gruyter, 1982, analyses its political consequences, while K. Borchardt, *Perspectives on Modern German Economic History and Policy*, Cambridge, Cambridge University Press, 1991, contains two revisionist chapters on the Great Depression and the collapse of Weimar. R. Boyce, 'World War, World Depression: some economic origins of the Second World War' in R. Boyce and E. Robertson, eds, *Paths to War*, London, Macmillan, 1989, provides a concise global overview of the Depression and its consequences. D. Abraham, *The Collapse of the Weimar Republic. Political Economy and Crisis*, Princeton, Princeton University Press, 1981, and M. Broszat, *Hitler and the Collapse of Weimar Democracy*, Leamington Spa, Berg, 1987, cover the collapse of Weimar. W. Patch, *Heinrich Brüning and the Dissolution of the Weimar Republic*, Cambridge, Cambridge University Press, 1998, is also an invaluable study of Brüning's chancellorship.

The Third Reich

There is an immense bibliography on every aspect of the Third Reich. I. Kershaw, *The Nazi Dictatorship: Problems and Perspectives*, London, Edward Arnold, 3rd ed. 1993, and K. Hildebrand, *The Third Reich*, London, Routledge, 1991, are good guides to the historiographical problems involved in studying the Third Reich. M. Broszat, 'A plea for the historisation of National Socialism' in P. Baldwin, ed., *Reworking the Past*, Boston, MA, Beacon Press, 1990, explores the problems of placing National Socialism's legacy and its place in the context of German history.

Good overall studies of the Third Reich are K. Bracher, *The German Dictatorship: The Origins, Structure and Consequences of National Socialism*, Harmondsworth, Penguin, 1973; N. Frei, *National Socialist Rule in Germany: The Führer State, 1933–45*, Oxford, Blackwell, 1993; and M. Burleigh, *The Third Reich. A New History*, London, Macmillan, 2000. An authoritative yet accessible study of the Nazi takeover of power in 1933 and of the Nazi regime is Richard J. Evans' two-volume work, *The Coming of the Third Reich*, London, Penguin, 2004, and *The Third Reich in Power*, London, Penguin, 2006. A briefer introductory study is D.G. Williamson, *The Third Reich*, Harlow, Pearson, 3rd ed. 2002. There are numerous biographies of Hitler. The classic is still A. Bullock, *Hitler. A Study in Tyranny*, Harmondsworth, Penguin, 1962, but the best and most detailed biography is I. Kershaw, *Hitler* (vol. 1, *1889–1936 Hubris*; vol. 2, *1936–45 Nemesis*), London, Allen Lane, 1998–2000.

For the administration of the Third Reich M. Broszat, *The Hitler State. The Foundation and Development of the Internal Structure of the Third Reich*, London, Longman, 1981, is indispensible. H. Mommsen, 'National Socialism: continuity and change' in W. Laqueur, ed., *Fascism: A Reader's Guide*, Harmondsworth, Penguin, 1979, is an interesting short essay on the Nazi regime. D. Orlow, *The History of the Nazi Party, 1919–1945*, 2 vols, Newton Abbot, David & Charles, 1971–3, covers the role of the party (including the SS) during the Third Reich. The development of the SS state is analysed in H. Buchheim, M. Broszat, H. Krausnick and H.-A. Jacobsen, *Anatomy of the SS State*, London, Collins, 1968, and R.L. Koehl., *The Black Corps: The Structure and Power Struggles of the Nazi SS*, Madison, University of Wisconsin Press, 1983, while R. Gellately, *The Gestapo and German Society*, Oxford, Oxford University Press, 1990, is a study of how the Gestapo functioned with the support of the German public. A useful book on Hitler's power in Nazi Germany is E.N. Peterson, *The Limits of Hitler's Power*, Princeton, Princeton University Press, 1969. I. Kershaw, *The Hitler Myth, Image and Reality in the Third Reich*, Oxford, Oxford University Press, 1987, deals with Hitler as an integrative factor in the Third Reich.

B. Koerner, R-D. Müller and H. Umbreit, in Research Institute for Military History, ed., *Germany and the Second World War*,

vol. 5, part 2, Oxford, Clarendon Press, 2003, is an immensely
detailed study of all aspects of the war economy. A more concise
study is R.J. Overy, *War and Economy in the Third Reich*,
Oxford, Oxford University Press, 1995. B.H. Klein, *Germany's
Economic Preparations for War*, Cambridge, MA, Harvard
University Press, 1959, and A.S. Milward, *The German Economy
at War*, London, Athlone Press, 1965, are dated, but still worth
reading. J. Farquharson, *The Plough and the Swastika. The
NSDAP and Agriculture in Germany, 1928–1945*, London, Sage
Publications, 1976, is the best analysis of Nazi agricultural policy.
The impact of the war on rural society is explored in J.S.
Stephenson, 'Nazism, modern war and rural society in
Wurttemberg, 1939–45', *Journal of Contemporary History*, vol.
32, no. 3, 1997. U. Herbert's, *Hitler's Foreign Workers*,
Cambridge, Cambridge University Press, 1997, is a key study of
the role of foreign workers and how they were treated by the
Germans.

P. Ayçoberry, *The Social History of the Third Reich*, New
York, New Press, 1999, and R.A. Grünberger, *A Social History of
the Third Reich*, Harmondsworth, Penguin, 1974, provide com-
prehensive overviews of German society during the Third Reich,
while D. Schoenbaum's perceptive *Hitler's Social Revolution*,
London, Weidenfeld & Nicolson, 1967, only covers the period up
to 1939. J.S. Stephenson, *Women in German Society*, London,
Croom Helm, 1975, and C. Koonz, *Mothers in the Fatherland.
Women, the Family and Nazi Politics*, London, Jonathan Cape,
1987, are studies of the role of women in the Third Reich. D.A.
Peukert's, *Inside Nazi Germany: Conformity, Opposition and
Racism in Everyday life*, Harmondsworth, Penguin, 1989, has
interesting sections on youth and the workers. M. Roseman,
'National Socialism and modernization' in R. Bessel, ed., *Fascist
Italy and Nazi Germany. Comparisons and Contrasts*,
Cambridge, Cambridge University Press, 1997, deals with the
question of how 'modern' National Socialism was. An excellent
study of German society during the war is M. Kitchen, *Nazi
Germany at War*, Harlow, Longman, 1995, and T. Charman, *The
German Home Front 1939–1945*, London, Barrie & Jenkins,
1989.

There is again a huge literature on Nazi anti-Semitism and the
Holocaust. D. Bankier, 'Hitler and the policy-making process on

the Jewish question', *Holocaust and Genocide Studies*, vol. 3, no. 1, 1988, and M.R. Marrus, 'The history of the Holocaust: a survey of recent literature', *Journal of Modern History*, vol. 59, no. 1, 1987, are invaluable guides to the intentionalist/structuralist debate. M. Burleigh and W. Wippermann, *The Racial State: Germany 1933–45*, Cambridge, Cambridge University Press, 1991, is the best overall account of Hitler's racial and eugenic policies. K.A. Schleunes, *The Twisted Road to Auschwitz. Nazi Policy towards German Jews*, London, Deutsch, 1972, and H. Graml, *Anti-Semitism and its Origins in the Third Reich*, Oxford, Blackwell, 1992, analyse the complex events that led to the Holocaust. L.S. Dawidowicz *The War against the Jews, 1933–45*, Harmondsworth, Penguin, 1986, states the intentionalist case, while M. Broszat, 'Hitler and the genesis of the Final Solution' in H.W. Koch, ed., *Aspects of the Third Reich*, London, Macmillan, 1985; H. Mommsen, 'The realization of the unthinkable: the "Final Solution" of the Jewish question in the Third Reich' and L. Kettenacker, 'Hitler's Final Solution and its rationalization' in G. Hirschfield, ed., *The Policies of Genocide*, London, Allen & Unwin, 1986, argue the structuralist point of view. D.J. Goldhagen, *Hitler's Willing Executioners. Ordinary Germans and the Holocaust*, New York, Abacus, 1997, analyses the attitudes of the German people towards the persecution of the Jews.

The best study in English of German foreign policy up to 1939 is G.L. Weinberg, *The Foreign Policy of Hitler's Germany* (vol. 1, *Diplomatic Revolution in Europe, 1933–36*; vol. 2, *Starting World War II, 1937–39*), Chicago, University of Chicago Press, 1970–80 . W.M. Carr, *Arms, Autarky and Aggression*, London, Edward Arnold, 2nd ed. 1979, is a much shorter account of the years 1933–39, while K. Hildebrand, *The Foreign Policy of the Third Reich*, London, Batsford, 1973, is a brief study of Nazi foreign policy up to 1945 from an intentionalist point of view. A.J.P. Taylor, *The Origins of the Second World War*, London, Hamish Hamilton, London, 1961, is still indispensible, as are A. Bullock, 'Hitler and the Origins of the Second World War' and T. Mason, 'Some origins of the Second World War', in E.M. Robertson, ed., *The Origins of the Second World War*, London, Macmillan, 1971. For Hitler's decision to invade the USSR see G.L. Weinberg, *Germany and the Soviet Union, 1939–41*,

Leyden, Brill, 1954; R. Cecil, *Hitler's Decision to Invade Russia*, London, Davis-Poynter, 1975; and E.M. Robertson, 'Hitler turns from the West to Russia, May–December, 1940' in R. Boyce and E.M. Robertson, eds, *Paths to War*, London, Macmillan, 1989. G. Wright, *The Ordeal of Total War, 1939–45*, New York, Harper & Row, 1968, and N. Rich, *Hitler's War Aims*, vol 2, *The Establishment of the New Order* London, Deutsch, 1973–74) cover German policy in occupied Europe.

General histories of the German resistance are provided by H. Rothfels, *The German Opposition to Hitler*, London, Oswald Wolff, 1970; T. Prittie, *Germans against Hitler*, London, Hutchinson, 1964; P. Hoffmann, *The History of the German Resistance in Germany*, Montreal, MacDonald & Janes, 3rd ed., 1996; and H. Graml et al., *The German Resistance to Hitler* Cambridge, MA, Harvard University Press, rev. ed. 1970. J. Conway, *The Nazi Persecution of the Churches, 1933–45*, London, Weidenfeld & Nicolson, 1968, concentrates on relations between the Nazi regime and the Church. I. Kershaw, *Popular Opinion and Popular Dissent in the Third Reich: Bavaria, 1933–45*, Oxford, Oxford University Press, 1983, explores the question of *Resistenz*.

Both Allan Bullock, *Hitler and Stalin: Parallel Lives*, London, Fontana, 1998, and Richard Overy, *The Dictators*, London, Penguin, 2004, provide excellent comparative studies of Hitler and Stalin and their regimes.

ITALY

R.J.B. Bosworth, *The Italian Dictatorship: Problems and Perspectives in the Interpretation of Mussolini and Fascism*, London, Edward Arnold, 1998, is the best guide to the historiography and debates on Fascist Italy. Alexander J. de Grand, *Fascist Italy and Nazi Germany*, London and New York, Routledge, 1995; MacGregor Knox, *Common Destiny, Dictatorship, Foreign Policy, and War in Fascist Italy and Nazi Germany*, Cambridge, Cambridge University Press, 2000; and R. Bessel, ed., *Fascist Italy and Nazi Germany*, Cambridge, Cambridge University Press, repr. 1997, contain some interesting comparative essays dealing with both Nazi Germany and Fascist Italy. A. Lyttelton, ed.,

Liberal and Fascist Italy, Oxford, Oxford University Press, 2002, contains 10 essays by experts on Fascist Italy, which form an excellent introduction to current research. John Pollard, *The Fascist Experience in Italy*, London, Routledge, 1998, is a useful collection of sources.

There are a large number of biographies of Mussolini. R.J.B.Bosworth, *Mussolini*, London, Edward Arnold, 2002, is both readable and a distillation of the most recent research. N. Farrell, *Mussolini. A New Life*, London, Weidenfeld & Nicolson, 2003, is a well-written, and on the whole sympathetic account of Mussolini. Denis Mack Smith, *Mussolini*, Weidenfeld & Nicolson, 1981, on the other hand is highly critical of both Mussolini and the revisionists. Ivan Kirkpatrick, *Mussolini, A Study of a Demagogue*, London, Odhams, 1964, is still worth reading.

Denis Mack Smith, *Italy. A Modern History*, Ann Arbor, University of Michigan Press, 1959, and M. Clark, *Modern Italy, 1871–1982*, Harlow, Longman, 1984, have good overview sections on Italy, 1918–45. A. de Grand, *Italian Fascism, Its Origins and Development*, Lincoln, University of Nebraska Press, 2nd ed., 1994; J. Whittam, *Fascist Italy*, Manchester, Manchester University Press, 1995; and M. Blinkhorn, *Mussolini and Fascist Italy*, Lancaster University, Lancaster Pamphlets, 1954, are concise general accounts of the Fascist era in Italy. A. Lyttelton, *The Seizure of Power. Fascism in Italy 1919–1929*, London, Weidenfeld & Nicolson, 2nd ed., 1987, is the most detailed study of the first ten years of Italian Fascism. P. Corner, *Fascism in Ferrara, 1915–1925*, Oxford, Oxford University Press, 1975; A. Kelkian, *Town and Country under Fascism: The Transformation of Brescia, 1915–1926*, Oxford, Oxford University Press, 1986; and F. Snowden, *The Fascist Revolution in Tuscany, 1919–22*, Cambridge, Cambridge University Press, 1989, are useful regional studies, which study the development of Fascism in a particular province.

There is a considerable literature on Mussolini's domestic policies, the development of Fascism and on its impact on the Italian people. Edward R. Tannenbaum, *Fascism in Italy*, Harmondsworth, Allen Lane, 1973, is still the best general account of the impact of Fascist policies on the population. R. Sarti, *Fascism and the Industrial Leadership in Italy, 1919–1940*,

Berkeley, University of California Press, 1971, looks at Mussolini's industrial policy. D. Thompson, *State Control in Fascist Italy. Culture and Conformity, 1923–43*, Manchester, Manchester University Press, 1991, is an interesting study of the regime's attempts to control the population. The attempt to fascistize the masses is examined in Victoria De Grazia, *The Cuture of Consent: Mass Organization of Leisure in Fascist Italy*, Cambridge, Cambridge University Press, 1981, and in T. Koon, *Believe, Obey, Fight: Political Socialization of Youth in Fascist Italy*, Chapel Hill/London, University of North Carolina Press, 1985. The best books on Fascism and women are V. de Grazia, *How Fascism Ruled Women, 1922–1945*, Berkeley, University of California Press, 1992, and P.R. Willson, *The Clockwork Factory: Women and Work in Fascist Italy*, OUP, Oxford, 1993. A good, but brief study on Fascism and the Italian workers is in Tobias Abse, 'Italian workers and Italian Fascism' in Richard Bessel, ed., *Fascist Italy and Nazi Germany*, Cambridge, Cambridge University Press, 1996. L. Passerini, *Fascism in Popular Memory: The Cultural Exeperience of the Turin Working Class*, Cambridge, Cambridge University Press, 1987, is a study based on memory and oral history. Fascism, as a new political religion, is analysed in Emilio Gentile (translated by Keith Botsford), *The Sacrilization of Politics in Fascist Italy*, Cambridge, Mass., Harvard University Press, 1996, while Ruth Ben-Ghiat, *Fascist Modernities. Italy 1922–1945*, Berkeley, University of California Press, 2001, discusses its cultural impact on Italy. Fascism's relations with the Catholic Church are covered in Richard A. Webster, *The Cross and the Fasces*, Stanford, Stanford University Press, 1960; D.A. Binchy, *Church and State in Fascist Italy*, Oxford, Oxford University Press, 1970; and J.E. Pollard, *The Vatican and Italian Fascism, 1929–32: A Study in Conflict*, Cambridge, Cambridge University Press, 1985.

C.J. Lowe and F. Mazari, *Italian Foreign Policy, 1870–1940*, London, Routledge, 1975, provides a very useful overview of foreign policy. R. Bosworth, *Italy, the Least of the Great Powers*, Cambridge, Cambridge University Press, 1980, and A. Cassels, *Mussolini's Early Diplomacy*, Princeton, Princeton University Press, 1970, cover the period up to the declaration of war. The events of 1939–41 are well analysed by M. Knox in three studies: *Mussolini Unleashed, Politics and Strategy in Fascist Italy's Last*

War, 1939–1941, Cambridge, Cambridge University Press, 1982; *Hitler's Italian Allies*, Cambridge, Cambridge University Press, 2000; and 'Expansionist zeal, fighting power, and staying power in the Italian and German dictatorships' in Richard Bessel, ed., *Fascist Italy and Nazi Germany*, Cambridge, Cambridge University Press, 1996. Useful studies on the Italian colonial empire are E. Robertson, *Mussolini as Empire Builder. Europe and Africa, 1932–36*, London, Macmillan, 1977, and D. Mack Smith, *Mussolini's Roman Empire*, Harmondsworth, Penguin, 1976.

Although dated, the best study of the Salò Republic is still F.W. Deakin, *The Brutal Friendship. Mussolini, Hitler and the Fall of Italian Fascism*, London, Weidenfeld & Nicolson, 1962. On the Fascist regime's treatment of anti-Semitism see Susan Zuccotti, *Italians and the Holocaust: Persecution, Rescue and Survival*, New York, Basic Books, 1987, and Jonathan Sternberg, *All or Nothing. The Axis and the Holocaust, 1941–43*, London, Routledge, 1990.

THE SPANISH CIVIL WAR AND FRANCO'S SPAIN

Raymond Carr, *Spain, 1808–1939*, Oxford, Oxford University Press, 1966, contains a good section on the causes and course of the Spanish Civil War. P. Preston, *The Spanish Civil War*, London, Fontana Press, 1996, and Filipe de Meneses, *Franco and the Spanish Civil War*, London, Routledge, 2001, are concise and invaluable guides to events and debates covering both the war and its causes. There has been much research on the economic and social causes of the war. A good introduction to this can be found in Martin Blinkhorn, ed., *Spain in Conflict, 1931–1939*, London, Sage Publications, 1986; P. Preston, ed., *Revolution and War in Spain*, London, Methuen, 1984; and P. Preston and A. Mackenzie, *The Republic Besieged. Civil War in Spain, 1936–39*, Edinburgh, Edinburgh University Press, 1996. More detailed studies of the causes of the war are P. Preston, *The Coming of the Civil War, Reform, Reaction and Revolution*, London, Routledge, (2nd ed.) 1994; Stanley G. Payne, *The Spanish Revolution*, London, Weidenfeld & Nicolson, 1970; and Richard Robinson, *Origins of*

Franco's Spain, Newton Abbot, David Charles, 1970. The classic, although by now somewhat dated study on the Civil War is Hugh Thomas, *The Spanish Civil War*, Harmondsworth, Penguin, 3rd ed. 1977. The Nationalist war effort is well covered in S.G. Payne, *Politics and the Military in Spain*, Stanford, Stanford University Press, 1967, and P. Preston, *Franco*, London, Fontana, 1995. R. Alexander, *The Anarchists in the Spanish Civil War*, London, Janus, 1999; B. Bulloten, *The Grand Camouflage: The Communist Conspiracy in the Spanish Civil War*, London, Hollis & Carter, 1961; and H. Graham, *Socialism and War. The Spanish Socialist Party in Power and Crisis, 1936–39*, Cambridge, Cambridge University Press, 1991, deal with problems facing the Republican government.

For General Franco's government at first in the Nationalist zone and then in Spain up to 1975, Stanley G. Payne, *The Franco Regime, 1936–1975*, London, Phoenix Press, 2nd ed. 2000, is by far the best general history. P. Preston, *Franco*, London, Fontana, 1995, is also a mine of information.

CONSERVATIVE AUTHORITARIANISM

S.G. Payne, *A History of Fascism, 1914–45*, London, Routledge, 1995; J. Held, ed., *The Columbia History of Eastern Europe in the Twentieth Century*, New York, Columbia University Press, 1992; Alan Palmer, *The Lands Between A History of East-Central Europe, 1815–1968*, London, Weidenfeld & Nicolson, 1970; and Elizabeth Wiskemann, *Europe of the Dictators*, London, Fontana, 1966, contain useful but short accounts of the authoritarian regimes that grew up in Europe after 1918.

EUROPEAN FASCISM

The first three chapters in S.G. Payne, *A History of Fascism, 1914–45*, London, Routledge, 1995, provide an excellent overview of a complex topic. In Walter Laqueur, ed., *Fascism, A Reader's Guide*, Harmondsworth, Penguin, 1979, and Roger Griffin, *International Fascism: Theories, Causes and the New Consensus*, London, Edward Arnold, 1998, there are useful essays on the ideology and origins of Fascism. E. Nolte, *Three*

Faces of Fascism, New York, Mentor, 1969, is a classic, which analyses the *Action Française*, Italian Fascism and National Socialism. F. Stern, *The Politics of Cultural Despair: A Study in the Rise of the Germanic Ideology*, Berkeley, University of California Press, 1974, is a readable study of the rise of Germanic *völkisch* ideology.

Glossary

Airlift The transport of food and supplies by air to a besieged area.

Anschluss The incorporation of Austria into Germany, 1938.

Appeasement The conciliation of a potential enemy by making concessions. The term is particularly applied to Neville Chamberlain's policy towards Nazi Germany.

Archives The records of government, which are deposited in the official government records and later open to historians.

Arditi Italian shock troops.

Armistice An agreement to end hostilities, so that peace negotiations can begin.

Arrow Cross Party A Fascist party founded in Hungary in the 1930s; it rapidly became a major political force, but was also divided between several different factions. Without German support it would never have come to power in 1944.

Aryan Originally a term used about Hindus, meaning a member of the highest cast, which first appeared in Count Gobineau's (1816–82) *Essay on the Inequality of the Races*. It was much used by the Nazis to denote ethnic Germans as opposed to Jews.

Autarky National economic self-sufficiency.

Axis Powers Nazi Germany's allies in the Second World War.

Blitzkrieg A lightning war, which would, to quote Hitler, 'defeat the enemy as quickly as lightning'.

Bolsheviks The Russian Communists. The term, which means majority, was originally given to Lenin's group within the Russian Social Democrat Party in 1903.

Bourgeois   Middle class.

Bureaucracy   National and local administrations, the civil service.

Capitalism   An economic system in which the production of goods and their distribution depend on the investment of private capital (money) with a view to making a profit. A capitalist economy is run by individuals, who wish to make a profit from their businesses or invested money (capital), rather than by the state.

CEDA   *Confederación Española de Derechas Autónomas*: Spain's major right-wing force, led by Gil Robles.

Central Committee   The USSR body that acted in the name of the Congress (q.v.) when it was not sitting.

Centre Party   Founded to defend Catholic interests in united Germany. From 1893 to 1907 it was the key party in a Conservative–Centre coalition, and it joined or cooperated with every coalition government in the Weimar Republic up to 1932. It was disbanded in 1933.

Cheka   Soviet secret and political police force set up to fight enemies of the revolution. Became the OGPU in 1922 and then later the NKVD (q.v.).

CNT   *Confederación Nacional del Trabajo*: the Anarcho-Syndicalist trade union in Spain.

Collectivization of agriculture   Abolition of private farms in favour of large units run collectively by the peasantry along the lines of Soviet agriculture.

Comintern   The Communist International, formed in 1919. Theoretically in the words of its chairman, Zinoviev, it was 'a single foreign Communist Party with sections in different countries', but in reality it was controlled from Moscow.

Commissar   Government minister in the USSR.

Communism   A political theory that envisages an inevitable revolution and the creation of a society in which private ownership of business and property is abolished. Everybody is paid according to their needs and gives to the community according to their needs.

Confindustria   Italian employers' accociation.

Congress   The most important meeting of the Russian Communist Party, where policy was laid down and Central Committee members elected.

Corporatism   The attempt to defuse class hatred by giving both capital and labour a role in running industry.

DAP   *Deutsche Arbeiterpartei*: German Workers' Party.

DDP   *Deutsche Demokratische Partei*: German Democratic Party.

Détente   A condition of lessened tension or growing relaxation between two states.

Depression, Great   The global economic slump, which hit Germany and Japan particularly badly, 1930–33.

Dissidents   Those who dissented from or who were critical of the official line taken by the state.

DNVP   *Deutsch-nationale Volkspartei*: German National People's Party.

Duce   Leader – Mussolini in Italy.

DVP   *Deutsche Volkspartei*: German Peoples' Party.

EOA   Agency for Welfare Activities in Fascist Italy.

Falange   Spanish Fascist party.

Freikorps   The volunteer groups formed in Germany to defend the government against Bolshevism and against the Poles in the east.

Führer   Leader – term adopted by Hitler to denote his absolute leadership over first the Nazi Party and then Germany as a whole.

Gau   A regional division of the Nazi Party.

Gauleiter   A regional Nazi Party leader in charge of a *Gau*.

German Labour Front   *Reichsarbeitsdienst*: formed in 1933 to replace the trade unions. Its leader was Robert Ley. The Strength Through Joy (KDF) and Beauty of Labour (SdA) were sub-organizations.

Gleichschaltung   Literally, coordinating or streamlining; the process of putting everything under Nazi control.

Gosplan   State planning commission of *Sovnarkom* (q.v.).

Gross national product   The total product from domestic industries combined with the earnings from exports.

Heavy industry   Coal, iron and steel production.

Intentionalists   Historians who emphasize the importance of the individual and personal intention in history (q.v. structuralists).

KDF   *Kraft durch Freude*: Strength Through Joy. The leisure organization of the German Labour Front (q.v.).

KPD   *Kommistische Partei Deutschlands*: German Communist Party. Founded in 1919 and banned in 1933; after working underground it was refounded in 1945, and amalgamated with the Soviet zone SPD (q.v.) in 1946 to create the SED (q.v.).

Lebensraum   Literally, living space, which Hitler hoped to gain for an apparently over-populated Germany in Russia. This was a key component of his foreign policy.

Left-wing   Political parties on the left, that is Liberals, Socialists and (far-left) Communists.

Liberalism   Belief in representative government and individual and economic freedom.

Martial law   Military rule involving the suspension of normal civilian government.

Marxism–Leninism   The political philosophy of the USSR deriving from Karl Marx and Lenin. Lenin adapted Karl Marx's teaching to the situation in Russia. Unlike Marx, he advocated the creation of a party dictatorship, which would have absolute powers – even over the workers.

Mittelstand   Literally, the middle estate. It denoted what in Britain was called the lower middle class: peasants, small businessmen, self-employed artisans and white-collar office workers.

Modernization   According to the German sociologist Max Weber and later German and American scholars, this involved first the emergence of a modern capitalist economy and bureaucracy and then a democratic national state.

Nationalism   A patriotic belief by a people in the virtues and power of their nation. Extreme nationalism, as in Nazi Germany or Fascist Italy, involves the desire to strengthen the state at the cost of its neighbours.

Nation-state   A state consisting of an ethnically and culturally united population, such as Italy and France.

NSDAP   *Nationalsozialistische Deutsche Arbeiterpartei*: National Socialist German Workers' Party or Nazi. In February 1920 the small German Workers' Party changed its name to NSDAP. In July 1921 Hitler was elected chairman. It was banned after the Munich putch but refounded in 1925. On 14 July 1933 it was declared the only legal political party in Germany.

NKVD   The People's Commissariat of Internal Affairs, formed in 1934 from the OGPU. It was a political police and was responsible for security, intelligence and all detention facilities (the Gulags). It was replaced by the MVD in 1946.

ONB   *Opera Nazionale Balilla*: Fascist Youth Organization.

OND   *Opera Nazionale Dopolavaro*: Fascist leisure organizations for workers.

OVRA   Italian secret police.

Partisan groups   Resistance fighters, or guerrillas, in German and Italian occupied Europe.

PCE   *Partido Communista de España*: Spanish Communist Party.

PCI   *Partito Communista Italiano*: Italian Communist Party.

Peasant parties   Parties representing the small farmers or peasants.

Plutocracy   Government by the very rich or by big business.

PNF   *Partito Nazional Fascista*: Italian Fascist Party.

Politburo   The Political Bureau of the Russian Bolshevik Party. It was the key decision making body in the USSR.

POUM   *Partido Obrero de Unificación Marxista*: a Spanish Marxist Socialist party independent of the PCE (q.v.)

Powers, Great   A term used to describe the most powerful nations, but 'power' can be used to describe any state.

PPI   *Partito Popolare Italiano* (*Popolari*): Italian Catholic Party.

Proletariat   Industrial working class.

PSI   *Partito Socialista Italiano*: Italian Socialist Party.

Ras   Originally an Ethiopian chieftain, but also applied to a Fascist gang leader, 1919–22.

Red Army   The army of the USSR.

Reich   Literally, empire. Hitler used the term Third Reich to describe the new Nazi Germany in1933. This term had come into common usage with the publication of Moeller van den Bruck's book, *Germany's Third Reich* in 1923.

Reichsbank   The German Central Bank, 1875–1945, which was responsible for currency issue.

Reichsrat   The upper house of the German parliament, in which the federal states were represented, 1919–33.

Reichstag   The lower house of the German parliament, 1871–1945.

Reichswehr   The German army, 1919–35. This was then replaced by the term *Wehrmacht*, which also included the air force and navy.

Reparations   Compensation paid by a defeated power to make good the damage it committed in a war.

Revisionist   Somebody who revises an accepted idea or policy. Hence a revisionist historian is one who challenges the accepted, orthodox historical arguments.

Right   Term used to denote parties stretching from Conservative to Nazi or Fascist (extreme right).

Risorgimento   Unification of Italy, 1859–70.

RKFDV   *Reichskommissariat für die Festigung des Deutschen Volksstums*: Reich Commissariat for the Consolidation of German Nationhood. This position gave Himmler responsibility for 'ethnic cleansing' in Eastern Europe.

SA   *Sturmabteilung*: Nazi storm or assault troops. The SA was originally founded in 1921 to protect party meetings. With the elimination of Röhm on 30 June 1934 it effectively lost its power to the SS.

Satellite state   A state that is dependent on and dominated by a Great Power (q.v. Powers, Great).

SD   *Sicherheitsdienst*: security service of the SS.

SED   The Socialist Unity Party of Germany. Created in the Soviet zone in 1946 through the amalgamation of the Socialist and Communist Parties.

Socialist   A believer in Socialism – the belief that the community as a whole, rather than individuals, should control the means of production, the exchange of goods and banking.

Socialization of the economy   Converting the economy from a capitalist to socialist economy, where industries are owned by the state, not individuals.

Sovnarkom   The Council of People's Commissars. In effect the government of the USSR (q.v Gosplan).

SPD   *Sozialdemokratische Partei Deutschlands*: German Social Democratic Party. It was dissolved by Hitler, but was re-formed in 1945.

Squadrisimo   The Fascist paramilitary movement.

SS   *Schutzstafel*: literally, protection squad. It was founded in 1925 to protect the leading Nazis. It played a key role within the Nazi Party, when Himmler was put in charge of it in 1929, and then, after 1933, in Nazi Germany. When Himmler established control over the whole police and security systems within the Reich in 1936, its influence was greatly strengthened. Its control of the police and then the occupied territories enabled it to play a dominant role in formulating the racial policy of the Third Reich (q.v. *Waffen* SS).

Stalin cult   The cult of Stalin as the great ruler of the USSR.

Status quo   The existing situation.

Structuralists   The name given to the school of historians who apply a structural analysis to modern history. When dealing with the Third Reich, they play down the role of the individual and place more emphasis on the German elites and the polycratic nature of the regime (q.v. intentionalists).

Syndicalism   A radical trade union movement; a belief in a society in which the trade unions are the dominant body.

Totalitarian regimes   Regimes such as those in Soviet Russia or Nazi Germany, which sought to control every aspect of their peoples' lives.

Transformismo   System of changing governments by winning over former opponents.

USSR   The Union of Soviet Socialist Republics.

Völkisch   Can be translated as 'folkish', but there is no real equivalent in English. The *völkisch* ideology preached the creation and preservation of a traditional Germanic, national and above all racial community. It was anti-Semitic, as the Jews were perceived to be a threat to the traditional Germany, and it formed an important component of the ideology of the Nazi Party.

Volksgemeinschaft   Literally, national community. This was to be created by unifying the population primarily on the basis of nationalism (q.v.) and race. By fusing nationalism with some elements of socialism, Hitler hoped to end class conflict and create a new national community.

Waffen-SS   Militarized or armed SS. A term first used in 1940. Three SS regiments were created after 1934, which formed the core of the *Waffen*-SS.

White Russians   The anti-Bolshevik and pro-tsarist forces in the Russian Civil War.

Index

revolution in the USSR
347–53

the Stalinist cult, 356, 368

and struggle for Lenin's succession,
64–70

as war leader, 450–1, 463–4

willingness to negotiate with Nazi
Germany after Stalingrad, 461

see also, Lenin, Bolshevik Party;
USSR

Stalingrad, 410, 412, 413, 450, 461,
463

Stambolski, A., 127, 131

Starhemberg, Prince, 136

State Defence Committee, (GKO)
450–2, 455, 472

Stauffenberg, Col, C., von, 424

Stinnes, H., 149–50

Strasser, Gregor, 188

Stresemann, 152–4, 159

Sudeten crisis, 30

syndicalism, 13–14, 22, 92–3

syndicates, Fascist, 110, 265

Szálasi,F., 375, 394

Tomsky, M., 69, 341, 343

totalitarianism, 2, 104–5, 112,
257–8

Transformismo, 88

trench experience, 17

Trotsky,L., 39–40, 45–9, 66–9, 74,
138, 337, 343–4

Turkey, 73, 477–8

Ukraine, 49, 460

United Opposition, 68

USA, 460, 463

USSR,
constitution of, 63–4
creation of, 63
foreign policy, 73–5, 357–363,
460–3, 477–481
and the Great Patriotic War,
449–464
and late Stalinism, 492–7
and the nationalities, 63, 459–60,
476
structure of government in, 63–4,
354–6, 452–53, 472–3

USSR and the Stalinist revolution,
333–6

see also Stalin, Lenin and
Bolshevism

Valkyrie, Operation, 424

Versailles, Treaty of, 147, 159,
148–9, 280, 439, 440

Victor Emmanuel III, King of Italy,
98, 99, 103, 108

völkisch philosophy, 10, 155

Volksgemeinschaft, 220–31

Wal Wal Oasis, 281

war
class, 44
Cold, 461, 477–81
Ethiopian, 276, 281–4
First World War, 8, 16–22, 33–40
Great Patriotic War, 448–66, 470
Korean, 480–1
Russian Civil, 35, 45–52, 50,
55–60
Russo–Finnish, 362
Russo–Polish (1920), 49
Second World War, 386–464; *see
also* Great Patriotic War

Wehrmacht, 390, 400, 450, 463; *see
also Reichswehr*

Weimar Republic
collapse of, 178–89
constitution, 145–6
and hyper-inflation, 151–2, 160,
169–70
legacy of the war, 142–5, 147
partial recovery, 158
and party politics, 160–1
threats to, 148–57

White Rose Group, 423

White Russians (Whites) 35, 46,
50–2, 53. 75

women (in the USSR) 60, 71, 352–3,
456, 457, 458–9; (in Nazi
Germany), 161–2, 418–19 (in
Fascist Italy), 268–9

workers
and Italian Fascism, 109–10,
264–6, 439, 442